# Watch the Birdie

*A Police Photographer's Story*

By
Alan Parker

CEREBUS
COMMUNICATIONS LTD.
No.2, Domalex House, 50 George Street, Walsall, West Midlands WS1 1RS

The photographs in this book were taken by the author, some are the copyright of the Metropolitan Police and are reproduced by the their kind permission.

*Front cover:*

*top left:* SAS entry team caught up in their ropes
*(courtesy of the Metropolitan Police)*

*top right:* Owl coming through church window

*bottom left:* Kingfisher

*bottom right:* Riot shield photographic team
*(courtesy of the Metropolitan Police)*

British Library Catologuing in Publication Data.
A catalogue record for this book is obtainable from the British Library.

*Bound and printed by:* Redwood Books, Wiltshire.

*Published by:*

Cerebus Communications Limited
No.2, Domalex House, 50 George Street, Walsall, West Midlands WS1 1RS

ISBN 0-9539539-0-4

# Contents

# List of illustrations

# Abbreviations

SP. ......................Special Police.
MP. ......................Military Police
SWO. .................Station Warrant Officer
Chi .....................Tea.
PTI. ....................Physical Training Instructor.
AWOL. ..............Absent without leave.
SNAFU. .............Situation Normal All F****D UP!
JAPIC. ...............Joint Air Photographic Intelligence Centre.
WAAF. ...............Women's Auxiliary Air Force.
RSM. ..................Regimental Sergeant Major.
CP. ......................Continuous Processor.
IVP. ....................Intravenous Pyelogram.
DCI. ...................Detective Chief Inspector.
MO. .....................Medical Officer.
HSF. ...................High-speed flash.
BTO. ..................British Trust for Ornithology.
SOCO. ...............Scenes of Crime Officer.
ESP. ....................Extra Sensory Perception.
NAAFI. ..............Navy, Army and Air Force Institute.
WAD. .................Cake.
WATCHIE..........Night Watchman.
LAC. ..................Leading Aircraftman.
CLICKS ............Kilometres.
OTT ..................Over the top.
PM .....................Post morteum.
VCR ...................Videotape recorder.
DFO ...................District Fingerprint Officer.
ATC ....................Air Traffic Control.

# Dedication

This autobiography is dedicated to Teresa and the children, who gave me the family support I needed throughout the difficult years, and to my friends and colleagues in the job, who I was privileged to work with.

To the memory of Dave Summers, Tony Mears and Alan McLean, who have passed on far too early and also my dear friends on the Isle of Inishbofin.

Lastly, to my wife Lisa, who has been a great sounding-board during my efforts to write this book over the last four years, and for reading and correcting the final draft.

To Sylvia & Peter
this tells most
of it!
Alan

# Chapter One

They say the older you get, the clearer your memories are of the earlier years, and yet, I have always been able to remember with great clarity, quite a few events which occurred around the age of three, and one in particular when I was just two years old.

We lived in a flat over the stables in Limehouse Police Station London, where my father was an officer in the Metropolitan Police Mounted Branch, and I distinctly remember being taken by him to a shop in what I now know as Commercial Rd Limehouse, to have my photograph taken.

Although I didn't actually know my picture was being taken, the situation was sufficiently stressful to cause me to pee myself, wetting my father's trousers in the process. I apparently got a right ticking off for this appalling lapse in manners, but I smile at the memory, when I see the resulting photograph, which still exists today.

Whenever my unruly behaviour around the flat got too much, I was incarcerated by my mother in a black, barge-like pram, parked outside on the landing, and held securely in limbo, by straps fixed with chrome snap hooks.

On the inside, the pram had a yellow basket-weave design printed on a shiny black background, which I was forced to regard at close quarters for many hours, until penance was done.

It wasn't until I saw this same design on the sides of 'fashion' Mini-Minor cars in the sixties, I realised what a lasting impression the design had left on my sub-conscious, and I still feel a sense of unease when I see that basket weave design today!

When I was four, my father, a hockey 'Blue' who played for the Police at Hendon, took me there to see the 1936 Hendon Air display.

I recall getting off the lumbering green coach that dropped us in Aerodrome Rd, and walking onto the airfield - where the Air Museum now stands, to see amongst other wonders, a bright red Fokker Triplane zooming across the field to 'bomb' a wooden fort in the centre, dropping his white powder bombs slap on target.

Although I was quite young, the highlight of the trip was being able to get really close to many of the aeroplanes, including one of the new Spitfires, which was specially on display there.

The whole show must have made a huge impression on me, as I have been an aircraft buff ever since!

It was about this time I was the cause of some considerable embarrassment to my father, concerning an incident in the station Patrol car.

As I was the only child living on police premises, young friends were hard to come by, and necessity being the mother of invention, I made friends with several local Chinese kids, who hung around the yard entrance from time to time.

It was singularly unfortunate therefore, that on one occasion, the station Superintendent should dash out with his driver to answer an emergency call, tyres screeching and electric bell ringing, to discover master Parker in the well behind the front seats, playing cops and robbers, with three Chinese kids!

Within a few months of this and other naughty incidents such as breaking office windows, or riding my tricycle under police horses awaiting parade inspection, we moved from the grim, sooty buildings of Limehouse, to the relatively open spaces of Becontree in Essex.

Here we had our own Council house, complete with fitted bath, in-house toilet, and even a garden.

No more tin baths in front of the fire here!

Despite these and other improvements in our habitation, we still had a glass globe suspended from the ceiling next to the electric light, containing a gas mantle which popped loudly when lit with matches. Talk about belt and braces!

It was now 1938, and I had a younger brother called Terry, just over a year old, who seemed to get all the best attention.

To record these and other events, dad, who was a good photographer, would take photographs of mum and us kids in the garden, using his Kodak Autographic Brownie camera.

I quickly learnt you could influence the content of the final photograph by what objects you carried with you, and the face you pulled whilst the photo was being taken, a fact also noted by my father, who took the necessary remedial action soon afterwards!

Because I had gone to day school in Limehouse since I was three, I was accepted into my new Roding Infants school at the age of five, under the stern tutelage of the Headmistress, Miss Jocelyn.

After a few months, a girl called Helen and I, were separated out from the others during reading lessons, as we were a couple of books ahead of the rest of the class.

I remember how odd it felt, the pair of us sitting either side of a small table set on the verandah in the open, it was as though we were outcasts.

We were very lucky as young children to enjoy an evening film show held once a week in the nearby Roding Junior school, where, sitting cross-legged on the floor, we watched silent black and white films about cowboys, the Inkpot man, and the exploits of Felix the cat, who just kept on walking, walking, walking.

It was all exciting stuff, even to watch the man put the lights up at the most interesting part of the story, and change over to the second reel of film, I was definitely hooked on filmshows!

At the end of the show, a great cheer would go up if the man who put the lights on announced, "Next week children, we're going to have a talkie!" It was an era of new discoveries.

In early December 1938, I was allowed my usual weekly visit to the silent cinema, on condition I met a neighbours' daughter who would take me across the busy main road into the school.

For some reason or other, as I waited on the pavement that night, she failed to turn up, so I carried on alone.

Being winter, it was already pitch dark, so I looked carefully both ways before stepping into the road. As there weren't any car headlights showing, there couldn't be any cars coming I thought, and off I went.

The next thing I remember was waking up in Oldchurch Hospital with my parents sitting next to my bed, obviously very upset about something or other.

Apparently whilst crossing the road to the filmshow, a car had hit me pretty hard, giving me a depression in my skull, the car's chromium stork motif on the bonnet with its long pointed beak, missing my head by inches!

I still have the dent in my skull to this day.

By a strange quirk of fate, uncle Arthur, mum's brother, was passing the scene on his bicycle, and as the ambulance men tucked me in on the stretcher, he noticed a pair of child's wellies sticking out from under the blanket.

He was sure he recognised them as the ones I usually wore, and dashed fifty yards to our house to alert mum and dad as to what was going on.

Somehow dad managed to rush out from home, and scramble into the ambulance, just as it took off for Oldchurch Hospital.

I made a good recovery and was allowed out of hospital on Christmas eve, and remember vividly, getting off the bus at Martin's Corner, and seeing snow flakes swirling through the bright yellow glare of hissing Tilley lamps on the coster-mongers' stalls. It was a magical time.

During the first few days of the war - whatever that was, I became aware of tension in my parents' attitude toward things going on around us, and my father's insistence on absolute silence, as he listened to the six o'clock news on our accumulator powered radio. Strange and serious things I didn't understand were obviously happening not too far away.

My next vivid memory at this time was seeing a large aircraft in the sky over Ford's by the Thames, being buzzed about by two or three smaller ones, and the sound of rapid gunfire coming from the planes - it all seemed very exciting to me, but this view wasn't shared by Mum and Dad.

I can't remember the exact date we stood outside Roding Junior school, but in the early morning sunshine, a large crowd of parents and children milled about, half on, half off the pavement, everyone unusually excited and fussing about.

Mums hugged and kissed their children, some of whom were crying whilst being ushered onto the large double-decker buses, leaving their parents standing anxiously in the street.

Naturally I went straight upstairs to the front, so I could wave to my mum in the street below, and of course to see exactly where we were all going.

Later, in a huge glass-roofed railway station, we were shepherded aboard a steam train, so long, that as we got on in the middle, you couldn't even see the engine down at the front.

By late afternoon, our excitement gone, we arrived in Reading wherever that was, and were allocated to local people as 'evacuees from east London'.

I experienced that peculiar cold feeling of 'un-belonging' drench me, as I was led into a strange house, with even stranger smells, and funny furniture. I didn't like this at all!

The woman of the house had a single child of her own, and obviously had every intention of doing her best for her new evacuee, but didn't appreciate the enormity of what she had taken on.

With little to do after school, except go out and enjoy the glorious weather, it wasn't long before several of us were hauled before the local bobby, accused of trespassing and scrumping from a nearby orchard - what on earth did they think those lovely red apples in an unfenced garden were for?

One evening, after returning home from school I was given tripe to eat for my dinner.

I hadn't even heard of the stuff before, let alone eaten it, but when I did, I found it nauseating.

I stubbornly refused to eat it.

It was produced warmed up for me the next day, and again I refused to eat it, and a terrible row with the woman ensued. Needless to say I was quickly packed up with my little suitcase and gas mask, and sent home in disgrace, unfairly labelled as an unmanageable little ruffian from the East-End.

Some months later, with wartime events taking place that mum still wasn't happy about, we went through the whole rigmarole again!

Red buses queued outside the school with engines running, tearful goodbyes and hugs from mums, and a check by teachers to see we still had our precious gas mask boxes hung round our necks.

With everyone pushing and shoving, especially those who wanted to go upstairs, we climbed noisily aboard our buses and moved off.

To us children it seemed to take forever, until the huge train got to wherever it was supposed to be going, but by late afternoon the name Exeter was called out, and one of the teachers collected a whole bunch of kids bound for something called Weston Super Mare.

Just before dark, we arrived at a little station called Kingsbridge, and, more asleep than awake, herded into a cold coach, to be told 'This is definitely the last part of the journey children, we're nearly there'

Quite a few of us were already asleep before the coach had gone very far, and it was a relief to hear someone say after the bumpy, winding ride, "We're here children, all get down carefully, and stand over there by the wall"

Wherever 'here' was, it was as black as pitch, not a light showed anywhere, and as we shuffled away from the coach, the road dropped away alarmingly down an incredibly steep slope, so steep, that as we stumbled forward in the darkness, we held hands to keep our balance.

Two by two, we were led forward into a tiny pool of torch-light held by someone whose clothes smelled of oilskins and tobacco. Another pair of hands held a clip- board, checking off the various children as their names were called out.

In front of Freddie and me - we had merely been put together for convenience, were Ronnie Steele and his sister, friends from Porters Avenue, whom I knew well.

Ronnie was sobbing uncontrollably, no doubt he was very tired and a bit scared like the rest of us.

"I don't want no boys, only girls" said a loud female voice in the darkness. "I'm sorry, there aren't any more girls, just this one and her brother".

" Oh all right, I suppose I'll take them two then."

Then it was our turn.

"I'll take these two yur" said a kinder voice, and a hand descended onto my head, guiding us out of the light and into the darkness again, while Freddie held on to my hand for dear life.

"Come on boyees" said the voice "We'm only a few yards to go and usn'll be indoors"

Quite suddenly the steep hill that threatened to buckle our knees levelled out, and we were on level ground once more, heading for a doorway where a dim light glowed faintly through deep blue glass panes.

"Are we anywhere near St Budeaux?" I asked, " I've got an aunt who lives there you know"

"It's not all that far away " replied the voice, and as the door closed, a blackout curtain swished into position, and a second light clicked on to reveal the source of the voice.

"I'm William, William Hannaford, and this is my mother, you can call her Auntie Vi"

"I'd rather call her Ma" I said.

"Alright then" said William " Ma it shall be, now lets get'n off to bed, you'm both like cocoa I take it?".

Not many of the youngsters dispatched to Salcombe that day were as lucky as Freddie and me.

Being billeted with the only butchers in town, we had plenty to eat, a lovely big three storey house to explore, and as the days and weeks passed, I knew I had been introduced into a world I never dreamed existed.

A heaven of sandy beaches, lots of boats, and dozens of seagulls - some so tame you could practically touch them as they stood on the low stone walls, the place was a paradise.

We hadn't been in Salcombe more than a few weeks, when a lone German fighter, a Focke-Wulf 190, buzzed the harbour, trying to bomb a large private steam yacht called the "Velda", assuming it to have some military significance.

In fact, apart from having a watchman on board who occasionally got up steam to keep it ticking over, the yacht never moved.

The German's bomb missed the ship completely, skipped on the water, and exploded on a promontory about 400yards from the Hannaford's waterfront home, demolishing a stone built shepherd's hut, but precious little else.

All in all, a bit of a flop.

A few days prior to this incident, William had introduced me to the mysteries of boat rowing, and on the day of the German attack, I had been idly sitting in the dinghy, trying to get the oars to stay in the rowlocks, whilst I pulled against the painter attached to a ring in the wall.

I had progressed to the point of aiming scraps of meat at the gulls yowling on the slipway, when a voice behind me called out "Hallo there" and turning, I saw the town doctor standing in Hannaford's yard.

"How about rowing me across to see the bomb damage then?" he enquired, "It won't take you long".

I suppose I must have agreed, because he hauled on the painter, got in, and pushed us off.

It was obvious to anyone with half an eye, that after half a dozen yards of very erratic progress, the oars jumping out of the rowlocks every few seconds, I was totally inept at the art of rowing.

"You haven't rowed a boat before have you?" said the Doctor, and quite undaunted, placed his hands over mine on the oars, and together we rowed out to see what damage the bomb had done.

Needless to say when we returned, I got a god-almighty rocket from William for my unauthorised use of his dinghy, let alone the worry my hour long disappearance had caused. He was severely narked.

I was only saved from further castigation by the intercession of the doctor, who said it had all been his idea, and I wasn't to be blamed at all.

It was quite typical of William and others I was to learn as I went along, that the incident would be completely forgotten with the admonishment.

However, I would now be taught properly about boats, ropes, oars, and all the other activities associated with water, so I shouldn't get into trouble in the future.

In a small, friendly community like Salcombe, the intrusion of some thirty street-wise London evacuees, was bound to cause friction, and it was only due to the local bobby; a formidable figure under an imposing helmet, wheeling his huge bicycle, that some level of discipline was observed around town.

Directly opposite Hannaford's shop was the town cinema, a small place capable of seating about a hundred people on bench-type seats.

The front two rows were meant solely for the use of children, and being so near the screen, it wasn't easy to take in all the screen at once.

The cinema was run by old Sam Goodyear, a stern, unsmiling man, who stood at the main door, personally head-counting the number of kids he let into his cinema, and when he reached twenty, that was yer lot!

Sometimes, when there were more kids than people, he would make an exception by allowing children to occupy any third or fourth row places left un-occupied at curtain up, but that was a very rare event.

As you stood pushing and shoving, trying to get that extra inch nearer the door for a spare place, you had to keep an ear cocked for the curtain-up music - the Minuet in G by Paderewski.

If you heard that playing, you knew the lights were going down and you might as well go home, there was no point in hanging around any longer!

Looking back on it, Sam Goodyear must have only had two records to in his library, as he always finished with 'Blaze away!' at the end of the show, no doubt to clear the place quickly so he could go home!

My acknowledged prowess in wicked evacuee practices, was crowned when I perfected the art of making 'pennies' out of thin slivers of slate, rubbed circular on concrete jetty walls.

With these, one could operate the penny slot machine, and get free tickets for the ferry crossing to the lovely beaches over at Portlemouth.

This lucrative practice came to a swift end, when the ferryman cunningly demanded payment in cash before boarding his boat, effectively killing the operation stone dead.

Freddie and I attended the junior school at the top of Salcombe hill, and on the way up, we used to twit old 'Strawberry nose' (nick-named by me) a most unfortunate man, who sat daily in the door-way of his cottage half way up the hill, regarding passers-by with a frightening stare, while muttering unintelligible curses.

He had a huge balloon-shaped nose, deeply pock marked all over, the result some said, of a shotgun exploding in his face during earlier poaching days.

It really did look like a huge red strawberry.

He used to swish his stick at you over the half-door, muttering curses and dribbling dreadfully down his chin as you went past, a really frightening man!

In the spring of 1941, mum somehow managed to get a permit to travel by train to Devon, and paid us a visit for a couple of days, bringing with her a new addition to the family, baby Anthony, who was a few months old.

Although it was good to see mum again after a year in Salcombe, the ties and memories of home were fading fast - I felt more at home where I was.

By the time we had been evacuated for two years, I had absorbed a great deal of country habits and values, which I certainly couldn't have experienced at home and I became more 'country' than townie, a most unusual metamorphosis!

Mrs Hannaford had some close friends, Police Sergeant Honeywill and his wife Margaret, who lived in the village of Sticklepath, way up on Dartmoor near Moreton-Hampstead, who came to stay with us in Salcombe once or twice a year.

In return, we visited them a couple of times during the summer, and once, in the depths of winter, when everything was deep in freezing snow, but only after William had somehow managed to get some petrol for his Austin 12.

I recall being as proud as punch when asked to go and bring in a small flock of sheep sheltering from the snow in a paddock half a mile down the road, and somehow managing to do it.

I didn't realise at the time it was a set-up, a test by the locals, who, knowing I was a London evacuee, expected me to fail miserably!

In the autumn of 1941, a heavy German air-raid on Ford's at Dagenham went awry, and as anti-aircraft guns in Parsloes park and Whalebone Lane somehow managed to make things hot for the enemy bombers, one of them unleashed his 250 pounder, straight towards our place at 86 Wren Road.

Just before that particular raid, Mum had gone to visit her mother in Barking,leaving dad at home, to potter around the garden. After the air -raid alert, dad waited by the front door until the bombers were overhead, before taking cover in our Anderson shelter, buried (as per specification), deep in the front garden, and heaped over with several feet of earth.

The German's 250 pounder clipped the corner of our roof, and penetrated deep into the house foundations before exploding, tearing a huge crater in the garden, into which toppled the corner of the house and a badly battered Anderson shelter.

Within minutes the local rescue team were on scene, digging furiously to see if there were any occupants left alive in the badly crumpled shelter, only to be greeted by a dirty, earth spattered creature, cursing incoherently at the Germans and their ruddy bombs. It was dad.

By some miracle, the blast from the bomb had gone away from the shelter, and bearing in mind the impact point was only ten feet away, the shelter had, by it's unique construction saved dad's life.

This incident was far from unusual, as in the next couple of years Anderson shelters proved time and again to be good protection to the occupants from everything but a direct bomb hit.

After a year or so, the trend of war began to swing the allies way, and Salcombe, like so many suitable sites on the south coast, was quickly overrun by British and American troops amassing their equipment for the final assault on France and Germany.

It was our turn to hit back now.

Every lane, field, or secluded spot that could hold guns, tanks, and lorries was in use, and all suitable civilian accommodation taken up as well.

The authorities announced that due to the massive build up of allied forces in the area, and fears for the safety of the evacuees in the event of German retaliatory air-raids, all evacuees were to be sent home immediately.

Within two days we were back home again, dumped into the greyness of war and austerity, with families we hardly knew, feeling like fish out of water.

Gone were the carefree days of sunshine and sparkling waters - and in their place, the uniform drabness of wartime suburbia stretching in all directions, putting a complete damper on my adventurous spirit.

Returning to school, I became acutely aware how far out of step I had become, compared to my contemporaries.

The missed months of schooling, when the Plymouth blitz refugees took over our little Salcombe school as living quarters, came home to roost with a vengeance.

I knew nothing about theorems, or past participles, but knew lots about birds and the countryside - it was obvious I had loads of catching up to do, but could I possibly do it?

We hadn't been back from Salcombe six months, when I heard from dad that Ma Hannaford had been buried alive when her house had been flattened by a German raider's bomb. Who knows what might have happened had Freddie and I still been living there?

She survived only by scrambling into a steel cage built under the kitchen table - a Morrison shelter, as soon as the warning siren sounded, it was all a bit of a miracle.

At school I was considered to be something of an artist, I could draw most of the Walt Disney characters with ease, and was pretty good at still life too, but bird drawing was a different matter altogether.

That required a good knowledge of anatomy, plus the fine detail obtainable from photographs or real life, to get anything like a realistic result, and I soon realised if I wanted to be any good at bird drawing, I had to do something about that.

It was about this time I became aware of the work of Eric Hosking, Walter Higham, George Yeates, and other prominent English bird photographers, whose photographs were appearing in books and magazines such as Picture Post, and my interest in photography began to blossom.

Our Secondary school, Park Modern, was situated within a quarter mile of large gravel pits backing on to Mayesbrook park Barking, a veritable paradise for water birds in such a built up area, and many dinner hours were spent wading the shallow waters searching for nests of Coot, Moorhen and Little Grebe .

As well as birdwatching, the possibility of being chased by the dreaded 'parkies' roaming Mayesbrook Park on their bikes just looking for trouble, added a distinct flavour of excitement to the proceedings.

Thus, each marauding schoolboy carried his shoes knotted by the laces around his neck whilst wading, essential for a quick getaway overland, if chased by the hated 'parkies'.

Sometimes the park-keepers worked in pairs in their attempts to catch us, coming in from each end of the lake in a pincer movement, hoping to trap us against the railings bordering the electric District line.

They failed lamentably to appreciate the daredevil spirit wartime events had engendered, which allowed us kids to execute a quick jump up between the iron spikes of the fence, skip across two sets of live rails (keeping a sharp lookout for oncoming trains) before dashing away on the other side of the tracks, leaving them shouting in fury.

It was about this time I remember dad coming back from work, and as soon as he got in, laying down the law about how he wished he was young enough to 'do his bit' against the Germans and help win the war.

Apparently he had been trotting his police horse nice and quietly down Lodge Ave; near Mayesbrook Park, and had stopped to speak to some soldiers in a large army convoy parked up there.

Out of the blue a German aircraft appeared, and buzzed the convoy, before circling round to give it a second look.

Everybody dived for cover, including dad, who hid behind an emergency water-tank built on the green, holding his horse by the reins.

The German pilot obviously thinking the convoy worth a bit of attention, gave it a squirt from his machine guns, causing dad's horse to rear up and break free, before galloping off into nearby Mayesbrook park.

Dad thought it less than funny to spend a couple of hours chasing the stupid animal across muddy fields in his riding boots, and getting himself rather dirty in the process.

Although I was glad he wasn't hurt, I thought the whole episode absolutely hilarious, and wondered if the German pilot really appreciated what he had done!

It was the 'done thing' amongst us schoolkids to collect shrapnel, bullet cases, shell nose-caps, and all other wartime detritus as souvenirs and status symbols, so when a Spitfire force-landed in nearby Parsloes park, we souvenir hunters descended on it like hungry vultures.

The authorities had left a lone soldier on guard at the front end of the aircraft brandishing his .303 rifle as a deterrent, but it was a simple matter to outwit him, by splitting our group into two raiding parties.

While one lot made tentative forays towards the front part of the aircraft, others at the rear helped themselves to anything they could lay hands on, and vice versa, and soon we had more toot than we could comfortably carry away.

One lad got a whole belt of machine-gun bullets, while I tore a huge chunk off the fuselage containing the RAF roundel, only to be challenged by a War-Reserve PC. who, entering the park in response to calls from the public, threatened to arrest me if I didn't take it back!

In one particularly concentrated raid on Ford's, the jerries dropped a huge number of incendiary bombs which missed their target, and fell into a sports field bordering Goresbrook Rd. and the A13.

Over the jungle telegraph, word quickly got round that bombs were there for the taking - all you had to do was walk over the field until you saw the circular tail fin sticking up through the grass, then, by wedging a couple of sticks under the fin as levers, pull it up.

Once we had a couple of bombs lifted, it was a simple matter to go to the nearest council house that still had a wooden gate left, shut the bomb-head in between the gate and the hinge-post, and while someone pulled the gate shut to hold the bomb in a vice-like grip, unscrew the tail section, and open the bomb.

This produced a beautiful cylinder of polished magnesium, about an inch thick and ten inches long, a highly prized souvenir amongst the lads which you could use to bargain for almost anything!

Looking closely at the bombs we dug up, I noticed the striker-pin, which was supposed to detonate the bomb on impact, had not been fully screwed into position, suggesting the bomb would never have gone off maladjusted like that.

Perhaps there was someone over there doing forced labour under the Germans who was sabotaging their incendiary bombs, I just hoped they never got caught!

Towards the end of my first year at secondary school, class 'streaming' was introduced, which resulted in one or two of our lot going in to 'A' class, most of the others including my friend Dave Summers and myself going into 'B', while the dum-dums ended up in class 'C'.

As most of us were well aware of everyone else's so-called educational achievements from previous terms' work, it all seemed fair enough to me, but it well upset some parents who thought it smacked of class distinction.

In direct contrast to most of the staff, our form teacher Peter Hayward was a pushover, his class lessons were a shambles from beginning to end - he couldn't control a thing.

Pen-nib darts stuck in the ceiling, and grains of rice were 'blowpiped' onto the necks of adversaries through glass tubing nicked from the science lab, and a level of 'who dares wins' pervaded the whole class.

Consequently, apart from being able to identify every Allied, German, Italian, and Japanese aircraft ever made, plus about a hundred English wild birds, complete with their Latin names, very little else was learnt by our lot during his lessons.

It wasn't a bright scenario.

Unfortunately poor old Peter was killed a few months later when a V2 fell on his flat in Barking, and we all felt pretty rotten at the way we had treated him whilst he was still alive, it just wasn't fair.

In his stead we got a fireball of a woman, Miss Haig, a Margaret Rutherford of a character, who straightened us out like a set of pipe-cleaners, and single-mindedly set about forging reasonable young men out of the load of rowdy, know-nothing hooligans she'd inherited.

She was ably backed by baldy Easterby our headmaster, who, black gown flowing and cane swishing, swooped around the school corridors like Dracula, avidly seeking out young offenders to whack with his cane. You certainly didn't tangle with him!

Although the allies were obviously winning the war, German retaliation in the form of flying-bombs, or 'doodle-bugs' as they were affectionately known, increased, and my mother fearing for our safety, arranged for Terry and I to be evacuated, this time to the remote village of Frostenden in deepest Suffolk.

We were billeted on a Mr.and Mrs. Schofield and their daughter, and while walking to school through vast acres of ripening wheat during the glorious summer of 1944, we seemed a million miles away from London, and all that noisy buzz-bombing.

Only the badly shot-up Liberators and Fortresses limping back from Germany, trailing smoke with engines stopped, flares signalling wounded on board, reminded us that a war was still going on out there somewhere.

The Schofield's semi-detached cottage that Terry and I had been sent to, was very old fashioned,and quite basic in its facilities, and I was amazed to see Mrs Schofield cooking our meals on a large double Valour stove, powered by paraffin and a wick!

In the evenings when it got dark, the only illumination was by a single, glass-funnelled, paraffin oil lamp, and when Mr Schofield decided to read his newspaper, Terry and I had to put our homework books away, and go to bed!

Quite suddenly, over a matter of days it seemed, the German offensive increased, causing Doodle-bugs to appear everywhere, scooting low over the countryside like predatory dragonflies, until the situation became identical with the one we had left London to avoid.

I wrote home to Mum and explained the situation, saying that Terry and I preferred to be bombed at home rather than here, and to my surprise we were returned to Becontree forthwith.

One morning as I got up to get ready for school, I heard the sound of approaching aeroplane engines, and looking out of my window, saw three Focke-Wulf 190's roar past our house at roof-top height, so close, I could clearly see the pilots at their controls.

Nose to tail they flashed across nearby Porters Avenue at chimney height before disappearing in the direction of Mayesbrook Park and Barking.

A few seconds later, there was a violent explosion, and by pressing my face hard against the window, I could just see a grey mushroom of smoke ascending into the air half a mile away.

"Mum, mum, they've dropped a bomb, I'm just going out to see what's happened", and before she could object, I was off on my bicycle, racing for the cloud of smoke that was already dispersing in the morning breeze.

In the middle of the road a large white scar seared the concrete, showing where the Germans' bomb had 'skipped' before carrying on through the front of a house in Stonard Rd. entering just above the front door.

You could see the toilet with it's lid still up, through a large hole in the front wall, and I wondered if anyone had been sitting on it at the time!

The bomb had passed through the house and out the other side, to explode inside a row of terraced houses behind, completely demolishing the lot, and killing a school friend of mine in the process.

This must have been about the last incursion by German aircraft into English air-space before the end of the war, incidentally, none of the three German aircraft returned home. We heard on the radio they had all been shot-down by Spitfires somewhere near Oxford.

The waves of in-coming doodle-bugs seemed to have slowed up a bit too, no doubt as a result of attacks by allied aircraft on their launching sites, but another and more insidious weapon began to take their place - the V2 rocket.

The first you knew of a rocket arriving was a god-almighty explosion on the ground, followed by another one high up in the sky.

The reason for this appeared to be that the rocket exceeded the speed of sound on its descent, breaking the sound barrier, leaving the warhead to plummet earthwards at an incredible speed and detonate on impact.

Sometimes in the early morning you could see a vertical vapour trail high in the eastern sky, followed a few moments later by a dull crump a few miles away, announcing the arrival of yet another of Hitler's self-styled 'terror-weapons'.

My school, Park Modern, was situated two miles from home, and as the activities of the German rocketry increased, it was announced that if any explosion took place whilst on our way to school, we had to go immediately to the nearest air-raid shelter and wait for the 'all clear' before proceeding.

This worked quite well in promoting safety, but on arriving at school, you didn't know where the heck your class was - they could be anywhere, although more often than not they were buried in the scaffold reinforced confines of our cloakrooms.

Here, a disembodied voice emanating from somewhere in front of hanging coats and schoolbags, declined totally uninteresting French verbs or mathematics, to an unseen, and couldn't care less class.

One morning I had just passed the last shelter before school, when there was an almighty explosion, followed by a blast of hot air that rocked me off my feet, sending dust and debris everywhere. About a quarter of a mile ahead a huge mushroom of smoke curled into the air, announcing another V2 strike, and yet strangely enough, there was absolute silence.

Nobody appeared on the streets to see what it was all about, and for what seemed ages, I was absolutely alone.

I ran to the end of the road, turned left into Lodge Avenue, and saw the houses near the entrance to Mayesbrook park, the same entrance I was about to use, completely destroyed, and on fire.

As I got to what had been the front of the first house, I came across three frightened children in blackened, tattered clothes, their faces masks of blood and dirt from flying debris.

They were just sitting by their front gate crying.

I pulled them towards the kerb away from the remains of the burning house, and sat them huddled together with their feet in the gutter, just as two men rushed up to see what they could do.

I can't remember what the men said exactly, but they must have asked who I was, and where I lived, because quite quickly I was sent away from the scene, and found myself crossing the park and heading for school.

Just before dawn in early April 1945, I was jarred from sleep by a tremendous roar and rush of air, which hurled dust and debris everywhere, and in the eery silence that followed, I heard a man groaning, "My legs, my legs".

Getting out of bed, I stepped onto a rubble covered floor, which sloped away at a most peculiar angle, and carefully shuffled my way across to Terry and Tony's beds to see if they were ok.

In the half darkness that had a peculiar glow about it, I grabbed them from their beds, and tucked them into mine, covering them with blankets off all three beds, I don't know why, I just did it.

I heard dad call from the landing outside our room "Are you ok in there? I can't open the door"

"Yes dad, were all ok at the moment" and realised that despite it being just about dawn, we could see quite clearly - the gas main in the street had blown apart, sending ten-foot flames licking skywards to illuminate everything in an un-earthly orange glow.

"Don't move about, stay exactly where you are, the floors aren't too safe" dad called from outside the door, so we all crowded into my bed together, snuggling down amongst the dust and grit.

Outside in the street, the man continued to moan "My legs, my legs" until his cries submerged into the general clanging of bells and shouting in the street, announcing the arrival of the fire-brigade and other emergency services.

As daylight gathered, I could see the whole front of the house had collapsed, leaving the contents exposed like one of those doll's houses with the front open, and I felt very exposed.

For some inexplicable reason mum had got dad to turn their double bed round, away from the outside wall the night before, and place its headboard against an inside wall.

The heavy, walnut-veneered wardrobe dad had put in the bed's place, now lay in splinters in the front garden, while their bed remained completely undamaged.

It was a marvellous escape for them, due as mum later claimed, to her 'ESP' telling her to move the bed when she did.

When I eventually managed to get a look outside, I saw the V2 rocket had landed about twenty-five yards in front of our house, digging a huge hole in the communal green, its blast funnelling down several neighbouring streets, helping to dissipate much of its explosive power. We were all very lucky to be alive.

The poor chap who lost his legs, had been standing at the bus-stop fifty yards away, waiting to catch the bus to work, and surprisingly, despite his serious injuries, survived to tell the tale.

It was pretty obvious we couldn't live in our house any longer, it was too unsafe, so we began collecting what we could salvage from the rubble, and stacking it in the front garden to take away.

I was surprised and quite disgusted to hear a patrolling PC.say to dad, that a couple of men had just been arrested for looting from damaged homes nearby, and we ought to keep a close watch on our stuff in case it went walkabouts too.

It was therefore singularly unfortunate for the gas man who, calling within an hour of the incident, entered our house un-announced, and proceeded to empty the electricity meter in the hall.

In seconds he found himself pinned to the floor by his throat, my irate father giving him a very rough time indeed, before throwing him out into the street, despite protestations that he was only doing his job!

It reminded me of a story dad told me when I returned from Salcombe, of a pilot who had been shot down, and parachuted into nearby Parsloes Park, where he had been set upon by some locals who thought he was German.

Hearing the man's unintelligible speech, dad thought so too, and promptly arrested him, hauling him up to Becontree railway station to phone for a police van to take him away.

It was only after RAF personnel from nearby Hornchurch aerodrome appeared, and vouched that the prisoner was in fact a Polish officer, the poor chap was released unharmed!

The next couple of weeks after the bombing were a nightmare, we really had to make-do, living like gypsies in the cloakrooms of nearby St. Erkenwald's school, and I hated every minute of it. Each family had a small area screened off by blankets suspended on ropes, and slept on three-tier metal bunks placed along the cloakroom walls.

When the husbands came back from work at night, and had whatever there was to eat, the lights went out and everyone went to bed. God help any kids that made unnecessary noises that kept the men awake!

After a couple of months of this, we were allocated the up-stairs half of a semi-detached house in Barking, and spent the next two years squeezing round each other, and the piles of salvaged chattels we hadn't the space to use, until our old house was repaired.

During the school summer holidays of 1945, I was rummaging through our side board, which was still buried under a mountain of packages and parcels, and came across Dad's old Kodak Autographic Brownie camera, its shiny black leather case, and brass fittings giving it a really purposeful look.

When dad returned from work I asked him to show me how it worked, knowing that in his early days with the army in India, he had been a very good photographer.

"I'm afraid it's a long time since I did any photography" he said, "I've forgotten all I used to know,-anyway you can't get the film for this size camera any more".

"Well how about this one then?" I said, bringing out an old, red leatherette-covered Box Brownie for his inspection.

"Ah, well that's a different matter, you just put the film in, wind it on, and press the button, I believe you can still get the films for these."

"Can I have it to use then? " I asked. With a nod he agreed, and the seed was sown.

In 1946, at the tender age of fourteen years, I and my friends were sent forth from the relative security of secondary school, to try and find work, competing with men who had just returned from the war.

It didn't seem real, and certainly wasn't easy, there was nothing us kids were any good at anyway.

A guardian angel must have convinced the members of some selection board or other, that my artistic talents were worth developing, and I was offered a place at the South East Essex Technical College in Barking, to study art for two years - an offer I gladly accepted in the light of such hostile working conditions!

Dave Summers, my schoolmate had found it impossible to get anything other than basic manual work, and I didn't fancy joining him on a cold building site casting lintels with the rest of the 'lads', even though the money was supposed to be good.

Mixing concrete didn't seem to fit in with what I thought I wanted to do.

Like most youngsters leaving school and in need of money, I did a paper round each morning before going to college, and collected 10/- a week (50p) for my labours, which was enough to buy one film a week, and have a couple of bob left over for chemicals.

There was just one place near Barking - a typical pre-war Chemists' shop with dark wooden shelves supporting bulbous glass jars with pointed stoppers full of blue or green liquid, which sold 120 size films.

The only snag was, they were ex-RAF aerial films, slit down and re-rolled onto old backing papers, and because of the film's thickness, it behaved like a steel spring when unrolled for development!

Despite this drawback, I could at least get out and take some photographs with Dad's old Kodak box camera!

During our forays into the countryside around Upminster, Dave and I had been allowed access to a small farm adjacent to the 14th century barn in Hall Lane, where a large colony of Jackdaws inhabited rows of very old Walnut trees.

Each tree contained several large holes, and it occurred to me after reading an article by Eric Hosking, that here, amongst the Walnut trees, there must be a nest hole we could line up a camera on, and take some bird pictures.

Sure enough, after a bit of a search, we found one eight feet above ground that looked about right, and if the birds came back to nest in it next spring, we could be in business.

Although I was at College, and Dave was still working on the building site, we went bird watching together most week-ends, and a friendship grew which was to last many years, and survive one or two rather hairy escapades as well!

In the spring of 1947, Dave and I returned to the farm at Upminster and began building our first 'hide' for bird photography in the Jackdaw colony.

A mountain of turfs discarded by the farmer was laboriously carried to the site of the Jackdaw's nest, and arranged in a four- foot square pile, six feet away from the base of the tree, until it reached a point nearly level with the nest hole.

Over the next couple of weeks we watched the Jackdaws' reactions to our hide from afar through binoculars, and were pleased to see the birds took no notice of our construction at all.

So far, so good.

With barely concealed excitement, we watched and waited during the next week, until the young jackdaws could be heard calling from inside the hole, indicating we could now start photography. The camera was carefully placed on a nice flat turf, and I squinted through the tiny ground glass viewfinder, to line it up with the nest hole.

Satisfied with the view, I asked Dave to cover me with a piece of tarpaulin, and scatter it with grass, so the Jackdaws wouldn't know I was there, and leave me to it.

It wasn't long before the adults returned to feed their young, taking not the least notice of the addition to the turf pile a few feet away, and as the bird stood outside its nest hole, I gently pressed the shutter - my first bird photograph had been taken!

During the hour I spent under the stifling canvas, I managed to take four shots before Dave came to let me out, this action being necessary so the birds wouldn't associate the hide with someone suddenly appearing so close to their nest.

On developing the film and contact printing it, I experienced what all nature photographers suffer throughout their working lives - the almost result!

This is where the concept is good, and everything appears to have gone down well, but the small print in Murphy's law subverts the whole process, and renders it fit only for the waste bin!

The shots of the Jackdaw were well exposed and reasonably sharp for the camera I was using, but I hadn't appreciated the blades of grass in the turf the camera was standing on, getting in the way of the lens, and partly obscuring the picture!

Such fine detail was not easily visible through the tiny viewfinder fitted to the primitive box camera, and by the time we were able to return to the Jackdaw's nest to correct the error, the young had flown!

Even so, a valuable lesson had been learnt, namely to check, and check again, Murphy was never far away!

Over the next few months I continued to try and master this new hobby, but with very little to go on, and no-one to ask for help, I made howler after howler.

Even though the summer had been good, the following winter was the coldest I remembered in ages, with bitterly cold winds and snow seeming to go on forever, and I can't stand the cold!

When we woke in the morning it was quite common to find our breath frozen into icicles on the eiderdown, and, once up and about, it was necessary to rub ice off the inside of the living room windows to see outside, despite a small coal fire burning in the room.

Coal was so hard to come by, it was virtually non existent, and when dad heard there was to be an allocation of a hundred weight per person at Barking goods-yard sidings the next day, he asked me to take our tall-sided wheelbarrow along and get some.

It was a good three miles walk to Barking, even using all the short cuts I knew, and dad's old barrow was a bit of a menace with its solid tyres in the snow and ice, but after an hour and a bit I got there - only to find the allocation already finished.

It hadn't even lasted until ten o'clock!

Knowing dad would be pretty mad if I came back with nothing, I took the hand shovel and started to rake up discarded rubble where the coal stock had been, and soon had the barrow filled with a mixture of sugar-lump sized coal, liberally mixed with snow and ice.

It was only when I went to move the filled barrow, I realised how damned heavy it was, I could hardly push it, it had to be pulled to get it moving at all!

To save bumping up and down the kerb each time I met a junction, I tried walking in the road, but the drifted frozen snow in the gutters made progress difficult, and it was necessary to keep out in the open road where traffic had partially cleared the surface.

The stops for recovery of breath and muscles, got longer and longer, and it was a great relief to see a little way ahead the sight of home, and rest.

Crossing the last main road before home, I was forced to let the barrow down over a kerb, and as I did so, the nearside wheel collapsed under the strain in a shower of rusty spokes.

We weren't going any further today!

Fortunately a man from the house outside which I had come to grief, called his neighbour, and together they dragged the barrow into his front garden. At least it was safe there.

Despite all this, when dad came home and heard the news, he got pretty annoyed, and blamed me for not taking more care of his rotten barrow on my way back.

I felt pretty narked about that, feeling that I had done very well to get anything from Barking in the first place!

I had recently progressed from using the ex-RAF wartime films, to the trying the new Selo Ortho films, as someone had told me you could develop these using a red light.

If you did so, you could actually see what you were doing whilst developing - it sounded too good to be true, but I thought I'd give it a try!

Without more ado, I bought a small packet of Pactum MQ developer, and some fixer, painted a 40 watt bulb red with some paint from the shed, and got cracking.

My first subject for this experiment was our black and white mongrel dog, who posed very nicely in the garden, while I made eight exposures and wound off the film.

The developer was warm - I don't know what the temperature was, we didn't have a thermometer apart from our clinical one, so in the cubby-hole under the stairs I unrolled the film from its backing paper, and began developing in the dish.

Like the man said, under the red light you could actually see the exposures coming up, and I see-sawed the film through the semi-circular dish and roller, for another minute or so.

After checking the image was visible through the back of the film - indicating the process was complete, I transferred the lot to the fixer and stabilised the image.

Now we would see just what this photography lark was all about! After a brief wash, I held the film up to daylight and was both amazed and puzzled to see our dog perfectly reproduced, but not in the negative form as I had expected!

There he was, just as in real life, white face, black body and tail, with a white tip on the end, how was that possible?.

It was only much later, when I showed the film to a 'proper' photographer the mystery was solved. I had slowly fogged the film during processing - due to the un-safe safelight, and had produced a completely reversed image of my subject.

I was a bit ahead of things with my accidental 'reversal' image processing!

Through a friend of my father's, I heard about a Camera club in Dagenham which welcomed beginners like me, so I decided to join, I wasn't getting anywhere floundering about in the dark so to speak!

Among the club's more prominent members was Mr. Wren, the man responsible for the superb filming of the blitz from the top of St. Paul's Cathedral during the air-raids.

From the high standard of his photographs, he obviously knew a heck of a lot about photography, so I approached him with my problems.

Fortunately he lived only half a mile from our home, and taking me under his wing, said if I cared to buy another Selochrome film and expose it, he would show me the proper way to develop it.

Furthermore, if there was anything on it that looked promising, he would also show me how to enlarge it as well!

The next weekend Dave and I were at our usual venue, the farm at Upminster, and I looked around for the sort of shots that might make an interesting photograph. By evening, I only had one shot left, and wondered what on earth I could use it on without wasting it.

On the edge of a nearby potato field under the Walnut trees, was an old seed-drill, a large wooden-wheeled piece of apparatus silhouetted perfectly against a lovely sunset. That I thought, would be my last shot.

I knew enough about taking pictures to know that in ordinary sunshine, the instantaneous shutter setting was quite adequate, but if the lighting was dull, a time exposure was required. Placing the camera on the ground, I tilted it upwards slightly by resting on a piece of stone, and engaging the time exposure lever, gave an exposure of ten seconds which I felt was about right.

Subsequently I was invited to bring my film to Mr. Wren's purpose-built darkroom, and my eyes were opened as to how a professional photographer really worked.

It was all wonderfully organised, and spotlessly clean.

With everything to hand, the film was quickly developed, and in the red light I saw the whole process from beginning to end, it was a real eye-opener.

"If you can come back one day next week" said Mr. Wren, "We'll enlarge one of these for you, they all look pretty good, especially the last one showing the farm equipment".

As I had made the enlargement myself, I was allowed to enter the print of the seed-drill in silhouette, in the camera club competition, and was more than delighted to gain second place from a dozen entrants in the beginner's section.

It was also from Mr. Wren I learnt that if you put a piece of tissue paper across the open back of the box camera, with the lens open, you could actually see the main point of focus - normally a disappointing six feet away, in glorious colour.

However, if you fitted a three dioptre spectacle lens to the front of the camera with sticky tape, the point of focus was now reduced to about eighteen inches, ideal for photographing flowers, butterflies, or even birds' nests!

To focus the subject accurately, I made a simple 'U' shaped probe out of wire, and fixed it to the front of the camera, so that when a flower or butterfly was between the tips of the probe, it was in focus.

Although the standard of definition gained from the meniscus lens was pretty abysmal compared to the stuff other club members were producing, I continued to get the odd second or third place in competitions, which made me feel I was at last getting to grips with this photography 'lark'.

As a result of all this keen-ness in my new hobby, I took a very basic photography course at the Technical College, run incidentally by a Mr. Parker, (no relation) which amongst other things, gave me the opportunity to do some contact printing and a little enlarging, thus gaining valuable hands-on experience and a 'feel' for the whole process.

There was a second hand shop in Barking which sold lots of things boys were interested in, such as model aircraft engines, Hornby trains,roller skates, sheath-knives and so on, but one item took my interest above all others, a Perma Plus camera.

This peculiar looking, wedge-shaped camera took photographs at different speeds, depending on which way you held it, due to its weighted shutter.

Held horizontally it fired at 1/50th second, vertically at 1/150th, and finally 1/450th when held in the opposite direction,the specification which interested me the most.

I had been watching some dirt-track riders practising on the clinkerbeds near Ford's by the A13. and I desperately wanted to get some shots as they skidded round a curve, dust and ashes flying, it looked really spectacular.

The price of the second hand Perma was £6.10 shillings, but as I only received 10 shillings a week from my paper round, I was quite a bit of cash short.

Would dad buy it for me, and let me pay him back over twelve weeks until I was square?

Unfortunately not, he had other commitments that required all his immediate savings, and a loan was out of the question, but he did sympathise greatly with my disappointment.

# Chapter Two

During the years since my return from Salcombe, I had written to William and Ma Hannaford a couple of times, expressing my desire to see them again, especially as I understood Ma was now pretty frail, and not mobile at all, but William's return letters hadn't seemed too keen on the idea.

As the August holidays were now in full swing, my mother, always one to suggest something out of the ordinary said. "Why don't you just cycle down to Salcombe and see the Hannafords for a few days, you could always go on to your aunt Kath's place in St. Budeaux if you're stuck".

I thought about it for a while, and looked at some pre-war road maps we had of the route to Devon - a whacking 240 miles to Plymouth which seemed a hell of a long way, besides, where would I sleep?

I also remembered hearing from someone that you should never go back to a place that has given you such special memories, it never works, perhaps I ought to forget the whole thing and go somewhere else?

However, things were given an strong nudge in the Devonshire direction when I came second in a National road safety poster competition - the prize for this noble effort being a new 26" Rudge Special bicycle.

Now that I had the means to make the trip to Salcombe more safely, I felt I really had to go.

The eventual journey to Devon was hard physical exercise, but quite uneventful really - I reached Salisbury at the end of the first day, and checked in to a B&B, before pushing on to Salcombe the next.

Traffic on the A303 was quite spasmodic, and along the great open stretches like Salisbury plain, you were lucky if you saw more than one or two cars in an hour.

It was great to be able to stop and photograph whatever took your fancy, without any hassle, or just sit down to admire the view. I felt as free as a bird!

On my arrival in Salcombe, it was quickly apparent there was no room for me to stay at the Hannaford's place, partly due to Ma being bed-ridden, but mainly due to the fact that William had sold the whole business to a London family, while he and Ma now occupied a small flat above the shop.

William explained, he felt that working in the shop, plus coping with the delivery rounds was getting too much for him at his age, and he wanted to slow down, so he and Ma had moved into the little flat upstairs.

To make ends meet he now worked part-time in the very shop that had been the family business premises for over 60 years.

So much for going back to re-live old memories!

I soon found a pleasant B&B in Shadeycombe, a quiet place near the very spot we had got off the coach from Kingsbridge as evacuees several years before, and used that as a centre to explore the countryside around.

Since I was now really into birds and photography, I just had to visit the magical Bolt Head, to see for myself the cliffs where all the gulls in Salcombe apparently nested.

I mentioned this idea in passing to William, who threw up his hands in horror, saying the area was far too dangerous for someone to visit on their own - I should wait to see if there were others who might want to go there, and join them, for safety reasons.

But me being me, I decided it couldn't be all that dangerous, and would go on my own anyway.

Over the next few days I got to know the cliffs pretty well, and found lots of Herring Gulls still nesting even though it was mid- August, with many large chicks nearly ready to fly.

As I climbed down to their nesting area, anxious calls of the gulls overhead caused the chicks to tuck their heads into sea pinks or rock crevices in an attempt to hide, leaving their big legs and rear-end sticking into the air in full view. It looked quite funny and made an interesting photograph.

My last day in Salcombe was a beauty, blue skies, with glorious sunshine sparkling off the water, just as I remembered it from years gone by, so I decided to walk the cliffs from Bolt head to Bolt Tail, a distance of about six miles, as a fond farewell.

I hadn't been to Bolt-tail since 1942. when the beach was mined against German invasion and out of bounds to everyone.

I thought it would be nice to see what it looked like now, free of all that wartime clutter, there might even be Terns nesting there.

About halfway along the walk, I stopped in the bright sunshine, to photograph the scene where a couple of Gannets dived from a height of fifty or sixty feet into the sea below to catch fish, their white shapes clearly visible below the surface.

To get a better view, I scrambled off the path and onto a huge boulder sticking out of the steep shale slope, and stood there, photographically framing the view far below, king of all I surveyed.

Suddenly, and without warning, the boulder rolled out of the shale cliff, just like drawing a tooth, and rumbled down the sixty degree angle slope, with me, head-first in hot pursuit.

In that weird slow motion action, peculiar to situations of sudden danger, I saw the boulder in front of me lazily hit the final lip of rock in a whip-crack of white smoke, and slowly disappear from view towards the sea below.

The next instant I felt a harsh tearing in my right thigh and both arms, before coming to a swift halt in mid air.

Far below, a huge waterspout erupted as the boulder crashed into the rock-filled sea, sending Herring gulls wheeling and calling from the cliffs in panic.

In a daze I hung head-down, yo-yoing slowly up and down, while my brain came back into real time, trying to figure out what the hell had just happened.

Very slowly I turned my head to the right, and saw two rusty strands of barbed wire wrapped around my arm, which then seemed to continue somewhere down my right side, while my left arm was held into my waist, also trapped by strands of barbed wire.

It seemed like ages, I just hung there gathering my wits, before deciding I had to do something about the silly situation.

By some miracle my glasses were still in place, at least I'd be able to see what I had to do next, whatever the hell that was!

With only my knees and lower legs touching the rocky cliff edge, and the rest of me in space, I thought how the hell do I get out of this one?

Very gingerly, in case the rusty wire broke, I pushed with my arms against the restraining wire, and scrabbled sideways with my knees, in an attempt to draw myself back onto solid ground.

The fact that I was hanging head-down at 45 degrees didn't help much, but luckily my toes found a grip on something, and I slowly bent my knees, doubling up until my elbows rested where my knees had been before, and I lay gasping on solid ground.

It was a good job I was pretty fit from cycling and climbing, otherwise I don't think I could have managed the awkward manoeuvre at all!

Gently I untangled the barbed wire from my arms, thankful I was wearing a thick pull-over, which had helped reduce the lacerations a bit, and sat back to look at the wire strands which had undoubtedly saved me from serious injury, or even death.

For about a hundred yards at this point, the cliffs had angle iron posts driven into the shale, with two strands of barbed wire running along the contour, remains no doubt, of the defences against possible invasion during the war.

An incongruous thought passed through my mind that the men who put the wire up years ago, would never have thought their work would be crucial in keeping someone in, rather than out!

I made my way back up the steep shale slope, miraculously finding my camera wedged in the Sea-Pinks, and continued towards Bolt tail, William's dire warning flooding back into my mind - he was right, it was bloody dangerous!

Deciding that discretion was definitely the better part of valour, I told no-one about my lucky escape, and quickly forgot all about it.

Back home once more, I finished my time at college, and with the two subjects of art and basic photography under my belt - or so I thought, began my assault on the advertising world in the city of London.

Full of confidence and hope, I did the rounds over the weeks, only to find the said world didn't really require me at all, I was quite, quite, surplus to requirements!

As a stop gap however, my father got me a job with a friend of his, working as an apprentice welder in Plaistow - so much for the arts!

For a year I buckled down, and tried to learn a trade which gashed and crushed my hands, burnt my clothes, covered me in oil and paint, and entailed a six-mile cycle ride in each direction along the A13, all for the princely sum of 25/- (£1.25).a week!

I had never worked so hard in all my life, lift this, push that, help Fred dismantle that boiler etc; the job was intensely physical, and I was often completely knackered at the end of the day.

Strangely enough the instructor at night-classes I attended after work, said he thought I had a flair for gas welding, and should study hard to make a serious go of it, but I had my doubts.

For the umpteenth time, I took a day off work to hawk my portfolio round the London agencies, and was eventually successful in getting the promise of an interview in a month's time, when the studio boss returned from a trip to Europe.

In the meantime, I carried on with the welding, working with characters whose dinner-time relaxation varied between seeing who could throw a 56lb weight the furthest in the work yard, or playing three-card brag for cash, using an oily pack of cards so worn, you could hardly distinguish their face values!

A few days before I was due up town for my art interview, we were in a smoke-filled workman's cafe near Prince Regent's Lane Plaistow, having a cuppa, when one of the lads mentioned the place had a second or `knocking-shop' upstairs (whatever that was).

A few minutes later, a chap who had been upstairs to the afore mentioned `shop', returned through the curtained door of the main cafe, and smilingly dropped something into a workmates half finished mug of tea, without being seen.

Moments later, the unfortunate man drained his tea, to discover an offensive rubber object lying in the bottom of his mug!

With a terrible roar, he exploded like a mad man, sending all and sundry diving for cover, as he fought to get his hands on the laughing offender just leaving the front door.

I had been sitting on the end of the bench next to the gangway, and as everyone got up, fell to the floor between a mass of legs and boots, lucky not to get my head kicked in!

As we made our way back to the lorry, I innocently enquired what had caused the terrible uproar in the cafe.

Back came the foreman's laughing reply, "Later son, later"

My art interview in London the following week was a success, I was to be taken on as an apprentice artist after giving my present firm a week's notice - the welders could now go jump in the lake!

My new workplace, Wadham Artists studio in Wardrobe Court, Blackfriars, had eight very talented commercial artists, all sitting at their own special easels, complimented by a small photographic studio, which undertook all the black and white copying of artwork and lettering, using a wooden half-plate camera for the job.

Apart from learning how to draw commercially, I was introduced to a technical camera with movements for correcting perspective, double dark-slides, retouching of negatives and prints, and the technique of using black and white prints oversprayed with colour, to produce superb colour originals.

It was all quite new and exciting.

The down side of the job was that although I saw, and took in everything there was to see, I was never given any drawing of my own to do, just fetching tea, and delivering art work to clients around London such as Harrods, Selfridges, and Gamages.

The devil finding work for idle minds to do, I soon twigged that if I asked the Italian cafe owner downstairs to give me six very strong cups of tea for the lads break, I could water the pot down from the hot water tap in the toilet and end up with the twelve cups the studio really required, pocketing the difference.

This practice undertaken twice a day, throughout the week gave a big boost to my meagre income, but brought howls of disgust from the artists, who slated the Italians' tea-making efforts as a load of crap!

Quite often I was asked to deliver urgent artwork to the agencies' head office in Curzon St. which meant I got the bus from Blackfriars to Piccadilly Circus, and walked down Piccadilly past Clarges St. to White Horses St. passing through Shepherd's market before entering Curzon St.

There was a small butcher's shop in the market which sold Quail and Lapwings' eggs in baskets, and had bunches of cock Pheasants and Woodpigeons hanging up, hook through beak, for sale.

In addition to these delights, I got to know on a visual basis, some of the ladies of pleasure who sallied forth from various doorways as I passed through the market, intoning "All nice an' clean an' fresh, the first today, how about it dear?"

The day to day management of the art studio was taken firmly in hand by Mr.Brewer, a rather pedantic, military looking chap in his fifties, who sat in a little office day after day, only appearing amongst the rest of us at the beginning and end of each day.

Any communications regarding the flow of work, had to be made to him personally in his office.

Each evening, he would stride purposefully from his office, complete with beautifully folded, rapier-like umbrella and jauntily tilted bowler hat, growling a gruff `goodnight' to anyone who happened to be nearby.

This religiously followed chain of events, hadn't gone un-noticed by Laurie, a middle-aged, laid -back artist, who made it quite clear from his politically left of left views, he didn't give a fart for the jumped-up manager, and devised a cunning way to take him down a peg or two.

One evening, as I got back to the studio from delivering art work to Selfridges, I noticed everybody was still in their places despite the time being a few minutes after five, what was going on?

Suddenly I saw Laurie giving me frantic hand signals to attract my attention, and when our eyes met, he put a finger to his lips requesting me to keep schtumm. What was he up to?

From where we sat, it was easy to see Mr. Brewer take his brolly and bowler off the hat stand, clap the bowler to his head, adjust it carefully in front of his mirror to the correct angle, before wheeling smartly out the door.

As soon as he was out of sight, I asked Laurie what was going on, but he refused to tell me, saying "Just be here each evening before we go home, and I think you'll join us in a laugh at our manager friend"

The next evening at five o'clock, everyone was busily engaged in something or other, whilst furtively keeping an eye on old Brewer's office.

This time he took a little longer to get his bowler at the right angle of dangle, but eventually satisfied, he emerged with a gruff goodnight, barely audible through his moustache.

"It's beginning to work!" Laurie said with a laugh, "A day or two from now and he won't know if he's bored or counter-sunk, that'll learn him"

Still none the wiser I went home, wondering what intrigue they were hatching, but as I was the only one `not in the know' I would just have to wait to see the outcome of this peculiar situation.

Next day, at five o'clock sharp, with everyone still at their places, Brewer reached for his bowler and brolly in the time honoured fashion, but seemed to have considerable difficulty in getting the bowler to sit properly, and it was a minute or two before he appeared at the door, looking quite flustered and annoyed.

We didn't even get his usual gruff goodnight, something was obviously upsetting him.

Stan said to Laurie, "How much longer do you think you can get away with it, surely he'll twig there's SOMETHING wrong soon, then we'll be in the shit!"

"I reckon another day should do it " replied Laurie, " If it doesn't go then, I'll give up!"

Hearing this, I was absolutely bursting to know what they were up to, but nobody was going to tell, I'd have to be patient and wait.

The next day being Friday, I thought whatever they had planned must happen today, otherwise it would be too late, the week-end would be here, and I'd miss it.

Just after half past four, Brewer announced that he was off early, and we could follow as soon as we had cleared our work, something I had never experienced since I started there, that sort of generosity wasn't in his nature.

He reached for his brolly and bowler in the usual manner, but after tipping the bowler forward at the correct jaunty angle, it just sat ludicrously on he top of his head.

It just didn't fit anymore.

Muttering to himself, he took the bowler off and carefully examined the inside, but there was nothing amiss there, and he was just putting it back on his head for another try, when there was a loud pop, and the lid came off, leaving him standing there with the rim in his hand.

"What the bloody hell's going on?" he roared, "Who's been interfering with my hat?"

At that, Laurie and some of the others burst into fits of laughter, someone saying "What's the matter, your head getting too big, or is your bowler shrinking?"

Shaking with anger, old Brewer threw the remains of his bowler into the waste basket, and stormed out the office hatless, thundering down the stairs like a madman.

"What did you do to old Brewer's bowler?" I asked.

"Not a lot" answered Laurie with a grin. "I found a nice thin piece of piano wire at home which I reckoned would fit nicely under the bowler's black ribbon. I thought if I tightened it just a twist a day with my pliers, we could have some fun seeing Brewer trying to get it on, but I didn't expect the wire to cut right through the bloody thing!

In early 1950, a visiting rep; whom I was friedly with, knowing of my frustrated artistic endeavours, suggested I contact a firm he visited in Holborn, and take my portfolio of work with me.

If my face fitted, and my work was ok. I might actually get a job drawing ads. and more to the point, I would get more money too!

An interview was quickly arranged, and again, I was lucky and got the job, but Wadham studios were pretty narked about the whole kaboodle, muttering something about unfair poaching of their junior staff.

Ark's Publicity in Holborn, was one of those firms which gave you an instant feeling of belonging the minute you stepped through their door. It was as though the place was one big happy family, which indeed it really was, and I quickly found out that Alec Guinness the actor had recently left there, and was still sorely missed.

From the directors down through the art dept; the space buyers, copy writers, even old Mr.Spriggs in the basement, who just tied up and despatched parcels all day, everyone seemed pleased just to be there.

I was placed under Bill White, head artist and ex-Royal Marine, who spoke immaculate Oxford English, but with a wicked sense of humour that belied his stern six-foot, fifteen-stone appearance. Bill was the most genuine and heart-warming man I was ever to work with, and amongst his many talents, could recite the coarsest of limericks with such immaculate eloquence and delivery, they sounded pure Shakespeare!

Work was now a pleasure, and I enjoyed being given simple drawings to do for advertisements appearing in the National press - it was great to see my work in print at last!

Just as I was beginning to settle in, my stint of national service loomed on the horizon, and Bill suggested that rather than just being cannon fodder, I ought to go for a trade of my own choosing, something like photography, how about it?

It certainly made sense to me.

All too soon the day of my departure from Ark's arrived, and the sorrow at leaving such a good firm, was tempered by the promise that I would be more than welcome to my old job on return to civvy street, if I wanted it.

# Chapter Three

The following week, my registration for national service at a recruiting centre in Wanstead, exhibited all the signs of a Whitehall Theatre farce, as I sat waiting for the professional-looking, hard-bitten army sergeant to finally speak.

"Name?" he barked.

"What do you think you want to do?" was his next question.

"Photography please".

"Ho! - photography as a National Serviceman? no chance!" his expression suggested that it would be far easier for me to crawl through the eye of a needle.

"I'm willing to volunteer for three years if I can get it " I replied.

His face changed like magic.

"Good lad, take the King's shilling will yer?" and pulling out a form from his folder, stuck my name on it and said, "Take this 'ere, to that officer in there" and pointed me in the direction of a room at the end of the hall.

After signing another form, and shuffling off to take a rather protracted written examination with about a hundred other young lads, we were all told to wait quietly until our names were called, and NO smoking!

After an interminable wait a voice bawled 'SILENCE!'

"When I call yer name, git over 'ere" intoned a lucid army corporal.

"An' when I call the second lot, git over there," he said, waving his pencil at the far end of the hall.

And the reading began.

The first seven names were read out in double quick time, our corporal shouting "Right you lot, Royal Navy - get mobile!"

Next, about thirty names were read staccato fashion from the same sheet, "Right - RAF you lot, - move to the end of the 'all NOW!"

"The rest of you lot are Army, so you can stay where you are fer the minute".

A bitter voice shouted "I wanted to join the Navy, why can't I?" another said, "I wanted the RAF, not the bloody army".

"Shut-up you lot, do as you're told" said an RAF officer, and order was quickly restored. We did exactly as we were told.

The Officer I had gone to see asked if I had done any photography in civvy street, and bending the truth a little, I said "Yes of course".

"Ok then, what I'll do is send you for a trade test to one of our trade centres, you can attend RAF Chigwell if you like, that's near you, and if you satisfy them, we'll put you forward for photographic training, ok?".

I felt as pleased as punch with the way things were going so far, but rather apprehensive about what questions I might be asked at RAF Chigwell when I eventually got there.

The funny thing was, having lived in the area for quite a few years, and knowing Chigwell pretty well, I wondered how on earth I could have missed seeing an RAF Station with its runways and hangars all these years?

The answer was quite simple.

RAF Chigwell was just a collection of Nissen huts, all painted blue and hidden away behind tall iron gates at the back end of nowhere!

When I arrived, like a visitor from outer space, I wandered in through tired looking gates, hoping someone might help me, but there wasn't a soul in sight.

One of the nearby huts had its door open, swinging gently in the breeze, so I walked across, opened it fully, and shouted inside, "Anyone there"?.

"There's no need to shout" said a voice, "I'm over here, what do you want?".

In the shadows, broken only by sunlight filtering through a wired-glass window, I saw an RAF Corporal, his back to me, slowly sweeping the floor, raising millions of dust particles that glittered like diamonds in the sun.

"I've come for a trade test in photography please"

Without even turning to look in my direction, or interrupt the steady sweep of his broom, the Corporal nodded his head left, towards a bench containing a huge enlarger. "What's that?"

"An enlarger" I replied confidently.

"Good, and what's that there?" he said nodding toward another bench in front of him.

"It looks like a long-lens aerial camera to me" I replied.

"Good", he said, "And what's that?" nodding to his right.

"A print glazing drum, a safelight and contact printing box"

He turned round, and with a smile like a teacher hearing the correct answers from a star pupil, said "Great, you've got 'em all right, give us your documents and I'll send 'em off for you right away - tatty-bye". And that was that.

It's a sad fact of life that anyone who has been in the mob easily re-calls horror stories related to square-bashing, and the harsh initiation into the peculiarities of service life, and we were to be no exception to that rule.

At Cardington in Bedfordshire, we were marched here, doubled there, kitted out, medically examined, (cough please), until after three days of processing we were 'em-bussed' outside Cardington's gi-normous airship hangars, 'entrained' at the camp railway station, and 'de-trained' at RAF Henlow, where within minutes of arrival, our feet didn't even begin to touch the ground!

The hideous exit from a warm bed for wash and breakfast at 0530, (It was still dark outside and snowing for God's sake!) and the fact that we had some right herbs amongst our number who couldn't even make their beds, and fell on the floor during the night, made everything seem so unreal!

I thought it was a nice touch by some thoughtful soul to provide neat bundles of firewood next to the stove, so that when we came in from a day's training, we had some means of keeping warm.

It was also enlightening to see how some people grabbed a bed in the darkest corners of the billet, as if to hide and keep out the way, while others like myself with an eye on comfort, chose a bed near the coke-bunker and stove, and enjoyed the warmth of the fire.

At lights out, it was surprising how snug your bed felt after half a dozen of the lads had sat on it all evening, talking about this and that!

The downside of this coveted situation was, whoever delivered the week's ration of coke to the billet, always seemed to spill lots onto the linoleum floor, which had to be grafted on hands and knees to assume a mirror-like finish for inspections, and of course my bed-space was next to that gritty coke bunker!

Our new life was hard but fair, although it did pose a rather nasty shock for some. The drill Sergeant's rancorous language, honed over many intakes to perfection, was designed to turn the rabble in front of him into a cohesive unit as soon as possible.

One tirade began "When I says jump up, jump up, an' when I says come down, come down, an' gawd 'elp any man what comes down before I says so!" caused me to snigger audibly, earning me an earbending tirade six inches from my face, and a double round the square, with my rifle held at arm's length above my head.

In the exceptionally bitter and snowy weather, a hundred men were reduced to using the one unfrozen toilet still available, kept operational only by the continued presence of a Valour oil-stove and a steady succession of warm bums.

A society leveller if ever there was one!

Once the terrible weather had abated and the toilets became usable again, the powers that be, decided it would be as good a time as any to re-decorate the lot, even down to new door handles and SINK PLUGS - I mean, what selfish prat would nick the old ones just to make sure HE had one? Just about everyone I reckoned.

This we were told, would serve two purposes in one fell swoop, 'A' - to give the tatty toilets a long overdue face-lift and re-furbishment, and 'B'. obliterate the dreadful graffiti that adorned the plaster-board walls of the bogs from top to bottom.

'They' weren't going to allow the sexual deviations depicted thereon to remain visible, as they were deemed to be in very bad taste.

Furthermore 'they' certainly weren't prepared to tolerate remarks depicting the dubious ancestry of senior officers and drill-instructors to remain there either, THAT was prejudicial to good order and discipline!

'Anyone, but ANYONE', droned the Flight-looey at morning parade, 'Who is found to have written words or drawn on the newly matt-painted walls will be guilty of destruction of Air Ministry property, and will be dealt with accordingly'

This dire threat obviously carried a lot of weight, and coupled with lightning inspections of the toilets by snoopy drill instructors, allowed the walls to remain in pristine condition for quite some time.

That is, until one week-end when there were few staff about, and a lot of the lads were away on their first 48 hour pass, then the devil struck with glee!

Going in to 'trap -one' I saw some Philistine had written at head-height on the clean wall, 'Masturbation' in inch-high black letters.

Fearing I might be cornered and questioned by one of the predatory drill-instructors, I rapidly moved into trap two, which was still in pristine condition.

The next day out of curiosity, I looked into trap-one again, and now beneath the offending word was another, this time it said 'Copulation' and I smiled, thinking here we go again, punishment be damned, someone wasn't scared of their threats at all - the instructors would go bananas!

Like a snowball rolling down hill, additions to the list in trap one grew daily, and soon we had 'Flagellation', 'Titillation', 'Initiation', and even 'Birth of a nation'.

I must admit I curled up in helpless laughter when after a few days the list reached the floor, ending with the words 'Paddington Station'. There were definitely some right wags about!

Whilst 'bulling-up' for a particularly critical billet inspection, the clannish 'northerners' in their half of the hut, steadfastly refused to clean anyfurther than halfway down the billet, insisting that the 'southerners' do the other half, even though they outnumbered us two to one, and the whole place nearly came to blows!

Despite this simmering tribalism, we all became well acquainted with that lovely service idiom which says 'If it moves, salute it, if it doesn't move, pick it up, and if you can't pick it up, PAINT IT!' and we splashed pots of white paint over everything.

Ten weeks later as the final passing out parade drew to a close, rifles crashing in unison and bayonets flashing in the sun, my parents, along with countless others must have asked 'Is this really our grotty, horrible little son, the one who left home a short while ago. How come all this spit and polish and discipline in so short a time?'

Obviously the age of miracles had not entirely passed!

Sergeant Savoury, (As in tasty, remember that lads!) our billet sergeant now addressed us for the last time in his capacity as our mentor.

"No doubt those of you wot have brains will remember the care for your personal well-being, wot resulted in them neat bundles of firewood being stacked ready for your use when you arrived?".

"And some of you might also remember the little exercise we gave you in dismantling them old packing cases, and constructing the neat little picket fence wot surrounds your billet today?

Well, I want you to feel the same compassion for the blokes wot follow you, by dismantling the fence and chopping it up into neat bundles of firewood, and placing it by the stove, ok?".

Turning on his heel to leave us to it, he called over his shoulder "And if you should be so heavy booted as to spoil the polished lino floor wot you have carefully produced over the last ten weeks, I wouldn't be surprised!"

Our penultimate day at Henlow became a real comedy, when, marshalled ceremoniously in front of our trade selection officers we sat in rows waiting to see what the hell fate had in store for us next.

The place was buzzing with more than a little anxiety - rumour control had it you never got the trade you asked for, just some crap they wanted to dish out or get rid of, so we all sat grimly awaiting our call.

"Ah yes, 429 Parker AC, civvy street artist eh? said my no-nonsense Flying officer, "Well I've got an interesting choice of trades for you here, and, because of your previous art experience, I've managed to obtain for you as first choice,camouflage painting of aircraft - how do you feel about that?".

"No, sorry Sir, that's no good, I'm down for photography, that's all I want".

"No you're not - anyhow, to get into photography you have to volunteer for five years, and there are no vacancies for training at the present time".

"Well Sir, I'm not doing camouflage painting, even though I was an artist in civvy street".

"Right, your second choice" he said with voice hardening slightly "Is with the Air-Sea Rescue group, luckily you'll be based at Hong-Kong".

I felt like saying he must be nuts or something, what the hell would I want spewing up on a boat in Hong-Kong harbour?

"Sorry Sir, it's just photography".

"Your last choice," he grated," and you MUST pick one of the three I have offered you is—- trainee aero-engine mechanic at St Athen in South Wales "

I couldn't help it, I just burst out laughing, and my Flying Officer friend got pretty mad.

"You obviously don't appreciate the work that goes into selecting the trades I've made available to you Parker, you must choose one of these trades I've offered you NOW, you are NOT going to get photography!".

"I took a trade test at RAF Chigwell" I volunteered, "And was told that if I passed it successfully, I would be given trade training in photography, if that's not on, I'll go back to National Service and take my chance, we haven't been attested yet you know".

He went several shades of purple and grabbed the phone.

"We'll soon settle this!" he shouted, "Give me HQ records" he barked, and after a few minutes said "Yes that's right, 4051429 Parker A C, says he was promised trade training in photography, subject to a trade test".

A long pause.

"Oh it was, was it, he can go forward then?"

He slammed the phone down, and glared at me in ferocious thought. "I don't know how you managed it, but you appear to have been successful in getting photography".

He stamped my papers, muttering to his sergeant about a rail-pass to somewhere called Wellesbourne Mountford, before shouting "Next!" at the top of his voice.

I stood up, gave the customary salute to an officer holding the King's commission, and silently thanked the nameless Corporal at Chigwell who had really made my day!

Arriving at Wellesbourne village, I was directed by one of the locals towards a country road which he assured me did pass the RAF camp, and off I went in the weak January sun, humping my heavy kit-bags, hoping the camp wasn't too far down the quiet country road.

After about a mile, and still no sigh of the ruddy camp, I came to the conclusion there must be some idiot specially employed by the Services - possibly a sadist or madman, who deliberately builds the camp you have been posted to, a muscle wrenching couple of miles from the last public bus-stop.

This is particularly gutty when you are humping a heavy load of kit.

My eventual reception by the SP's at Wellesbourne was cool, almost indifferent, and came as an anti-climax to the hectic days of highly personal attention we had been used to at Henlow.

A couldn't care less SP. dumped two of us into a billet amongst a load of other lads who were half way through their ten-week photographic course, and that's how Tony Mears and I became the only two nerds to get into RAF photography at that particular time.

Apparently Tony had been a full-time wedding photographer in Wisbech Cambridgeshire, and like me had taken a trade test and been accepted. And yet everyone we subsequently spoke to, told us there was a complete block on photographic recruiting - why?

The brains at Wellesbourne told us it wasn't practical to start a new photographic course with just the two of us on it, so we had to wait while someone higher up sorted it all out.

In the meantime they would happily find us something else to do, which seemed about par for the course.

At this point the 'system' dealt me a nice poke in the ribs, just because my name began alphabetically with 'P' and not 'M'.

There were it seems, just two prestigious positions vacant for non-course people at that particular time - 1. SWO's runner and general message carrier for the Station Warrant officer, and 2. general duties, ie, whatever shitty job had been left undone for ages, which would keep a body occupied indefinitely.

'M' Mears got 1. and 'P' Parker got 2.

This grossly unfair situation was to persist for several rotten weeks, with Tony enjoying the fat-cat job complete with bicycle, while I endured chores like loading coal into sacks for the officers quarters, cookhouse duties, and digging over the CO's garden.

This last gem was awarded just two days before the start of the new course - which we were promised would include Tony and myself plus some others, but at this stage they wouldn't say who.

In the meantime I was told to prepare the CO's garden by completely removing all the rough grass, and get it ready for seed planting.

The CO. wanted a good job done, and I was to take my time.

Looking at it, I reckoned the last time the plot had been used for plants, Pontius wasn't even a bloody trainee pilate let alone aircrew, the ground was a rotten mess of dead weeds and tangled grass.

In a pretty foul mood I plunged the spade into the soil for the first dig, and to my surprise found the going far easier than I expected, I could turn the whole sod over in one go, completely burying grass and weeds, and presenting clean virgin soil to view.

In double-quick time, the whole 20'x30' garden was converted from a wilderness, into a neatly turned, grass free garden, to which the returning CO expressed his appreciation at a job well done.

Not even the hawk-eyed SWO thought to ask where the expected turfs might have been dumped for disposal, or how the hell I'd managed the job without a bloody wheelbarrow!

It just shows you can fool even the experts some of the time!

Anyway, for the remainder of my time at Wellesbourne I kept well cl;ear of the CO's garden, just in case the buried grass started to re-shoot, and the SWO remembered the name of the nerd he'd given the prestigious job to!

Again, like a script from a Whitehall farce, the course organiser decided that because there were no new recruits in the pipeline, (surprise, surprise) and Tony and I had been wasting our time for weeks, he would commence the course as promised, with us two 'chaps' - plus four WAAFs, all of whom had failed their photo courses earlier in the year, what a gas!

My last day on 'grottijobs' detail, before starting the photo course started most unusually, when I was given a clapped out bicycle, and told to deliver several messages about camp, starting with the officers' mess, about a mile away.

I had only pedalled a hundred yards or so when the cotter-pin holding the pedal arm slipped, making the bike impossible to ride, and to save walking, I scooted it the rest of the way to the officer's mess in the bright morning sun.

Having delivered my first message to the officer in question, I returned to the bicycle rack outside the officers' quarters, and found a much newer bike than mine parked alongside my old heap. Without hesitation I took it.

I certainly wasn't delivering the remaining messages on foot for any clown if I could help it - trudging around camp was far too strenuous for that!

The next port of call was the guardroom, with a message for Chiefie Glasgow, NCO. I/C the dreaded SP's, a bastard if ever there was one!

He didn't even have the grace to look up and acknowledge my presence at the counter, just stuck out his hand and took the envelope without a word - what a pig!

When I came out of the guardroom I could hardly believe my eyes, some bastard had already pinched my new bike, and I'd only been in the guardroom a few minutes!

All was not lost however, there was just one very nice bike left in the rack, so I took that, after all, all's fair in love and war, and I still had several messages to deliver!

Twenty minutes later with my last message handed over, I returned to the photographic section and dumped my nice new bike in the rack alongside a couple of others resting there - you never know, I might need it again soon, it certainly beat walking!

About half an hour later whilst watching one of the lads dry some urgent aerial films, I heard raised voices somewhere in the distance, and wondered vaguely, what the heck was going on, why would anyone need to shout, was there a fire or something?

Eventually the voices quietened, and I continued watching the film coming off the machine, counting the minutes until the NAAFI bell would ring, and we could all slide off for chi.

Suddenly Tony Mears appeared in the doorway looking very agitated, and came over to me saying quietly in my ear "Did you do the rounds this morning delivering the personal messages around camp?"

I said I had, and asked why he wished to know.

"Did you deliver anything to the guardroom?"

"Yes, of course I did, why?"

"Well, some idiot took chiefie Glasgow's personal bike, and other people have complained of losing theirs too, what did you get up to?"

When I explained what had happened, he looked horrified, and took a shaky step backwards.

"Chiefie Glasgow said if he ever finds out who stole his bike, he would have him crucified and thrown to the dogs, I had a hell of a time explaining it wasn't me, bearing in mind I've had that particular job for the last few weeks!"

I laughed like a drain, and thought, serves the bastards right for giving me shitty jobs all the time, although I did feel quite sorry for poor old Tony.

It was something he would never have done in a million years!

It was still very cold, especially at nights, and the miserable issue of coke delivered to our billet for the comfort of twenty men soon ran out, despite being supplemented by wooden, photographic paper cores looted from the section, plus anything else we could lay our hands on, that would burn.

It got pretty desperate when no more gash wood could be found, and inventiveness came to the fore as we removed alternate spindles from the backs of billet chairs, and strengthening blocks from inside the heavy wooden kit boxes located under each mans' bed.

Any port in a storm to keep warm!

In conjunction with these activities, straws were drawn to see who would run the gauntlet of the SP. camp patrol or any alert NAAFI staff, to steal buckets of coke from the nearby cookhouse compound.

Naturally the NAAFI had more than enough coke for their cookhouse boilers, but it needed a commando-like squirm to get under the barbed wire, and place the knobs of coke one at a time in a bucket lined with a towel.

This was absolutely essential if a quiet, successful operation was to be achieved.

It wasn't unusual to discover another filcher on the other side of the pile, only given away by a trickle of coke running down his side of the mound, or the accidental clunk of a coke knob in his bucket! It was all good cloak and dagger stuff!

Word quickly spread amongst other huts, that it was easy to get extra coke from the cookhouse compound, providing you were careful, and during the next few days the NAAFI pile shrank visibly.

This must have caused the miserable cookies to ask the SP's to keep an eye on it, and forays under the wire became an extremely hazardous operation, even with our lookouts posted on the nearby roadway to avoid detection.

In one of my bird-watching forays between our billets and the adjacent farmland, I had discovered a derelict wash-house, probably used by earlier servicemen when there were more billets than now, which was gently disintegrating in the severe weather.

The old place, about twenty feet square, minus doors and windows was partly screened by tangled elderberry bushes, and wasn't immediately visible from the road unless you were actually looking for it.

One evening about nine-o'clock, when the fire was on its last knockings, someone moaned "What are we going to do now? There aint no coke for another two days, and there's nothing else to burn, we can't even chance the bloody cookhouse any more, life's getting really grotty"

"There is one possibility we might just consider" I said hesitantly.

"About fifty yards from here there's an old wash-house on its last legs, it hasn't been used in yonks, AND it's made of wood. Perhaps a raiding party could find something useful in there?"

"Well as it's your flippin' idea" said one, "I suggest you go and look at it, although

I don't know how you're going to deal with bloody great planks of wood"

Huddled in their great-coats, they looked at me expectantly without saying anything more, so I grabbed the fire-shovel off the billet wall, and went into the darkness, heading towards the old wash-house.

It didn't take long to find, but prowling round in the stygian darkness made me feel like some kind of burglar, what if the SP's had guard dogs out, and I got caught?

Swallowing my fears, I placed the end of the spade behind the lowest skirting plank at one corner, and levered gently.

With a grinding squawk of rusty nails it came free, and I stood motionless, straining my ears like hell to see if there was any response to the noise. There was none.

Emboldened by my immediate success, I levered again, and quickly had the whole twenty-foot skirting plank lying on the ground.

So far so good.

Returning to the billet like a successful stone-age hunter, I dropped the plank outside the door and walked in.

"Well?" said my erstwhile critic, "I suppose it was a no go?"

"No, not at all, if a couple of you lazy buggers come outside right now and help me break up a plank, we can all enjoy a decent fire for the rest of the evening"

Like hyaenas around a carcass, they broke up and completely devoured the huge length of pine planking, whipping it indoors before prying eyes had a chance to see what was going on.

"Someone make sure there's no splinters outside to give us away please" I called, and in minutes we had a lovely roaring fire.

The wood we hadn't used on the fire was carefully hidden in the space under our billet, and used the following evening, but by nine o'clock we were in the same position as before, with nothing left to burn.

"Hey, Alan, do you think its worth another trip to the wash-house, after all if we've had the plank off one side, we might as well even it up and take one off each of the other sides, what do you think?"

"I think you're stark-raving nuts" said Tony. "If you're caught, god knows what will happen, it's theft you know"

"Well I'd like them to try and find the evidence then!" said one wag, "If you show us where it is Al, we'll do the rest, you can just disappear"

Armed with the trusty spade, four of us made our way to the old wash-house, where I pointed out the result of my last incursion into Air Ministry property.

"Right, you can buzz off now and leave us to it, we know the drill and will be extra careful"

Our ration of coke arrived shortly after the last foray, and combined with wooden cores looted from the section, we were self-sufficient once again.

However, the best laid plans of mice and men often come to grief, and it wasn't long before some blabbermouth spouted where the combustible material could be had, and when I visited the wash house a week or so later, most of the walls had gone.

Despite my initial misgivings, the photo course went pretty well, Tony's previous professional experience, plus the almost personal tuition from Chiefie Cross our Flt/Sgt instructor, made even the dimmest WAAF feel confident they could pass their exams this time, which of course they did.

Those weeks on the photo course were a period of exploration and discovery, not least, the delightful Pub at Loxley, from whence many an intoxicated gaggle emerged, billet bound, walking the farmer's fields and ducking under barbed wire, to avoid the guard-house, where the hated SP's sat, just waiting for trouble.

The SWO, and his little toady, F/Sgt. Grommit, seeing the obvious decline in our physical condition, (their words, not ours), decided to organise a Saturday cross-country run for the benefit of all those not in possession of a current 48hr pass.

Everybody, but everybody was in, no excused boots this time, no slackers, no scivers, it was a massacre!

Saturday dawned, a dull, cold, lifeless day, and immediately after breakfast we were herded into several 3 ton Bedfords, and whisked away down the road towards Warwick, with explicit instructions as to how we were to cover the eight little miles back to camp.

As we set off on the return trot, a PTI corporal in front, and some prat to organise things at the rear, it started to rain, and in no time we were completely soaked through.

Through rain-splashed glasses I thankfully noted Wellesbourne village jog into view, and our straggling mob splashed its way noisily past startled shopkeepers and onto the camp approach road. In the bustop layby, a stationary RAF truck sat with its engine running, the exhaust making clouds of steam in the cold air.

"Did you see who was sitting in there out of the fuggin' rain the rotten bastards?" said a voice up front, "It was the bloody Station Warrant Officer (SWO) and his mate Sgt.Grommit, trust them not to get their bloody feet wet"

"Never mind" said a chirpy voice, "Once we get back in and cleaned up, the morning will be almost gone, and we'll be free of the usual Saturday bullshit session"

"Too right" said another.

It turned out however we weren't getting off that easily at all. After washing and changing, a smiling Grommit appeared at the billet door and shouted, "Right you lot, get fell in outside in yer Ponchos, we'll be marchin' across to the 'angar so the SWO can have a few choice words in yer ears - DOUBLE!"

It transpired that the object of the SWO's immediate displeasure was a group of four bods from the tail-end of the run, who, for reasons far beyond his understanding, had decided that running about in the rain getting wet was a mug's game, and had hailed a passing country bus.

Unfortunately for them, it disgorged its passengers right in front of the waiting RAF lorry, and they were nabbed 'in flagrante' so to speak, by the SWO man himself!

"There will be no sports afternoon today" the SWO intoned sonorously, as though imparting some rather sad news.

"Instead there will be a little billet inspection for everyone at 1500hrs, and as for you four " his eyes scoured the crestfallen group in front of him, "You will report to the Guard-room in full kit, on the hour, every hour, six 'till ten, tonight and Sunday night, just to make up for the exercise you sadly missed today".

Sometime during the following week I saw a poster announcing that due to recent postings, budding musicians were required to volunteer for the parade band, and all hopefuls should present themselves for selection in the music room that Friday, after tea.

Amongst all the guff about the care and responsibility of one's instrument and the need to practice with it in your own time, I noticed a magical one-line statement which read:-

'All musicians will be awarded an extra 48hr pass a month, to compensate for instrument practice in their own time.'

In very quick time I attended the selection meeting, got issued with my bugle, and began to blow - I could use the extra 48 as well as the next man!

As a result of becoming proficient enough to play 'Semper Fidelis' and one or two other bits and pieces, us 'new lads' were expected to play along with the others as we marched on morning parade, and of course the prestigious monthly station parade too.

As these parades followed immediately on the heels of breakfast, our nicely polished bugle, complete with its red and gold tassle had to hang on coat hangers in the entrance to the cookhouse, presenting a great temptation to some inventive wag, far too good to miss.

As Corporal Ross led the band off, flourishing his mace and white gloves, we swung down the road towards the square striking up the first notes of the tune the lead trumpeter told us to play - or at least tried to.

All I got was a treacly gurgle and a plopping noise, as a piece of toilet tissue flew out of the end of my bugle and hit the man in front, followed by splodges of gooey red liquid.

I was completely gob-smacked and hadn't a clue what was happening, and someone nearby let out a loud snigger.

Trying not to draw attention to myself, I carried on as though nothing had happened, keeping the bugle to my lips, but not blowing, while the lads on either side gave me wide-eyed stares of disbelief, as they continued to blow.

In a crash of drums we arrived on the main square, where the Wing Commander stepped to the front of the parade, and prepared to raise the flag, and take the salute

"Trumpeter, sound the still!" shouted the parade officer in the clear morning air, and immediately the Wingco threw up his arm in salute, and the flag began to rise.

Corporal Ross, who hadn't played 'til now, brought his bugle to the 'raised postion' and began the first notes of the 'still', calling everyone's attention to the rising flag.

All that came out however was a slurping gurgle and a strangled squeal, followed by the same gooey red liquid I had suffered. What the hell was going on?

The flag puller looked as though he didn't know whether to laugh or cry, the Wingco stiffly at salute, screwed his eyes to one side desperately trying to see what the hell was happening to his parade, while the lead bugle frantically stepped in and completed the remaining bars of the still.

Corporal Ross looked as though he had just shit himself.

They never did find out who poured the tomato ketchup into our bugles, and although I thought it a smashing gag, it was a bit too near a Courts-Martial offence to be repeated!

During a spell of walkabouts round camp in the improved spring weather, I chanced on the site of the old wash-house, and although I was certain I had the right place, there was no sign of the tiled roof sticking up over the elderberries. Where had it gone?

I soon found out.

Pushing through waist-high dead grasses and thistles, I looked into a cleared area between the elderberry bushes, to see the roof of the wash-house lying on the ground, looking for all the world like a 'lost' archaeological ruin buried up to its gutters in the grassy soil.

Some people just couldn't leave anything alone!

One morning after tea-break, I was in the photo stores, drawing a wide angle lens for the S4.camera, when I met Sergeant Alan McLean, a photographer on the squadrons, recently returned from service in Germany.

He told me he had been out there several years, and enjoyed aerial work immensely, but coming back to the UK, even for a short while, was a real pain in the butt.

He explained he was 'time-ex' in a few weeks, and would be looking for a photographic job in civvy street, but he hadn't a clue as to what he might find there.

Little did I know that I was to meet him again in 1958 under quite unusual circumstances, and when I least expected it.

Eventually we came to the end of our course, and passed the exams with flying colours - and were told that the two previous courses which had been held back for reasons unknown, would receive their final postings, along with ours, on completion of the forms provided.

The said forms were a record of everything we had achieved to date, plus the usual rank, name, and serial number, but at the bottom we were asked to state our preference for either a home, or an overseas posting.

In the meantime we all went home on a 48hr pass, each of us clutching our Serviceman's ration card, which allowed us to buy extra items of food, especially meat.

My mother said that apart from anything else I was always welcome with the ration card, as that was the only time the family had a decent meat-joint for the week end!

Back at Wellesbourne we eagerly discussed our hopes and fears concerning future postings, and names like Leuchars, and St Athen, seemed hell-holes to be avoided at all costs!.

From various discussions I had with others, it seemed that most people wanted to go abroad either to Germany or the Far East, while Tony and I, who had things we wanted to do in England, preferred a decent home posting.

In a voice totally devoid of emotion, a young Pilot-Officer began reading our list of postings, to the accompaniment of gasps or groans, as the various recipients learnt their fate.

Needless to say Murphy had a field-day that day as everybody got home postings, except Tony and I. We were bound for Egypt!

Our pre-embarkation camp turned out to be RAF Hednesford near Cannock, Staffordshire, a peculiar place where most people seemed to please themselves what they did during the day, disappearing completely from view between meals.

The parade ground on which we all assembled, sloped an incredible 20 degrees from the horizontal, and only saw human activity at meal times and so-called pay-parades, the rest of the day the camp seemed quite deserted.

After a couple of days wandering around on my own, I spotted a bunch of lads disappearing into a large underground bunker, where some enterprising erk had managed to turn on the electric lighting. Here in peace and quiet the lads played cards, or odds and evens throughout the day, totally undisturbed.

Others, far less enterprising, played a desperate game of hide and seek with prowling higher ranks, hiding in empty lockers or store-cupboards as the hunters searched the billets.

After all, the clowns were only looking for someone they could lay hands on, and give a rotten job to.

One of the lads, Ginger Horrocks got himself in bad schtook with the woman F/Sgt in charge of the shrubbery clearing detail, as they stood awaiting their final instructions.

The other lads had all been issued with machetes and bill-hooks to attack the rampant foliage, but Ginger stood out like a sore thumb, hands in pockets carrying nothing.

Our WF/Sgt, built like an all-in wrestler, and twice as nasty, confronted Ginger in an aggressive pose and demanded loudly, "Where's your chopper?"

"In me trousers of course" replied Ginger with a grin, but the humour in the snappy-catch answer was lost on the dominating woman, who promptly called in the SP's and had him carted off for gross insubordination!

Within a week of arriving, we were sent home for the weekend, which was one way of getting rid of us, as there was so little for anyone to do, and no money to do it with.

Even the paying-out officer was in transit, and new to the camp, announcing to the grumbling pay parade he didn't have the facility to draw money to pay people with anyway!

Our final return to camp on Sunday evening turned out to be a right madhouse, as the last train for Rugeley Trent-Valley, disgorged its hundreds of swaddies from three grossly overloaded, ancient coaches, just below the camp gates.

Submerged in a welter of shouts and oaths, the solitary ticket collector tried manfully to stem the human tide and collect his tickets, but most of us stuffed his hands full of cut up Woodbine packets, bits of thin card resembling passes, mickey-mouse IOU's, anything that would get us through the barrier, and up the steep path to the camp rear gates before midnight.

Like cinderellas, we were all trying to avoid the dreaded AWOL.

The black night sky unloaded a miserable downpour of rain which soaked everything, and with hundreds of trampling feet churning the soil into mud, it became a fierce struggle to ascend the slippery path to the camp gate.

Once inside, I could see in the distance the building where we had carefully stacked our kit-bags before going on leave, now brightly illuminated by outside lights.

The place seemed to be a scene of utter confusion, with men pushing, and shouting, and I wondered what the hell was going on.

On the muddy ground in pouring rain, a hundred or more kit-bags lay in a hideous pile, some with their contents strewn over the ground, everything getting wetter by the minute.

A voice nearby said "Some silly bastards came back earlier and were so pissed out of their minds they couldn't find their stuff, so they threw everyone else's outside while looking for theirs, and this is the result".

In minutes there were over a hundred of us gathered around the pile, pushing and shoving, getting in each other's way while searching for our kit. it was chaotic.

I shouted out "If a couple of us read out the numbers on the bags we pick up and there's no answer, we can pass them along a chain and stack them in the doorway again, those who hear their number called can grab their bags and go, how about it?"

People seemed to agree, so I took first bash with a couple of well-built fellers, and started calling out serial numbers.

I said to Tony "Keep next to me, and if ours come out I'll pass them to you, and we'll shag off sharpish, and leave the rest of them to it, ok.?"

After half an hour's grotty work in the pouring rain, I was lucky to find both Tony's and mine, and we sloped off leaving the rest of them to sort it out. It looked a right bloody circus in that lousy weather.

If we could have found the clowns that perpetrated the rotten deed, we probably would have killed them!

That wasn't the end of the evenings' fun however.

As Hednesford was a transit camp, no-one seemed to have thought about allocating the returning troops any billets for the night, and the duty SP's didn't give a monkey's about it either!

Taking the bull by the horns, we chose the nearest hut and booted the door in, piling inside to escape the pouring rain.

Naturally there was no electricity on, the fuses having been looted aeons ago by previous raiders, but as usual, some genius with the requisite initiative and knowledge, inserted a penny or something between the make and break, and we were away.

There were of course no palliasses or even enough beds to go round, so it was a case of fully dressed in wet great-coats - to take the sting out of the wire mesh beds or the cold hardness of the floor, and get your head down.

Join the RAF and see the world - ha! What a joke.

After a couple more days in the mad-house, we finally got the go, we were to travel by train to Liverpool and the docks, then by Bibby Line, the SS.Devonshire, to Gibraltar, Malta, Tripoli and Cyprus, before reaching Egypt.

It sounded great.

Just before going to Hednesford I bought myself one of the new Ensign Selfix 16 on 120 folding cameras, fitted with a 3.5 Ross Express lens, and was taking pictures like they were going out of fashion. I wasn't going to miss a thing!

# Chapter Four

On board ship it was the typical service SNAFU situation, 2300 men packed into a ship meant to carry 800, which seemed about par for the course. Nothing really changes!

Our first test of endurance was the Bay of Biscay, where it was said, many a strong man was brought to his knees, and I can well believe it!

As darkness fell, a howling wind lashed the waves into a fury, causing the ship to roll sickeningly from left to right, and the bows to plunge up and down, giving the whole ship a wicked corkscrew motion.

It wasn't long before the first swaddies began puking up like good-uns, and the for'ard toilets were awash in a sea of half digested carrots and potatoes, not a pretty sight!

Next morning at reveille, very few heads rose from the horizontal, but because I felt slightly better than others, I appointed myself chief galley-hand, and staggered aft to collect breakfast for the few survivors on our table.

Although I didn't particularly enjoy the erratic motion of the ship, I was ok. provided I looked straight ahead, that is, until I suddenly got the smell of fresh bread from the galley, and I suddenly felt very queasy.

The sea-going crew had been at pains to show us how to `stow' a hammock, but conveniently forgot to tell us about the `spreader' a wooden device absolutely essential if you wish to get in and out of the darn' things without strangling yourself in the process! They laughed themselves sick watching our antics before trying to get some sleep!

It got so bad at hammock-hanging time, with twenty odd rope-ends knotted round the same pole, that many of us just slept on the floor, or on the deck outside, it was a damn' sight easier! Eventually our ship passed the rock of Gibraltar and entered the Med. ploughing slowly through blue seas in glorious sunshine, leaving us nothing to do except sunbathe and play cards.

One beefy character who had commandeered the best sunning spot near the fo'castle, fell asleep on his chest, his porcine white body slowly turning pink in the hot sunshine.

One of the lads, a right wag, tore a sheet of paper from his exercise book, and with a penknife cut out a very rude four letter word in the middle, and laid it gently on his back.

The gag soon became the centre of attraction, and even the non-coms whose duty it was to keep order on deck smiled, bets were taken as to how long it would stay in position to give the desired effect.

We needn't have worried, it was a windless day, and our friend slept like a log, long enough anyway for the rude word to be transferred boldly to his skin in the middle of a lighter coloured square.

At first he laughed because everyone else was laughing, until it eventually got through his puerile brain, that he was the cause of so much hilarity.

In a fury he grabbed one of his friends and made him say what the hell it was all about.

It was the best gag of the trip.

It took us sixteen days to reach Port Said, and when we finally got there, it was our misfortune to spend another two days entombed on board in the stifling heat, before being `de -shipped', and `en-trained' into decrepit wooden railway carriages, like so many exhausted cattle.

These delightful carriages were pulled by an oil burning loco that must have seen better days well before the war, but with all the stops pulled out, and to strains of military music played over the Tannoy system, it somehow managed to haul us out of the station.

Within a few yards of moving off, the train made a sharp`U' turn, so tight, the rails cracked and banged in the sleeper shoes, like rifle shots, while black belching smoke from the loco's chimney rapidly obscured the scorching sun, it was a right circus!

As we slowly gathered speed, streetwise arab boys jumped onto the running boards, snatching sunglasses, watches, and even hats from unwary servicemen, anything to make a few bob from the hated British swaddies.

The quite bizarre train journey from Port Said to Moascar Garrison sticks fast in my memory for several reasons, not the least being the huge glassless windows which admitted furnace-like blasts of hot air from the surrounding desert, and secondly the basic device that passed for a public toilet.

This consisted of a cubby hole at one end of the carriage, with the remains of a door swinging from its hinges, and a rotting, gaping hole in the floorboards, through which the sleepers of the track could be seen flickering past.

The ancient train naturally banged and swayed about on its clapped out springs, and as previous occupants must have suffered from aggravated Montezuma's revenge, or `Gyppo-gut' as it's known out here, it wasn't surprising that the immediate surroundings of the aperture were liberally splattered with faeces and toilet paper. There was no doubt that one's `aim and fire' technique had to be honed and synchronised to the train's erratic motion, if a successful shot was to be achieved!

During the journey we were soon introduced to the bland rip-off techniques employed by the more sophisticated Egyptian vendors, who, on boarding the train at a short stop, dispensed cold drinks and sweets with an engaging smile, promising immediate change for the dozens of 100 and 200 piastre notes tendered by the innocent swaddies, only to disappear rapidly as the train pulled out of the station, keeping all the lads' change!

It was late afternoon when we `de-trained' at Moascar, and `em-bussed' in grubby 3-tonners, heading for somewhere called El Hamra, arriving just as the evening meal was being served.

It looked a right dump.

"Right you two, into that tent over there with the others, and wait until you're called about your postings" Tony and I were told, and with a roar, our 3 tonner clattered away in a cloud of choking dust.

Two figures eventually appeared at the tent entrance, the leading one proclaiming, "My name is Warrant Officer Baldwin and this is F/Sgt Hughes, which of you lot are the two new photographers?" Tony and I indicated our presence.

"You'll both be going to JAPIC HQ at Deversoir in a couple of days, incidentally, where the hell have you been, we expected you here weeks ago?"

I was absolutely gobsmacked at this, and couldn't believe my ears, how the hell could we have any influence over what the RAF decided do with us?

Was he really nuts, or had the sun just cooked his brains?

Fancy asking us where we had been, it must have been obvious!

Deversoir turned out to be a huge RAF camp situated on the west bank of the Suez canal, just where it enters the Great Bitter lake from the north, with lots of sand and hundreds of date palms.

Surprisingly it all seemed fairly civilised, with proper buildings, roads, a cinema and a couple of shops gently sizzling in the hot sun.

Perhaps it wouldn't be too bad here after all?

Tony and I were dropped off outside the photographers' compound, a circle of five Nissen huts, half buried in the sand, completely surrounded by a six foot high, barbed wire fence.

Apparently earlier in its history, the place had been home to a contingent of WAAFs - hence the barbed wire fence, consequently the photographers who lived there were nicknamed the ``Waafs', or `Poofies' by the rest of the camp.

As new boys, Tony and I were rapidly absorbed into the duties of the section, mainly due to the high volume of work undertaken, dealing as it did with all aerial intelligence flown in the Middle East, from Crete to Cyprus, Iraq to Hormuz in Iran, and along the southern Russian border.

In those first days, whilst being indoctrinated into the various section duties, one event firmly etched itself in my memory, which concerned the mosaic copying room.

This room, which was about twelve feet square, contained an old 15x12 wood and brass copying camera, its two-foot long bellows and massive lens denoting a piece of apparatus from pre-war times.

It sat on a large trestle, which had wheels at the base, allowing the whole camera to traverse the floor on two steel tracks.

The Corporal given the task of educating us into its use stated "We adapted the back so that apart from copying the 8ft, square aerial mosaics, like that one pinned to the wall there, it can be used as an enlarger too".

He went on "It uses a cold cathode system of lighting that clips easily on the back when printing, in fact we're going do a job with it now, so you can join in and help - just take your shoes and socks off". I looked at him in amazement, but his expression was quite serious, so I did as instructed. "Douse the lights Nobby" he called, and we clicked into stygian darkness.

"See alright yet?" the Corporal demanded.

"Just about" I replied.

"Well then, help Nobby fix that roll of bromide to the wall, now that I've focussed up the image, and we'll get cracking and make a print. The exposure's quite a long one, and we've a fair number to do".

After about twenty minutes, waving his hands here and there for shading purposes, he considered the exposure to be sufficient.

"Ok, this is where you come in, grab the opposite side of the print to Nobby, and lay it carefully on the floor in front of the camera".

"Right, now, weigh the corners down with these lead weights, keep 'em right on the edges of the paper so's they'll stay there until the paper has lost its kink".

I tried desperately to think how on earth he was going to develop an eight foot square print like this on the floor, but there was no time.

"Grab this soft broom and be ready to move when I say" he said and promptly emptied a couple of buckets of liquid across the print.

"Right go!" he shouted, "That's developer down there, shift your arse and keep the brush moving, Nobby'll do the same from his side".

After a minute or so another couple of buckets of developer sploshed down, while Nobby and I scrubbed backwards and forwards like a couple of matelots onboard ship.

"Ok, standback, we'll give her a quick rinse before the fix."

and more buckets of liquid crashed down, to the accompaniment of loud gurglings in the background, suggesting the surplus liquid was draining off outside somewhere.

"Right now the fix, and you can start scrubbing again, make sure you keep it even, you can stand on the print now if you want to, but go easy".

"Lights on!" and Nobby and I stood back to admire our efforts sweating profusely as the wall thermometer showed 90 degrees Fahrenheit.

"She don't look half bad at all" said Corp. "A nice wash down with some fresh water, and we can all shag off for some chi".

While Nobby did the honours with the water, I rested my elbow on the back end of the camera trestle, suddenly noticing a large German eagle and Swastika badge fixed to the back of the camera. In the area just below the Swastika was a serial number, in a classic continental typeface.

"What's this German insignia on the back of the camera then corp." I asked.

"Oh that? The story goes we captured it from the jerries after Tobruk in the last war," he replied, "And good job too, we ain't got anything of our own out here like it that I know of".

A few weeks after settling in, we were informed that a snap AOC's (Air officer Commanding) inspection was imminent, apparently he liked to test his operational airfields' response to an emergency, and we were next in line.

Because Deversoir was such a large camp containing major runways, plus dozens of out-buildings and hangars, I felt it would be difficult to take people by surprise, so how this chap expected to test our responses, seemed a bit of a mystery to me.

There had been a traditional way of warning all ranks in photographic that the NAAFI wagon was outside the main door, and if you wanted chi and a wad before supplies ran out, you had to get in line bloody quick!

The signal for this mass exodus from various parts of the section, was the vigorous shaking of a large, highly polished fire-bell which normally sat splendiferously on it's bullshitted plinth in reception.

It had never been used for any other purpose as far as anyone knew.

On the appointed day, the AOC managed to arrive on camp with the minmum of fuss and detection, eventually driving up to photographic just before ten.

Catching the nerd behind the counter unawares - he was probably reading a Hank Janson paperback or something, the AOC grabbed the firebell and gave it a prolonged shake, intending to observe just how long it took photographers to respond to his fire alarm.

Within seconds, bods who had been idling out of sight, flashed into life, and poured through reception like a tide, nearly knocking the AOC and his aide off their feet in the rush.

His smile of satisfaction at such a marvellous response, was immediately wiped away, when he walked out the door to see a line of mug waving swaddies pushing and shoving in the sand, eyes straining for a glimpse of the promised NAAFI wagon.

It soon became apparent that there wasn't a tea-wagon, and voices of anger and frustration began to rend the air.

"What tosser sounded the fuggin' tea bell then?" said one.

"Is this a joke or something, if so I'll have someone's guts fer garters!" shouted another, and it was only when someone said "Fer gawds sake don't turn round!" people saw the AOC on the top step, arms akimbo, and face like thunder.

"Get back to your work stations immediately!" he bellowed.

"There will be no Naffi break this morning until I find out who is responsible for this gross misuse of emergency service equipment" And that was that, until lunch-time.

In this strange, new environment, time passed quickly, and I soon became an established hand at the various jobs needing to be done, but one thing continually bugged me - my inability to drive one of our service vehicles.

There were definite perks to be had if you could drive, like getting off camp to nearby Fayid, or Ismailia, without the hassle of waiting in the heat for the crowded hourly bus, but as far as I could see there didn't seem to be any opportunity on camp to learn the art.

Just prior to my first trip into nearby Fayid, I had been astounded, and somewhat pleased to hear from mates who had already discovered its delights, the place boasted both a Harrods and Selfridges, obviously things weren't quite as basic out here as I was beginning to believe!

When I eventually saw the mud-brick hovels on either side of the Bailey bridge spanning the `Sweetwater' canal, I roared with laughter. On weathered wooden boards, hand painted signs declared `Selfridges' and `Harrods, store to his Britannic Majesty', the latter proudly displayed upside-down alongside an `Out of bounds to Servicemen' sign. What a load of nerds!

I'd get my own back on those friends of mine later!

Ismailia on the other hand was quite a large town situated fifteen miles north of Deversoir, still exhibiting numerous signs of French influence in its architecture, even boasting a branch of Gordon & Gotch, a firm I had bought art materials from, when working at Ark's Publicity in London.

My second visit to the fair town of Ismailia on the 16th October 1951 however, was one which would stick in my mind for many years, not just because of the new 8x34 binoculars I had bought for £12, but for something entirely outside my control.

Just after four o'clock in the afternoon I wandered slowly back into French Square, and boarded the single decker bus signboarded for Deversoir - it wouldn't be leaving just yet, so I could sit back and relax, just like the Sudanese bus driver and his mate asleep on the grass outside.

Suddenly the musical `ching-ching' of brass cups striking together like the Hari Krishna mob, heralded the imminent approach of the sweetmeats and water seller, plus his performing monkey.

Sensing a possible sale to either the Sudanese crew or myself, he quickly took up a pitch in the lee of the bus, and began his act. The monkey was made to perform rapid somersaults to the clinking of brass cups held between the vendor's finger and thumb, and as it looked a great local atmosphere shot, I raised my camera to record the scene.

I had just taken the first shot, when the vendor seeing me filming from the bus window, screeched `Baksheesh, baksheesh! pushing his cupped hand to the open window and demanding money.

Naturally I had picked up enough Arabic during my short time in Egypt to answer him, `La, inta yallah', (No, you go) but this only provoked a violent stream of abuse, amongst which I certainly recognised references to my ancestry, and a likeness to certain defaecatory substances.

Almost immediately there was a sudden increase in the shouting outside, and I noticed out of the corner of my eye, the Sudanese bus-crew nipping away quickly under the trees.

Then, before I could really appreciate what was happening, half-a-dozen Egyptians crowded into the forward door, shouting, "English bastard, you no photo Arab - we kill you", and began to pile on board waving sticks and knives.

Transfixed by the speed of events, I could only gaze stupidly at the mob piling into the bus, and it was only when the nearest attacker was a seat or two away, I jumped up and raced to the back of the vehicle.

Fortunately for me it had an opening back door, held fast by two large chrome handles which weren't locked.

To this day I don't remember opening that door at all, I do recall however, hitting the tarmac of French square at the run, accidentally heading the wrong way for safety, by going towards the Arishia native quarter, instead of the waterfront road.

I was in deep trouble.

On the first corner I came to, an Egyptian Policeman in white suit and red fez, leant on his Lee Enfield rifle, talking to some locals. I raced up to him and said. "Can you help me please, these men are after me".

"No speak English" he said with a leering smile, and turned his back, to continue with his conversation.

The mob now about a dozen strong, were right on my heels, so with renewed vigour, I cut across the next corner of French square, and galloped down the east side, away from Arishia and entrapment. Glancing back over my shoulder to see what was happening. I was horrified to see several of the shouting mob were now on bikes and rapidly gaining on me, I was caught now for sure.

In desperation I veered left out of the square, and shot down a narrow side street, jumping through a couple of women with woven baskets containing chickens and vegetables, and after a hundred yards, came out onto the waterfront road by Lake Timsah. The bikers hadn't been able to follow me as quickly, due to the clutter in the street.

A married families bus, a Bedford 3 tonner with canvas top and slat seats was cruising past, having just left its appointed stop a few yards away, and hadn't picked up full speed yet - it was my best chance to escape.

In a last burst of energy I raced alongside the rear, and hurled myself up the iron steps at the back, before collapsing into the nearest seat, puffing like a grampus.

The serviceman conductor came across to me with a grin and said, `I don't know what your hurry is mate, this isn't the last bus back to Deversoir you know, there's still one leaving French Square shortly'.

It was some time before I could get my breath back, and explain why I was in such a damned hurry, which caused his face to drop in alarm, and he shouted to the driver, not to stop for anyone.

I learnt on my eventual return to camp, that one unfortunate soldier had been chased by the mob in Ismailia, cornered by the railway station, and stabbed to death, so in French Square I had experienced a very, very, narrow squeak.

The abrogation of the Canal Zone Treaty by the Egyptians really began in earnest that day, and the normal infrastructure of life in the zone we were used to, fell apart dramatically.

As things began to hot up both locally and internationally, the volume of aerial reconnaissance increased tremendously too, and everyone worked day and night, in mind-clogging shifts, to clear the huge backlog of photographs.

Until now, I had been able to roam freely along the shoreline between Deversoir and Abu Sultan, watching migrant, and local species of birds in safety, totally ignored by the local fellahin, who probably thought I was `macnoon' (mad) anyway, but all that quickly changed.

This ideal situation was knocked on the head after a gun attack on one of our guard patrols by Egyptian terrorists - and as a result, personnel could only venture out of camp if fully armed.

Trying to keep a 303 rifle hitched on your shoulder, while focussing binoculars on a distant bird wasn't my idea of a relaxing time, especially with the temperature well over the 100F mark, so I reluctantly decided to give birding a miss for a while, and join the lads in their daily swim in the Suez canal.

This pastime required very little effort from anyone, and was therefore quite debilitating, in fact blokes were dying on their feet from mind-blowing boredom between duties.

Celebrating the `feast' of Christmas in 1951 was a pretty miserable affair, guard duties on the airfield were running at one night in three, the Canal zone itself was buzzing with over 90,000 men instead of the usual 30,000, and what was probably the biggest gripe for many, the abysmal lack of beer and food available to celebrate the so-called festive season!

In an attempt to inject some semblance of festivity into a desperate situation, some clown in the Zone HQ. organised a New Year's dance for the troops in the Fayid area, but didn't bother to think how several hundred swaddies were going to dance with six young Wrens from HMS Osiris, or the few hard-faced NAAFI women who bothered to attend!

As it turned out, the swaddies needn't have worried about the situation at all, the Wrens were off limits to anyone who wasn't an officer, and the NAAFI women were already spoken for!

When the cheers and hoots of derision greeting the few men seen dancing together had waned into an uneasy silence, the whole shindig suddenly disintegrated into a fist swinging punch-up, leaving the hated SP's as the only ones seen to be enjoying themselves.

By the end of March it was warm enough to go swimming in the lake again, and having seen the Hans and Lottie Haas' film about life under the Red sea, I was dead keen to give this new sport a try, it looked really exciting.

A few weeks later I found a recent exchange and mart-type magazine, in which a firm in southern Ireland was selling off ex-German submarine escape apparatus at a good price.

It was exactly the same as used by Hans Haas, which he said could be used to a depth of thirty feet on oxygen alone, without causing serious trouble.

This sounded fine to me, as I didn't expect to go deeper than that around Deversoir anyway, so I sent off for one.

Several weeks later, a weighty parcel arrived on camp, bearing Irish stamps, and I was the proud possessor of the only underwater breathing kit in the whole of the Suez Canal!

The Gestetner copy for the assembly and use of the equipment was a bit sparse, but with only a pressure bottle, airtight breathing bag, soda-lime canister, and mouth-piece stamped with German eagle rampant over a swastika to hand, there didn't seem a lot to get wrong.

The next problem was to try and get hold of a face mask, there weren't any in the zone, although we did hear they could be bought in far off South Africa, but nobody had an address to write to.

There was only one thing for it, I would have to try and make one from bits and pieces around camp.

I found if you took an aerial-film tin, and cut a hole in the bottom, leaving a ledge all round, and glued it into a short section of Mosquito aircraft rubber inner - tube, this would do for the main body of the mask and head strap. A disc of perspex cut from a crashed Typhoon cockpit canopy, and glued into the shallow ledge at the bottom of the tin, would do for the window, and we were in business!

As for oxygen, the one ton pressure bottle supplied was easily filled by colleagues servicing the squadron's Meteor jet breathing apparatus, but the replacement of soda -lime in the canister (useless once it has absorbed air and changed carbon dioxide into water) was giving me insurmountable problems.

There was just nowhere one could get sealed soda-lime crystals to re-charge the canister in the Canal Zone, it was as scarce as rocking-horse dung.

A self-professed chemist in the section suggested that caustic soda pellets were near as dammit the same as soda-lime crystals, so why not try those?

I soon found out why not, when I inadvertently allowed sea water past the mouth-piece, down the breathing tube, and into the canister containing the caustic soda.

From a depth of about ten feet I shot to the surface choking and blowing like a spouting whale, lungs full of caustic fumes, and mouth burning like blazes!

After that fiasco I did away with the re-circulating aspect of the kit altogether, and relied on pure oxygen released into the bag.

When I felt the oxygen was getting stale, I released it through a side valve before allowing fresh oxygen in from the pressure bottle. It all seemed to work just fine.

Our main relaxation after work - swimming in the canal, was becoming a bit of a bore, the same old thing day after day was enough to send you nuts, so some of the lads invented the chicken - run game, ie: seeing just how late you could leave your swimming dash across the hundred-foot wide canal, before the huge tankers ploughed through on top of you.

The poor lookout or whoever was on duty, blew the ship's klaxon furiously, as we disappeared from his view beneath the tanker's bow, only to re-appear waving like idiots as the ship swept monstrously past.

This practice attracted so much bad press from the Canal company lookout staff, that all bathers were ordered to leave the water when a whistle sounded the imminent approach of a large ship.

No one of course said anything about AFTER the ship had passed, and another new game was invented.

When large tankers and liners passed through the canal, their massive propellers thrashing half out of the water, they virtually filled the centre of the canal, taking a huge volume of water with them as they entered the Bitter lake.

If you were mad enough to dive in when the stern was just opposite, you were sucked along at about eight knots, tight up behind the ship's propeller, unobserved by anyone on board, as the ship ploughed its way towards the Bitter lake a hundred yards away.

You then swam leisurely back to the jetty and waited for the next ship to come along. It seemed that as one scheme to combat the deadly monotony of our existence paled, another took its place, and that's probably how our group of six, came to plan our `great escape'!

The inspiration for this caper came from watching `Seven graves to Cairo', or some such film, whereby a trek across limitless sand wastes eventually leads to freedom.

"We'll need two water bottles each, some army type puttees to keep the sand out of our boots, suitable headgear, sun-glasses and a couple of good compasses" said our self-appointed leader, "And a plastic bag to put our stuff in to keep dry, whilst we swim across the canal" said another.

The plan was to start at first light, about 0400hrs, and taking a bearing from the Canal watch - tower, strike off into the Sinai as far as we could get in three hours, leaving a cache of water buried under various markers for use on our return.

In the cool air of early dawn all went well, and we quickly crossed the railway-line that runs parallel to the eastern shore of the lake, and ploughed on through stone covered desert, hard as concrete, towards a small ridge of dunes ahead.

We reckoned we were making about five miles an hour, give or take a bit, and after the first hour buried our first water bottles under a large pile of stones as a marker.

"We should be able to find that one easily enough on return" said our leader, and off we went again. At the conclusion of the second hour we repeated the procedure, and looking back, we could see our footprints stretching away into the soft drifts in a fairly straight line. It had been a doddle so far.

We felt pretty confident the whole trek was going down well, and felt really pleased with ourselves, there was no doubt we should have been on the film set to show how it was really done!

It was now 0630hrs, and under a warm sun, the temperature began to rise quickly, causing the night dampness in the sand to evaporate quickly.

"We'll go on for the last hour as planned " said our leader, "But we must start back no later than 0800hrs - we don't want to get caught out here in the real heat of mid-day, that's for sure".

A couple of miles ahead lay a long sandy dune, capped with black sun blasted rocks and stones, probably undisturbed since Moses' walk through.

"If we can make the top of that ridge by the time we have to quit, we can build a cross or an arrow out of rocks and stones up there, you never know, we might spot it on one of the training sortie films one day, then we'll turn back for home"

Surprisingly it took us more than an hour to reach the top of the ridge, and another half an hour to make the arrow. "I'm shagged out" said a voice "Me too" said another, "How about a little kip before we go back?"

"I don't think that's a good idea at all" I said, "You won't feel any real benefit resting in the sun, and your muscles will begin to seize up too"

My advice fell on deaf ears, and three bodies flaked out on the hot sand, desert bush-hats tipped over their eyes for a short kip.

"Come on you lot you've had your half hour's rest, let's get mobile!" barked our leader, and after a lot of moans and groans they all got vertical. Plodding along steadily we made fair progress, our watches indicating we had now been on the go for an hour, and must be pretty near our first water cache.

To our great relief and not a little pride, we spotted the cairn at once, although to be fair, our outward tracks were still plainly visible in the drifted sand.

As we downed the warm, but welcome water, I wondered what would happen if we couldn't find the other two caches, would it prove serious like it always did in the cinema? My unspoken fears concerning the location of the second cache became a harsh reality, when at the conclusion of our timed second leg we just couldn't find it.

We cast around in several arcs, searching for some time without success, it was a worrying mystery.

Although we were on the reciprocal compass bearing of our outward journey, the scenery didn't feel right either, even our tracks had disappeared from the sand. We would have to go thirsty for the moment.

Our group of six was now strung out into two groups of three, with about twenty five yards between each, the last lot were definitely feeling the strain.

"Come on you lot, don't fall behind, we've only got about five miles to go, it's a doddle".

Not quite a doddle I thought for some.

The hot sun in Egypt had never really bothered me too much, I could wander quite happily in temperatures well over a hundred degrees fahrenheit with no shirt or sunglasses on, which must be my Burmese ancestry coming out, but for some of the others it was no joke at all.

At the end of the next hour we stopped again, hunting around for the last water cache, but like the previous stash, it couldn't be found. "I just don't understand it" said our leader "I've taken good compass readings all along, and have timed our progress more or less right, and yet there's no sign of it, we'll just have to carry on without it"

With everyone feeling pretty dehydrated, we breasted a slight dune, and saw the railway track shimmering in the haze a mile ahead, and noticed that despite keeping an accurate compass heading for the return trip, we were inexplicably a couple of miles south of the canal watch tower we had used as a marker on our way out. It was most puzzling.

By now,it was 1300hrs and reading 44C on our thermometer, and as we had told friends in the section we expected to be back before 1300, I hoped no twit had raised the alarm to say we were overdue and missing!

We sat with our feet in the Bitter lake for a while, waiting for the second group to catch us up, and when they did, it was obvious they weren't going any further just then, they flopped out on the shore, completely exhausted, unable to move a muscle.

They would have a swim in the lake to revive their bodies, before returning to our original crossing point, so it would be some time before they set off again.

We could go on ahead if we wanted, just to make sure no-one spilled the beans regarding our late arrival.

In our hot and tired state, the relative coolness of the canal crossing was an absolute delight, it hadn't been such a bad trip after all, but it had taken much longer than we thought. It was past 1430 as we crawled ashore, so we could be in the kacky-poo already!

Fortunately for us, a couple of fellow conspirators were anxiously awaiting our arrival on the jetty as we landed, while the other erk, who might have blown our late arrival, was asleep on his pit, typical, but at least we were home and safe!

A few days after our mad desert jaunt, I sent off for a 1/4 plate Soho reflex camera I had seen advertised by Westminster photographic in London, but because my father was anxious I shouldn't buy a pig in a poke, he asked a friend of his in charge of the photographic section at New Scotland Yard to look it over first. Apparently everything was ok. and the camera eventually arrived by forces mail in Egypt two weeks later.

In common with a lot of 1/4 plate and 9x12 cameras sold at that time, an RFA (roll film adapter) was included which had a metal, knife-edge fitting - not a lot of use really when the camera used wooden book-slides, with block edge fittings!.

Unable to use the 120 size roll-film holder, and necessity being the mother of invention, I made a jig from two strips of thick card pinned to a wooden, print trimmer, and cut odd lengths of 9" wide panchromatic aerial film, into 1/4 plate sheets to fit the book slides. I could now go out and see what my new acquisition could do!

On the marshes at Deversoir there were, amongst a host of migrant species, a couple of pairs of resident Spur-winged Plover, a species very much like our Lapwing, which I thought would make an ideal first subject for my camera. I knew they had not been photographed at the nest in Egypt before, so I waited hopefully for them to breed, and perhaps give me the chance of making a photographic`first'.

It only took a couple of days using the binoculars to locate the plover's nest once the female was sitting, and when you knew where to look, she was amazingly obvious.

The nest, a mere depression in the sand, contained four heavily marked eggs, and was situated just above the high flood level of the marsh - quite vulnerable to any rising water level, so I kept a close eye on it.

Fortunately the marsh was rarely if ever visited by Europeans, and out of bounds to Egyptian workers anyway, so I decided to erect a small hide about twenty feet away from the nest, and see how the birds re-acted to it.

I dug a small pit about 30" square and two feet deep, put a brown canvas cover on poles over the top with just sufficient height to clear my head, and the job was done. I could now sit on the ground with my feet in the hole, my upper body camouflaged by the canvas, thus keeping the hide to an absolute minimum height.

I walked back to the RAF Medical centre some 150 yards away, and sat down to watch the birds' re-actions to my hide through binoculars. On cue, the female appeared about 50 yards from the nest, and after checking all was clear, walked straight to the eggs and sat down, resuming incubation.

The hide had been accepted.

A few days later, after checking that all was still ok. with the Spur-Wings, I decided a short session in the hide should be ok. and managed to convince one of my colleagues to put me in the hide, and wait nearby for a while to see that all was well before he left.

Our pre-arranged signal was that a piece of red cloth would appear at the back of the hide if all was not well, and he would promptly come and let me out. If no cloth appeared within a quarter of an hour, he could come back for me in an hour, by which time I should certainly have got some photographs.

Once in the hide I settled down, full of excitement at the prospect of photographing my first Egyptian species at the nest, and within minutes the plover appeared, hesitated briefly to look at the hide from thirty feet, before walking to the nest and settling down. So far, so good.

As I was some twenty feet from the bird, its image on the 1/4 plate screen using the standard 6" Ross XPress lens was a bit disappointing, nevertheless I released the mirror gently, and using the Luc Shutter on the front, gave 1/30sec at F.32.

The bird didn't bat an eyelid.

I managed to take several more photographs before I was released from the hide, and out of interest, walked over to the nest to show my sceptical colleague what it was all about.

Arriving at the nest site I was alarmed to see the water level of the marsh had risen quite a bit since my last visit, and the eggs were now only six inches away from wet sand.

I had intended to move the hide a bit closer to the nest when the bird had got used to it, but now to save the nest, could I do the opposite, and move the nest nearer the hide?

So as not to disorientate the bird too much, I made a new scrape only six feet away from the old one, moved all the little stones and shells that the pair had collected, and placed them round the eggs, offering a silent prayer that the bird would accept my substitute nest in its new position.

From the medical centre we watched anxiously as the plover returned, but she walked straight back to the nest without hesitation and sat quite normally, we couldn't believe it!

Apart from a quick check of the nest through binoculars at tea break, I wasn't able to get down to the hide again for nearly a week, by which time it was obvious I had done the right thing in moving the nest, as the old site was completely saturated and the new one was in danger of going the same way.

This time I took the bull by the horns and moved the nest to within ten feet of the hide, it was now fifteen feet from its original position, would the bird accept such gross interference? To my great relief she did, and on my next session in the hide I managed to get some really good close shots, and felt quite pleased with myself!

Unfortunately at this point, action by local terrorist groups put everyone on full alert, and I sadly missed the hatching of the plover chicks - I was buried deep in the bondoo (outback) on the far side of the airfield, guarding the ruddy bomb-dump!

I can assure anyone, anywhere, that there is nothing more soul destroying than to spend several days, miles away from everyone else, making sure some native doesn't nick or interfere with a load of dirty great bombs gently sizzling in the noon day sun!

There was little obvious wildlife in these baking, desolate wastes only the chameleon, swaying gently from side to side, as he weighed up his chances of snatching a praying mantis, or the huge hornets that seemed to chase you from pillar to post (for your moisture?) moving in the heat.

The Hornets' football-sized nests hung from palm and thorn thickets in their dozens, definitely deterring anyone from venturing off the paths between the bamboo clumps.

Jarring one of those buzzing citadels into life could well prove fatal!

Tension between the `occupying forces' and the Egyptians now manifested itself into desultory guerrilla strikes on the outskirts of various service camps and installations.

They also strung wire across the roads to decapitate unwary drivers and motorcyclists, and forced a complete blockade on any fruit or vegetables reaching the camps via our local suppliers, and giving us a pretty hard time of it.

Guard duties at the rate of three days on, three days off, combined with a heavy photographic workload, got up everyone's nose, and people's tempers were beginning to fray rather badly.

Life wasn't even a sick joke anymore!

There was one character whom I shall call Marsh, who made a point of firing off ammunition every time he was on guard, at real, or imagined intruders, friend or foe, he didn't give a damn.

I made his acquaintance twice, each time, way out on the perimeter of the airfield, where his post, atop a two-storey building set fifty yards off the peri-track, was only approachable through the centre of a ten-foot high bamboo thicket.

From the peri-track you could see his searchlight swinging backwards and forwards over the parapet of sandbags, casting a beam of light in the most erratic fashion.

"It's ok". said the corporal posting us from the Bedford truck, "Lazy bastard is probably laying down reading, he moves the light about by jerking his foot through a loop at the end of a long rope, mind you, I should call out your name and number loudly as you approach, he isn't particular who he fires at!"

As I entered the darkness of the bamboo thicket, I felt suddenly very naked and scared, especially now the gharry with its engine running, was out of sight and sound.

I'd seen the rows and rows of white crosses in the military cemetery in Fayid, and had vowed not to end up there if I could possibly help it!

"Marsh, Marsh it's me, Alan Parker, 13 squadron photographic, do you hear me?"

I stood stock still while waiting his reply.

Not a sausage, and what was worse the light had stopped swinging.

"Marsh, Marsh, you stupid bugger, do you hear me, I'm here to relieve you, it's second shift, and the gharry is waiting"

The only sound was the grating clack-clunk of a 303 bolt being worked, as someone put one up the spout.

"You'd better advance carefully into the light Parker or you're friggin' dead meat" said a voice I didn't recognise.

"Just stand still while I check you through the binocs, then you can come on with your gun held at arms length by the front sight"

Out of the rickety doorway and into the night, stepped a character straight out of the western backwoods, dirty, untidy, and carrying his rifle at the port like Davy Crockett, ready for action.

"Weren't scared were yuh?" he leered, "Can't be too careful y'know with all them terrorist bastards about.

Keep yer eyes peeled, and the light movin', see yer again sometime maybe" and he was gone.

A few weeks later, I was sent on a short detachment to 42 Field survey, Royal

Engineers, at Fayid, to learn Lithographic map-making, which was the end product of some of our aerial photography. The move away from our relatively large camp at Deversoir to the smaller engineer's camp, showed graphically how the food shortage was hitting a lot of the small camps scattered throughout the canal zone.

The Engineers' NAAFI was closed - it had nothing to sell, consequently the RSM organised a `paupers' Naafi at the back of the cook-house, where hungry swaddies could find something, anything to eat, including left-overs and scrapings from the cook-house bench.

I fondly recall being introduced to a stiff breakfast `porridge' made from iron-hard army biscuits, pounded into powder with a wooden mallet, and served with powdered milk and no sugar, yuk! - it was revolting, and had the consistency of cement.

Travelling anywhere off camp necessitated carrying a 303 rifle or Sten gun, and moving about in parties of three or more for security.

Despite these restrictions I managed to wangle my way onto various gharries taking equipment into Fayid a couple of times a week, and I was able to visit the Hospital gardens, an area of about 5 acres, given over to producing vegetables and fruit for British servicemen incarcerated in nearby Fayid Hospital.

In these gardens an army officer, Lt Col:Brownlow had got his engineers to build a 60ft long, 30ft wide Heligoland trap, which was capable of capturing large numbers of the thousands of migrant birds passing through the area during spring and autumn.

The Cairo Museum supplied the necessary rings, ringing pliers, books and identification manuals necessary to ring, and record the species that were trapped, and left the rest up to service enthusiasts.

An old looking, but relatively young in years Egyptian gardener by the name of Bulos was in charge of the gardens, and was always very helpful, especially in diverting irrigation water from the infamous Sweetwater canal, and pumping it into the mouth of the Heligoland trap to help us trap dozens of various warblers, Buff-backed Herons and other interesting species. It was all great stuff.

One morning, relieving myself at the Engineers' communal open air toilet, affectionately known as the `desert rose' I suddenly experienced an excruciating pain, and started to pass what looked to me like pure blood.

It was like pissing razor-blades.

"Ho! ho!" said one wag facing me across the large metal funnel embedded in the sand "We all know where YOU'VE been then, dipping your wick down the brothels at Suez eh?"

Knowing full well I hadn't indulged in anything of the sort, I stared in shocked horror at the crimson stream pouring into the desert rose, thinking, what the hell is wrong with me?

In considerable agony I staggered across to the MO's office, and reported sick, feeling a right prune describing why I was there at all.

“Ok. airman, get your kit into stores, and I’ll have you down the hospital in Fayid pronto, if it’s the clap, you’re on a charge for being unfit for duty, so you’d better be kosher!”

# Chapter Five

At the British Military Hospital in Fayid, I was quickly bunged into a ward with tough army swaddies, who wanted to know what a walking-wounded RAF pouftah like me was doing in their midst.

I said I didn't know what the problem was, but when I did, I'd let them know.

For a couple of days I was prodded and probed, while the doctors tried to analyse the continuing agonising expulsion of blood each time I urinated.

"There's no doubt about it, it's Haematuria - blood in the urine", one said. "We'll have to do an IVP, that's where we inject you with 100 ccs of X-ray sensitive dye, and take several X-rays at intervals to see if your kidneys are ok, we'll also continue with the anti-biotics, ok?"

"How did I get this condition then?" I asked.

"Oh, it's probably an infection from flies you've picked up somewhere, it's hard to say with all the dirt and filth out here" and off he went.

Fortunately my bed was near a large, ever-open window, which kept me a little cooler during the heat of day, but the venue was a source of great amusement too. Each day at about ten o'clock, an arab stood quietly outside the window, the top of his head just visible above the window cill, calling out in a sonorous voice, "Ebbrytin, ebbrytin"

After the third day of this peculiar behaviour, I asked one of the lads from the Lancashire Fusiliers, a long time resident of the ward, what the old boy was saying.

"He's saying 'everything, everything' when you get out of bed, you'll see he's got a big tray supported by a strap round his neck.

The tray is full of junk, because the rotten bastards who have been in here before, asked him if he could get this or that, or something stupid they didn't really want.

When he finally got it, they denied asking for it, or left the ward early, anyway that's how he's ended up with everthing, and that's what he's trying to sell"

When I got back to the Royal Engineers I was cured of the horrible lurgies, but still suffered from a feeling of tiredness which wouldn't go away, despite a good nights' sleep.

Once or twice I didn't hear reveille, which seemed to upset the tent Corporal, and he put me on a charge for failing to rise at reveille.

I don't think he was entirely happy that the RAF were being treated with a little more decorum than the bullshine riddled Engineers, and decided to even things up a bit.

The second Lieutenant who heard the charge, sensing the feeling behind the action, gave me the option of accepting his punishment, or having the charge entered on my service record.

I happily accepted his.

Unfortunately this turned out to be as an active member of a gang responsible for digging new ten-year bogs around camp, something I hadn't quite reckoned on.

These 'ten year bogs' were merely a trench dug in the desert, three feet wide, twenty feet long and fifteen feet deep, with toilet seats erected over them, serving as receptacles for human waste, until they filled up.

It is only when you beginto dig in the ruddy desert you find its only the top layer that is sand.

A foot or so down the terrain changes to the consistency of concrete, and can only be dug out with a pick-axe!

When I arrived on the scene, I was handed a shovel, and told to get to the bottom of the pit and shovel the loose stuff into a basket on the end of a rope, until the bottom was clear.

I could then start pick-axing the bottom loose for the next man.

It was a bit claustrophobic at the bottom of the narrow pit, and whilst shovelling rubbish into the basket, my shoulders and elbows got badly scratched coming into contact with the rough, stone encrusted sides of the walls.

To add considerably to my discomfort, those 'colleagues' engaged in operations at the top, inadvertently scuffed bootfulls of loose sand into the pit, coating my head and sweaty body in a thick layer of gritty sand, causing me to sneeze repeatedly.

At the conclusion of my hour's stint, I was recalled to the top, where I emerged looking like a flaming Yetti, glasses so covered in dust and sweat I could hardly see to stand up.

"Ok. that'll do for your stint, get yourself off to the showers for a clean up" said the Corporal in charge, and I shuffled off to get my towel, leaving them to their fun and games.

I reckoned if I could get the sand out of my ears, I would more than likely hear reveille next time.

There was a dramatic incident one evening, when a group of Engineer swaddies came back from Fayid, worse for wear from booze - in itself unusual as the stuff was in short supply, and decided to un-hitch the huge regimental 6" shell-case from its bullshit display case at the camp entrance, and drop it down the nearest ten-year bog.

This act of blasphemy was quickly picked up by the dreaded MP's who, on learning which bog the shell case was in, persuaded one of the Egyptian cleaners to go in after it, the ten pounds bribe being met from the pockets of the offenders.

When the poor chap emerged from the evil smelling bog, clutching the shell-case to his stinking clothes, he was hosed down by the fire crew, and given a clean change of clothes.

Sooner him than me!

As they say, nothing stands still, and it wasn't long before my stint with the Royal Engineers was over, and I was back at Dev. with a vengeance.

The local situation fluctuated between downright aggravation as the terrorists blew up our water supply, then the aerial film library, or caused mayhem by trapping married families in their Ismailia rented accommodation.

To put the last situation right a hundred or so Lancashire Fusiliers and us RAF bods piled into three-tonners and descended on Ismailia at gun point, it was almost open warfare, and we crunched them like matchwood.

It seemed to me that anyone not partaking in terrorism or downright non-collaboration with HM. forces, indulged in the national past-time of nicking anything that wasn't securely nailed down or closely guarded.

The place was rapidly becoming a zoo.

My normal weight prior to the troubles had been twelve and a half stone, but because of the severe lack of food, and my recent illness, I was down to eleven stone, and, like everyone else in the zone, constantly hungry.

I could count my ribs with my eyes shut!

Life at Deversoir was definitely at it's lowest ebb, and we really felt the pinch, it couldn't go on like this much longer without some very serious trouble errupting.

I thought it the height of stupidity to allow young Egyptian lads to come into camp each day to cook, dhoby, and clean out our billets, when they could see the name and patrol area of every swaddie by looking at the SWO's list on the Guard-room wall. Failing that, it didn't take any great intelligence to know who was on guard duty, by remembering whose webbing they had just blancoed!

We might just as well give the whole population free rein of the damned place, and let them take what they liked. It was crazy!

Despite having been warned by the terrorists not to co-operate with the English, most of the young lads continued to roll up for work, they were desperate not to lose the little money they got working for us.

There was no other income available.

It wasn't surprising therefore, that due to our naive lack of security, the odd Egyptian truck was man-handled quietly across the sand at night, the perimeter wire clipped, the truck filled with goodies spotted during the day, and the whole lot driven smartly away to be sold in the Suez kasbah!

In retrospect I know this sounds completely mad, but one day as we sat drinking our tea at afternoon break, Ginger broke the silence by saying "Do you know I haven't had a crap for four days now, do you think there's summat wrong with me?"

Dave, his close friend, never known to be bested in anything immediately replied "Nah! that's nothin' unusual, I haven't been for five"

"You lying bugger!" said another, "I saw you at the bogs this morning, I was there".

"Aha!" said Dave "I WENT there but I didn't do anythin', so I beat old Ginger here"

"Well I haven't been for four days, but I bet I can beat five, maybe even six" said Ginger, and that's how the competition started.

Within a short time, several of the lads were claiming alarming records as people tried to beat the total, which now stood at eight days, but of course you never knew if anyone was cheating by slipping away quietly to the bogs during the night!

Anyway it certainly provided a hilarious distraction to the monotony rampant around us.

During a bit of horseplay with the lads one evening, I managed to break my glasses, and as we had no ophthalmic services at Deversoir I was told to go to BMH (British Military Hospital) Fayid and get some new frames immediately.

I enquired how in the present circumstances I was to get there, bearing in mind there were no Service buses running, and we were supposed to travel around armed, and in threes?

"Don't be awkward lad, just go there and get it bleedin' done will you? Scrounge a lift, fly, walk, swim, anything, but don't bother me" said our Chiefie with a pained expression.

The first lift I got was from a chap going to Abu-Sultan, only a few miles down the road, not very far, but better than nothing.

After that, I sat beside the road for an hour or so with my gun, watching a delightful Rufous Bush-chat, and thumbing various service vehicles that passed by, with no success at all.

I got off my butt and started to walk.

It was quite funny really, here I was, myopic, blind as a bat to anything more than six feet away, constantly turning round and round with my sten gun, listening for any Egyptian who might sneak up out here, and cut my throat!

As it turned out there were no suitable frames for my lenses in BMH Fayid anyway, the whole trip had been a complete waste of time - they would let me know when something came in.

On return to camp many hours later, having been without a bite of food all day and thoroughly cheesed off, I was utterly mortified to find I was on the SWO's list for wandering airfield patrol over the next three days.

How had that miserable bastard had got my name, I'd like to know?

Apparently the SWO required me to guard several million pounds worth of jet aircraft belonging to King and country, with or without the aid of my glasses, pronto. That's all I needed!.

My protestations to the SWO's office, the MO (Medical Officer) and anyone else I thought had a grain of common sense, met with no sympathy whatever.

'You're down for the duty and that's it - everyone has to do it some time or other, anyway it's too late to change the list now' was the mindless rejoinder I got.

Fortunately the other chap I was rostered with, (there were only the two of us!) understood my plight, and laughed like a drain. How could anyone expect a chap to guard millions of quids worth of property from terrorists, when he couldn't make out a 15cwt gharry parked a hundred yards away on the runway?

He said he would, for a small fee, be my eyes too.

The first day passed quietly enough - we found an old air traffic-control trailer to hide in, which made life a little easier.

At least we could get out of the 100F. heat, and read or doze alternately, whilst my friend kept a lookout along the peri-track for any signs of life coming our way in this god forsaken wilderness.

Apart from the groaning of expanding corrugated iron, the only sound to penetrate the stinging heat was the monotonous drooling of Palm Doves in the hangars, which was enough to send you to sleep anyway!

The second day was like the first, mind bending silence and crunching heat, we were so far away from camp even the flies hadn't managed to find us, but my mate's stickability was going, he had to go walkabouts or go nuts, leaving me and my ears, to keep out of trouble.

On the third day he disappeared as soon as we were dropped off at the edge of the airfield next to a small village consisting of four mud-huts.

I hadn't a clue where he went into hiding.

The village children, used to our casual patrolling and not giving a toss for HM Forces anyway, climbed the wire fence to collect dates from the palm trees on our side, which I certainly didn't mind, it was their country anyway.

On one of my perambulations the previous day I had picked up a nearly new .303 cartridge, lord knows who dropped it, and I toyed with the idea of popping it off, just to see if I could hit a target or something, even without my glasses.

Things were getting to the point where anything would do to break the sheer mind-bending monotony of the place, I could see quite clearly now how people went mad out here!

Just before midday I was searching the dispersal area for my absent colleague - I needed his presence to provide some relief from screwing up my eyes in an attempt to see things - when a Red-necked Raven landed on an old telegraph pole next to our hideaway hut, and started his sonorous croaking.

As he bobbed up and down croaking his challenge to an unseen rival, a wicked thought entered my mind; a pot-shot from my .303 would no-doubt make him sing a different tune, although with my lack of vision there was no chance of hitting him, but it would be fun to see him jump!

I released the magazine from my rifle, drew back the bolt, inserted the spare round, and slammed the bolt home.

Squinting my eyes down until they were mere slits, I managed to see the telegraph pole through the sight and took first pressure on the trigger.

At that precise moment, an RAF Landrover appeared from behind a nearby hangar, and screeched to halt twenty yards away, its image dancing and distorting in the heat like something seen through a watchie's coke fire.

In a sweat, I lowered the rifle to the ready position as the SWO and his satellite F/Sergeant, complete with youthful Squadron Leader, strode purposefully across the sand in my direction.

"You there, airman, we've had reports of intruder activity on the North perimeter, have you seen anything suspicious over here?"

As it was the SWO who reached me first, I dropped the rifle to my left side and threw them all a perfunctory hand salute.

"No Sir, nothing at all to disturb the peace" and at that instant I remembered that my rifle still had the magazine off and the bolt cocked, would old hawk-eyes notice?.

"Where's your colleague?" the Squadron leader asked .

"I saw him a few moments ago down by dispersal Sir" I lied.

"Well keep your eyes and ears especially open from now on, you never know what to expect next" said the SWO, and they turned round, piled into the Landrover, and sped off.

I really had to agree with the SWO, you never did know what to expect next, another second and they would have thought they were under attack themselves!

By the autumn of '52 both Tony and I agreed we were extremely cheesed off with the lousy conditions everyone was having to endure at Deversoir, and things were very near exploding point.

The frequent guard duties, long queues of scruffy men at the cookhouse, which continued to serve exquisitely lousy grub laced with galloping paratyphoid laying hundreds low, plus gross overcrowding in our billets, meant life was becoming a real crock of shit.

Out of 1000 men served by the disgusting Greek cook in our cookhouse, only myself and three others managed to escape the dreaded plague of paratyphoid, and the bogs were beginning to overflow.

Due to the continuing food blockade by the Egyptians, I was still running a stone and a half below my normal weight, and resembled a brown bag of bones, which wasn't so different from everyone else really.

Like most of the lads on camp, the only real 'top up' came when a food parcel arrived from home, then it was like Christmas for a day or two.

Quite often you'd come back to the billet from a stint of night-time guard duty - which had immediately followed a full day's work, to find you had no place to sleep.

Your bed and locker had gone, and the hut was full of RAF Regiment or Army bods with their piles of kit, kipping all over the floor, it was disgusting.

One day a notice appeared on the section notice board, stating that vacancies existed for two LAC's in the mobile field-processing unit at Kabrit, an airfield some thirty miles south of Deversoir on the shore of the Bitter lakes, and I said to Tony, how about it, surely it was worth a shot?

Anything but anything, was better than Dev. at the moment, so both Tony and I volunteered, and were dispatched forthwith - two volunteers were worth a hundred pressed men anyday!

In complete contrast to the daily apathy and drudgery of Deversoir, the lads at JAPIC Kabrit were a fiercely independent and dedicated lot, serving 6 and 13 Squadrons' daily photographic needs with gusto, and a high degree of professionalism.

The photo unit consisted of two Multi's and a CP - large mobile box trailers capable of multiprinting thousands of prints and continuously processing miles of aerial film day or night, plus large bright offices for laying out the aerial reconnaissance photographs after printing.

A 3 ton Bedford water-bowser was also on hand to feed the machines with enough water to wash all the films and prints.

The atmosphere of urgency, coupled with a massive output of high quality photographs (the machines ran at twice the speed of those at Deversoir) of politically interesting places, made the section a good place to work in.

We were engaged in first-line squadron service, with intelligence flights over Iraq, Iran, Saudi, Egypt, Crete and Cyprus occurring on a weekly basis, which were affectionately known by us as 'milk-runs'.

There were some lively and interesting characters on the aircrew side too, not the least was F/Sgt'Tiger' Bates, who had flown Gladiator bi-planes in the battle of Malta, during the second world war.

Whenever he touched down from a sortie, the cockpit hood would fly back, to reveal 'Tiger' standing up in the cockpit whooping like a banshee, riding the plane like a jockey on horse-back!

Other pilots who shall remain nameless, but carried the King's commission, felt themselves above this sort of childish horse play, but when Tigers' photo runs were laid out on the checking room table, his flight line over the target was as straight as an arrow, while some of his critics' work resembled a dog's broken hind-leg!

For some reason I could never fathom, it was common practice to take aerial films after our initial print, back to Deversoir for further multi-printing, by using one of our Meteor 6 jets as transport.

The journey would have taken about forty-five minutes by car, and although it was obviously quicker by jet, the difference in cost must have been enormous.

If you were a strongly built character, and were standing in the wrong place at the right time, you could be shanghied into the passenger seat of the Meteor, and a couple of heavy film tins dumped into your lap - a free ride in His Majesty's jet to deliver some of the day's work, what a gas!

After a particularly heavy day of printing, I was the recipient of one of these 'freebies', and thus experienced my first flight in a modern jet aircraft, and what an experience that was!

With a muffled roar and a continuous hard shove in the back, we were off, and I became acutely aware of that plasticky, sickly smell that seems to pervade cockpits of most modern aircraft.

Within seconds of take-off, I glanced out of the cockpit window to see the Bitter lake shrink to the size of a blue postage stamp in a sea of golden sand - it was quite frightening!.

"Hold on to your hat Parker," came a gritty voice over the intercom, "We're going down to look at some of those ships in the lake", and with that, the sky became sand and we hurtled down to God knows where.

With violent G forces tugging at my arms, I held on to the heavy film tins for dear life, as we barrell-rolled down the centre of the lake, skimming upside-down past tankers, cruise ships, and a French destroyer.

"Let's go round again and have a look at the Frenchman" said the pilot, and in a flash, the film tins tried to crush my knees, as we did a steep climb before rolling off the top.

"We'll pass the Frenchman on the starboard side - coming up now!" said the voice.

"There, did you see them all waving?". and before I could reply the world reversed itself, and we were climbing up-side down, sand and odd bits of rubbish from the floor cascading past my face onto the hood.

"We'll stooge around for a few minutes just to use up some of the fuel, the runway at Dev. is cracking up and doesn't like heavy loads, you still ok. back there with those films?

I must have given some assurance that all was well, although I didn't really feel it, my fascination for aircraft which had burned so strong over the years, had just taken a very nasty knock!

There was no doubt that three and four 'G' turns plus the negative 'G' of rapid descent, did nasty things to my ear balance mechanism, and I felt quite nauseous.

"We'll just do a little loop-the-loop for practice" said the disembodied voice, "Hang on to the tins Parker, here we go!"

As we got to the point where your feet begin to go over your head, I felt myself yelling in fear, and opening my sweat-filled eyes saw, over the pilot's shoulder, the Bitter lakes far below like little blue puddles. Like a locomotive out of control, we raced for the ground and I expected we would gradually level out to make for Dev. and a landing, but no.

As we reached the bottom of the terrifying helter-skelter, he pulled back the stick, causing me to sink through the seat, glasses sliding down my nose with the bone-crushing 'G' and we climbed like a rocket for a second go.

Again the terrifying inversion, and panic as things cascaded past my face towards the canopy, followed by the suicidal speed-dive towards the ground - I wasn't enjoying this at all!

Arriving at Deversoir, I felt a right prune as we taxied to a halt, hood back, and engines running, just to hand over two large tins of film, before turning around and heading back to Kabrit.

There must be easier ways of delivering films than this!

The work routine was tough, and not always inspiring,and sometimes we were so busy during the night, we were pleased to hit the sack during daylight hours.

Normally after breakfast at 0630, it was off to the portable trailers to mix and replenish dozens of gallons of chemicals, and run up our processing machines.

We would then stand down, until the first aircraft returned, (which they  timed to perfection with the lunch-hour) then, while the rest of the camp knocked off at 1300hrs for lunch and swimming, we shut the trailers to make them light-tight, and began our  processing and printing.

It was well known to our senior officers that refrigeration units fitted in the trailers for cooling had been perforated for ages, and were quite useless.

Without them the internal temperature soared to 110deg F. as we slogged away, and it was essential to take short breathers outside, to recover from the intense sweaty heat.

Apparently nothing could be done about the coolers, the trailers were obsolete, and no new ones were expected for yonks -  the erks would have to grin and bear it - typical!

It was quite a relief when the sun finally went down at 1830 and we could open the doors to work  in the cool of the night, without risk of fogging our materials.

If there was a complete 'milk-run' to process and print, we would be working in two shifts throughout the night, and the lot that came on at 0100 would close the doors again as dawn broke at 0400, finishing their work just in time to go for breakfast at 0630.

Naturally we used a hell of a lot of water with both processing trailers on the go, and someone had to take the three ton Bedford bowser to the camp mains and fill her up.

The water was then discharged into  huge circular canvas dams, which had suction pipes to feed each of the processing trailers.

Some weeks earlier, I had  mentioned to Tony, as he was one of the  drivers, I would like to learn to drive the bowser myself, and perhaps he could give me a few lessons, especially  as our regular driver had just been posted home, time-ex,

Thus with Flt/Sgt Tickners' permission and Tony's tuition, I became novice water-getter, and general NAAFI 'gofer' as required. Although the Bedford had a crash gear-box, and required double de-clutching to make a successful gear change, I soon got the hang of it, and was quite happy to charge back and forth as the situation demanded, complete with my prominent 'L' plates.

This blissful state of affairs might have gone on for ages, except for gross inattention on my part when returning to the billet one afternoon.

We had just completed a particularly heavy work load, and were coming up to the billets with  a dozen photographers clinging to the  bowsers' sides or sitting astride the tank, when I slammed on the anchors and  sent a great fountain of water gushing out of the top filler-hole, drenching everyone on board.

We all fell about laughing and got off.

This act of wanton abuse of RAF transport was witnessed by the garage Sergeant himself no less, who, when he finally became articulate, said he would see me in his office without fail the following day.

In some trepidation I duly presented myself to the garage Sgt's office, but for some reason, he was either too busy, or too pre-occupied to hand out the prescribed rollicking, he merely said "Have you got the Bedford outside?"

I replied I had.

"Good, get in and drive me round camp for a bit, I've got several calls to make and I can see for myself whether you're any good or not.

God help you if you're not!"

For the next hour we went here there and everywhere, reversing, into this bay, or driving down this or that narrow road between buildings, until he said "Ok, I've seen worse, get yourself down to the compound next Saturday morning, and prepare for a driving test, - I'll be taking you myself!".

When Tony and the lads heard what had happened, they fell about laughing, saying that I would certainly get a right going over from his nibs for my troubles, no doubt about that!

The dreaded Saturday duly arrived, and complete with Bedford, I presented myself at the compound for my baptism of fire, knocked on the office door and waited until an educated voice said, "Come in".

Behind the desk sat a young Pilot officer - National Service Commission by the look of him- reading of all things, a manual on vehicle servicing.

"Morning Sir, LAC Parker, re - the 3 Ton Bedford test"

"Oh yes Parker, how did you get on, pass ok. did you?"

It was one of those delicious moments when your mind races like a dynamo, and you hear your mind say, ' Do I or don't I?'

"Yes Sir, no trouble at all"

"Good show" he replied, "Nice to see all you chaps getting street legal" and with a flourish of his pen, signed my driving pass and banged the official station stamp across the middle.

I had done it!

Heart thumping, and with a grin as wide as Martha Ray's, I jumped into the Bedford and took off for the billets, not daring to look in the rear view mirrors, in case I saw the garage Sgt. turning up for work.

When I told the lads what had happened, they hooted with laughter, but the smiles were quickly wiped off all our faces by one of the SWO's grovelling little clerks, who, passing on his issue bike, told us maliciously that amongst next week's delectable treats, was a rare Station Commander's close kit inspection.

Miserable bastard, that was all we needed to make our day!.

The photographer's billets consisted of ten, two-man accomodations, which although pretty spartan in their furnishing, were better than the RAF Regiment lads across the way, who had to make do with tiny pup tents, pegged into the sand.

On the morning of the inspection, seconds before the dreaded ordeal, Chiefie Tickner gave the imperious command, "They've just left the RAF Regiment tent lines and are headed this way, STAND BY YER BEDS at once!"

A couple of doors away, 'Frenchie' Saunders sonorously parodied Chiefies command with his own 'Stand by yer beds, here comes the Air Vice Marshall, he's got rings up and down both arms, but he's only got one arsehole"

"Silence that man!" bawled Chiefie, and being the first hut in line for inspection, our daylight abruptly vanished, as the SWO, his toady F/Sgt; the Station Commander and his Staff officer, crowded into the open doorway of our small room.

"Ten - shun, ready for inspec - shun" bellowed the SWO, and they all squeezed in.

After nearly fifteen months in the Zone, much of the time taken up with either hard work, or just relaxing and trying to stay sane, this close inspection lark came as a bit of a shock.

Brasses had acquired an interesting patina, our webbing looked like old sacking, and our KD was patchy with dried sweat.

It had taken a lot of bull and dhobying to get it in anything like good nick in such short time, but we had managed it.

Tony being nearest the door was grilled first, and passed muster with no adverse comment.

Then it was my turn.

The SWO unrolled my neatly folded socks with the end of his pace stick, as though they were something dredged from the latrines. "These need replacing, see to it" and his brown-nose F/Sgt; wrote it all down in his little black book for future reference.

For what appeared an age they all stood there gazing at my bedspace with it's less than pristine kit, as though wondering what to inspect next.

"Ah-ha - wot's this then", said the SWO triumphantly, and raking around with his stick, pulled an underwater speargun from deep underneath my bed.

"And these?" raking out a pair of swim fins and face mask.

"Put this man on a charge F/Sgt;" he said turning and grinning wickedly at my discomfiture.

"Unauthorised equipment found during a kit inspection by Wing Commander Freeman - sah!"

"Just a minute Station Warrant officer" said the CO, and turning towards me said. "Parker, are you interested in underwater swimming, or does this kit belong to someone else?".

"No Sir, it's mine I have been interested in underwater swimming for some time - some of this equipment was purchased in South Africa"..

"See me in my office directly after the inspection will you Parker?" said the CO, and whispering something in the SWO's ear, moved outside to continue their mayhem next door.

As they disappeared out of earshot, Tony looked at me and grinned, "You're damned lucky not to be blind-folded and shot according to the look on the SWO's face - you ARE a bit of a nut leaving that stuff where the ferret would find it"

"I thought I had put it far enough back to be out of anyone's sight, trust him to spot it, wonder what the CO wants to see me about, a bit peculiar isn't it?"

"Don't have a clue" Tony replied, "But whatever it is, you've landed yourself in the kacky-poo again, that's for sure!"

Thankful the SWO man wasn't in evidence in his outer office, I made my way cautiously to the CO's office and knocked gently - I didn't want to tangle with the SWO man again so soon, once they knew your name and number, you were dead meat!

"Come in".

The CO's well modulated voice gave no hint whether this was to be crunch-time or not.

"Sit down will you?"

"I asked you to come and see me because at the end of this week I'm leading a small convoy down past Suez, along the Red Sea coast, to evaluate possible forced landing sites for our aircraft, it's a reconnaissance if you like, of course we'll be swimming in the Red Sea as well, would you like to join me?".

To say I was astounded to hear his words would be the understatement of the year, but before I could answer, he continued, "Of course I'd like the opportunity to borrow your spear gun, they are unobtainable here, or even in the UK as you probably know"

I heard myself say "No problem at all sir, I have a second gun I am building to my own design, I'll use that, you are welcome to the other one"

We carried on a short discussion concerning various aspects of underwater swimming, plus Hans Haas, before I was dismissed with the instruction "Be at my house at 0800hrs this Friday, with a fully fuelled and kitted out Landrover - you'll be driving me, my wife and our two children down to the Red sea. We'll be followed immediately by two Bedford three-tonners manned by the RAF Regiment chaps bringing all our food, water and kit, so we should be quite comfortable".

In a daze I returned to the billets, repeating to the waiting lads what the CO had said. They had all expected me to get 80 days over the wall with forty lashes and couldn't believe their ears - a friggin' seaside trip with the CO? It was a wind-up!

"But you've never even driven a Landrover before!" said one of the lads.

"And what's more to the point" said Tony," I know you can drive the Bedford well enough, but you didn't really pass your test you know, and you've never driven off camp yet, how are you going to manage?".

The enormity of the situation suddenly hit me like a bomb, how the hell WAS I going to manage, and everyone began hooting with laughter at the thought of me trying to get the CO and his family across the bondoo, followed by the ever faithful Regiment - would we ever return?.

I suppose it served me right for being a clever dick, I should have admitted not taking the test instead of saying I had passed, then I wouldn't be in this ruddy mess.

There were only two Landrovers on the busy station, so it was quite difficult to get to grips with one, and I only managed to familiarise myself with the gear pattern and where the petrol and water went a day before that fateful Friday morning.

I was far too wound up to eat anything before we left, so I skipped breakfast and wandered down to the transport section, hoping to find the Landrover available few minutes early.

I was told by the garage Sgt. the Landrover for the CO. was already out, and wouldn't be back until 0730, but there would be ample time for me to do a daily inspection on it, and re-fuel, before meeting the CO at 0800. - I hoped to god he was right.

Needless to say sod's law operated at full-speed that morning; and the lousy driver didn't return until dead on 0800, it all seemed to be going bolo before I'd even started!.

Like a demented demon I filled her up with petrol, plus the two Jerri-cans on the rear, checked the oil and water, and raced to the CO's house where everyone, including two truck loads of RAF Regiment were already waiting to go.

"Sorry Sir, the vehicle wasn't returned until dead on eight, that's why I'm a bit late".

"Never mind that now, let's get this stuff on board and be off".

His wife and two kids, plus a huge wicker hamper thumped into the open back of the Landrover, and the CO plonked himself down next to me.

"Right, off you go, and head straight across the airfield due south, I'll navigate and give instructions as we go along". Exhibiting far more confidence than I actually felt, I engaged first gear, let out the clutch and we were off.

We had only gone about a mile when the engine began to splutter and misfire, causing the CO to glance quizzically in my direction. The engine picked up again when I pumped the throttle vigorously, but we only managed to cover a 100yards or so before it started spluttering again, before finally dying completely.

"What's the matter Parker, are we out of petrol or something?".

"No Sir, I filled her up, checked oil and water, as far I know there's no reason for this"

At that moment a huge figure bearing three stripes, on whose shaven head sat the smallest beret I had ever seen, slammed to a dusty halt alongside, threw up a cracking salute and enquired, "What seems to be the trouble SAH?".

I chipped in "She's cutting out intermittently Sergeant, it sounds like petrol starvation to me".

He wheeled on the spot, called to one of his men in the first truck, and within seconds had the bonnet up and was deep inside territory which was absolutely alien to me. After five minutes of embarrassing silence, a voice under the bonnet called "Try it now Sir please", and the engine roared into life.

"Just dirty points on the electrical petrol pump SAH!" exclaimed the Sgt; and disappeared to the rear, in a cloud of dust.

It wasn't long before we were rattling through the dirty streets of Suez and heading along the coast road south, the route alternating between long stretches of desolate sand, hemmed in by the garish red cliffs of the Gebel Ataqa, or a cliff-hanging track hacked into the rock face of the Gebel el Bahariya, with the blue sea twinkling invitingly, a hundred feet below.

Just after mid-day we arrived at a place called Ma Swelim, a beautiful area of secluded beaches nestling between huge red cliffs that plunged almost vertically into the sea.

It was idyllic.

After a quick meal, everybody made for the sea, which to my amazement was so clear when looking through the face mask, I felt a distinct feeling of vertigo as I looked at the numerous fish and coral formations 60ft below.

Looking back on it, I don't remember anyone actually going off to look for likely sites for a forced aircraft landing, (as per the original instructions) but I do know everyone had a super time for a couple of days, swimming fishing and eating. I managed to harpoon a couple of fish with my new design gun, one being a grouper of about 30lbs weight, which we cut up and grilled on a drift-wood fire on the beach.

Although this part of the Red Sea was known to have sharks up to 3 metres long, (Hans Haas-'Under the Red Sea') nobody actually saw one, which was quite a relief.

I must have had the gods on my side though, because after I harpooned a large fish, I swam about with its carcass clipped to a trailing line, leaving an inviting trail of blood and fish essence behind me, for any scavenging shark to find!

Once it occurred to me the idiot thing I was doing, I made a bee-line for shore and got rid of it, I didn't want to end up like the sharkbait scenes we saw at the cinema!

The return journey to the zone was quite uneventful, but as we clattered our way across the stony wastes south of Kabrit airfield, the engine started to splutter and cough once more, just as it had on the outward journey.

Determined not to be embarrassed like the last time, I gave her full throttle and slipped the clutch a bit to keep her going, and finally made it back into camp.

Naturally Tony and the rest wanted to hear all the lurid details concerning our trip, what had happened, how many driving goofs had I made, how often we get lost etc: which I recounted in fair detail, until, savouring the best 'til last I said, "In fact, it all went so well the CO has asked me if I would care to go with him again in a month's time"

They just couldn't believe their ears!

Phrases like 'Jammy bastard' and 'He should have got jankers, not a bloody holiday' floated on the air, and we all trudged off to the Naafi and tea.

By the time the second visit to the Red Sea was over, I was practically 'time-ex, with only a few weeks remaining before repatriation to the UK - two and a half years of my life had simply slid away.

What would things be like at home after this sort of life?

Hearing the old Army song 'The long and the short and the tall' on the radio next day, I suddenly appreciated exactly what the songwriter meant when he said 'And back to their billets they crawl'.

We ourselves had just said sad goodbyes to lads we had lived with for more than two years, often under the most trying conditions and parting wasn't funny at all.

It was like losing your right arm.

For some reason not explained to us, the number of squadron sorties flown on photo reconnaissance suddenly increased from the norm, and while everyone else happily finished at 1300hrs, we had the usual business of standing by until our aircraft touched down, and then starting work.

This meant we had to split the section into two groups for night work again, something we had thankfully got out of the habit of doing lately.

Our processing machines were still breaking down on a daily basis, and poor old Johnny Hammerton our mechanic, had his work cut out to keep us operational, spares were almost impossible to get, and most replacements had to be made by hand.

On one occasion, the leader on a long roll of 9"wide film was just entering the last meths. and water rinse tank, when the hot air blower packed up, leaving 500'of film coming off wet.

The rest of the lads had just gone off to lunch, leaving me to deal with the last knockings, which would have been a doddle under normal circumstances, but as the film was still being driven at the front end where the developer was, I had to keep it all moving or have a disaster.

There was no time to organise a spindle across a tank of water to keep the film wet until it could be dealt with later, what the hell could I do?

In a bit of a panic I looked out of the open door of the trailer and saw a couple of chaps I knew on their way to lunch.

"Hey, come and give me a hand will you,? this is urgent and I'm in deep trouble"

They stopped and looked at me, uncertain whether I was quite all there or not.

"For god's sake come and give me a hand with this bloody film will you, otherwise I'm in it up to here!"

Sensing the urgency in my voice, they came over at the run, by which time I was being forced to walk backwards out the door, and down three steps to the ground, holding the wet film in the air in an effort to keep it off the steps.

"Grab this end of this film will you, keep it taut and walk slowly backwards, DON'T let it touch the sandy ground for god's sake" I said to the first chap.

"If you as No.2 take a grip on the edges after the next ten feet comes off and follow suit, I'll try to get our lads back from dinner to take over, ok?".

Like a madman I dashed to the cook-house and grabbed a couple of the lads as they finished their food, haring back to the trailer just in time to insert a couple more bods under the length of film grinding out of the trailer.

By the time Johnny our mechanic got the message and returned from the beach, I had six chaps all in a row, holding 60' of aerial film over their heads emulsion up, drying in the hot sunshine.

From anyone's point of view the whole episode must have looked absolutely hilarious, it was so totally un-professional!

Whilst I gave Johnny a hand to mend the film dryer, a spare man at the head of the line checked the film for dryness, and wound it carefully by hand onto a spool.

Thank God things were coming under control at last.

At this point Nobby Clark, our Flight-looey in charge of the unit cycled past on his bike, and seeing ninety-odd feet of precious aerial film being supported on the heads of a line of blokes all laughing and joking, asked what the bloody hell was going on.

Fortunately he saw sense in what we were doing, and left us to it. Nobody dropped the film or stood on it, and it dried a treat, but it had been a ruddy close thing!

The weather fell true to form throughout July and August - 120 degrees in the shade on the airfield,(what little shade there was) being quite common, and with some of the lads getting 'Dear Johns' now that two years' separation were beginning to take their toll, acute depression was evident within the section.

It was said by those that knew, there were two ways of getting home, one by boat, the other by plane, and although a couple of hardy lads had asked to be allowed to cycle back to the UK, most preferred to fly.

Therefore it was with great glee we heard the troopship 'Empire Windrush' had caught fire, and had been beached somewhere off Cyprus, making her un-available in the immediate future for trooping, and we were being given the 'privilege' of flying first-class to the UK.

We were to fly in an old Avro York transport which had apparently seen stirling service carrying food supplies to the Germans during the Berlin airlift.

Having lived so long in a hostile environment, where to survive mentally and physically you checked all the angles, it came as a shock to finally be off, and I felt a distinct feeling of 'escaping' as I looked at the taut faces of friends I was leaving behind.

It didn't feel right somehow.

One of the lads, 'Frenchie' - he of the rude 'Air Vice-Marshall' song, found the prospect of going home to an environment where he wasn't wanted, just too much to take, and signed on for another year in the Zone, just to be with friends he knew and liked.

I felt that was incredibly sad.

We were brought down to earth as ever, by a grizzled F/Sgt who, ticking us off his list, bawled at the top of his voice, "Come on lads, get yer arses in gear, she's not long off the Berlin airlift this one, did dozens of trips then, should see you home this time too, IF you're lucky!"

After a quick stop at El Adem, we flew on to RAF Luqa in Malta where we kipped for the night, before flying on next morning to Stanstead in Essex, arriving just after mid-day.

# Chapter Six

I reckoned we must have flown directly over my house on the way in, and said to Tony it was a pity we didn't have some parachutes handy! Stepping off the York, I was immediately struck by the extreme contrast between the cool, gently falling rain in an incredibly green Essex, to the dry, raking heat of Egypt, it was unbelievable.

However, with no time to stop and stare, we were loaded on to coaches,and bundled off round the North Circular to RAF Hendon, we were just so much service baggage.

I had thought naively it would be a matter of us checking in, getting a travel warrant, and we'd all be on our way home, but no, the RAF had other ideas. We filled in this form, answered questions about that, had a full medical examination, were allocated a modern dormitory where we dumped our stuff, and finally shepherded away for a meal.

You were still just a ruddy number mate!

"You will be issued with travel warrants in the morning, and should be away by 0900hrs" said a pimply faced little Junior Technician, "None of you must leave the camp area for any reason whatsoever - other than that, the rest of the evening is yours" Great, here we were just a few miles from home, and still unable to complete our journey after two and a half thousand miles!

It made the marvel of virtually `instant' travel from Egypt to England, a nonsense.

The following morning, the faces of fellow commuters on the underground from Colindale to the City, were something to behold. Grim and unsmiling, heads buried into newspapers, each one sat silently minding his own business, scowling at us occasionally, as though our laughter had somehow trespassed into their personal dungeon.

I strode out of Becontree station at the end of my journey, and began the mile walk home, the two kit bags over my shoulder, seeming to weigh a ton.

How peculiar the houses all looked, they were so close together, they were actually LEANING on each other! Everything I remembered about the place seemed to have shrunk, distances had telescoped, houses had got smaller, just like Alice in Wonderland after her drink, and then suddenly I was at my own front door, it was all so unreal.

An incredulous mum and dad welcomed me in, and although the house was the same size as everyone else's, I ducked my head as I went in - I felt as though I would bang my head against the door lintel if I didn't watch it!

After a great week's disembarkation leave I still had two months service to complete, and the RAF in its wisdom decided that my talents could best be used at Nuneham Park, an RAF station near Oxford, the HQ of JAPIC UK.

With a logic born of many years dedicated service, the Flight Lieutenant in charge of the section decided that as I wasn't actually security cleared for the station, I was technically an `outsider', and therefore unavailable for printing duties without infringing top security.

Looking at some of the film canisters in his office, and the codes they carried, I told him that the work they were printing was in fact flown by my last squadron, and that

I was well aware of their contents, having done the initial printing some months ago in Egypt myself.

No matter, was his inane reply, I wasn't security cleared for Nuneham Park, and THAT was the thing - anyway, for the eight weeks I still had to do, it wasn't worth his while starting any new paper work just for me.

He had a brilliant idea though, I could be seconded to special duties - the SWO and his merry men would surely find plenty to occupy my time!

I groaned - I was back where I had begun my service three years before, a `gofer' for anyone who had a shitty, stupid job to get rid of!

My return to a mindless `bullshine' regimen, after two and a half years of purposeful working, came as a nasty shock to say the least, and when my hard worn kit finally caught the official attention, five days jankers were awarded with ill concealed glee. "You can't walk around here looking like that, even if you were on the squadrons abroad, etc. etc.

The Flight-looey who checked me out on my last day was a real wag though, "I don't suppose you've given any thought about signing on for another five have you - you could probably make Junior Technician with your knowlege and experience?"

"You must be joking" I replied, "I've just been given five day's jankers after three years exemplary service abroad, under conditions that you lot here wouldn't tolerate for a minute, I couldn't possibly work with the mindless attitude that exists here for TEN times the cash or rank".

And that was that.

Like someone who has just got off a rush hour train and left standing on a quiet, deserted platform, I felt alone and vulnerable, what should I do?. What could I do?

I decided that until I found a job I really wanted to do, I would go back to Arks Publicity in Holborn, and pick up where I left off. That would do for starters.

I got a terrific welcome from everyone I knew, my old job back in the studio, and an enhanced salary, because I was 21 and now a `man' - what a lovely firm!

In no time at all, I slid back into the bubbling mass of commuterism, did my `nine till five' with the rest of `em, and went bird-watching with Dave at the weekends.

Despite allotting mum half my 12/8d a day pay,(61p) for the last three years, I had still managed to save a hundred pounds, which was enough to buy me a brand-new 150cc Excelsior motorbike. Travelling around Essex taking photos and bird-watching would be quite luxurious now compared to pedalling my trusty old bicycle.

It was about this time I had my little Ensign Selfix adapted to synchronise with the new `X' electronic flashes that were becoming available, flash-bulbs had always seemed clumsy to me, and in a second fit of monetary madness, I splashed out six pounds - a week's wages, on a 25 Joule electronic flash gun, which had a duration of a 1/000th. second.

It all worked off a 110 volt dry battery, and with its reputed short flash duration, I felt I should soon be producing masterpieces of bird photography in the mould of Eric Hosking!

Of course I hadn't yet heard of reciprocity failure - the inability of film to record as one expects, the small amounts of light given to it during very short exposure, but I was sure going to find out the hard way!

I was still pretty good at drawing and had done quite a lot of water colours of birds and scenes in Egypt, but now, having to draw to order, and adapt typographic layouts and lettering for press releases, I found it all rather stultifying. I knew I missed the hustle of active photography immensely, and things had to change.

Visiting Hainault Lodge with Dave one Saturday in July 1954, I climbed to a Kestrels nest we had been photographing from a nearby hide the week before.

Now the young were half grown, it was time to put numbered BTO rings on their legs, to see how long they lived, and where they might end up after fledging.

I had been off work with shingles the whole week, and I needed a break, hence our visit to the Kestrels.

Whilst I sat on a horizontal branch near the nest replacing the last young Kestrel after ringing, there was a loud crack and I somersaulted backwards through the air, and knew no more.

I `came to' at the base of the tree as Dave, who had shinned down the trunk like mad, asked breathlessly if I was ok.

"Yes I think so" and then shouted in pain as I quickly realised I had broken my right arm just above the wrist.

I stood up shakily, and Dave sensibly suggested we go to a hospital straight away and get it fixed.

The nearest was Oldchurch hospital, six or seven miles away - we could easily get there by bus, and I could leave my motorbike at the Lodge, it should be safe enough there, while we shuttled back and forth.

A couple of hours later, sporting a brand new plaster which stopped me putting my jacket back on, we made our way back to the Lodge. With my broken arm we'd have to call it a day, after all it's not everyday day you fall thirty feet out of a tree and walk away from it, so to speak!

"I've just thought" I said to Dave "You left your bicycle at our place, and came here on the back of my motorbike, how am I going to get us back home with only one arm, you can't drive can you?".

After his negative reply I said "Well, there's only one thing for it, I'll steer and work the clutch as usual with my left hand, you'll have to turn the throttle as I tell you from behind, we should manage to get home that way ok.".

It was quite a circus pulling away and stalling, shutting down the throttle, changing gear and jerking along, until we got the hang of it, but eventually we arrived back at my place in one piece.

My mother's re-action, after her initial concern was, "well you broke your left wrist mucking about with dirt-track bikes in 1950, and now you've done the other one, perhaps you'll leave it at that for now?"

I had a very difficult time explaining to the people at Ark's Publicity how on earth I managed to break my arm whilst in bed with a dose of shingles. I don't think my story of tripping over the back step, was entirely believed!.

Undaunted, I continued to go to work on the bike, solving the problem of being unable to twist the throttle by swapping the throttle and clutch positions on the handlebars. I could twist the throttle with my left hand and gently pull the clutch lever back with my right fingertips.

The only thing was, the throttle had to be twisted forwards to accelerate instead of backwards, which took a bit of getting used to at first!

Driving to work one day, I was nudging the lawful 40mph across Wanstead flats, when I noticed a Police motorcyclist in my rear view mirror. He kept just behind me for several yards, eventually pulling close alongside, glancing quizzically at the plaster showing on my wrist, and then at my handlebars.

As we came up to a zebra crossing a pedestrian walked out, so I revved, changed gear, slowed down and stopped. For a few seconds the P.C looked at me closely as I selected first for moving off, and as I pulled away smoothly, so did he, keeping pace alongside me for about a hundred yards.

Apparently satisfied that I seemed to have perfect control, despite my unusual layout, he zoomed away and left me to it, I had thought for a minute he meant trouble.

When the plaster was removed a couple of weeks later, it was like learning to drive all over again, with the controls returned to their normal positions, it just shows how we can adapt if we have to.

After two years with Arks, I began to feel it didn't matter whether I produced anything substantial or not, the firm was so big, and making lots of money, my presence was neither a plus nor a minus. I definitely had to go, and no messing!

In December 1955 I saw an advert in a national newspaper, seeking applicants for a medical photographer's post at Gt. Ormond St Hospital, Holborn, which incidentally, was just round the corner from my present job with Arks.

When I went round there for the necessary forms, I discovered the Senior photographer in residence was none other than Roger Wellingham, the same smart-allick who had gone `sick' at RAF Wellesbourne, so that he could dodge the next course he knew to be processors and printers, and get the following course of ground photographer, thus ensuring he had camera work all the time!

A right crafty-Clara.

Apparently I was one of six people selected for interview and must have made a reasonable impression, because I was eventually offered the job, which paid six pounds a week, a little better than Arks at five, but I was going back into full-time photography again, and that was great!

One thing I remember dear old Roger saying on my first day in the studio - he hoped I hadn't come into photography to make money, as there wasn't any, leastways not as a medical photographer, as I would very soon find out!

In the world of ornithology I decided I would like to continue bird-ringing on my own, and because of the expertise I had gained trapping and ringing birds in the Suez Canal Zone, I was accepted by the British Trust of Ornithology as an `A' ringer straight away, which allowed me to trap and ring birds for scientific research purposes in the UK. without supervision.

In a BTO magazine I read that a Dr. Eric Ennion was running week - long ringing courses, on how to trap waders, and sea birds at a place called Seahouses in

Northumberland, and wrote off to see if Dave and I could attend that autumn. He replied we would be more than welcome if we could make the long trip, as he had plenty of work lined up.

The first week in August saw Dave and I set off on my trusty 150cc up the A.1 to Northumberland, but with two great blokes and all our gear on board, the little bike found it hard going, and it was ten hours before we finally got to Seahouses.

We had a marvellous time though, and learnt many new trapping techniques, not the least a method known as Bat-fowling, where you swung two bamboo poles joined together in the shape of a Gothic window, with the middle filled with loose netting, at bushes where birds were roosting after dark.

With a bicycle torch strapped to your chest, the birds flew towards the light when disturbed, and were caught between the poles in the loose netting. It seemed so simple and quite exciting, especially as you didn't always know what you had caught until it was examined back in the laboratory.

A couple of days spent on the Farne islands ringing scores of Lesser black back gulls, and evenings spent catching flightless Eider ducks as they came ashore to drink, were real eye-openers.

Dr. Ennion had devised a method of catching the moulting, flightless Eider ducks, by hiding between the rocks at low tide, and allowing the birds to walk past to drink at a fresh-water stream further up the beach.

Once the birds were past, people ran out and caught as many Eider by hand as they could, before the birds made it back to the sea again.

Naturally, success depended on the speed and skill of the catchers, and only a few birds were caught on each occasion.

I reasoned that if I diverted the stream through a right angle, making the Eider come further up the beach to drink, and laid out an old tennis court net I had found between the diverted stream and the sea, all we had to do was pull up the net with guy ropes once they were past, and snaffle the lot!

That evening as daylight faded, we anxiously watched a large flotilla of Eider appear off shore, and then make their way cautiously up the beach to drink.

I had managed to persuade nearly a dozen people to help release the birds from the net in the event of our being successful, and we all waited breathlessly for the ducks to cross the netting and start to drink.

Almost as though they suspected some trick, most of the birds hesitated to cross the net at first, but as one or two crossed and began to drink, the rest followed like sheep. I was situated on the right hand guy line, and Dave on the left, and the signal to pull, would be a flash on the torch in his direction as soon as the birds were in the catching area.

As the torch flashed and the net came up, pandemonium broke loose, ducks went everywhere, but anticipating the Eiders might try to bolt round the open ends of the net, I had helpers get there first to keep them bottled up.

Dr. Ennion, who had been briefed in what I hoped to do was ready and waiting in the observatory with data sheets, rings and scales, so that as the birds came in, they were checked, ringed and weighed before being put into soft hessian sacks and laid on the floor to settle down.

By the time everything was complete, we had a total of thirty-two Eiders, far more than had been caught at any one time previously, it had been quite a success.

Everybody took a couple of sacks apiece and walked down to the waters' edge to release the birds - it was essential to let them all go at the same time, so the group could stay together for safety reasons. At the end of our stay Dr. Ennion was so pleased with our general efforts he reduced our bill by a substantial amount, and said we were welcome to return to Seahouses anytime we liked!

As Dave and I were well known to the Hainault Lodge hospital staff for our bird-watching and `accident' activities, we were invited to a Christmas party in 1956, given by the nurses at Oldchurch Hospital Romford, and it was there I met the young Irish girl who was eventually to become my wife.

Until that time I had firmly resisted any temptation to get `bogged down' with girls - I had seen far too many of my friends turned `inside out' and diverted from their masculine pursuits to let that sort of thing happen to me!

The party was a great success, and afterwards Teresa and I met quite a lot, and when she got `posted' to Hainault lodge, it couldn't have been better.

During the next few months we got to know each other pretty well, and I felt she was the girl for me, but what did I have to offer her as a potential husband?

The upshot was, I now had to stop shilly-shallying about, and buckle down to a profession that could support us both in the event of our marrying, the regular job at Ormond St although poorly paid, was only a start.

My initiation into the very precise world of medical photography was taken in hand by Roger, the Senior photographer, an excellent tutor, who seemed to know not only how to photograph the various obscure parts of the human anatomy, but the latin names for all the bits as well!

These lessons were supplemented by day classes, held by the head of St. Bart's hospital photographic department, and night classes at the Regent St Polytechnic, under the tutelage of Ms Margaret Harker - all in all, a wealth of education and instruction!

In my spare time, I read quite a few travel books, and in particular, accounts of bird trips made to Eire in the 1920's by the great naturalist Ussher,

It seemed from his vivid descriptions of birds and places, Ireland was a terrific place to visit, wild, unexplored, and teeming with sea-birds, besides, if I went there, I could call in on Teresa's family at the same time, and button- hole her dad regarding our plans for future marriage!.

The outcome of all this Irish stuff was that I set off in June, armed with trip-tyque, travel carnet, and visa, on my trusty 150cc motorbike, heading towards Fishguard and the ferry. The bike was unceremoniously hoisted aboard the Irish ferry in a rope sling, and dropped into the hold like a sack of spuds, no roll-on, roll-off ferries here!

Once in Eire the magic of the place soon took hold, the country was wide open and virtually free of traffic, in fact the only other motor bikes I saw, were those belonging to the chaps who crossed on the ferry with me!

It didn't take long to reach Loughrea, Co. Galway, where Teresa's family lived on a two-hundred acre farm, in fact there was more difficulty in locating the farm just outside Danesfort, than any other part of the journey.

The patchwork of farm fields surrounded by drystone walls, seemed to go on for ever!.

Feeling just a little incongruous visiting future relatives, dressed in my motorcycle gear, I turned off the little bogside road through very impressive wrought iron gates - a fairly typical feature of houses in the area, towards a large white house set on a small hill some distance away.

There was little to see except sheep feeding in the fields, which went on for miles and miles, overlaid with mellow calls of Curlew in the boggy fields. It was all very quiet and rural.

My reception by the family was cool, but courteous - I was formally introduced to everyone by Teresa, - who just `happened' to be home on leave for a few days.

I felt like one of those young men in films, who presents himself for examination in front of the stern head of the family, but in this case things turned out to quite differently.

As soon as the initial awkwardness disappeared, conversation began to flow, and things got a lot easier. In no time at all, the roast goose dinner was pronounced ready, cooked the traditional way in a sealed iron pot suspended over an open peat fire, and it tasted delicious!

When the meal was finished, I fondly imagined myself buttonholing Teresa's father to acquaint him with my intentions of marriage, but no, as soon as we got up from table, he grabbed his hat and walking stick, and legged it out the door like a good `un, not bad for a chap of seventy-one! By the time I was free to leave the room, he had disappeared completely, and for the next hour or so, he played find- me- if- you can, over most of his farm.

Eventually I cornered him among some haycocks he was building in the home meadow.

"Can ye make a rope?" he enquired, squatting on the ground amongst the loose hay, and starting to work with his hands.

"I'm sure I can if you show me" I replied.

"Ye twischt it like this" he said, in that peculiar way they speak locally, "An' when ye have done a bit, ye hold it down with a rock like this, and make some more"

He proceeded to tease the loose hay into a substantial rope, twisting it round his fist into a strand and keeping it tight. When he had made a couple of feet, he weighed it down on the ground with a large stone to stop it uncoiling, while he twisted some more.

I got stuck in, and once I got the hang of it, had little difficulty in producing two ropes, each about fifteen feet long, which he sat patiently waiting for.

"Right now, tie a rock on the end of the rope and throw it over yonder rick" - a conical pile of hay about ten feet high built round a central pole, "Keeping hold of the free end" he added with a grin.

I did as I was told, and he did the same, but at right angles to me so the rick was held down like a hot-cross bun.

"Now the wind can't blow the hay away" he said by way of explanation, "We've got three more ricks to do before dark, so we'll have to hurry"

"I want to marry your daughter Teresa" I blurted out.

"Oh" he said non-commitally, "What do ye do fer a living then?"

"I'm a medical photographer at a London hospital" I replied

"Can ye support my daughter as well as she is now, - her education cost a bit ye know" I was quite puzzled by the inclusion of her education into the conversation, but hastily agreed that I could, although to myself, I earnestly hoped that my new job would eventually lead to an increase in salary to make it all possible.

We finished the haycocks as lowering clouds brought on spitting rain, telling us the day was done, and retreated into the warm security of the house.

An anxious Teresa pulled me aside as I entered.

"Did you ask, did you ask him?" she whispered anxiously.

"Of course I did, but he didn't say yes and he didn't say no, I imagine he'll speak to your mother and you about it later, then you can tell me!".

Supper was a pretty formal affair, with lots of body language belying the actual words being spoken, and soon it was time to go - I had to find a room at the Railway hotel in Loughrea before everyone closed up and went to bed!

Teresa suggested I carry on with my proposed trip to the islands of Inishbofin and Inishshark the following day, and call in on my way back home to England, she would then tell me how things had turned out.

I still had a full week to go before returning to the ferry at Rosslare, so I took off as Teresa suggested, ploughing across Connemara, following the muddy road through Maam Cross and Oughterrard towards Clifden, taking photographs as I went.

Beyond Oughterrard the unmade road was lined in places with large oil-drums, no doubt an invaluable aid to travellers facing the prospect of disappearing forever into the stark wilderness!

After a couple of hours crossing some of the wildest, grandest and most desolate scenery imaginable, I rolled into Clifden, made famous by Allcock and Browns' epic trans-atlantic flight, and asked the way to Cleggan, the jumping off point for the islands.

`Ye can take the low road by way of Claddaduff or the high road, it doesn't matter which',I was told.

`They're both on the far side of town'.

By pure accident I found myself on what I hoped was the `high' road, a muddy earth track meandering along the cliffs, with nothing much in sight for miles, but it didn't seem right somehow.

As I progressed, I saw in the far distance a small cottage which the track appeared to be heading straight for, and as I approached I could see two people talking at the front gate.

As I got closer, I realised the track must lead straight to their front door, and I felt a right twit bursting in among them, an absolute stranger out of the blue!

However at the very last moment, the track did a sharp right turn at their front gate, and meandered off into the distance again - I was saved from embarrassment!

As I changed gear and took the bend, almost touching the two at the gate, they stopped talking and stared vacantly in my direction without a trace of surprise. "Good afternoon!". I yelled, and continued without pause, feeling like some weird visitor from outer-space.

After such a long drag through pretty demanding terrain, the track finished with sudden abruptness, and I was rolling down a short-steep hill towards the sea and a jetty. I was in Cleggan.

Parking the bike on the tiny quay, I anxiously waited for someone to appear and perhaps tell me when the boat to the islands was due, but there wasn't a soul about - it felt like the end of the world.

After an hour I spotted a fishing boat way out to sea, its little mizzen mast swaying from side to side as it rolled in the following sea, and I thought how tiny it looked in the sheer immensity of it all, and I start taking pictures.

The boat when it eventually arrived, turned out to be my long-awaited transport to Inishbofin, the `Northern Ranger'

The locals called it the `mail boat' and I suppose it was, but to me it was a jack of all trades, French-style fishing-boat, and pretty small at that!

A couple of passengers appeared from no-where, and put their goods on deck squatting down stoically by the open hold, where I joined them. The lack of any facilities except the tiny wheel-house, and a strong fishy smell emanating from the hold, told me it was definitely a working boat!

On arrival at Inishbofin I was made most welcome at the hotel, and found that my hosts, Michael and Margaret Day were in fact distant cousins of Teresa's family! It was only years later I learnt that everyone was a distant cousin of someone in this part of the world, it was no big deal.

Over a welcome dinner, I mentioned to Michael my hope of visiting Inishshark whilst I was on `Bofin, and he replied that if I attended the hotel bar that evening, I would be introduced to a man who might take me over in his currach the following day, wait a couple of hours, and bring me back again in the evening. It sounded just the job to me.

In the little building that served Inishbofin as a bar, a solitary electric bulb pulsated to the rhythm of a diesel generator somewhere, amidst a sea of tobacco smoke, and that's where I struck a deal with `my man'.

I was to meet him on the jetty at nine thirty next day, and he would take me across to the island of Shark for a few hours if the weather was suitable.

The next day, complete with binoculars, camera, sandwiches and drink, I arrived at five to nine on the jetty and waited for `my man'. I waited, and waited, and by twelve o'clock decided that something had gone sadly wrong, and although the weather was fine, the trip must be off.

Not wanting to waste precious time, I spent the afternoon exploring aand photographing Bofin, and noticed that as I came up to various crofts along the track in the West Quarter, doors would close, and curtains would `twitch', but I never saw a soul to speak to. I would have to ask Michael about that.

His eventual explanation was quite simple, the coastguard back on the mainland made it his duty when communicating with his opposite number on `Bofin, to give him a run down on any strange characters coming their way, and in his view, I was definitely one of those.

I had been observed using expensive binoculars on the jetty at Cleggan, looking all around and taking photographs, and therefore couldn't be trusted, I might even be someone from the government checking up on things!

As the news quickly spread, people feared the worst, I could just be a government agent - there was illicit poteen to be had on the island if you knew where to go, so it was safer if people kept a very low profile while I was about.

In an attempt to rectify this awkward situation, I asked Michael if he would kindly spread the word that I wasn't an agent, just a photographer, and would love to sample some of this poteen stuff myself given half a chance!

The next day, walking along the jetty I recognised `my man' from the bar, leaning against the side of a currach, and casually smoking his pipe.

As I drew near he called out "Are ye ready to go then? it'll be a lovely day"

I was too flabbergasted to ask what the hell happened to yesterday, and settled for the fact that we would at least be going today, `tomorrow' was obviously a very debatable item!

"It'll cost ye four pound" he said as we started to ease the light-weight Currach into the water, and I felt a bit put out at that, I had expected it to be about two pounds, four was a bit steep.

With a weeks' holiday still to go, I had to watch the pennies, things were surprisingly expensive in Ireland.

"Ok.then" I replied, but felt I was being `had over' because I was a stranger. Outside the harbour, we cut through a sparkling green sea, with Arctic terns screaming overhead and Razorbills surfacing nearby, and headed for Inishshark at speed, the outboard motor fitted to the lightweight tar-and-canvas craft, sending us across the sea like a bullet.

With just one family left in residence, the Laceys, the island was a naturalists' heaven, but for the Laceys, existing in their low -roofed cottage with only their animals for company, it must have been very hard, especially throughout the long, dark winters.

I was intrigued to see Festy Lacey cutting his sparse barley crop by hand sickle, although the fields here seemed far better than those on Bofin, and possibly well suited to mechanisation, I doubted if anyone on Shark could have afforded the machinery to do such jobs.

All around us sea birds flew in their hundreds, Fulmars, Razorbills and Kittiwakes, while overhead Choughs cracked their rifle-shot calls, overseen by the lordly Peregrine falcon. It was all anyone could ask for.

I arranged with my boatman to be back in three hours, and set off to explore the island, and soon found it would need several days, not hours, to see and photograph half the islands' birds.

All too soon my time was up, and I had to leave this unique habitat and return to `Bofin, but I'd return in the future that's for sure!

A couple of days later, with feelings of real regret, I said goodbye to the Days who had treated me so well, and boarded the fishing boat for Cleggan, vowing Bofin hadn't seen the last of the bird-watching Englishman by a long chalk!

To counter this exciting interlude, visiting Danesfort on my way home was a bit of an anti-climax, Teresa told me her dad thought I had the makings if I put my back into it, but her mum was dead against me, I was English, and that was the end of it!

Returning to my other world of London, and Gt. Ormond St, I was soon back into the swing of things, learning how to decipher consultants' dreadful handwriting and abbreviations, so that we could interpret their wishes and photograph the correct part of the patient's anatomy they wanted recorded.

There was one lovely incident where an indignant surgeon swept into the department like the Mad Hatter, waving some photographs of a child's ear in the air shouting, "Yes,yes, a lovely set of photographs for someone, I don't know who, pity it's not the nose I asked for!"

It was pure theatre, and obviously a dreadful mistake of the highest order!

There was a very strict pecking order to be observed when dealing with the hierarchy of the hospital, from Mr. Dennis Browne, Senior surgeon a lovely man to work for, Mr. Wylie McKissock, brain surgeon, a brilliant eccentric prima donna but a real shocker to work with, all the way down to those who knew what they wanted, and let you get on with it, relying on you as a professional to get the best results from their work.

After about a year I was considered competent enough in my photography to be on call for the main theatre, recording whatever the surgeon on duty there required. The department's only camera for this demanding work was a Rolleiflex with Proxar close-up lenses, and a Rolleiflash, using PF5 flashbulbs.

I didn't particularly like using these small flashbulbs as they had a couple of nasty features, one being the occasional broken wire at the base,(which you didn't notice), which gave no flash at the critical time, or if you placed the bulb in the gun before cocking certain shutters, the bulb went off in your eyes, - not very funny.

The worst scenario was if the bulb had air inside, it would explode on firing, splattering glass fragments everywhere, despite the bulb being coated in a protective plastic film.

Having watched Roger at work a few times I felt the results he got from his flash pictures were a little harsh, due to the strong highlights reflecting off shiny tissue, so for my own use I made a diffuser out of some opalescent plastic, which clipped tightly over the flash gun reflector, giving out a soft diffused light.

This arrangement did mean however, the reflector had to be unclipped each time a new bulb was inserted, but the resulting photographs of brain, or shiny tissue without harsh highlights were in my humble opinion, well worth the effort.

On one occasion I was glad beyond measure I had used the diffuser over the flash gun, when, during a close-up shot of open heart surgery showing a hole in the heart repair, the bulb exploded.

The surgeon whose face was about a foot from mine, fixed me with his steely blue eyes and said icily from behind his mask, "I sincerely hope for your sake that none of that went into the heart, or we're finished".

In a sweat, and shaking with trepidation, I carefully retreated from the operating table, and shook the remains of the bulb into a special disposal bag held by the theatre sister, carefully wiping the diffuser and reflector with damp wipes, before inserting a new bulb.

Looking across at the surgeon and his team, I waited for him to see me, and speak.

"I particularly want this aspect recorded before closure, but can you guarantee this bulb won't explode too?".

"No Sir, I can't, it almost certainly won't but I'll keep a bit further away and not directly over the chest cavity".

"Ok then, but if there's another bang like the last one to shatter my concentration, you'll be well advised not to be in this theatre a split second afterwards, AND I shall be speaking to your head of department about this matter, as soon as we have finished here".

The second shot went off ok, and I left the theatre with tail between my legs, reeling at the thought that I could so easily have been responsible for a child's chest being full of glass fragments, and a certain horrible death.

Back in the department I related the incident to our head, Mr Martin (pincher), and asked why we didn't have an electronic flash unit for this kind of work, it certainly made sense to me after my dreadful experience.

"I take your remarks seriously Parker" he droned, "But we haven't had an incident of this nature in the past, anyway, leave it with me and I'll discuss it with the finance committee at the next budget meeting".

Needless to say during the two years I remained at Gt; Ormond St, no electronic flash equipment was forthcoming for this kind of work, but I managed to avoid using flash for heart ops. altogether by using a much faster colour film under the existing theatre lighting.

A short while after this event I got an urgent call from `pincher' to attend one of the small side-theatres, to record a new technique being developed for restoring the hearing to children born without any connection between the outer ear and the inside of the skull.

An eminent visiting surgeon was about to undertake the corrective operation, and I was to record each stage of the proceedings for use as lecturing material afterwards.

I felt this was a situation where the Rolleiflex and flashbulbs would be quite ok, so in I went, waiting to be given my orders by the great man.

All went well for the first half an hour or so, during which a large patch of skin was removed from the child's thigh, and retained on a small stainless steel drum studded with tiny spikes, just like a miniature musical box.

The surgeon made a half inch diameter hole in the centre of the ear into the skull, and then took the piece of skin tissue off the drum, and wrapped it carefully round a plastic tube about 1/2" in diameter and 2" long.

"I'm going to insert this tube with the tissue wrapped around it into the aperture I've just made through the ear. I want you to photograph the aperture first, then the tube being placed in the aperture, and finally when it's in position, being stitched in, got all that?"

"The idea is that we line the aperture with tissue taken from the child's thigh, so that it doesn't gradually close up as the surgery heals". I duly completed the initial photograph without trouble, until we came to the point where the tissue on its tube was about to be offered up to the aperture in the ear.

Time after time, as it went in, the tissue rolled back down the plastic tube, as the edges of the aperture were a tight fit for the tube.

The anaesthetist and theatre sister were obviously beginning to get a bit anxious as the time slipped by - we had been in theatre well over an hour, and still the tube and tissue had not gone in.

The great man was sweating and barely controlling his exasperation, when for the umpteenth time the tissue rolled back, like a sock being pushed down a leg.

I couldn't contain myself any longer, and although I knew in the hierarchy of things, I was a mere microbe, I heard a voice I recognised as mine say, "Excuse me Sir, may I say something to you?".

His eyes flashed at me over his mask, and a steely voice said "Well?".

"I know it's not my place to speak to a surgeon, least of all when he's working, but I think I can see a way round your present difficulty".

The dye was cast, I was in shit street now - even the theatre sister gasped. I stood absolutely still.

"Oh you do, do you, perhaps you would care to give me the benefit of your undoubted experience?" I swallowed.

"Well Sir, each time you insert the tube and tissue into the aperture, it gets rolled off because of the tight fit you obviously need.

If you were to spilt the nylon tube down it's length before you affix the tissue, you can crush the tube down a little to allow it to go in, and the natural spring of the nylon will allow it to expand, and fill the aperture again".

In absolute silence, the great man split the tube with a scalpel, re-affixed the tissue, offered it up to the aperture while crushing it down, and in it went!

I took the remaining photographs as he directed, finishing off with the job beautifully stitched into position - it had been a long morning.

"Thank you, we've finished now, I shan't need you any more" he said, and with that I left the theatre at full speed, wondering what sort of rollicking I would get for such unmitigated impertinence.

Back in the section `pincher' asked me how it had all gone - had I managed to get the photographs the visiting surgeon required?.

When I related what had happened in theatre, his face went the colour of putty, and he wailed, "You actually SPOKE to a surgeon, without being spoken to first?, - my God Parker you certainly ask for trouble, I don't quite know how I'm going to deal with this, you'll probably get your notice".

Needless to say nothing happened, and we didn't hear a word from the surgeon either - not even a thank you for the photographs.

I never found out if my impudence had been forgiven or not, maybe he even thought my split-tube idea a good one after all!

It was during this time, the summer of 1957, that Roger, our Senior photographer left the department to take up a teaching post at a College in Kenya.

I thought at the time he was mad to take such a gamble, despite a very tempting increase in salary and rank. I felt the country was too unstable to base a career on, but off he went, and I was left on my own, while the Hospital advertised for a replacement Senior photographer.

Although my work was extremely varied and interesting, the call of the wild began to twitch my soul, and I arranged to visit Ireland and Inishbofin again, this time for ten days taking Dave Summers along for company.

The bike trip across Eire was, like last time, exhilarating, the warm sunshine made riding through the open countryside a pleasure, and in no time we were in Loughrea, visiting Teresa and her family for a few hours.

That evening Dave and I stayed in the little Railway Hotel in Loughrea, having a few convivial drinks with the manager and locals until midnight, but still managing somehow to be up and away at first light, bound for Inishbofin and the birds.

This time the route across Connemara didn't seem quite so bad as last time, someone seemed to have filled in the biggest pot-holes, and paint the oil drums along the route white.

Even the weather stayed fine enough for me to take some good photographs of the fantastic mountain scenery.

On `Bofin, I introduced Dave to Michael and Margaret Day, plus one or two other people I knew from my last visit, mentioning that apart from exploring `Bofin thoroughly, we both wanted to visit `Shark a couple of times as well, as it was such an interesting place for birds.

"Well now" said Michael, drawing me slightly aside, "There's a little matter of last year's visit to Shark I want to discuss with you" and I tried desperately to recall what I might have done to upset someone that still festered after a year?

"First ye'll both be my guests at the bar this evening, everything's on the house. Secondly we all apologise for the way `your man' charged for the trip across to Shark last year, he's been told about that, and put right,"

It was then I realised `my man' must have boasted to his friends how he got four quid from the English fella, and had subsequently come a cropper from the Days for being greedy - it was great to see the country code of fairness was still alive and kicking.

"If ye think ye can row my punt across" said Michael, "Ye're welcome to borrow that, and ye'll be free to come and go as often as the weather allows."

I told Michael that I was no stranger to rowing, and was well aware of the dangers of coastal waters, having lived in a Devon fishing town for some time during the war.

"Right-o then, but as I said watch the weather, and be careful, I don't want the Guarda coming over here looking for two missing English fellas".

Michael's `punt' was a sturdy twelve-foot clinker built boat, similar to ones you would expect to see on the Serpentine, rather long and narrow, but of much stronger construction, essential to cope with the rough coastal seas.

The next morning, Dave and I set out in brilliant weather to row the two and a half miles to Shark, the sun shining from a cloudless blue sky, and making the sea twinkle like diamonds.

There were a couple of small islets on the way to Shark which we landed on and explored, finding and photographing nests of Arctic Tern, and Oyster-catcher, it was all turning out really super.

Pulling the punt up the tiny slipway on Shark, Dave and I walked the few yards to Lacey's cottage, where Festy leaned over the half-door, awaiting our arrival.

"You've come back again then?" he enquired as we shook hands, "Didn't expect to see you here again, leastways not so soon".

He gave us a run down on the birds he recognised, including the news that a pair of Choughs from the island, had built their nest on the fireplace in a nearby cottage, a most unusual site.

"Would ye like a drink before you go off, it's a hot day and ye'll be thirsty" he said, disappearing into the gloom of his cottage, returning with two cups without handles, but full of milk.

He looked on approvingly while we sampled his hospitality, but I nearly gagged at the first draught, it was milk alright - probably goat's, but it was buttermilk, ugh!

Somehow, with a smile that belied the alarm bells my taste buds were ringing, I gulped the buttermilk down, said our farewell, and plodded up the hill past the old school, heading for the cliffs on the far side of the island.

We had a fabulous time, Peregrines chattered overhead, Greater Black-backed Gulls yowked noisily as we made our way through their nesting areas, colonies of Fulmars, Storm petrels, Kittiwakes and Razorbills were everywhere, in fact it was just the stuff you read about in bird magazines.

I glanced at my watch to see how the time was going, and saw it was four o'clock - we had been on the island for nearly six hours, and the wind was getting up.

The sun had slowly lost its brilliance, and now had a `brassy' look. It was time to go.

By the time we had covered the three-quarters of a mile back to Lacey's cottage, the wind was gusting strongly with dark clouds piling in, and it was obvious we hadn't a minute to lose if we were going to make it back to `Bofin before it all went pear-shaped.

Striding down the steep slope from the school, we came abreast of Lacey's cottage just as he appeared at the half-door

"If ye're thinking of leaving at all, ye'll have to leave right now, I lost two boys in weather like this a few years ago, they were swept into to the Stags of `Bofin beyond".

He pointed away to the vertical cliffs of `Bofin barely visible in the rapidly failing light.

"It's ok Mr. Lacey we ARE leaving, and right this minute!" I replied and we ran to the punt, threw our stuff aboard and pushed off.

As soon as we cleared the little breakwater, a squall drove the punt sideways into a huge area of kelpweed which fouled the oars, making rowing extremely difficult.

I cursed and swore as we were driven more and more off our intended course by the fierce winds and cloying weed, and I understood exactly what old Festy Lacey meant.

Keeping the sweep of the oars as shallow as possible, I finally managed to clear the tangled kelp, but the winds had driven us a hundred yards to leeward of a direct course for `Bofin harbour, and we were heading straight for the dreaded Stags.

I looked at Dave. "Give me a sight with your arm on the bearing for Bofin harbour,

I'm getting disorientated with only `Shark to look at" I shouted into the wind, and Dave in the stern, pointed well off my left shoulder into the wind.

"God, is it that bad?" I remember saying, and slewed the punt round to follow his directions, but as I did so, heavy seas coming in from my left began to broach the boat, drenching us both with icy cold spray.

"I'm not going to be able to maintain this direction with the sea coming in like this, we'll roll over for sure, I'm going to have to turn into wind away from Bofin, and do a series of tacks to get us back in line with the harbour"

Dave didn't reply, but sat grim-faced in the middle of the rear seat, clutching the sides of the boat fiercely as we rolled and juddered in the rushing waves.

In a fury now, the wind really began to blow, hitting us with severe gusts like physical blows, tearing the tops off the waves in spume, as they grew higher and higher in the fading light.

I was beginning to get a bit worried.

Due to the huge waves it was only possible to turn the punt round through a hundred and eighty degrees and tack, when we were on the top of a massive rolling wave.

To attempt it anywhere else on the wave would have rolled us over, especially if we were caught half-way through the manoeuvre.

I had completed our third or fourth tack, and was heading out towards `Shark again, when Dave pointed over my head and shouted in terror "Look!"

We were at the bottom of a dark green, glassy trough, and, bracing the oars against the rowlocks, I turned to see what was causing him so much concern.

I soon found out!

A huge wave about fifteen feet high was rolling and creaming towards us, and it's approach slope some fifty feet long, black and menacing was already under our bows.

As though in an express lift, the punt rose to meet the crest and I thought god, this is it, but somehow the nose of the punt punched through the spray, and roared down the other side like a roller coaster, straight towards the foot of the next wave, which looked just as big.

I had never seen waves as huge as these, and doubted whether we could stay afloat much longer, it was absolutely crazy.

"Dave, if I can't make decent headway in the next few tacks, I'll have to let her run towards the stags - we'll have to jump over the side and hang on, I can't think what else to do".

He looked at me as though I was mad, and yelled "I can't swim!"

I couldn't believe my ears, everybody could swim, especially if they damn' well had to.

"Make your way towards me, and grab an oar then, perhaps the two of us will make a better impression on it".

"I can't row either" he wailed.

Shit I thought, now's a bloody fine time to find out, I'd just have to get on with it then, for both our sakes!

I can't remember how many more tacks I made, it was certainly about thirty, spinning the punt round on the top of huge waves, and rowing like mad down the other side, until at last I felt we must have made enough sideways travel, to shoot for Bofin harbour, and home.

During the last hour or so, the wind had moderated slightly, and the torrential rain hammering down like stair-rods had flattened the waves a little, making the punt a bit easier to row.

During our battle with the broaching seas, Dave had been bailing like mad in a desperate effort to keep us afloat, the water inside the punt was well over our ankles most of the time, and quite worrying.

He must have been having some effect though, as the water didn't seem to get any deeper, but it was obviously going to be a close run thing!

My arms felt like they had been torn from their sockets, and huge blisters on my palms had bled, covering my hands with a sticky mess that looked worse than it really was.

Once inside the protection of the West Quarter, and `Bofin harbour, the rough seas became more manageable, only a two foot chop with `white-horses 'flicking off the tops indicated the havoc still going on outside.

Feeling absolutely knackered, we tied up at the jetty alongside the Northern Ranger and hobbled towards Day's hotel just a few yards away, or at least tried to - after several hours tossing about on the sea, the ground just wouldn't stay still!

Suitably washed and cleaned, plus a change of clothes, we cheekily seated ourselves in the hotel dining room, hoping there might be a chance of a bite to eat, although the eight o'clock dinner was a long time gone.

As Michael came towards us from the kitchen, I said apologetically, "I know we're late, we've only just got back from Shark, is there any chance of something to eat?

His jaw dropped, and he stared at us in blank amazement.

"Ye've just come across from Shark ye say, in the last while?"

"Yes" I replied, "It WAS a bit hairy, and Festy Lacey was quite right in saying if we left it any later we wouldn't be leaving at all, and would have to stay the night".

"My god" he said, turning round and calling to his wife Margaret, "Did ye hear that, the two lads here have just brought the punt across from Shark in this weather, it's a miracle they made it at all, none of us would dare be abroad in this kind of weather".

And with that, he asked Mary to get us something to eat, while he disappeared out the door.

The bar on Bofin obviously served as a community centre for the whole island, despite it being only a small out-building, but I thought Dave and I ought to drop in there directly we finished our meal, to meet some of the locals again.

It was nice to converse on topics of mutual interest like politics and such, and of course they all knew far better than we did, where the birds we were interested in, could be found.

As we pushed open the door, the hubbub of conversation within faltered and died, and all eyes swung in our direction.

The Guinness and spirits had obviously been flowing for some little time, and the gently pulsating, generator powered light-bulb, glowed a dull orange through the thick tobacco clouds descending from the ceiling.

“Come in lads, come in and welcome” said Michael from behind the bar, “We all want to hear about ye’re trip across from Shark this evening - and of course what ye would like to drink?”.

I recounted the incident just as it happened, and when I had finished Michael said “That’s amazing, none of us would have gone out on a day like this, not from choice anyways, so drink up, there’s plenty more waitin’ where that came from” and from then on, we could do no wrong.

There were at that time, about a hundred-plus souls living on Bofin, and as the word spread concerning the two mad English bird fellas, the punt trip, plus other additions, we were greeted with smiles everywhere, and even challenged by the local darts champions to a game of 301.

Now when I play darts, I either have a session where everything clicks with uncanny precision, and I can hit anything I choose, or deadly inaccuracy where I can only hit the board.

Dave on the other hand was a good steady player, who could be relied on to make reliable progress under any pressure.

One evening, in front of a smiling and expectant bar crowd Dave and I faced our opponents, one of whom, the `deadly Mulcahy’ adopted the pose of a hunter about to launch his javelin, with the same deadly accuracy!

The first game was a doddle, we wiped the floor with them, I was on that winning streak where everything seemed to click, and Dave held his end up admirably.

The second game we also won by a comfortable margin, and I could feel our friend the`deadly Mulcahy’ was beginning to get a bit narked, as he shot me several hard glances between throws.

As Dave and I squared up for the third game I felt it go, almost like taking my coat off, and no matter how I tried, I couldn’t hit a thing.

They won handsomely. It was two -one in our favour.

“How a bout a final game, just for the hell of it?” I volunteered. Needless to say my form remained absolutely dormant, and they won again by a fair margin.

Everyone was smiles, the guinness flowed, and I’m afraid both Dave and I returned to the hotel quite a bit worse for wear.

We did manage to go back to Shark again, this time in a fishing boat, and after landing, spoke to our friend Festy Lacey again. He had feared for our safety seeing the punt’s erratic progress, and was glad to hear we had made it back safely,

All too soon the wonderful days were gone, and it was time to leave Bofin and the friends we had made, and make our way back to the rat-race that living in London is all about. It all felt horribly wrong to me, we shouldn’t be chained to such a treadmill way of life!

Back at Ormond St I found I was expected to work on my own now that Roger had gone, although I was occasionally helped by `pincher’ when he could be found.

The work load for some reason increased considerably, not only did I have the normal intake of patients, and post mortem specimens to do, but there were quite demanding sessions in the theatre, using stills and 16mm cine.

There were also slide and film projections for consultants’ lectures and hospital `teach-ins' to do - I was rapidly becoming a jack of all trades, all for a mere six quid a week!

It got so busy that `pincher' got permission to place an urgent ad. in the photographic journals for a projectionist, which would allow me to get on with the rest of the work without that particular hassle, which was something.

The result of this little exercise was, the chap they employed to do the projection and lecture-sldes but nothing else, was paid 30% more than I was, despite the fact that until he came, I did both his job and mine. Terrific!

During one particularly miserable lunch-hour in November when it was too wet to go out for a walk, I sat reading a daily newspaper in the studio and saw an ad which said,`Civilian photographers required to work at New Scotland Yard'.

I didn't know in detail what sort of work they did, but it couldn't be that much different from what I was doing now. I was quite competent in photographing operations and pathological specimens for the doctors and professors, and felt confident I could deal with the odd dead body or two I might encounter at the Yard. Anyway they were offering £9 a week against the £6 I was getting at Ormond St, so it was worth going for, especially as I hoped to get married next year!

I had known Teresa for nearly a year now, and felt sure enough of our relationship to ask if she would marry me, and she had agreed. If I got the Scotland Yard job at £9, plus her small salary of £4 a week as a Staff-nurse, we might just have enough to get a place of our own. I kept my fingers crossed.

After my interview at New scotland Yard in November, Teresa and I waited on tenterhooks until well into the new year without hearing a thing, and with our proposed February wedding drawing ever nearer, we seemed to be stuck in limbo.

We had both wanted to get married in England, but Teresa's dad said if we would go over to Eire for the wedding, he would pay for everything, and as some of my family were able to travel, and Teresa's mother was not, we reluctantly agreed.

My dad hated travelling, and said if I didn't mind too much he'd rather stay at home, but mum, and brother Terry said they would come, just to make sure I wasn't entirely alone in a foreign country!

It was February 10th, and Teresa had just gone ahead to Danesfort specially to help her family with the lambing - apparently it was snowing like the clappers, and everyone was having a difficult time.

Extra hands were more than welcome.

A few days later, Mum, Terry and I arrived at Loughrea railway station, our quaint little `coffee-pot' engine, had struggled manfully to pull the two-carriage train through deep snow covering the branch line from Athenry.

Everything was covered in deep snow, and things looked pretty bleak, not exactly the best weather for a wedding!

Mum was suffering badly from her Meniere's syndrome after our flight from Heathrow, (chronic nausea and sickness from imbalance in the ears) but Terry and I felt ok, so after seeing mum put to bed with disprin and a hot water-bottle, we had a few drinks with locals at the hotel bar, before retiring at midnight, after all it was my wedding day tomorrow!

I suppose I had been asleep about half an hour, when there was a loud tapping on the glass of my ground floor bedroom window, from the outside.

I didn't know where the heck I was for a minute, but through the haze of a rudely disturbed sleep, I heard myself say "Who the hell is it?" and squinting at my luminous watch, saw it was a quarter past twelve.

"Is that you?" intoned a rich Irish brogue.

"Yes" I replied idiotically, still not being fully awake.

"Well this is me, Johnny yere best man, see ye in the Cathedral presbytery at half nine, bring the ring with ye, and don't be late goodnight". and he was gone.

In the morning, someone thoughtfully provided a taxi to take us to the Cathedral, which although only a quarter of a mile away, was impossible to get to without wellies, due to the deep snow.

Mum had recovered a little from her nausea, and went with Terry into the Cathedral, while I tried to find my best man Johnny, whoever he was, the night visitor and family friend Teresa had specially asked for.

Johnny Monaghan turned out to be an easy-going, middle-aged, ruddy faced man, who owned a large farm at nearby Cahernagharry, and was well known to everyone.

He also found time to drive the ramshackle local school bus, and do the many odd jobs about town.

I took to him instantly.

"Ye know" he said within minutes of our meeting in the Cathedral entrance "Ye are a lucky man to get Teresa, I was going to marry her meself"

I was too lost for words, to make a suitable reply!

To say that the whole of Loughrea turned out to see this upstart English fellow marry a local girl might be an exaggeration, but the fact that people lined the short route from the Cathedral to the main road, one or two deep in the flurrying snow, was extremely impressive to say the least.

With everything happening in a whirl, it wasn't until the photographs were being taken - by Terry and myself on my little Ensign Selfix, that I realised Teresa's mother wasn't there.

In tears, on what should have been her wonderful day, Teresa told me her mother had said she felt unwell, and had gone into Galway hospital last night, but was apparently quite comfortable.

We could visit her after the reception, on the way to our honeymoon if we wanted to - I could hardly believe it!.

After the reception, we said our goodbyes to everyone, especially Teresas' dad, who was a real brick, and jumped into Johnny Monaghan's not too-new car, for the hairiest ride into Galway it is possible to imagine!

He would insist on turning round to tell us some facet of the wedding he found interesting, whilst negotiating a fast right-hand bend, barely skimming the dry-stone walls on his off-side!

I tried to explain the folly of this style of driving, only to be told grandly, "To be sure, there's not much traffic uses this road anyway".

As I knew the exact time we left the reception, it was easy to see by my watch that it took just thirty minutes for us to cover the twenty odd miles to the hospital in Galway.

Nobody was more pleased than me to leave Johnnys' car in one piece, as several times during the ride, I felt sure we'd never arrive safely!

The maternal greeting at the hospital was for me, an anti-climax, Teresa had kept her wedding dress on for her mother to see, but I felt there was more joy and admiration from the staff and patients on the ward, than was demonstrated by her mother.

I felt pretty mad at what I perceived to be a definite snub on her part, and somehow managed to curb my tongue and not say something I might later regret.

Nevertheless, we said our goodbyes and continued our journey, enjoyed the honeymoon at Dun Laoghaire, and returned to the nuts and bolts of trying to start a new home during an English winter in Romford.

It was our second day in the new flat, and things were beginning to settle down a bit, when Teresa said to me "You won't forget to take the wedding film to work for developing and printing when you go back will you?"

Suddenly I realised I hadn't seen the camera for some time.

Where the heck was it?

A frantic search of our few belongings revealed nothing, it was gone.

Then I remembered our early morning return journey on the first underground train of the day. I had put the camera on the seat next to me with our luggage, and must have got off and left it behind!

A frantic call to the lost property office soon revealed some honest person had handed the camera in, and it was mine if I cared to pay 10% of its value - and they somehow valued it at fifty pounds.

I only paid thirty pounds for it brand new!

It was either that or no wedding photos, so I had to cough up five pounds -nearly a week's salary, and thought it sheer bloody robbery to pay so much money to get one's own property back.

Meanwhile, there was still no word from Scotland Yard saying whether my application had been succesful, and like others in a similar position, I began to fear the worst.

A month went by, by which time we had found a much nicer flat in Ilford, before we finally got the news we had been waiting for, I had the job - could I start as soon as I had given my present employer notice?

You bet!

The first day of my new job dawned in glorious spring sunshine and I ascended the imposing stairway of New Scotland Yard's main entrance full of beans, only to be told very firmly by the patrolling PC. that this was the COMMISSIONER'S entrance, and only meant for senior officers!

Other ranks and civil staff like me, were expected to use the `back-hall', a dingy, dimly-lit foyer round the back, which smelt like an old Victorian library.

After a short wait, I was escorted by a clerk to the photographic section on the sixth floor, and ushered into the presence of the head of dept. Det.Supt. Percy Law, who reminded me more of a top business man than a policeman, with his smart suit and handkerchief tucked into his sleeve.

His first words to me were a bit of a shock, "You may have been directed to come here today at half past nine Parker, but we start at eight o'clock sharp, so don't be late in the future, and by the way, we don't allow anyone to bring their private camera to work, you'll find out why, as you go along, ok?".

I'll get Det.Inspector Dickinson here to show you round the section and introduce you to everybody - any problems, come and see me, but not between one and two o'clock, that's when I'm asleep and my door is shut!"

In the corridor outside Percy's office the first person we bumped into was Alan McLean. Insp. Dickinson started to say, "This is Alan McLean........"

I said "Yes I know, we met several years ago in the RAF as photographers, but I didn't know he was here too, what a co-incidence". Insp; Dickinson went on "Alan is the first civilian we have taken on,and you're the second, so follow him, and you won't go far wrong!"

Those first few months at the Yard were, looking back on it, rather frustrating, and a bit of an anticlimax to all that I had expected to see and do.

Although I was learning new lighting techniques concerned with fingerprint and Ultra-violet photography, the general standard of photographic equipment was well below that which I had been used to at Gt.Ormond St. and I couldn't figure out why.

Comparisons are odious I know, but I was pretty depressed when, after being there six months, I was asked to go and photograph the scene of a fatal road accident, using a Kodak 1/2 plate Imperial camera, without even a shutter to its lens, just a cap!

I had been used to using either the 5x4 MPP or a 9x12 Plaubel Makina Press at the hospital, both good quality cameras, light-years away from the old Kodak 1/2 plate!

The photo section at that time only possesed two half - plate cameras, one with a Kodak Ektar lens in an Epsilon shutter, half a dozen 9x12 s with 6.8 Goerz-Dagor lenses, and a reasonable MPP Mk 1. which sat locked in a cupboard in the governor's office.

I was told it was a `Sunday' camera, and used for special jobs and murders only!

One morning Inspector Dickinson (Dickie) called for me and said, "Come along young Parker, we're going to see how good you are at unidentifieds, get a 9x12 camera and some slides, load 'em, grab a flashgun, and we'll be off to pastures new, ie. Southwark Mortuary".

I found out from Alan whilst loading my slides, that `unidentifieds' consisted of taking a full face and side face of a deceased person, so the negatives could be contact printed for inclusion in the `Police Journal' which featured missing people, etc.

"Don't forget" Alan warned me "The two heads must be the same-size on the negatives for contact printing side-by-side, so don't change your bellows extension between shots".

As we walked in to Southwark Mortuary I got for the first time that characteristic whiff, common to all mortuaries wherever you go - disinfectant mixed with a bad-meat smell.

You can't escape it, and you never forget it!.

"This is one of our new chaps, a Mr. Parker " Dickie greeted the mortuary keeper cheerily. "He's come to do the unident out of the river, can you get it out for him?".

"Certainly guv: where do you want it, on the floor or on the trolley?".

"On the floor will do" said Dickie.

"We can always twist his head round to do the side view, provided of course it isn't too stiff!

"Oh no" said the mortuary keeper, "It isn't too stiff at all, quite the contrary really," and as the tray came out of the freezer on to the floor, I could see just what he meant.

The grotesquely bloated and disfigured face was anything but stiff, in fact it appeared to be on the point of disintegration, and the smell was stomach gagging.

Dickie watched me closely as I set up the 9x12 camera and tripod directly over the foul smelling face, no doubt expecting me to have problems.

I made the facial image on the ground glass screen about one and a half inches tall, remembering that I had to get the much wider lateral view, the same-size on the next film.

Buried under the focussing cloth, and trying not to breathe in the revolting smell, I heard Dickie say,

"Do you smoke young Parker?".

I came out from under the cloth to see Dickie and the morticians smoking like chimneys in the far corner of the room.

"No I don't - not yet anyway" I replied, and they all burst out laughing.

"You fuggin' soon will lad" said Dickie, and I could see his point.

From one of the small windows at the rear of the photographic section you could just see down Richmond Terrace where it leads into Whitehall and the Cenotaph. In the tall Plane trees lining the road, hundreds of Starlings gathered for their nightly roost, seeking the comparative warmth of the city, while below, a tide of commuters hurried homewards without an upward glance.

While I was watching this evening spectacle, Alan came up to me and said, "You wouldn't believe what I've just found in an old cupboard, do you recognise this?" and he produced an old flash-powder gun, complete with its tray and thumb lever, which actuated a flint wheel and fired the powder.

"Good lord, I thought those had gone out with the ark, is there any powder to go with it?"

"No, but would you believe there's a box of those huge percussion caps used to fire the flashpowder on a different type of gun"

"I think we can have a bit of fun with a couple of those if they still work, can you show me where they are?"

The paper caps were about half an inch across, with a large blob of blackish explosive material in the middle.

"If we wait until just before finishing time, I'll let one off on the back window-sill overlooking Whitehall - should make the Starlings jump a bit if they hear it"

"You're nuts" said Alan, "Someone in the building will hear it and wonder what the hell is going on up here"

It was quite dark by a minute to five, and the Starlings well bunched in their hundreds, clattering and wheezing their tinny chatter, as the hammer came down on two of the caps on the window-sill.

Even I was surprised at the bang the caps produced, perhaps it was channelled by the narrow passageway between the buildings, anyway, the chattering birds stopped immediately, and in the short silence that followed, the pitter patter of hundreds of defaecating birds could be heard, before they took off in a roar of wings.

People hurrying home beneath the birds must have been covered in it!

I must confess to repeating the same anti-social act a couple more times, before it became too risky to continue, someone was bound to complain!

I was quite often employed as a `gofer' within the section, but in the process learnt a lot, watching other Police officers at the variety of forensic tasks the section undertook. One of the more senior officers, P/Sgt. John Merry, was an excellent photographer and instructor, but unfortunately had a terrible disposition towards the drink.

God help anyone who spoke to him without being addressed first, if you did, you soon learnt the lineage of your ancestry in blistering terms, if you hadn't suspected it already!

On one occasion I had been seconded to work with John, to learn how to photograph a difficult fingerprint in blood on a mirror, and as we went up to the front door of the house in Streatham, he explained the technique we were going to use.

Once inside the house, the lady asked if we would like a drink while we were working, tea or coffee?. Like a flash John replied "Don't touch the stuff myself, but if you've a whisky to hand, that would go down rather well".

When he got his drink, he turned to a framed picture of Jesus on the wall and said, "Cheers J C". and took a sip.

I cringed with embarrassment at the lady's shocked reaction to this exhibition of poor public relations, and was very glad when we were finished, and out the door.

One of the first big murder scenes I covered with P/Sgt `Bing' Foreman, concerned the stabbing to death of PC Summers in the Holloway road, by a chap called Marwood.

I was allowed to take some of the scene photographs on the MPP 5x4 myself, print, and present them in folders as Court exhibits for the trial, where Marwood was eventually found guilty of the murder, and hanged.

In those early days we seemed to get at least a murder a week, and a fine old time was had by police, trying to keep the press photographers and reporters away from the scene of the crime. Nowadays, the average murder barely warrants a mention in the press, or T/V, let alone an attendance by press photographers, how times change!

I had noticed that from our place on the sixth floor of New Scotland Yard overlooking the Embankment, some of the wintering population of Black Headed Gulls could be enticed to our window ledge, by throwing out pieces of bread.

Having got the birds used to this method of feeding, I made it my business each morning before 0800 to get bread scraps from the downstairs canteen, and, armed with a boxful of BTO. No.2 rings, try to grab the excited birds as they scrambled for food just outside the window.

I asked Alan if he would help by tossing the bread very close to the sash window, while I waited, arm poised, to grab the nearest gull. Naturally there were a lot of misses, but over the next few days I managed to catch half a dozen, which made me think there might be an even better way of doing the job.

Armed with my briefcase stuffed full of bread scraps, I went each dinner hour to the centre of Westminster bridge, and proceeded to attract the gulls with the food.

I found if I threw the bread just a little way in front of me, the swooping gulls could be caught by hand in mid-air, either by their breast feathers or wing tip, and quickly but gently held, before attaching the requisite BTO (British Trust for Ornithology) ring.

Most times the gull just gave a few vicious pecks while it was being dealt with, othertimes they squawked as though they were being murdered.

I found the only way to quieten them was to stick your finger between their mandibles, and let them vent their anger on that!

One of the interesting things that came to light as I got more proficient in trapping was, I sometimes saw a gull with a ring already attached, and by carefully watching and waiting until it came round for its share of the food, I could catch that particular bird, thus gaining valuable `re-trap' information.

One bird I caught on two occasions had been ringed as a nestling in the midlands eight years before, and was still going strong. One of my own ringed gulls was later killed by traffic in the centre of Oslo!

When the gulls got wise to my predations on the bridge, I nipped into St. James' Park, and carried on trapping from the little bridge over the lake there, sometimes to the consternation of passers by, who weren't convinced I wasn't up to something really diabolical.

I sometimes stooped to the low practice of catching gulls attracted to food thrown by other lunch-time strollers.

On one occasion I caught a right screecher, who refused to be quiet, his squawks sending every gull in the park spiralling into the sky, leaving the park completely empty, except for ducks!

It was quite funny to see people staring at the sky, wondering why the heck all the gulls had suddenly disappeared.

During that first winter of hand-catching, I managed to catch a over a hundred gulls, and thought it might prove a useful way of finding out just where the gulls we observed in London came from.

During 1959 Alan and I were joined by other civilian photographers, and the section began to take on a more balanced outlook, as all the new civil staff were professionally qualified to British Institute Standards, while all but one of the police staff had learnt their photography by rule of thumb.

There was a standby rota amongst police staff for night call-outs which was arranged on the basis of whoever was not tied up that night copped the duty, but now that Alan and I were able to do the duty as well, a regular rota was drawn up.

This meant that during the week or weekend, once every ten days or so, you were liable for whatever job came in, anything, anywhere, anytime and I remember well, the first night call I got.

An Essex PC knocked at my door just before midnight and said, "They want you to go to a fatal accident over at Edgware, I'm to take you to Chadwell Heath Police station where a Met. pool car will take you to the Yard to pick up your gear, ok?"

These peculiar arrangements were necessary, due to the fact that I lived near Romford, which was a few miles outside the Metropolitan Police boundary, and special permission had to be obtained from the Yard for a Police car to leave the Met. and pick me up direct.

It seems ludicrous by today's standards, that I then had to go into the Yard, pick up my camera kit, and be taken to the scene of the accident, which by chance we might have passed on the way in! However, that night we eventually got to Edgware Rd. A.1, near the junction with Spur Rd, and I left the nice warm car at 0130hrs, stepping into a bitterly cold night, with black ice underfoot, and the air full of sparkling ice-crystals.

As I walked towards the waiting traffic patrol car, I was horrified to see there were no street lights anywhere nearby, they had finished a hundred yards back.

We were in virtual darkness!

"Where do you want to start then guv?" said the genial traffic PC, "The road's pretty quiet now, I've got PCs with lights and signs both sides of the accident, so we can start whenever you're ready".

He told me that two cars had collided head-on at speed, spun round on impact, separated, and come to rest some distance apart. There had been dead in both cars, but they had been taken away earlier.

I walked up to the first car which was a black Vauxhall, and attempted to form a mental picture of the scene, so I could take some sensible photographs.

The basic rule was that you took a long view, and medium-distance view from each direction, using available light only, noting the exact position from which each photograph was taken, and then take as many close-ups of the damaged vehicles as necessary, using flash to show damage detail.

"Where on earth is the second car?" I asked the PC.

He nodded into the gloom. "About thirty yards ahead, after they hit, they spun away from each other on the ice, a fair old distance".

Bloody hell, in virtual darkness, long shots were out of the question - they would have to be done in daylight later, but I could just about manage the medium distance shots using the big PF100 flashbulbs to light up the foreground, coupled with a sufficiently long time exposure for the rest.

Even as I fired the flashgun holding three PF100 flashbulbs, I realised it wasn't going to work, the air was full of swirling frost crystals, and the flash just bounced back off like a reflector.

With a patience borne of many years duty, the Police crew stood by, while I thought what the hell to do next, I knew I had to try something, but what?

It was then I noticed the Wolseley traffic car had two searchlights mounted on its roof, perhaps I could use one of those?

I lined up the police car to one side of the camera, and closed the lens to F.11, and carefully opened the shutter on the 5x4. Over my shoulder I called the RT operator to switch on one of the lights while I `painted' the roadway, verges and crashed car with the moving light beam, giving a minute's exposure.

Changing the double-dark slide, I doubled up with a two-minute exposure, just to make sure.

I repeated the whole procedure from the opposite direction beyond the second car, before finishing both cars in close-up with PF 60 flashbulbs.

Despite the cold, I was sweating with the effort of plonking up and down between the cars, and, ramming the last dark-sheath home looked at my watch - an hour had gone by since I started, where the hell had the time gone?.

"Finished then guv?". enquired the friendly PC.

"Yes, thank god." I replied. "Where are the cars going, in case we need further photography, and who is the Duty Officer at the nick dealing with this accident please?"

On my way back to the Yard in the comparative warmth of the car,(It was the practice in those days to process your films before going home) I hoped fervently that I had done the right thing, if not, my head would be well and truly on the block for all the wasted time and effort!

In the darkroom I anxiously lifted the lid off the Kodak 3 litre fix tank, and saw to my great relief, good density images on some of the plates - at least I had something!

The painted light exposure of two minutes paid off handsomely, no sign of the aerial frost crystals at all, due to the long exposure, whereas the flash exposure was quite useless, just a grey square of density, with a few indistinct highlights in the middle.

All the flash close-up shots of the damaged cars were ok. too, I felt quite relieved.

I got home just after 0500hrs and crashed into bed, Teresa complaining that I had darned cold feet, and ought to have got myself a hot-water bottle!

Getting into the Yard in those days by 0800, meant leaving home no later than 0700 on my trusty 150.cc Excelsior - the same bike I had taken to Eire years before, so getting up at 0630 after only an hour and a half of sleep, left me feeling pretty groggy.

By 10 o/clock that morning my 12x10 black and white glossies were swishing about in the cascade washer, and looking pretty good - I was well pleased, especially with the long shots.

"Hear you were out and about last night then young Parker" said Dickie, leaning over the print washer, and looking at me with a condescending grin. - "Think you'll like the job then?"

Picking up one of the road shots he said,"These look good, how did you light it with no street lights about, and the vehicles that far apart?".

As nonchalantly as I could, but secretly chuffed to hell inside, I replied calmly, "They happened to have a spot- light on the roof of the Police car, so I used that to paint the scene - with all that frost in the air, flash was no good".

"There's hope for you yet" he said smiling, and walked off hands jammed into trousers pockets, for tea.

I felt very happy that I appeared to have `scored' one, and kept the end up for us civvies.

In January 1959 Teresa and I celebrated the arrival of our first child Bernadette, whose birth I learnt about under quite unusual circumstances.

The redoubtable John Merry and I, plus a fingerprint officer were attending an armed robbery scene at a jewellers' shop in Burlington arcade, Piccadilly.

John and I were deeply engrossed in photographing some difficult fingermarks on glass, when a fashionably dressed woman speaking in an awfully far-back voice intoned, “Is there someone here by the name of Mr. Parker?”.

“Yes” I replied “That’s me”.

“It’s your office calling, apparently I’m to tell you that your wife has had a baby girl, and you are to go home immediately” but before I could reply, John butted in “You’d do anything to get out of a ruddy job wouldn’t you Parker you lazy bugger, I suppose you’d better get off then”.

The shop woman’s face was a real picture.

Our new head of department, who succeeded Percy Law, had, by the dint of continuous report writing, and meetings with finance the branch, managed to purchase six, Super Cambo 5x4 camera kits, complete with standard and wide-angle lenses, Weston meter, Kobold flashgun, a dozen slides, and a substantial Bilora tripod - we were out of the dark ages at last!

We could now ditch the poor old 9x12’s, and really get cracking - it was going to be great.

Until now we had been driven to scenes of crime by a faithful band of pool-drivers, most of whom would go anywhere, anytime, and sit in the car reading the paper until you finished.

Others like Jock, who appeared to hate the job all the time, would curse and swear at Dickie for sending us out, especially when it was nearly their `going-home time’, but all that was about to change.

One driver I had a lot of time for was`R’ who, on leaving Yard and turning left down the Embankment towards Charing-Cross, would surreptitiously unscrew the large chrome nut in the centre of his steering wheel, and as he passed the PC. on duty there, remove the steering wheel from its spline, and wave it out the window to his colleague as we went by.

After completing this madcap manoeuvre, he would quickly replace the wheel and turn off the ignition for a few seconds, before re-starting the engine again, causing a build-up of unburnt petrol vapour to accumulate in the exhaust box.

On re-ignition this vapour would explode with a tremendous bang, causing the pigeons under Charing-Cross bridge to fly out in sheer terror!

Coupled to these gags, driver `R’ trotted out one particularly exasperating habit - usually when he’d finished reading his paper, and had nothing else to do, except annoy the photographer.

He would wait until you put your camera and flash boxes down behind the car and opened the boot, and then with devastating accuracy, catch the exact the moment you lifted the boxes up to put them in the boot, and drive ten yards down the road and wait for you to catch up.

If he felt particularly frivolous, he would do his party trick more than once, which sometimes left me in a pretty ragged mood.

All this was to end however with the acquisition of four new Minivans, making us virtually independent of the Police vehicle pool, but as I only had a motorcycle licence at the time, I was sent on a five-week driving course to the famous Hendon Driving school, the first `C’ department `civvy’ to be trained there alongside Police officers.

It was quite an experience. I particularly enjoyed the long night drives, and chuntering round the busy City, whilst the work-outs on the skid pan were both demanding and scary.

Slippery situations you would rarely meet in the course of normal driving, became familiar after an hour or so on the oily slick, especially when reinforced by the caustic remarks of the driving instructor, when things went pear-shaped!

The technical instruction given to us students, explaining what actually went on under the bonnet and chassis was extremely thorough, finishing up with a pretty stiff theory and practical exam, which strangely enough, I thoroughly enjoyed.

At the conclusion of the course, I scored 89% and came third out of a class of twenty - I felt quite chuffed!

Pity I hadn't had that level of tuition and practice years before when I drove the CO down to the Red sea in Egypt!

It was about this time my brother Tony was making noises about settling in New Zealand, and I thought with Terry in the Royal Navy on detachment to Australia, I would be the only grown son left in the UK. and it felt a bit strange, perhaps we should emigrate too?

Teresa and I had been house-hunting for weeks, and had at last found a nice, two-year old, semi-det.in Collier-Row going for £2300, all we needed was the deposit of £230 and we were away.

"Well if that's all you need" said Tony just before leaving for NZ. "I can lend you that, no problem, pay me back when you can"

It was a lovely gesture, and one which we were very pleased to accept.

Now that I was able to drive to jobs on my own, I began to meet, like others in the section, a level of hostility from certain Police officers who believed for some reason, that we `civvies' were out to steal their jobs.

There was also the occasional CID officer who was `out on enquiries' and not available when you turned up to do his particular job.

They either had an important `meet' somewhere, (usually a pub) or just left it for someone else in the office to organise, usually the female civilian CID clerk.

If there was no-one in the office to assist you, due to prior commitments, it was necessary to attend the scene alone, and because we carried no Police identification, access to some premises was extremely difficult, especially if they happened to be a bit anti police, due to the offence.

To counter-balance this situation though, there were many officers who saw the service being offered by extra photographic staff as a godsend, and seized the opportunity with both hands throughout the whole of their service, and the `job' benefitted accordingly.

One day I mentioned the problem of proving our identity at scenes of crime, to our head of department, who immediately bristled and exhibited a reaction which was to become all too familiar during my early years of service,

"There is no way laddie that this job is going to give you a warrant card or anything like it, so's you can go around impersonating a police-officer.

You'll just have to find a police officer to accompany you, no matter how long it takes".

You wouldn't expect that from your own boss would you?

Thinking back on those times, I have a lovely mental picture of a visit to the old Hounslow nick, when it stood isolated and folorn in a sea of re-development rubble.

Brian Bellingham. and I had arrived to do a job which required two photographers, and were greeted at the back door of the station by a very fat, six-foot PC, who, arms akimbo, demanded with overbearing pomposity "Who might you be?".

Brian who was just in front of me, drew himself up to his full 5' 6" and said cheekily "I might be the Commissioner, but I'm not! We're here to work with the district fingerprint officer on a job".

"Right sonny, well you just wait where you are, and I'll find him for you, only policemen are allowed in here". He was pathetic.

For our summer break, Teresa and I decided we would go across to Eire in response to her family's repeated requests to see Bernadette our first baby.

I must say I wasn't entirely overjoyed at the prospect, bearing in mind our previous experience after the wedding, when certain aspects of family behaviour left a lot to be desired.

It was really a bit hypocritical I suppose, but nevertheless to try and keep some semblance of family unity, we decided to go.

It was a tough schedule by any standards, trying to catch the Irish mail train in London by 1930 - already bursting at the seams with hundreds of returning paddies, then to transfer at 0100 in the morning to the Irish Mail ferry at Holyhead, so as to arrive in Dun Laoghaire, Eire by 0630.

Dozens of passengers then had to make a mad dash to catch a local train to Westland Rd. Dublin, where you hoped to catch the 0900 train to Galway in the west.

The 0900 was the only train of the day crossing Eire to Galway, so if you missed it, you'd had it!

On the night we chose to travel, the Mail train managed to lose an hour during the journey north, causing the Mail boat at Holyhead to await our arrival, and consequently sail late.

I suppose the skipper did his best to make up for lost- time, but despite his best efforts, we arrived at Dun Laoghaire at 0830, leaving us barely thirty-minutes to cover the distance to Westland Road, which normally takes forty-five minutes.

As it appeared about sixty people were expecting to travel on to Galway from Dublin, I button-holed the stationmaster at Dun Laoghaire, and asked him if he would kindly telephone ahead to Westland Rd. and get them to hold the Galway train pending everyone's arrival.

Like a good chap, he said he would, and off he went to make the call.

The rail journey into Dublin was made at an infuriating snails' pace, so unless the Galway train was held in Dublin, we would all miss our connection, sure as eggs.

As the platform at Westland Rd, came into view, it all looked ominously deserted and quiet, except for a very obese chap in a peaked cap, studiously examining his clip-board.

I walked up to him and asked, "Excuse me, did anyone get a message that the boat-train had been delayed, and that passengers for Galway would be a bit late?".

He raised his head and looked at me as though I was the last person on earth he expected to see.

"Yes we did, and as I'm station master here and have a time-table to run to" - he stabbed his finger at the clipboard, "I got the train away on time. The Galway train is shown down here as leaving at 0900, and that's when it leaves".

"But as it's the only train to Galway, except an evening train that gets into Woodlawn at about midnight, couldn't you have helped all these passengers here catch the 0900, after all it's still only 0920".

"What happens on your British side of the water has nothing to do with me, we run the Irish rail to time, and that's it".

"And you don't give a damn about the crowd you've left here then?" I countered.

"No, you'll just have to make other arrangements". he said and turned to walk away.

"Just a minute mister!". I said loudly "If that's your attitude, I want an immediate refund for the rest of my journey on Irish rail NOW, and we'll go on by car"

"The office for re-funds isn't open yet, you'll have to wait" he smirked.

After a whole night's travel and feeling quite prickly, this was just too much to take.

"You'd better get that ruddy office open right now mister, otherwise I shall be seeing someone a lot higher than you with a serious complaint on how you treated your passengers arriving at this station today!" I said angrily.

He looked at me quizzically for a second, and could see I was ticking like a meter - it wouldn't take very much to make me to explode.

"Follow me". he said tersely, and marched off towards the administration buildings.

"All those who want a refund for their spoilt journey, come this way" I said to the crowd, and about a dozen people tagged on behind, as we made our way up the steps to his office.

In ten minutes flat he produced a harassed woman clerk, who opened her till, dishing out the requisite money all fingers and thumbs, before we walked out to the main street, looking for somewhere to hire a car.

Now that I'd burnt our boats, I only hoped to god we could hire a car or something to finish our journey!

Ryans' car hire turned out to be the only people anywhere near who could help us, and then it was only with a Volkswagen beetle, it was all going to be a bit of a squeeze.

Bearing in mind there were three adults, (Teresa's sister Phyllis had come along too) plus one child, and enough luggage to sink the Titanic, Ryans had to supply us with a roof-rack to carry the three large suitcases because the silly bonnet-stow area was far too small!

The journey across Ireland to Loughrea was completed without further incident, and we arrived at Danesfort just after lunch.

The only snag with the whole caboodle now was, I had to have the car back in Dublin for 0800 Monday morning, and as today was Saturday, that meant I would have to return it tomorrow, Sunday, unless I wanted to be up with the lark on Monday morning!

It was decided I should leave for Dublin directly after Mass on Sunday morning, get to Ryan's about midday, and park the car in their lot, push the keys through the door in an envelope, and return. It sounded simple enough.

When I eventually accomplished all that, I looked around for some form of transport back to get me back to Loughrea, but apart from some lads leaning on a wall waiting for the bar to open, the place seemed deserted - I'd have to start walking.

My first lift from a kind lady visiting some friends, took me as far as Lucan, not a great distance but at least it was a start.

Half an hour later, a chap took me through Leixlip and on to Maynouth, and as it was only just two o'clock, I felt I wasn't doing too badly at all.

A rattle-bang farmer's truck took me to the outskirts of Mullingar, and as I stood there wondering whether to walk or wait, a large road-going tractor towing a combine harvester appeared, the driver smiling and waving in a friendly manner as he went past. No good hailing him, where would I sit?

I walked for nearly an hour before the next lift took me as far as Athlone, on the way passing our friend with the tractor and harvester who was still going well. In Athlone I began walking in the direction of Ballinasloe, only to be overtaken after a mile or so, by our friend in the tractor and harvester, who waved in my direction once again.

It now began to rain steadily, and fortunately a good Samaritan took pity on me, and gave me a lift through Ballinasloe before dropping me off half-way to Loughrea, I was nearly back!

A few minutes later I heard the approaching sound of an engine, and prepared to thumb what I hoped was my last lift, when, like an oft re-curring bad dream, that blasted tractor and harvester came into view, passed noisily, and turned off down a side road. If only I had been able to get a lift from him back in Mullingar, I could have travelled most of the way in one go!

The rain that had decided to christen my journey from Dublin, carried on in dribs and drabs for several days, before finally settling in to a continuous downpour that flooded every damn thing in sight.

It was so bad even the sheep crowded round the buildings in the home pasture, and the ducks cowered in the barn entrance, to avoid getting foot-rot!

There is no doubt about it - if people are confined on top of each other in absolutely horrible conditions, and the social acceptance level is tricky enough to start with, behaviour cracks rapidly appear.

Half-way through the second week of our `holidays' I felt the atmosphere becoming so strained, I said to Teresa "I'm sorry love, I feel we ought to cut our losses and go home, at least it won't be raining there all the time!" and so under a bit of a cloud, we left.

Arriving in England, I felt really pleased to be back in our own little place again, even though we still hadn't got around to carpetting the stairs!

Meanwhile at the Yard, I continued to gain experience at scenes of crime, and was really enjoying my work, I felt as though I was beginning to get somewhere in life at last.

On January 1st, 1960 at about 0400hrs I received another visit from the local Essex bobby, asking me to get myself down to Kings Cross nick to meet Alan, who was already there photographing the scene of a night-watchman's murder on a building site.

It had been a bitterly cold night, with everything buried under six inches of snow, which made riding the bike into the Yard a bit hairy, but by driving with my feet down to steady the bike, I got there without coming off, grabbed a dozen loaded darkslides, and dashed in my minivan to Kings Cross nick.

I received directions from the station officer how to get to the murder scene and set off, but because of heavily drifted snow, I could only get within about twenty-five yards, before the mini `bottomed-out' and refused to go any further.

Rather stupidly I had left my wellies with my bike at the Yard, and as I hopped out in my shoes to find Alan, the snow came up to my knees, and I knew I was going to get horribly wet and cold.

A PC. indicated where I could find Alan, and for the next hour we worked with the officer in the case covering the scene, finishing off by photographing a bum impression in the snow, where the suspect had jumped off a tall fence and sat backwards, before getting up and running off.

The Superintendent running the inquiry called across to us from the site office saying "I'm off to Kings Cross mortuary now, when you've finished here, join us for the PM which is set for ten o'clock, be as quick as you can, we don't want to keep Dr.Camps, the pathologist waiting".

Alan turned to me with a wry smile of resignation and said "I'm glad you brought those extra slides down, I've just run out of film despite using the changing bag once already. I don't know about you, but I could murder a cup of tea and a wad, I'm freezing".

"Me too" I replied " I didn't bring my wellies with me, my socks and trousers are soaking, I'll be glad to get out of this rotten lot"

As we pulled up outside St.Pancras mortuary, I heard beautiful honking calls of geese trumpeting through the cold bright air, and looking up, saw a skein of grey geese at about 200' flying due west. Wild geese over Camley St N.1? How absolutely incongruous!

The warmth of the mortuary was more than welcome after the last couple of hours in the cold, but to us as photographers, it was a damned nuisance.

We had to wait for our lenses and other bits and pieces to warm up sufficiently to lose their condensation, before we could even think about starting work.

With the body laid out on the floor, Alan focussed up to do the full-length shots, fully clothed front and back, before the next stage, which would be unclothed front and back as well, to show any injuries.

Everything was going fine, I was passing Alan the next slide after he had changed the flash-bulbs, and putting his used slides well aside, so we knew exactly where we were, and pretty soon we were well into the job.

While Dr. Camps and the mortician worked, instructions came at odd intervals such as "Photograph this for me will you?" or "Can you record this please?" while police officers huddled in a corner by the door, smoking cigarettes held discreetly behind their backs, like naughty school boys.

The Superintendent, catching the pathologists eye, walked across the mortuary floor to enquire if Dr. Camps had any further information to impart, regarding the exact cause of death.

"Shouldn't be too long now Supt. W. we're nearly finished, then I can tell you for certain"

Just before twelve o'clock Dr. Camps walked across the mortuary and joined the group by the door, speaking quietly to the Superintendent before motioning them to follow him.

They all disappeared from sight.

Thankfully Alan and I sat down on the camera cases, and took stock of our situation.

We had just about enough film left to finish the job, provided Camps didn't go mad with the `diddly bits' and with a bit of luck we might even be away by lunch-time.

So far we had endured a pretty rough start to the day, with no breakfast or tea break, we were absolutely starving, cold, wet and tired, and needed a rest.

As no-one had re-appeared by 1230, I wandered off to try and find out from someone what was happening next.

I found the mortician with his feet up, having a cuppa and reading his newspaper in front of a gas fire.

"Where have they all gone?" I asked.

He looked up from his paper, and almost as though it were a second thought, replied. "Oh, they've all gone off for lunch somewhere, probably the pub round the corner, should be back soon though".

To say I saw red would be an understatement, I was bloody boiling! I couldn't understand how people you were supposed to be working closely with, could `up and disappear' without having the grace to say `we're taking a lunch break now' and give us a chance to do the same!

I went back to Alan and told him what I'd discovered, and he was pretty disgusted too.

We couldn't leave the place now to get a bite to eat, it was too late for that, they might return any minute. We had to stay put.

"I know what we can do" I said. "I'll go down to the shops at Kings Cross, and see if I can get a bite at a take-away or something, I shouldn't be long, you can stay here and cover if they come back"

Just opposite the main railway station stood a little ABC cafe, which luckily was still open, but almost empty of food.

All they had left was two steak and kidney, and two pork pies. "I'll take them all" I said to the startled man behind the counter, "Just heat them up and I'll take them straight away".

Back at the mortuary I re-joined Alan, and handed him his half the spoils in a paper bag.

"I don't suppose it matters where we sit and eat really, the whole place is probably jumping with germs, let's just wash our hands and eat sitting here on the camera boxes"

"Sounds alright to me " said Alan, "I'm too bloody famished at the moment to worry much where the hell I sit".

I suppose we had started on the second of our pies, when the murmur of voices announced the imminent return of Dr.Camps and his party to the mortuary.

"Good god." he gasped as he saw us, "What on earth is going on here, why are you eating in my mortuary, doesn't the sight of all this stuff put you off?".

Still ticking from the cavalier way in which I felt we had been treated, I chanced my arm and replied. "If we had been told that you were all going off to lunch leaving us behind, we might have been able to go and get something to eat for ourselves."

"It may not have occurred to you that we have both been up since before daybreak, with no breakfast not even so much as a cup of tea!"

He recoiled at my outburst, and I saw a look of annoyance cross the Superintendent's face. Oh boy, I thought, I've done it now! With an emphatic flourish, and apparently dismissing my tirade, Dr. Camps put on his protective apron, and, not giving Alan or me a second glance said, "Let's carry on then shall we, that is, if you have finished your lunch, and are not too tired"

The rest of the work was carried out in a fairly strained atmosphere, conversation being limited to instructions as to what needed photographing, and when.

"Well, that's it," said Dr.Camps, "Cause of death, severe fractures of the skull, and multiple lacerations to the face, I'll send you my report as soon as I've seen the photographs".

He turned quickly, took his apron off, and disappeared out of the mortuary without a word to us, closely followed by the police staff.

"You didn't go down too well with the D.Superintendent" said Alan. "You know how they have to kow-tow to the pathologist and give him a bottle to get their report as soon as possible, we'll have to make extra sure we're waterproof with our stuff, and get it out in double quick time".

Needless to say the photographic side of the job went down well, but for years afterwards whenever I did a job with Dr. Camps, he invariably greeted me with, "Ah yes, you're the chap who eats steak pies in my mortuary. I hope you can last out better this time!"

In those first years the sheer variety of jobs we were expected to cover, meant that your basic technique had to be good.

There were no second second chances, especially with the fingerprint and laboratory staff up your tail, and there were times of course when you just had to fly by the seat of your trousers to get a result.

During a particularly bad bout of winter smog, when London people were dying in their scores, Dickie sent me to do an unident. at Hammersmith mortuary, a grotty little job we had all done countless times in the past, but still necessary.

This time though, as I walked in to the outer yard of the mortuary, I was greeted by the sight of numerous bodies stacked one on top of the other, covered by white sheets.

There must have been at least thirty of them outside the building, what the heck was going on?

Squeezing through, I pushed into the short corridor leading to the mortuary room, passing more bodies stacked head to toe, two or three high along both walls, faces touching feet in an intimacy never known in life.

In the mortuary itself, a solitary figure frantically cut and sawed, preparing some of the sixty or so scattered bodies around, for the pathologist's examination.

It reminded me of a scene from an ancient Egyptian embalming house!

"Hello there, can you help me please?"

He looked at me across a sea of bodies, his arms up to the elbows in some unfortunate's abdominal cavity.

"What do you WANT?" he said in a tone that reeked of frustration and exasperation.

"Met.Police photographic, I've come to do an unident out of the river, any idea which one it might be?"

His gaze became almost maniacal.

"There's bloody hundreds 'ere from the smog epidemic, take yer pick, help yer self - just DON'T bother me with anythin' ok?"

I saw his point, and, realising that this was not the best time to bother the poor man, beat a hasty retreat back to the Yard for lunch.

Our night call-out system had improved tremendously now that we had our own minivans, but they had to be left at the nearest Met.Police station to our home, in my case Chadwell-Heath about five miles away, so a Met. or even an Essex car would still have to come and pick me up.

Because I wasn't on the `phone to give detailed directions, a Police car calling at night stood a good chance of picking the wrong house in our quiet Close, even though they had my correct address written down.

I knew my immediate neighbours were getting a bit umpty being called out of bed at ungodly hours, just because the police got the number wrong.

If we wished to stay friends with our neighbours, I would have to get on the 'phone a bit sharpish, even though there was a two year waiting list for new subscribers, how could I possibly manage that?

About this time I received a night call to attend a fatal accident in St James' Rd. Southwark, where a bus and a private vehicle had collided in the snow, killing a passenger in the private vehicle. It was a crisp dark night, with clear sky and good street lighting, which, combined with the snow on the ground, meant the scene was quite well illuminated.

On completion of photography, I made notes of what detail I could see in the shadows, and how much of the rooftops I could see against the skyline, (so that my final prints would be neither too dark, or too light) and went home.

Subsequently I got a call from the Inspector at Tower Bridge Police station, saying he was delighted with the photographs and what they showed, he felt a conviction for causing death by dangerous driving would be quite easy to demonstrate with these.

Eventually the case appeared at the Old Bailey, and I was summoned by the defence to prove my photographs, and after prosecuting counsel had formally elicited my personal details, the court proceeded to hear my evidence.

"A nice set of photographs Mr. Parker, we can see a remarkable level of detail for night-time, taken by flash I assume?" said defence counsel.

"No Sir, the only flash we use is when recording details of damage to vehicles or property, all road scenes are photographed using available light, unless otherwise stated".

"You mean to tell me that no flash was used to record these road scenes at all?"

"No sir, none, they are the result of a straightforward time-exposure" He thought for a minute, and then said, "How long was this time exposure?" and immediately the alarm bells started to ring, perhaps I should have left it at a straightforward `no' instead of being honest.

"In this particular case twenty seconds"

"Ah ha!" he pounced "So therefore my client could not possibly have seen the scene like this, unless he had sat in that junction for twenty seconds?".

I groaned inwardly, I could see just where this conversation was leading.

"No Sir, that is not the case at all, the reason for the twenty second exposure is because the lens aperture has to be made smaller to get things sharp over the whole range of the photograph, which results in the exposure going from a fairly instantaneous one like the eye sees, to one of twenty seconds.

The resultant photograph however is as true a representation of the scene as it is possible to get, using today's film and printing papers".

"Would you say then you could see more in these photographs than could be seen at the scene at the time then?".

"Only by the fact that you can study the photographs for as long, and as close as you like, while the driver having the same viewpoint at the scene, might only have a second or two to appreciate the same view" I answered, not feeling at all happy at the way things appeared to be going.

Eventually after a few more unimportant questions I was free to go, and wondered what the jury would make of it all.

I soon found out, as a quite irritable Inspector came on the `phone to tell me they had lost the case they had fully expected to win, and he didn't think a great deal of my photographs after all!

About a year later I got an urgent call to attend the appeal Court in the Strand, where the court had temporarily recessed awaiting my attendance for questioning.

Not knowing which case of mine was being heard, or what it was about, I duly presented myself at court, and was quickly ushered before the newly convened assemblage.

I took the oath, gave my details, and anxiously awaited what was coming next. A barrister stood up and looking straight me straight in the eye said "You may remember appearing before me at the Central Criminal court last year, and when questioned about these photographs, your answer is a matter of record", he waved a sheaf of papers in the air.

"Would you please look at exhibit one, and in particular photographs 1-4. Would you say you can see more in the photographs than you could see at the scene at the time?, just answer YES or NO".

And the trap was sprung.

"I can't answer....." I began, but he crashed back, "I said just yes or no Mr. Parker, and that's all I wish to hear"

I started again addressing the judge this time, "My Lord this isn't a question of yes or no it's ....." and again I was stopped dead in my tracks, this time by the judge himself.

Over his half-glasses he said. "Mr. Parker, learned counsel has asked you a question to which you must answer as required, will you please do so?"

I looked down at our prosecuting counsel, but he had his back to me, and refused to look in my direction.

The whole court waited in silence to hear my answer.

I gave learned defence counsel the dirtiest look I could muster, and in a voice which I hoped showed resentment at the answer I had to give, said "Yes".

What I SHOULD have said was `If my answer is as you say, already a matter of record, may I please hear it?'

The split-second I said the word Yes, counsel said "Thank you very much Mr. Parker, you may now leave the court". and that was that! I vowed that in future I wouldn't be manoeuvred into such an unfortunate position again.

The case remained lost.

A few months later I was involved in another case, where the defence produced photographs of their own, and to rebut them I attended the scene of the incident to take police photographs. It concerned a sports shop in Upminster where the venue consisted of the front shop and two smaller rooms behind.

If you stood in the middle of the second room where a chair had been strategically placed, a person standing in the toilet in the far corner of the third room could be seen quite clearly in a mirror on the wall.

This mirror, angled at 45 degrees was originally placed, so that a person using the toilet could see a customer at the front shop waiting to be served, and could respond quickly.

The owner of the shop however, had placed some sports clothes on the chair in the second room, and calling miss `X' to pick them up, exposed himself indecently whilst giving her instructions, knowing that he would be seen by her in the angled mirror.

The young lady had naturally gone home and complained to mum, who had gone bolo, and called police.

Following the normal practice amongst police photographers, I used a standard focal-length lens to photograph this particular situation - I wanted the scene recorded as the human eye would see it, without the distortion of a wide -angle lens, as details described by the complainant were crucial in proving the offence. During photography I used the local CID officer as a guinea pig, and stood him where the girl had described, but with his hands crossed over his groin to simulate a penis.

I could see the officer's fingers quite clearly in the mirror as I took the photograph, and I felt quite happy with the shot. The rest of the shop, plus the chair were quickly done, and we left the scene.

Several weeks later in court, after the CID had submitted my photographs to the magistrates, I was asked to look at photographs submitted by the defence, and as I went through them I could see their photographer had used a wide-angle lens on a 35mm camera, probably a 28mm, which had the effect of showing a wider view of the room than I had, but also in the defendant's favour, showed a tiny mirror on the wall, with no image in it at all.

In fact the mirror looked like a black light switch on the wall!

I explained to the magistrates the reason why they couldn't see the effect described by the girl in the defence photograph, and why you could see it in mine, confirming that we had been scrupulously fair in showing the scene as it actually was, without any lens distortion.

This was also confirmed by the CID officer whose hands appeared in our photograph, and the case was won.

The poor defence photographer, who wasn't actually called in to prove his photographs, got a right rollicking from his brief, for not making him aware of wide-angle lens distortion!.

Away from work I fondly hoped that 1960 would be the year I might be able to get stuck in to some bird photography for a change, but the gods planned differently. Week after week the weather remained dull and windy, with copious amounts of rain crashing down, and I achieved practically nothing.

The one thing I did manage though, which had nothing to do with photography at all, was to buy a 500cc. AJS motorcycle combination in lovely condition with 17000 miles on the clock, the family and I could now get mobile without having to rely on public transport.

It was going to be great.

By the end of May the weather still hadn't improved, and with nothing available for natural light photography, I decided to have a go at photographing Sand Martins underground - a bit of a technical problem as it hadn't been done before, but at least I wouldn't be dependent on the sun for illumination!

Sand Martins build their nests by digging a small tunnel three or four feet long into a tall, sandy bank, and then excavating a small nesting chamber at the end.

I figured that if I could dig a large hole in the top of the bank to one side of the nest, and get down to nest level, I could get myself and camera inside, cover the whole lot over with thick material to make it light-tight, and take pictures of the birds at the nest using flash.

This method of photographing sand martins hadn't been tried before so it was suck it and see. I watched the Sand Martin colony as they excavated their various tunnels, and when I thought the birds had reached the egg-laying stage, picked a tunnel at the extreme edge of the colony, to keep general disturbance to the minimum.

The site I was working was a landfill rubbish-tip, with plenty of junk material nearby to use, and because it was regularly patrolled by guards with dogs, was relatively secure from outside disturbance by people.

After carefully measuring the length of the Sand Martins' tunnel by using a thin reed stem, I transferred the measurement to the ground above the nest and commenced digging.

When I knew I had dug below the level of the martins' nest, I carefully excavated sideways until I came across the nest chamber, a bed of grasses and white feathers holding four white eggs. So far so good.

I carefully sealed up the exposed nest with soft clay, and squared off the pit to about four feet square, putting two discarded bed frames side by side over the top as a roof.

Over these I put an old carpet ten feet square, liberally covering it with sand to camouflage the site, and weighted the whole lot down with house-bricks round the edges.

It was now up to the gods whether the martins would accept my new `wall' to their nest chamber, or desert, I fervently hoped they would accept.

About fifty yards away from the colony I sat down quietly in the grass, watching the martins' tunnel through binoculars and waiting for the birds to fly in.

After half an hour, a single martin shot in at high speed, and didn't re-appear straight away or even during the next ten minutes, so it looked like success at the moment.

I left the area, feeling highly chuffed with my efforts so far.

A week later I returned with a specially made sliding door set in a wooden frame, which I fitted over the re-exposed nest chamber, fixing it to the sand with long wire pins, and making the whole thing light-tight once more with soft clay.

If you slid the wooden panel to the right it exposed the nest to view, if you slid it back to the left, the nest was hidden in darkness again - it all seemed to work ok.

All I had to do on my next visit, was to clamber into the hide by lifting one corner of the carpet, and once inside, make the place dark again, slide the wooden door across to reveal the nest, and hopefully begin photography.

Because the distance between the nest and the camera position was just over two feet, I borrowed Alan's Rolleiflex camera, with Proxar close-up lenses to take my pictures, even so, the final image of the nest in the viewfinder was pretty small.

The weather continued to be dull and wet, so wet at times I wondered how the martins found enough insects to feed on, nevertheless my first session in the hide was marvellous.

The four young martins were a just few days old, and in the dull light filtering down the tunnel, I could see them barely two feet away, snug in their bed of warm feathers waiting to be fed. Despite having put on heavy, warm clothes, I was quite cold sitting on the damp sand, and realised now why the martins built such a well insulated nest - there was no warmth in the ground at all!

It was a revelation to see that as the adults returned down the nesting tunnel, they blocked off all the light, which was a signal for the young to raise their heads and call for food.

A peculiar state of affairs, when one considers they were now in virtual darkness, and neither adults or young could see what was going on!

It was only when the adult bird came fully into the nest chamber, that a dull light could once again illuminate the scene.

I took several flash photographs using small PF.1 bulbs, which didn't seem to distract the birds at all, but I had to remember to close my own eyes at the moment of exposure, so that I could see in the dim light afterwards, what was still going on.

Initially it took about ten minutes for my eyes to see detail in the nest chamber, but once I had gained low-light vision, I was amazed at just how much detail I could discern, not only in the nest, but what went on outside the nest entrance too.

If anything flew close to the nest entrance, an image of it briefly flickered across the back of the nest chamber, and I could tell whether it was a sand martin or a pied wagtail by the colours. I was absolutely amazed when a Cabbage-White butterfly landed at the entrance to the tunnel, and was depicted upside-down on the back of the nest-chamber, in full colour!

It was obvious to me the nesting tunnel was acting like a camera obscura, and creating an image in the darkness, something I had never expected in my wildest dreams!

I wasn't able to return to the Sand Martins for nearly a week, due to heavy overtime at work, but it was no great loss as the weather was still pretty awful, with dull skies and heavy rain the order of the day.

When I next got in the hide, I could see the young were now quite large - it wouldn't be long before they were flying, and the delightful experience would be over.

The first change I noticed since my last visit was, that darkening of the tunnel when the adults approached, now caused the young to run towards the entrance in an effort to be fed first, leaving me looking at an empty nest! I would have to get shots of them now before they all disappeared outside.

During my time in the hide, the rain continued to fall heavily, consequently feeding visits by the adults got less and less, and I was on the point of giving up for the day, when suddenly I felt something touch the top of my head.

I tried to look up to see what the devil it was, but couldn't move my head backwards, the carpet-covered bedframes were pressing on my head and getting lower by the second!

Suddenly a stream of cold water ran down my neck from above, and I realised the sand covered carpet must have absorbed so much rain, the whole roof was being driven into the pit by the sheer weight of wet sand!

Quick as lighting, I whipped Alan's camera off the tripod, closed the sliding door to the martins nest, and scrambled for the exit in the corner, only to find it had disappeared!

In a bit of a panic - the bed frames were now touching my back, I dug furiously beyond the edge of the bedframe until I saw daylight and scrambled clear, just as the whole lot gently caved in.

It had been a pretty close call, and I had almost been caught like a grape in a wine press, under a huge pile of wet sand.

Not very funny!

It was on the longest day of the year, and a pretty dull and wet one too, that Janette was born at home, putting paid to any further ideas concerning bird photography with a new baby to help look after.

I had taken a week off work to get things straight at home, and now that everything was running ok. went back to the Yard, only to find I was attending five or six crime scenes a day, and covering about a hundred miles around town in the minivan, the place had gone mad.

Coupled with leaving home at 0630 to get in by 0800, and leaving the Yard around 1730 to get home and help Teresa, the situation left me dog-tired at the end of each day.

On December 10th at 1845, Murphy decided to have his last wicked fling of 1960, maybe because he hadn't anyone else to bother at that particular moment.

I was riding the 500 AJS home from work as usual, and had just left the main road with its good lighting, and turned down a secondary road with no lights at all, putting on dipped headlights for better vision.

Suddenly, in the headlights' beam I saw a large lorry wheel straddling the centre of the road, and swung the bike hard right to avoid it, and knew nothing more.

Apparently, the driver of a large flat-bed lorry delivering goods to a farm, had misjudged his turn into the farm entrance, and had got out to get assistance, leaving the tail end of his lorry stuck across the road.

The lorry, which had been travelling towards me, had its front lights obscured from my vision by being inside the farm gates, while it's offside tail-light, on the far side of the vehicle, was completely out of sight too.

The AJ's sidecar hit the lorry's rear-nearside wheel dead centre, slewing the bike viciously to the left under the lorry's tailboard, shearing everything off at tank level, including me.

At the same instant I hit the lorry, a car immediately behind me and about to overtake, piled into the whole tangle, while I flew over the back of the lorry, landing on my head ten yards down the road.

A motorist coming towards the accident from the opposite direction saw what he thought was a pile of rags in the road, and toyed with the idea of putting his wheels either side of it, before deciding it was too big, and stopped.

I'm jolly glad he did, because the bundle was me!

The two Police officers who subsequently attended Oldchurch hospital to get a statement regarding the accident were out of luck - I couldn't remember a thing.

My glasses had been smashed into my left eyebrow and broken, while the haematoma on my left cheek was so big I couldn't see round it, but my head seemed to be head ok.

It was lucky I had always worn a crash helmet, even though they weren't compulsory at the time, without it I would almost certainly have been killed.

Needless to say Teresa was pretty worried by my non-arrival from work, and scared witless when police eventually arrived at the door, accompanied by a breakdown lorry which thoughtlessly dumped the remains of the bike and side-car on the drive.

The next day with more of my wits working than before, I heard one of the nurses say `Did you know you have a briefcase under your bed - would you like me to check what's in it for you?'.

When she opened it, a few papers came into view plus Alan's Rolleiflex camera - and suddenly I remembered - I had asked to borrow it again for a couple of days - god, was it still in one piece?

Apparently the briefcase had been thrown clear when the sidecar disintegrated on impact, and had lain in the middle of the road until found by police. whilst clearing up.

It was nothing short of a miracle that both camera and I had survived.

This was now the second time I had been in Oldchurch hospital after an accident, just before Christmas, and I hoped Murphy wasn't setting a precedent!

Despite all the kerfuffle, Christmas turned out to be pretty good all round, and although still suffering some stiffness from the crash, I looked forward to whatever 1961 might bring.

I certainly wasn't going to give up riding motorbikes just because of the accident, I thoroughgly enjoyed motorcycling.

For my sins I was put on night-call standby over the new year, and mentally prepared myself for the worst.

No doubt there would be the usual murder to see the old year out, plus a couple of nasty fatal accidents as drink took its usual toll, but I wasn't prepared at all for the silly job that came in on new year's eve.

Due no doubt, to the current festive season, a warehouse in north London had vast stocks of beauty preparations and cosmetics stacked on its premises, protected by a security man watching intruder alarm warning lights in his control room.

In the main storage area, stacked goods were protected from theft by an infra -red beam system, running round the inside walls from floor level to just over head height.

The system had obviously worked very well over the years, until some wag discovered that if you entered the building through a window higher than six feet, and jumped across the narrow gap between the window and the stacked goodies, you missed the sensitive Infra -red beam entirely, and no alarm was raised!

On this particular evening, a lady whose home and small back garden backed on to the warehouse, saw to her amazement two Police officers helping a third scramble through a top window to gain access to the factory.

She immediately went to her phone and dialled 999, reporting the incident just as she had seen it, adding that as her husband was in charge of security, she knew Police had specific instructions to call him first, before making any attempt to enter and search the premises themselves. The lady continued to watch the scene, while awaiting the result of her 999 call, accompanied by her husband.

The PC who had gone into the factory soon re-appeared at the top of the window, and began dropping packages to his colleagues below, before climbing out onto the shoulders of his two friends and dropping to the ground.

As they appeared round the front of the factory, and got into their vehicle, a Panda patrol car screeched to a halt alongside theirs, and asked what was going on.

The three PC's declared they had just intercepted a couple of thieves at the rear of the warehouse, who, after being challenged by police, dropped their loot and ran off, leaving the officers to pick up the stolen goods and bring them into the nick.

Unfortunately for them, they didn't know the security man and his wife had clocked them entering the factory earlier, and had reported exactly what they had seen.

My brief was to photograph the scene from the lady's back window showing what she and her husband had seen concerning the entry. It all sounded pretty straightforward and simple - night photography held no qualms for me, especially after some of the hairy jobs I had done over the years!

There was no doubt at all, you could see an officer in his black uniform against the dirty yellowish bricks of the wall, I had an officer on hand to demonstrate that very point, the only problem was, there was no lighting anywhere, only a dull pinkish glow emanating from sodium lights in the street at the front of the factory some fifty yards away.

I got the officer to stand by the lower window and remain perfectly still while I made four exposures at 5.6 the widest aperture I had, one at 50 seconds, another at a minute, the third at 1-1/2 minutes, and the last at 2 minutes. On completion I said to the lady, `I'll process these tomorrow and if they're ok. I'll do a print for you both to look at, to see if you agree it shows the scene as you saw it, ok?'

When I processed the films next day I was mortified to see only the faintest image on the two minute exposure film, the rest were virtually blank - I would have to go back and try again!.

The next night I took our Linhof technica with it's 3.5 lens and gave two exposures, one of 5 minutes, and the other at 10, although without the police officer standing in this time - he couldn't be spared.

On development the ten minute exposure was fine, it produced a print which visually matched the scene at the rear of the factory, and the lady and her husband said it was spot on.

When the officers charged with the offence were shown the photograph of what the witnesses had seen, two pleaded guilty straight away, while the third elected to go for trial, taking his chance with a jury.

When I eventually gave evidence in court and explained that no extra lighting had been added to the scene to take the photograph, I prayed we wouldn't have a re-run of the previous fiasco about the exposure time necessary, and kept well off the subject. Explaining the necessity for a ten minute wait with the shutter wide open would have sounded quite ridiculous!

As the number of crime jobs escalated - we eventually covered over 2700 in 1961, it became necessary to advertise for more staff to cope with our increased workload, and after a prolonged delay, several new faces appeared.

One of the new arrivals was Hugo, a tall, well-spoken heavily built chap, naturally good natured and quite inoffensive, but definitely the wrong sort of chap for the grotty disgusting jobs we had to do. It was possible he might change in the future, but his general naivetÈ and good manners wouldn't last long against Dickie & Co, with their notorious piss-taking and barrack-room humour.

During his initial indoctrination into the workings of the department, he was asked to get left-handed mops from stores, take copies of fingerprints to non-existent fingerprint officers working in the complex below, or clean his developer stained hands with neat Potassium Permanganate crystals, (Which made his hands ebony black) and wave them at the sunlight to remove the stains. He was only told at clocking off time, when everyone else was scooting out the door, that Pot.Metabisulphite NOT sunlight would get the stains off, but only after some very hard scrubbing!

Hugo took all this ribbing with good humour and a smile, which only made Dickie & Co. more determined than ever to have him over, somehow, sometime, but definitely.

Because we worked closely with fingerprint branch, we often received a severed hand or piece of skin tissue for photography, to show in detail the loops and whorls that made fingerprint identification possible.

One day, while Hugo was being shown the ins and outs of photographing these specimens, he expressed his disgust at the process, saying he didn't go much on the idea that he would be expected to undertake such horrible work one day.

Dickie, hearing of Hugo's aversion to having to handle `dead bits', even with rubber gloves on, decided to give his leg a good pull, and sort him out.

"Right Hugo" Dickie said one morning after tea, "Get a 5x4 MPP camera on a tripod over to this bench here, plus a couple of 500W lights, I'm going to show you how to photograph a body specimen properly using a scale for size. then you can have a go yourself".

Hearing this conversation, a couple of us hovered nearby pretending to be busy, but really intent on not missing whatever Dickie was up to.

In very slow time Hugo set up the MPP, plugged in his lights, and went off to load some slides.

"Ok. then Hugo - the first thing to remember is, we don't photograph anything like this, unless we have a scale included in the field of view, otherwise we can't print it back to same size can we?"

"Also we need a clean white dish to put our specimen in, we don't want the bench all mucky do we? and while you're organising that, I'll fetch the specimen we're going to do".

By now Hugo was in a pretty nervous state, jigging up and down next to the camera, as Dickie returned with a package in plain white paper, sealed inside an official clear plastic bag.

"Right now Hugo, I want this specimen photographed from both sides, we'll do one side first, and check that your focussing and exposure are ok. before you carry on and do the other side entirely on your own, alright?".

Hugo gulped an affirmative, and watched as Dickie wearing protective gloves, took the white paper package out of the plastic bag and opened it up. It contained a large, reddish -brown piece of flesh about twelve inches long, six inches wide and weighing about two pounds.

Flopping it into the dish, Dickie pulled it into shape so that it was flat, and placed a white plastic ruler just below it for a scale.

"Ok. then Hugo, get the camera in front of it and let's have a look when you think you've got it sharp - jump to it!".

I looked at Alan and Frank questioningly - it certainly didn't look like any specimen I had ever seen, and there were no particular anatomical features I could recognise on it either.

Under the MPP's focussing cloth, Hugo mumbled and sweated, racking the bellows this way and that, but not having a great deal of success.

"Let me have a look Hugo, you don't seem to be having too much success there" and with that, Dickie dived under the cloth, tweaked the camera in to focus, and they were ready to go.

"There you are Hugo, now just stop down to F.22, give it what the lightmeter says, plus a bit extra for your bellows extension, then go and develop it.

Call me when you've got a result".

On his return Dickie obviously thought the result was good enough to carry on, and said to Hugo "Ok. now turn the specimen over and we'll do the other side".

Hugo went pale.

"Come on Hugo put the gloves on and turn the specimen over, we haven't got all flippin' day!"

Hugo stood transfixed, gazing stupidly at the specimen whilst flapping a solitary rubber glove ineffectually in the air.

"Oh for god's sake come here" said Dickie in exasperation "All you have to do is pick it up and turn it over, can't you even do that?"

Dickie grabbed the specimen from the tray with bare hands, and turning to face Hugo said "Anyone would think there's something wrong with the bloody thing -look it's quite clean, see?" and with that, he put it to his mouth and took a huge bite out of it.

Hugo yelped in disbelief, and dropped the glove, bolting into the gent's toilet gagging, while we all laughed like drains.

Dickie the old wag had brought his pet dog's meat out of the fridge, and used it as a specimen, and poor old Hugo had thought it was a piece of human anatomy!

Happily, he did eventually see the funny side of the gag, but only much, much later.

We in our turn managed to get the better of Dickie from time to time, and one day when he had completed a prestigious job, he came striding out of darkroom No.1 saying to no-one in particular "Yep, they look pretty good to me, even if I say so myself, they should do nicely"

Alan looked at me and said "What do you reckon he's been up to then?"

"Haven't a clue, but whatever it is, he seems highly satisfied with the job, let's go and have a look"

In a 3 litre Kodak wash tank, a metal frame containing a dozen 5x4 slides washed gently in the cool water, before being put in the cabinet to dry.

They were some shots of the Assistant Commissioner on his horse.

"How about a little gag with Dickie just to spice things up a bit?" I asked.

"If it's another one of your daft tricks, I don't want to know" said Alan moving away, "Just tell me when it's going to happen, and I'll watch from a long way off, in case of shrapnel"

I took Dickie's frame of slides carefully from the wash in No.1, and put them to wash in darkroom No.2, replacing them with a spare rack containing discarded 5x4 slides from the waste bin.

All I had to do now was to turn the cold water off, turn on the hot water and wait.

In just a few minutes the emulsion on the plates began to frill and loosen at the edges, before floating to the top of the wash-tank like ribbons of black weed.

It was definitely time to be somewhere else!

It wasn't long before Dickie, whistling a happy tune, returned to the darkroom to put his slides into the dryer.

It was even a shorter time before a roar of despair and anger rent the air, followed by "What stupid son of silly bastard turned the hot water on in No.1 darkroom and ruined my negs, there'll be bloody hell to pay for this!"

Giving him a few more seconds of terminal blood pressure I said "It's ok Mr. Dickinson, your negs are safely washing in No.2, We're washing off some old slides in No.1 to use as 5x4 film-holders in the enlargers"

A small smile began to break at the corners of his mouth, and, with hands on hips said "Ok. you bastards, I give you that one, but mark my words I'll have you for that, just see if I don't" and off he went whistling into No. 2 to see to his negs.

That was Dickie, and I liked that.

During the spring of 1961 Dave and I decided that as this was probably the last year the Rooks would nest at Hainault Lodge due to the lack of livestock farming in the immediate area, and destruction of winter habitat, we would make a last effort to colour- ring all the young Rooks produced, so that we could check other nearby Rookeries and see if any turned up in subsequent years.

Every year since 1954 Dave and I had climbed to over a hundred nests at the Lodge, number-ringing the young birds to find out how long they lived, and how far they travelled after leaving Hainault.

It had been an immense task, which entailed climbing over twenty trees, some fifty feet tall and quite dangerous, due to their dying branches.

Because all the young Rooks in a tree were not ready for ringing at the same time, a second visit to most trees was necessary within a few days, to make sure we accounted for every nestling. It was hard physical work.

By the end of April, we had managed to complete the half dozen nests that had produced young so far, but one nest in a huge oak still required climbing, and it was a real stinker.

The first Saturday in May dawned bright and clear, without any sign of rain, and because Dave wasn't free until the afternoon, I decided to go to the Lodge on my own and finish ringing the young Rooks in the tall oak.

As I got ready to climb the tree, a 200 year specimen with bark as hard and shiny as a Brazil nut, I realised I had forgotten to put my rubber boots in the van.

Both Dave and I had, over the years favoured short rubber wellies for `free-style' tree climbing, as they gave a glue-like grip on the bark, unless of course the trees were wet, or covered in green-mould.

This time, having forgotten my wellies, I had to climb in my normal walking shoes, which, having leather soles slid off the hard oak bark like skates on ice, but they would have to do.

I managed by using my arms more than anything else, to reach the first weight-bearing branch fifteen feet up, and then scramble to the main branch some ten feet higher, before stopping for a rest. There was no doubt I would have to take it easy, my shoes gave virtually no grip on the iron-hard oak, and as an experiment I took them off to see if climbing in socks was better - it wasn't, the tree was far too rough!

By careful climbing I reached the nest, some seventy feet above ground, and colour ringed the four young Rooks, feeling quite pleased with myself at having managed it.

It was remarkable when looking towards London from this height, to see clearly the curved dome of St. Paul's cathedral ten miles away, it certainly didn't look that far in the bright sunshine.

Slowly and carefully I made my way down the tree until I reached the last large branch before the bottom, and sat astride it.

I only had thirty feet to go, and the job was done.

As I stood up to begin the last descent, my shoes, which were now shiny after heavy contact with the tree, zipped from under me, and in a blurr of leaves I fell into space and knew nothing else.

I was on the beach at Salcombe, with the steady roar of the surf in the background, and the sunshine bouncing off the water dappling my eyes through closed lids.

It was all so warm and peaceful I didn't want to open my eyes or even stir, but gradually the shushing of the distant surf, became rustling of leaves in the breeze, and I opened my eyes to see a blue sky through a canopy of oak leaves.

Where the hell was I?
Slowly I turned my head to the left and saw my watch, it said half -past three.
Gradually, a picture came into my mind about Rooks and the oak tree, then, I remembered looking at my watch before starting my climb to the nest - it had been one-thirty, where had the rest of the time gone?.
Puzzled by the whole thing, I made an effort to get up, but nothing happened.
I tried again, conscious that my brain was sending messages to whatever bits did the necessary to get things started, but nothing stirred.
Oh god, what wasn't happening?.
Slowly my brain began to clear, and I realised with a jolt, that I could no longer define the leaves and branches in the canopy above, my glasses had gone, and what was more I couldn't move anything except my head and eyes.
Exerting all the strength of mind and body I could muster, I gradually rolled over from my back onto my side and rested, the exertion utterly exhausting me.
After a short rest, I tried again, screwing everything together in a mighty effort to get my body to respond to my brains` command, and rolled on to my chest, face pushed firmly into the acrid leaf mould.
This was absolutely crazy!
Ever so slowly - it seemed to take forever, I drew my arms under my chest and began to lever upwards and backwards letting my knees bend, until I lay crouched on the ground, head between my arms like a supplicant to Allah.
After a long rest I had enough strength to raise my head and look immediately in front of me, where I saw a glint of sunshine on glass.
Screwing my eyelids down to the minimum, I managed to focus on one-half of my glasses which somehow still contained a lens, at least I would be able to see a few things now!
Looking at my watch again I saw it was now four o'clock, half an hour had gone by, and I still hadn't managed to stand up, let alone discover what damage I might have done to myself.
Using both elbows I managed to crawl over to the remains of my glasses, hook the single arm over my ear and hold the lens frame in place like a monocle.
Now at least I could see where I was going - things were improving by the minute!
Puffing like a grampus I crawled towards the base of the oak, and sat with my back against it, noticing that where I had fallen, a large tree-root about four inches thick broke the surface of the leaf-mould.
This must have caught me across the small of my back at the moment of impact, and was no doubt responsible for my inability to jump up and run about.
I was lucky not to have broken my back or been totally paralysed!
Feeling stronger by the minute, I crawled on hands and knees to where I had left my van, pulled myself into the seat like a roaring drunk, and rested. It was now five-o'clock,
Through a mind fog I realised I should have been home ages ago, I'd told Teresa I wouldn't be long, ha! that seemed a bit of a joke now!
Feeling definitely groggy and worse for wear, I started the van, and drove slowly out of Hainault Lodge down the hill towards home. I only lived four miles away, so

it would be ok. provided I took things easy.

Feeling a right prat, I tottered through the front door just as Teresa was getting dinner ready for the family.

She turned, saw my face and said "Oh my god, what have you done now?"

I explained I had fallen out of a tree - yet again, so she sat me down, took my pulse and temperature, and checked for any obvious breakages.

These Staff-nurses were something special.

"I'm going to call an ambulance" she said "you've got a temperature of 102F, and you could have internal injuries I can't check for - you are a bit of an idiot you know".

In due course the ambulance arrived at the front door, giving all the neighbours a good `nosey', wondering no doubt, what all the fuss was about.

Relating the whole sorry incident to the accident emergency staff at Oldchurch hospital, made it sound quite stupid, I mean, what on earth was a fully-grown man doing thirty feet up a tree in Hainault forest anyway?

The accident staff were their usual model of efficiency and procedure, examination, X -rays, the lot, until satisfied that I wasn't going to peg it in the immediate future, they put me into a crisp sheeted bed, and told me to lie still.

Two days later a bespectacled Doctor accompanied by his entourage, and the unsmiling ward Sister, consulted his notes at the foot of my bed, before saying in a voice loud enough for the whole ward to hear "So this is the chap who fell out of a tree in Hainault forest is it? ha! ha! What were you doing up there, bird watching or something?, ha! ha!"

I disliked him immediately.

I was incarcerated there for a week, happily I hadn't ruptured my spleen as had been suspected, but had damaged my fourth and fifth lumbar vertibrae, for which carelessness I pay the sore penalty today.

Returning to work, I was put on inside duties for a while, not out of any sympathy for my ravaged body, but as some sort of retribution for dodging work, `idling my time in hospital' whilst everyone else had been under heavy pressure, I was told.

Dickie in the meantime, had been given the task of teaching overseas police officers the basic requirements of forensic photography, and his six week courses at Hendon Police College were interspersed with visits to Fingerprints and Photographic at the Yard, to broaden his students' experience.

One particular group of students consisted of officers from Belize, Egypt, and various parts of Africa, who had a fair knowledge of English, and one hoped, sufficient savvy to take in what they were being taught.

In the middle of the week Dickie would breeze in to the section with his usual bonhomie, accopmpanied by his band of students, and announce that he was off to tea with the guv'nor - would we all chip in and look after his students by demonstrating what we were doing while he was away?

Of course we would.

I was on washing and drying, dealing with hundreds of 12 x 10 prints that cascaded into the wash from the darkrooms, squee-geeing, and placing them on the Kodak glazing drum to dry - not very interesting at all really.

Alan said he would demonstrate a document he was copying, and Frank would show them a complete scenes of crime 5x4 kit after his tea break. I could fetch up at the rear, by demonstrating the highly technical bit - the art of washing and drying.

After half an hour or so, I heard Alan approaching with the students, and after introducing the motley crowd, announced he would leave them in my tender care as he was now off to tea with Frank.

Unbeknown to the students, I had placed a row of quarter-plate prints of prisoners' faces on the glazing drum, wound it round so that the prints were just out of sight, and stopped the drum. Nearby I had four other blank quarter-plate sheets of paper swishing about in the wash.

After a spiel about processing and the need for thorough print washing - as seen at Scotland Yard, I switched the glazer back on, and started to demonstrate the amazing new Kodak glazing drum. "This remarkable and versatile machine does not require a lens to take photographs" I began, "If you watch closely you will see that I am about to put four sheets of plain bromide paper on the drum, so"

They all stared intently at the glazer.

After a short period of time the previously hidden photos came slowly into view, and I continued "Yes here they come, now we have four very good prisoner's photographs, dry, glazed, and ready to go into the picture library, how about that?"

There were murmurs of admiration all round, and wonder on the faces of several, as they scribbled it down in their notebooks for future reference.

One African even asked if he could take down full details of the machine, as he felt his department would require one straight away!

Several days later Dickie returned to the section, and without hesitation marched straight across to where I was working and said without rancour, "I suppose you think that was bloody funny do you? For goodness sake have a laugh do, but remember I've got to undo your little gags, it's bad enough getting the bloody knowledge in, in the first place".

A few weeks later Dickie introduced yet another crop of students to the section, and we did try very hard not to mislead them in any way, but one opportunity proved just too good to pass up.

I was working with Jim, a fingerprint officer, on the viability of obtaining better fingerprint identification from a decaying body. Very often under these appalling conditions, the surface skin has entirely disappeared, leaving only the flesh below, but this still has that persons' unique fingerprint on it, and it was this impression we were trying to reproduce accurately.

In his previous employment Jim had been involved in specialised latex research, and it was this expertise he brought to bear on the current problem.

He found that if you coated the flesh thinly with a special latex compound, it could be carefully peeled off after hardening, creating a new `skin' plus fingermark, which we could handle more easily.

It could also be subjected to various lighting techniques, to provide the best photograph for comparison and identification purposes.

I had just got to the point of photographing the latex skin, this time using transmitted light instead of oblique lighting, when Dickie introduced a fairly high-ranking African Police officer, saying what we were doing would be of great interest to him.

I explained the technique we were using, and got him to look through the camera viewfinder at the `new' fingerprint.

He then asked if he could see the original hand we had used for the experiment, for comparison.

The hand was duly brought from the fridge in a plastic bag, the seal undone, and tipped out on to an enamel dish for our friend to inspect.

His nose wrinkled a bit at the musty smell emanating from the decaying hand, but after an examination of its ridge characteristics with a magnifier, and comparing it to one of my prints off the `skin' looked up and said.

"This looks a pretty good result to me" and turning to Jim asked, "What do you feel about it, have you got enough here for an identification or not?"

Jim replied he thought we were doing quite well, and was off to do a magnified comparison, to ascertain that very point.

I continued with my experimental trans-illuminating of the latex skin, which seemed to offer far greater control over lighting contrast than oblique lighting, when our friend, who had been quiet for some time said, "Out of interest, what happens to the hand when you are finished with it?".

I turned to him, and as non-chalantly as I could, said "Oh, it's usually disposed of, or we can keep it ourselves, in fact if it's not too decayed it makes a good soup"

His eyes were a picture, like two great gob-stoppers in a sea of ebony. "You don't mean you actually EAT them do you?"

"Well not actually the meat, by it does make a fine soup, I was going to cook this one tonight - would you like me to bring you some soup when I come in the morning?".

I could see he didn't know what to believe or do about it all, so I made an excuse to develop my film, and walked off.

When I returned, our African friend had gone.

"I heard that, you wicked bastard". said Alan "If he goes and tells Dickie what you've said, he'll go bolo, you know what happened last time".

The following morning I arrived at the section bearing a small thermos flask, and placed it on the bench where Jim and I were set up, and started work.

As luck would have it, at around ten o'clock Dickie arrived with his students, including our African chappie, who smiled in acknowledgement and walked across to see how we were progressing.

"Good morning" I said. "I didn't forget you last night you know, I've brought some soup specially for you to try" and with that I unscrewed the thermos and poured some hot cockaleekie soup into two nearby mugs.

"Here you are, this one's yours" I said and took a large sip from my mug, passing the other to him.

With an incredulous stare and a shout of disgust, he took off like a rocket, fortunately, Dickie was too occupied with the rest of his students to notice anything unusual, and we all fell about laughing like mad.

Although we were very busy, and flying around London like loonies in our Minivans, there was great camaraderie all round, especially on the days we were in developing and printing together.

I felt that quite a lot of our whacky behaviour was an escape mechanism, a necessary counter to the terrible and disgusting sights we had to see and photograph at first hand.

Dickie, who was taking a mid-term break from his students, and with us practically every day now, was I observed, a creature of certain predictabilities.

Regular as clockwork, he returned from lunch at one o'clock, strolled down the corridor talking to whoever was his companion, and if any piece of litter was in his way, be a film wrapper, or accidentally dropped carton, he would swiftly kick it into touch out of sight.

No doubt a habit left over from his service training, if you can't see it, it doesn't exist.

There was, amongst other paraphernalia in the studio, a 40lb weight, the sort with an inset grip-bar, obviously belonging to a weighing machine, which was used whenever a heavy counter balance was required during difficult photography.

Co-incidentally, one of the lads had celebrated his birthday that day with a large chocolate cake, which he cut up and dispensed among the staff, leaving the empty box discarded on a nearby bench.

I said to Alan "If we put the 40lb weight in the chocolate box, and left it in the corridor just before one o'clock, do you think Dickie would belt it one, and stub his toe?"

"You must be conkers" replied Alan. "Dickie will go absolutely mad, I just wouldn't do it if I were you".

However,the more I thought about it, the more attractive the joke became, and at five to one, the trap was set.

Most of the lads waiting to go to second lunch were in on the gag, and took up strategic positions in doorways and behind curtains, to observe the action, but keeping well out of sight.

On the dot, Dickie appeared with Sgt.McMacken, walking briskly down the corridor, hands jammed into trousers pockets, deep in conversation about something or other, until they came to the discarded box.

Without breaking step, Dickie placed his left foot alongside the box, and in true soccer style hoofed it strongly with his right, the subsequent crunching impact being quite audible throughout the studio.

The box naturally never moved, and Dickie, brought to a shuddering halt, laboured mightily to continue his stride despite a definite limp to starboard.

"I bet that was that f*****g Parker!" he gritted to Mc.Macken but true to his stoic nature, he never remarked on the incident all the years I knew him. That was Dickie.

It's funny how some things can go badly wrong without your knowledge, and its only later, when they finally come home to roost with a vengeance, you fall in.

That's exactly what happened to me after photographing a particularly nasty murder in Highbury Vale.

I received a call over the air to attend Aberdeen Gardens, where a young girl had been found dead in the front garden of a derelict house, apparently the victim of a sex murder.

On arrival, I found the place secured by Police, and the press being kept at bay by hard pressed officers.

The DI. greeted me with a look of relief and said "Glad to see you Alan, we've got a nasty one here, I want you to get your pictures done as quick as you can, the Doctor's already been to certify death, and I've got the pathologist lined up ready and waiting".

"Can you tell me anything about it?" I asked.

It was essential in my opinion to get as much information at the off, to save taking photographs that might delay proceedings, or be of no value at all.

"All we know at the moment is, that she's a young girl who has been stripped of her underwear, been sexually assaulted, and appears to have been strangled".

"Ok. I'll cover the body from all angles, including close-ups of the marks on the neck, and the immediate area round the body, then it's all yours, I should be about twenty minutes".

I got cracking, and soon came to the bit where I wanted a view of the victim from the top of the short flight of concrete steps leading to the front door of the house.

"Can I have everyone out of the front garden please?

I'm doing a wide angle shot showing the last few steps, the victim, and a general view of the garden towards the front gate, I need it cleared"

In seconds the area was clear of Lab: personnel and police officers, but I could still see a few pairs of feet through the gap between the bottom of the privet hedge and the ground, but as time was passing, I decided to let it go, and took my shots.

"Is that it then?" called the DI.

"Yes." I replied "You can all come back in now, I've got everything I think you need, but there's something I'd like you to look at though".

He walked over to where I stood at the victims feet, her legs spread, bare feet resting on the second step up from the bottom.

"It might not have struck you as you've been busy elsewhere, but the steps under her feet are covered with a sheet of old newspaper, which has been here for ages, it's so brittle from weathering it disintegrates at the touch, if she'd been raped here, the newspaper would certainly have been torn, as you see it's quite complete, I've got it all in the photograph"

"Quite the little detective today aren't we" he said with a grin, "Anything else?".

"Well yes there is, but I don't know whether you'll want to hear it, in view of your jealous attitude" I countered.

"I know it's a bit off, but if you look closely as I did when I was focussing the camera, you will see that there's a Dandelion growing right in front of her wotsit.

There's no way that flower would be undamaged if she'd been raped here, and besides that, there are twin dust tracks coming in through the front gate onto the smooth asphalt of the drive, which look like pram tracks to me, perhaps she was brought in and dumped here?"

"Thank you professor, thank YOU!" he said mockingly, "You just stick to taking your little snaps and we'll get along fine" and turning away with a smile, left me to put away my gear.

It had been policy in the department for some time to get officers to call and sign for their initial six sets of crime photographs, because in the past, when asked in Magistrates and other courts for copies to be handed round, when perhaps only one or two copies had been brought along, the cry of mitigation went up `Sorry sir, photographic haven't given us sufficient copies'.

The resultant snotty letters from the judiciary and other aggrieved parties, had resulted in the aforesaid tightening of procedure, which in this particular instance was to save my bacon.

About a month after the murder, I got a surprise call from our Chief-Superintendent, head of Branch, known affectionately as `bladder-head', to present myself at his office IMMEDIATELY with my diary, a hard backed 12x10 book which chronicled my every working minute, from signing on, to booking off.

Frantically I checked to see if it was up to date, and ruled off after the last entry as per instructions - everything seemed ok. and whistled myself down to the holy of holies and knocked on the door.

"Come" droned a bored sounding voice from the other side.

I felt the intonation was intended to give the impression that some hitherto unapproachable being, like the Wizard of Oz, was deigning to set eyes on me, before signing my execution papers.

I went in.

Sitting with the boss and examining something, were two other people I didn't know.

"May I see your diary please Parker?" said the boss, and nodding to his left, "This is Det.Chief Supt X, and his Det.Sgt Y. from C.1. who will take notes, please sit down".

Bloody hell, take notes I thought, this sounds grim, and my stomach tightened in anticipation of the action, whilst my mind ran ice-cold through all the permutations of possible disaster.

"Ah yes, here we are" said the boss stabbing his finger at one of the pages, "It was you then, what have you got to say about the murder scene at Aberdeen Park then?".

I went through the whole saga from beginning to end, while the C.1. Sgt. scribbled in his notebook.

Bloody unfair I thought, they've had all the time to prepare whatever it is they want to spring on me, including their own man to take notes, while Joe soap here has to get it right, first-time, with no friend to turn to!

After about twenty-minutes the boss said, "Ok. what I want you to do now, is to show these officers the signed form of the officer collecting the scene photographs, and then they'll want to question you further".

When we got to the C.1 office, I sat down in front of the Ch. Supt. while his Sgt. sat behind me out of sight, jiggling his clip-board containing statement forms

"Now then" he began, "Let's go through it all again so I've got it clear in my mind" and I thought, `No mate, what you want is to trip me up, find something different the second time round, but you're going to have to do better than that'.

When we finished he said, "Ok. Det. Sgt. Y. will read your statement back to you, and if there's anything in it you don't like, or feel is wrong, we'll make a note of it as we go along" This was duly done, and I signed it, getting pretty annoyed by now at being treated like a suspect for something.

"Do you mind telling me what all this is about, what the hell's going on?" I said, and with that he whipped a 12x10 print onto the table between us and said, "This picture appeared in the German publication `Der Stern' recently, did you or did you not take this photograph?"

There plain as day, was the colour shot of the murdered girl with her legs apart, the very one I had photographed at Highbury Vale.

I stared at the photograph for a few seconds before saying "Yes it's the shot I took, but it's not my photograph"

"What do you mean it's not your photograph, you took it didn't you?"

"Yes I did, but if you were a photographer, which you obviously AREN'T - (I emphasised the word nastily), you would know that despite having white borders and being pretty sharp, the degrading of the whites tells me this is in fact a copy print"

His mouth opened, but nothing came out for a few seconds, then like a whiplash he came back, "Exactly what do you mean by copy print, did you or did you not make this print?"

"No I didn't" I replied, and as I scanned it closer, a detail in it hit me like a sledge hammer, causing my adrenalin to surge like an electric current.

It was as clear as day!

There in the centre bottom edge of the print about an inch and a half long, and projecting into the picture area by about a quarter of an inch was a black crescent - and I knew exactly what it was! I laughed in relief.

"You must realise Parker this is no laughing matter, you could be facing very serious charges" but ignoring his remarks I obeyed a totally sub-conscious command to turn the print over to see the back.

I quickly reached for the print and began to turn it over, getting just over half-way through, when his hand slammed down to stop me. Unfortunately his action was a fraction too late, and only served to complete my movement, and the back was exposed.

There, in the middle was a two-inches high black rubber stamped logo, inside which read `Press copyright, not for release'

I looked the Ch. Supt. straight in the eyes and said in a fury, "You lousy bastards, you might have told me!".

Embarrassed as hell, and now in a conciliatory tone, he replied "You weren't meant to see that, I'm sorry, please tell me what you were saying about it being a copy".

I wasn't going to let him off the hook that easy and thought angrily, you've given me a rough time, now I'll dish some out'.

"As I said before, you're not photographers and therefore can't be expected to think like one, but you ARE supposed to be Detectives, what do you make of that black crescent at the bottom of the picture then?".

They both had a look at it through a Sherlock-Holmes type magnifier, but could make nothing of it.

I wriggled with glee.

"I can tell you EXACTLY what it is, it's the tip of a man's shoe, the welt, this photo was copied by someone holding it down with his shoe on the floor, someone who is professional enough to copy a colour picture, hand-held whilst it is still in the album"

I could see they weren't convinced, but I didn't care, I had made my point.

To cover this new development, I had to make a further statement clarifying what I had just said, and when they were satisfied I went back to the section, still feeling pretty mad.

For a couple of months I heard nothing further regarding the incident, until one day I saw Ch. Supt. X's. name in an article in a Police magazine, and I thought `they were quick enough to pounce on me for an explanation, but haven't come back to let me know of any subsequent developments' - bloody typical!' so I rang him for a meet.

As I sat down in his office, I could see he wasn't particularly keen to see me, but I pressed ahead anyway.

"What have you discovered in relation to the photograph of the murdered woman you thought I had sold?" I asked bluntly.

Looking down at his desk before looking at me he said "We've now got to the bottom of it, and as far as we are concerned you're in the clear, so you don't have to worry any more about it".

I sensed he was a bit on one foot, so I banged in again.

"I'm afraid that's not good enough Sir" I answered "I want to know how a photograph of mine turned up unofficially in a German newspaper, so that we can guard against a similar incident occurring in the future"

He regarded me closely for a few seconds, and said tersely "I can only tell you that the Det.Supt. in charge of the case received the six sets of photographs exactly as you said, but allowed a press photographer friend to see them whilst they were in his office together - that's when one of the prints was copied".

I was gobsmacked, how could anyone be so stupid?

"We interviewed the press photographer concerned, who initially said he was standing next to you when you took your photograph, and in fact this was HIS photograph not yours, what do you say about that?"

"Well apart from myself there was no one else in the garden at the time, the DI.will verify that" I replied "I had it cleared for photography, anyway I remember there were people outside the privet hedge when I took my pictures, one of whom was moving.

I doubt we could both have got exactly the same leg position by coincidence, he's lying" and that's as far as I got.

A few weeks later I saw in an issue of the Police Gazette that the Det.Supt.X concerned with the illegal copying of my photograph had put his papers in, and had resigned, which I felt was about right for the grief he'd stirred up.

The sordid background to this tale of murder was, that the murdered girl was one of three prostitutes living in a flat not far from the murder scene.

She was also the mother of a delightful young child.

Apparently, a furious row had broken out between the three girls concerning the child, which resulted in the natural mother being strangled by the other two.

When the ponce who ran the girls came back to the flat and saw the murdered girl, he apparently flipped, saying they were in deep shit now.

While he figured out how to get rid of the body, he took it to the pram-shed lock-up at the end of the garden, and left it there. After two days he came up with the idea of dumping the body somewhere to make it look like a sex crime, and to make the whole thing credible, had sex with the corpse, so that police forensic examination would show the presence of semen in the body and deduce rape.

He then took the body in a child's pram and wheeled it after dark to Aberdeen Gardens, where dumped it in a front garden.

End of story.

On a much lighter note, one afternoon I got a call from the office saying I had to be at Waltham Abbey Police station at 0700hrs sharp the following morning, as there was going to be a early morning raid on an address, followed by a visit to a secluded piece of ground near the river, where Cannabis drugs were known to be growing.

As I drove into the tiny yard of Waltham Abbey Police station at the designated time, I found my way blocked by a large flat-bed lorry surrounded by police officers all wearing wellies.

I got out of my van and approached the officers, who were in the process of dropping the tailboard, to reveal dozens of Cannabis plants loaded into the back.

"Excuse me" I said to the Inspector standing by, "I'm Mr. Parker from SO.3 Photographic, I've come to do a drugs job here this morning" and as I looked past him at the plants the officers were unloading, an uneasy thought crept into my mind.

There were laughs all round at my words and the Inspector said with a grin "You're too late Mr. Parker we've already been and done it, but you can photograph these here if you like"

Having got up extra early to do this particular job, I wasn't in the mood for piss-taking at my expense, so I replied "You know of course you have to show as well as prove continuity with cannabis plants found at a location, and now you've dug them all up, the defendant can allege you got them from anywhere".

It wasn't strictly true of course, but his grin faded away and was replaced with a look of uncertainty.

"Have you had the Lab. liason officer take some leaves as samples, as well as a whole plant from the site as an exhibit?" I asked. "No I haven't" he replied,

"I didn't think you lot would be here for ages yet, so I told the troops we'd go and get the job done as soon as they came on at six o'clock"

"Well as far as I'm concerned you've blown it, by digging the plants up before we could prove photographically where they were growing, especially as they were probably protected by all this transparent plastic sheeting you have here"

"Can't you just photograph them here as they are, after all, you record the one-or two plants we seize from peoples houses when they're at the station?".

"This isn't just one or two plants is it?" I countered.

"This chap is obviously producing cannabis in a big way, no, the only way I can see out of this is, if we nip back to the scene where you dug them up, and we quickly re-plant them for the camera"

He looked at me very closely to see if I was taking the mickey,

"Do you think we could do it?" he asked.

"If we get a move on, we might get the photographs taken before they all start wilting" I replied, and the look on the faces of his troops was a delight to see.

"You're friggin' joking aren't you guv?" wailed one, "There must be a hundred plants here".

"No I think he's right, that's what we'd better do" said the Inspector, and they started to re-load the lorry with the few plants they had already dumped off.

I don't think I have seen a funnier sight than a group of police officers attempting to re-plant cannabis plants and screen them with plastic sheeting - it was all I could do not to press the shutter and record the scene for posterity, but I daren't!

The winter of '62 was a pretty trying time for Teresa and I, not only was she getting close to having our third child, but the job schedule at work was very heavy too.

I didn't do less than ten hours a day for weeks, and with an hour and a half journey home at the end of it all, I felt pretty exhausted.

By now it was only a couple of days to Christmas, and everyone was in festive mood, and on Teresa's ward, staff were at the bare minimum.

Only a few Scottish nurses remained, who would take their leave in the new year. The Scots Sister in charge of the ward was one of those people who obviously did her job quite efficiently, despite having a grim appearance, but I never saw her smile, or have a friendly word for anyone.

Teresa was written up in her notes to have the baby turned whenever it was appropriate, but for some reason in the latter stages this wasn't done.

Because she was in some physical distress, the sister gave her morphine, which reduced the effects of the pain, but sent Teresa into a state of drowsiness.

Throughout a whole day Teresa was kept sedated on morphine, and left in bed shut off behind a curtain, and she remembers calling for help but no-one came.

It was only several hours later, when a junior doctor making his visit to the ward, routinely swished the curtains to one side, and found Teresa lying there unconscious, that things got done.

He summoned emergency help immediately, and picking her up from the bed in his arms, ran towards the lifts and the emergency theatre.

In theatre, the emergency team did an immediate Caesarean section to save the baby, accidentally cutting into Teresa's bladder as they did so.

It was, as they said later, touch and go whether they could save both mother and child, but by a small miracle they achieved just that.

I was so relieved when I heard by phone that all was well, despite a Caesarean, that I didn't consider the implications of what little I had been told.

It was only a couple of days later, when I got some of the story from the young doctor who had found Teresa behind the curtain, I began to understand what had happened.

To say I was hopping mad was the least of it.

I demanded to know what action was being taken against the ward sister responsible for Teresa's, outrageous treatment, only to be told she had been sent off to another hospital.

During the next few weeks I sought advice from a solicitor, with a view to claiming damages for negligence, but he informed me that his enquiries had shown the young doctor who found Teresa in distress had left quite normally to work in Australia, and the notes covering Teresa's treatment could not be found.

It was stonewall.

Christmas as such, was a pretty glum affair.

I was visiting Teresa and new baby Stephen daily, managing to get Bernie and Janette looked after by my parents and a relative, but coming home to a cold deserted house, where everything lay just as you left it eleven hours before, was a bit grim.

On boxing day it started to snow, and it kept snowing practically every day for the next six weeks, it was murder, and extremely cold!

I got into a routine where I got up at six, arrived at the Yard by eight, finished at five, home by half-six, cooked a meal in the frying pan, whilst I washed and changed.

Then a frantic dash to the hospital by seven-thirty see Teresa and the baby until eight-thirty, and back home by nine-thirty.

Once home, I struggled to light the fire, which would give me some hot water for the morning, huddling over it in my top-coat in an effort to keep warm.

By eleven o'clock when it was time for bed, the fire was really working well, and it was a pity to have to leave such comfort!

The snow continued to fall day after day, making the roads extremely treacherous, and it was only because our minivans had front-wheel drive we managed to get anywhere at all.

On one occasion I was working late, but fairly near home, and decided I wouldn't go all the way back to the Yard, just to get a train back home again, I would drive the van home, take all my photographic gear indoors, and leave early in the morning to be in by eight.

As darkness fell, it began snowing again, and by the time I reached home the snow was a foot deep everywhere, and virtually undisturbed.

I tried to get the van onto our drive, but couldn't locate it under the white blanket, so I left it out front on the hard frozen snow, and got ready to visit Teresa.

The following morning, after a freezing hard night and more snow, I went out to the van,loaded up, and got in.

She started first time, and on full choke I eased out the clutch and prepared to move off. Apart from a slight rumble, nothing much happened.

I depressed the clutch, shifted to neutral, re-engaged first, and tried letting out the clutch again.

Apart from a slight rumbling noise, she still didn't move.

Leaving the engine running, I got out and had a look all round, and it was only after I saw grooves in the snow under the front wheels I realised all four wheels were in the air!

The Mini-van was sitting on its belly on a platform of solid snow, virtually immobile!

In desperation I cast around for some way to get the car moving, when Paddy O'Sullivan, a neighbour turned the corner on his way to work.

"Do you think you could put your shoulder to the van and give me a push onto the road again?" I asked.

"Sure an' all, that'll be no trouble with the both of us" he replied, and together we gave an almighty shove, and it began to move.

"One more like that, and I think we'll have it" I said.

But it was only with both of us pushing, and my leaving it in gear with the wheels turning, that we managed to get it clear of the ice, and mobile once again.

I eventually got to work alright, but missed the embarrassing situation of being late by a whisker!

After all those weeks of bitter cold, the weather improved a little, and the snow began to melt.

Teresa had also begun to make a good recovery, and was feeling much stronger now.

Speaking to the surgeon who actually performed the Caesarean, he told me it had been a very close thing, a few more minutes delay and I would have lost them both.

As the year progressed, we all got more and more involved with scenes of crime work on our particular divisions, and as mine covered an area stretching from the City, east to Romford, bounded by the Thames in the south, and stretching north to Barnet in a semi-circle, there was work aplenty.

One of the problems when working with local Police officers, especially as I now kicked off from Collier-Row, was that on your own manor you were considered `their' photographer, but at less visited stations you were still regarded as an uncertain element'. Your best friend as you entered the CID office was almost certain to be one of the women typists, who would offer you a cup of tea, and try and find the officer requesting your attendance.

One or two stations still had the reputation of housing a belligerent officer, who, on learning of your arrival would say `What's the Job coming to letting you civvies in to do our job etc."

It was quite `down-putting' and seemed diametrically opposed to the stated purpose of our being employed by the police as professionals in the first place.

It was quite some time before I remembered to use a phrase my dad taught me when presented with this sort of nonsense, which went `I've got a Police whistle at home, but they don't let me do Police duty'.

The effect of this reply was often very gratifying!

There were of course lots of officers who, appreciating the professionalism on tap, and the speed at which their jobs were delivered, never hesitated to call us throughout their entire service, but more importantly, thanked us for a job well done.

In August 1963, a group of villains decided to hold up the London bound Mail train at Sears Crossing near Leighton Buzzard, making off with £2,600.000 in used bank - notes, and severely injuring the driver Jack Mills.

Because the heist was such a huge one, the Yard were called in to help, and soon we were inundated with sacks full of paper and Monopoly money discovered at various hide-outs, which had to be chemically treated for fingerprints before being photographed. Eventually the work produced dividends, and suspects began to appear, resulting in twelve being charged with taking part in the robbery, and nine going to prison.

As a celebration, the head of SO.3 Branch, Gerry Lambourne invited all those who had taken part, to join him in a meal and drink at his home in west London.

I didn't know it at the time, but that visit, and the hour or so I spent explaining various watercolour techniques to his wife, an amateur artist, were to be amongst the most productive of my whole career at the Yard.

Soon afterwards,`Yorkie' Hayes, one of the original police photographers at the Yard when I joined, was given the job of covering a prison escape which had just taken place at Wandsworth, but when told that there would be some climbing shots to do, asked if I could go along to give him a hand, he knew I was a dab hand at climbing!

We arrived at the prison, and ushered through a road block, into a road which ran alongside the prison wall, where a large removal van partly blocked the road, surrounded by Police and men in smart suits.

In bright sunshine Yorkie and I completed the necessary ground shots, and were then asked to get a view from the top of the very high wall, looking down into the removal van, the path the prisoners had taken whilst escaping.

After climbing the inside wall, the prisoners had aapparently leaped down through a large aperture in the van's roof, onto a pile of mattresses stacked inside, which then broke their fall.

"This is where you come in" said Yorkie. "They've sent for a long ladder to get you on top of the wall, take the 5x4 up with the wide-angle lens, and get a couple of shots of both sides, especially looking down into the van".

Willing hands placed the ladder against the wall, and I began my ascent, gripping the MPP 5x4 by its press grip, and grimly hanging on to the ladder with my left hand. I think the wall was about twenty feet high, but it seemed a lot higher, and when I got to the top, I could see we were going to have problems.

The wall had a pointed top, not a flat one, so I couldn't walk along it to position myself over the roof of the van as I had expected.

I called down to Yorkie that I thought we needed one of those road-lighting service towers on the back of a lorry to do the job properly, and surprisingly Det.Supt.Jack Slipper in charge of the case agreed, sending for one straight away.

As I balanced precariously on the pointed wall, trying to show the position of the van relative to the wall, I could see and hear the dozens of prisoners at their cell windows cat-calling and booing, dragging their mugs backwards and forwards across the window bars and making a hell of a din.

One prominent face at the nearest window to me shouted louder than the rest, "I hope you fall off and break yer fuggin' neck, you bastard" and a prison officer in the yard below shouted back, "I know who you are X, and you'll be on bread and water for a week," at which there was raucous laughter all round.

After half an hour or so, the Wandsworth Borough Council lighting examination and servicing vehicle arrived, and I was dismayed to see that it comprised a collapsible wooden tower arrangement on the back, instead of the metal one I had imagined.

"Right where jerwannit guv?" asked the old boy driving it.

"If you can get it fairly close to the front of the removal van, I'll start from there, then we can work our way alongside and do a couple of shots to finish off".

Good as gold, he got in position for the first shot, and then commenced to wind the whole tower into the air by hand, whilst I stood on the top platform waiting to arrive at the correct height. I was just a little higher than the wall top, when a voice called out from below, "That's yer lot mate, that's as far as she goes".

"Ok. then that will have to do, I'll take this shot then we can move along" I was conscious that the whole shebang was the centre of attraction, and hoped to god nothing went wrong, otherwise the distant press photographers, and the world at large would have a field-day.

"Right I've finished this one, we can move along now" I called to the old boy, who hearing this, wound me laboriously down to the ground, mumbling and grumbling.

Once we were in position for the next shot, he laboriously wound me back to the top again, and I took the second photograph in quick time.

I looked over the edge of the wooden platform, to see my man sitting dejectedly on the running board of his lorry, obviously not the least bit happy about all this up -and -down stuff.

"Hullo there" I called down, "How about you carefully moving the truck forward alongside the van with the tower raised for the next couple of shots, it'll save you winding me up and down all the time?". His face relaxed its dejected look, and took on one of relief and concern.

"You'll 'ang on tight now an' won't fall orf?" he enquired, "If you was to 'ave a haccident it could cost me, me job".

"Don't worry, just take it gently - I'll hang on and we'll be ok." I replied.

He got in and started the engine.

As he let out the clutch, the vehicle moved forward but the tower lagged behind, due to the three telescopic sections bending like an elephant's trunk. I grabbed the tripod and camera with one hand, and held for dear life to the guard rail with the other, as I felt sure the rickety tower was about to snap off somewhere in the middle.

When we got to the next position for photography I yelled for him to stop, and I've no doubt he thought he did a nice gentle one, but once again the lorry did one thing, while the tower continued forward, swaying wildly and doing something else.

Fortunately we were exactly above the hole cut in the van's roof, and I took the requisite photograph, which couldn't really have been taken in situ, any other way.

"Right, last one" I called down, "Take it a bit easy on the starting and stopping will you, this thing shakes like a jelly up here".

"Right mate, yer got it" he replied, but the result was just the same as before. How I didn't come to grief I don't know, but at last the job was done, and I was safely on the ground once more.

Only later did we find out that the successful escaper from Wandsworth Prison, was in fact the notorious Ronnie Biggs.

During the latter half of `63, I had been involved with the Flying squad several times, and had got to know one or two of the squad pretty well, especially Johnny Vaughan, who, knowing of my interest in ornithology, asked if I would be interested in submitting a design for the new Flying-Squad tie.

The suggestion currently occupying favourite position, was of a Golden Eagle swooping down on its prey, symbolic I was told of the squad pouncing on the villains, so I got scribbling.

A few days after I had submitted my initial sketches, I was summoned to the office of the big man himself, head of CID, and told that one of my sketches had in fact been approved - would I go ahead and provide a finished drawing, so the tie manufacturer could start at once.

Having had previous experience of what I considered ornithologically `correct' drawings being altered by others after submission, I was apprehensive that the final result would be a travesty, especially as my design would be interpreted by mechanical stitching!

I needn't have worried though, the final job was as good as I could have wished, and the Squad tie remains, some thirty years later, a much cherished item within the service.

A couple of weeks after Christmas `64, I got an early Sunday morning call, directing me to an address just off Piccadilly, where a large safe-breaking job had just been discovered. I left Teresa and the kids and roared off in the Mini-van, cursing my luck that I hadn't been left free for at least part of the Sunday, even though it was a dull, wet, rotten day.

At the address I found a solitary PC. huddling in the doorway of an internationally known jewellers, trying to shelter from the cold, pelting rain.

"SO3 Photographic here, is the officer in the case about?"

"No, they've all gone back to West-End Central nick, they said when you've finished though, you have to go up and see the DCI for further instructions".

Setting up and using the 5x4 technical camera was always a bit of a bind in good conditions, but in this rotten weather it was a drag to get everything out of the van, and down into the basement where I had to work.

Why is it I thought blackly, most of the jobs you get to do, are either on the top floor of a block of flats, down some dingy basement, or in a dirty stinking toilet?'

Maybe it was just sod's law.

Grumbling to myself, I struggled down the steep spiral staircase with the kit, the tripod catching and banging on each step as my arms grew tired under the weight of the gear.

At the bottom, a huge steel door six feet across, and three-feet thick, shaped like the breech of a huge gun, stood slightly ajar, allowing just enough room for someone to squeeze past.

Inside the vault, I could see a narrow room about twenty feet long, lined on each side with rows of wooden shelves, covered in hundreds of brown, paper-wrapped parcels.

On the floor squashed and broken by people's shoes, were dozens of ladies rings, diamonds, emeralds, and sapphires - someone must have been in a heck of a hurry, to leave that lot!

The photography was awkward, due to the fact that I only had a three-foot gap between the shelves to work in, and the massive door was no help at all. Thank god for the 65mm wide-angle lens!

I scooped up the rings at the completion of photography, and placed them in a neat pile on the nearest shelf, thinking that here I was having hell's own job to get a mortgage to buy a house, yet in my hands was the means to buy at least two such houses for cash!

From the door inwards, the shelves on both sides had been cleared for a distance of about six feet, so it seemed the thieves might not have got away with very much, but what was in the parcels that made them bust in here in the first place?.

Being nosey, I carefully peeled the neatly wrapped brown paper off a couple of the parcels revealing a glint of gold.

Gold cigarette boxes, gold cigar boxes, gold containers of all sizes and descriptions, it made my eyes water to see so much dosh! Putting the gear away I fought my way back upstairs, and rested to regain my breath in a large room at the head of the spiral stairs.

This was obviously the polishing and cleaning room, and in its centre sat a huge, well scrubbed wooden table, surrounded on three sides by closed wooden wall-cupboards.

The fourth side appeared to contain store-rooms built into recesses under the pavement overhead. I wandered over to one of these store-rooms, and carefully pulled open the wooden doors, revealing a cupboard crammed full of silverware, old packaging, and a couple of old suitcases.

The Hotel labels on the suitcases intrigued me, the lettering being in the style of the old Toulouse-Lautrec posters, obviously well pre-war.

The dozens of silver candelabra and other objects inside, all hopelessly jumbled together, were covered in a substance black as pitch, in fact the surface deposit was so advanced it felt like rust to the touch.

I wondered how many years the stuff had lain shut away there, and where the people who had entrusted it here for safe keeping were, perhaps long gone?

On the street again, I loaded the van, and bade farewell to the lonely, soaking PC. who asked me plaintively to remind the Station-officer that he would like to be relieved for breakfast. Speaking to the investigating team at West-End Central, I discovered that the estimated loss to the jewellers for the little bit of shelving which had been cleared, was in excess of £250 000 - in that case, God knows what the contents of the whole room must have been worth, it must have been millions!

In November we celebrated the arrival of Phillip our second son, but were disconcerted to find that he suffered from a double hernia. After each feed he would be ok. but the moment he started to cry or hic-cough, abdominal pressure caused his bowel to force its way through the stomach muscles like two hard lumps the size of plums.

It was of course a simple matter to gently massage them back through the abdominal wall, but any subsequent internal pressure brought them popping out again!

Just before Christmas we were visited by a friend of Teresa's who knowing we had a new baby, brought her two children along, but failed to mention that her eldest was already suffering from whooping cough!

It was only after she had been gone some time, and Phillip had contracted the cough, we found out she was to blame - and to say I was hopping mad, would be a gross understatement!

After a week of virtually sleepless nights, being on night-call, trying to get enough food into Phillip to keep him healthy, and holding his abdomen in as he coughed from the dreaded whooping cough seemed a never ending nightmare.

In desperation, Teresa said we should take Phillip to Oldchurch hospital and see if we could get him admitted for immediate abdominal surgery - without some help we were fighting a losing battle!

The Sister we saw on emergency was one of those hyper-efficient, no-nonsense professionals, who seem to have lost the ability to listen when ordinary people say something, and poo-poohed Teresa's suggstion that Phillip be taken in for surgery.

Passing her hand peremptorily across Phillip's abdomen she said.

"Really I can't understand what you're making such a fuss about, there's nothing here at the moment, just keep a binder on him between feeds and he'll be fine. Come back and see us again in three months if things haven't improved".

At that moment the Sister was distracted for a few seconds by a nurse asking about another patient, and Teresa, looking straight at me, gave Phillip's toes a good squeeze. Naturally the poor little devil yelped like a good 'un and the two hernias popped out like monsters from Aliens.

"Oh my goodness!" Sister said seeing the two straining shapes "We certainly shall have to do something about this!" and swept off to make the necessary arrangements for Phillip's immediate admission.

Both Teresa and I had been so exhausted by the last couple of week's shenanigans that we had forgotten what a luxury it was to sleep the whole night through, but the immediate relief didn't stop me from falling asleep twice whilst driving home from work in the van.

Even though each incident lasted only a few seconds, it was enough to give me a nasty feeling as to what might have happened.

The appalling thing was, that I didn't know I had gone to sleep, it was only when the car tyres began rattling against the off-side curb, that I awoke to the terrible situation of driving head-on towards oncoming traffic!

Phillip had his hernia operation almost immediately, and on Boxing day, Teresa and I went in to see him, although we had celebrated a good Christmas with the rest of the family, we had all missed the new addition, and wanted him home.

As we entered the children's ward, we were greeted by a probationer nurse, who told us that she was the only one on duty, but we could go and see Phillip for ourselves.

There were about twenty children on the ward, some of them recovering from recent operations, and yet the only nurse on duty was a white-belt, an unqualified nurse. I was amazed.

I suppose we had been with Phillip only a few minutes when he woke and started to cry.

Teresa gently stroked his head and remarked that he was sweating on his face, and appeared to have a purple rash round his mouth, and on his face and neck.

His crying increased in intensity, and suddenly his body arched upwards, supported only by his head and feet, and he vomitted. For a couple of minutes he intermittently arched himself in spasms, before collapsing back onto the cot sweating and crying.

At that moment something came back into my mind from my days projecting consultants' slides at Ormond St. Hospital - could this be meningitis?

I ran to the office where the White-belt nurse was writing her notes and yelled "Get the ward Sister here at once, I think our child has meningitis!". She looked at me as though I were mad, but didn't move.

"Would you get someone over here right away, a doctor, anyone, it's urgent!"I shouted.

She quickly turned to the phone and dialled a number.

Without waiting to see what she did next, I ran back to where Teresa was trying to calm Phillip, who was still crying and arching in stiff spasms. A few minutes later deputy Matron descended on the ward like a Panzer tank, and with a face like thunder demanded to know what all the fuss was about.

I started to explain our fears, and at that moment Phillip went into spasm again, sweating, and retching, obviously in serious distress.

As soon as she saw his condition, Matron turned on her heel and went straight to the phone, her tone of voice indicating a fair measure of urgency.

A couple of nail-biting hours later, a doctor came to the waiting room and told us that they had done a lumbar-puncture on Phillip, and were proceeding with the necessary antibiotics to combat meningitis, adding it was lucky they had been able catch it so early, a couple of hours delay could easily have proved fatal.

Later, Teresa said it was extremely unfair that a baby of three months should suffer a double hernia, whooping-cough and meningitis one after another, but if he could pull safely through that lot, he should be able to beat anything!

It was quite a worrying time for both of us.

As winter retreated, and a sunny spring fought to establish itself, we decided a holiday in Ireland during the summer of 1965 might be a good idea - we could split our time between Inishbofin, a place I had long wanted to re-visit, and Teresa's family home in Loughrea, they apparently wished us to visit them again despite the last fiasco.

It was necessary to thoroughly check and fit-out our old A35 van for the Irish trip - with two adults and four children on board, and being in a place where spares might be difficult to get, I couldn't leave anything to chance.

The months flew by, and soon it was time to leave for the ferry at Fishguard, a pretty long trip for the family cooped-up in such a small vehicle, but once across into Ireland, we could take it a bit easier.

Loading the car for the crossing between Fishguard and Rosslare was a doddle, compared with the first time I came, when they slung my motorbike aboard in a rope net!

This time we drove over the side of the boat on a special ramp, and, turning a sharp left, drove completely round the deck to end up facing the point where we had just come aboard - this was real progress!

We had the luxury of a cabin for the night crossing, so we would all be fresh for the journey across Ireland and Connemara the next day. It wasn't very far, about 150 miles or so, but baby Phillip was still only eight months old, and needed a fair amount of attention.

Getting down to some serious driving, we were soon passing through Galway, Oughterrard, and on to Clifden, and the last push for Cleggan and the boat. Teresa and the children had no idea what the boat journey to `Bofin was like, and were quite worried when they saw the tiny thirty-foot Northern Ranger rolling and pitching it's way towards Cleggan and the harbour.

As we were the only passengers going to `Bofin that trip, the boat picked up the mail and a few parcels from the nearby pub, and put to sea almost immediately - the skipper said the wind was rising, and it would be a bit rough out there soon.

Although the distance from the mainland to `Bofin is about six miles, it seems a hell of a lot further on a small boat in such rough seas. By the time we were half-way to `Bofin the sky had darkened, the wind gusting strongly, and waves were rolling past the boat six feet high, their tops skittering away in foam.

"I think ye had all better come in the wheel-house" said the skipper, "It's a wee bit crowded, but better than being out there in the wet"

Leaving our suitcases wedged behind crab-pots and other deck fittings, we all piled into the tiny wheel-house, Teresa holding on to Bernie, Janette and Stephen, while I held Phillip wrapped in a shawl in my arms.

"Don't worry about the weather" said the skipper with a smile, "Once we get in the lee of `Bofin and into the harbour, it'll be quite calm, it's always a bit rough just here".

The boat, built French-style, was rising into the oncoming seas like a bird, shooting the foaming crest before dropping into the next trough like a stone, shuddering at the bottom before ploughing into the next wave - it was all a bit scary for the children.

The only way I could keep my balance whilst holding onto Phillip, was by jamming my head firmly against the wheelhouse roof, and standing legs braced against the rolling of the boat, which became quite exhausting after a while.

Through the gathering dusk, and just off the starboard bow, I could just see the low-lying shape of Inishbofin, it wouldn't be long before we ran into the lee thank God, my arms were nearly falling off with fatigue.

The tide was at low ebb when we arrived, and our boat had to anchor off the jetty, leaving us to transfer into a dinghy for the few remaining yards to shore.

I thought grimly, this will be fun transferring everyone over the side of the boat into a bobbing dinghy, but due to the patience and help of the skipper, plus the chap in the dinghy, it was achieved without disaster.

All we had to do now, was to step ashore over the round, polished stones exposed at low tide, nastily covered in places by slippery green weed.

As I made my first step ashore, I slipped and filled my shoe with ice-cold sea water and thought dammit, I might as well stay in the water and man-handle the others ashore, I couldn't get any wetter! There was no point in ending the day with one of the children cracking their skulls on a rock!

After the rigours of travel, the next couple of days soaking up the sunshine on lovely sandy beaches, plus the generous hospitality of our hosts the Days, made it all worthwhile - I could get very used to this!

I mentioned to Mike Day that I would like to visit Inishshark again if possible, to see the cottages where the Laceys and the Murrays lived, and of course re-visit some of the fantastic sea-bird colonies which bred there.

"The Laceys had to leave since you were here last" Mike said. "It was so bad one winter with one of them ill, and the sea so high, we couldn't get them off for several days. It was decided to move both the Laceys and the Murrays across to the mainland".

"In answer to your question though, three of the men are going to Shark tomorrow to shear their sheep, if ye've a mind, ye might go with them".

And so it was fixed that at eight o'clock next morning I would accompany Austie Coyne, Pat Mannion and Pat Burke across to Shark for the day, we might be a bit late coming back, depending on when the work was done, but not to worry.

With the sun sparkling on a flat sea, I said goodbye to Teresa and the children - they were all off for a picnic with the Day's children by the Lough - and set off for Shark in one of the large sea-going Currachs, the long sweep oars uniquely held on their thole-pins by a twist of rope.

During our first hour on Shark, I helped the men get the sheep penned in front of Murray's deserted cottage, and when they were ready to start shearing with hand-clippers, bade them farewell. Under a bright blue sky I climbed the hill past the old school towards the centre of the island, this time it was going to be great!

Choughs spiralled overhead - a pair had made their nest on a ledge over the fireplace in a nearby cottage, dozens of Greater-black backed gulls got up from their nests in the short wiry turf, while along the cliff-edge, Fulmars glided on plank-like wings, eyeing me closely.

In the stiff breeze a Peregrine falcon challenged my presence with its harsh chatter, saying I was much too close to its nest and young for comfort. Where else could you enjoy so much nature at close hand?

I climbed halfway down the cliffs on the seaward side of Shark,and watched in amazement the hundreds of Kittiwakes nesting on the stack of Youghil, discovered a large colony of Storm Petrels nesting in the crumbling earth slopes above horrendously steep cliffs, and photographed grumpy Razorbills nesting in the cracks and crevices between huge boulders.

By late afternoon, almost like a re-run of the time Dave and I were here last, the wind began to rise, and storm clouds rushed in from the west like galloping horses. This dramatic scenery was after all, the last bit of land before America, and typical Atlantic seaboard, prone to getting very nasty when the weather changed.

Great gobs of rain spattered the bleached granite rocks, which absorbed it like blotting-paper, and the warm sun disappeared as though it had never been.

`Time to go' I thought, no doubt the lads back at the landing would be anxious to get back to Bofin before things got any worse.

I legged it as fast as possible in the direction of Lacey's cottage, which after crossing the centre of the island, was all downhill, and although it only took me a short while, the wind was blowing half a gale with heavy rain driving horizontally by the time I arrived. It was getting really nasty.

From the darkness of Lacey's cottage door, a craggy head appeared in the slatting rain and shouted in my direction - it was Austie Coyne.

"We're all in here" he called "Come in out of the rain and have some tea".

It was the first time I had been inside the cottage since Tom Lacey invited Dave and I in for that drink ten years before, and it was amazing to see the place looking as though it was still occupied.

Above the fire, on a shelf, were various pots and packages, including tins of Baking soda which had burst, spilling their contents around, plus tins of sugar and salt.

Close to the fire, which some enterprising soul had lit to make the tea, was a multi-forked stick still held socks and things for drying, although they were covered in dust and cobwebs, and had been there for ages. It was incredible.

"How come all this stuff is still here like this?" I asked.

"When we came to take them off, they only took a suitcase and what ever else they could carry" said Pat Burke.

"They left everything else just as it was" and looking up into the darkness of a shelf high over the fireplace, I could dimly see the outlines of an old Malodeon - a small accordion, also covered in cobwebs, it was like being in a time-warp.

"How are we going to get back in this weather then?" I asked Austie.

"We won't" he replied flatly. "We might get off tomorrow though" he added thoughtfully.

Immediately I thought of Teresa and the children who expected me back that evening - oh lord, she'll have to cope with that lot on her own, and I felt rather guilty at sloping off for the day.

"We've got enough for a couple more cups of tea, but nothing left to eat, how about you?" said Austie.

“I’m afraid I only had a couple of sandwiches from the hotel” I said “And I finished those at lunch-time”.

“Oh well, we’ll have to make do on tea until this clears, won’t hurt us none for a while”. Obviously these chaps were used to surviving under these basic conditions from time to time.

Someone had managed to pull a pile of turfs from the roof of a nearby hut and bring them in to fuel the fire, at least we shouldn’t be cold during the night.

It was obvious looking around the small room, there was nowhere to lie down - we would have to sleep sitting up in Festy Lacey’s rough home-made kitchen chairs, and as anyone knows who has endured the comparative comfort of an airport lounge, sleeping in a chair is lousy under the best of conditions, but with these chairs?

Before we settled down to doze, I decided it would be great to record the scene for Teresa to see when we got back, so I dragged Alan’s Rollei - which I had borrowed yet again, out of my Rucksack and set it up on a tripod with the Metz flash to take a shot.

The room was really small, about ten feet square, and the camera only had a standard focal length lens, so I had to get inside a small alcove opposite the fireplace to get Austie and the two Pats together in the one frame!

I suppose most of us have wretched memories of the war, getting up out of a warm bed during an air-raid, and hiding in the Anderson shelter situated below ground in the garden.

Then you were expected to sleep on bunks where the steel strip supports nipped your skin, and the ice-cold, corrugated steel walls ran with condensation.

Under such miserable conditions you rarely got a good night’s sleep, and I felt this particular night was going to be just like that!

I must have dozed and woken a hundred times, getting colder and more cramped each time as the night wore on, and was more than glad to see Austie stirring himself to get the fire going again.

It was 0600hrs.

Outside, the wind roared just as it had done the previous evening, squalls of rain hurled themselves horizontally with demonic force as if trying to tear the cottage up by its very roots.

It would take hours for this lot to abate, even if it started now I reckoned, and Teresa, if she isn’t anxious for my safety, will be hard put to cope another day on her own with the children in such restricting weather.

We had only had a couple of cups of strong tea for breakfast, so by midday I was getting fidgety and quite hungry. The others, dozing by the fire in total resignation, looked more like dead bodies than men,being totally immobile.

I felt absolutely brassed off looking at the peat fire and cob-web covered walls, and said to no-one in particular, I was going outside to see what was happening.

Austie’s eye opened briefly, and he gave me a totally uncomprehending look, before sliding back into unconsciousness. He wasn’t totally against the idea, but obviously didn’t think much of it either!

Hanging on to the latch, I stepped outside, and ran straight into a wall of roaring, buffeting wind that blew me sideways off my feet, before dumping me on the ground breathless.

I just couldn't believe the wind could assume such physical force, and showing a little more sense the second time, I crawled along behind a low stone wall before putting my head up to see what the storm was doing.

Immediately the wind whipped my glasses to one side, and I grabbed them frantically, before turning out of the wind to look in the direction where Inishbofin was supposed to be. It didn't exist.

In the shrieking gale, huge waves pounding cliffs on the Atlantic side of Shark, were sending long streamers of spume flying overhead across the island, before dropping into the sea between Bofin and Shark.

The sight was absolutely incredible, the distance the air-borne spume travelled was over half a mile, and showed nature in the absolute raw, powerful, and rather scary.

Rather sheepishly I fought my way back to the cottage and let myself in, looking more like a drowned rat than a human being.

"Can't see much out there" I volunteered, "The wind is so strong you can't even look over the low wall, is it often like this?"

"Not all that often" said Austie "We're just a bit unlucky that's all".

The three men began talking amongst themselves while I warmed myself by the fire, so I didn't really pay much attention to their conversation, until a prominent voice said,"Ok. then, that's what we'll do".

It was Austie, who then took a large cast iron pot from beside the fire - one discarded by Festy, and handed it to me, saying, "Get ye down to the little beach near the landing jetty if ye can, ye'll find a fresh water spring runs into the sea there, dig a small hole to collect the water and bring it back here - and mind you don't get blown all the way to Bofin!" he laughed.

Bending double, I made for the jetty fifty yards away - I didn't have to walk, I was propelled along by terrific gusts of wind that drove me to my knees more than once.

All I had to do now was find Austie's little spring.

At last, I found what I thought was the right place, and using a piece of flat rock, dug into the sand until I had a hole two feet across and a foot deep.

It didn't take long to fill, and after getting rid of a potful of dirty brown stuff, I scooped up a cleaner second lot, and I fought my way back to the cottage, arriving at the door on my knees.

I was just in time to see Austie with a young sheep held between his knees, grab its jaw, pull its head back quickly, and slit its throat with a large folding clasp-knife.

Blood spurted in a carmine stream to one side as Austie clamped the struggling sheep tight between his knees, but soon its struggles ceased, and the animal was dead.

Inside the cottage they hoist the dead sheep by its hind legs, and lashed them to a beam, while Austie got cracking with his trusty knife, gutting and skinning the animal in a thoroughly professional way.

He'd obviously done this sort of thing many times before!

Meanwhile Pat Burke had put my pot of water on the peat fire, where it was already sputtering and hissing, so it seemed with just a bit of luck we might be eating soon.

Austie removed a hind leg from the slaughtered sheep and dropped it into the pot, followed by various bits of offal, and soon the whole lot was bubbling merrily over the fire, and smelling really great!

I had never eaten large chunks of fresh lamb cooked without salt, served on a communal plate before, but being pretty hungry, I ate arab style with the rest, and got stuck in.

In no time flat the meat and offal disappeared, and we all felt a lot better with the hot food inside us.

As daylight faded, it became obvious we'd be spending another night in those damned uncomfortable chairs, and even with a good turf fire, the second night seemed colder than the first, it was getting beyond a joke.

The following morning we were up and about at six, and a more scruffy band of tramps you wouldn't find.

Our faces were smoke blackened from puffing up the turf fire, and with the shortage of water, nobody had washed.

Our clothes were filthy from dust and cobwebs festooning the inside of Lacey's deserted cottage, and you could say we looked a right scruffy mess!

The wind continued to gust with great force, although not quite so violently as the two previous days, and you could, if you crouched behind the wall, hold the binoculars steady enough to see the storm lashed Staggs of Bofin a couple of miles away.

At least that was something!

Bending nearly double, I struggled up the path beyond the old school of Shark, and found a vantage point looking westward towards the open Atlantic where gigantic waves rolled in like ridged hills towards the island, the scene was absolutely incredible.

Stretching out to sea from Shark was a succession of waves mind-boggling in their immensity and power, and although it was difficult to gauge from this distance with binoculars, I reckoned each wave was over thirty feet high, with a hundred feet or so between crests.

How on earth had Chay Blyth and his colleague managed to row across the Atlantic and survive in seas like that?

Back in the cottage breakfast was just about ready, boiled Lamb's liver and tea, needless to say it slid down a treat - I was starving!

At lunch-time we boiled up more large chunks of lamb, and washed it down with plain strong tea as there was no milk left, we had used the last at breakfast.

Huddled by the fire, we waited impatiently for the wind to drop, but it seemed to clatter and roar with undiminished strength, and I reckoned we might easily spend a third night in those bloody chairs!

At three o'clock I went outside to check the weather, and noted the wind appeared to be blowing from a different quarter now, and a bit less strongly, was the storm beginning to blow itself out at last?.

Encouraged by these apparent signs of moderation, I scanned the harbour entrance of Bofin, which was now just visible through high seas and flying spray, in the hope I might see some form of rescue on the way, but nothing moved, not even a gull.

By four o'clock the wind had dropped considerably, and Austie was of the opinion that if it continued to improve before lightfall we might even get off today - I hoped to goodness he was right!

After half an hour my eyes got tired of looking at the same stretch of wave-tossed water through the binocs, I was beginning to imagine all sorts of things - a boat on the way - which turned out to be a gull, a peculiar wave crest that looked like a powerboat, until eventually one black and white shape remained constant for several minutes - it WAS a boat!

Like an exited schoolkid I ran back to the cottage shouting the news "I think there's a boat coming!"

Austie replied "Well now, if that's the case we'd better clear up here and be ready for it, there's a lot to get aboard before we leave".

Looking through the binoculars again, I could see the boat was in fact a Currach driven by a large outboard motor, skimming the waves like speedboat, sending up sheets of spray as it leapt from wave to wave towards Shark.

At its present speed it should be with us quite soon, and we'd be leaving our island `prison' at last.

Gathering all our bits and pieces together in cardboard boxes and sacks, we took them down to the jetty, along with huge bundles of raw wool trimmed from the sheep.

There were also the two sheep dogs, and the most surprising thing to me - half a dead sheep! I hadn't realised how much meat the four of us had eaten during our enforced stay!

When our rescuer arrived at the little jetty, the sea-swell was still bad enough to cause a four-foot rise and fall of the boat inside the tiny harbour, and it took a lot of skill and luck to get everything safely on board.

The dogs had no trouble at all of course, and were aboard in a flash.

"No doubt ye'll enjoy a drop o' the hard stuff" said our rescuer, and passed over a small bottle of scotch, which went the rounds as we all took generous swigs.

Things were feeling much better already!

Back on Bofin, and re-united with Teresa and the family, I learnt from Mike Day, the coast guard had been alerted as to our plight, and if we had been forced to stay another night on Shark, they would have got the helicopter from Dublin to take us off next day, they were that concerned for our safety!

For the next couple of days the family pottered happily about the beaches, and exploring Don Boscoe's Castle at the entrance to Bofin harbour, while I sat back with binoculars watching a pair of Oystercatchers which were obviously nesting on the nearby shingle spit.

It didn't take long to pin them down, and I showed the children the heavily mottled eggs as they lay on their camouflage bed of lichens and stones.

"Why don't you have a go at photographing them while we're here" Teresa said. "We can all be at the far end of the beach, and let you get on undisturbed if you like"

I hadn't really thought of doing any nest photography whilst on holiday, but as she had suggested it, I rustled up a few poles and some sacking and soon had a hide thirty feet away from the nest, which the birds soon accepted.

"If we all go back to the hotel for lunch, we can came back here afterwards, and move the hide a bit closer for photography" I said, and we all trooped off to Day's Hotel, absolutely starving, hoping for something to eat.

After lunch, Teresa saw me into the hide, and I sat on an old upturned bucket, squinting through the 200mm lens on the Pentax, waiting for the Oystercatcher's return.

Within fifteen minutes the bird was back and sitting, so I carefully released the shutter and took my first photgraph, the bird took no notice at all.

I had arranged with Teresa that she let me out of the hide after an hour, by which time I should have all the shots I wanted of the sitting bird, and now having taken twenty shots, I sat back and relaxed, waiting for my time to run out.

Suddenly to one side of the hide a couple of Turnstone waders appeared, one bird leading the other to a spot ten feet away from the Oystercatcher's nest.

As the second bird caught up with the first - I could see it was the male, a wing-shaking, trilling display broke out, the first bird crouched on the ground, while the male bird mounted, and began copulation.

As the birds parted, the male started to scrabble with his feet in a little hollow in the rocky soil, forming a nest scrape, sending dirt flying in all directions.

I had never expected to see anything like this in the British Isles - I knew the Turnstone wasn't a British breeding species, so was this for real or what?

For several minutes the pair called and displayed at the scrape, before my attention was drawn to the Oystercatcher, who stood up quickly and ran off towards the sea.

Teresa was obviously coming over to let me out of the hide.

I explained what I had seen, and walked over to where the Turnstones had been making their nest scape, showing Teresa the site, it was a great pity we had to leave tomorrow, I may have

of been able to record the first nesting of Turnstone in Ireland!

Our eventual journey back to England - it sounds as though you're miles from home and have an international journey to complete - was a matter of slogging it out on the roads until London came into view.

There was no doubt in my mind, that the far west of Ireland, was as remote and different as you could possibly get within a few hours of London, about as foreign maybe as Tibet!

Just before Christmas, when armed robberies seemed to increase as the villains get their pocket-money together for a happy new year abroad, there was a particularly nasty bank robbery in Ilford, where a gang of four got away with thousands of pounds in cash.

Brian Smith and I who were not far away, were directed to the bank, and getaway vehicle respectively, while Flying Squad officers continued to chase the villains around Ilford.

Brian joined me at the bank as soon as he had done his bit, and together we waited for the officer in the case to return with further info.

We were just about to ring our own office and let them know the state of play, when the bank manager called us to answer a phone call from the local police station.

Apparently there were new developments, the squad car hunting the villains had managed to track them to a house in north Ilford, and burst in as they were counting out the cash on the kitchen table - a right`fair cop.'

Would we get round there right away, and do the necessary?

At the address we were met by a couple of Squad officers who quickly showed us round the scene, and said, `Would we photograph the money first so they could get the loot checked in at the nick as an exhibit, leaving us to get on with the rest?

The stacks of notes were just as the villains had left them, divided into four equal piles, but not obvious in detail as to how the money was made up.

It was common practice for us to gently `fan-out' notes so that it was possible to see in the final photograph, just how many there were, what denomination, and many of their serial numbers, to obviate any allegation of theft or malpractice afterwards.

As soon as this was done, the lads scooped up the cash, sealed it in an exhibits bag and headed for the door like long dogs. "Typical innit? said Brian, "Death or glory boys, they nick the villains and leave us to plonk around on our own to do the necessary, if we miss something of importance, who gets a bollocking? We do"

It took about half an hour to cover the place photographically, but we still had the loft to do - one of the villains had been found hiding up there behind a water-tank, where it was all dark and grotty with cobwebs.

"I'll go up if you pass me the gear" volunteered Brian, "I'm smaller than you are anyway, so let's get on with it"

It's no fun trying to focus a 5x4 Monorail in a dark cramped loft using a torch, whilst trying not to put your foot through the ceiling, but somehow Brian managed it.

I saw the flash go off a couple of times, and knew Brian had got his shots and was just about done.

Once we got the gear down and stashed away, we could both Fox-trot Oscar to Ilford nick, for a nice cuppa and a wad.

"Al, Al can you hear me?" came Brian's muffled voice from the depths, "You'll never guess what I've found up here"

A few moments later his bald head, dusted with black cob-webs appeared at the loft hatch, followed by a hand clutching a fistful of paper.

"When they discovered that bloke hiding up here, they must have called him to come down, without checking him out, I bet he left this little lot up here for collection later on", and extending his arm towards me, showed a huge fistful of notes.

"Bloody hell!" I said,

"Christmas HAS come early this year hasn't it?" said Brian with a smile.

"Yeah, but not for us unfortunately, I bet the Station officer will go potty when he sees this little lot, especially with an extra entry and signatures to account for in his property book"

It wasn't the first time, and certainly not the last by a long chalk, that such goodies were dangled invitingly before one's eyes, but it had long been a rule of mine never to get involved, I had a wife and family to look out for, besides, you never knew whether some wicked bastard had clocked it before, and was setting you up!

Although death in its many forms formed a large part of our work, there was from time to time, an incident that made you think afresh, how bizarre life can become.

There is little doubt that the ability to detach oneself from the immediate horror of the situation is extremely helpful, and as I often say when questioned about my work, I can often see more in my final photographs, than I remember at the time of taking them, because the subject doesn't register on your mind in quite the same way.

On this particular day, I had been asked to go to a small furniture factory in Hackney, where a chap had been found dead in unusual circumstances in his woodworking shop.

A doctor had already attended to certify death, and photographic were required as usual to record the deceased in position, before his removal to the mortuary.

I saw the dead man laying at the foot of a circular-saw bench, and noticed the ceiling was dripping with congealed blood, splattered in a straight line down the middle, even over the lampshade.

Approaching the deceased I saw that he had apparently put his neck to the large circular-saw blade, and practically severed his head, not only that, there was a huge cut into his skull just above the left ear through which brain tissue could easily be seen.

Bloody-hell I thought, the poor devil must have had two attempts to kill himself!

I thought of the state of mind he must have been in to continue to commit suicide after inflicting such a dreadful injury at the first attempt, it was a sobering thought.

I can't remember exactly when during 1966 I heard part of the tapes, but it was during the trial of Ian Brady and Myra Hindley, the sadistic moors murderers. Apparently everyone who was in the section at the time had been asked to go to early lunch, and a session held behind closed doors, presumably to see if there was any audible information, apart from the voices, that could be gained from the tapes.

I had returned early from a job that had been expected to last all day, and had wandered into an unusually deserted section which was un-naturally quiet. Suddenly I became aware of a child crying, followed by the most soul-searing moans and cries of terror I can ever remember hearing, - it made my stomach crawl.

The sounds seemed to be coming from the guvnor's office.

The crying started again, followed by heart-rending moans and screams which seemed to reach into my very being, what the hell was going on?.

It soon became apparent after a couple of stop-starts, I was hearing a tape recording, but of whom? I gathered something was going on that I wasn't supposed to hear, and dumped the camera gear next to my locker and went out, I couldn't take any more of that!

I felt terribly depressed and shaken by what I had just heard, as the father of a young family, it hit me hard to hear such screams of terror, far more than any of the dreadful sights I had encountered in the job so far.

It seemed to me, pure bloody evil.

I later found out the tapes were part of the evidence against the torture and murder of young children by Brady and Hindley, and to me, defies any normal human feelings.

One Sunday in September I was on weekend duty, and just after lunch got a call to go to Wembley, where there was a suspicious death.

It was a lovely warm sunny day, the first for quite a while, and it would have been super to enjoy a quiet day with the family forgetting rotten jobs for a change, but then I was on call.

Arriving at the address, I got out of my van and approached the small group of police-officers standing by the front gate.

"Hello there, I'm Mr. Parker SO.3 photographic, what have we got then - and what the hell is that awful smell?".

"Oh you'll enjoy this one!" said the Uniform Inspector, "It was so bad in there, one of my lads used a whole can of special deodorant, just so we could look around, it's still a bit yukky, but better than it was"

"You're not calling the Lab out on this one then?" I asked - I always liked to have a brief look at the scene if it's forensically possible, to give me an idea of room size, lighting, and position of the body etc; before starting photography.

"No, there's no suspicion of foul play on this one" said the Inspector, "Just record the scene and body for us, and we can all go home for tea"

Inside the neat semi, I was hit by a smell so nauseating, it caused me to gag almost immediately, and I quickly reverted to the old trick of breathing through the mouth, and not my nose.

Turning left into the living room, I saw a man hanging by his neck from a short rope fixed to a hook in the ceiling, while around him were arranged a multitude of mirrors and lights - a typical restrictive masturbation, or`hanging-wanker' as we wickedly described them in the office.

The man had rather cunningly fixed a large hook into the ceiling - normally hidden by the lamp-shade, and suspended himself from it by a rope round his neck, standing tip-toe and watching his masturbatory actions in mirrors placed nearby.

Unfortunately for him, he had passed out before he could release himself, and died of strangulation.

He had apparently been dead three or four days, and the heat from the lamps, combined with the central heating, plus a lovely day, had made the place an oven.

His face, arms and legs were covered with huge blisters, some of which contained nearly a pint of fluid, while the advanced disintegration of the body, plus excreta running down his legs, gave the impression of a rough tree, complete with its roots fixed firmly to the floor.

Gagging in the revolting stench, I recorded the scene in double quick time - but had to come out a couple of times for air, much to the merriment of the officers waiting outside.

There was no way anyone could take that vile mixture of rotting flesh and gagging deodorant spray for even a short length of time! The final shot required me to take a close view, showing the detail of the noose round his neck, which meant I had to squeeze between the body and the settee, bringing the obscenely tortured face to within a few inches of my own.

It was decidedly grotty.

Within minutes I was ecstatically pleased to announce to all and sundry that I had finished, they could do what they liked with their rotten body, I was off for some fresh air and a good wash!

Like all good things however, the day wasn't over yet, there was more grot to come.

I had only been home an hour when the phone rang again - this time it was a fatal accident, vehicles in position on Hammersmith flyover. Here we go again!

The accident was memorable in that a grey A35 van, the same type that I used to have, had run into the back of a five-ton lorry broken down on the flyover, the offside rear end of the lorry had torn the whole nearside of the A35 van away, killing the two passengers on that side.

By the time I finished photography it was getting dark and a cold wind was blowing, but I didn't mind that too much - the fresh air was diluting the the last traces of the previous job's rotten stink from my clothes!

A year later, on a similar weekend duty, I received a call to a fatal accident, vehicles in position, in Porters Ave, Dagenham, and was intrigued to find on arrival, a grey A35 van smashed into the rear of a parked lorry, killing the driver's son and his friend as they sat on the nearside.

The occupants had all been returning from a wedding reception before coming to grief in such tragic fashion.

I was about half way through photography, when a man appeared at the scene with a paraffin lamp, saying he wanted to illuminate the rear of the lorry as the normal lights had been destroyed in the accident.

As I finished, and told the chap he could now place his lamp in position, I said, "Do you know it's a bit of a coincidence, I photographed an accident similar to this, involving a lorry and A35 van on the Hammersmith flyover about a year ago".

"Even more of a coincidence if you like" he said. "That was me at the Hammersmith Flyover at a year ago, and this here is the same flippin' lorry"

I just couldn't believe it, two A 35's into the back of the same lorry? But it turned out to be quite true.

The photographic section was beginning to grow in numbers as we were allowed to advertise for more civil staff in respose to the ever increasing work-load, and we were now twenty strong.

For the first time in Police history, members of Civil staff went on a promotion board with a Police officer, contesting the post of Principal Photographer, or Det.Inspector, depending on which side of the fence you were on.

There is no doubt that this was a critical point in the future structure of SO.3 and if only the senior Police officers on the board had the foresight and guts to do what should have been done, then Alan McLean the senior civilan would have been `made' over the non-qualified, Det.Sgt Adams.

If this had happened, the whole emphasis of civilianisation within photographic would have been on a proper, progressive footing.

As it was, with Det.Sgt A's promotion we lost any chance to lead the section for the next twenty years, and in consequence suffered a warped and divisive regime, of `them and us'.

Now that I was earning good money, especially with extensive overtime, Teresa and I decided to leave our first home, bought at two years old in 1959 for £2300, and plump for a brand new three-bedroom, detached house, with 100' garden, price - £5950, a mile or so away, on Collier-Row common.

We had only been in the new house a week before my next weekend duty came round, and to make things easier for relatives, friends, and the `job', I transferred our original phone number to the new address.

However, being so fiendishly clever did not allow for the `keen' Police drivers at Chadwell-Heath, who thought they knew where I lived, and continued to knock-up the occupants of our old place, who grumpily told police our new address, and sent them on their way.

That wasn't the end of the matter either, because, being on a new development, the officers still managed to find the wrong house, despite having the right address.

At about half-past five one Sunday morning, I got a knock on the door from a full-of-beans PC. who breezily announced "Mr. Parker? -good, they've got a body in the gents' toilets in Piccadilly Circus Underground, he's got a syringe stuck in his leg, and they want you there NOW, so they can clear away, and open the place to the public, ok?"

With a grin of satisfaction at getting me up so early on a Sunday, he whisked me off to my van parked at nearby Chadwell-Heath. Naturally, having been in our new house such a short time, we hadn't got to know the neighbours yet, in fact the new development of ten houses had only six occupants so far, so it wasn't really surprising we were all strangers.

Returning home from the Piccadilly job, I had just finished lunch, and was thinking how I might tackle the jungle of a garden, when our next-door neighbour introduced himself over the rudimentary fence.

"Hello there, I'm Ron your new neighbour, you must be Mr.Parker, tell me, what the hell do you do for a living that gets the old Bill knocking me up at half-past five in the morning, rabbiting on about dead bodies in toilets at Piccadilly circus?".

When I explained what I did, he grinned and said, "Well I'll have to watch meself then, won't I, can't be too careful these days, incidentally did you know the infamous Tibbs family live just round the corner?"

Because of my known enthusiasm for 16mm cine work - I had my own Bolex reflex and sound projector, I was quite often given the task of screening obscene films seized by the obscene publications squad.

They didn't have a projector of their own, or indeed anyone with the expertise to use one, so quite often I would have to black out our studio and project dozens of porno films, whilst officers attempted to identify the participants, or locations where the films were shot.

After several months of these bizarre screenings, I was told I was now considered `bona-fide' by the various officers I had met on the squad, and would be accompanying them from time to time on daytime raids as they seized pornographic equipment and materials. I was to take photographs of everything they found.

It sounded an interesting development.

As we got to know more and more about the fine detail of our Civil Service job, and the way it `dove-tailed' into the police service, it became apparent we civvies were missing out on one or two aspects which could be financially helpful, if only we could get them implemented.

Alan pointed out one to me which concerned the use of a private phone, stating that `If the phone was installed at the behest of the department, for the department's use, then the installation and rental costs were the responsibility of that department'.

"Hey, that looks like me" I said to Alan. "I wasn't on the phone before I came here, and it was certainly installed by our Civil office, with their influence getting me priority installation for police calls, I'll have a go and see if I can claim for the installation and rental"

"You'll need to quote the requisite Estacode Civil Service reference number for that, but go ahead, write a report and the best of luck to you, mate!"

Not being a typist, I had the necessary report typed by our divisional office, signed it, submitted it through my head of department for consideration and payment, and waited.

I waited for nearly six weeks before enquiring from our head of department what progress if any, my report might have made.

"Don't worry laddie, these things take time, you'll just have to be patient"

I waited a further month before enquiring again, this time to be told "It's still with the Civil staff office, but I'm sure you'll have your answer soon"

Too bloody right I did, in a brief message from the guvnor, I was told to present myself downstairs to the head of SO.3, old bladder-head himself, who would give me an official answer to my report forthwith.

`Come' replied the pained intonation to my knock on the door, and in I went.

"Ah yes, Parker..... I'm telling you very strongly, that your request for payment for telephone installation and rental charges has been refused, and should you persist in attempting to claim such payment, not only will you jeopardise any future promotion you might have, but your present employment with us as well, good morning!" and with that he picked up some papers, and prepared to leave the room, indicating the `interview' was at an end!

It reminded me of a story dad told concerning his brush with an overbearing sergeant whilst serving with the 16th. Irish Lancers in India.

Apparently his sergeant, taking a distinct dislike to dad for some unknown reason, and dad being regimental middle-weight boxing champion, and well able to take care of himself - insisted dad tidy his tent and bullshine his boots, as some sort of punishment.

Dad tidied the tent as required, but also consigned the said boots to the burning stove in the middle of the tent, as he considered the whole thing an `un-lawful order'!

Needless to say when the sergeant asked to see his boots, and dad repiled they were in the fire, he went absolutely bolo, but had to swallow it, as there was little else he could do.

However, dad had to watch his tail like a hawk for the rest of his time!

I must admit I felt a bit like that now.

Having not had the courtesy of a written answer to a properly submitted report, I felt it wasn't right to tell me I had to watch myself, or face the sack.

For twenty years I paid the rental on the phone, but made sure I used the job's phone to ring home whenever I found it necessary!

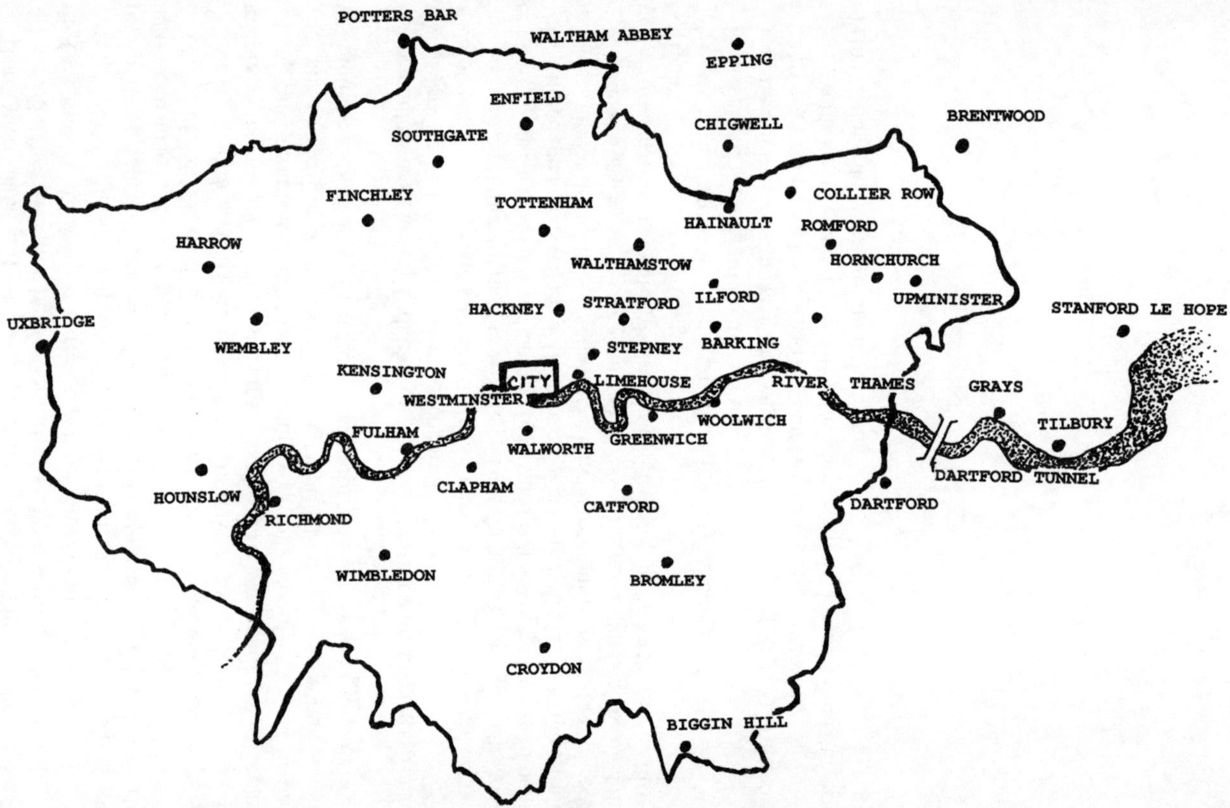


Metropolitan Police area of London

# Chapter Seven

One morning whilst engaged on fingerprint copying, I received a call from the 'Obs-pubs' lot downstairs, telling me to be ready in half an hour for a porno raid in the City, near Aldgate. It was quite exhilarating dashing through London's back-streets in a couple of squad cars, before roaring into a magazine distribution warehouse yard, and nabbing everyone in sight.

The officers seemed more than pleased with their latest captures, and left me to record the set-up, while they took the suspects back to the nick for statements etc: It was all straight forward 5x4 photography, showing the loading bays with a few boxes of porno books ready for despatch, offices controlling the operation, but that was about it, certainly nothing too extreme.

During the early months of 1967 I went on three more raids, each time arriving shortly after the premises had been raided by police and searched, but apart from recording the general layout of the place, there was nothing particularly pornographic to record.

On the next raid, I arrived just as the squad were leaving, and approaching the PC. On duty guarding the door, I enquired if there was anything special the squad had asked me to photograph.

"No, so long as you inform their office when you've done, then they can give the keys back to the owners", the PC replied. Once inside, I saw the premises were just like other offices I had been in recently, except this time there were obvious gaps on shelves, and cupboards yawning half empty, suggesting various items of property had been recently removed, whatever they were.

It didn't take long to do the job, and after putting my gear away in the car, I went back into the building determined to find something that would indicate the premises were being used for pornographic purposes.

I found nothing.

How come I thought, is our intelligence so bad, or the crooks too smart, that we weren't getting to photograph any incriminating evidence like tapes and equipment in situ? With the sort of ESP that has got me into awkward situations in the past, I went back inside and searched again, this time rummaging under a counter at the side of the main office. Tucked hard against a side panel, and well out of sight of a casual search, was an 8mm cine film in its new cassette.

Back in the office I quickly processed my films, and while they were washing, had a quick look at the first few minutes of the 8mm cine film on the projector, yep, there was no doubt about it, classic hard porn. What was also very interesting, I recognised during the opening scenes, a garden which featured some unusual fencing and garden furniture in the background. Not only that, I recognised some tattoos on a participant's forearm, as the points of evidence proven against a north London defendant, convicted of porno material seized the previous year.

When I had made up my albums of prints from the latest raid, I took them to the squad office, and asked if I could have a word with Mr. Moody, who was head of 'obs-pubs' at the time, but was told 'Sorry, I'm afraid he's not available at the moment, what's it about, can I help?'

"You might be able to" I replied "It's about the premises I attended at 'X' yesterday - I may have found something quite important".

"Oh yes, I was on the team that went in there, what is it?"

I produced the 8mm cassette, and described how I'd found it under the side counter. "Not only that" I volunteered, "On the film I recognised not only the scene where the opening shots were taken in north London, but one of the participants as well, the tattoos on his arm are a dead giveaway for that particular defendant"

"You'd better leave this with me" he said, "I'll inform Mr. Moody when he comes in, no doubt he'll follow it up and get in touch with you"

A couple of weeks later I received another call from the squad, this time to photograph items that had been seized in a raid, and by chance met the officer I had given the 8mm film to.

"Hello there, any developments on the 8mm film I gave you last time we met, did Mr. Moody have anything to say?"

He gave me a blank look of non-comprehension.

"You know, the film I found under the counter after your raid on 'x', I gave it to you in the office".

"What film? you never gave me any film, I certainly don't recall receiving any film from you, otherwise you would have been asked for a statement, you must be mistaken" and turned away.

To say I was shaken by his abrupt reply, was a chronic understatement, I just didn't get it.

I couldn't figure out why he denied ever receiving the film - until very much later, when I heard about the large sums of bribery money accepted by police officers from the 'Mifsud/Silver' porn syndicate in London! Not only was Bill Moody himself heavily involved, but the head of C.1. Commander Wally Virgo was accused of taking back-handers from the syndicate as well, how rotten can you get?

After this awful revelation, my views on the integrity I had expected from senior officers in the job took a steep nosedive, and I became very cautious of people I met until I really got to know them. In a sea of unspeakable treachery to the job, a lovely little 'buy-back' scheme had been operating in Obs-pubs, whereby obscene material seized by police from one address, was offered for purchase to rival operators, for resale at another.

Now I could see why I had failed to photograph anything of a pornographic nature at the premises we raided, it was a long time gone! That coincidentally, was the last assignment I had with Obs-pubs for quite some time, until in fact, after the new Commissioner, Sir Robert Mark went through the job with a fine toothcomb, and George Fenwick was in charge of Obs-pubs - but that's another story!

In May I had a telephone call from my friend Ray Connor, Oologist par-excellence and ultra-diligent Det.Ch/Inspector of the Company Fraud squad, asking whether I would like to accompany him on a trip to Eire, searching for nesting Roseate Terns in Wexford. After that, we could cross over to the island of Innishbofin - a place I had described to him earlier when we had been discussing Peregrine Falcon, and then perhaps go on to Co. Mayo, to look for nesting Scoter. It sounded marvellous, but could I afford the time to go, bearing in mind the short time we had been in our new house?

Teresa, like the super wife and friend I was lucky to have, said yes, go. Aunt Anna in London would stay and keep her company while I was away, anything not done by then would have to wait until my return.

Although Ray probably wouldn't agree in the least, I would describe him as a fanatically focussed person, homing in on whatever he was engaged on at the moment - to the exclusion of almost anything else. Not that he is consciously selfish, it's just that he has no time for distractions away from the main object of his particular attention. Bearing in mind I am virtually the opposite - I function intuitatively most of the time, and after leaping, tend to sort out any problems I encounter on the way down. The thought of spending two weeks with him in the close confines of a car scouring the wilds of Eire for birds, sounded potentially explosive!

Later I said to Ray, that under normal conditions you could expect a visit to Ireland to produce about three days' rain in a week, and we must go prepared, but this time Murphy perversely pulled out all the stops, and did the complete opposite.

The week before we left, and during our first few days, it was so hot the authorities banned people in the Wexford area from washing their cars due to a WATER-SHORTAGE, and we had to drive with all the windows and sunroof open, just to keep cool!

Initially, we visited Lady's Island not far from Rosslare, but the Roseates weren't nesting there this year, in fact they were nesting in great profusion on a small sandy island in the middle of the estuary, in the nearby Slobs.

In this fantastic venue, we stayed for two days photographing and observing over two-thousand Roseates, a hundred Sandwich Terns, a few Common, and over twenty Little Terns - it was really great and I was able to use the 200mm lens on the Pentax and Kodachrome film to good advantage. Despite commuting backwards and forwards through dusty, bumpy lanes between our digs and the estuary, my old Cortina estate coped pretty well, occasionally groaning under the weight of cameras, hides, camping gear, and I crossed my fingers hoping she wouldn't break down.

With a fair bit of ground to cover, we reluctantly left the exhilarating tern colony, and made our way across country to Clifden in Connemara, where the weather rapidly changed back to its old miserable self, making visibility and travel difficult in a continual downpour of rain.

It was nearly dark by the time we were able to consider where we might stay for the night, but luckily a kind farmer directed us to a cottage just outside town, where he assured us a great meal and a couple of good beds would be available. He was right, it couldn't have been better.

Picking up our gear next morning, and bidding the landlady a grateful farewell, Ray and I stepped out into heavy rain, before setting off for the wilds of Connemara in search of Scoter. It was then I noticed the long streaks of black goo trickling along the gutter in the pouring rain, and thought 'Oh god, we've got an oil leak somewhere, perhaps the differential's gone, we're in the kakypoo now!

Because there wasn't enough room under the car to see what was at fault, I started the engine and drove carefully for a few yards, putting two wheels on a slight bank, which gave me just enough room to crawl under the car, provided I lay in the gooey mess. The underside of the car was relatively dry, and I could see no sign of dripping oil to indicate where the problem might be, until a drop of liquid splashed on my face and I smelled petrol.

Looking at the petrol tank an inch above my nose, I saw the bottom was covered with drops of liquid, all oily black in colour, and as I rubbed one with my finger, a tiny jet of petrol squirted onto my face, burning the skin, what the heck was going on?

With my finger I carefully rubbed a couple more oily drops off the tank, and each time a small jet of petrol followed, turning the black rubber underseal into a treacly goo. Now I knew the source of the oily streaks in the road!

'We've got a bit of a problem here" I called to Ray. "The petrol tank's got a leak in it, and of course we filled up with eight gallons last night, so we aren't going anywhere until I fix it"

It became obvious on closer inspection what the real problem was - Fords in their wisdom had stamped the inside bottom of the tank with a series of longitudinal grooves, no doubt to give the tank added rigidity under load. Some time after manufacture, water had got into the tank, and settling at the lowest point, ie: the grooves, had steadily corroded the metal until all that kept the petrol in, was the rubberised underseal on the outside!

The landlady was quite surprised to see us back on her door-step so soon, but readily complied with our request for buckets to drain the eight gallons of petrol from our leaking tank.

In short time we had four buckets brim-full, standing by the roadside covered with newspapers to keep the rain out. With the petrol tank now empty, I rubbed away the soggy underseal to reveal not just two or three pinholes as I had expected, but literally hundreds! The whole length of each of the four grooves was perforated like a colander!

"I just can't think at the moment what we can do to put this right' I called to Ray, 'I shouldn't think there's a Ford agent this side of Dublin who has a spare Cortina petrol tank, let alone us being able to get hold of it"

At this point the landlady piped up from the shelter of her front door saying "If ye want to fill some holes in metal, and for it to be petrol proof I've got just the stuff. It's a new thing just out called Plastic Padding, I'll go and get it" She quickly returned with a large yellow tube, and handed it to Ray.

"They say that'll do the trick, and now's the chance to prove it" she smiled knowingly. I looked at Ray, who grimaced back with a look of - well, you've got nothing to loose, better try it - so I got cracking.

Having read the instructions, I found you had to 'key' the stuff into the repair to be effective, and there was no-way I was going to key it into the myriad of tiny pin holes without some help. Taking the bull by the horns, I used a small Phillips screw-driver to punch a series of larger holes through the myriad of pin holes, until the bottom of the tank looked as though it had been hit by a shotgun. I hoped to god I was doing the right thing!

The stuff proved easy to work with, and soon I had all the holes nicely filled, and while waiting for it to go off, I refitted the drain plug, which on tightening, felt as though it too, wouldn't take much to twist out of the surrounding rusty metal.

"Ok. now's the time for the nitty -gritty" I said to Ray. "I've done the grotty bit, perhaps you can bend your arms for a while and pour the petrol back in to the tank, while I check underneath - and keep your fingers crossed for a small miracle!"

As the second bucket went in, followed by the third and still no sign of a leak, I began to thank this marvellous Irish landlady who, in the middle of nowhere, just happened to have a tube of this miracle stuff to get us mobile again, it was just unbelievable!

It wasn't too long afterwards we rolled on to the little quay at Cleggan, and under clouds you could almost reach up and touch with your hand, waited for the mail boat to take us across to Inishbofin. I always enjoyed that trip on the Northern Ranger - it was the last stage before experiencing the incomparable beauty and excitement of being back in the real wilds once again.

Once ashore on Bofin, I could see that little had changed since my last visit, people had got older, others had left or died, but the utter tranquillity of the place alongside the rasping calls of Corncrakes, remained the same as ever.

At the hotel, the Days welcomed us both in their usual friendly way, and soon stories of past exploits were being re-lived over a pint or two of best porter in the bar next to the hotel.

It was great to be back.

On our first crossing to the island of Shark, I found a piece of slate propped against the low wall in front of Lacey's cottage, on which Mrs. Lacey had scratched, 'Visited my dear home July 1966 - God bless all'

It was sadly to be her last visit to Shark, as she died shortly afterwards in her new home on the mainland. I really felt for these kindly people of the earth, and the hard lives they led, who, with little of their own to share, had made me so welcome in the past, it was all rather sad.

In bright sunshine Ray and I began the steep climb to the highest point of the island, passing the derelict schoolhouse, and the roofless little church, poignant reminders of a community swallowed in the mists of time and ravaged by countless Atlantic storms. On the tops, we trod a lush carpet of green grass, kept in bowling-green condition by the rabbits and sheep, on which a large colony of Greater black-backed Gulls were nesting, and I was clicking away with the camera as though I might not come here again.

In typical fashion the Black-backs yowled and dived at us ferociously, flicking our heads with their wings, as we made our way through their nesting area towards the cliffs, we were definitely the intruders here!

Reaching the cliff top at last, we stood for a while looking at the boiling sea below, reeling, as powerful on-shore winds bucketted up the cliff-face, making balance on the cliff-edge precarious, so we sat down. In sunshine that was almost too much for the eyes, we scanned the surrounding cliffs through binoculars, checking out the plank-winged Fulmars and scudding Razorbills, whilst listening for any sign of my old friends the Peregrines.

Almost immediately the female responded to our presence with an agonised 'Hek-hek-hek-hek!' of alarm, and swung overhead in the stiff wind, a majestic anchor-shape of power against the bright blue sky. It wasn't difficult to spot the nest once you knew where to look, and she appeared to have a couple of half-fledged chicks in residence already. Perhaps this time I would be lucky enough to get some photographs of this magnificent bird and her chicks.

Around us gulls and Fulmars soared effortlessly in the strong breeze, while in the crevices between boulders and rocks, Razorbills and Black Guillemots grunted their alarm calls, complaining at our intrusion as we made our way towards the Peregrine cliff.

Starting at just above sea-level, I made my way up the first hundred feet or so with little difficulty, until I reached a huge gently sloping triangle of rock about sixty feet high, and thirty feet wide at the base. I was positioned at the lower right-hand corner, and could make no further progress towards the nest, which was situated at the apex of the triangle.

I would have to traverse the triangle from right to left, and climb the rugged left side, it was the only way up. Fortunately, there was line of grasses and sea-pinks growing right across the base of the triangle, about three feet up from the bottom, indicating a 'fault-line', which would enable me to cross the face and ascend the left side of the triangle to the nest.

I was going to make it.

Egged on by the exhilarating calls of the Peregrines, and without ropes, I leaned against the rock face and turning my feet sideways, began the traverse, using the vegetation growing in the fault line as support. In no time I was across and scrambling up the steep incline, until at the top I saw it - the Peregrine's eyrie!

At my approach, the two young peregrines flopped on their backs and presented four sets of wicked-looking talons for my inspection, but I declined to be raked at that moment. Just seeing them at such close quarters was reward enough, the last nest I had climbed to was at Salcombe, some ten long years ago.

Initially the climb had been intended as an exploratory one, and I had left my camera and rucksack with Ray - if I wanted to record the peregrine chicks, I would have to come back tomorrow and do it then, it shouldn't be too difficult now I knew the route. As I made the awkward return traverse across the triangle, I thought, why is it, that it seems far easier and more natural for me to move from right to left, than the other way round, perhaps it's because I'm right handed?

The next day we borrowed Michael's punt again - the same one that got Dave and I to safety once before, and I rowed steadily across a bottle-green sea to Shark. Overhead the harsh 'kee-er!' calls of Arctic terns, and 'Peep-peep' calls of Oyster catchers gave a deep feeling of being miles from all that crazy urbanisation. This time we had come prepared with a couple of hundred feet of light climbing rope, in case the approach to the Peregrines from the bottom proved too difficult the second time.

Even on remote Shark, Peregrines don't make it too easy for intruders to approach their young!

With Ray waiting on the cliff-top above me, I climbed again to the point where the huge rock triangle was bisected by the vegetation-filled fault line, and prepared to cross. As I put my foot on the first clump of sea-pinks, it gently rolled out of the rock and bounced down the near vertical cliff to the sea a hundred feet below. I was puzzled, it hadn't been like that yesterday.

I got down on hands and knees and looked closely at the fault-line which I had imagined to be a product of the whole rock splitting and shifting backwards, leaving a one or two inch ledge on which the sea pinks and grasses were growing. How wrong I was!

In fact the whole length of the fault-line was as far as I could see, merely a crack in the vertical rock face. I had traversed both directions yesterday on the strength of vegetation growing out of that crack!

There was no way on earth I could expect the twice abused vegetation to support me a third and fourth time, and for some time I looked for a way round the impasse, but there was none.

It could only be done by ropes from above.

From high above me, Ray's voice penetrated the roar of the surf, wanting to know the reason for my delay, and my reply that I couldn't do it again, must have made little sense after yesterday's rapid jaunt across the face. Re-united half an hour later on the cliff top, I breathlessly explained the problem, and Ray agreed the only sensible way was to descend by rope, and he proceeded to clip a carabiner on to my rope belt for an immediate abseil.

We set the ropes so that I had both a climbing rope and a safety rope, and all went well until I got to a point about ten feet above the Peregrine's eyrie, when I only had about fifteen feet of climbing rope left.

Like a lot of birds of prey, the peregrine had chosen a site under a slight overhang, as protection against the weather, which meant that if I abseiled over the overhang, I would be left dangling in space about three feet out from the nesting ledge, at the end of my ropes. Not a pretty thought!

Ray and I had agreed beforehand on a progamme of whistle blasts to communicate my needs to him, one blast for tie off, two for let it run, three for I'm moving back up and so on, and so far everything had gone well, despite some repetition of whistles when the wind and sea roar, made hearing difficult.

After negotiating the overhang, I swung on the rope like a pendulum until I got my feet on the ledge, and slackened the rope a little to sit down. I was very conscious I only had a foot of rope left through the Carabiner to keep me anchored to Ray above. I would have to watch it.

The Peregrine chicks were delightful, and I sat three feet away while they gradually accepted my presence and settled down. It was a moment to savour and record on film. All too soon it was time to go, and I went to the end of the ledge to see if there was any way round the overhang - but it looked pretty hairy and un-inviting. Pulling on the short length of line between me and the overhang, I tried climbing up, but when I got to the point where the rope went over the rock lip held down by my weight, I couldn't get my fingers under it for the next stage of the climb, and I had to retreat.

I tried a couple more times without success, blowing on the whistle from time to time, to let Ray know what I was trying to do, but it was useless. I knew that if I untied myself from the ropes and made my way to the end of the ledge to try a free ascent I was committed. I had no signal arranged with Ray for what I was about to do, and knew it wasn't very bright of me to try either. Fortunately the rocks on Shark are eroded granite, some smooth, some razor sharp, but mostly rock solid to the grip without crumbling, ideal for climbing.

I blew on the whistle to let Ray know I was still coming up, and thought he would wonder what the hell was going on when the rope didn't move, and there was no apparent weight on it, but it was the best I could do right then.

At the end of the ledge there was an almost vertical rock face riven with cracks and splits, into which one could get hand-jams and toe holds, which looked as if it might lead to the ledge above, I'd give it a go. Sweating profusely, and not entirely from the warm sunshine, I traversed the riven section and hauled myself on to a small outcrop slightly higher than the peregrine's overhang, the backs of my hands raw from hand-jamming, and legs trembling from exertion.

Craning my head backwards, I could just see Ray's head as he leant over the cliff far above me.

"Could you drop the ropes down above where I'm standing now?" I shouted in to the buffeting updraught, and to signal his understanding Ray gave a long blast on his whistle. After about five minutes two ropes came snaking down the cliff in a shower of dirt and stones, and I tied on again, using the carabiner as a safety hold for my ascent.

At the top I met a very relieved Ray, who quite rightly berated me for casting off like that, and then pointed to a solitary figure making his way slowly down the track towards the tiny harbour.

"Who on earth is that?" I asked, totally gobsmacked, "As far as I know we're the only people on Shark today, what did he want?"

Apparently during the time Ray and I had been blowing our whistles, the sound had carried across the calm sea to a fisherman checking his lobster pots a mile or so away, and thinking that someone might be marooned or in trouble on Shark, had come ashore to see if he could help. I felt quite embarrassed that we had inadvertently been the cause of inconvenience to this good man, when he had no doubt far more important things to do.

During the next couple of days I photographed Arctic Tern, Common Gull, Chough, Fulmar, and Storm Petrel at the nest, it was all exhilarating stuff, and I was sorry when it was time to leave and make our way up north to Lough Conn, County Mayo, in search of the Scoter duck Ray hoped to find.

In lowering clouds we passed Kylemore and its famous Abbey, on through Westport and Castlebar, where the bleak countryside just got wetter and more miserable, although a smile did cross our faces as we roared through a village called Pontoon. In this heavy downpour we felt sure they'd ruddy soon need one!

We decided to use Ballina as our base of operations, and for a couple of days, under scudding clouds and pelting rain, searched Lough Conn from end to end, eventually finding a couple of the Scoter duck nests Ray had set his sights on. Personally, I was more than glad to call it a day, and after a good nights' kip, begin our long journey back to the UK.

# Chapter Eight

Presenting myself for work at 0800 after our exciting, but all too brief holiday, was the complete opposite to the idyllic freedom of roaming Ireland, and I found it difficult to settle into grotty scenes of crime work straight away.

Things lifted a little when it was suggested that because I was still the only one in the section qualified to use cine equipment, and a regular user of my own 16mm, I was designated to fly in a Hughes 300 helicopter to obtain traffic-flow data on cine film. This was quite an interesting project in that the cine camera was coupled to a variable framing rate control, which allowed you to take a series of 'still' pictures on 16mm film. The film was projected on a variable speed projector, thus producing a 'time-lapse' effect on the screen. It was all rather clever.

On the first day of the trials, I presented myself at Battersea Heliport with my equipment, to be met by what I call the 'silly' response from a police officer, reporting as a 'civilan' to use the helicopter facility with my camera.

The police observer - who normally accompanied the civvie pilot on every flight, refused point blank to be left behind - even though the Hughes 300 was obviously a two-seater aircraft. Therefore the three of us, plus my bulky equipment, had to try and squeeze into the tiny cockpit.

As you couldn't film through perspex without losing definition, I asked the pilot to remove the passenger door from its hinges, which although giving me fantastic visibility, made me feel distinctly vulnerable!

Obviously I had to sit on the outside so I could point my camera at the traffic below, and although my waist harness was fixed by a steel wire to the helicopter's cabin, I was left sitting on one cheek, my left buttock and thigh hanging outside the cockpit into fresh air!

As the pilot started the engine, I was switched on the time-lapse controller - which was driven by a twelve-volt supply obtained by crocodile clipping two leads onto the helicopter's external battery, just outside the cockpit.

Jokingly I said over the intercom "I hope I don't draw too much current with my camera and cause the engine to conk out in mid-flight" which immediately brought a look of withering disdain from the disgruntled police observer.

The first flight over central London was both exhilarating and a little frightening, I had never been in a chopper before, and yet here we were skimming over all the places of interest I had known for years, seemingly able to touch the sides of buildings like the GPO tower, as we floated past.

The resulting film was quite a success, we had flown up and down Oxford street, Park Lane, Regent's St. and Knightsbridge, filming at the rate of one frame per second, and when we projected the results at half normal speed, they were stunning. Traffic flow, or the lack of it was well demonstrated, as well as various hold up sites, plus their 'knock-on' effect. So much so, I was asked to continue with the experiment over the next few weeks.

I was amazed at how much detail one could see from the air, at 600' altitude over

Hyde Park Corner, I could easily see Woodpigeons waddling along feeding in the grass, and distinctly saw a man bend down to pick up his dropped cigarette packet from the footpath, it was quite remarkable.

A couple of flights were also made at night-time, which made orientation of your position difficult whilst looking through the viewfinder, although the traffic flow and congestion could easily be recognised by looking at the headlights and stop-lights of the vehicles below. It went off rather well, and eventually provided some very interesting results.

We had just completed the final flights, and were analysing the latest results on the projector with Traffic Division officers, when we heard the helicopter with two crew on board had failed to clear the landing strip at Battersea on take-off, and had plunged into the Thames!

I thought of the hours and hours when THREE of us had stooged around the City filming, and thanked my lucky stars nothing like that happened whilst we were over Oxford St or Hyde Park Corner!

Back on Divisions, covering my old patch of 2 and 3 District, I was called one day to a massive safety deposit breaking near Stratford, where police were anxiously awaiting my arrival, before starting forensic examination of the scene. Looking through the main door, I could see the inside of the huge safety-deposit room was in complete chaos, Between iron bars that separated hundreds of deposit boxes from the public access area, I could see the floor ankle deep in papers, boxes, files and bric-a-brac. The only way in to photograph the boxes appeared to be the one the thieves had used - a large hole cut through the steel gate with an oxy-acetylene torch.

To save themselves from being burnt on entry, the thieves had covered the cut ends of the bars with wet sacking, and it couldn't have been all that long ago either, as the metal was still warm to the touch. Sliding head-first through the hole, I had one of the CID chaps pass my 5x4 camera, flashgun, and tripod through, and started work, showing the overall carnage, and in particular the numbers of boxes which had been forced, and those which had not.

After about twenty minutes I finished my photography, and as I walked back to the hole where the officer waited to take my gear through, I accidentally kicked a round tin, which clattered across the floor, before its lid came off.

Inside I could see a tightly rolled bundle of paper, which on examination became a roll of fivers held tight with an elastic band. "What you got there then young Alan?"said my waiting officer. "Looks like a roll of loot" I replied. "They were in such a hurry to get out, they missed this little lot"

"Give it to me, I'll take care of it until the exhibits officer starts his list"

"No, for safety's sake I'll leave it here on the floor next to its lid - when they come do to the exhibits they'll find it in situ, then were covered - it's been recorded on film anyway" I often wonder what happened to that cash - there must have been at least a hundred notes in the roll, a terrible temptation for someone with itchy fingers!

A short while later I was called to a Post-Office breaking in Islington, where the thieves had given the poor old safe a right bashing. They had drilled holes in the front, driven chisels into the door cracks from the sides, and slogged away at the handles and locking gear with a sledge- hammer until they sagged.

It looked a total wreck.

No doubt, as night slid away and a new dawn approached, the exhausted thieves had given up in disgust and gone home. I did my photography on the safe, and while the fingerprint officer did his powdering, I shot off a couple of interiors to show the entry point, and the table where the hard working, would-be robbers had made themselves cups of tea.

Behind me 'prints called out "All finished Alan, there's nothing here for me but smudges, you ready to go?"

"Yep, no problem, let's go"

As I picked up the gear and made my way to the front door where a PC. stood on guard, a silly thought entered my head.

"You sure there's nothing on the safe to interest you 'prints?"

"No, as I said they're all smudges really, nothing of interest to me"

I walked back to the shattered safe, grabbed the remaining twisted brass handle, jerked it down hard, and the door swung open!

"Hells bells" said 'prints, "How did you know that was going to happen?"

"I didn't know at all, it's just a funny feeling I had. I thought how hilarious it would be if all they had to do to get in was turn the flippin' handle...and bingo"

There was no doubt about it, fingerprint photography at scenes of crime was often extremely difficult to do, either because of the background colour, the texture the mark was on, or the sheer difficulty of getting a 5x4 camera in front of the mark you had to record. When it was impossible to get the 5x4 in front of the mark, I reverted to the smaller fixed-focus 'CRL' camera we carried, which gave a same-size image on film, without the need for focussing.

To overcome the time consuming aspect of fingerprint photography, Ernie, one of our 'boffin' photographers working in collaboration with fingerprints, did some experiments using a clear, low-tack tape, which was rolled over a fingermark previously dusted with aluminium powder, and then lifted.

This lifted tape was then applied sticky-side down onto a transparent plastic film, sandwiching the mark permanently between the two materials. Now we could lift marks at a scene and bring them safely back to the Yard for photography and examination by experts, and, more importantly, save the poor old photographer yonks of time trying to get a result!

The technique was no good however for blood or grease marks, which still had to be recorded by the expertise of the photographer at the crime scene. Although photographic and fingerprints were both part of SO3. the fact that 'prints had over a hundred staff to our thirty, meant that their senior staff felt they were the important section, and photographic were there primarily to service their needs.

They certainly weren't keen on us undertaking any photography which took staff away from fingerprint work, and into areas they regarded as less important. They failed to see that Press and Public relations, aerial photography, and many other aspects of police work, were essential to expand the police photographer's skills.

When the question arose as to how the newly lifted marks were to be photographed in bulk, it was a senior fingerprint 'expert' who decided how he thought it should be done, while Ernie, our qualified Senior photographer - who had worked hard developing the system, was really hard pushed to get his technique in the frame.

In the end it was a matter of a qualified photographer understanding how the job really needed doing, as opposed to someone who thought they did, before the new system began to take off.

As our numbers of staff increased, so to did the number and complexity of jobs we were expected to do, and, despite the churlish reaction by the odd police officer - who still thought we were a threat to their safe little hidey-hole jobs, we managed to make a good impression on most people as we went along.

One example of this 'difference' came about purely by accident, and served to show that in some cases, just being very good at your job, can be dangerous.

We were asked to do a photographic 'obbo' (observation) on a particularly nasty criminal, where police could send only one of their camera operating staff, due to several officers having to  attend court that day.

At the conclusion of the operation, the Det.Chief Inspector running the show, asked to see the photographic results, so that with the contemporaneous notes taken by his officers, he could evaluate which villain was doing what. Within a short time of our shots being delivered, we received an urgent phone call from the Ch.Insps' office requesting an immediate meeting of all participating officers, to discuss the outcome of the operation.

Once seated in his office, the first remark by the Ch.Insp: was, yes, we seem to have hit our target smack on the button, which was good, but why was there such disparity in the detail between people depicted in their officers' photographs and ours?

Looking at both sets of pictures, it was immediately apparent that apart from a difference in print quality, our grain-size was better, and we had less subject movement in the frame, all in all the sort of results you would expect from someone who fully understands film uprating techniques, development juggling, and quality printing.

The meeting concluded with the Ch.Insp. saying he was well pleased with the results so far, but next time SO3. would be invited to occupy the prime photographic position too, which went down like a lead wellie with the D/Sgt who had turned in the less than professional results!

One Friday afternoon I had just finished my days' printing, and was fondly thinking that if I slid off now, I could just beat the rush-hour traffic, when a call came from the duty office - would I care to put my head round the door for an urgent late job?

"It's a suspicious death at a flat in Leyton" the duty officer grinned in my direction. "The Pathologist isn't being called at this stage, so it shouldn't take you too long, ok?"

"What about the late-turn photographer, why can't he go?" I asked hopefully.

"He's already on a job and won't be free for a couple of hours yet, anyway it's on your manor, and you can do it on your way home".

"Thanks a bunch!" I growled, and stonked off down the corridor generating the beginnings of a foul mood.

At that moment I saw Smithie, one of our Senior Photographers coming down the corridor, obviously making moves to slide off home too.

"You leaving soon?" said smudger hopefully "Wouldn't care to drop me off at Romford or somewhere nearby would you?"

"I've got a sus-death to do at Leyton on my way home, you can come and carry the gear for me, and I'll drop you off afterwards if you like".

I could see his brain working - was it worth a half hour's grotty job, to be dropped off at Romford for free, or should he forego the pleasure, and pay the quid or so it cost on the train?

"Yeah, alright, let's make it quick though, I've had a real grotty day that's done my brain in, and remember it is poets day today! (Piss off early tomorrow's Saturday)

Pushing the Mini hard, I managed to get to the address in just over thirty minutes, where a patient PC. surrounded by noisy mickey-taking kids, was trying to preserve some semblance of law and order.

"Cor, I'm glad you've arrived guv, I'm missing my grub break waiting here, how long do you think you'll be?"

"If it's all straight forward, about twenty minutes or so, give or take a bit"

"That's great, ok. if I contact the nick and arrange for the funeral bods to take the body away?" and getting the nod, off he went leaving smudger and I at the mercy of the shouting kids.

Inside the old fashioned house, smudger and I saw the deceased laying on the floor in the kitchen/lounge, surrounded by several large mirrors propped against chairs, and a variety of lamp standards - all switched on.

"Ello, ello, wot 'ave we got 'ere then?" smudger growled in a music-hall parody of the phlegmatic British Bobby.

"I 'ope as 'ow it's not one of them sexual perversion jobs, I don't think I should be 'ere to be corrupted!"

Focussing the 5x4 on the body I said "Stop messing about and give me that flash-gun will you - you were the one who wanted to get finished quick and go home". The poor chap on the floor was probably in his late fifties, and had only his shirt on, which was tucked up round his waist. By his foot was an old-fashioned flat iron weighing a couple of pounds, which was connected to his penis by a length of thin rope.

"Bloody hell" said smudger "He wasn't behind the door when they gave out todgers was he? Do you think he was trying to make it longer by hanging the flat-iron on the end, or was it some kind of forfeit?"

"I'm damned if I know smudge, all I know is that once I've done this next shot, plus a couple of room shots to show the mirrors and lamps, we can have it away on our toes, now be a good chap and lift the penis over, so that I can see the underside and how he tied the knot will you?"

"And just WHAT do you expect me to turn it over with then, clever-cloggs?" he snorted at me in mock disgust.

"Use your pencil dammit, and don't be so bloody churlish!"

"Use your own friggin' pencil!" he shouted back, and we both burst out laughing at the incongrous situation we must have presented. To give smudger his credit he did find something to flick the poor man's penis over with, and the job was done.

It had been apparent for quite some time that we had outgrown our allotted space on the sixth floor of the Yard by the Thames, and a move to new premises was imminent. I had always enjoyed working next to the river though - there was always something of interest happening on the river with ships and things, or the myriads of tourists who thronged the Embankment on most fine days.

The 'new' Scotland Yard was situated in Victoria St. and looked from the outside like a huge egg-box with windows, about the only saving grace as far as I was concerned was, it backed on to St, James' Park, probably the best park in London for watching birds!

As we were a department that needed a fast response to emergency calls, we had been allotted special places in the basement for our vehicles, but the 'brains' of the outfit had compensated for this gift, by allocating us the seventh floor of an eight storey tower, one floor higher than in the old Yard! So much for progress.

Apart from having to instal a special water supply for the whole floor, and electricity points in sufficient number to run our equipment, the new place was great. At last we had space to instal automatic processors and printers, a special fingerprint photography area, several large darkrooms, and a huge studio.

We hadn't been in the new premises all that long before I thought I detected a hardening in the attitude between our senior police staff and the civilian photographers, suggesting a sort of 'new-broom' syndrome was coming.

Naturally the top four places of guvnor, deputy, Det/Insp. and Det/Sgt. were all held by police, but it was becoming clear that the top echelon of civil staff, Alan Mc. myself, and Frank, equating in rank to Det/Sgt. would soon be looking for a career structure that would allow us to go forward into the future.

It was discovered one day during a serious conversation on this very matter with Alan Mc., that the guvnor had in fact offered to make Alan up to the rank of Principal photographer, equal to our Det.Insp.A, but Alan fearing he would be 'rocking the boat'(?) declined, and a chance for a substantial rise in the ranks for civil staff was lost.

In the general scheme of things, there was no doubt Alan was an appeaser, a fence-sitter, Frank was mainly a 'yes' man, and I'm afraid I was considered a bolshie bugger - not afraid to speak my mind, so perhaps we weren't ready for middle management just yet?

During most of 1967 I had been far too busy with work to get involved in much serious bird photography, and 1968 seemed to be going much the same way. In late April I managed to do a survey of bird species present on nearby Gobions Farm at Collier Row, and found to my surprise I had a pair of Kestrels and three species of owl, Tawny, Little and Barn owl, all breeding virtually on my doorstep!

When I mentioned this to the farmer he informed me that his brother who ran an adjoining farm just across the A12, had a pair of white owls there too, perhaps I could do some photography on them after I came back from work?

I just didn't have enough time at the weekends!

Because of my experience with 5x4 cameras at work, I decided I would like to use that format myself, but there was no way I could afford to buy one, even a third-hand MPP Technical camera was beyond my pocket, so I decided to build my own.

I managed to collect enough bits and pieces to build the body-work, but didn't have the necessary bellows or lens, how could I afford to get hold of the expensive 4" square bellows needed to connect the two ends together?

"No need to buy them, at forty quid a set, they're far too expensive", said Pete Sherrif, one of our new photographers.

"I'll show you how you can make them yourself, it's an education, but it'll save you lots of cash"

Over the next couple of days I learned how to fold a sheet of leatherette into corrugations, holding the folds together with washing-line pegs, until sufficient length was made, before glueing the whole lot together with Evostick.

I must say, the hardest part was making a spring back for the film plane, so that I could use 5x4 double dark slides and a focussing screen, but at last it was done.

All I needed now was a lens and shutter.

Sorting through the second hand equipment in Brunnings,Holborn, I came across an 8" Kodak Ektar lens fitted to an Epsilon shutter, which, priced at £5 seemed a bargain, so I bought it.

It turned out to be one of the finest lenses for outright definition I was to own for many years.

On the Collier-Row farm, I built a 20' high steel scaffold hide to photograph the Little owl, as I knew it would raise its young first - the Barn owl could wait, because after incubation, their young wouldn't fly for about eighty-six days, which would take me through to the end of August.

The Little owl turned out to be a delight to work, and I got some nice shots on my home-built 5x4, but I felt that if I could adapt the camera to take a roll-film back, I could save myself a lot of energy, carrying bulky dark-slides up and down trees.

The Barn owls I photographed later were a different kettle of fish, nesting in the top of a 25' high dead Elm stump, way out in the middle of a fifty acre field, and difficult to get to.

I knew there was a small possibility of roving youngsters spotting the hide scaffold poles, so I kept construction to the absolute minimum, using just two upright poles, and two horizontal poles to reach across to the tree.

To gain access to the hide, you had to climb the twenty-foot scaffold poles by bracing the outside of your wellies against the vertical poles and climb up by the strength of your arms - I thought that should eliminate all but the most agile of young climbers!

Because I felt my little 25 Joule Metz wasn't up to the job of photographing the Barn Owls, I asked one of the lads at work if I could possibly borrow his Mecablitz 502 for a while, hoping to use the Metz as a second slave unit.

The 502 was certainly a far more professional piece of equipment - twice the power of my old Metz, and used a re-chargeable lead-acid battery that lasted an hour and a half, even when switched on continuously.

My first attempt on the Barn Owls was during warm, dry weather, and the hide support poles were quite dry and shiny, which made an ideal grip for my wellies. In no time, I was sitting in the hide, hauling my gear up by rope and bucket, and settling in.

It was 1930hrs and still quite light, but working on my own I had to be in position well before the owls were out and about.

At 2100hrs I heard the muted screech of an owl, and saw a white shape float past in the gloom - it must be one of my owls returning. Fingers crossed, and heart pounding, I glued my eye to the peep-hole in the hide, waiting to see the bird arrive at the nest, when suddenly the hide gave a slight tremor, and I heard a sharp metallic 'ting'.

A few seconds later the hide gave another little lurch, and a barn owl suddenly appeared, landing next to the nest hole before scrambling inside, to the accompaniment of loud hissing from the hungry young.

About thirty seconds later, the owl's head appeared at the nest entrance, and looked carefully around, before flying off into the night for further hunting. Now that I knew the owls were happy with the hide, and the flashgun poking through the hole at the front, I felt I could confidently take a photograph next time one returned - I felt quite sure of success.

Forty minutes later the hide gave another sideways lurch, accompanied by a metallic 'ting', and I suddenly realised what was happening. When I built the hide, I used 20' poles for the uprights and 12' poles for the horizontals, which passed either-side of the tree and crossed over at the back, where they were lashed together.

As the hide was six feet from the nest and the tree was about two feet thick, that left four feet of scaffold poles sticking out behind the tree. It was on this backward projection the owls were landing, hence the noticeable lurch at my end, and the metallic 'ting' was the sound of their claws striking the pole!

I now knew exactly when to expect the owls, and had plenty of time to switch on the flash before the second lurch indicated the bird was now on its way round to the nest.

I switched on the 502, and a few seconds later the hide gave a second lurch as the owl took off towards the nest, when suddenly it gave a loud screech, and flew off to a nearby branch, giving low calls of alarm. After about twenty minutes the owl flew hesitantly to the nest, dropped food inside to the young, and beat a hasty retreat, still cursing volubly.

As I was sure nothing had changed since the bird's first successful visit, I had to check outside the hide to find out what the bird was objecting to - I'd get nowhere until I sorted that out!

Balancing precariously in pitch darkness on the horizontal poles connecting the hide to the tree, I inched my way towards the nest and looked back at the hide to see what the trouble could possibly be. After a few seconds I saw it, but couldn't figure out straightaway what the devil it was - a soft pink glow filled the front of the Metz flashgun like a malevolent eye, and quite naturally the Barn owl didn't like it.

The pink glow was undoubtedly the cause of the bird's alarm.

Back inside the hide before either of the owls returned, I took the flashgun away from the front of the hide and had a close look at it by torch-light.

I had long been aware that the neon light on the back, indicating the flash was ready to fire, was a problem at night-time, and had masked it off with black tape. Unfortunately I had completely overlooked the fact that the internal chromium reflector on the 502 wasn't a light-tight fitting, and light from the neon in the flash-head was leaking past the reflector and being amplified by the diffuser, hence the pink glow.

Without a screwdriver to dismantle the gun, I was stuck, I'd have to fix it at home, so I quietly packed up the gear and waited for the next visit by the owls, which was perfectly ok. now the flash wasn't in view. Disappointed with the way things had turned out, I slid down the vertical hide poles like a fireman on call,picked up my gear, and walked back to my bike.  It was just before midnight.

There was a simple lesson I had learnt thoroughly when attempting to photograph suspects on surveillance jobs - always put yourself in the suspects' position, and examine your camera position from his, minutely. If you are unhappy about anything at all, then he will be too. I had slipped up.

Suspects are in many ways just like the wild animals you are trying to capture on film, and really I should have taken a bit more care in checking the Barn owl set-up after dark.

Although I, like everyone else in the section was extremely busy at scenes of crime during the day, I managed to scoot down to the Barn owls on my bike twice during the week, usually Tuesdays and Thursdays, getting back home about one-o'clock in the morning, cold and stiff from my time in the hide.

As I cycled along the deserted roads towards home, I sometimes wondered just what a patrolling Police car might make of the situation, stopping a chap with a large bag of camera equipment on his back, and carrying a tripod over one shoulder.

"Excuse me sir, what exactly are you doing carrying this equipment, at this time of night?"  The ensuing conversation could have been quite hilarious!

# Chapter Nine

Whilst waiting developments at a particularly nasty murder I was covering in Hackney,I struck up conversation with a press reporter I knew from the Daily Express. He asked me, amongst other things, if police work was the only kind of photography I did.

When he heard about the bird photography I undertook in my spare time, he asked if he could see some prints, and we arranged a 'meet' at the Daily Express office in Fleet St. for the end that week.

When we eventually met, he looked at my photos and said "These Barn owl shots are great, is the bird really as scarce in the London area as you say?"

I gave him all the background information on Barn owls currently available from records of the London Natural History Society - which I belonged to, and he seemed very interested, saying if I left it all with him, he would draft an article for submission to his editor for publication.

I had all but forgotten the meeting, when during the last week of October 1968, I received a call from the reporter saying his article on Barn owls in London was appearing as a half-page in the October 30th issue of the Daily Express.

He hoped I would be pleased with it, and would no doubt find a good use for the £100. cheque he had enclosed too!

As I set off for work on the 30th, I wondered what the article would say, and how it had been presented - more importantly, what would be the re-action of my colleagues at work?

As I entered the office, there didn't seem to be any one about, which was strange as I was already a few minutes late, when suddenly, a loud raspberry rent the air, followed by "Who-hoo's the bird-man of the Yard then?" and I suspected the absolute worst!

In fact, apart from the melodramatic caption, 'Murder in Romford - but the suspect is known' and a certain 'consumerised' presentation of Police photographer and Ornithologist, the article wasn't too bad, and I was quite pleased.

Dave Shapland, the colleague who had lent me his 502 flashgun and thought he'd seen the last of it, was pleased to see the article too, and asked if he could now have his flashgun back, as he had forgotten what it looked like!

With the money from the Express article, I was able to by my own 502, plus a slave unit, and I felt I was now getting enough gear together to tackle a wider variety of birds in the future.

All in all, I felt it had been a highly successful venture.

One day in January 1969, I had just finished a crime job near Hornsey, and being quite close to Eric Hosking's home, called in with the intention of discussing details of the equipment he had used years before, to trigger his high-speed flash units.

I had no knowledge of electronics whatsoever - I wish I had been interested as a youngster, then perhaps I wouldn't have to ask every question from the bottom up, but in the event, Eric wasn't able to help very much at all.

Like me he wasn't much into electronics, and after use, the triggering device had been put away somewhere and forgotten.

He couldn't explain, and I couldn't see, how a small box of components could project a beam of (?) at a point on the ground, so that a bird flying through it triggered the camera.

I had of course seen this triggering equipment demonstrated by Eric at a Kodak exhibition in Kingsway years before, but I couldn't remember how it worked.

It was always a pleasure to call on Eric and Dorothy, you were always made so welcome and given tea, during which Eric would enthusiastically show you some of his latest shots, and discuss the pros and cons of various cameras and techniques, without the slightest air of condescension or 'side' at all.

You could learn a helluva lot just by listening to him.

At the Yard I had discovered an old Dawe 'Liteflash' unit tucked away amongst old junk in the back of the camera store-room. It had two flash-heads fitted with Mullard LSD3. tubes, which I remembered from my days at Ark's Publicity, when we handled the Mullard account. The duration of the flash was I recalled, a healthy 1/5000sec, fast enough to stop most birds in flight, provided of course you could catch them at the right point of focus, hence my recent visit to Eric concerning a trigger.

There was no doubt this particular aspect of bird photography was an exciting one, but very demanding, A pity I knew so little about electronics - I would need to learn some basics fast, and apply it to birds as Eric had done, and his results were really superb. Although it was still early spring, we were enjoying a fine spell of weather, so I suggested to Teresa the family might like to spend the next weekend at Bradwell on the wild Essex coast for a change, watching birds and taking photographs.

Our quarters were to be in the reasonably appointed warden's hut, which had bunk beds, cooking and heating facilities, but an outside toilet and wash room.

Although the kids gave the expected 'thumbs down' to the venture - they couldn't see the sense in leaving a comfortable home for this old rhubarb, but despite the opposition, we had a wonderfully relaxing couple of days, entertained by the skirl of calling Redshanks, and the wild calls of Terns.

Within months however, the local authority built an access road to the beach at the far end, so that Bradwell atomic power station could be built, leaving the public free now to walk the beach from end to end, ensuring the demise of the nesting Little Terns.

One lunch-time I was in the canteen with Alan Mc.Lean when a call came for me to return to the duty office for a late turn crime scene. 'There's a big job at this address in west London, go there right away will you? 'Nipper' Read Det/Supt. in charge of the case is waiting, so you'd better get your skates on'

At the scene it was pretty obvious which house was the focus of media attention, by the frantic activity outside, as reporters and photographers jostled for best position.

I knew D/Supt.Read. well from a couple of jobs I had done with him in the past, so I walked over and asked what the score was.

"This is a pretty big drugs bust" he said "Where a rich American's daughter has been consorting with some low-life criminals, both in the States and here, selling hash.

We've recovered seventeen plastic sacks full of the stuff from this address, so we want the place photographed from top to bottom before fingerprints do their bit, so kindly keep your hands in your pockets, Ok?"

It was a large rambling house occupying three floors, with loads of rooms everywhere, some in use, others quite obviously empty.

I started at the front door and worked my way in, first room on the left, next on the right, second on the left, kitchen, hallway from both ends, the usual stuff, and then moved upstairs followed by Mr. Read.

"I particularly want this bedroom covered in detail, this is where we found most of the plastic sacks, and also those letters which you can see on the bureau over there, cover them too, they're most important"

As soon as he left, I set up the 5x4, and shot from each corner of the room, plus the letters on the bureau, which I also recorded in close-up so they could be read easily.

These would tie-up visually when the letters themselves were produced in court as evidence.

When I had finished, I went over to the double bed where I had seen a Nikon 35mm camera laying in the centre of the crumpled bedspread, its front lens badly smashed.

Whilst I was examining it, Mr. Read appeared in the doorway and asked whether I had finished, as he wanted Fingerprints to start their investigation as soon as possible.

"Yes, I've done my bit" I replied. "Could I ask 'prints to dust this Nikon camera first, so that I can have a close look at it please?"

With his consent, 'prints gave it a going over, but apart from a few smudges, there was nothing in it for them.

Picking it up, I saw the film counter showed that over twenty of its thirty-six exposures had been taken, so there should be an exposed film in it.

"Sir, you notice the lens on this camera has been badly smashed, I think we ought to remove any film in the camera, to avoid damage by fogging, or glass fragments, whilst its in police custody"

Mr.Read. looked at me questioningly for a second, and then smiled.

"You think there's a distinct possibility of that happening if we don't take some action to prevent it?"

"Yes Sir, I do" I replied, hoping he wouldn't say, 'Isn't the shutter or mirror supposed to stop that sort of thing happening?' but he didn't.

"Have a word with the exhibits officer and make sure you have the film given a separate exhibit number from the camera, and that you have taken possession of it, that way we're covered" he said, and left me to it.

Stepping out of the lift the following Monday morning, after a grotty week-end - which had included two night-call fatal accidents and a murder, I felt I needed some sort of a boost to get me going. The thought of ploughing on until next Friday, when I would have worked two weeks without a break, seemed just then, slightly impossible.

After processing my scenes of crime negs, I started on the 35mm film taken from the Nikon at the drugs bust, if sod's law was on our side for a change, we might find something useful on it.

As the film came out of the wash spiral, I could see we had plenty of good exposures, some showing a young woman in front of an American style home, others showing the same woman with a group of male friends outside another house, and glory be, the woman and friends posing against a wall, along which were displayed plastic sacks similar to those we recovered from the drugs bust!

How stupid could some people get?

On receipt of my phone call, Mr.Read. came hot-foot into the section and looked through my prints before smiling.

"Gotcha! that's her, and you're right, those ARE the sacks we recovered from the address, and photographed in America too.

We're going to need an extra statement to cover this lot Alan, I'm extremely glad we decided to remove that film for safety reasons!"

Much, much later at Crown court, I stood before defending Counsel, flown in specially from the States, explaining to the jury, the album of photographs I had taken at the scene.

"Now Mr. Parker, I'd like to ask you about a certain camera you say you examined at this address" and I thought, here we go.

"You say you removed a film from this camera for safety reasons?"

"Yes Sir, that is correct.

"What reasons were they?"

"I was concerned that because of the smashed lens, the camera might have glass fragments in it, and of course light could get in and fog the film"

Counsel turned away from me to address the court. "And I suppose the Commissioner in his generosity asked you to develop and print the film for us too?" His tone was both condescending and admonishing.

I smiled and said "Yes Sir, that is correct"

"No further questions of this witness my Lord" Counsel intoned, and shuffled his papers irritably before sitting down.

The outcome of it all was that we won the case, and various bodies ended up in prison.

Shortly after this episode, I had a letter from mum saying that she, dad, and Greg were a bit fed up living at the Sir John Soanes Museum in Holborn, and were out and about looking for somewhere new to live. .

I took all this with a pinch of salt, after all hadn't she been the motivation behind the projected emigration to Rhodesia - change of mind, stay put - the actual emigration to New Zealand - two and a half years there, before returning to blighty again, and just after that the move to Holborn, houses in both Ilford, and Clacton on sea in Essex?

No, I felt this was just another bit of fidgety-foot, which would blow itself out when the present wander bug finally ran out of steam.

I may have kidded myself with these thoughts, but cicumstances were about to prove me completely wrong.

In August, Teresa and I decided to take the kids on a week's holiday to a working farm near Crediton, Devon, where the brochure said they could have 'hands-on' experience with all the animals, and machines - it should be a really good experience for them.

A few days before we were about to go, mum phoned to say she had finally found the place to 'end to their wanderings'- a cottage in a little village called Walkhampton, near Princeton on Dartmoor. I just couldn't believe it, THAT was a real change from London with a vengeance!

Our holiday farm at Crediton wasn't all that far from Walkhampton, just across the moors really, so we planned to have a look-see while we were pottering around the countryside, I was curious to see what 'Valhalla' really looked like!

Our holiday was great fun, alternating between farm animals and trips to the beach at Exmouth, and with the sun behaving itself perfectly for a change, we were sorry when Friday came along and it all had to end.

"Let's go and have a quick look at the cottage nanna wants to buy' I said to the kids. "It's up on the moors near a great big prison, it shouldn't take us long, then we can make our way home".

We had barely got home that evening, when the phone rang.

It was mum - could I possibly hire a large removal-type van and get it round to the Soanes museum for next Friday evening?

They had exchanged contracts with the vendors and were expecting to move in to their new cottage by next week-end.

Ruddy marvellous!

By sheer coincidence I had recently photographed a heavy break-in on an industrial estate near Barking, where the manager said if ever I needed a large lorry for a job, he'd give me a good price, and with Mum's request for a van ringing in my ears, I went back there to try my luck.

We were lucky - yes, I could have his five-ton box-lorry over the week-end, provided it was back in the yard before 0800hrs Monday morning, and as good as his word, only charged me a day's hire for the whole week-end.

"Who is going to drive this removal lorry then?" mum asked when I told her the news over the phone.

"I'm afraid it's a self drive job to keep the cost down, anyway, there shouldn't be any hassle, I know the route blindfold, we've just come back from there".

I would much rather have had the week-end resting at home with the family, instead of charging around the west country in a dirty great lorry!

Just to complicate things however, my old friend Murphy chuckled out loud on Thursday, and delivered his double whammie.

"Hello Alan, dad here, just to let you know that mum has been taken into the Middlesex hospital with a severe attack of Meniere's, and we're still only half packed, I don't really know what we're going to do"

With my mind racing overtime at this gob-smacking news, I said. "Don't worry dad, carry on packing, and we'll see how mum is before we go, if she is still unwell then, she will have to follow down later"

Somehow I managed to get away from work at 1630hrs on Friday - which in itself was no small miracle, and dashed to the industrial estate in Barking, arriving just as the old man was closing the yard gates.

"Hold on, hold on, I've come to pick up a box-lorry for the week-end" I shouted, and he turned towards me in mid-action, without the slightest expression crossing his face.

“That’s it over there then” he said, nodding over his shoulder, “The blue one” and as I looked, my heart sank to my boots, I hadn’t imagined it would be so huge - it looked like a block of flats. “Are you sure that’s it?”

“Yup, that’s the one, boss said a chap might be pickin’ it up Friday, gotta be back ‘ere eight o’clock Monday though, right?”

I left my old Cortina in the corner of the yard, and climbed cautiously into the cab of the huge lorry.

There was at least four feet of empty space between me and the near-side passenger door, I’d need a pair of binoculars to see into the nearside flippin’ mirror!

“Don’t fergit she’s a diesel” the old chap shouted as I drove gingerly through the gates, muttering a silent prayer of thanks to the previous driver for leaving the van pointing in the right direction.

I had a distinct feeling of deja-vous as I set off along the A12 towards town, and re-lived the panic I felt when driving the Landrover for the first time in Egypt with the camp CO. Fortunately I was still able to double de-clutch, and by the grace of God, and various patron saints, I arrived safely at Holborn Kingsway.

All I had to do now was negotiate the narrow turning into Lincoln’s Inn Fields - without taking the ornate gas lamp off the wall, and I was there.

To say I was disappointed with what I found at the museum would be an understatement. Dad in his anxiety had been fully occupied visiting the hospital, and consequently little or no packing had been done since he phoned me on Thursday.

It was chaotic.

Greg was only a young lad, and couldn’t be expected to do much, except scavenge around and make sure we didn’t forget anything, while dad helped me get the remaining stuff into tea-chests.

It was midnight before we got everything to the top of the stairs, and there were still four flights of spiral iron stairs to traverse before reaching ground level.

This was going to be tough!

Picking the heaviest tea-chest containing the crockery, saucepans and stuff, I said to dad. “I’ll take the awkward side going down backwards, you lift your side to follow me, and we’ll take it step at a time”

On the top step, I slid the box to its balancing point and said to dad, “Ok. lift now” and prepared to move to the next step.

Nothing happened.

“Obviously you weren’t ready dad, ok. ready, lift”.

Again nothing happened.

“What’s the matter dad, can’t you get a grip on it?”

“I can’t do it” he replied stern faced.

“What do you mean, you can’t do it?”

“I can’t lift it, I just can’t do it” he said quietly, and suddenly I saw him as a very tired man.

I was really gobsmacked, I couldn’t take this in. Here was my dad one of the strongest men I had known from boyhood - he could bend a six-inch nail with his bare hands, telling me he couldn’t lift his half of a tea chest!

“Ok. there must be one of those two-wheeled trollies around, we’ll put the tea chest on that, tie it on with a rope so that it doesn’t fall forwards, and I’ll let it down step at a time, you and Greg can bring the trolley back up again between you for the next load”.

This was the first indication I ever had, that age really was beginning to get the better of dad, and I must say it shook me up quite a bit. You tend to think of your dad as everlasting.

It took an hour to get the stuff down to street level and into the van, by which time I was pretty exhausted, and we still had two hundred miles to drive!

Fortunately my years of driving round London for the police now paid off, I knew exactly which route to take with the huge van, and soon we were bowling down the A30 towards Salisbury like experienced furniture removers!

Dad and Greg were squeezed into a couple of small sleeping places in the back, lying on some carpets and a small settee, leaving just enough room for me to close the tail-board.

Meanwhile, up front, I was left to drive in solitude, hoping to god I wouldn’t fall asleep.

I wouldn’t say driving the 5 ton van was a doddle, it just seemed to get easier the more miles we covered, and by the time the lights of Exeter appeared, I was feeling pretty confident all round. We had managed to travel without any nasty incidents this far, and I fervently hoped things would stay that way!

After Exeter, I decided to take the A30 to Whiddon Down, turn off at the A382 for Moretonhampstead, and go straight across Dartmoor to Princetown and Walkhampton - it seemed a nice straight route without any complications.

As a grey dawn broke, concentration on driving became more difficult - in my tired state, trees and foliage merged with the early morning mist in a kaleidoscopic blur, and sharp bends came up with mind- jarring suddenness.

It was definitely time to call it a day!

A road sign loomed ahead, Yelverton 4 miles - and as Walkhampton was about two miles out of Yelverton, we must be nearly there thank god!

Inching the lorry round an acute right-hander into the narrow road, I eased down slowly into the village, remembering at the bottom of the hill by the village cross, I had to do a sharp left-hander up to the cottage.

The time was 0530 - I had been up since 0630 yesterday and working at the Yard before starting this crazy jaunt - no wonder I was feeling light-headed.

Friends had agreed to be at the cottage by 0600 to give a hand unloading, and as we were early, I hopped down from the cab to let dad and Greg out for a breath of fresh air, before settling down for forty winks.

It seemed that I had only been asleep a few seconds, when I heard the tail-board go down, and a gaggle of voices muttering in the background as to what they should do first.

It reminded me in my half awake state, of the incident where an oversize Alice is lying down in the house with her foot jammed up the chimney, and the villagers are noisily egging Bill onto the roof to gain entry via the chimney - absolutely hilarious!

It was agreed they would unload the settee as soon as possible, so I could have a couple of hours kip on it, before returning to London.

This week-end, being a Bank Holiday weekend, was bound to be extra busy on the roads, so the sooner I was away the better.

Just before mid-day, I was woken with a hot cup of tea and bacon sarnie, which I woofed down, before climbing aboard the monster and waving goodbye, making my way down into the village and passing the memorial cross on my offside.

I had gone about fifty yards, when it began to seep through my befuddled brain - a cottage on a sharp bend, and the tall earthen banks, they weren't quite what I remembered coming into the village, perhaps I had gone wrong somewhere?

Pushing on a few yards further in the hope that something familiar would click in my brain, I became annoyed and worried when I couldn't find anywhere I could turn round - I was definitely in trouble.

As I couldn't turn, I had to go on - there was no way I could back this monster down a sharply curving lane with no-one behind to see me back.

As I pushed on, the lane got narrower and narrower, and the earthen banks on either side got higher and higher, until they were above head height. This was getting crazy!

With a shudder, the lorry stalled to a halt as the ends of the heavy bumpers bit into the banks, in a shower of earth and stones. I looked in the side mirror to see if there was anyone behind me, only to find the mirrors had folded inwards under pressure from the bankside vegetation.

"Bloody, bloody hell!" I heard myself shout, and immediately had a mental picture of the lorry stuck for ever, like a beached ship, in this bloody lane.

In a fury I banged the door handle down to get out, only to find the door wouldn't open, the banks on both sides held the doors firmly shut!

"Oh shit, shit, shit" I yelled in frustration, and thought if the lads at work could see me now, they'd laugh their ruddy nuts off!

Winding the window down fully, I was just able to squeeze through between the cab and sharp-smelling fern and brambles on the bank, and reach fresh air. God, what a mess!

I walked up the lane about thirty yards, and came to a farmyard gate on the right-hand side which was far too narrow to turn in to, I couldn't use that, I'd have to go on.

Still the damned lane didn't get any wider, but after another fifty yards, it ran out onto an open area on top of the moors, from where I could clearly see traffic on the Princeton road half a mile away to my right, just where I was supposed to be.

There was a nasty problem with the open area however, it was liberally sprinkled with large chunks of Dartmoor rock, sticking up through the wiry grass like anti-tank defences. I'd really have to watch the tyres driving amongst those!

Back at the lorry I had to walk along the top of the bank until I was opposite the hidden door, slide down feet-first until I found the open window, and force myself in.

I felt a right prat - it was a good job there was no-one around to see my silly antics.

Starting the engine, I gave it lots of wellie, and forced the bucking, grinding lorry up the lane, hoping there weren't too many rocks and stones in the banks to score the sides of the vehicle.

At last I made the top, and began the delicate job of turning her round, I just couldn't afford to get a puncture up here!

Talk about three-point turns, this one must have taken twenty three, backwards and forwards dodging those damned rocks until at last I was facing the right way again.

With a sigh of relief I re-entered the lane and began my descent, the grinding of the bumpers not so bad this time - I must have gouged deep grooves on the way up, making the going easier, and I gently nosed past the farm gate I had passed earlier.

At that precise moment, a one-ton van appeared, pushing up the hill at a fair rate of knots, indicating with frantic hand gestures he wanted to turn into his farmyard.

This was getting like a bloody French farce, here I was sweating like a pig, having almost got out of one of the grimmest and daftest situations in a long time, and I was expected to reverse up the hill, to let this fruitcake into his friggin' farm!

It was all getting a bit too much.

I couldn't use the mirrors, they were still folded in, so I wanged her in reverse, gave it buckets of wellie, and juddered blindly backwards. Somehow, I managed to get far enough back for the chap to enter his yard, and he swept past, giving me a puzzled look, wondering no doubt, what the hell a huge lorry like that, was doing in a place like this!

When I got back to the village cross, I realised I should have turned right on leaving, instead of keeping straight on, but I put it all down to a tired brain, and thankfully aimed for London and home.

A scene of crime job I did just after the Devon holiday was of interest in that it showed a need for some kind of collation of job details from one area to another. I don't suppose there would be a tremendous amount to be gained overall, but it did show how one person's observations could help solve a crime somewhere else.

I had been called to the Bow Rd. fly-over near Stratford, to photograph a vehicle index number scratched on a concrete slab by a construction worker.

Apparently he had witnessed a hold-up robbery from his position on high, and identified the robbery vehicle index as 'ABC 123', a blue Transit van, cleverly writing the number down on the only place available, a concrete parapet thirty feet above ground.

When I heard about the description 'blue Transit van' I informed the officer in the case that I had photographed a similar hold-up scene in north London a couple of weeks before, and the index of the get-away blue Transit then was 'ABC 124', one digit different from the number I had just photographed.

Naturally he was very interested, and contacted the other officers, informing me later he had been able to tie the two jobs together, to the point where fingerprints found on a typed letter, were common to those found on both vehicles.

It had been decided to phase out the 5x4 as a crime scene camera, and replace it with a 6x7 rollfilm one. This would certainly make life easier handling the smaller kit, but what about the film format change?

After a week's trial however, I became very impressed with the new Pentax 6x7's though I did miss the Cambo's movements, and the ease of handling large format cut-film during procesing and enlarging.

Having passed the imposing Bank of England building more times than I'd had hot dinners, I was intrigued to get a call to go there one day, and meet officials who wanted a gold ingot photographed in close-up for identification purposes.

It was nice to be able to park right outside the BofE, and take my gear in through a side entrance, leaving the Mini in the care of a tall City of London PC. - no chance of a ticket here!

Once inside, the officer in the case and I, plus various officials made our way deep inside the building, until we came to a huge room with prison-like iron bars running the length of one wall.

Behind these formidable bars lay row upon row of gold ingots, stacked higher than one's head, there must have been thousands and thousands of them!

"If the photographer will just step this way" intoned a dispassionate official, "I'll have the ingot in question brought out to you".

One of the gates was opened with a key that wouldn't have looked out of place in the Tower of London, and in an officious little ceremony, two uniformed attendants - one at each end, brought out a gold ingot and stood before me.

"Could you put it down on this sheet of brown paper while I fix the camera on its tripod please?" Placing a millimetre scale parallel to the bottom of the ingot for accurate sizing in the final print, I disappeared under the focussing-cloth of the 5x4, much to the amusement of a watching attendant, and focussed the image.

We were still using flash-bulbs as our source of artificial light, so I clipped a PF5 into the Kobold flashgun, and took my first shot. As soon as I had completed the top surface of the bar, I walked round in front of the camera, and bent down to turn the ingot over. There was a unique identification stamp mark on the reverse side, which had to be done as well.

As my hands reached out to touch the ingot, the bank staff moved forward as one man, and a voice commanded imperiously, "Don't touch that sir, we'll do whatever moving is necessary"

I felt their concern was a bit over the top, but I suppose it made them feel important.

Lighting the other side was quite a simple matter to show the Rand origin and number, and I was done.

The ingot was taken away in the same ceremonious manner, and we left for the exit, escorted by our stern-faced friends.

I had the heavy Cambo kit and tripod in my right hand, and the large wooden box containing flash-guns, PF5 and PF60 bulbs in my left, and because we were being scrutinsed extremely thoroughly by a guard we were approaching, I leant over to the left as though the flash box was extremely heavy.

"Excuse me sir" the door guard said. "You appear to have something heavy in your box there, may I see what's in it?"

I suppose I shouldn't have taken the mickey really, but I said. "If it's gold bars you're looking for I haven't nicked any"

"That's ok. then sir, you won't mind opening the box for me will you?"

With the lid open, he was presented with two flash-guns sitting on a sea of flashbulbs.

"Would you mind emptying the case, item at a time sir please?"

As the police officer hadn't noticed my accentuated lean to the left suggesting a heavy load, he was mystified by the whole episode, and as the last bulb joined the pile on the floor, leaving the box obviously empty, the door guard said. "Thank you sir, you may put them all back now, and proceed"

As we returned to the sunshine of Threadneedle St. the officer turned to me and said. "Officious little bastard wasn't he, wonder what got into him?"

One of the best aspects of being a Police photographer is that wherever the scene is, you have virtually carte-blanche access to the action, a position of extreme privilege, leaving pompous officials and members of the press fuming behind Police lines. Such a situation occurred after being called to a particularly heavy safe-blowing in Hatton Garden, when it was rumoured thieves had got away with hundreds of thousands of pounds in precious jewels, leaving the poor dealers wringing their hands in agony.

How soon my life, could they get back inside, to assess the extent of their losses?

Fingerprints had marked off the footprints they wanted protected for photography, and were awaiting my presence (for a change!) so they could start dusting the actual scene of the blowing.

"You'll have some fun in there" said 'prints, "I've had a quick look in through the door - you'll be up to your neck in rubies!"

"Pull the other one!" I replied. "Anyway, if you push off out of it, I can get started - the sooner I'm done the quicker you can get back in"

After recording the foyer, and security access to the premises, I moved inside, and once behind the security screen I could see what 'prints meant. The huge safe, big enough to hold two or three men, stood in a sea of chaos, its huge steel door gaping drunkenly, bearing the marks of a searing explosion.

The lads had obviously done a good job.

To help contain the explosive charge - probably Polar Amon, the thieves had stacked bags and bags of uncut rubies and emeralds in front of the door, and covered the whole lot with office carpets, and anything else they could lay hands on, to deaden the explosion.

After the big bang, the place was awash with rubies, emeralds, and finely shredded carpet, which hung in spider-web like festoons over everything, it was most bizarre.

When I had finished photography, I called the officer in the case, and asked if he wished me to photograph in close-up some of the stones littering the floor, which were ankle deep in some places.

"No, if you've got the place covered as usual that'll do me fine, these stones are practically worthless so I'm told, until they're cut and polished.

They're not worth a light as they are, in fact you can help yourself to a couple as a memento if you want"

I picked a couple of the red and green crystals off the floor, and looked at them closely, yes, he was right, they looked for all the world like pieces of coloured plastic.

It just shows how uninformed you can be, and can't always appreciate what's involved in another person's professional expertise, until it's explained to you.

# Chapter Ten

Sometime later, in January 1970 I think, I met a Traffic Division Sergeant - Peter Etheridge, who although a very amateur photographer, was dead keen to improve his photography, as he was a member of the RSPB and a keen bird-watcher.

During the next few months, he contacted me several times with a view to accompanying me on any field trips I might do, but having worked on my own for years and got used to it, I wasn't too keen on the idea.

However he did have a permit to visit nearby Walthamstow reservoirs, and, due to his prompting, I also acquired one, and together we visited the place a couple of times during the year. The reservoirs held many kinds of wildfowl, and was an area unique to London, especially as it had a large breeding colony of Herons on two small islands.

I well remember seeing Eric Hosking's photo of Herons taken at Walthamstow some years before, and wondered if I could do something similar.

However, looking at the steep-sided main island one day, I thought it would be a huge undertaking to get a camera level with some of those nests high up in the trees, I'd have to forget it for now.

At work,the sheer number of crime jobs, plus the grottiness of situations we often found ourselves in, was obviously having an effect on my subconscious, and for a while I was listless and disinterested in things, in fact pretty depressed.

Teresa, no doubt sensing the reason for my attitude - although I never discussed any of our grotty jobs with her, suggested I go and see the quack for a check-up.

The Doc, one of three Irish brothers practising in Romford, and knowing quite well where I worked, was quite forthright in his diagnosis.

"You are suffering from chronic debilitation. I am recommending you take a week off from work to relax, go bird-watching, anything, you'll feel much better after the break"

I thought he was beeing a bit far out, but it sounded fine to me, I had found a nice Skylark's nest with young at Fairlop gravel pit, plus a super Little Grebe's nest on a small pond, both ideal for photography - I'd have a go at those during my time off.

The weather was bright and sunny, and with no worry whether I could get my photographs done in the usual narrow time-slot of a week-end, I did well.

The photographs of the Skylark chicks running out from the nest to greet the returning adult were some of the best I had done to date. The Little Grebe too, a perfect sitter on its floating nest, produced good shots of the young trying to get on to the female's back, after hatching.

The good weather held all week, and it was a great wrench to go back to the Yard on Monday morning, knowing nature was still happening out there, but without me!

That autumn I competed for a bursary offered by Kodak on any project connected with photography, and chose the subject 'high-speed photography of birds'.

I must admit I knew very little about the subject, except what I had gleaned from reading Erics' and other peoples' notes, plus speaking to people in the flash industry like Hadlands.

Their equipment was good, but I found it wasn't meant to be portable and used in the field, so that was out.

The only other suitable flash gear I knew of were the units used by press photographers, which gave a 1/5000th sec. duration - sufficient to stop most wing movements, but rather heavy and cumbersome to use.

In due course I received the inevitable letter from Kodak, 'We are sorry to inform you that you have been unsuccessful in your application for a bursary etc...' and although I felt disappointed, I decided there and then, I had to get into this new form of bird photography somehow.

That June I got a telephone call from Eric Hosking - would I like to go to an address in Avondale Square, Old Kent Rd. where a Kestrel was apparently nesting in a window box on the sixteenth floor of a tower block. He couldn't attend himself as he was busy elsewhere, but I might get something useful.

A couple of days later, after finishing a robbery job near Tower Bridge, I visited the Avondale towerblock, went up to the sixteenth floor and rang the door-bell.

It was answered by an elderly couple who readily agreed to let me see the site, once I showed them my ID. and the source of my information.

What came next was quite incredible. The couple asked me in, and took me into the living-room, where they pointed to a window box just visible through the net curtains.

"There they are" said the man, "If you go any closer she'll leave. We can sit and watch them through the glass from a foot or two away, but they won't accept strangers".

The sitting female Kestrel looked at us through the gap in the curtains, stood up, and slid off the nest into the upstream of air past the window-ledge.

"There you are " said the man. "I told you, she don't like strangers, she won't come back until you're gone"

I got down on hands and knees in the lounge, and looked at three young kestrels plus an addled egg, from a distance of three inches - it was incredible.

Why should the birds choose such an unusual site?

"You say you're from the Police" said the woman, "The young lady in the flat next door is a police officer, perhaps she'll let you take some pictures from her place opposite, you never know"

I thanked the kind couple for their hospitality and left.

In for a penny, in for a pound, I rang Holloway Police station where the WPC. was stationed, and explained as best I could, who I was, and what I wanted to do regarding the Kestrels.

She was naturally a bit sceptical about the whole thing, and to gain her confidence, I suggested she ring me back at SO.3 on the Police network, to verify my identity.

The upshot was, that I could come and see her the following Saturday, and if she was satisfied with my answers to her questions, she would let me take a few shots there and then, she didn't want her boy-friend thinking he had a secret rival!

Working from the WPC's bathroom window, I only managed to get a decent view of the Kestrel's nest site by supporting the Pentax S1A and 200mm Optomax lens on a tripod, set up rather shakily in her bath!

Naturally in the hour that she allowed me on my first visit, neither adult returned, all I got was a few shots of the nest and chicks.

"How much longer will the birds be nesting there?" the WPC. asked. When I explained that the chicks were only about a week old, and would require another three weeks to fledge, she wasn't too impressed.

However with great generosity she finally said. "I'll tell you what, I'll give you a spare key, and you can come and take photographs over any week-end I'm not here, provided you ring and check with me first, I'm not having my boyfriend getting any wrong ideas"

It sounded a more than generous offer, which I was glad to accept. I managed three Saturday visits to the WPC's flat, and got some quite unusual photographs of the adults and chicks, on both 5x4 and 35mm, one of which has been published nearly a dozen times in bird books over the years.

The name Stephen Dalton had surfaced several times, both in conversation with Eric Hosking, and with some of the lads at work. Our lads were photographic students of his at Croydon College, where they said he did a very good instructing job. There was no doubt he seemed to have his finger on the pulse in this high-speed photography caper, and was obviously someone I would have to talk to, if I wanted to get any further.

From conversations I had with various people, it appeared that Stephen Dalton had been the winner of the Kodak bursary I had applied for earlier, and had gone from strength to strength since then, having a marvellous picture of a Barn Owl in flight published as a result of his initial efforts.

There was no way I was going to progress to that sort of standard without some practical input - I just had to go and have a chat with Dalton.

The upshot of all this, was an invitation to call in on him at his home the next time I was in the area, but as he lived in deepest Surrey at the time, this wasn't easy to arrange.

However,after work one Friday evening I made my way through the rush-hour traffic and headed south to Dalton's place, eventually pulling up outside a large country house deep in the countryside. I felt distinctly awkward presenting myself at the door, wondering how I was going to put my request for help, without appearing to be scavenging, but the door opened, I said who I was, and was made welcome.

It didn't take very long to exhaust the scant sum of my knowledge of high-speed flash, and after a cup of tea, Dalton asked me if I would like to see his studio and high speed flash set-up, which had been developed in conjunction with Ron Perkins of the Farnborough College of Technology.

As it stood he told me, his equipment represented the state of the art in HSF units today.

On a large table-top in his upstairs studio, Dalton showed me the layout of his system, with small flash heads connected to power units by substantial cabelling, similar to the system used by Hosking in the early fifties.

"This stuff is all powered by mains electricity" I said. "How do you get on when you want portable power in the field, aren't you restricted to using heavy car batteries?"

He replied at present that was the case, but there were other batteries available which weren't so heavy and awkward, which did the job, but were quite expensive. It seemed to me that this whole form of photography was quite expensive, perhaps far too expensive for me to pursue!

After an hour or so I thanked him for his time and trouble, and prepared to leave. I could see from some slides he showed me of flash tests using his pet Little Owl, that this was an exciting field to explore, and hoped somehow I might just be able to get into it.

“Tell you what” Dalton said as we went back downstairs, “I’ve got an old Dawe Liteflash two-head unit I don’t use any more, it’s a bit dangerous at times, but it would do to get you started.

It’s yours for ten-quid if you’re interested”

Naturally I was very interested, and diving under the stairs he hauled out a unit similar to the one in the stores at the Yard, but in a far tattier condition.

“You’ll need to get it checked and overhauled first, we’ve had a few troubles with it in the past, but it should do you for a year or so, until you get something better”.

On the way home I ran over some of the tests I might do, to find out just how good the unit was - then I remembered I hadn’t asked Dalton in what way it was supposed to be ‘a bit dangerous’, what did he mean by that?

There was no doubt its speed would only be 1/5000th sec. - it used the same Mullard LSD.3 tubes I was already familiar with, but at least it would be a start.

Due to the usual pre-Christmas level of crime, it wasn’t until the new year of 1971 I was able to get stuck into further testing of the Dawe HSF unit, to find what it could really do.

The power unit was quite heavy to carry, although the flash-heads were comparatively light and easy to handle, despite being at the end of heavy six-foot cables.

Those connecting cables I knew had to be perfect and without cracks, as they carried the high voltage from capacitors in the power pack, to the flash-heads, which at 3000 volts DC. was decidedly lethal if earthed!

By one of those peculiar co-incidences, one of the lads at work mentioned he had seen in his hobby mag, a circuit for making a photo-diode trigger, used to detect an object passing through a light beam, and thought it might be useful to me.

Mightn’t the gadget be suitable for detecting moving birds too?

As I was a dum-dum in the art of electronics, I said if I got the parts, would he make one up for me to try? A couple of weeks later, he produced a weird looking jumble of wires and things mounted on a piece of circuit board and said, “Well, that’s it, what do you think, pretty good eh?”.

“How does it work then?” I asked. “It all looks rather fragile to me”.

He explained, if I focussed light from a torch on the front of the diode, and passed my finger through the beam, interrupting the light, the circuit would collapse and a contact normally held open would be closed, thus making a circuit.

To test it, I had to rig the trigger across the end of a cardboard tube, and find a subject to travel through it, and set it off. What I needed was bird willing to act as a guineapig, which might prove difficult unless.... yes, we DID have a tame Budgie who was allowed to fly about the lounge from time to time.

HE would have to be my guinea pig!

It took a fair time to set up the camera and trigger, but at last all was ready, and to dis-approving looks from the children, Billy the Budgie was taken from his cage, and offered up to the open end of the cardboard tube.

Without hesitation Billy went down the tube and shot out the end into a bright light and discharge crack, as the flashes went off. It all appeared to work just fine.

Billy swooped up to the curtain rail, chittering loudly in consternation at such harsh treatment, the iris of one eye already becoming smaller due to the bright flash light.

He wasn't too keen on that!

Despite Billy's misgivings, I managed to get him to trigger off two more shots, and finish my Kodachrome film, so it could be sent off for processing immediately.

The results when they came back were very illuminating - the exposure was correct for the distance the flashes were set from the subject, but on two of the shots I had just the rear half of Billy, only the first shot showed him completely in frame, how come?

I was now entering a phase where I had to calculate not only where the bird would be when the flashes went off - allowing for its flight speed, but more importantly, allow for the magnetic plunger release time, and the mechanical delay time of the shutter from the moment the beam was broken,

This could easily equal the time it took a bird to travel across the camera's field of view, hence the fact I only captured half the bird in my shots.

There was more to this high-speed lark than I first thought!

# Chapter Eleven

There were occasions attending certain scenes of crime, when an unexpected 'spin off' could prove quite useful, and one such occasion came after attending an arson at the Chigwell Country and Golf club.

As I completed my photography of the fire- damaged lounge, Sean Connery and Bobby Moore, co-owners of the club, came in to see the extent of damage for themselves, so I slid off.

Having time to kill whilst the SOCO did his examination, and then explaining his findings to Connery and Moore, I wandered outside, to see the extent of their grounds.

The drive leading to the club was shared with a cattle-breeding farm next door, owned by Mr. Norwood of butchers' chain fame, and seeing one of his farming staff nearby, I asked if there were any owls on the farm premises.

"Yes, I reckon we have, leastways we often see the little brown 'uns sitting in that old oak over there, and occasionally a white owl round by the barns" This was really good news.

"Is it possible for me to come onto the property and see just where they are, and maybe take some photographs in the future?"

"You'll have to take that up with Mr. Norwood down at the 'ouse, 'e may say yes, and then agen 'e mayn't"

After speaking with a very 'protective' Mrs. Norwood, I eventually met the man himself, who after close questioning of my intentions, reluctantly agreed I could look for the owls, with the proviso that I reported my presence to his manager each time I arrived, - he didn't want strangers walking around his property at will, which seemed fair enough.

Ringing in to the office on completion of the job, I was told to 'have lunch', which meant of course I could have a quick look round the farm there and then, to see just what it contained.

I tramped round the hundred acres or so adjacent to the home paddock, and found the farm to be quite ordinary in its' bird population, but there were signs of Kingfisher on the river Roding which ran through the property, and a Little Owl in the aforesaid Oak.

This could turn out to be interesting later on in the year, and with a bit of luck, I might even discover the whereabouts of the reported Barn owl too.

It was about this time I unexpectedly bumped into Dave Summers, I hadn't seen or heard from him since our last sojourn on Inishbofin, and of all places to meet, we met on a Central Line train when I was bound for Snaresbrook Crown Court.

We only had time for a short chat before I had to get off, but I did learn that he had met a young lady, and was hoping to get married soon.

He was still teaching youngsters part-time at a school near Leytonstone, and hadn't managed to settle into a solid full-time job yet. At forty years of age, I thought he was cutting things a bit fine.

With the demands of work more than filling the day, and only the short time left at week-ends to be with the family, the remaining months of 1970 rolled away, and suddenly it was New Year.

Hooray for 1971 and all it might bring!

They say, see the old year out with a bang, well the new year certainly came IN with a bang for Robert Carr, Employment Minister at his home in Hadley Green, Hertfordshire, as persons unknown placed two bombs against his house wall, and blew a hole in it.

At the scene I met Major Harrison - one of those fabulous characters who defuse bombs left about by murderous morons, just as the morning mists were beginning to lift, yet the Press were there in their dozens already! Although he was a stern and taciturn man, Harrison was, as I already knew, a smashing chap to work for, and under his instruction we got on with our work, piece by piece.

Kept back only by the railings in front of the house, the press shouted their "Turn this way please, or hold it like that please" commands as flashguns popped, taking pictures that would no doubt banner the dailies throughout the country.

It was like being a celebrity.

A month later I received in the post, a newspaper cutting sent from my brother Tony in New Zealand, stating in the 'Auckland Star' that after the Carr outrage, Britain feared it might inherit the US. spectre of bombing violence, and a photograph underneath showed a photographer at work recording the bomb scene.

Despite the fact that I had not seen Tony for a couple of years, and I was sporting a full set of whiskers, he recognised the photographer in the picture as me!

During April we had the experience of yet another kind of bomber, one who was sophisticated enough to wire up the car of Jimmy Tibbs, relative of 'those round the corner' at Collier-Row, so that when he turned the ignition key of his van, sticks of gelignite next to the engine exploded, giving him and his small son a violent shock.

A second explosion against the Tibbs clan went off just a week later - this one supposedly a bad gas leak in their Canning Town café. It seemed to me that things were beginning to hot up against the local criminal fraternity, which could only mean more work!

In July I had to do another job at Chigwell, funnily enough concerning pollution of a small stream feeding into the river Roding not far from Norwoods' and the Chingford country club.

The owners of a small engineering works had allowed a highly toxic effluent to drain from their premises into the stream, causing serious pollution, and the local river authority were taking them to court, via police evidence.

It didn't take long to do a couple of shots showing the vile green effluent, plus the dead Minnows etc; left upturned in its wake, so I took the opportunity to wade along the stream for a hundred yards or so, to see if there was any sign of Kingfishers, and on a small bend where the stream formed a deep pool under a four foot bank, a recently occupied nesting hole.

The site was incredible, I knew that Kingfisher were sometimes very crafty in selecting their nest sites, but this was quite remarkable, the stream was so narrow you could jump across it with ease! Without further pollution, I might be lucky enough to have the birds back next year to breed. It would be a case of re-visiting the site at intervals, and keeping my eyes open until next spring.

Towards the end of July I was called into the office of our newly appointed guvnor Nick C. and told that I was being given the responsibility for producing and directing a film on the Police use of CS. Gas, a subject regarded as a political hot potato.

The broad script had already been written by a Chief Inspector, all I had to do was interpret it into a twenty minute film, and have it ready for the big-wigs to view by the end of September.

Dave A. who was now second in command, leaned forward over Nick C's shoulder and said "You do realise that you are to DIRECT this film and not film it, I don't want you to even touch the cine camera, you'll have Dave Teague to do that, do you understand?"

It was said in such a peculiar way, I got the distinct impression I was being 'used' somehow - he knew how keen I was on cine filming, having shot and edited hundreds of feet of my own stuff, but had never been allowed to film anything within the section.

So why was I being considered for this project at all?

Nick went on. "You'll have the undivided attention of the D.11 Firearms Unit, all twelve officers, during the last week in August, and that's ALL you'll have, because that's the only time they'll be free, so you'd better get cracking right away"

I came out of the office with my head buzzing, I had a budget of twelve-hundred pounds to get a cutting copy to the viewing stage, twelve 'actors' I hadn't met, and Dave Teague as cameraman, junior to me in service, but pushing hard to get higher!

What a lovely situation!

The Chief Inspector obviously knew his stuff, but hadn't a clue as to where we could stage the sensitive set-up, which required Police to chase and contain armed criminals in a hostage situation, plus the use of CS. gas to persuade the nasties to surrender.

Apparently CS. gas blowing down-wind could adversely affect people quite some distance from the scene, therefore the venue would have to be very carefully chosen, if we were to avoid serious complaints from joe public!

Over the next couple of days Dave T. and I sat down with the Chief Insp. and got stuck in, trying to interpret into sensible visual terms, what he wanted to say concerning Police use of this highly controversial substance.

We scoured dozens of inner London areas for a suitable location to shoot, but without success, until I remembered the huge derelict area of Woolwich arsenal from my bird-watching days, and decided to try for that.

We would have a helluva lot of red-tape to undo before we were successful in getting permission, but it was worth a try.

Due to the sensitive nature of the job, plus pressure from top police 'brass' associated with the project, we got permission to film at Woolwich within a matter of days. I could hardly believe our luck, and started on my shots list immediately, before someone changed their mind!

The 'powers that be' decided we could use the roads and buildings of the arsenal in close-up to disguise exactly where we were, and use our CS gas with great care, but we still needed to find a venue for the realistic hostage building, where the actual discharge of CS. gas wouldn't be seen on film.

Returning to the Yard through Limehouse one day, I noticed a four storey block of flats boarded up ready for demolition, which, after a furious bout of phone calls, I managed to get the Council to loan us for our hostage scene, and we were ready to go. It was now the third week in August, and my schedule for completion was getting a bit too tight for comfort.

I can tell you without doubt, that the remark made by that wonderful film director Sir David Lean, 'Unless you know right down to what the actor had for breakfast, you can't begin to interpret a scene properly' is true - he was dead right.

I had lived with that bloody script day and night for the last three weeks, and I knew every shot in my head, and a good job too, as Dave A. had invited himself along to see how things were progressing, and checked my every move.

I had managed to persuade Engineers Branch to lend me one of their 60ft.'Cherry-pickers' to do the elevated and downward panning shots, and so on a bright and sunny morning in late August, the 16mm Bolex began to roll.

I had of course marshalled my shots so that we didn't keep people waiting who weren't needed, but the continuity I hoped and prayed for as regards the weather didn't happen at all.

On the third day of shooting, the skies began to cloud over, giving a different colour cast to the interleaving shots taken earlier in bright sunshine, and by Thursday it was blowing strongly and spotting with rain.

I just hoped we could cut the various outside scenes together without it being too obvious that in one shot trees were swaying about, and in the next they were quite stationary!

The scenes where the CS. gas canister was lobbed in to flush out the villains went without a hitch, and nobody was unintentionally affected by the gas, which fortunately dispersed in the wind.

At the Limehouse venue things went well too, and where we did have to suggest the presence of CS. gas, we used a red smoke canister to give the desired effect. Everyone was kept happy.

Despite Dave A's insistence I mustn't even touch the camera, I made it my business to check every shot through the viewfinder before shooting. If it was my film, then it was my responsibility how it looked too, and full control over the shot obviously meant 'hands on' here!

Only one or two cut-aways and location shots were needed to complete the shots list, and I left Dave T. to get on with those, while I started editing on the Steenbeck machine.

It had been agreed that the diagram showing the spread of CS. gas over an area, would best be shown by animation, and a couple of evenings were spent in the quietness of the studio, camera mounted upside-down, firing off one frame at a time, to produce the forward animated movement the script required.

It all took time.

During the third week of September I was called over the Tannoy to go to the guvnor's office immediately, it sounded urgent, what could it mean? I soon found out.

Behind his desk in an attitude of regal power sat Nick, with his ever present satellite Dave A. half a pace back, impassive behind his right shoulder.

Without any pre-amble, or voice modulation whatever Nick said loudly "I'm reading the riot act to you Alan, I want that film finished, and I want it finished immediately!"

I couldn't believe my ears, Nick had always been a good natured sort of chap, blow up the odd time, but would forgive a mistake immediately afterwards, and never refer to it again - what had caused this nasty outburst?

I looked beyond his shoulder to where Dave A. stood unbending, facial expression frozen into nothingness, his blue eyes like cobalt rivets. Aha! now I knew the reason, Brutus had been at it again!

Plunging in with both feet, furious at what I felt to be a stab in the back, I said, "I don't know WHAT you've been told guvnor, but we're doing quite well, the editing is nearly finished, and the sound-track is complete, however if you're not entirely satisfied with my progress I'd be quite happy to give it over to whoever you nominate, and I'll go back to scenes of crime tomorrow"

Nick jolted back in his chair at that, no doubt he was expecting some craven excuse or argument, but he didn't get it.

"There's no need for that extreme course of action Alan, just keep me informed on a daily basis how you are progressing that's all I need to know - you can go now"

In a thoroughly depressed mood I went back to the editing room, where I met a suspiciously subdued Dave T. and I wondered just what had been going on behind my back?

The close working contact made with the lads in D.11 Firearms unit, was for me, the highlight of the whole project. They were a real riot of laughs, and could be depended upon to see the funny side of things in almost any situation.

Their friendship and trust was to be of great value to me over the intervening years, especially during a serious siege situation that was soon to come.

The CS.gas film turned out to be quite a success, and was used for training purposes by several Police Services across the country. Its success enabled SO3 photo section to form its own official 'film unit' with the necessary budget and equipment to undertake small film productions.

However, for reasons best known to those who promulgate them, I was never asked to join the unit, and possibly to rub salt into the wound, Dave Teague was eventually put in charge of it all.

I was out.

# Chapter Twelve

Back on my old manor once more, I soon got into the swing of things, and in a matter of days it seemed as though I hadn't been away. Christmas came and went with its usual alacrity, and in no time it was spring, with jobs in the open air becoming a little more pleasant to do.

Perhaps it was becoming known to the section hiearchy I was enjoying myself too much - over the last six months or so, I had accompanied Shaw Taylor, filming the sequences to be used on TV's 'Police 5' each week.

I knew most people in the section had seen my work on television, and although I got a few plaudits, some I felt, were not a little envious at my apparently cushy job.

On the other hand somebody may have genuinely believed I was the man for this newly created, prestigious job, and nominated me. Anyway, the guvnor, Nick C. called me in to his office, and said that a Senior photographer was required to staff a new post at the Detective Training School, Hendon, supplying visual aids support to the two resident artists there. That person was to be me.

I was to have within reason, all the studio kit I required, plus a new 35mm Nikon F, with a full range of lenses, and a dark-room fitted out to print black and white work, from 5x4 down to 35mm, and my own office.

It was like going back to basics again, really great!

The new journey from home to Hendon was quite a long one, but I did get the difference in mileage allowances which the extra journey incurred. It wasn't much, but it was something to offset the increased petrol costs my old Volks Caravanette was incurring.

At the Training School there was a marvellous full-size swimming pool too - available to staff during the dinner hour, plus a superb gymnasium, and a large canteen where the meals were surprisingly good. My offices were next door to Walter and 'Cookie' the two Hendon artists, and it was a simple matter to set up a copy system in my studio, so that their art work placed beneath the camera could be turned into visual aid slides with the minimum of delay.

I found it quicker and cheaper to knock off as many copy slides as were required at the taking stage, rather than make an original, and ask the lab. for dupes later on, and I soon had a good rapport with the teaching staff, who gobbled up my material like it was going out of fashion.

As I still had the 16mm Cine on board for the weekly forays with Shaw Taylor, I happily continued doing the job over ensuing weeks until one day, Dave A. rang to say that my new post didn't attract the filming overtime he noticed I was putting in for payment.

A detachment like mine from the Yard didn't warrant it - I was forbidden to accompany Shaw Taylor from that very moment, and he would send someone up to reclaim the cine camera immediately. What a nasty piece of work he was!

I decided in the light of developments taking place at the Yard, I would dive in and fill my boots whilst at Hendon. I might as well make the most of whatever fate offered, and what it didn't offer, I would try and provide for myself. It was no good crying over spilt milk.

The weeks soon passed, and once my presence was known on the estate, requests for photography began to roll in. Needless to say Dave A. gave me a right dressing down after hearing that I was taking photographs 'off the site', and was only put in his place by Insp.W. who said I was operating under his specific instructions, as his script called for certain venues to be photographed, which didn't exist on the Hendon estate.

Dave A. was distinctly narked.

I had until that moment, taken all my colour films back to the Yard for entering in the special Hendon requisitions book, before having them posted on to Kodak for processing. They were then returned to me direct at Hendon.

Whilst taking a couple of days off for leave, I asked our Hendon clerk to send some films off for me, which she did, but mistakenly put the photographic section at the Yard as their return address, instead of Hendon.

When I returned to Hendon full of beans on Monday morning, I hadn't been in five minutes, before the phone rang - it was Dave A. Would I come in to the Yard as a matter of urgency, and see the guvnor?

Oh. shit! what little surprise had they in store for me now?

As I walked towards the guvnor's office, I saw one or two colleagues faces look my way and grin sympathetically, there was obviously something in the wind I didn't know about!

I knocked and waited.

"Come in" said a voice that was obviously Nick's, and in I went, clocking Dave A. standing in his usual position behind Nick's right shoulder.

"Sit down, I want to show you something I consider to be very serious" he said in an icy voice, and my heart sank to my boots.

"I'd like you to explain these" he said, laying out a row of colour prints I'd taken, all showing houses for sale, with the estate agent's name prominently displayed in the foreground.

"I don't know what you mean, explain them, they're all part of a job for the school, what's the problem then?"

"You mean you haven't taken these for private use, for estate agents to use in private house purchase?"

I nearly fell through the floor in stupified surprise.

"You mean you actually thought these were buckshees, you really thought I would be THAT stupid? Is that the level of trust you place in your staff?" I was really boiling!

"If you're telling me this is an official job, how is it being used then?" he went on. I explained it was all part of a scenario where a member of Hendon police staff played the part of an unscrupulous estate agent on CCTV, who was to be filmed looking down at houses for sale pictures lying on his desk.

"If you're not satisfied with my explanation, you can easily ring Ch. Insp. W. at Hendon, he'll confirm what I've just told you, and I don't think your accusation of mistrust is very nice at all"

Nick turned, and glared icily at Dave A. and I knew once again the source of my troubles. I would seriously have to watch my tail with that bastard around!

"OK. you can leave, but continue to put all your films through here, I want to see all the stuff you're doing, ok?"

It was like a re-run of the CS. gas film scenario.

As I about to leave the section, Dave A. called me into his office and closed the door.

"I have been checking on you, and I'm not satisfied about some of the things you're doing. You may like to know I've built a wall round you, you won't get over, you're finished, you're going nowhere in this department!"

Although quite shocked at this injudicious revelation, I felt that as he was dishing out the hard stuff, I could at least reply in kind, although I didn't really want to.

"Well if that's your strategy, you'll have to work bloody hard at it, I'm not scared of you, you're pathetic, I'll be here long after you're gone!" and turned and left him to it.

In the general office, several lads raised questioning eyebrows as to my fate after the inquisition, but I just smiled and left them guessing. Its amazing how fast bad news travels when you don't need it!

It wasn't long of course before it became impractical for me to send all my films to the Yard for 'scrutiny' - work schedules didn't allow for that sort of delay, and ChInsp.W. had to get on the blower to Nick, and sort it all out.

"You might like to know I'm supposed to vet all your films young Parker when they come back from processing. How am I going to do that if you don't have a booking-in book for me to see?

Anyway I don't suppose I'd have the time to peruse it even if you had one" he mused.

What a lovely chap.

The 'pace' of life at Hendon certainly took some getting used to, gone were the days of tear-arsed bustle to get jobs out in time, instead, things proceeded at the leisurely pace one would expect from a centre of learning, before slowly coming to a satisfying conclusion. I could certainly get used to this!

As things hotted up in town with bomb scares and such, the lads were sorely pressed to provide the 'on-call' cover required at the Yard each night until midnight, and I offered to join the roster, hoping to ease the load, and make a few bob as well.

Dave A. curtly dismissed my offer with the explanation that as I was on official detachment, and totally divorced from the day to day running of the section, I wasn't eligible. I was dead.

Part of a Police Cadet's training consisted of a week's hard physical training course at a place called Pen y Gwyeth in Wales, and was designed especially to extract confidence and teamwork from the men.

As one might expect, the course instructor having his camera with him, took a few shots in Wales to illustrate what they did, and with the artists' help, made a display for the foyer of the cadet school.

The shots weren't bad, but they did lack the bite of professionalism that better equipment and experience could produce, I resolved to see if I could change all that.

Now that Hendon training school had its own photographer on site, dozens of projects were presented for consideration, the driving school needed to update their slide-talks to students, the scenes of crime and fingerprint section required an update too, so did the physical training lot, even the estate office wanted buildings and roadways recorded, and so it went on.

I was happily inundated with interesting projects that would keep me busy for months!

There was a large wooden hut about forty feet long situated on the edge of the sports field, which was about to be demolished to make way for a newer construction. This hut had a very interesting history in that it had been the flight-hut of the American Flying Tigers, a squadron based in the UK. before the war, and flying out of Hendon.

Before that, it was sited in Trafalgar Square, from whence troops were served their last cuppa, before embarking for the front in 1914-18. It certainly needed photographing for posterity before its sad destruction.

Life proceeded at a far more leisurely pace now, I wasn't on late-turn or weekend duties - and was therefore able to devote a little more time to bird photography, especially on Saturday afternoons, after the necessary home chores had been done.

I had recently been reading a book on birds photographed in the London area, and had noticed again the colour photograph of Herons at their nest in Walthamstow reservoirs, taken by Eric Hosking. The date of the photograph was quite a few years earlier which set me thinking, it might be possible to approach the Water Board people, and despite the obvious difficulties I noted earlier, ask permission to build a hide on one of their islands, with a view to updating London's Heron photography.

I drafted what I thought was a suitable letter to the Waterworks HQ in Roseberry Ave. Islington, and awaited their reply. Surprisingly, I received an answer in just over a week, containing a questionnaire, wishing to know my experience in nature photography, suitable sponsors, and when I might wish to commence the work if permission was given.

Eric Hosking was his usual helpful self in such matters, and gladly wrote to the Water people, giving them all the assurances they needed from a world prominent bird photographer, and fellow member of the London Natural History Society.

After receiving Eric's letter the Waterboard people told me I had been successful in my application, and requested I attend a meeting at Roseberry Ave. with one of their senior managers.

He wished to discuss in detail what I wanted to do.

At the conclusion of the discussion I remarked that I had never set foot on the main breeding island, and would like to do so, to enable me to select a suitable place for a pylon hide.

"Do you mean you would have to build some sort of tower to get up to the nests for photography?" the manager asked.

"Yes, it is usually made from steel scaffolding, and is braced against other trees or supports to stop it falling over, I have a contact where I can hire some at very reasonable rates"

"We couldn't possibly let you bring outside materials on to the reservoir site" he said in a slightly aggrieved tone, "We would have to take full responsibility for building the tower ourselves, we wouldn't want any accidents to happen you know"

I could hardly believe my ears, here was a chap practically demanding to do the donkey work, which I had fully expected Peter, myself, and any other interested volunteers, to struggle with for weeks, before completion.

"We have a photographer of our own you know, and I would expect him to be able to use the hide, whenever it suited the Company to do so"

"That's a perfectly natural request, but I must insist he tells me whenever he wants to use it, there are certain procedures you must follow going in and out of the hide, without which, we could seriously disturb the Herons. We would be castigated throughout the whole country, if there were any desertions due to our activities"

We arranged to meet on the bank near the main colony the following Saturday, with a view to rowing across, and seeing just what might be done. I was getting quite excited at the thought of sitting high up amongst the Herons next spring, and taking plenty of photographs, I could hardly believe it!

Collecting Peter from his home, we trundled off to Walthamstow in the Volks Caravanette, complete with my old fibre glass dinghy on the roof, just in case we needed it. Fortunately though, our friend from the Waterworks HQ. was waiting with his own ferryman and dinghy when we arrived, and it was a simple matter for him to row us the hundred yards to the island, and scramble ashore.

The sides of the island were quite steep, and the trees, most about forty to fifty feet tall, were crowded closely together in sandy soil, and interspersed with tangled Elderberry.

It wouldn't be easy to clear a working space for the pylon.

The Herons had finished their breeding for the year, and therefore we weren't a disturbance to them, but through the leafy canopy we could see dozens of used nests, any one of which would make a good site for photography.

"I think we ought to keep the hide to one side of the main colony" I said. "We don't want to create any obstruction to their flight-path into the colony, and also by being a little to the south, we'll have the sun on our right, and behind us for most of the day"

"Ok. so you think this is the tree you'll be working on" said our Waterworks man, "I'll mark it with a piece of chalk so our chaps will know which one it is when they come to put up the scaffolding".

"Yes, but as the tree goes up pretty straight, the base of the hide needs to be just here" I said marking the stump of an Elderberry growing ten feet away from the tree,

" This will give us about fifteen feet distance between the camera and the nearest nest, which is about right, it should be great"

Our man then went on to discuss how the hide would be built on top of the scaffolding; they had plenty of old green canvas we could use, and he would make sure that a ladder would be built up the outside, so we would have an easy climb to the top.

Things were panning out extremely well.

"The Herons normally return to breed at the end of January/early February, so the hide must be completed by the end of December at the latest" I told our man.

"That's no trouble, we'll begin in October and be finished in a couple of weeks, so the December deadline is fine"

Because of various job commitments at Hendon, I wasn't able to visit the reservoirs for a few weeks, but as it was now the first week in September, I thought I'd better ring Peter and make a date for us to check the site again before the Waterworks boys got cracking.

However, before I could get around to it, Peter rang me.

"Have you been over to the reservoirs lately and seen the hide? If not I think you ought to get over there as soon as possible, they're putting the top on it, and its just about finished"

Oh god I thought, they were supposed to tell me when they expected to start, so I could be on hand to see things were done properly, after all, with their own waterworks labourers doing the job, anything could happen!

The next morning I rang Hendon and said I wouldn't be in until midday, and made a bee-line for the reservoirs, hoping the construction gang would still be working there.

As I pulled to a halt on the bank opposite the heronry, I could see two bods standing inside the canvas covering on top of the hide, their arm movements suggesting that they were putting finishing stitches along the top edge.

I blew the horn, and waved my arms, indicating I wanted to come across, and in slow time one of them descended the tower, got into the boat, and began to row across.

"Hallo there, I'm the photographer you're building the tower for, can I come over and see how you're getting on please?"

Without a word he held the boat on the oars while I got in, and began the return journey in silence.

"I thought someone was going to tell me when you were going to start" I said, "You've certainly got on faster than I expected"

"I don't know about that, all I know is that we were free for this couple of weeks, the scaffolding was handy nearby, so were told to get on with it"

As we crunched ashore I had a funny feeling that all was not well, and in a few seconds my gut feelings were proved dead right.

There, at the rear of the scaffolding stood the Elderberry stump with its chalk mark as plain as day, while the front of the scaffolding appeared to grow from the base of the Heron's tree! Looking up the magnificent steel structure to the leafy canopy, I could see the nearest Heron's nest barely four feet away from the front of the hide. What the hell was going on?

In a minute flat, I was up the steel ladder, superbly constructed from short lengths of scaffold pipe, and into the roofless hide, where the second man was sitting on a box, drinking his mug of tea.

I walked to the front of the hide and looked out to where a huge stick nest swung lazily in the breeze four feet away - I just couldn't believe it!

"What do you think of it then" said the man putting his mug down, "A pretty fair job eh?"

I swallowed hard to restrain my scream of frustration and said carefully, "Who on earth said the tower had to be built as close to the tree as this? I distinctly said it had to be no nearer than that chalk-marked stump down there, and that hasn't been done. This is just plain crazy, and won't do!"

His anticipatory smile froze, and his eyes hardened in disbelief, "What won't do?"

he said "We've built it just as the guvnor ordered, it's finished now, and that's that"

"What do you mean it's finished? apart from being totally in the wrong position its' NOT finished, what about the roof, - how did you think we were going to photograph the Herons without a roof on top?"

"We thought you would sit on a stool or something, and rest your elbows on the edge, pointing your cameras over the top"

"And what about the birds seeing US?" I queried.

"Oh, we didn't think they'd mind, considering all this steelwork around"

"Well I'm sorry to disappoint you after all your hard work, but its got to come down, and go back to the point I indicated, otherwise I'm certainly not taking responsibility for it, let alone using it"

"You mean you want us to take the whole bleedin' lot down, and put it up again a few feet further back?" he said incredulously.

"Yes I'm afraid so, I'll have a word with your boss at Roseberry Ave. as soon as I can get to a phone, but there's no doubt about it, its got to come down"

He walked to the rear of the hide where his friend was just making a slow appearance at the top of the ladder.

"Did you 'ear that 'arry, its all got to bleedin' come down and be put up again further back"

"Nah, I don't believe it" said Harry, and without stopping for a second, continued a measured retreat down the ladder.

When I managed to get through to the office in Roseberry Ave. and speak to the chap who marked the trees with us, I asked why the hide had been put closer to the tree than I originally suggested.

"Oh, that's easy" he replied, "After our little chat, I got out one of Eric Hosking's books - very interesting it was too. He says that one of the most important aspects of good bird photography is to get a large image of the bird on your film in the first place, so I moved the hide nearer the nest to help you, ok?"

I thought I did very well explaining why his marvellous efforts on my behalf had fallen flat, and he eventually conceded, that in the light of possible repercussions if the fault wasn't remedied, he would tell his chaps to re-site the tower as soon as possible.

I distinctly made a point of keeping a very low profile while the rebuilding went on, and checked construction only after the waterworks chaps had gone home.

I thought it would be far easier that way.

It was during January 1972 that I got a letter from David Cobham, a film director who worked for Anglia TV. saying he understood I had a hide on Herons at Walthamstow Reservoirs, and as they were doing a film about nature in a town environment, could he send his camera crew, Ron Eastman and wife, to join me when I got started?

Naturally I had to seek clearance from the water people, who said it was ok. provided they got a mention in the credits, and of course they wouldn't be liable for any damage claims that might arise from ATV. When we eventually spoke, Ron Eastman told me he was mainly interested in action shots showing adults feeding the young, so would I have a couple of nests lined up which would give the best shots, before he turned up.

In February, Peter and I anxiously watched the herons as they took over last year's nests for the coming breeding season, and noted with satisfaction they weren't avoiding the area around the hide in their nesting deliberations. It all looked pretty good.

Knowing my interest in birds of the middle-east, Peter told me of a talk with slides, being given by a young chap called Rumsey recently returned from the Caspian Sea where he had been trapping migrant waders. It sounded too good a talk to miss, and I arranged to join him at the Woodford RSPB group meeting the following week.

The talk was indeed very interesting, reminding me strongly of my own trapping and ringing experiences in the Canal-Zone, Egypt, where the knowledge of treading new ground, with little previous work to refer to, gave one a great sense of exploration.

After the presentation, I made a point of talking to Stephen Rumsey, as he mentioned the whole trip had been sponsored by the Churchill Trust. Out of interest I asked what was involved in attaining such a fantastic award.

"If you give me your name and address I'll make sure you have all the literature you want sent to you - anyone is free to apply, you don't have to be an expert in your subject either you know"

I questioned him further, and the more I learned in that short time, the more determined I became to have a shot at the scheme myself. I had always wanted to visit the southern part of Iran, and see for myself the vast lakes and marshes crawling with wildfowl, ever since I had seen the area on our aerial intelligence photos way back in Egypt.

There was also the matter of Persepolis, that wondrous city I had only read about, destroyed by Alexander the Great in his great push to Afghanistan in 32BC. If I could get to see that whilst surveying the wildfowl, it would be the trip of a lifetime, no doubt about that!

Photography from the Heron hide at Walthamstow was a real treat, we had four nests immediately in front of the hide, the closest being twelve feet away, which, with the 200mmm lens gave a frame-filling view of the birds as they stood by their nests.

The downside however was the cold weather, which at fifty feet elevation, seemed colder than at ground level, and we often left the hide unable to feel our legs and feet.

At the training school, work slowed considerably now that I had completed most of the lectures for the instructors, and I was able to take things quite easy, in fact I was usually home by 1730, something unheard of on when attending scenes of crime!

A couple of weeks later I received a package from the Churchill Trust, containing all the information on the organisation I might need, its aims, its trustees, and last year's list of the categories from which one could apply for a fellowship, it was quite an eye-opener.

"You sound very enthusiastic about this Churchill Trust thing" Teresa said, seeing me reading all the relevant bumpf,

"Do you think you're qualified enough to stand a chance of being selected, besides what category would you apply under when travelling to Iran?"

"You're governed by the categories set out each year according to this literature, unfortunately there's nothing down here in either ornithology or travel that would suit me this time. I'll have to apply under the adventure heading or something similar in October, but I am going to set out in detail what I would like to do, and see what happens" I replied.

Now that spring was well and truly with us, I was itching to find a subject I could photograph with the fast flash, and with this in mind, re-visited the little stream at Chigwell to see if there was any sign of the Kingfishers, and there was. Last years nest had tumbled into the stream when the bank crumbled under winter spates, but there slap-dab in the middle of the newly exposed clay bank was this years' tunnel. It couldn't be better.

Opposite the nest, and about six feet away, I drove a short length of natural fence-post into the shallows, knowing it would be irresistible to the Kingfishers to perch on after they sped round the bend towards the nest. With a bit of luck I should be able to photograph them perching on that, especially when they were feeding their young.

At the Heronry, things were still going well, I had quite a few shots of Herons feeding their young, and had shot a hundred feet of 16mmm film on my own Bolex cine, just to see what sort of fist I made of it. Surprisingly for such a short sequence, it turned out rather well.

Sharing the hide with Ron Eastman was a revelation in how a good cameraman and his Arri should work together, achieving those stunning shots we all admire so much on TV. He seemed so laid-back about it all, and yet I knew from his superb film on the life of the Kingfisher, how different images came together under his skill at the end.

I also learnt in detail how free-lance nature photographers were treated by organisations such as the BBC, and if his experiences were anything to go by, it wasn't an occupation to pursue as employment, especially if you wanted to earn good money at the end of it all!

In early April I decided to set up my diode trigger on the Kingfisher's nest, to see if I could possibly get the fast mobving bird in mid-flight. It took me a fiddling half hour to set up the Pentax and photo-diode trigger between the wooden post and the nest entrance, mainly because the sun was shining smack onto the diode and masking the light beam, making it difficult to see when I was on target.

Having got everything set up at last, I walked away and left the Kingfishers to do their bit, although really, it was such a Heath-Robinson set-up I wasn't expecting any results at all.

An hour later when I returned to the site, I discovered the camera had in fact gone off, but with what results?

Without thinking I waded through six inches of water as I brought the flash unit ashore, suddenly remembering the capacitor charges up to 3000 volts DC. and I hadn't remembered to turn the unit off.

That mistake could have been decidedly lethal had there been a short circuit anywhere!

In actual fact the unit was quite dead, either the battery had gone flat, or some component was extremely kaput, whatever it was, everything was ominously inert, but a single frame of film had been exposed!

During the next week I visited an electronic flash repair chap I knew in Wallington, who told me he would certainly have a look at my flash unit, but as the unit was over twenty years old, he couldn't guarantee its performance for much longer, what could I do then?

The next day at Hendon, I heard that my offers of photographic assistance to the

Cadet training wing had borne unexpected fruit - I was asked if I would like to accompany the next group of cadets travelling to Penn-y-Gwyeth, in Wales, to record their progress at rock-climbing, canoeing, and general training activities?

Wouldn't I just!

At the end of that week, my roll of Ektachrome film containing the Kingfisher came back in the post, and with feverish anticipation I zipped through the slides until I found it - yes, there it was, in glorious colour, wings fully spread, a female kingfisher just in front of the nest hole. And quite sharp too.

By some small miracle I'd done it!

The next week's trip to Penn-y-Gyweth was all that I could have asked, bright sunshine, blue-skies, and a freedom to take whatever photographs of the cadets I thought best. All in all, the job turned out to be my some of my best colour-print work to date.

Most of the photography was on medium format, 6x6 colour neg, and the resulting exhibition of 20"x16" prints went down rather well.

Throughout most of 1973 I was left to get on with my work at Hendon with few intrusions from the Yard, and I really began to enjoy the leisurely pace the college offered. I could plan my work in detail and take my time, with the eventual satisfaction seeing it turn out just as I wanted. It was very satisfying indeed.

Not only did I have enough stills work to keep me fully occupied for months, but I got an intro to the CCTV studio on the complex, which produced low-band productions for the college's use.

Here I gained an insight into a whole new world of photography, based on electronic imaging, it certainly seemed the way to go.

One day at Hendon there was an incident which showed how close Teresa and I had become telepathically over the years. We were both quite used to the phenomenon in our daily lives, but this one was a real corker.

I was standing in front of my class, re-iterating the difficulties of fingerprint photography on mirrors, when I became aware of a voice in my mind saying 'Give me a call at home'.

It was Teresa.

I said to the class "Excuse me for a minute will you, I have to ring my wife and see what she wants" and I noticed a funny look cross the faces of a couple of my students.

Dialling home, I heard Teresa say, "Good, that didn't take long, I'm in trouble and need your help. I've got several women friends here at the moment, we're looking at the slides you took recently in Ireland, only the projector has stopped working - I think its the bulb, how do I change it?

I must admit even I was surprised to hear that, she seemed so sure I would pick up her thoughts and act on them.

"I told the women here you would ring shortly and help me sort out the problem, but they can't make out how we did it"

"I don't think it would help much if you did explain" I answered, and got down to telling her how to fix the problem.

Returning to my class, I was about to continue, when one of the lads said "How did you know your wife wanted you to ring her, was it pre-arranged or what?"

"No, it was just a case of telepathy, that's all" I replied and we dived back into the lesson.

For quite a few years now, Teresa and I had this 'thing' where we could communicate across a room, or at a distance without any problem, although she was the better 'sender' whilst I was the sensitive 'receiver'.

That month I sent off my application for a Churchill Fellowship for the second time, but shortly after we were into the first days of 1975, received the same conciliatory letter as before, - I had been unsuccessful this time, but please, don't give up, do try again. I most certainly would!

I had been at Hendon training college for just over two years now, and was really used to my regular life-style, when Nick C. the guv'nor decided that as the post was comfortably 'up and running', my duties there were at an end.

I was to be re-placed by someone else.

Nobby Clark, one of our new young photographers would be my replacement, and I would be free to return to my old duties at scenes of crime. Naturally, having got extremely used to a very comfortable and orderly way of life, I wasn't that keen to give up all I had achieved. Far from being the incarceration I'm sure Dave A. expected it to be, I had fashioned the posting into a widespread visual aids tool, which included regular flights in the force helicopter, and trips to the provinces.

Losing all that was a bit of a wrench.

They say bad things come in threes, and a few weeks after losing the Hendon posting, I got news that Nick C. our boss had dropped dead while visiting friends at the American embassy.

With Nick's controlling influence removed from the scene, and Dave A. now in charge, and awaiting up-grading to Superintendent, it was sure going to be a tough time ahead for some, no doubt about that!

Within a few days of my return to the fold, I received a telephone call from Ray Connor, erstwhile Det.Ch.Insp. Cannon-Row police station, currently teaching fraud techniques at Peel House - asking would I care to have lunch with him, as he had an interesting proposition to put to me.

Knowing Ray pretty well, I knew it would be something to do with ornithology, but didn't expect in the least, the unusual proposition he eventually came out with.

'Would I be prepared - with the obvious extensive knowledge I had of photography (his words not mine) to undertake the photography of birds' eggs for a prestigious publication, that would eventually appear in about seven volumes?'

Naturally, I said a cautious yes, I was interested, but there were many problems concerning both the photography and final printing of the egg shots, which were crucial to the success of the whole project.

"Yes, I appreciate that, but are you willing in principle to undertake the photography, while I organise the selection of the specimens to be photographed?"

"Yes" I said with some misgivings. I could see all sorts of land-mines looming in the future, snags I felt sure he hadn't considered or didn't even know about, but he wasn't taking no for an answer. As we got up from lunch to return to our respective offices, he added as an aside. “Oh, by the way, the eggs will all have to be reproduced same-size, without shadows or reflections, and be photographed wherever they are kept, private collections, museums whatever, ok?”

“You must be ruddy bonkers Ray, do you know what you’re asking? I replied. “I was only just beginning to sort out in my mind, the technical problems involved, assuming that all the eggs would be brought to a central studio set-up, but now you say that’s not the case, I’m worried”

Ray continued, “There’s no way people will allow me to take their eggs away from a collection for photography, they’re far too precious for that, you’ve got to do them in situ”.

With that bombshell ringing in my ears, we left Canon Row canteen, and on my way back to the Yard, I tried to think how on earth I could tackle this horrendous problem without making a fool of myself. A few days later Ray called in at the Yard, leaving me a box of twenty eggs of various species, which I had asked to experiment with.

Apparently some plates in the volumes would have four or six life-size eggs displayed on a page, whilst others would have over ninety!

“When do you think I can see a test result then?” said Ray as he was leaving, “And by the way, don’t forget, we don’t want any highlights or shadows associated with the eggs, just the plain eggs themselves”.

It was all I could do in the name of friendship, not to say something VERY, VERY rude.

During my dinner hour, I set a large sheet of plate glass across two wooden chairs in the studio, and spread a sheet of light brown art paper on the floor directly under the glass as a background.

Using one of the heavy-duty Gitzo tripods, I set a 5x4 MPP camera directly over the glass and focussed on an area marked out in grease pencil that represented the 10x8 page size of the volume.

All I had to do now was place the eggs on the glass, and we were away - or at least, that’s what I had worked out in theory.

Murphy operating through HIS laws though, had very different ideas.

For illumination I placed a 500watt lamp on either side at 45 degrees, and a separate lamp lower down to illuminate the background. It all seemed to be going ok. until I began placing the eggs on the glass, where, after a few seconds, the eggs started to roll and spin in the warmth of 1000watts of heat!

Ignoring for the moment that I couldn’t get the eggs to line up properly, I made a couple of test exposures based on meter readings, to see if at least that was correct, and also that I had sufficient depth of field to cover the largest of the eggs.

I hoped to god nobody wanted to put a Wren’s egg next to a Swan’s egg otherwise we were going to be in dead trouble!

I felt the only way this job could be done as a portable set-up, was to construct a tower from aluminium tubing, where the bottom level was the background, the middle level the subject plane, and the top surface the lens plane. Once I got a good result from the crude chairs and sheet-glass set up, I could measure the distances involved, and transfer them to the proposed aluminium tubing tower for further photography.

Struggling with the problem of the eggs moving about, I tried anchoring them in position with stamp hinges, but this didn't allow for fine movement of the eggs when lining them up.

Then I tried a spot of Cow gum on the underside of the egg, but this was apparently unacceptable to the purists, who feared for the safety of their delicate little specimens!

Finally I tried transparent plastic washers, bought from the local DIY, which supported the egg invisibly and securely from underneath, especially when it was being nudged gently in to position for photography.

The use of transparent washers worked perfectly well for the medium sized eggs, but fell down badly where the edges of the washer protruded beyond the object, such as the tiny Wren's egg. It also didn't work particularly well with the huge Golden Eagle or Black-backed Gull's eggs either, as the large eggs failed to sit satisfactorily on the small surface, and rolled off.

There had to be a better way of dealing with the problem than this!

One day I was working with Ernie in the studio, photographing some 'lifted fingerprints' on tape, which was now standard practice in the Met. and gaining acceptance in provincial forces as well as the USA. During a break in operations, I idly picked up a roll of the 'low-tack' sticky tape we used to lift the fingermarks, and as one does, unrolled a small section of the tape whilst talking, and smoothed it back onto the roll again.

Suddenly it struck me, it really was low tack, could this be the stuff I had been looking for to photograph the birds' eggs on? Would the tape allow me to place eggs on its sticky surface and roll them gently into position without smashing them, and how neutral would it photograph, using transmitted light?

The answers to all these questions after some tests was yes, it was perfect, all I had to do was ask the manufacturers if they produced it in rolls 12" wide, and get them to send me a sample.

The product came from Wales and was made by a company producing huge rolls of the stuff, designed to cover newly made thin sheet steel. The low tack 'skin' apparently stopped the metal from rusting, but was VERY expensive to buy.

Like the good people they were, the company sent me the 'throw away' end of a 12" roll, which was more than enough for my needs, and I would be able to use a fresh sheet for each egg plate in all the volumes of 'Birds of the Western Palearctic' we photographed. There's no doubt in my mind at all, that without that low-tack tape, we would have been struggling to find a fool-proof system to keep those darned eggs in place, for years!

During October, with things still pretty busy at scenes of crime, our section experienced a scenario that was to become quite familiar to us in the following years - the siege situation.

One Sunday in Knightsbridge, the Spaghetti House restaurant became the scene of some serious contention, when three black men committing a robbery, took eight whites hostage, holing up in the basement store-room and refusing to come out.

For a day or so police communicated with Davis, the leader of the gang, by megaphone through the closed door, while outside the lads from D.11 Firearms kept the basement

A.1 secure, so tight, not even a cockroach could get out.

SO.3 were asked to provide a photographer at the restaurant on continuous standby, to record whatever might transpire during the siege, and on the second day of the siege it was my turn to attend. As I entered the premises I was told to be absolutely quiet, as one of the lads from the sneaky-squad was trying to pick up conversation using a microphone and a recorder.

The mikes had been inserted into the ventilation system, and also down a hole quietly drilled by hand in the ceiling above the store room, with the intention of listening in on Davis and Co.

Whilst we were waiting for further hostage conversation to take place, D/I. H. in charge of the D.11 group said out loud in obvious frustration, "I wish we could see just what the bastards are up to in there, it's so frustrating only hearing what they're saying"

With the picture of the chap quietly drilling the floor to insert the miniature microphone still fresh in my mind, I said to D/I. H. "If you really want a chance to see what's going on in there, there is a way, but I don't know how good it will be"

"Well don't stand there like a big prat, if you really know a way, tell me!"

"I used to be a medical photographer before I joined the job, and during surgery the surgeon used a gadget called an endoscope, fitted to a TV monitor, so that he could see inside the body before cutting into it, if we had one of those inserted through the ceiling or wall, you could then see what's going on"

"Where can we get one of these gadgets then?"

"Well, I know the Senior photographer at the local hospital quite well, I could start with him, and see perhaps, where we go from there"

"In that case, I suggest you get your arse on it right away, and don't come back without it!"

It took me nearly an hour to explain to the hospital authorities what I wanted a portable endoscope for, but once they had spoken to police control outside the Spaghetti house, the device appeared like magic, and I was on my way back to the scene of the siege. Once the device had been demonstrated in the restaurant, the technical boys got cracking and fitted it up, so that D. 11. could see whatever the probe might reveal in the basement, via an upstairs monitor screen.

All they had to do now, was painstakingly drill through the ceiling again, without alerting Davis and his mates below as to what was going on, and quietly insert the endoscope.

I didn't return to the scene for two days, by which time the endoscope was working well, and Bill Harper one of our photographers, was recording on a 5x4 camera direct from the monitor screen, incidents of police interest taking place amongst the hostages in the cramped basement store-room below.

Unfortunately, halfway through the afternoon, Bill called out "Hey, the ruddy picture's disappeared" and we were without our covert eye. Something had gone seriously wrong.

The man on the mike said "I'm getting conversation which suggests Davis has discovered the probe, and he's stuffed the hole with a piece of wet paper. If you want further pictures, you'll have to drill a new hole somewhere else"

In the course of the next two days various holes were quietly drilled, and observation maintained until, like cat and mouse, they too were discovered, and put out of action by Davis and his mates.

Keith Maughan, one of our photographers on the cine team, had with D.11's permission, rigged up a 16mm Bolex camera at the foot of the stairs, pointing straight at the store-room door six yards away.

In the event of a shoot out, civil staff would be naturally kept well out of harm's way at the top of the basement stairs. Therefore the only sensible way to film what was happening by the store-room, was to fix a mirror on the newell post, and run an electric release up the stairs from there. Using the reflected image in the mirror, we could easily see and film what was happening in the basement without risk of being shot.

By Thursday night things were obviously coming to a head, and control felt they needed detailed photographs of the whole basement area, including the store-room door, before deciding on their next strategy.

I had the job of crawling carefully round the area with the Nikon and wide-angle, staying out of the line of fire directed at the store-room door, while behind me, my D.11 friends, fingers taking first pressure on their triggers, lay ready to obliterate the door in the event of anything moving whilst I worked.

"Tell me when you want to take the store-room door Alan" said D.I H. "But if I say DOWN! you do it instantly, the amount of lead passing over your head will be terminal!"

I took the necessary photographs and passed the film to a police motorcyclist, who took it to the section straight away for processing and printing. Back behind protective sandbags I breathed a sigh of relief, happy that a potentially hairy situation had gone down without incident - it was nice to have a reciprocated trust with the D.11 lads.

It was now approaching 0400 hrs Friday morning, and all the signs were, that something was about to break.

"They are going to release the hostages" someone said, and I asked permission to crouch at the head of the stairs, so I could look in the mirror and trigger the cine camera as they started to come out.

"Hands on your heads and walk straight towards me" I heard DI.H shout as the first hostages appeared, and I looked down the stairs towards the mirror to see what I was about to film.

The mirror wasn't there!

Knowing I only had a hundred foot roll of film in the Bolex, which would last a couple of minutes on continuous run, I held fire, and let the hostages come up the stairs to safety.

"Ok. the rest of you, throw out your guns NOW, and come out!"

I pressed the electric release, and prayed that whatever was going to happen, would happen quickly, so that the damned film didn't run out before the end. I couldn't see a ruddy thing!

I heard the clatter of what I thought was a firearm hitting the tiled floor, and H's voice commanding immediate compliance with his instructions.

"That's two of 'em" I heard someone say, then there was a loud bang as a gun went off.

The two prisoners were bundled roughly past me up the stairs and cuffed into immobility, while D.11 officers rushed the store-room door. It appeared that Davis had shot himself - fortunately not seriously, perhaps intending to avoid live capture, and was taken away in an ambulance. I retrieved the Bolex cine camera, and asked out loud if anyone knew what the hell had happened to our mirror.

"Yeah, sorry about that" said one. "I needed to be able to look round the corner at one point, so I took it off the post and tied it to a stick, here it is, thanks a lot"

There had always been political demonstrations going on in town over the years, and it had long been job policy for us to cover these 'demos' without 'showing out', and take photographs of characters who either committed offences against the public order act, or were thought to be implicated in orchestrating any subsequent disorder.

Dressed as no-one in particular, we would tag along with the demo, picking off likely faces in the event of things going pear-shaped later on. It was amusing after a while to photograph the same old 'rent a mob' faces appearing, this time representing some contemporary body or other, shouting objections and waving banners, while their side's photographer photographed us for their records. We would smile and acknowledge their efforts as they 'clocked' us, while we in turn recorded them - it all seemed uncommonly well behaved at times!

Sometimes of course it all went badly wrong, and you had to watch your back, plus that of your colleagues, to make sure you weren't 'taken out' by hooligans assuming you were a police photographer recording their anti-social behaviour!

Although we would probably 'cough' to being police photographers when challenged by someone in an official capacity, it was strictly taboo to infer that we were press, TV, or any other media agency, just to pacify angry demonstrators. It was far better to back off, and slip back again later if you could.

It was now a couple of weeks before Christmas, and jobs were beginning to get grotty again. There were far too many nasty little villains out there doing wicked things to earn a few bob for the festive season, and I needed something to give me a lift. When I arrived home Teresa greeted me with a smile as usual, and said "There's a letter for you from the Churchill Trust people, I hope it's not another - not today thank you"

Yes, I thought, that's all I need to complete my day, and ripped open the envelope.

'Dear Mr. Parker, would you please make arrangements to attend this office regarding your recent application for a Churchill Fellowship visit to Iran. You will be meeting members of the Council of the trust ....' I didn't read any further at that point, I just shouted 'whoopee' and gave Teresa the good news - I hadn't been turned down flat this time, but I did have to face the top trust brass in a searching interview regarding my plans.

How well would I cope with that?

Christmas came and went in its usual frenetic way, a mad rush to get seemingly important things done, while the whole spirit and reason for the occasion, seemed to get lost somewhere in transit.

In February 1975 I attended Queen's Gate Terrace, London, as guest of Lord O'Neill of the Marne, chairman of the Trust Council, and took my place nervously on a single high-backed chair, ominously placed at the point of focus for seven or eight eminent members of Council.

I was pleased to see the chairman of this particular interview was none other than Sir Peter Scott, artist and naturalist par excellence, and felt that here at least, was someone I might have some rapport with.

Sir Peter opened the interview in a gentle, friendly fashion, explaining that all the board wished to hear, were the aims of my proposed fellowship, how it could benefit both Britain and the country I wished to visit, and exactly how I had prepared for it, both logistically, and mentally.

I gave my carefully rehearsed spiel covering the importance of wetland conservation to the world's wildfowl population, and the effects of mis-management or ignorance, on the chain of wetland reserves stretching from Iran across Europe to the UK, and noted that Sir Peter smiled and nodded in apparent agreement. I had obviously scored a small hit there.

One by one, each of the Council members put their searching questions and waited patiently for my answers, which I found quite nerve wracking. The questions weren't necessarily linked to the project as such, but covered aspects of local politics, problems of language, and how the final report was to be written up and distributed to interested parties etc; they really gave me the works.

One prominent member who had given me a fair going over earlier said. "I see from your CV you are a bit of an artist, can you draw birds?"

"Yes sir, I can, I have drawn them for many years now, but don't find them easy at all, I'm certainly not in the same class as Sir Peter here"

He persisted. "Yes, yes, but are you any good at it, have you managed to sell any?" I felt he was trying to un-nerve me a bit, but before I could think of an answer, Sir Peter cut in.

"Tell me Mr. Parker, do you paint in oils, or water colour?"

"Water colour only sir, I haven't mastered the technique of using oils yet"

"And what happens if you make a bad mistake working in watercolours then?" said Sir Peter.

"I'm afraid it's into the waste-bin, and start again"

"Ah well," said Sir Peter, "If I make a mistake in oils, I can just wipe it off, or correct it there and then, and carry on, which I feel makes you a better artist than me in that respect, don't you agree?"

I just smiled in relief, and said nothing. What a lovely man!

"That's all then, thank you for attending this interview, you will be informed of our decision in due course. Thank you again, and good morning" and with that I was outside.

For better or worse it was done. The die was cast.

# Chapter Thirteen

Back home, I went through the whole scenario again with Teresa, trying to assess whether or not I had given the right answers, or had hopelessly fudged it, and the more I thought about it, the less sure I was of success. One thing bothered me though, if by some chance I was successful, I wouldn't be informed before mid-March, and yet my homework had shown we ought to be in Iran at the END of March if observations were to be undertaken on the wetlands wildfowl, before they migrated. How could I get over that hurdle?

I spent a couple of dinner-hours buried in the basement of a map publishers near the Yard, looking through sheets of 1:100000 ordnance survey maps of Iran - it was amazing how much of the place was empty desert, and ominously marked 'unsurveyed'.

It also brought home to me the fact that Iran was roughly four times the size of France, and was a damn' big place to go wandering around in, confined to a single vehicle!

In early March I received a letter bearing the logo of the Churchill Trust, and with shaking hands tore it open.

'Dear Mr. Parker, it gives me great pleasure to inform you that you have been successful in your fellowship application to travel to .....' I didn't read the rest just then, I just sat pretty stunned while Teresa said "Well done, that's the first bit under your belt, now the REAL work starts"

What wheels of fate had I just set in motion with my successful application? Only time would tell.

I spoke to Major-General Lascelles the Director General about taking up my fellowship, pointing out that the main thrust of the trip was to count and identify the wildfowl present on various wetlands, which was best accomplished at the end of March, or the beginning of April at the latest. I couldn't possibly be ready in time this year, could I hold it over until 1976?

His reply was that as long as the fellowship was taken up within a year, he couldn't see any problems, and I should go ahead and plan my trip on that basis. I reckoned it would take at least six months to get everything ready, plus finding a suitable vehicle, I also had the unenviable task of informing my employers that I would require three-months off to go bird-watching. Bird watching?

How the hell would Dave A. re-act to that?

Alan Mc. was naturally quite excited at my success, and congratulated me sincerely, but some of my colleagues, not understanding the prestige that a fellowship brings both to the recipient and his workplace, thought the whole thing a whacky idea just to get off work!

The trust announced that I had been awarded the princely sum of £1,360, based on my estimated costs, and suggested I write to as many businesses as possible, seeking sponsorship for my project. It was a good job I had a new portable typewriter, as I was going to be very busy writing begging letters for some time to come!

Over the next few weeks I managed to post over a hundred letters and CV's to various sponsors, each accompanied by a two-colour hand-out, outlining the aims, and route of the expedition. I also made innumerable phone calls to various suppliers, who might be able to help with food supplies for our trip. In the main, replies were quite supportive, and sometimes generously helpful, while others, hit by tough economies of the times, said they were no longer able to donate in any way, but wished me well.

A lady friend of Teresa's, who worked in the local Nat. West. bank, suggested I write to their head office for a donation, saying they had a scheme to help deserving causes like mine, and to my surprise, they came up trumps. Their letter said that I could at my convenience, draw a cheque for £200 from my local branch at Collier-Row, provided I would be willing to give a talk to interested senior staff on my return. As I had been giving talks on birds illustrated with my own slides for a couple of years now, that was no problem to me at all. They were on!

The question as to who would accompany me on the trip had been hovering in the background for some time, in fact, ever since I received the letter at Christmas asking me to attend for interview. Peter had said he definitely wanted to come, and would even take un-paid leave if necessary. I knew he wasn't an experienced ornithologist, but could take an accurate description of a species he didn't know if necessary, so that was something.

He was also a police traffic driver, and therefore fully competent in car maintenance, and well able to take his share of the driving duties involved, so we were ok. there too. If he came, all I would need was someone who was initially a very good all-round mechanic, then a naturalist, cook, gofer, or whatever, to fit in with what I wanted to achieve on the trip of a lifetime. Who was he?

I planned to take the Hovercraft from Ramsgate to Calais, drive through Belgium to Germany and Austria, into Slovenia, Croatia and Yugoslavia, through Bulgaria and Turkey into Iran. By the time we reached the capital Teheran, we should have covered 3,765 miles and the vehicle would already be in need of a service!

Although we were quite busy at work, grotty jobs were tempered by the thought of the exciting trip ahead, and it was surprising how many people I met during the course of my work, contributed in some way or other to the progress I was making.

The head of the Cadet training school at Hendon, immediately offered the use of any of their camping gear I might need, and another chap in security, introduced me to Lt/Col, Blashford-Snell, known fondly as 'Blashers', of the Engineers Regt, and the Scientific Exploration Society.

Blashers was to become a good friend and mentor in the difficult field of preparing an expedition and vehicle to go off into the backend of nowhere and survive.

Regarding a vehicle, I asked Peter if in his travels round the capital, he would keep his eyes open for something suitable, and I would do the same, but it would have to be in good nick to stand up to the 12,000 miles of hard going we expected to give it.

All sorts of people were approached to become sponsors, with the proviso that their product would without fail, be mentioned in any follow-up literature, and their company logo be displayed prominently on our expedition vehicle. As the days went by, the corner of our lounge at home began to look like a boot sale, as the sponsor's products came rolling in.

Bringing me back to earth, Ray rang to say he had the egg photography tower under construction, and it would be finished in a few days. Had I got the lights ready for it, so that we could go down to Gloucester and start work on an egg collection belonging to a Major O'Neill in a weeks' time?

Earlier I had made up two sets of 500watt lamps in aluminium reflectors, one pair to illuminate the eggs, the other two for the background. Now I asked Ray for the tower, or egg-rig as I called it, so I could do some final lighting tests before jumping into full scale photography.

I must admit I wasn't happy about my ability to produce the high standard of photography required, especially when taking the camera to the eggs, it was definitely the wrong approach, but there was nothing I could do about that!

We had been invited to stay at O'Neill's place overnight Friday, so we could get cracking first thing Saturday morning, and hopefully finish by tea, it was going to be a real baptism by fire this one!

After breakfast, the old boy started sorting through his collection with Ray, who, knowing which specimens he wanted beforehand, soon had twenty or so eggs ready to place on the glass subject platform. There is no doubt, that without the low-tack sheets the job would have been horrendous, as it was, it took ray an hour to line up the eggs perfectly, whilst I checked him on the 5x4 camera's grid-etched glass screen. What I had failed to appreciate in deciding to use 500watt tungsten lighting as opposed to flash - which I didn't have anyway, was the heat generated by 2000watts of lighting in a relatively small room.

After an hour of fiddling and twiddling to get the specimens lined up, the room temperature on the old chaps' thermometer was reading 27C. and he began muttering something about his specimens being adversely affected by the heat!

We managed to get several pages of eggs photographed before taking a break, and Ray, who was as red as a beetroot and sweating profusely, certainly needed it, he was getting a bit edgy.

There had to be a better way of working than this!

A few days later, Peter rang me at work full of excitement - he had found the vehicle he felt was just the job for us, a one-owner 2800cc petrol LWB Landrover, with just 12000 miles on the clock, and selling for £720!

The previous owners Barnardo's Homes, had been using it to pull a large promotional trailer around the countryside, and had upped the braking spec. to hydraulically assisted. It was apparently a real beaut. but how on earth was I going to find £700 cash needed to buy it? The cash couldn't come out of the grant, there just wasn't enough, I had trimmed everything to the bone as it was.

In desperation I rang the Churchill trust office who must have had experience of these problems before, and asked to speak to the chairman, Lord O'Neill of the Maine, acquainting him with my problem.

"I don't think that will be an insurmountable problem" he said, completely undeterred by my request. "I'll arrange for you to have a draught for that amount, on the understanding that on your return, you either sell the vehicle and repay the trust half the advanced figure, or keep the vehicle, and repay the trust yourself, it's entirely up to you"

I must admit I had never received such magnanimity, coupled with a pleasant matter of factness ever before, and was quite taken aback.

I had fully expected horrible complications, but there were none.

I had to think about the photography I wanted to do, and the equipment I could muster for it - I had an oldish Pentax S.1A, and an SVS, one fitted with the standard Pentax Takumar lens, the other with a superb 200mm Optomax, very good for general bird work. I also had a 400mm F.4 lens, which could at a pinch be coupled to a X2 converter, but I had never found the loss of definition converters entailed, really acceptable.

For general photography I needed a good 6X6 format camera, and with the cash provided by Natwest, I decided to buy the new Kowa 66. complete with standard and 200mm lenses. I would dearly have liked the 50mm wide-angle lens too, but that was out of the budgetary question, I couldn't have everything!

In the meantime, Peter had taken the Landrover into the police Trafpol garage at Leyton, where it sat while we decided what modifications it would require for the trip. It had to be capable of carrying three months dried foodstuffs in the back, plus all our equipment, and provide sufficient space for the third person to sleep, while the other two were navigating and driving.

It would be a tight squeeze fitting everything in.

At Leyton police garage, the senior manager Keith, a friend of Peter's was all ears when he heard about the project, and said straight away he'd come along given half a chance. He obviously had the necessary mechanical knowledge I required, and had been away camping on many occasions, and alhough he wasn't a naturalist, that might not matter too much under the circumstances.

One evening just as I was leaving the Yard, I bumped into 'blashers' who asked me how things were going with my Churchill Trust application. When he heard the trip to Iran was well under way, and I'd bought a Landrover vehicle, he patted my shoulder and said. "Come and see me at the Guards' depot in Chelsea next week, I've got a couple of items there you will definitely need for your expedition vehicle, you won't get by without them"

I duly presented myself at the depot in my little green police Mini, and found the indomitable blashers buried in some store or other on the far side of the square.

"Ah, come in young Alan, I won't be a minute here, then we can go and get the goodies I've put aside for you, I presume you've got transport?

At a cracking pace, the short, but sturdy blashers whizzed through a couple of passage-ways before stopping at a small store.

"They're in here" he said, and threw open the door to reveal two sets of vehicle leaf-springs, and a large petrol tank.

"You'll find these invaluable out there in the desert, they're heavy duty rear springs, and will see you through thick and thin, the extra fuel tank might just save your bacon too"

Blashers commandeered a couple of muscular young chaps to bring the springs to where I had left the mini, while he and I did a bow-legged walk carrying the tank between us.

"God, is that all you've got?" said blashers eyeing my Mini with apparent disdain, "Oh well if that's it, that's it, put 'em in lads" and the massive springs clumped alongside my photographic gear, followed by the large fuel tank, virtually driving the mini to its knees.

"Before you go, I've managed to get you a few compo rations in sealed containers, they contain enough to keep you going for a while in the event you get lost or something, they could be very useful".

It was a good thing there were no Trafpol lads about as I made my way slowly back to the Yard, with the Mini's wheels all but disappearing into the wheel arches under the crushing load. As I bumped cautiously into the entrance, I said a few prayers and hoped the suspension could take it, a nasty collapse here would be most embarrassing!

The next day I was able to deliver the springs and tank to Leyton garage, and have a close look at the 'customising' being done on the Landrover by Keith and Peter - it was beginning to look rather good.

During the following weeks, four extra spotlights were added to the front, a second spare wheel bolted on the bonnet to compliment the one on the rear door, air horns fitted which produced ear-crushing decibels, and side windows put in. A padded couch was built across the vehicle, and partitioned from the rear compartment, giving the third man somewhere to sleep. Finally, the extra petrol tank and springs were bolted on, until the original vehicle was hardly recognisable.

While all this was going on, Teresa had been experiencing quite severe bouts of what the doctor described as 'indigestion' and suggested she start a fat-free diet, to see if that would help, but apart from milk and cheese, she had always eaten a normal diet, and it didn't seem to be the right answer to me.

Christmas came and went with its usual alacrity, and we were well into January when Murphy's bombshell hit us right on the button. Keith, our mechanic and helper par excellence, announced he wouldn't be coming on the trip after all. His wife, realising that things were rapidly coming to a head, put the screws on - no buzzing off to Iran for three months holiday and leaving her behind, he had to stay at home!

I felt so sorry for him, all his expectations, and conscientious work down the drain, but the position was just as serious for me, what could I do at such a late date?

Teresa had a pretty good solution to the problem, "Why don't you advertise for someone with the skills you require, I'm sure there's lots of people out there only too willing to come on a trip like this. All you have to do is find the right method, in fact I listen to Pete Murray's 'Open House' most days, he's just the sort of chap you should approach with this particular problem"

Out came the old typewriter, and a resume of the expeditions' aims and problems were listed for Pete Murray's perusal.

"Yes, I think that will do fine" said Teresa, "I'll just sign it as though it's from me, and you can post it straight away - we haven't a moment to lose".

I was begining to feel a bit embarrassed at work, due to the time and telephone calls the project was taking up, and when the invitation came from Pete Murray to be interviewed on the BBC. concerning the trip, I thought I had better clear it with Dave

A. the boss, as anything emanating from the Yard without specific authority, was strictly verboten!

"Just remember" he said "You can talk on bird matters or anything else you like till the cows come home, but you can't even begin discussing what you do here, ok?" I agreed.

The day of the broadcast arrived, and after presenting myself at BBC. reception, I was whisked to an upstairs room, where Pete Murray sat studying some papers at a large table.

"Come in, come in do, sit yourself down while I go through this stuff, we've got plenty of time"

I looked at the clock on the wall, which showed ten-to-ten, I knew his programme went out at ten o'clock, which didn't seem a lot of time to me. When was he going to go over the questions he intended to ask, and give me a chance to formulate some answers?

He continued to go through his papers, sitting on the other side of a large microphone suspended over the middle of the table.

"Two minutes Mr. Murray" said a ladys' voice from somewhere out of sight.

"Ok. love we're just about ready to go - you're ok. and comfortable aren't you Mr. Parker? just relax and I'll lead you into the questions, there's nothing to it, Ok. here we go"

The opening music started to play, and in a daze, as though from a long way off, I heard Pete Murray go through his opening spiel, and suddenly I heard him say "And this morning we have with us Mr. Alan Parker, a Photographer from New Scotland Yard, who is leading an unusual expedition to Iran, tell us about it Alan"

I heard myself talk about the aims of the expedition, and the importance to society that good management of Wetland resources meant, and began to feel a little more at ease as things went on. I was still pretty annoyed though, that he hadn't quickly run through his questions, to give me an idea what was coming next.

"Tell me Alan, in your job as Photographer at the Yard, there must have been a few instances where something really funny happened, can you tell us about them?

I felt an ice-cold lump form in the middle of my forehead - what the hell was he on about, funny things? Didn't he realise our job was deadly serious, and more often than not you were seeing the shitty side of life, and sometimes near to tears?

I began to formulate an answer, and was finding it difficult by the second, when he quickly saw I had problems.

"OK. we'll take a break there, and after this piece of music we'll come back to Alan and his expedition to Iran..."

Over a dead microphone I said "I'm sorry, I really can't think of anything that's funny in my job, only the sort of humour that gets us through a revolting situation - which is a bit off really, and unfit for general consumption, it acts mainly as an escape mechanism"

He gave me an odd look, and said "Never mind, we've got plenty to talk about, especially the loss of an important member of your group at such a late stage, we'll concentrate on that"

**Plate 1: Female Rook on nest, Hainault Lodge Essex.**

**Plate 2: German submarine escape apparatus, Kabrit, Egypt.**

**Plate 3: Original Bromide-paper fingerprint camera, Scotland Yard.**

**Plate 4: Catching and ringing gulls, St.James' Park, London.**

**Plate 5: Sand Martin at underground nest, Essex 1960.**

**Plate 6: Adult Heron and young, Walthamstow Essex.**

Plate 7: Self at Spur wing nest and hide, Egypt.

Plate 8: Spur wing Plover at nest and eggs, Egypt.

**Plate 9: Young black, pick-pocketing, Notting Hill carnival 1976.**

**Plate 10: Early police helicopter and traffic-flow camera.**

**Plate 11: Tinker making pots and pans, Inishbofin, Ireland.**

**Plate 12: Mick Mannion Austie Coyne & Pat Burke, Inishark.**

Plate 13: Going out on a raid, leaving Helen in van, Hackney.

Plate 14: Male Kestrel and chick, 16th Floor, Avondale Square, London.

Plate 15: Barn Owl with mouse, Collier Row, Romford.

**Plate 16: Tomb of Cyrus the Great, Pasargardae, Iran.**

**Plate 17: Detail of frieze, Persepolis, showing wheel and tyre.**

**Plate 18: Pushing the Landrover through to Sharanjan village, Iran.**

**Plate 19: Presentation of Churchill Fellowship medal by Queen Mother.**

**Plate 20: Riot photography training, using petrol bombs. Me on the right!**

**Plate 21: Black with weapon, facing S03 photographer, Tottenham riot.**

Plate 22: SAS assault group on Iranian embassy roof.

Plate 23: SAS member caught up in ropes, Iranian siege.

Plate 24: Salim, leader of terrorists, killed by SAS during siege.

Plate 25: Lord Snowdon's visit to S03 crime-video section.

Plate 26: Self, video filming murder scene, Epping Forest Essex.

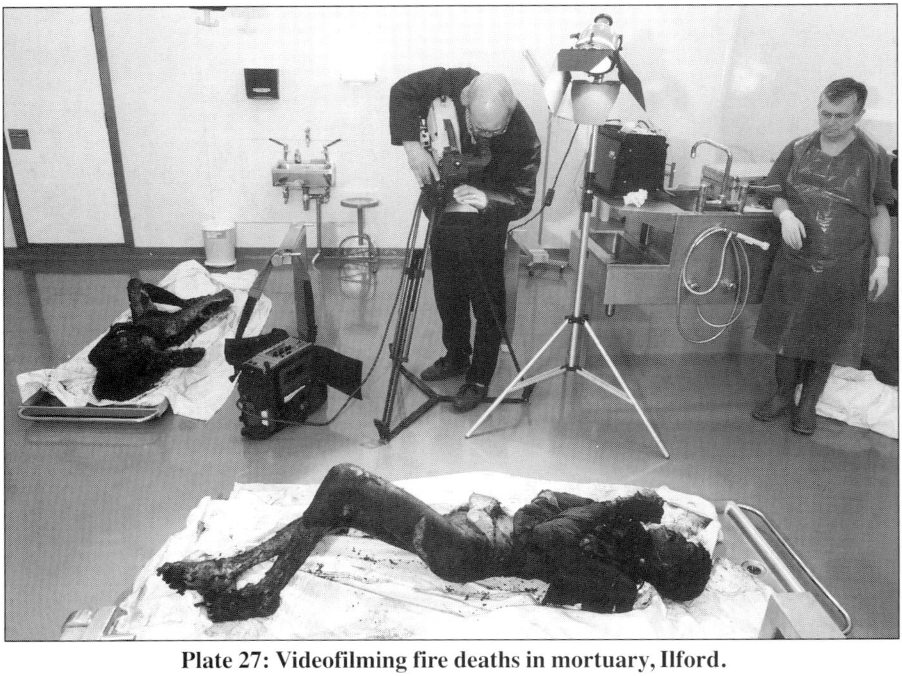

Plate 27: Videofilming fire deaths in mortuary, Ilford.

Plate 28: Videofilming scene of Clapham train crash.

Plate 29: Aerial view of Purley train crash.

**Plate 30: Videofilming scene of Purley train crash.**

**Plate 31: 'Playing the fool' - arson scene at my old college.**

The rest of the interview went quite well, and with a sigh of relief I heard him say "So if you have any ideas which can help Alan out at this stage, I'm sure he'll be pleased to hear from you" and immediately the next break arrived, complete with soporific music.

"There, that wasn't so bad was it? I think you did extremely well, thank you very much for coming in" and he stood up, shook hands, and motioned to a young lady, who took me smoothly towards the exit. Boy, was I glad to get out of that place!

I suppose it was the best part of an hour before I walked into the section, going over in my mind the answers I'd given to Pete Murray, the better answers coming more easily to mind, now that the pressure was off.

"You're a ruddy nice bloke you are, the chaos you've caused here during the last half hour! Do you think we've got nothing better to do than answer the damn' phone for you? Here - there's a list of sixty odd people who want to speak to you right away about your trip!" and with that Pete Skitt shoved a sheaf of papers into my hands, and disappeared. What the hell did he mean?

I soon found out!

As I had explained on the air, Keith our mechanic had to drop out for personal reasons at virtually the last minute, leaving me with the difficult job of finding a replacement, and dozens and dozens of people listening to the programme had rung Scotland Yard straight away, offering to go along in his place!

The very last thing I had wanted - undue hassle with the boss regarding the trip, had materialised with a vengeance, and our three-phone duty office was inundated with calls by the dozen!

"We've just had a call from the Met. Police Laboratory at Lambeth" said John, who was now manning the phones in the duty office. "They've had over a hundred calls regarding your trip, they're going barmy, and want to know what the hell it's all about"

It was one of those times when you wish the ground would open and swallow you up there and then, but I just had to apologise to those who had taken the names and addresses of the callers, and buy tea and cakes all round!

It took me nearly a week using both post and phone to sort the serious applicants from the plain ridiculous, and I was eventually left with twenty possible names. It wasn't going to be easy to select one successful applicant from this lot.

There were, as one might expect, hardly any applicants with natural history experience, and only a few with the mechanical know-how sufficient to get us out of trouble in the desert - would I have to compromise somewhere? I managed to see most of the hopefuls in town, leaving three or four to contact me when they were free, but I didn't see anyone who clicked immediately.

Was I being too critical in my search?

One of the last applicants was Dick Smith, a chap who had just left the Hampshire Police after ten years service, and was looking for a challenge before deciding what to do next. He had worked on Landrovers all his service, was a frequent outdoor camper to various places such as the Brecon Beacons with his wife and kids, and seemed a very good prospect indeed. When I rang him to arrange a meet, he volunteered to come to see me instead. He felt we could discuss things better that way.

The huge pile of contributions from sponsors was getting a bit out of hand in the dining room, and resembled a chaotic church bring and buy sale. We had the new soft leather trekking boots from Clarke's, zip-up padded driving jackets, and all our vehicle lubricants from Duckhams, medical supplies and first aid kits from Boots, plus water-purifying pump and filters, fluorescent 'stick' lights that clipped to battery terminals for emergency lighting, sleeping bags and inflatable mattresses, cutlery and plates, and a huge pile of dried foods and camping gear. The list seemed endless, but it was all essential stuff.

John Prior a neighbour, turned up trumps, letting me have three of his camping 'portaloos' to use as hides for bird photography, and what was to prove the most useful contribution of all, a double petrol-burner stove which had accompanied his sons on their driving trip to Lake Chad in Africa.

The cadet school at Hendon had generously provided me with a four-man tent, complete with welded-in floor, which was easily erected on an aluminium 'A' frame, and held secure by four sensible guy ropes and a fly-cover. We could certainly camp in comfort in that.

Dick Smith and his wife arrived on Sunday, and we had a long talk about the things I hoped to achieve on the trip, plus what might go wrong with our Landrover whilst in the wilds. He seemed very much at ease, and was obviously an extremely practical chap, I liked him straight away. "I see you've got the tent up in your garden, do you mind if I have a look, I'd like to see the sort of gear you'll be taking.

It wasn't a very nice day, cold and damp - you could see your breath on the still air, but the bright yellow tent offered a promise of something better to come.

"Yep, she's pretty good, very reliable design, and a doddle to put up, you won't have any trouble with that I can tell you"

As we turned to go in, and I looked across at Teresa, who unobserved by the Smiths, smiled, and put her thumb up. I tended to agree with her, he was definitely the right chap for us.

"You know of course you'll be expected to provide £100 cash of your own for personal spending if you're selected, the rest of the cost is down to me"

"No trouble at all, I just want the chance to come along and get stuck in, that's all"

When they had gone, Teresa and I both agreed that he seemed eminently suitable, and unless someone else could top his undoubted ability and enthusiasm, he was our man.

# Chapter Fourteen

On the matter of visas, I deliberately left the Iranian embassy until last - I felt that if I cleared all the other obstacles out of the way first, I would feel happier on the home straight with the end goal in sight.

As embassies go it was a vast improvement on many, but it still took two-hours for the line of applicants to be slowly devoured by a grey haired, iron faced woman, who certainly wouldn't have looked out of place in the Kremlin.

"I see you want to visit Iran by driving there in your own car, in that case you will need to fill in this, this and this, before I can issue a visa, read the papers carefully as you will have to leave a bond with us equal to three times the vehicle's value"

"Why is that?" I asked quite shocked.

"In case you are short of money, and want to sell the car. We don't want people making a lot of money by selling their cars, just because they are expensive to buy in Iran"

"What happens if we have an accident or break down and are unable to bring the vehicle out with us?" I asked.

"That would be your problem, you would have to see what you could arrange with the local authorities or police at the time" I felt she was getting a bit ratty with my questions, and was already looking round me, to speak to the person behind.

"One more question please, you say I have to leave a bond for three-times the value of my vehicle, how do I find out what the value is?"

With a face like Medusa, she grabbed a book from a drawer in the desk, and without looking up started to open the pages.

"What make and year is your car?"

"It's a 1972 long wheel-base Landrover" I replied.

"That's valued at £7000 here" she said looking up with a completely expressionless face.

"But I've only just paid seven-hundred pounds for it a little while ago, which is the accepted second-hand market price here"

"That may very well be so, but if you want to take it into Iran, you'll have to lodge a bond with us for three-times our valuation, thank you - next"

I reeled away from the queue, still clutching my fistful of un-processed papers, wondering how I could have got this far, only to be dashed by bureaucracy! How on earth could I get round this one?

The immediate answer of course was to go back again to the source, where they MUST have met this sort of situation before - the Churchill Trust.

"What you must do" I was told "Is to approach your Bank and ask what the insurance premium would be to guarantee a bond of that figure. You can then approach the embassy with that guarantee, which they will almost certainly accept"

I breathed a huge sigh of relief that there appeared to be some way round this impasse, and made an appointment to see my bank manager the next day.

"As you are a house owner, and in a responsible job, I think we can accommodate you in this, and the fee will be quite reasonable too, only £125 for three months"

Armed with the requisite bond guarantee, I again took my place in the Iranian embassy queue, and awaited events.

"I came here the other day, and enquired about a visa, and the question of taking my vehicle into Iran. You quoted me a figure of £21000, for which I have a bank's bond guarantee, is that ok?"

"I remember you" she said. "When exactly are you going, and what date will you be leaving Iran?"

"Well, we're leaving the UK on March 20th, and expect to be in Teheran about a week later, probably the 27th, and we are booked on the return ferry to the UK on June 10th, so I suppose we'll leave about the 1st or 2nd of June"

"In that case you won't need this " she said pushing the bank bond back across the table, "If you're in the country for less than three months, the bond isn't necessary" I could have fallen through the floor! Why on earth hadn't she made that point clear at the beginning, and saved me a lot of trouble and headache?

With cold efficiency she dealt with the visas, accepted the fee, and I was done, free to travel to Iran and back without let or hindrance, or so I fervently hoped!

There was however one major hurdle still to cross, namely, the transportation of both Peter's and my photographic equipment through the various borders and customs, without attracting some tax or other, or heaven forbid, total confiscation!

Through one of the lads in special branch I heard that if I listed every piece of equipment we were taking, and had it certified by my head of department, the Home Office would stamp it as bona-fide, keep a copy for themselves in the event of a dispute. We should then be able to travel through the various customs posts without any problem.

I duly listed every bit of kit we had, make, type and serial number, and presented myself to our head of department Dave A. requesting that he might endorse it for me.

"What exactly do you want me to do with this list then?"

I explained that as my head of department, I wished him to sign the list as being my personal property, so I could take it to the Home Office for official endorsement. It was a guarantee that I was the true owner of the equipment, and intended to bring it all back when I returned from the trip, thus avoiding duty.

His face suddenly went white with anger, and he stood up, waving his arms and shouting loudly "How do I know this list of equipment exists, I haven't seen any of this stuff, how do I know you've even got a mortgage (?) I'm not putting my name to this list, no way!" and he thrust the list back into my hands, and sat down.

Shocked at this un-expected reaction to my request, I left his office in a daze, coming face to face with Alan McLean in the corridor.

"Well how did you get on then, get it signed ok?" he grinned.

When I told him what had happened he said "Oh no! give it to me, I'll have a word with DI.Paddy O'Neill downstairs in fingerprints, as Gerry Lambourne's number two, he should be able to come up with some sensible solution to this nonsense"

Just before three o'clock that afternoon I got a call to go and see Gerry Lambourne, Commander in charge of both SO.3 fingerprints and photographic, and to bring my list with me. I knocked and went in, to see the boss sitting behind his desk, pen poised over a mountain of correspondence.

"What seems to be the trouble Alan, I hear you're having problems getting some sort of list authorised, what is it all about?"

I explained what was required by the Home Office in this instance, and showed him the list of equipment we intended to take to Iran.

"Are you sure without any shadow of doubt, this list is correct, because if my signature is on it at the Home Office, I want it perfect"

"It's absolutely correct Sir, you have my word on it, I'm only embarrassed that I have had to come to you to get it done, I thought my own head of department could have dealt with it quite adequately"

In an expression of honest opinion, not often experienced between a senior Police officer and a civilian, he replied, "I know just what some of you chaps have to put up with from THAT man, I've experienced it myself on more than one occasion. If you'll give me the list I'll sign it for you right away"

Despite his undoubted disappointment at not being able to come on the trip, Keith continued to work with Peter on the Landrover, eventually producing a really professional job. It had a full-length roof-rack which took five jerri-cans across the front, four with petrol, and one of Duckham's oil, with enough room left to stack all our bulky stuff such as tent, hides, tripods, cooking utensils and petrol cooker, plus a neat ladder up the back for easy access.

Behind the two front seats Keith had finished off the full-width sleeping compartment, which allowed the third man to sleep in the fashion of a space traveller, knees slightly drawn up and his back at a slight incline. For protection against bulky gear in the back crashing forward in the event of a collision, a steel mesh barrier had been welded across the interior.

During the last week of re-furbishing, Peter had made up bull-bars from 1-1/2" water pipe, which was meant to give protection to the lamps, radiator, and 5 gallon water containers mounted between the wings. As a finishing touch, he then added a diamond mesh grill over the main lights, to give protection from flying stones, but this addition was later to give us un-expected problems when crossing Yugoslavia during some very heavy snowstorms.

Over the years I had given several talks to the Woodford Green branch of the RSPB, and I was booked to appear at the end of January, for an illustrated talk on woodland birds. It all went down ok. and at the end of it, the group leader announced that I was off quite soon to Iran with Peter, one of their members, on an Ornithological expedition, and hoped I might have something of interest to show them on my return.

I replied it was a Churchill Trust sponsored trip, and outlined briefly what we intended to do there, and the meeting broke up. In the foyer of the venue, various people congratulated me on the talk and slides, and one or two mentioned the envy they felt, knowing I should be going on such a marvellous trip abroad.

Peter in the meantime, had gone to the other side of the foyer near the exit, and was talking to a group of about six people, and as I said goodbye to my lot,I wandered over to join Teresa, who was standing there, listening whilst Peter spoke to his friends.

Suddenly I heard Teresa say "But it's not YOUR expedition, it's Alan's, and he is taking you along, not the other way round!" and I wondered what the hell had caused such an outburst.

It was totally out of character for Teresa to react like that, it just wasn't her.

The bemused, and obviously embarrassed people moved away from the scene, to reveal a red-faced Peter nervously facing a very up-tight Teresa.

"I think you ought to have serious talk with your friend Peter here" she said. "From what I just heard, the Iranian trip is mainly due his efforts, you only played a minor role in organising the trip."

I thought, Oh god, that's all I need at this stage of the proceedings, and grabbed Teresa's arm, saying to Peter as I brushed past "I'll speak to you, later"

On our way home Teresa said "I think you're going to have trouble with that chap, I don't want to put the damper on things, but you wait and see" and I felt instinctively she might be right.

There was no way I could alter the arrangements now though, it was far too late for that, I'd have to soldier on, and play it by ear. What a lovely way to start an expedition!

With the last of the applicants seen, there was no doubt in my mind that Dick Smith, the Hants policeman, was the chap for the job, and I telephoned him to say so. It was obvious by his voice he was over the moon, and he eventually told me it really was a miracle that he had applied at all.

Apparently he had been taking a friend to hospital at the time of the Pete Murray show, and had only heard part of the broadcast, and not being able to do anything about it just then, put it out of his mind. When he got home that evening, his wife Jo, who had also heard the Murray show, urged him to do something about it right away if he wanted to go. There and then he wrote a letter, asking to be considered as the third man, but not expecting to be lucky. It had been as close as that.

With my Churchill funds, we made our purchase of carefully selected foodstuffs from a large bulk-selling warehouse in Chadwell Heath, the manager kindly allowing us over two-hundred pounds worth of goodies at cost, on a 'once only' basis. We had boxes of dried meats, dried fruits, rice, powdered potato, loads of made-up meals sealed in foil, such as chicken supreme, beef stroganoff, steak and kidney etc. and I thought with all this stuff, we're going to live like kings!

Quite suddenly it seemed, the time to go was upon us, only one or two odds and sods needed sorting, and we were ready to leave. The local press were giving us good coverage, and attended the ceremonial handing over of the Natwest £200 cheque outside the bank, our Landrover in the background boldly sporting Natwest's distinctive logo.

Several weeks before, Brian Bellingham one of our photographers on the sneaky squad, had promised me the loan of a Nagamichi casette recorder, which he said was far better than my old Sony, and rang me to say that it would be ready for collection at St. Mary Cray police station the day before we were due to go.

I MUST pick it up, and sign for it, as he was out of the country for a couple of weeks. If I didn't, it might 'go walkabouts' which would cause him no end of trouble with stores. It sounded a bit of a dog's dinner to me, but as he had kindly arranged it, I thought I'd better go and pick it up.

It was now March 20th, the day of our departure, and various friends and relatives had come to the house to see us off, yet it didn't seem real somehow. After prolonged hugs and kisses, plus a few tears, we piled into the Landrover, and roared off, waving like mad.

It was just twelve o'clock, and as we were due to catch the last Hovercraft of the day at 1630 hrs, it seemed we had loads of time to spare for the journey. Peter kicked off with the driving, and as we cleared the Blackwall tunnel I reminded him we had to call in to St. Mary Cray and pick up the tape recorder, otherwise I was in trouble. "No sweat, it's more or less on our way, and as you shouldn't be in the nick more than a few minutes we'll be ok."

It was a glorious sunny day, the first for some time, and everyone and his uncle seemed to be enjoying it too, not the least the traffic in the vicinity of Orpington and St. Mary Cray. "Where the hell have they all come from?" said Dick in frustration "At this rate we'll have to really push it once you've picked up the recorder, otherwise we'll be cutting it fine"

I collected the recorder in double quick time and in a haze of exhaust we roared away, there was an hour and a half left to make Ramsgate.

By four o'clock we were just approaching the outskirts of Ramsgate, and getting a bit anxious at how little time we had left to reach the harbour and get ourselves on board, as everything was conspiring to slow us down.

"This damned traffic!" shouted Peter in sheer frustration - all we could do was hope joe public would get out of the way, and give us a clear run at it.

With less than a mile to go it was 1625hrs - five minutes to sailing, and I felt sure we'd blown it. As we breasted the rise before the Hoverport, we could see in the far distance our Hovercraft leaving the shore in clouds of spray, it had gone.

"Bloody hell, that's buggered it!" I shouted "We've missed the damned boat, I don't know what we're going to do now!"

"We'll just have to go to the Hovercraft office, and find out the time of the first crossing tomorrow" said Dick, and I laughed ironically. "Isn't it ruddy marvellous, a year in the planning, and we can't even cross the channel on the day we're supposed to, do you think we'll get to Iran at all?"

The staff in the office were very sympathetic to our plight, but could only say we would definitely get on the first ferry in the morning at 0800, all we had to do was be there! After the concentrated push of the last couple of hours, the stillness and quiet of the Hoverport, now everyone had gone was a crushing contrast, and I wondered how we could spend the next fifteen hours before the next day's sailing?

With devastating logic Dick said "We can't put up the tent and kip here on the quay, and we can't sleep comfortably in the vehicle, so we'll have to find a bed and breakfast for the night, any ideas about that?

Remembering what my old dad had taught me years ago - when in trouble go to the nearest nick and ask for help, I said "Yes, what we'll do is, find the local nick and see if they can recommend anywhere nearby to stay, we don't want any further agro in the morning".

"If you think that will work, let's give it a try" said Dick, but Peter mumbled something about looking in the telephone directory and seeing what could be found there. We found Ramsgate nick without too much trouble, and being the instigator of the idea, I was nudged forward to do the necessary.

"Good evening" I said to the PC. behind the counter. "I wonder if you can help me, I'm Met. Police, and my two police colleagues and I have just missed the last Hovercraft by a few minutes due to traffic. We can't catch the next one until 0800 tomorrow, have you anywhere nearby you can recommend for bed and breakfast to get us out of trouble?".

"Yes, as a matter of fact I can help you, we've got a chap who runs a 'half-way' house not far from here, I'm sure he can help you out, here's his details".

Armed with the address, we charged through the back streets of Ramsgate, and found the place in a quiet side-road, not too far from the Hoverport, all we needed now was to be lucky.

I knocked on the door and waited for someone to answer.

"Good evening, we're looking for a bed and....." I stopped in mid sentence and looked at the man who had answered the door.

He chipped in "Hallo Alan, what on earth are you doing down here?" and I was looking at Det.Con. B. retd. whom I had known and worked with on countless occasions at Southwark Police station in the Met. What an un-believably small world!

I soon told him our tale of woe, and with a grin he replied, "No sweat, park your vehicle over there, get your two mates, and we'll go down to the local for a couple of swift halves to celebrate, it's been a long time, no see" Needless to say the evening turned out to be an extremely pleasant and convivial one, and we rolled into bed just before midnight, in a very jovial frame of mind.

Not wishing to have repeat performance of yesterday, we were up at 0600, breakfasted on eggs and bacon, and roared down to the Hoverport office at 0715, determined not to mess things up for a second time!

I presented my paperwork to the smartly dressed lady behind the counter, and confidently awaited whatever action was necessary to get us on board. "I'm afraid this isn't any good you know, you were scheduled to go yesterday, and today is the 21st, you'll have to pay again"

I didn't think I was hearing this. "What difference does that make, if you've got space, as you appear to have, why can't we just get on and go?"

"Ah, you see yesterday being the 20th was the last day at the cheap rate, which you obviously paid for your journey, today being the 21st is at a higher rate, you'll have to pay for new tickets".

I really began to think there was some genie hell bent on not letting us get abroad without a fight.

"How much will that be?"

"Well, the three of you, plus your vehicle, that would be another twenty-five pounds"

"Look, we missed the darn ferry yesterday because of heavy traffic, and we're trying our best to get to Iran, I just don't have £25 in English money at the moment. I changed all our cash into the currencies of the various countries we'll be passing through, couldn't you just stamp the tickets and let us on board?"

One of her colleagues who had been listening to our conversation, came over and whispered in her ear, nodding in my direction.

"Well I suppose I could, it's irregular, but in the circumstances it might be possible"

She went across the room, picked up a phone, and spoke to someone obviously senior to herself, before coming back to me with a half-smile.

"It seems we CAN bend the rules a little, but it's quite exceptional, I wouldn't count on it happening again in the future if I were you" she said and stamped our tickets to sail.

Dashing outside, I waved the tickets at Peter and Dick, scrambling aboard the Landrover as it eased down the slip towards the waiting Hovercraft - we were on our way at last!

The journey across the channel was pretty quick, far better than a conventional ship, and we arrived in Calais at 0900hrs, with the odometer reading 13152 miles. It would be interesting to see just what it read on our return in a few weeks' time!

With Dick driving, we headed across France into Germany, and using the agreed formula of two hours driving, four hours rest, pushed hard to reach Wurzburg by 2030hrs. To say it was cold would be a gross understatement, the temperature was minus 10C, and the frozen snow crunched underfoot like someone munching celery as we walked around the car, not the best of conditions to stop for a roadside meal.

It was our first practice at cooking beside the road, consequently it took a little time to locate the right food and get the hang of the petrol stove. I soon discovered that thorough heating of the atomising jets was essential for efficient burning, unless you wanted a miniature version of a flame-thrower burning half your hair off!

The weather was still pretty bleak with nearly two feet of snow blanketing the Eisener Alps, and the ropes securing our gear on the roof were frozen so stiff it was impossible to retrieve anything from 'up-top' until it had melted, so we pushed on.

Things began to improve a little as we approached Graz around mid-day, and brilliant sunshine sparkled through the frosty air putting some warmth into the vehicle. On leaving Austria and passing through customs into Yugoslavia, I pocketed the paperwork and passports, and quickly made my way back to the Landrover, it was damned cold weather.

We left Maribor as dusk fell and continued towards Zagreb, the scudding sleet turning occasionally into heavy rain, making driving really hazardous, and identification of the route quite difficult. In view of the horrible weather conditions we agreed to try and find a motel or something when we got into Zagreb, hoping to make up for lost time the following day.

It was 1830hrs when we finally crawled into Zagreb, and like most cities at this time of day, it seemed to be full of rush-hour traffic at its worst.

For half an hour we went round and round in the darkness, not knowing which route to take, either to find somewhere to stay, or just get out of town, it was really exasperating. Quite by accident we ended up behind a vehicle, whose driver was just getting out and locking his car. It was a slim chance, but I'd try and buttonhole him for help, it was hit or bust, we had to do something!

"Excuse me, do you speak English please?" I asked hesitantly - the thought of meeting anyone here in this place who understood a word of I said seemed slightly ridiculous.

"Yes, little"

"We are lost, we don't know where we are, we want to find a place to sleep for the night, can you help us?"

"I meet English soldier in war, I like - good friend, you got cigarette?"

With just such a situation in mind, Peter and I had stashed a small stock of cigarettes and sweets on board which we now put to good use.

"Thank you, I like English cigarette, you follow in car, I take you hotel"

There was no doubt we would never have found the place on our own, but on the outskirts of town, not far from a sign indicating the direction of Beograd, our next destination, he stopped outside a reasonable looking single storey hotel, and got out of his car.

"This hotel good, no trouble here, food good, bed good, ok?"

With a grateful shake of hands, and another pack of cigarettes, we said goodbye to our rescuer, who said as he got into his car, "I like English - good soldier, good cigarettes ok?" and disappeared into the rain-soaked darkness.

Inside the hotel, with a dozen people sleeping together in a large room, it felt like a drab YMCA, but despite the loud snores, we managed to sleep through most of the night. After a rather spartan breakfast at 0700hrs, we gladly warmed up the Landrover and headed for Beograd. It was snowing like the clappers already.

Crossing the open wind-swept country between Sava and Novska, the snow came down like mad, and in no time it was a foot deep everywhere, and the road disappeared from view. To make matters worse, the windscreen wiper motor packed up, and I had to operate the driver's wiper by the little manual handle, so I could see where the hell I was going.

Although we were doing a good 30-40mph in appalling conditions, I was constantly passed by huge articulated lorries roaring past in clouds of freezing slush, which coated the front of our Landrover with ice, until we resembled a mobile igloo with a small peep-hole in the front.

"I think we'll have to get out and knock some of this ice off fellas, it's so clogged round the front end, I can feel it restraining the wheels against my steering"

For a couple of miles we struggled desperately to find a safe place to pull off the road without sliding into the deep ditch which ran alongside. With twenty-tonners passing us each way at speed, there was no way anyone could stay on the road and work without being wiped away, it was too hairy.

It took our combined energies to hack the ice off the front bumper and wheel arches with a spade, but Pete's bull-bar, with diamond mesh grill over the lights proved unassailable, the ice was packed solid and the headlights quite invisible.

"We'll just have to drive using the spot lights on the bumper and keep them clear as best we can" Dick said. "We'll be up cat's creek for sure if we don't show some lights for'ard"

By 2000hrs we felt we'd had enough of battling against the weather, and just outside the town of Nis, pulled off the road by a railway bridge and lit our stove for dinner. All around us, tall pines rose from steep snowy slopes which threatened to crowd the narow winding road out of existence, while overhead an inky black sky sparkled with incredibly brilliant stars.

"Bloody hell", said Dick stamping his feet. "It's certainly brass monkeys weather init? I'll be glad when we get somewhere a bit warmer than this"

Whilst Peter got the meal going, I croc-clipped the fluorescent strip -light to the battery terminals, and attached it to the side of the vehicle. It was much easier when you could actually see what you were supposed to be cooking!

Away from the fluorescent light, my eyes soon got used to the inky darkness, and I noticed something glinting amongst the trees on the slopes above us. Then something else caught my attention a few yards further to the left. "Hey, look up there, there's something glinting in the light, it could be the eyes of some animal or other"

Dick came alongside, his feet scrunching in the deep snow. "Yeah, probably foxes or something and they can smell our grub - they're probably hungry too"

Suddenly, there was the loud scream of a vixen.

"See, what did I tell you, just a couple of foxes sniffing our grub, Pete must be doing something right!"

I had long been able to imitate the call of a vixen pretty well, and to tease the animals above, I gave my best call, and awaited results.

Not a lot happened.

Over the next few minutes I repeated my calls - much to Peter and Dick's amusement, but eventually in answer, the number of twinkling eyes increased, until we had four or five inquisitive foxes drawing ever closer to the car.

"Don't you think you should give it a rest?" said Peter. "If you don't pack it in, they'll be down here like long dogs, pinching our dinner"

The group of foxes, up to their bellies in snow, yelping and whining a few feet away, didn't know quite what to make of it all, so I stopped teasing them and joined the others in a welcome hot meal.

# Chapter Fifteen

The bash across Suva plain towards Bulgaria was awful, with alternate snow and freezing rain making the driving really difficult, and we breathed a sigh of relief as the customs post with Bulgaria loomed into view.

Perhaps we could take things a bit easier now. Entering the low wooden building with its under-lit rooms and corridors was a bit depressing, and things weren't made much better when I found myself in a queue with a dozen lorry drivers, all waiting for the customs man to do his bit.

An unsmiling little man, with a swarthy complexion and mexican moustache nonchalantly took our passports and demanded I hand over the equivalent of three pounds for each traveller, because, he explained, we were just passing through his country and not staying anywhere or spending any money. This was a Bulgarian rule.

When I had handed over the money, our little man continued in very bad English to say that as I had paid the fee to enter his country, we as tourists, were now being given the equivalent of three pounds in petrol coupons, which we must use before leaving Bulgaria. Perhaps things weren't so bad here after all!

On arrival in Sofia, it was necessary to fill up with petrol for the next leg of our trip into Turkey, and I felt now would be a good time to cash in the coupons, and save a few bob.

The garageman filled her up, and I noted the price, but was at a loss to know how I could deduct the value of the coupons customs had given me.

I waved the coupons under his nose, but he pushed them aside, tapping the price indicator with his finger and demanding money. Feeling just a bit narked at his obvious lack of understanding, I said "Coupons AND money, coupons, coupons!"

He looked at me as if I was mad, grabbed my arm and pulled me along to the next pump which served diesel fuel. Pointing to the coupons, and then at the pump he said something I didn't understand, but got the message alright, the clown at customs had given me diesel coupons, assuming we drove one of the heavy international transport lorries.

A fat lot of good they were to us in our petrol Landrover!

As a cold, grey dawn broke, the road ahead became visible through the murk, and we began to pick up speed. In the far distance I could see we were about to catch up with the last vehicle in a monster convoy of lorries, which for some reason appeared to be stationary on the road. Stopping a few yards behind the last one, I got out and stood on our bonnet, hoping to see what the problem might be, but could only make out the next mile of road leading toward the Turkish border completely solid with heavy lorries. Some of the drivers were trying to keep warm by huddling round blazing lorry tyres set in the middle of the road, others just sat in their cabs.

What the heck was going on?

An English driver from Yorkshire told us the border had been closed for a week - nobody had been allowed through, there was some internal dispute or other which hadn't been resolved yet.

We would have to wait like everyone else.

At that moment a Volks Caravanette roared past, weaving its way between burning tyres and parked lorries, the driver looking as if he knew exactly what he was doing, and where he was going.

"Ok. Dick you drive, follow that Volks and we'll see what happens, perhaps he knows something we don't"

At the head of the three-mile lorry queue was a large customs building, and an open space where no vehicles had been allowed to park. Our friend in the Volks was there in earnest conversation with an indifferent looking customs man. After a few minutes of agitated talking, our man began waving his arms up and down and getting very excited, before climbing back into his Volks and roaring off in the direction he had come.

Definitely not a lot happening there!

It was 0630hrs and brightening slowly. We had been sitting in the Landrover looking at the deserted customs post for an hour and a half now, and we were getting umpty. The only sign of life anywhere was three uniformed chaps making their way slowly along the border wire towards the large building in front.

"I suppose they're going in for their early morning cuppa" said Peter in a voice that echoed our sentiments exactly.

"Yeah, well I hope they ruddy well choke on it, while we're sitting here biting our thumbs, the bastards" said Dick.

A few minutes later, an enormous shiny Limousine pulled up in a cloud of dust on the Turkish side, and a large, well dressed man, with smart overcoat on his shoulders - his arms weren't in the sleeves, got out, and strode rapidly into the large building like a tank.

Through the window we could see the electric effect his presence had on the staff within, as they flew around in all directions, trying to make like they had something important to do.

"Hells bells. did you see that?" I said. "He's the chap we need to speak to about getting through this lot, I'm going over there to see if I can talk to him, perhaps he can get us through"

"You can't do that" said Peter, "We're still in Bulgaria, and that's Turkey over there, you'll get arrested"

"Well, anything is better than just sitting here, so I'm off, keep your eyes peeled, and if I give you a wave to come on over, bring the car with you"

Showing more confidence than I really felt, I ducked under the drop-bar and stepped onto the board-walk that ran round the building, looking for a door that approximated to the window where we had seen our man go in. Through the first glass door, I could see Mr. Big, elbows on the table, a glass of black coffee held delicately between his fingertips, giving controlled vitriolic hell to several of his sub-ordinates, just out of my view.

I waited for what I felt was an opportune moment, and knocked on the door. He looked at me as though I was the last thing he wanted to see at that moment, but made no motion to beckon me in or go away, so I grasped the door handle and went in.

“Excuse my interruption please, we are three police staff from London, and have an appointment in Teheran, could you possibly tell us when we can expect to be let through the border?”

For what seemed to be an eternity he just stared at me, not saying whether he understood or not, then turned to one of the customs officers standing nearby and let fly another string of foreign words.

The man jumped to attention, and obviously agreed to whatever Mr. Big had said, marching towards the door where I stood, beckoning me to follow him outside.

I looked at Mr. Big, who hadn’t moved an inch during all the kerfuffle and said “Thank you very much sir for whatever help you have given us” and quickly left the room, trying to catch up with our friend who was already half way across the compound.

He called to someone of lesser rank emerging from another building to join him, and began an earnest conversation with the new man, pointing at me, then at our Landrover sitting just outside the compound.

Our friend then hurried back to the office to re-join his Mr. Big, leaving our ‘new man’ to lead me to an open air check point, consisting of a couple of rows of 50 gallon drums, between which traffic was supposed to move for checking.

“You bring car here, everything out, we look, I come back” and off he went before I could say a word. There was only a single scaffold plank supported across two oil drums serving as an unloading table, and there was no way we could get even a quarter of our gear onto that, what the hell could we do?

I walked through the now open barrier and went across to Dick and Peter, saying I thought I’d done it, but we had to let them check the contents of our vehicle before we could finally go through.

“You mean they want us to unload ALL the stuff we’ve got in the back? you gotta be joking!”

“I tell you what we’ll do”, I said. “We’ll unload enough odds and sods for them to see the remaining contents in the back, and tell them it’s all food. If we take our time unloading, we might get away with it”

It was half an hour before our ‘new man’ returned, glancing at the bits and pieces on the plank before going round to the back of the Landrover to check what was in there.

“Out, all out” he said waving his arms for added effect, and turned to go.

“All this is food - mangerea. “I said pointing with my finger into my mouth. He stopped, turned back to the vehicle, and looked closely at the dozens and dozens of packets and boxes of dried food.

Stabbing his finger at the nearest package, he said. “Open”

He had picked one of the waterproof, survival ration boxes donated by Blashford-Snell at Chelsea Barracks.

A knife soon had the covering off, and the box open. Inside were individually wrapped packages of survival rations.

“Open” he said pointing to the first package inside, and with a few cuts of the knife it was open. Inside were various portions of food wrapped in separate wrappers, and amongst them was a small circular tin, about 2” across and 1/2” deep.

"Open" came the imperious command, and I realised he thought he might be onto hidden drugs of some kind, and he wasn't stopping now! Using an army folding tin-opener on my key ring, I soon had the lid up, and he stuck his finger in, and licked it.

It was meat paste!

He spat it out with great distaste, and said. "Ok. you go to office with passport now, ok?" and it was all I could do not to burst out laughing with relief. With our gear neatly stacked away once more, Dick pulled up outside the passport office, while I went inside to do the necessary paperwork. In a small office, behind a tall Pickwickian desk sat a solitary figure, who proceeded to copy all the details from our passports into a large ledger using longhand. As he finished, he looked up at me, smiled, and demanded the equivalent of a pound for copying each of our passports into his book. I felt this was blatant extortion.

"I no have Turkish money here, go to bank, only English" I lied.

"English Ok. I change" he said without losing his condescending smile, and I had to dig in to my small contingency fund to get our passports back.

Weatherwise it was still pretty cold, the countryside looked pretty bleak and inhospitable as we headed for Istanbul, the only bright spot being the sight of our first White Storks on their return migration to Europe, many of them walking beside the road, obviously far too cold to fly!

Our route along the fast asphalt road to Izmit and Adapazari was downright dangerous most of the time, our right-hand drive vehicle needed to get into the oncoming lane for the driver to judge for himself whether it was safe to overtake. With locals careering down the hills towards us at 60mph, we hadn't the acceleration to overtake the slower transporters in front, and had to jump back to suffer their choking diesel fumes for a few more miles!

Once clear of Adapazari and heading for Ankara, we made better time, in fact we had to, as the accompanying traffic pushed us into speeds we thought far too fast for the zany road conditions.

Somehow we managed to arrive safely in Ankara at 2300hrs, just a sixteen hour run from the Bulgarian border, which I felt was pretty good going. Pushing on through the night and into a wintery dawn, the scenery didn't appear to have changed all that much since yesterday. Desolate snow covered country lay all around, and we saw very few people. Ornithologically things were brightening up a bit though, there were a couple of Griffon vultures, and both Spotted, and Lesser Spotted Eagles, dozens of White Storks, and scores of Calandra Larks, I suppose that was something.

Near a place called Durulumus we pulled off the road under a stand of bare Poplars, trying to find some shelter from the bitterly cold wind to cook ourselves a meal. It was a purely automatic gesture to give our bodies the necessary sustenance, there was no pleasure in it at all.

During the rest of the night we whizzed through Erzincan and Erzerum, before starting up the so-called 'road' just before dawn to the 7000' high Tahir pass. The scenery here was out of this world, absolutely fantastic, and reminiscent of scenes from the Arctic as we made our way up the icy track between snowdrifts 15-20' high.

At the top, well above grey clouds, we basked in brilliant dawn sunshine and stark blue skies, and although it was well below freezing, it felt like a glorious spring day in England.

Naturally we stopped to take photographs of this fantastic scene, and spotted the first of the day's migrant birds flying towards us a few inches above the snow. There were dozens of Shore Larks, Rock Buntings, White Wagtails, Linnets and a few Stonechats, all looking a bit out of place against the dazzlingly white background. Some of the Linnets and Buntings dropped into patches of sparse vegetation poking up through the snow, and I saw a couple of white foxes trying to stalk them, despite being up to their bellies in deep snow. Life must be pretty tough up here.

With the migrants now coming over the summit in ever increasing numbers, I asked Dick and Peter if they would care to stop and make a quick cuppa, while I walked ahead with my binoculars, revelling in the gorgeous sunshine and unique bird watching event. They could catch me up along the road later.

At first it had been unusual for us to see the odd twenty-tonner, either off the road and hopelessly bogged down due the driver falling asleep, or lying on its side after the nearside wheels had gone into a ditch. I suppose our tally must have reached at least a dozen by the time we got to the Tahir. However here on the summit, and as far as I could see, before the road disappeared from view, were another four lorries, two from the UK, one Hungaro-camion with its distinctive yellow tarpaulin, and one from Teheran.

All vehicles appeared to be intact, even though they were leaning at a steep angle, or on their sides, but what was most intriguing, the loads didn't appear to have been stolen at all.

I took photographs of the vehicles, purely to show the people at home this quite unbelievable sight, and carried on down the road, trying to identify the streams of migrant birds breasting the pass, now the clouds below us were rapidly dispersing.

I suppose I had covered about a mile, and photographed another three vehicles abandoned in the roadside snows, when I heard the approach of our Landrover, signalling the end of my stroll.

"All these lorries abandoned like this" said Dick. "It certainly makes you think, how did the drivers get rescued, and doesn't anyone miss the goods that were supposed to be delivered?"

Peter replied "I don't suppose anyone can do much about it up here in the winter, they probably have to wait until the spring weather before it's possible to tow them out, there must be a fortune in insurance claims for someone"

"The funny thing is, that last one over there has a hole cut in its canvas cover, and I'm sure I saw smoke coming out of it, someone must be living in there" I said.

"Don't be a dope" Peter replied, "Why would anyone want stay up here in this god-forsaken freezing place if they didn't have to?"

We were to learn the answer to that some time later when talking to fellow travellers. We discovered that bandits hid out in the abandoned lorries for weeks, waiting to ambush vehicles coming over the pass in the snow. Drivers finding their way blocked by some obstacle or other, got out to move it, only to be confronted by bandits brandishing guns and other weapons, demanding their money and valuables.

Apparently we had been extremely lucky not to have been robbed as our fellow travellers had been!

After the Tahir, the 'road' to Iran split in two, our track, almost totally destroyed by lorry wheels pounding ruts a foot deep into the morass surged east, while other huge transporters ground their way westwards a quarter of a mile away to our right.

The surface of our track had been pounded into a series of never ending 'waves' by the repeated action of lorries, and some of the ruts were so deep our differential bottomed, causing the Landrover to lean over alarmingly. There was no doubt if we were to come a cropper out here, it could be rather serious!

After several miles of tortuous driving in four-wheel drive, the track slowly improved, and the countryside levelled out into a huge basin containing a large shallow lake about ten miles long. It looked to me as if it had formed from the run-off from Mt. Arrarat which dominated the skyline on our left, its twin snow-covered peaks glowing salmon pink in the late afternoon sun.

For several miles a row of stout fence-posts bordered the 'road' on our left, newly strung with several strands of barbed wire.

We thought this a bit peculiar as there didn't seem to be that much out here worth protecting, what was it all for?

Suddenly, a little way ahead I spotted a large tarpaulin cover laying in the middle of the road, and called to Dick in the navigator's seat, "Hey, do you see what I see? a lovely piece of canvas which could make good hide material for our bird photography, how about we stop and pick it up?"

"Oh alright if you must, you're always on the look-out mumping some damn' thing or other, some poor bugger loses his lorry cover, and all you want to do is cut it up for hides, whatever next?"

I pulled to a halt just short of the canvas, and Dick scrambled out into a cloud of dust to retrieve it. Suddenly from under a camouflage net draped over vegetation, a 15cwt. truck roared towards us, its soldier occupants yelling like banshees and waving their rifles, as they pulled alongside us on the other side of the wire.

"Let's get the bloody hell outa here!" yelled Dick as he dived for the door, and I gunned the engine with everything she'd take in first and second.

Peter's head appeared groggily from the kip-couch demanding to know "What the hell's going on out there?"

"Don't ask, just keep your head down while we make rapid tracks!"

As the road was pretty bumpy, I angled away to the right onto unused ground, where the Landrover picked up better speed, although on our nearside, the soldiers were still pacing us in their truck shouting for us to stop.

They MUST be flippin' joking!

I hoped there wasn't a gap in the wire ahead where they could punch through, and use our track, if there was, we'd be well and truly in it.

Ever so slowly we began to pull away from their truck, and I feared in their frustration they might pop a couple of shots off in our direction, but thankfully they didn't and we escaped.

Thinking back on it later, I wondered whether the canvas had been left as bait for some unwary lorry driver, creating a diversion from boredom for the troops, or was there another insidious reason?

Clearing the Customs border post at Bazargan was a doddle now we had the hang of things. All it needed was a quick look round to identify the most senior-looking policeman, show him our English passports, tell him we were with the British police, which was enough to get us through in 45 minutes flat, miles ahead of the noisy, milling horde that jam-packed the smelly waiting hall.

It was now goodbye Turkey, hello Iran!

# Chapter Sixteen

Outside the border post in the chilly darkness, I felt quite chuffed that we had got through so easily, and drove the Landrover across the enclosed yard separating Turkey from Iran towards the general exit, which consisted of three stone arches, two smallish ones flanking a large, lorry-sized one in the centre.

Naturally enough I aimed for the convenient one in the centre, which was blocked by a chain and padlock.

I looked across at a couple of guards who were leaning against the wall smoking, and pointed to the chain. One of them pushed off the wall, and came slowly up to my door, saying something I didn't understand, pointing to the smaller arch on the left.

"He wants you to use the arch on this side" said Dick, who was occupying the navigator's seat. "What's wrong with him letting us through this one" I said. "Is he daft or something?"

At this, Peter who had been having his kip in the rest couch, poked his head up between us and said, "I dunno about that, but we're going to be hard put, to get our top load through that pointed arch, I bet it's only meant for small cars"

I indicated our rooftop load to the man, and pressed my hand on my head to indicate the arch was probably too low, but this seemed to trigger off a loud out-burst of words, which brought several of his compatriots onto the scene as well. Waving their rifles and shouting like idiots, they ordered me to back up, and use the arch on the left - there didn't seem to be much else to do but give in at that point.

"If I go one side, and Peter goes the other, we'll guide you through, and tell you when to stop if you have to" said Dick, "That way we should be safe, despite these awkward buggers"

Nodding, I carefully centred on the small arch and eased forward, Dick and Peter standing either side of the arch, waving me on.

"Stop, for crying out loud stop!" shouted Dick. "There's a bloody great hole under the arch, about eighteen inches deep, they've chucked some rocks in to try fill it, but it's still bloody hairy."

I got out to have a look at the obstacle, and could see it was caused by a succession of cars leaving the concrete edge of the yard, bumping down onto the wet earth under the arch, and spinning their wheels before driving away. No wonder they had to drop rocks in the bottom, you could get stuck in there for ages!

"Just look at this too" I said bending down to examine the chipped and scarred concrete lip on the edge of the hole, "I bet half the cars that go through here get their exhausts ripped off as well, I suppose they think it's a bloody great joke"

"Well whether they think it's a joke or not is immaterial, can we get our vehicle across, without damage?"

"I reckon if I let the front wheels down slowly over the edge, you two can use torches to see how much clearance we have under the exhaust, and if that's ok, how close the tail-end comes to the lip, as the bottom end goes in".

Bearing in mind we were only just starting our trip, and still had a hell of a way to go, serious damage at this point could be potentially terminal.

Concentrating hard, I let her down inch at a time, and thanked god we were fitted with vacuum assisted brakes, she held beautifully.

"Alright here!" "Ok, here too", came reassuring calls as the front wheels bottomed on the rocks, at least we were halfway across.

"Take her forward gently and we'll see how the back end goes"

As the rear wheels went over the edge, gravity and weight came into play, and the tyres slid down the concrete wall unchecked. There was a resounding crash as the tow-ball clipped the edge of the lip, and we were through.

"Well at least we didn't do any damage - no thanks to those stupid bastards" said Dick, and they both climbed aboard for our first journey onto Iranian soil.

Our supper, cooked a few miles down the road was chicken supreme, with boiled rice and carrots, a fitting celebration for having got this far without serious incident.

The road into Maku was unlike anything we had experienced so far, even in Turkey. It consisted of a sheet of ice several inches thick, dusted over with a fine covering of fresh snow, and no matter how carefully you tried to steer, the vehicle just wandered and jiggled over the scalloped ice, entirely at the mercy of fate.

Incredibly, at one point while passing through the 'centre' of town, we were actually higher by two or three feet, than the pedestrians shopping on either side of us at the busy roadside stalls!

Under such hairy driving conditions, I had visions of losing control of the steering, and slowly toppling over the side onto the people below, it was all rather scary!

Once clear of Maku, there was another steep climb along an icy, rutted 'road' in total darkness, until we reached the summit at 6890' before starting the long run down to Khvoy and Tabriz.

As if to keep our attention concentrated on the road and its various hazards, we passed our hundredth abandoned lorry, incidentally an English one, and wondered just how many more wrecks we would see like that, before we got to Teheran.

It must be costing someone, somewhere an awful lot of money.

One of the signs we quickly learned to interpret on the road, was the conglomeration of black skid marks a short distance ahead on the excellent tarmac surface. They definitely meant trouble!

At odd intervals the road would be criss-crossed or bisected by natural cracks, produced no doubt by geological forces acting against this man made structure. These cracks ranged from annoying ones, one or two inches across, to the downright dangerous ones six inches across and a foot or more deep.

Hitting one of these at speed with our load on board would probably have torn the wheels off, hence the need to observe the frantic skid marks of previous travellers, and take heed!

While squatting next to the Landrover drinking my tea, I experienced that weird sensation of being warm on my back which was facing the bright sunshine, and shivering on my front, which was still in deep shadow, it was most peculiar.

"We've got problems here" Dick called out during his daily inspection. "Oil splashes on the rear-offside tyre, which generally means we've lost an oil seal, I'll have to deal with it before we can move on"

It was a real education watching Dick at work; in no time flat he had the vehicle jacked up, wheel off, and was grubbing around between the brake hub and half-shaft, up to his elbows in grease.

"Alan, if you can get a fire going with some twigs, grasses and stuff, I'll have these shoes ready to burn the oil off, we must get them clean again, before we put 'em back"

It was an hour before the shoes had cooled sufficiently to handle, by which time Dick had everything else under control, and was waiting to put them back on.

"I reckon this Landrover must have stood unused somewhere for quite some time for that seal to go, it was a bit perished on one side, good job we had some replacements"

By mid-morning we had reached Myaneh, where we saw the largest single rookery to date, probably 200 pairs, their nests built in Black Poplars, and jammed firmly against the trunk of the tree, one above the other looking so un-Rook like, I just had to take photographs.

It seemed during the long haul from the Turkish border towards Teheran, that whenever we stopped by the roadside to eat, or attend the needs of nature, the scenery hadn't changed a bit since the previous stop. The same forbidding scrub desert continued mile after mile with mind-bending monotony, and I was glad when we passed Qazvin and on the last leg towards Teheran.

I suppose it was good old Murphy's law that we should arrive in Teheran at 1800hrs just as everyone was shutting up and going home. It seemed unlikely we would find anyone who knew where the Department of the Environment's offices were, or had even heard of them, especially at this late hour.

We had come to a halt at the beginning of the Eisenhower road, almost opposite the remarkable Shahyad Arya Mehr monument, surely one of the world's most beautiful structures, a superb blend of Iranian architecture and modern building techniques.

Seeing it now, lit by warm, artificial lighting during a glorious sunset, it looked exquisite.

Suddenly, I spotted a European-type face amongst the passers by, and leapt out of the Landrover to bend his ear.

"Actually I'm American, and work out of town for Aramco, I can't really help, but if you go to the Bel-Air Hotel, which is a couple of miles away from here near Ferdowsi Square, you might find someone around to help you. All the Brits go there"

That advice eventually proved of little use, the place was deserted, but someone directed us to the nearby Hotel Parisa where he thought we might have more success. While I was in the hotel trying to find someone I could converse with, a European chap came in and said. "Are you with the Landrover outside?".

I replied that I was.

"I've just seen the Churchill Trust sticker in your window, concerning your trip to Iran, there's a chap staying at this very hotel, Mike Hutchinson, he's an Ornithologist, and might prove very useful to you, I'll go and get him"

I just couldn't believe our luck, it looked as if we were getting off to a good start after all!

That evening turned out to be a great success, our new friend Mike was a mine of information, and having recently returned from the Lake Bakhtigan area with an Iranian colleague, told us the going down there could be pretty rough. After hours of talking, laughing, and downing at least six pints of lager each, everyone was a bit the worse for wear. I do remember though, being party to teaching Mike's Iranian friend that 'Up your bottoms' was the 'in' thing to reply, when a toast was proposed, and wishing I could somehow be present when he eventually used it!

As our vehicle was parked in a side street by the hotel, we drew straws for who was going to sleep where. I drew the shorty, allowing Peter and Dick to use the hotel, while I shook down on the kip-couch. The next morning I was jolted into life by Mike hammering on the car like a maniac, informing me that everybody started work early out here, and it was 0600 already.

He didn't see why, just because we were visitors, we should be treated any differently!

Although it was Sunday, that didn't count for much in a Muslim country, where Friday is the all important day - we could still go to the Department of the Environment just round the corner, and meet our contact, Lindon Cornwallis, the English ornithologist employed by the Iranian Conservation department.

He'd be working there as usual.

I made a mental note that we had parked just off the Takhte-Jamshid Ave, with lots of side streets around called this or that allee, and memorised a few of those too, so that I could find my way back later, the area was quite confusing.

In the Department's office, situated in Villa Avenue, it was a simple matter to locate Lindon, and after introductions all round, we spent most of the day with him, gaining up to date information on our projected visit to the Bakhtigan/Tashk Lakes complex, the species we were likely to see there, and any recent sightings of the Humes' Tawny Owl I was particularly interested in.

The one thing I wanted to mobilise straight away, was a document written in Farsi, the national language, stating who we were, what we were doing, and under whose authority we were doing it. I hoped it might smooth the way in the event of our being stopped by local police or the military. Lin was very helpful and drafted what we wanted there and then, and because we were special visitors, mentioned that it would be ready the following day.

Although this might seem quite normal to us, he asked us to bear in mind that an officially headed document of this nature, drafted, typed and signed in less than three days, was little short of a miracle, it normally took a week!

After our hectic weeks' journey from the UK, we had to find some accommodation in town to sort ourselves out, catch up on some much needed dhobying, and contact Mr. George Haddad, the general manager of 'Skol' International's bottling plant. He was one of my initial sponsors and would take us round the factory, before supplying some free samples of their beverage to 'help us on our way'.

"There's no need for you to look for accommodation" Lin said. "I've just taken a newly built flat in Tajrish, that's the northern part of town near the mountains. My wife and I haven't moved in yet, so you can all stay there until you're ready to leave, there's plenty of room"

It was a super gesture which was really appreciated.

The route to Lin's flat in Tajrish via the fantastically busy Bandar Pahlavi Avenue - which seemed to meander on for miles and miles, was an education in itself.

Through a sea of hooting cars, and scurrying humanity, overlaid with loud religious wailing from hidden speakers, the journey could only be described as an entirely unique experience in motoring!

There appeared to be no road rules whatever, taxis carved you up from all directions, changed lanes abruptly without signalling, disgorged passengers in the fast lane, and even entered one-way streets if it suited them. Amazingly, no-one seemed the least put out by the mayhem, except perhaps us visitors!

I got a little tired of being patsy in the middle, and for the next couple of miles, leant on our outrageous air klaxons whenever things got too bad, with devastating effect. By some miracle we located Lin's flat and piled inside - it was nice, but I thought a bit skimpy in its construction, and a tad expensive at £400 a month, but he didn't seem to think so.

The next day was given over to two projects only, the first, 'acquiring' our official document from the Environment Dept, and secondly, locating the Skol bottling plant and Mr.George Haddad. With the chaotic traffic conditions we had already experienced in Teheran, and being 'new boys' in town, I didn't think we'd manage much more than that. Returning to town down the madhouse that was Pahlavi Avenue, I found it far more rewarding to 'aim' the Landrover aggressively in the direction we wanted to go, accompanied by screaming air klaxons, rather than try to manoeuvre. People must have thought we were 'military' and slowed abruptly to let us through!

After a four hour wait, Lin was able to hand over the document detailing our business in Iran, and also give the latest information regarding water levels at Lakes Bakhtigan and Perishan, which was very important as we needed to know what to expect. Then it was off to the Skol bottling plant on the North Karaj road, to see what George Haddad might have in store for us.

George kindly treated us to lunch before showing us around his large bottling plant, it was apparently quite a good set-up (according to Dick who knew a bit about engineering) but there was dreadful sloppiness in respect of certain repairs, essential to maintain the efficient running of the plant. At the conclusion of our tour, George presented us with a couple of flat-packs of Skol Lager, sufficient he said, for us to have a can a day each for two months!

Dick, as ever a man with his eye on the main chance, noticed the bottling plant boasted a vehicle inspection bay, plus a two-ton hydraulic jack, and asked if we could possibly borrow their facilities to service our Landrover, before moving off into the back of beyond?

It was a good job we did, because during the inspection Dick found the hub-spline on the rear offside wheel badly worn, and in need of immediate replacement. Naturally we carried a couple of spare half-shafts, but hadn't thought it necessary to include spare hub mounts.

Learning of our problem, George whistled me off in his little Dyane CV, to Khosh St. - the address of Landrover spares Ltd. Teheran - which I had noted down before leaving the UK. in case of emergencies such as this.

While I was away with George, Peter and Dick stripped the whole assembly down, and were ready and waiting for the new hub when I returned. It had cost £20.

In just two hours from start to finish, the job was done, and so impressed were the Skol staff, with both the scale of our intended exploration, and the speed of repairs, George questioned Dick regarding his qualifications and relative experience, with a view to offering him employment with Skol Teheran at the end of our trip!

The following morning, 31st.March, we carefully re-loaded the Landrover with our mountain of goods, before making a plan of where everything was stacked - we didn't want to be hunting around for something in a hurry, not knowing where the heck it was!

I checked our petrol in the Jerricans on the roof and the vehicle's two tanks - we only needed to fill our secondary tank to be completely full. With petrol in Iran selling at only 6 Rials (6p) a litre, we could now fill up anytime and virtually forget the cost! The odometer showed that since leaving Calais we had covered 3765 miles, which worked out at 538 miles a day for seven days, which I thought was rather good going.

Leaving Lin a note of thanks for his kind hospitality, we entered the crazy stream of traffic fighting towards the centre of Teheran, trying to keep an eye out for the road leading south that would take us to Saveh, but in this traffic, finding the right route seemed well-nigh impossible.

The last pink glow of sunset was just disappearing as we roared through Saveh towards the next town Delijan, and it became necessary to put on all six headlights to scan the bumpy road ahead. The lower spots were particularly useful in this situation, as they cast shadows across even the shallowest pot-holes, allowing us to avoid them in good time.

Despite some very rough road conditions, we covered the 280 miles to Esfahan by one o'clock in the morning, and although it was the early hours, the place seemed unusually lively. Rows of blazing lights festooned the trees and lamp-posts along the Chahar Bagh e Abbasi Ave: and small groups of people wandered about everywhere talking. The map showed we were making our way towards the Seeyo-se-pol bridge, and the Zayandeh river, which we had to cross to get out of town, and yet at this early hour, we were in a steady stream of traffic, crawling along at about ten miles an hour!

Bright green taxis pushed and hooted to get passengers to their destinations, and we smiled when we realised they were all British Hillman Hunters, although out here they are called 'Peykan'.

Crossing the Zayandeh river, we turned hard left, and drove a short distance along a small roadway lined with poplars, looking for somewhere to park and have a short kip. We had been on the road for twelve hours since leaving Teheran, and felt so whacked we decided to sleep where we were in our seats.

The three of us were rudely awakened at 0530 by slamming car doors and raised voices, and fearing we were about to be descended on by police or military, piled out into the first light of dawn.

To our surprise we found ourselves surrounded by loads of cars and people, some setting up cooking facilities on the pavement, while others disentangled themselves from blanket rolls on the grass where they had been sleeping. It was all very laid back.

Suddenly it dawned on me. It was Friday, and of course a public holiday in Iran, which accounted for everyone and his uncle being out and about so early!

Because everybody around us seemed to be cooking or eating something, we decided to do the same, before driving back over the Seeyo-se-pol bridge to see where we could park up, and do a bit of sight-seeing.

The only place we could find straight off, was a dusty vacant building lot directly opposite the sumptuous Shah Abbas Hotel, Esfahan's equivalent of the Hilton, a bit unusual, but it would have to do.

Esfahan is without doubt, an incredibly interesting place to see and explore, but with only a few hours at our disposal, a lot of things had to go by the board, so we started at the 'centre' and walked about from there.

The main square, probably the world's biggest maidan square, has a wonderful bazaar on its northern side, a 400 year old Shah mosque on the south side, the beautiful Lutfollah mosque and dome on the east, and the resplendent Ali Qapu palace on the west. It was an area you could spend all day exploring, and still not see it all.

On the corner of an alley leading from the bazaar into the square, a local chap was cooking kebabs over a bed of charcoals, kept red hot by the draught from a large electric fan, hooked up to a nearby shop. It looked so comical I just had to photograph the scene, with the chap laughing and posing as I clicked the shutter. You could see the next lot of skewers ready to go on the fire, and behind them, a pile of fresh meat waiting to be cut up for the next load. It smelt delicious.

"I bet you haven't noticed that" said Dick, pointing to a dejected looking goat tethered to the far end of the table supporting the barbeque. "That poor bugger is the next in line for the chop, I wouldn't care to be in his shoes" and made a rasping noise as he drew his finger across his throat.

I could see our man watching us closely, and decided in the interests of diplomacy, I wouldn't take a photograph of the sacrificial goat, it all seemed a bit macabre now, and not quite so funny. We managed to inspect dozens of stalls and shops but refrained from entering any of the mosques because of our tee-shirts and shorts. I didn't think it a wise thing to do.

By two o'clock we were hot and tired, and only wanted to get back to the Landrover for a beer and something savoury to eat, rubbernecking certainly requires a high level of stamina.

"Where shall we go to cook our meal then, any ideas?" Peter said.

"Don't see that we have to go anywhere other than where we are if we don't want to" replied Dick.

"We can put the stove behind the Landrover out of sight of passers by, and sit in the easy chairs as though admiring the view while the food's cooking, how about it?"

And so, just across the width of the Shah Abbas road, in full view of a meticulously dressed major-domo, complete with turban, sash, and embroidered cape, we prepared our meal of steak and kidney pudding. His expression on seeing us, was not that of a happy man.

After our meal, some might say we added insult to injury by sauntering into the beautiful foyer of the Shah Abbas - the clump of our expedition boots muffled by the opulent white Persian carpet, to post our postcards home by using the hotel's exclusive postal service!

Looking round, Dick spotted a barber snipping away in his sumptuous glass panelled studio, and declared his intention to go in for a quick trim, which Peter and I agreed he obviously needed. While he was doing that, Peter and I would nip into the immaculate gent's cloakroom and have a quick wash and brush up, and rinse out our stiff, sweaty socks, you couldn't pass up a chance like that!

As we got ready to leave Esfahan, I found myself thinking that travelling through wild open spaces and being self sufficient for a long time made entering town almost unbearable, and yet leaving town to head off into the great wilderness once more, produced a slight feeling of apprehension, which was somehow difficult to define.

It didn't make sense to me at all.

Leaving Esfahan, the striking city of domed mosques and artistry, we pointed the car towards Shiraz, some 300 miles away, and went by way of the Pol-e-Shahrestan bridge, reputedly 14th century and the oldest bridge in town.

Seen at close quarters it appeared much as one would expect. It certainly looked very old, even the turgid green water gurgling under it like treacle looked old, but what made us laugh was the sight of two Iranians stomping huge Persian carpets into that dreadful water, in an effort to get them clean!

On the river-bank, dozens of rolled carpets stacked in neat pyramids dried in the sun, while nearby, another couple of chaps beat the hell out of some newly dried carpets with long canes, sending clouds of fine dust into the air.

"I must get some photographs of the Esfahan patent carpet-cleaning Company at work" I said, "This is just too good to pass up"

There was no doubt, the system must work out satisfactorily in the end, and the clients be satisfied with their 'cleaned' carpets, otherwise these chaps wouldn't be doing it now, but it all looked a bit 'iffy' to me!

# Chapter Seventeen

The road to Shiraz was for the most part very good, having only a few sections where we HAD to keep our eyes peeled for tell-tale, black skid marks indicating trouble ahead. Pushing on hard, we reached a dusty little town called Abadeh just before sunset, a carbon copy of so many towns we had passed through, and a few miles on the other side, decided to stop and make camp.

This was the first opportunity we had to put the tent up since leaving home, and it all went very smoothly, the aluminium `A' frame making the whole thing ridiculously easy despite the wind. Due to the strong winds, we had pulled in to the lee of a stony ridge for shelter, rather essential up here on the bleak 6600' plateau, where snow still clung to the nearby hilltops, making everything feel extremely cold!

After a substantial meal, we climbed into our sleeping bags fully dressed and settled down to write-up the day's notes, serenaded by distant yipping foxes, and the mournful call of a Little Owl. Earlier, Peter and Dick had laughed like drains at the sight of me blowing my air bed up by mouth, but my resultant night's comfort compared to their twisting and turning on the cold hard ground, made it all worth while.

The following morning dawned chill and bleak, a distinct contrast to the comparative warmth of Esfahan, and although we were awake at 0630, nobody stirred until 0830 when the sun began to appear at long last.

Peter and I were clearing away breakfast, and Dick doing his daily inspection, when he called out oil was leaking down the inside of the rear off-side tyre again. The seal BEHIND the bearing was faulty this time, it would all have to come down again!

Peter and I got the vehicle jacked up, while Dick got out his tools, and I left them to get on with their unenviable job in the bitterly cold wind. Having nothing to occupy me for a while, I wandered across to a couple of small natural hill caves in the direction I had heard the Little Owl calling last night, you never know he might be at home.

Judging by the acrid smell and droppings on the floor, the caves must be used to pen sheep or goats, and as I reached the far end amongst a pile of boulders, a Little Owl scrambled into view, tumbled out the entrance in a hurry, and disappeared over the hill.

Ok. lads, she's all fixed" grinned a happy and relieved Dick, and we piled into the vehicle to get out of the sharp wind and relax, after all, it was his turn to drive. From the navigator's seat I watched him pull the starter several times, but apart from the engine turning over normally, not a lot happened. This was most unusual - she had always gone first pull so far, what had gone wrong?

Grumbling a bit in the cold wind, Dick got to work, checking the plugs and air-filter, even the coil was exchanged for a spare, but still the engine showed no signs of life.

Suddenly Dick got back in to the vehicle with a grunt, pulled the knob changing the fuel supply from auxiliary to main tank, tugged the starter and the engine roared into life.

We must have used the very last drop of petrol in the auxiliary tank when we arrived, and as Dick said with a funny grin, it's amazing how the obvious can be so easily overlooked!

The road to Dehbid was surprisingly good and a pleasure to drive on, despite being very close to the 13,000' snow-bound Kuh-i-Bul range. Occasionally we were passed in this back end of nowhere, by klaxon blowing juggernauts, reminding us that roads were still the only way of moving heavy goods quickly through south Iran, so get out of my way you Ingloustan slowcoaches!

Although my fellowship was ostensibly to study the species and numbers of wildfowl we might find in the wetlands, plus, trying to establish positive breeding of the Humes' Tawny Owl, I always had in mind the possibility of visiting the archaeological sites of Pasargardae and Persepolis if I could.

The stories of Alexander the great, and the fantastic kings of Persia, had stirred my imagination vividly since childhood.

Descending the barren hills from Dehbid to the desert floor, we turned off the road onto a stony track, which led further and further into a bleak natural basin about ten miles across, where in the distance we saw the shapes of buildings, and a tall, single column.

It was the remains of Pasargardae, the wonderful city built by Cyrus the Great, founder of the Achaemenian empire 2500 years ago, and it lay quietly before us.

I stood deep in thought before Cyrus' tomb, trying to envisage the motivation of the great man who had accomplished such history shaping events aeons ago. What circumstances had produced a magnanimous ruler of an empire which, continuing under Xerxes and Darius, would stretch from India to Europe, and include the defeat of Iraq and even the mighty Egypt, twice - it had all started from here, which seemed so incredible.

In the middle of the stunted columns stood a complete single column, forty feet high, and perched ludicrously on its top, a huge White Stork's nest complete with sitting bird.

There wasn't a great deal of the original site left, a few stunted columns, set on a vast levelled rock base, a curious Zoroastrian fire pillar, and away to one side, a huge stone-block construction, a hundred yards long, twenty yards deep, and sixty feet high, known as Solomon's Throne, an impressive but puzzling ruin.

In the gaps between six-foot blocks making up the construction of Solomon's `throne', at least four pairs of Lesser Kestrels competed for nest sites, making an excited din with their calls. Nearby a couple of Little Owls chased Short toed Larks in and out of the boulders, while overhead a Golden Eagle soared in company with a smaller Long Legged Buzzard.

Ornithologically things were beginning to get very interesting indeed.

The wan afternoon light was beginning to fade as we hit the road again, and checking the maps while Peter drove, I knew we wouldn't get far before needing to find somewhere to park the tent.

Out here in the wilderness, it was far nicer to be sure of your site in daylight, rather than hoping for the best in the dark!

"This should do us nicely" said Peter as he swung off the road, splashing through a shallow stream, and heading towards the back of a rocky basin flanked on all sides by steep sixty foot cliffs.

"We'll be as snug as bugs in a rug in here, and we'll have the place to ourselves!" Both Dick and I laughed at that, apart from the few people we saw in the small towns we passed through, plus the odd juggernaut, we might as well be the only people left on earth!

The next morning, the third of April at 0530, the strident calls of a Cuckoo from a ridge high above camp chased us from our beds, and as a bonus the sun came out too! The rocky basin we had chosen for our camp appeared to be a natural `stop over' for many species of birds, and we soon identified Red-rumped Wheatear, Blue Rock-Thrush, Chough(nesting), Pied Wheatear, Red Fronted Serin, Rock Sparrow, Chukar, Desert Finch, Red-rumped Swallow, Crag Martin, Saker Falcon, and the nicest for me, a beautiful Ruppell's Warbler, an old friend from Egyptian times.

As we moved off next day, I noticed we had been camping near Klm.116 and made a note of it, in case we ever had to locate the spot for the Department back in Teheran.

The next `town' on the map was called Saad-atabad, and from somewhere near there, a track branched off across open country to the villages of Arsinjan, and Aliabad, eventually ending at the shores of the Daryacheh-i-Tashk, and Bakhtigan lakes, our first wetland goal.

The map indicated we had roughly twenty miles to go before reaching Arsinjan, and probably another forty after that to the lakes, depending on the amount of snow and rain falling during the winter, which would naturally define the limits of the shoreline. Lin had asked us particularly to watch for any bird species as we passed through the Pistacchio woods of the Arsinjan reserve.

With so few people visiting the area, records were sparse, but vital.

After leaving Saad-atabad, the road degenerated into a dusty track, the bleak terrain stretching away as far as the eye could see, with barely a bush or tree to break the monotony. The only habitation we came across was a walled plantation, enclosing about twenty acres planted with almond trees.

The surrounding mud-brick wall was about eight feet high, and the only way to see what was on the other side was to stand on the Landrover's roof. The sight of hundreds of flowering almond trees in the bleak terrain was a complete anomaly, and certainly would not have existed without careful protection and watering.

Pushing on, we began to pass large oak trees every fifty yards or so, and it gradually dawned on us that this must be the Arsinjan forest Lin had mentioned. It was pretty obvious that Teheran's idea of what constituted an Oak forest, differed considerably from ours!

Many of the oaks had tremendous girths, but were relatively short - it was obvious that constant pollarding had kept their height down to 20-30', causing the top growth to become an impenetrable tangle of fine branches.

Following the track closely for several miles through the `forest', an irrigation stream gurgled along a stone-lined channel, pumped from goodness knows where, and at one point where it had flooded out onto a small patch of ground, two Green Sandpipers chased after insects!

Within a couple of miles, the oak trees thinned rapidly and finally disappeared, leaving us to clatter along a dusty track through stony wastes, the far mountains shimmering in the bright sunshine ten or twenty miles away to our left.

Arsinjan village when it appeared, turned out to be a collection of mud-brick houses lining each side of the track, where the only thing of note, was three pairs of White Storks nesting very precariously in a small scraggly tree. We saw several Humes' Wheatears, a few Swallows, and over 100 Swifts zooming backwards and forwards over a boggy piece of ground, but not a living soul.

For the next thirty miles we bumped along, leaving a huge dust-cloud behind us, until we came to Alibad, which, if it were possible, was more rustic than Arsinjan. This time we actually caught sight of someone, an old chap, whom I asked in dreadful Farsi `Daryacheh Tashk, Daryacheh Bakhtigan?' and he nodded, pointing in the direction we were heading, at least that was alright! The situation felt for all the world like Alice in Wonderland, where the nearer we got to Bakhtigan, the further it seemed away!

Gradually the mountains on either side fell even further back, the 7000' Kuh-i-Kum on our left became a low smudge on the horizon, and as dusk fell, it became obvious we were on a downward sloping plateau heading for the lakes, surely they couldn't be far away now?

With all lights blazing, we carefully navigated the bumpy, pot-holed track, hoping to god we wouldn't end up axle deep in the lake, when in the headlights, a mud-brick wall suddenly appeared, then another, and another, so close we could easily reach out and touch them from the vehicle.

"What the hell have we here?" said Dick in an exasperated voice. "We seem to be in someone's ruddy backyard"

Creeping forward in first gear, we passed close to several houses, before finding our way blocked by a raised dyke wall - that was obviously it for the day, we weren't going any further.

"I reckon that's it then fellers" I said. "Let's get out and see what we can make of the situation" and on inspection found we were between a maze of ditches and dykes, the nearest six feet wide, and about eight feet deep, filled with water.

"There's no point in blundering about in the dark" said Peter. "I think we ought to camp here for the night, and sort out where the hell we are in the morning. We're all hungry and need a meal, let's do it here"

With the Landrover practically filling the space between the surrounding dykes, the only space left to erect the tent was behind the vehicle, knocking the guy lines into the mud-brick walls for support, it all seemed a bit of a mess!

The next morning our pleasant dreams were interrupted by the religious chanting of a man passing close by our tent, urging his flock of sheep and goats along with clicks and whistles. They trotted and stumbled over our badly deployed guy lines, practically bringing the tent down, it was quite a circus. Tumbling into bright sunshine at 0530, we were horrified to see we had parked slap in the centre of the only track leaving the village on this side, forcing the villagers and their animals to go round our tent to get to their fields!

Without a backward glance, or word of admonishment, our chanting man continued through a small gap in the dyke wall with his flock, and disappeared from sight. We had better get the hell out of here fast!

Whilst I was on the Laandrover's roof packing down the tent, I looked around, and noticed the shepherd had crossed the dyke in front of us by traversing a huge circular concrete pipe, which filled the dyke from side to side, leaving the deep water to flow through its middle. It was something we just hadn't seen in the dark last night.

"Ah ha, that's obviously our way out then" I said, and pointed it out for Dick's benefit. "I'm glad it's your turn to drive Dick, you can do the necessary and we'll guide you across, it'll be as easy as pie"

Dick obviously felt it was ok. too, but I noticed the middle of the pipe was a foot higher than the ground on either side, and to make matters worse, the pipe was only six inches wider than the the track of our vehicle.

I could see us slipping off the ruddy pipe into the dyke if we weren't careful! With Dick's accurate driving and our frantic arm-waving, we were soon across the dyke, and trundling beside the sparkling waters of Lake Tashk.

It was time to stop for breakfast.

We had parked a few yards from the muddy shoreline, and it was a simple matter to get out the folding chairs, and sit with binocs and telescope, trying to identify the myriads of wildfowl just off-shore. First off, there were hundreds of Flamingo, some only 200 yards away, with the water barely half-way up their tarsus - the lake must be very shallow round here!

Around the Flamingoes were White Pelicans and Spoonbills, 200+ Ruddy Shelduck, 3000+ Widgeon, 200 Shelduck, 5000 Teal, 1000 Pintail, and hundreds of Garganey, Shoveller and Pochard. We also counted 1200+ Tufted Duck, and several Ferruginous Duck, all in all a staggering sight!

A wonderful bonus for me, was the sight of 10 Red-Breasted Geese taking off and flying against the purple backdrop of the nearby mountains, it was just like a Peter Scott painting!

There were also great rafts of wildfowl we couldn't identify or even guess at as they were too far out, and could only estimate their numbers by counting an area, and multiplying it into the main mass.

All in all we felt the total number of wildfowl present to be not far short of 50,000 birds.

There was a regular track running along the muddy shoreline, suggesting village traffic passed this way, and it wasn't long before we saw some of it. Three 100cc. two-strokes clattered towards us bearing the most gi-normous loads of twigs and branches I had ever seen strapped to such small machines, the pile was a foot higher than the driver, and about four feet wide!

To keep the front end down, the driver had to sit on the extreme tip of the saddle, and trail his feet along the ground in an effort to keep the bike upright in the slippery mud!

As they drew alongside, they stopped their engines and started to talk to us, no doubt asking who we were, and what we were doing. Having only the barest command of Farsi, we could only answer, "We Ingloustan, parander-shanas" (bird-watchers) and point to our binoculars. The sight of the three men and their bikes was so funny I couldn't resist taking a couple of photographs of them, plus some of the villagers who suddenly appeared from nowhere. There was even one herdsman who carried a couple of newborn goat kids in his motor-bike saddle bags, so they could keep up with the main flock!

While they were all jabbering away amongst themselves, I switched on my portable tape recorder, hoping to record a bit of local atmosphere for the people at home to listen to.

Looking up, I saw one of the group eyeing me closely, no doubt thinking something diabolical was going on, so I shut off the recorder, re-wound the tape, and played back the recorded conversation.

The effect was astounding.

All conversation ceased, as everyone tried to hear the sounds coming from the tape recorder.

Suddenly one of them pointed to a friend and said something like `Hey that's you talking isn't it?' and they all crowded round trying to hear themselves on tape, it was a real circus.

I held up my hand and said, "Hey, hold it a minute" pressed record, and motioned one of them to start talking directly into the microphone.

After that I had a hell of a job to stop them talking and singing continuously and possibly wearing my batteries out, they just loved hearing themselves `on the radio'as they called it. After a while they got the message, and prepared to move off, leaving us in peace.

Two of the chaps who hadn't got off their bikes for fear of losing their load, kick-started their machines and pulled slowly away, slipping the clutch like mad so as not to stall the engine. The third fella pulled in the clutch, kick started the bike, and as he let the clutch out the merest fraction, the bike stalled.

He must have done the same thing half a dozen times, causing us to smile at his dilemma. Perhaps we should give him a shove?

"No, I'll tell you what we'll do" said Dick, "I'll clean all that caked mud off the clutch release, and adjust the clutch lever so's it will work properly, then he'll be ok"

"Well the best of luck to you Dick!" I said. "I don't think they'll appreciate you mucking about with their bikes, they probably don't know any better, best leave well alone"

"You know me and things mechanical, I can't stand by and see something like that all to cock, I'll give it a go"

Waving his arms about, and pointing here there and everywhere, Dick finally managed to get the chap off his bike, although the looks he got from the hard faced Iranian, suggested he thought Dick was trying to pinch his wood!

With two villagers supporting the bike and its load, Dick got cracking with his tools, and soon large chunks of mud fell off, exposing a crankcase that hadn't seen the light of day in years.

"Just look at the state of this stretched cable" said Dick. "It's a bloody disgrace, it's got no adjustment left, I don't know how he got this far"

"He's looking at you a bit mean-like" mumbled Peter. "I only hope you can get it going again after all this, otherwise our heads might roll"

"No worries, as soon as I've trimmed the cable, greased it up and got some movement on the release lever, it'll be fine, just like new!"

Ten minutes later Dick stood up, wiped his hands mechanic-like on an oily rag and said "Well there you are chum, all finished and no charge to you, it's on the house"

The man hesitated, he didn't know what Dick had been doing, or why, all he knew was that these Ingloustanis had got him off his bike, when he should be on his way home. With a grim expression, he re-mounted the bike, kick-started the engine and pulled the clutch in fully as he had been doing for weeks, and clonked it into first gear.

Because it didn't stall immediately he let the clutch out, he glared furiously in our direction, you could actually see the cogs in his brain going round - what the hell had we done?

Revving furiously, he let the clutch out a little more, and still the bike remained motionless. His expression changed to anger as he revved again, letting the clutch out about half-way, and still the bike refused to move. Both Peter and I looked anxiously at Dick, for his re-action to the scene.

Still holding the throttle half open, the Iranian relaxed from his taut riding position, and let the clutch lever go, he'd had enough of these interfering Ingloustanis!

Suddenly the bike reared like a frightened pony as the fully engaged clutch bit, and our friend threw himself forward to bring it under control, before wobbling along the track at a high rate of knots, shouting furiously as he finally disappeared.

I'm afraid we laughed like mad.

"I told you it wasn't wise to interfere, I don't suppose he'll thank you in the least for that" I said, and we all went back into the tent.

Just before sunset, thousands of wildfowl began streaming into view from the eastern end of the lake, dropping down into an area between our camp and a small island a couple of miles offshore, and soon the water became black with roosting birds. We started counting again, and confidently arrived at a total of in excess of 50,000 birds, it was fantastic.

As darkness fell, the fiercely bright stars came into view, and the only sound to be heard was the continuous muttering of thousands of wildfowl across the still waters, it was very relaxing.

At 0430 the next morning we were roused from deep sleep by the tent flapping wildly in great gusts of wind, and heavy rain drops smacking onto the flysheet, which continued unabated for half an hour, and then silence.

Half asleep, I crawled out of my sleeping bag at 0600 to the liquid calls of Nuthatch and Blue Rock Thrushes, when the wind suddenly sprang up again, driving huge black clouds off the far mountains towards our camp. The temperature dropped quickly, and torrents of ice-cold rain crashed down, reducing visibility to less than five yards, turning the lake margin into a quagmire. It wasn't very nice at all.

As suddenly as it had started, the rain stopped, the wind died away to nothing, and everything went very quiet.

Without warning, and like a raging demon, the wind returned with a terrific crash, threatening to tear the tent out of the ground and driving rain horizontally into everything.

For an hour and a half we huddled in the tent, waiting for the storm to abate, occasionally unzipping the door a little to make sure that all was well with the Landrover. Then, like someone throwing a switch, the rain died away to nothing, the wind fell, and weak sunshine came out, ending an astounding sequence of events.

In an attempt to warm ourselves up with a nice hot cuppa, everyone made a dash for the Landrover, at least we'd be warm and dry in there with the Calor gas burner going! After half an hour, we nipped out, downed the tent, collected our bits and pieces, and prepared to move along the shoreline to a site offering better shelter, we could get another crashing downpour any minute.

About a mile further on, we came to a deep gorge in the cliffs, which had a grassy knoll at its entrance and looked far more secure than the last place. We re-erected the tent there.

Whilst making ourselves comfortable, numbers of Wheatears, Shrikes and Desert warblers flicked around the camp, while overhead Kestrels and Egyptian vultures jockeyed in the strong up-currents of air whistling between the 100' cliffs.

It looked as though we might have found a good site.

Getting out the telescope, we sat and did another wildfowl count, producing much the same figures and species as yesterday, lake Tashk is obviously of great importance to wildfowl, both for feeding and roosting, and needs a lot of study to evaluate its potential fully.

The following day I decided to try and tape some of the bird calls we were hearing, and that was when I discovered I had left my parabolic reflector at home - a bit of a disaster that, the bare mike on it's own was pretty useless!

Amongst the tumbled boulders that littered the floor of the gorge, over a dozen `pied' Wheatears flicked backwards and forwards, some agitated at our presence, others carrying food to hidden nests.

It took me several minutes to realise that amongst the fairly obvious Hume's, were two Mourning Wheatears, which demonstrated we would have to be very much on our toes, carefully checking everything we saw. I sat down in the lee of a huge boulder and watched a Hume's wheatear carrying food towards a pile of shattered stones, and quickly found the nest containing four fully fledged young. I got my camera and took a couple of photographs for future reference.

The thought crossed my mind that having found both Nuthatch and Wheatear with young during the first week in April - much earlier than I had expected, what other species might we be too late to find nesting in the days to come?

Watching a couple of Egyptian vultures overhead, I noticed they were making repeated flights into a cave 200' up our gorge wall - it certainly looked worth investigating as a possible nest site, I'd have to investigate.

As I climbed the wall, several Ruddy Shelducks scrambled off the ledges, their nasal `Aargh-aargh' calls echoing down the gorge as they flew towards the lake and safety. Their frantic exit caught the attention of a passing Golden Eagle, who changed direction and planed rapidly after them along the rock face, wings crooked back for maximum speed. From my position fifty feet away the eagle was a magnificent sight, but this time he was unlucky, the Shelducks were well away.

The cave wasn't that difficult to reach, but apart from dozens of Desert Sparrow nests jammed into every possible crevice, there was no sign of Egyptian vulture activity anywhere, despite the cave floor being sixty feet long, and fifteen feet wide. I was about to climb down when a loud twittering caught my attention, and I noticed several small Swifts zooming in and out - where had they come from?

Re-tracing my steps, I found a colony of 60+ Little Swifts at the end of the cave, their nests of dried grasses and feathers stuck to the roof of the cave in any convenient hollow or crevice, so well camouflaged as to be almost invisible at first glance.

The birds whizzed round my head screaming shrilly, popping in and out of their almost invisible nest entrances, with no apparent concern, despite my standing there taking photographs.

When I reaching ground level again, I continued up the gorge for half a mile, noting the walls were about 700' high with a surprising variation in their make up. In some places rank grasses and thorn bushes jostled for position on dizzy shale escarpments, while in others, slabs of featureless rock soared cathedral-like into the sky, interspersed with wind eroded buttresses and crumbling sandstone bastions.

In this seemingly quiet and lifeless habitat, I discovered a bird whose agility on rocks and ledges had to be seen to be believed. It was the Chukar Partridge.

When disturbed from a ledge, the bird flew rapidly along the gorge, and after about thirty yards veered sharply at ninety degrees, heading full speed towards a sheer rock-wall.

In the last few inches before collision, and in one magical movement, the bird brakes, touches down, and runs rapidly up the vertical wall to a small look-out point, calling `Caccaba-caacaba' as though laughing out loud.

Quite a bit different from the French Partridges I knew back home!

Back in camp, I was spooning down the last of some tinned peaches, when I noticed a small brown, long-tailed bird making its way cautiously through nearby thorn bushes, calling `Ter-zit, ter-zit' and I recognised an old friend from Suez Canal days 25 years before. It was a Graceful warbler, and it was carrying food.

The bird was typically bold in its actions, just as I remembered it, and I found the nest within five minutes. It was a typical ramshackle collection of straws and grasses wedged in the middle of a viciously spiked bush. It contained several small young.

Although it was almost unnecessary, I put up a hide six feet away, and got in with the 200mm lens and electronic flash to record this delightful little bird. In an hour, I had taken half a dozen shots, showing the bird entering and leaving the nest, but due to a steadily rising wind - just like yesterday, I dismantled the hide and joined the others in an evening duck count before the impending storm broke.

Due to the extreme distance of most birds from shore, binocs were virtually useless, and the tripod mounted telescope became our only hope of successfully identifying sspecies. As before, huge rafts of Widgeon, Teal, Shelduck, Pintail, Shoveller, Pochard and Tufted duck dominated the scene, interspersed with Flamingo, Spoonbill and Pelican, I had never imagined so many wildfowl being together in one place, as they are here!

The rising wind veered considerably, and was now driving straight into our gorge, making life very uncomfortable - it was time to move again in the hope of finding an even more protected spot. That however, turned out like jumping from the frying pan into the fire, as we drove slowly along the muddy lake margin in the direction of Gumoon village.

Ugly black storm clouds rolling off the distant mountains discharged sheets of heavy slanting rain, closing visibility down to a few miserable yards. Peter, who was driving, complained it was almost impossible to hold the Landrover in a straight line under such slippery conditions, and despite being in four-wheel drive, we slithered this way and that, as though on ice.

If anything, the downpour increased, but we pressed on in the hope of finding somewhere better to stop, anywhere that offered a decent bit of shelter, but in this weather it didn't look good. In one or two places the locals had placed large mats of twigs and branches on the mud, enabling them to cross small streams running into the lake, which we were only too pleased to use, but I had this gut feeling we weren't improving our lot by going on.

I felt we were driving into a no-win situation that wasn't ever going to turn to our advantage. Over the next couple of miles, the steep cliffs on our left got closer and closer, until we were forced to drive with our offside wheels continuously in the lake, and were only saved from bogging down by the locals' use of branches and twigs to pave the way.

Directly in our path a low spur of rock jutted into the lake, causing us to mount its rocks with our nearside wheels, leaving the offside ones half submerged in water as we carefully navigated the hazard. Once or twice Peter looked questioningly at Dick and I, as the vehicle leant at a dangerous angle towards the lake, but he carried on. Things weren't looking too good.

"I'll get out and recce ahead before we go any further" I volunteered, and dressed up in an effort to keep out some of the rain. This definitely wasn't the sort of weather we needed or expected - roll on summer!

Fifty yards in front of the Landrover I came across a huge boulder, the size of a London bus, which had toppled from the cliff completely blocking the track between cliff and water - we weren't going any further along that route for sure!

The bottom of the lake at this point consisted of soft grey mud, totally incapable of supporting the weight of our vehicle if we tried driving round the rock, besides, further reconnaissance beyond the boulder showed another rock spur blocking the way entirely. We would have to go back.

As if to emphasise our dilemma, the weak daylight faded to a dull grey murk, and the wind rose in fierce gusts, driving ice cold rain horizontally before it like bullets. Through my rain spattered glasses I couldn't see a thing, and stumbled about like a drunk, in the mud. What a flippin' mess!

"Ok.Peter, if you turn her round, Dick and I will keep our eyes peeled for hazards while you take us back, and may god bless all who sail in her!"

The hairy bit came whilst turning round, how far could we risk going backwards into the lake to get opposite lock, without bogging down? I was conscious that we all held our breath as Peter manoeuvred to and fro, it would be disastrous to get stuck now.

In two hours of the worst weather conditions yet encountered, we recovered the ground made over the last two days, despite the lake rising at least 6" and covering our outward tracks completely.

In complete darkness and belting rain we somehow managed to find the little village at the end of the Arsinjan trail, and stopped to see which way we should go.

"If we can find the way out of this place, we ought to give it best and move on" I said.

"Bloody good idea" muttered Dick.

As if in a bad dream the vehicle lurched between a maze of mud-brick walls absolutely running with water, our six headlights cutting a swathe through the stygian darkness and lashing rain, until we came to an apparent dead end by a dyke. Definitely a touch of the deja-vous here!

Dick and I got out, immediately sinking to our boot tops in thick clinging mud, and all but losing our balance in the treacherous goo.

On our left a flooded field containing a couple of mud huts began a few feet from the vehicle, while the same appeared on our right. In front, a glistening mound of mud, similar to a load dumped from a cement lorry, completely blocked our way.

Where the hell was out?

In the cold pouring rain, Dick and I discussed with Peter what the heck we could do next, when a faint voice called from beyond the mound of mud, and a couple of storm lanterns swung into view.

Who the heck would be out on a night like this?

Over the mound, and into the glare of our headlights emerged the figures of two men, swathed against the rain, their storm lashed voices obviously enquiring who we were, and what we were doing.

In my best Farsi I shouted "Ingloustan, Ingloustan, paranda shanass, go Shiraz" ( English birdwatchers-going to Shiraz)

"Ok. Burro, burro, (Ok. go, go,) said one, beckoning us forward to the mound and waving his lamp, while his friend did the same.

I thought they must be nuts or something, there was no way out there, just a mound of water saturated mud.

Standing either side of the mound they swung their lanterns, calling intermittently `Burro, burro!' and I thought I must go and see what on earth they were on about.

Through rain splashed glasses I saw the mound of mud was in fact, another of those concrete pipes dropped into the deep dyke, only this one was covered with six inches of gooey mud, hence the `mound' appearance.

"You must be bloody joking!" said Peter, after I told him what I had found. "We'll never make it across in this rain"

"If Dick and I stand on the six inches to spare either side as you come across, we'll try to make sure you're in a straight line, if she starts to slide sideways we'll yell for you to stop before she goes in!"

"Thanks a bunch" said Peter, and let out the clutch.

At the first attempt, the front wheels spun as they met the muddy concrete pipe, causing the Landrover to wander to the right, almost pushing Dick into the dyke.

At the second attempt, with a bit less throttle, plus the two Iranians and ourselves pushing like mad, we got the Landrover onto the middle, leaving Peter to inch her carefully down the other side, and across. It had been a very close thing!

Thanking our Iranian friends for their selfless help, I took the wheel from Peter, who had done well to get us back this far, and we splashed off in the direction indicated by our friends as leading to Shiraz. It was 1930hrs and raining like mad.

With all lights blazing in an effort to see something in the pelting rain, I followed the narrow ribbon of track which hopefully would take us to Shiraz, some fifty miles away, while Peter took a well earned nap in the kip-couch.

Dick was supposedly navigating.

The waterlogged track snaked backwards and forwards following the contours of the barren land, dipping into hollows and gulleys that gushed with running water, it was like driving along the bed of a small river!

Under our powerful lights, the faint trail appeared greyish against the darker colour of the untrodden soil, while the water-filled dips and pot-holes remained ominously black by comparison.

Some of the dips in the track were so extensively flooded, pools 50 yards long had formed, with no indication as to whether they were an inch deep or six feet! I just had to carefully edge the Landrover into the water and take a chance, hoping the track continued opposite the place where I eventually came out!

It was a really weird sensation inching your way through dark water, unable to see the ground on either side, dreading a lurch that would say you had gone in too deep, so I tried to put it out of my mind.

I soon lost one of our low spotlights when it thumped against a rock or something under water, but they hadn't been as good as I had expected out here anyway, casting worrying oblique shadows on rough terrain, and making the ground seem worse than it really was.

The windscreen wipers groaned away endlessly - not one of Landrover's better features, just about keeping the windscreen clear, and I had to drive with my nose jammed against the windscreen to read anything of the way ahead.

For the next three hours I ploughed through flooded gulleys and racing torrents that virtually obliterated the track, and it was demonstrated to me time and again, that without four-wheel drive, we wouldn't have got anywhere under these dreadfully demanding conditions.

Driving in continuous pouring rain after dark had dulled my senses, and I became slightly mesmerised, concentrating on the unfolding track ahead.

It was some time before I finally realised there were one or two stars in the black sky ahead, the clouds had gone, and the downpour finished. At least that was something.

The red glow from my digital watch indicated it was 2300hrs, and by my reckoning we should be nearing the Shiraz road at a place called Zarqan, but as all place names are written in Farsi, signs were useless unless you could ask somebody where you were.

Suddenly Dick nudged my arm - he must have woken from his `navigating' and pointed to tiny vehicle headlights moving along an invisible track miles ahead. We had made it to the Shiraz road! The sweet relief in quitting that bloody awful track, and being able to drive along a smooth tarmac road once again, was a marvellous lift to the senses.

A few clicks down the road towards Shiraz we found and all night cafe serving coffee and sweet cakes, where we made real pigs of ourselves, and the smiling proprietor a little bit richer.

It was only a few miles now to the city of nightingales and roses, neither of which was much in evidence at one o'clock in the morning, so we found ourselves a quiet lay-by and parked the vehicle as best we could. It was bitterly cold.

# Chapter Eighteen

We were woken by the rumble of passing traffic at 0530, and thought it might be a good idea if we could locate one of the campsites shown in our INTO (Iranian National Tourist Office) guide, for a wash and brush up, and maybe even a meal. I had managed to get a few street maps of Esfahan and Shiraz whilst we were in Teheran, and now it paid off, the maps showed an INTO campsite a few miles down the road, we might just be in luck.

The imposing green painted gates were firmly closed, and a black beretted, uniformed person sat immobile in his little hut, oblivious to anything other than his newspaper.

I finally got his attention, and he reluctantly came across to the gate.

"We are English tourists, can we come in?"

"Not before 10 o'clock"

"How much does it cost please?"

"Two hundred and fifty rials a day each, (£2.50) without hot water, that is reserved for chalets sleeping seven people or more"

"Have you any eating facilities here"

"No, you eat in town, or bring your own"

He was still rambling on about something or other in ludicrous detail, as I backed away and got back into the Landrover.

"No joy there fellers, we'd better continue into town and see if we can find the Iranian Wildlife Department office, perhaps they can help us".

Just before the steep descent into town, there was a fresh water fountain running into the equivalent of an old London horse trough, which we commandeered for a while, trying to make our selves a bit more presentable and sweet-smelling, in case we had to meet someone important.

Although we knew the name of the street the Department's office was located in - the Karim Khan-e-Zand, there was a whole minefield to cross when asking the first person you met, how you might find it.

In Teheran I had found the average Iranian had no idea how to interpret a two dimensional map into his three-dimensional surroundings. I developed a technique whereby I approached modern dressed Iranian girls, usually finding them fluent in either German or French, and got the information I needed that way.

Because I had achieved some earlier success in this technique, I was 'volunteered' to try it again now, so taking a letter with the Department's crest and address printed on it, I approached a couple of girls I saw, and pointing to the address, asked where it might be.

Smiling acknowledgement, one of the girls scribbled down how to get there on my piece of paper and handed it back to me, before continuing on her way with her friend.

It was only when I looked at the paper to interpret her instructions, I found she had written it in Farsi!

This minor problem was soon overcome by tackling some girls just leaving a religious school nearby, and as one of them spoke French, we soon got the directions translated.

In no time we were knocking on the door of Mr. Hooshang Adami, head of the Department, who, on finding who we were, benevolently made us welcome.

We were invited to put our Landrover in their secure yard, and make ourselves at home in their 'guest room' where three beds and a hot water shower were ours for the taking. Much cleaner, and I hoped sweeter-smelling, I presented Mr Adami with our precious Teheran document, which outlined who we were and what we hoped to do during our stay in the Province of Fars.

He positively beamed with delight, telling us he was honoured by our presence, and wished to know all we had done and seen, since leaving Teheran.

"Ok. all that sounds very interesting, I shall now get our friend Majid, a field botanist from Meshed to take you for a meal, and then show you round our city of Shiraz, I'll see you all later".

Following our botanist, who spoke passably good English, into the busy street, we entered a large restaurant to sample some of the delights of Iranian cuisine. Chelo-Kebab, charcoal grilled lamb, with rice and butter - Fesenjan, Chicken cooked in a sauce of pomegranates and walnuts, followed by glasses of strong tea and Iranian unleavened bread, it was delicious!

Majid was obviously no stranger to Shiraz, and took us on a guided tour through the maze of rambling bazaars, showing us pottery, brassware, leatherwork, jewellery, glittering clothes from India, and exotic foodstuffs and spices, so strong they took your breath away. There was even a shop selling stereo tape recorders with Dolby noise reduction, something we were still waiting for in the UK.   It was all here.

By 1800 feeling pretty exhausted from the continual rubber-necking, we made our way back to the Department and said a grateful au-voir to Majid, who had gone out of his way to be a good friend and guide.

After the last couple of days waking up to nothing more devastating than bird-song, it was a shock to our system to be woken at 0730 by the roar of city traffic and crowing cockerels, and it took us a few minutes to figure out where the hell we were. After breakfast Mr. Adami came into the room, asking if all was well, and I took the opportunity to ask him if he would kindly return our document, as we expected to leave Shiraz at two o'clock that day, bound for Lake Perishan with Majid.

"No trouble, I'll have it ready for you, come to my office when you are leaving, it will be there"

At two o'clock I tried to locate Mr. Adami, only to be told he had left the Department that morning, and wouldn't be back until later the next day, which was damned annoying because without our document, we could easily be in trouble running around on our own.

Un-graciously perhaps, I felt he had held on to our document for personal use, perhaps to impress other departmental staff concerning his dealings with the 'big-house' in Teheran, I don't know, but I didn't get it back.

It was a good thing we had Majid along as guide after Shiraz, I'm sure we wouldn't have made the journey through the extremely mountainous country as easily as we did - out here, was definitely the back of all beyonds, and it was very easy to get lost.

After what seemed an age, we arrived at a small, dusty Iranian 'town' hilariously named Kazeroun City, which looked to us like a frontier cowboy town after the gold had run out!

With the sun getting low in the sky, we set off on the last leg, passing through a narrow gap between shops and houses, and along a bumpy pot-holed dirt road which Majid assured us DID lead to Lake Perishan, or Daryacheh Famur as the locals called it. Eventually our headlights showed the track petering out on a small promontory, where a sign in English and Farsi indicated we were in a nature reserve, and must repect all wildlife found there.

In a night made bright by the full moon, we erected the tent under twinkling stars, while a warm wind blew across the water bringing the reed beds alive with a soft rustling sound, it was a great place to camp. It was only after we had finished our meal, we became aware of a peculiar continuous rasping sound, rather like the muttering of massed waterfowl, and after searching around, found it to be the monotonous grating calls of thousands and thousands of frogs, plopping about in the mud.

The next day we were up just as the sun cleared the snow covered mountain ridges opposite, with the drooling, melancholy calls of Crested Larks for company, and surveyed the scene for the first time in daylight, it was breathtaking.

A few yards from where we stood, a six-foot wide dyke ran fifty yards across the marsh into the lake, and hovering over it were a pair of Pied Kingfishers, whose trilling calls drew my attention to their newly excavated nest-hole in the bank.

In an attempt to evaluate our surroundings for birdlife, I suggested we ought to explore the large marshy area between the track we had arrived on, and the water's edge, half of which was under wheat cultivation, the rest rough grasses and sedge set in a sea of oozy grey mud.

Setting off together, we were soon amongst a myriad of birds, several pairs of Black Headed Wagtails held nesting territories, as did dozens of grating Clamorous Reed Warblers. There were also Cattle and Little Egret, Ruff, Squacco Heron, a dozen or so White Tailed Plover, crowds of Kentish Plover, Redshank, Greenshank, Glossy Ibis, Spoonbill, Night, Common and Great White Heron, the latter apparently non-breeding birds without their plumes, but with a black-tipped bill, probably wintering here from China.

Through-out the next couple of hours under a blue sky and brilliant sun, we continued to log the fantastic array of species this part of the lake contained, Marsh Harriers, Purple Heron, Little Grebe, Widgeon, a raft of a hundred Pelican, and to overlay it all, well over a thousand Coot, individual birds dotting the water every few yards.

Pushing our way through a dense area of reeds about five feet high, we all jumped in fright as a huge wild boar the size of a Shetland pony, got up from his muddy wallow, and charged across the shallow lake in a welter of spray, scaring off hundreds of birds.

Returning to camp at mid-day, we found a local Game Guard, an Iranian named Zamit-Kesh sitting outside our tent next to his motor bike, scanning the lake through his binocs. He greeted Majid in Farsi, and it transpired they knew each other from a visit some years before. Majid told us that Zamit came from a village on the other side of the lake called Sharanjan, and travelled about the reserve on his dilapidated Honda two-stroke motorbike, keeping some sort of law and order.

He was, according to Majid, quite well up on birds, and when I showed him the Collins Field Guide, Zamit was able to point out many of the species we had already seen, plus one which we hadn't found yet, the rare White-Headed Duck. He indicated it could be found much further down the lake on the far side.

Translating their conversation, Majid told us that Zamit would now return to his village, and come back across the lake in his punt to show us the birds he knew, it all sounded very promising.

Within an hour I saw him poling his way effortlessly across the lake, and it appeared from the length of his pole, the water was eight to ten feet deep in most places, but often a lot less. When he arrived, we saw his punt was a sturdily built, flat bottomed craft without a keel, and of rather basic design. With enthusiastic bravado I volunteered to have first go with the paddle instead of the pole, to see how it handled.

I soon found it impossible to paddle the craft in a straight line due to its banana shape and lack of a keel, and quickly realised why Zamit preferred to use his pole! It was all he could do not to laugh, as we made our way across the lake in a series of curves!

On return to camp Zamit said 'Hodofez' - goodbye in Farsi and began poling for home, he had things to do. When we had finished our evening meal, Majid offered to show us where to get fresh water, something that had been bothering me ever since we arrived at the lake - it was surprising how much we got through in our day to day living.

The source of the water was a spring three miles down the track, which gurgled from the base of a 500' cliff and ran into a small enclosed pond, the bathing place of ladies from the nearby village of Pasgard.

It was the only place for miles around where any trees grew, and due to the freshwater spring, its plantation of Casuarinas was quite dense, in fact it was the daytime roost for about 200 Night Herons.

On the way back with our precious water, we passed through the tiny village of Ayuzabad, where we were greeted by shouts of "Manchester United!" from a group of young lads playing volley-ball over a fishing net stretched between two poles. What the heck did lads out here know about Man.United, and more importantly how did they know we would understand their greeting?

Zamit came over again the next day, and left us his punt to explore the reed-beds on the far side of the lake near Sharanjan village, indicating he preferred to stretch out under the fly sheet of our tent, and have a good kip. The reed beds on the far side where the mountain range dropped steeply into the water were appreciably different from those on our side. Growing in fifteen feet of water, the reeds were already ten feet high, making them twenty five feet tall from their roots!

There were dozens of Great Crested and Little grebe about, and a pair of Black-Necked Grebe, whose nest I found containing three eggs. This delightful bird was seen several times skulking through stands of reeds, its golden ear tufts and dark head blending perfectly with the sun-dappled stems. In the quiet back waters between the tall reeds and the rocky shore, we came across nine of the rare White Headed Duck, five males and four females, all of whom disappeared into the reeds at our approach, despite us being nearly a hundred yards away. They certainly are a difficult species to get close to.

After a couple of days, we began to settle in to a routine, and although we were seeing lots of birds of the area, it was obvious most of them were migrants - it was still too early for local nesting species. Despite that, it didn't take me long to find my first Clamorous Reed Warbler's nest which contained four eggs, but as it was built over deep water, photography was quite out of the question.

One morning, just as we were about to go down to the shore line, Mr. Adami, plus an entourage of his friends descended on us in a Department Landrover, causing us to play host with tea and coffee for an hour, while recounting everything we had seen and done since we arrived. I asked him about our document, and he apologised profusely, saying he had forgotten to bring it with him, which reinforced my original suspicion that he wanted to keep it for prestige reasons.

Everything we said of note was taken down in a little notebook by Mr. Adami's No.2, and no doubt the talking would have gone on for ages, but for the arrival of Zamit, who, on seeing his boss from distant Shiraz drinking coffee with the 'foreigners', sat unobtrusively to one side, but didn't miss a word of what was being said.

They seemed genuinely interested in seeing something of the birdlife on the lake, so I suggested that Mr. Adami and some of his friends might like to accompany Zamit in his punt to see the spoonbill colony, which would get them out of our hair for an hour or two. The fat one, who apparently didn't like boats, we parked in a newly erected hide on the Pied Kingfisher's nest, saying he should sit in there quietly for an hour or so, carefully timing the birds' arrivals and departures for our records! Eventually they all piled into their transport and left for Shiraz, it was a relief to see them go.

Zamit strongly insisted through Majid, that his side of the lake at Sharanjan was worth looking at too, and although the species we saw here each day would be difficult to beat, it was decided to give Sharanjan the once over, just to keep him happy. I'm sure it was more of a prestige thing for him, to be able to bring the Ingloustanis across the lake to HIS village for a visit!

That night I experienced a peculiar happening which was far and away above the normal things I had become used to over the years. I had long been accustomed to sometimes knowing what a person was going to say next, or knowing in a few minutes time I was going to meet someone I knew in a totally unexpected location, but this was something quite different.

We had all gone to bed about 2230hrs, feeling pretty whacked after a long day, when suddenly I sat bolt upright in my sleeping bag, and said out loud, 'Teresa's in trouble, what on earth does she want?'

I had woken Dick with my outburst, and he turned to me grumpily, saying "What do you mean she's in trouble, who is in trouble, are you dreaming or something?"

I looked at my watch glowing clearly in the dark, and saw it was 2330. I had been asleep an hour. Why had Teresa's anxiety come through so clearly and woken me, as though she had called my name out loud? It took me an hour or more to relax and finally go to sleep, but in the morning, the first thing I did after breakfast, was to write a letter to Teresa asking what the problem was, why had she 'contacted' me at 2030hrs

English time?

There was no doubt something was seriously wrong, and we'd only been away a month!

As we needed more fresh water, it was decided to combine that chore with a short visit to Sharanjan, so our campsite would have to be completely cleared. At the police post by the waterhole, I could give my letter to the driver of the Toyota pick-up 'bus' who took passengers into Kazeroun City and beyond.

Along with other shopping chores he would post it in Shiraz when he got there. It was our only contact with the outside world.

It felt funny pulling up stakes from our delightful campsite, the place had been a good home to us during the last few days. Peter said he wanted to row across the lake with Zamit in the punt, leaving Dick to lead the way in front of the Landrover, astride Zamit's little two-stroke bike.

It was a slow, bumpy three miles to the waterhole and Police 'post', and when I arrived, Dick was already supping tea from a glass with the Police Sergeant and his two men. The Post was a sagging four-man tent that had seen better days, dumped folornly by the track near the village of Deh-i-Pul. It was obviously the 'nerve centre' and passenger collection point for miles around.

A dozen yards away the Toyota bus sat waiting for customers, and I pulled alongside to give the driver my letter for Shiraz which he accepted with a grin. At the police post I could see Dick talking to the inhabitants, so I pulled off the track and walked across to see what was going on in the tent. Inside, the Sergeant and his men, plus a Kurd in national head-dress were all standing talking, while a glass of dark tea passed from hand to hand in friendly fashion.

"Come in and have some tea old chap!" grinned Dick in his best upper-class English accent. "Although none of us understands a word the other chap is saying, we're getting on fine, by the way did you manage to hand your letter to the bus driver?".

Nodding the affirmative, I was duly presented with the glass recently drained by the Kurd, now refilled with strong tea and lots of black stalks swirling about in the bottom. Putting a brave face on it I took a cautious sip of the brew and groaned - it was horrible!

"I don't like tea without milk, or without sugar it's just not on" I growled at Dick, my mouth crawling as if I'd just bitten on a sloe, "Haven't they got any sugar?"

The Sergeant must have guessed something was wrong, and pointed to a screwed up paper bag on his little table, then pointed to his mouth at the same time.

Looking into the bag I saw various lumps of crystallised brown stuff, and suddenly fell in, it was sweetener for the tea - the same stuff we kids used to call 'hokey-pokey, penny a lump' sold by street vendors from a tricycle cart before the war!

The Sarge nodded, and said "Kand, kand" and I knew immediately what he meant, it was weird having a hidden memory like that brought to light after all these years. I popped a large piece into my mouth, and gritting my teeth, swigged the tea round it before swallowing, and somehow the stuff didn't seem so bad after all.

Having completed our obligatory tea - I think the glass went round three times, I made excuses to leave, and tucked in behind Dick down the bumpy track to Sharanjan. Within a mile or two the track deteriorated into a rocky footpath, winding between dry stone walls, so narrow they threatened to tear the free-wheel hubs off the front wheels, I had to watch it.

The walled track ran for some distance along the lake margin, and at one point dipped sharply to become a water filled trough fifty yards long. Dick, in a moment of bravado lifted his legs and ploughed through on Zamit's bike at speed, only to come a cropper as the ignition flooded. With a loud blare on the klaxons I surged past him, sending a bow wave up to his knees, I didn't dare ease down in case the water got too deep and I stalled too! Looking back in the mirror, I was amused to see him making a very rude gesture at me, indicating his great displeasure.

A mile further on, the track took a sharp turn to the right, far too narrow to navigate, and I had to demolish by hand, a small section of drystone wall to get the Landrover through.

Eventually a cluster of mud-brick and stone huts appeared, one of them proudly flying the Iranian flag, which turned out to be the schoolhouse, the best building in the village. The others were so poor and primitive, I wondered how on earth people managed to live in them.

They were built of large stones forming a three-foot high wall round a large hole in the ground, thatched over with whole Palm fronds, the cut ends being lashed together at eaves level on the top row of stones. To gain entrance, you walked down a couple of earthen steps to the interior, being careful not to bang your head on the roof!

The village consisted of about fifteen huts, all tucked into the lee of a huge overhanging cliff, which looked as though it would come crashing down at any minute, and because there was nowhere nearby to leave the vehicle, I drove on, passing a crowd of women and children, who silently monitored my progress.

A few yards beyond the last hut, I stopped the Landrover on the only piece of boulder-free ground I could see, and got out.

Immediately my nostrils were assailed by the smell of decomposing flesh, a smell I was extremely familiar with from work, and I looked around to find the cause.

It didn't take long to identify the source of the smell. It came from a sarcophagus-like construction a few yards away, which obviously contained the remains of some recently deceased person, in fact there were quite a few of these 'above-ground' coffins dotted about, I must have stopped in the middle of their local cemetery!

Looking at the situation a little more closely, you could understand why this form of burial had come about, the ground was so rocky you couldn't dig more than a few inches down, and because arable land was precious for crops, it wasn't going to be wasted on the dead, hence the stone sarcophagus!

Zamit had loaned us his punt again, so we could explore the reed beds on this side of the lake, which were in complete contrast to those on the other side, due to the fact that the water shelved steeply from the rocky shore-line to a depth of twenty feet or so, in which acres of ten-foot high reeds grew. In the quiet backwater between the reeds and cliffs, seven White-Headed Duck swam cautiously amongst dozens of Little and Great-Crested Grebe, while in the reeds dozens of Little Bittern, Clamorous Reed-Warblers and the odd Black-Necked Grebe milled around, it was like a quiet bird reserve.

We paddled for about a mile in the backwater between the shore and deep-water reeds, seeing in close-up, a bird that was new to me, the Cetti's Warbler. There were also Slender_Billed Gulls, Moustached Warblers, and on low exposed mud banks, Spotted Redshank, Greenshank, Common Sandpiper, Snipe, and more Little Bittern, the place was a gold mine!

From somewhere not too far away the repetitive beat of a drum assailed our ears, and as it went on and on without pause, it gradually became annoying. We tried to think what it could mean, had we upset the natives, were they telling their friends 'red indian' style about us, or was it something else?

Dick was just squaring breakfast away, while Peter and I got our cameras ready, when Zamit arrived on foot. Sitting cross-legged in front of the tent, he started to explain in a mixture of Farsi, bad English and drawings in the dust with his finger, the drum was a signal that a wedding was about to take place, would we like to go along as guests?

I had often thought in the past that Zamit, or 'Mellors' as I sometimes called him,, understood a lot more English than he let on, and probably used that fact to advantage when we were talking amongst ourselves, anyway, he was certainly able to get his message across this time.

Naturally we all said yes, and arrangements were made for us to attend that evening. We would have to go on foot into the mountains, and the journey would take about an hour, but we would see an interesting facet of Iranian country life, plus the wedding. That evening, returning from a marvellous day on the lake, we were met by a crestfallen Zamit, who informed us that the bride's mother had been knocked down by a car in Kazeroun 'city' that afternoon and suffered a broken leg. This unfortunately meant postponing the wedding ceremony and all the celebration arrangements until she was better.

As a consolation however, we were invited to an evening meal with three young Army schoolteachers, presently teaching the village children of Sharanjan, would we please come?

# Chapter Nineteen

The next morning we were quickly packed and ready for the return journey to our original campsite, but not before I had done what I promised to do last night - take a couple of photographs of the teachers and their pupils in front of the school. At eight o'clock, under a scorching sun, twenty pupils and their two teachers faced my camera, to the obvious amusement of the whole village, who laughed and giggled out loud, hiding their mouths politely behind their hands.

One of the schoolteachers asked if we could take a visiting gendarme back with us, and drop him off at Pasgard near the watering hole, and naturally we agreed - it was apparently the highlight of his day. Occupying the navigator's seat, he sat bolt upright looking straight ahead, a smile of satisfaction on his face, as we pulled away through the crowd of smiling onlookers.

There were two villages between Sharanjan and Pasgard, the first we hadn't a name for, the second we knew as Paul or Pol, so I decided to ask our friend its name as we drove past. To make things as easy as possible as I knew he spoke no English, I said "Me, Ingloustan Ok.?" He smiled and nodded, and feeling I had crossed the first hurdle picked an onion off the floor and said "Iranian sib, sib?" He smiled and nodded, saying 'sib, sib' at least we had that much right. Next I picked up a plastic bottle containing water and said "Ab ab, Ok.?"

All smiles he enthusiastically agreed 'Ab, ab', and made as if to drink. Boy I thought we're really doing well here, now for the cruncher, and pointing to the village that was just coming into view, enquired "Village, Deh?" He looked at me without the slightest comprehension, so I tried again, going through the things I had said before, this time adding a couple more, Daryacheh - lake, Kuh - mountain, Namak - salt, just to reinforce the idea. "

Village, Deh?" I enquired again feeling I was rapidly losing this one, especially as the village in question was now out of sight.

"Ah Deh!" he exclaimed getting the message at last "Deh, do Kilometer" (village two kilometers away) and both Peter and Dick curled up with laughter, while our friend resumed his fixed gaze through the windscreen, a huge smile of satisfaction on his face.

At the gendarme post we dropped our friend off, and were immediately invited in to share some more tea, the one glass passed among six men, it was so strong that despite being sipped round a large knob of kand, it put fur on my teeth! After the third glass of tea, we made our apologies, and, removing the five-gallon containers from the front of the vehicle, began to fill them with crystal clear water bubbling from the base of the nearby cliff.

In the morning it was sunny but overcast, and with heavy snows still covering the mountains opposite, it looked for all the world as though we were in Canada or North America. On the lake more than 300 Coot paddled around offshore, in company with 70 Pelican, a few Flamingoes, dozens of Teal, Marbled Teal, Widgeon and Mallard.Red-Crested, while Pochard chased backwards and forwards, often fighting furiously in the intensity of their courtship displays.

To try and give a complete picture of all that was happening is almost impossible, crowds of birds were using the lake both for feeding and as a migration route, some residents were taking up breeding territories, while others were over-wintering, it was a huge kaleidoscope of wildlife virtually undisturbed by man.

While Peter was using the 'scope I scanned the immediate marshy area, watching the Black-Headed and Corn-Buntings singing their territorial songs from prominent perches, and it was while watching a particularly active Corn-Bunting, I noticed a pair of Black-Headed Wagtails carrying food into a large clump of sedge. On investigation, I found their nest deep in the sedge containing five small young, and I felt we should be able to get some good photographs using a hide.

As the day had started so well, I thought I'd make a special effort for lunch, and dug out on some beef stroganof, potatoes and beans, to be followed by tinned strawberries and cream, it should all be rather scrumptious!

I had just shouldered one of John Prior's portaloo hides, and preparing to walk out to the Wagtail's nest, when three van loads of laughing, shouting Iranians descended onto our camp-site, immediately turning the place into a Butlin's holiday camp.

What the heck was going on?

It suddenly dawned on me it must be Friday again, the Iranian weekly holiday, this lot must have come all the way out from Kazeroun city, or maybe Shiraz for a break, but wherever it was, they completely destroyed our idyllic day.

Their main occupation seemed to be sitting in the warm sunshine, talking in small groups and brewing up pots of tea, or rushing down to the shallows half a mile away, to splash and swim in the lake, scaring every wild bird for miles!

The Black-Headed Wagtails' nest was on part of the marsh the Iranians weren't at all interested in, so I was able to erect the hide quite easily and get a bit of photography done.

I was using my new Kowa 66 with it's 200mmm lens and mecablitz flash, and by 1600 I had taken several photographs of both birds, feeling quite happy with the way things had gone. Picking a moment when I could see both birds were well away from the nest feeding, I quit the hide, and made my way back to camp.

I was amazed to see our Landrover and tent completely surrounded by a crowd of noisy Iranians, who appeared to have abandoned their normal reserve with strangers, and were taking sweets and biscuits from Peter and Dick, as though they were going out of fashion!

It looked like Hampstead Heath on a bank holiday.

After an hour or so of looking into everything we were doing, they suddenly decided to leave, and with smiles and handshakes all round, they were up and away in about two minutes flat - it was quite remarkable. The funny thing was, when we went round the far side of the Landrover nearest the tent, we saw a small boy rubbing his eyes and beginning to cry.

He'd fallen asleep, and been left behind!

It took a little while to calm him down, and the offer of a few sweets soon stopped his tears, but what the heck were we supposed to do with him, trot down to the gendarme post and report one lost child?

The situation was resolved half an hour later, when one of the trucks that had been with us earlier, screeched to a halt by our tent, and a scolding mother leaped out, grabbed the kid by the arm and yanked him into the truck, without so much as a glance of thanks in our direction. Funny lot.

With a speed that was quite surprising, the sun slipped behind the mountains beyond Famur, and plunged the area into sepia coloured darkness, which wasn't really black at all. Now that we had our camp routine established, it was a simple matter to switch on the fluorescent light attached to the Landrover, and start cooking the meal. Unfortunately the slight rise in temperature seemed to trigger a vast increase in the number of night-flying insects, and we were tormented by bugs of all shapes and sizes attracted no doubt by our light.

There was only one sure avenue of escape - the Landrover. Quickly picking up our plates and cutlery, we shut ourselves inside, spraying copious clouds of insect aerosol around, wiping out the foolhardy marauders who managed to nip in.

Coughing and spluttering, we cursed the damned mossies, and watched with glee as the last ones curled up and died under the onslaught of man's superior technology.

After the meal we were listening to a couple of tape casettes I had transcibed from LP's, when Dick pointed in horror to the windscreen and said "Cor, look at that flippin' lot!"

As we got into the vehicle, I had hung the fluorescent strip-light above the rear view mirror, where it must have acted as a beacon for all the insects in Perishan. The whole width of the windscreen for a depth of two inches up from the bonnet was a seething mass of mossies, piled up like a snowdrift, and struggling to get in!

The next morning quite early, Zamit arrived on his pop-pop, asking if we wanted to explore further down the lake towards Famur, but I had already discussed with Peter and Dick, the advisability of moving on to look for Hume's Tawny owl further south, returning to Perishan when more birds should be nesting.

Zamit looked very disappointed at our refusal to go, and said he hoped to see us when we got back, which I thought would be in about two weeks' time.

To say the track out of Perishan towards Famur and Ferouzabad was awful would be the understatement of the year - if it had been at all wet, I'm sure no wheeled vehicle would have made it. The hard clay ground was hideously rutted and cracked, meandering between irrigated fields of tomatoes and wheat, and the muddy edge of the reed-filled lake, with its boggy shallows.

Gradually the 'track' angled away from the lake, wandering across stony wastes towards a group of thorny trees surrounding an occupied mud hut, but no-one came out to see who we were.

It was mid-afternoon when we came upon a slightly better track, one half going to Famur, the other to Kazeroun city, and as we needed to fill up with petrol, we chose Kazeroun.

KC, as we called the motley collection of shops and buildings, was a friendly, but slightly incongruous place you just couldn't take seriously at all. Probably the most useful place for us was the 'Ali-Baba Hamburger & Sandywich Bar' on Main St.

where we had a gastronomic fill-up to save cooking that evening.

Re-fuelling at the hand-pump was easy.

Just keep going until everything was full, and in short time we had twenty gallons on board, costing £4.50, enough to give us roughly 800 miles travel at 18 mpg. Bandar Abbas our next main stop, enroute to the Persian Gulf and Hulmes' owl certainly wasn't as far away as that!

Without incident covered another 50 clicks, traversing rocky desolation so extreme in it's geography, it was hard to believe it could just go on and on. At the top of one tall escarpment I caught a glimpse of water far below, splashing along a rocky gully which contained the only vegetation in sight. I hoped it wasn't too far off the road for us to get to, as we all needed a cooling dip!

Ten minutes later we screeched to a halt a few yards above the sparkling water, the track had in fact ended up quite close to the gully, and the streanm was relatively easy to get down to.

Without a word, everyone made a grab for towel and washbag, and dashed down the boulder strewn scree, to see who could be first into the water.

With the thermometer showing just over 32C. initial contact with the icy tumbling torrent was a violent shock to the system, but Dick being a macho bugger, stripped off and jumped straight into the rushing waters, laughing and shouting like a madman.

After half an hour of lazily dangling my feet in the rushing cool waters, I began to look closely at our surroundings. We had descended several hundred feet from the ridge-top where I had first spotted the water, and were barely a quarter-way down to the valley floor far below us, and yet here was a stream belting out from rocks near the TOP of the mountain - how come?

Our climb back up the hot crumbling shale slope to the vehicle almost cancelled out the advantage gained from the cooling waters, but we had to move on, Firuozabad and places beyond were calling.

Some people say it is better to travel than to arrive, and in the case of Firouzabad I think that's very true. It turned out to be a typical dusty little Iranian town, which elicited no comment from us except a definite no no.

The track from Firouzabad to Qir, ran between two mountain ranges the Kuh-i-Surkh, and the Kuh-i-Khureh, both well over 7000' high, and although rocky and barren, had odd clumps of Casuarina and thorn bushes growing from cracks and crevices bordering the road. It was all extremely hot and desolate.

A few clicks before the town of Qir, we came to the first signs of serious habitation, a petrol station - which in itself was a bit unusual out here, as most fuel is dispensed through a hand pump fixed to a 50 gallon drum. Opposite the petrol station a cluster of comically shaped houses, shaped like giant concrete mushrooms, with a stalk on the roof, dominated the scene. The place looked to me like an experimental military development, and was certainly in complete contrast to anything we had experienced so far in Iran.

As we had nearly emptied our main tank, I thought it would be a good idea to fill it up again, rather than lugging one of the jerricans off the roof, I suppose I was getting a bit lazy.

Out of the corner of my eye I saw Dick aiming his camera at the peculiar buildings opposite, but was busy counting out the right money for the 44 litres we had taken on board to really take much notice.

As started to pay the man, I noticed an immaculately dressed army sergeant hitch up his holstered revolver, and start walking across the road in our direction, talking loudly to a colleague.

Although we had only been in Iran a short while, and our grasp of Farsi was negligible, I readily translated his 'Nis ax! nis ax!' as meaning 'no photographs' and it was obvious we were in the serious position of having pointed a camera at some military establishment, a situation we had been very careful to avoid so far.

The Private followed the Sergeant across the road, and in poor English asked us to accompany him through the gates of the establishment, to speak to his commanding officer.

Not feeling confident at all about the outcome of such a manoeuvre, I replied "No. we are Ingloustan tourists, we had not taken any photographs as the sun was against us, and I didn't want to meet his commanding officer either'

After several excited verbal exchanges, during which I cursed that I didn't have our document from Teheran to produce, the sergeant finally accepted our assurance that no photographs had been taken, and marched briskly back to his camp.

I watched them go with a sigh of relief, having re-learnt an invaluable lesson, if in doubt about photographing something 'iffy' - don't do it!

The weather was comparatively mild that evening, and we were able to get our meal cooked and eaten in the open without feeling cold, things were obviuosly improving, the further south we went.

The following morning while I was preparing our porridge and banana breakfast, Dick announced during his DI. of the vehicle, we had an oil leak on the near-side rear hub, which meant stripping the whole lot down and burning brake shoes off again.

It would also mean using another one of our precious oil seals, definitely a touch of the deja vous here! With practised skill, Dick made short work of the grotty job, getting us under way again by 1100, and we headed for the Mand river, which our map indicated lay only a few miles ahead.

When the Mand finally appeared it was an awe inspiring sight, half a mile wide, it's main stream now confined to a boiling, rushing cascade fifty yards wide in the centre, the margins heavy with tamarisk bushes ten feet high. The bed of the river was littered with whole trees, logs, branches and boulders all piled together in chaotic confusion, demonstrating the mighty power of the river during its winter spate from the mountains.

Like the Loire in France, and other similar locations, there were vast shingle banks exposed between the areas of debris and water, where new spring growth was trying to make a comeback. Tamarisks and other plants all leant at 60 degrees angle, testimony to the strength of the rushing water on it's way to the sea.

Spanning the entire width of the Mand at this point was a newly constructed steel and concrete bridge of elegant proportions, without which, a journey to the opposite bank would have been impossible.

It was decided that as it was such a grand spot, we would put up the tent nearby, relax for a few hours, and have a quick dip the swirling river before our evening meal.

Later,from the sanctuary of deep sleep, we were woken abruptly at 0230 by the loud flapping of canvas, and heavy raindrops spattering the tent.

Through the partly zipped door, I could see the green eerie glow of sheet lightning as it flickered continuously along the nearby mountain ridges.

We were obviously in for some rough weather.

Within half an hour, the full force of the storm hit us, making the tent buck and twist like a live thing in the violent gusts of wind, while the driving rain slashed horizontally across the stony ground, soaking everything.

Almost as suddenly as it had started, the storm died away, and everything went quiet. Half an hour later it hit us again, in fact every hour or so, until 0800, when a watery grey dawn showed itself timidly, as though in recompense for the terrible night.

By 0900 the wind had fallen away completely, a blue sky appeared, and soon afterwards the sun came out, giving us a chance to get outside, and check all was still ok.

Before we could even get breakfast started, the weather changed again into low scudding clouds and heavy rain, driven by gusts of wind so strong, small stones were lifted into the air.

For half an hour nasty squalls ranged along the river, developing into black, ball-clouds, riddled through with flickering lightning, a complete contrast to the scene only a short while before.

The surrounding terrain was now so wet and waterlogged, we decided to stay where we were, in the hope that conditions might improve the next day, and buckled down to make our selves more comfortable until then.

The next day we piled out of the tent just after dawn to find another grey day, with the threat of rain heavy in the air, but as the track seemed driveable, we decided to push on after breakfast.

# Chapter Twenty

At 0900 in very heavy rain and low cloud, Dick eased the Landrover off the bridge and up the steep rocky incline that led to the distant town of Lars, it all seemed distinctly yuksville.

On our right, black clouds rolled down the mountains almost to ground level, and the rain, driven horizontally by furious gusts of wind, turned the desert soil into a sea of slippery mud.

Our route to Lars turned out to be terrible, with thick mud obscuring the track surface for so long we didn't know if we were even heading in the right direction!

Despite being in four-wheel drive and treating the throttle like an egg, it was difficult to keep the Landrover going forward in a straight line, and several times we ended up with the back end chasing the front, as though on ice.

Through the pouring rain we tentatively identified a miserable collection of mud houses as the village of Deh-Kuh, (mountain village) and ploughed on across the Kurdeh plain towards Lars.

Barely visible through the rain, pinpricks of light showed ahead, foretelling the imminent appearance of Lars, a small town that boasted a beautiful blue, mosaic-tiled mosque, which dominated a short section of modern, well-lit dual carriageway.

These carriageways, a first-class copy of their European counterparts, are found in many Iranian towns, and would appear to be built, to facilitate traffic movement within the most impressive part of town ie: the mosque, shops, bazaar etc.

Unfortunately a little way out of town, they come to sudden stop, leaving the unsuspecting traveller to drop a bone-jarring 6" onto the desert floor, wondering where the hell the road has just gone!

With a weak setting sun only half an hour from darkness, we felt enough ground had been covered to warrant a break, and piled out to look around, and take some photographs of the elegant blue mosque. On a wall opposite the mosque sat three men, all in their thirties, who looked wordly wise enough to me, and I felt it might be a good idea to confirm through them, our exact route to Bandar Abbas.

The reason for my question was that the exit road seemed to fork into three directions just after it left town, which one was ours?

"Sallom alaykum" - peace to you, I intoned to the three men, and pointing to the three tracks leading out of town said "Ingloustan tourist, burro Bandar- Abbas?"

Not a flicker of comprehension passed their countenances, so I tried again, this time using my three fingers to indicate the three tracks ahead, intoning questioningly, "Bandar Abbas, Bandar Abbas?"

They looked at each other, and gabbled something in Farsi, and turning to me, one indicated with his finger the left-hand track of the three.

As a final check I asked again, using my finger angled to the left, does that track go to Bandar Abbas? and he nodded in agreement. At least we had that sorted out!

Thinking about it as we moved off into the failing light, I had a nasty recollection of reading somewhere, that eastern people tend to agree with you out of courtesy, rather than offend by correction, and I wondered if we were about to take the right route after all!

Once under way, the track quickly degenerated into a muddy swamp, liberally sprinkled with half buried rocks, causing the Landrover to bounce and judder towards the distant mountains in a series of spine-jarring jolts, which I feared would damage the casings of our tyres.

It got so bad, we turned on all the headlamps in an attempt to follow the barely discernible route in the gathering darkness, and I felt we were really taking too much of a chance.

By 2000. Dick reckoned he'd driven as far as he dared, without risking collision with huge boulders which loomed out of the darkness, when suddenly the wheels bit deep into fine sand and we slammed to a halt.

The resulting shock wrenched the steering wheel from Dick's hands, and we stalled inches away from a boulder as big as a London bus!

"Right, that's bloody well it for tonight" he shouted in frustration, and we agreed, come hell or high water enough was enough!

In total darkness, apart from our headlights, the tent went up, a cup of tea was brewed, and we hit the sack just as we were, exhausted.

As in a dream, and from somewhere a long long way away, I heard the sound of rushing water, overlaid with the excited calls of a Kestrel, and, lifting the skirt of the tent aside, I squinted upwards through half-awake eyes, at a narrow slice of blue sky framed between very tall cliffs.  Where the heck were we?

In a state of awe, and just a little shock, we got up and looked around as best we could. The way ahead beyond our huge boulder was a sea of smaller boulders filling an apparent cul-de-sac. Only feet away from the tent, an icy torrent tumbled football-sized boulders along a river bed, noisily clacking and banging against each other, certainly barring travel in that direction.

We were stuck!

"Before we do anything about anything" said Peter, "How about getting some porridge on the go for breakfast, I'm starving".

"Yeah" said Dick. "It was your idea to follow this route, and it appears to be a bit of a balls up, so I reckon it's your turn to do breakfast" and with that level of logic, I was left to get on with it.

The water rushing down the gorge looked pretty clean, so I filled the kettle and made some tea, only to find the finished brew tasted heavily of soda. It was so disgusting we threw it away and used the water on board, passing it through the Safari filter pump for safety. At least that was guaranteed to be clean!

The track we had failed to see in the darkness last night, took a right turn just before the huge boulder, and meandered between various smaller boulders towards a large undercut cave a hundred yards ahead.

"I think we ought to do a foot recce to see just what happens ahead, looking at the tracks between the rocks, there have been some four-wheeled vehicles through here previously, but not many"

"Ok. Dick" I replied, "You and Peter go ahead and have a dekko, I'll put away, and warm up the vehicle ready to follow on through, when you give the word"

Ten minutes later they re-appeared, saying the track did go on quite strongly for some way, things didn't look like a dead end, but they couldn't be sure. The immediate snag was that a few yards ahead the track went over a large spur of rock, which would put the vehicle over at a tricky angle, but if that's the way the track went, we'd have to give it a go.

I inched the Landrover backwards out of the sand-trap, and turned into the sea of boulders, marvelling we had got as far as we had last night, this was all definitely very hairy.

Our route lay through a sea of boulders ranging from cricket ball to football size, all beautifully rounded and polished by the tumbling action of the river, and I wondered if those three jokers sitting on the wall in Lars really knew if this route led to Bandar Abbas or not!

For most of the morning, at little more than 8mph and in four-wheel drive, we bounced along the river bed, crossing and re-crossing the surging stream a hundred times, as it snaked down the gorge, it was damned hard work.

There was no way you could hang on to the steering-wheel and drive, the front wheels were juddering and banging over the boulders so violently, the wheel-spokes spun viciously this way and that, cracking unwary fingers extremely hard.

You just had to let the wheel spin through your hands, and try to slow it down a bit, holding the rim.

At one point, crossing the river for the hundred and umpteenth time, with water about eighteen inches deep, I had just got to the half-way point, when several large boulders rolling downstream in the turmoil, hit the wheels with resounding crashes, and I began to slide sideways.

With the vehicle acting like a small dam, the build up of water on the upstream side began spurting in the door bottom, and I'm sure it was only the ruggedness of Landrover's design that eventually got us out of that particular mess.

After covering nearly 20 miles in this fashion, the track gradually moved away from the river bed, and ascended a high ridge from where we could see, about twenty miles ahead, a chain of mountains identified from the map as the 8000' Kuh-i-Hormuz - we were well off our intended route!

There was a further ten miles of rugged river-bed down the other side to follow, before we could start climbing the pass between the Kuh-i-Hormuz and the Kuh-i-Gardish Siah, where for practical purposes we might have well been on Mars!

Dark soaring mountains surrounded us, and an indigo sky contrasted with the searing glare bouncing off rocks and cliffs, which appeared to have been there since time began. The fantastic swirl of colours in the rock strata was amazing, blues, greens, deep terra cota, grey and black, while in some places a greeny copper oxide colour stained the rocks and cliffs like a modernist painter's palette.

I think we all felt the immense power of the place, and the insignificance of our miniscule presence there, and in a futile attempt to record the scene, I took a couple of photographs, but even on wide-angle I couldn't capture the half of it.

Our descent through the gradually sloping foothills was by contrast, relaxing and pleasant, and reminded me of pictures of a Kenyan game park's rolling acres of sparse grasses, dotted here and there with flat-topped thorn bushes ten feet high.

The area appeared to be a haven for shrikes, dozens of Great-Greys appeared to hold territories already, and were chattering their alarm calls from the tops of thorn bushes. Scattered among them were dozens of Isabelline, Woodchat, and Masked Shrikes, it was really marvellous.

The terrain was unusually smooth beneath the waist-high grass, and we were able to bowl along at thirty miles an hour quite .omfortably, although I did wonder what would happen if we hit an unseen crack or fault in the earth at that speed!

We passed a couple of tiny villages that were really a collection of mud huts without any inhabitants, and made our way down the broad valley towards the confluence of two rivers, the Rud-i-Rasul and the Rud-i-Kul. We were now only 50 miles short of Bandar Abbas, the furthest point east of our Iranian journey.

Renewing our dash through the grasses, Dick took up a forward viewing position by sitting in the spare wheel on the bonnet, which gave him an excellent view for'ard and the benefit of cooler air, but made vision rather difficult for me.

Suddenly he banged his fist on the windscreen, shouting "Stop, stop!" and we screeched to a halt in a cloud of red dust.

A few feet in front of us, a sunken dirt track crossed our path from left to right, and after consulting the map, we all agreed that as the sun was moving to the end of it's arc on our right, we ought to turn left, as Bandar Abbas was in the bottom left-hand corner of Iran when facing south - basic navigating stuff this! The track wasn't bad as surfaces go, hard packed earth littered with small stones and rocks, and we were able to reach speeds of 40 mph, leaving behind a huge cloud of dust that hung in the still air, long after we had passed.

One or two side roads were seen as we roared along, but the blue painted signboards pointing to the villages were written in Farsi, and not a lot of use in telling exactly where we were. We guessed the identity of two places we passed through as being Kichal and Isin, the latter being large enough to sport a petrol station of sorts, where we took on 100 litres for 540 Rials, or £5.40p, what a snip!

With its usual speed, darkness fell as we left Isin, and far away in the distance could see the flame of a gas burn-off stack in a refinery, which, as we got closer illuminated the nearby hills in an erie glow. The road surface now improved considerably, and we were able to accelerate up to 40mph. keeping it there for just over an hour, until a twinkling sea of lights heralded the imminent approach of Bandar Abbas.

In stark contrast to the virtual silence we had enjoyed during the last few days, a nightmare cacophony of car horns and blaring incantations assailed our ears, and a garish smell of cooking, intermixed with a sticky-sweet aroma, and sewage invaded our sense of smell, it was all extremely basic.

It didn't take long to find someone who understood enough English to direct us to the least disreputable hotel in town, where for £6 the three of us could occupy a large single room in relative privacy.

With sweeping gestures, a small, filthy looking youth ushered us into the 'best' room, deftly flicking on a 12" portable black and white TV. for our appreciation.

On it's screen, unrecognisable highlights and shadows chattered away in Farsi, competing for cogniscence with a ferocious snowstorm of interference, a sight too bizarre for words! The room however was fitted with a refrigerated cooling unit and a couple of ceiling fans, which made the place delightfully cool, and as an added bonus, the floor was reasonably clean as well!

It was quite impossible to get the car close to the hotel - there was the usual footway, plus a two-foot wide concrete storm drain, and a row of bedraggled palms out front, so we covered the windows and locked the car, bringing everything of value into our room.

Our particular section of storm drain had a character all it's own, and I suspect no water had passed through it since the last winter rains. Every few feet or so, piles of vile garbage disintegrated in nauseating mounds, sending out the most stomach-curdling stench, while just behind our Landrover the blackened, rotting remains of a dog snarled horribly in the rictus of death.

While Peter and Dick sampled the delights of the shower somewhere upstairs, I started the evening meal, at the same time cleaning my camera gear of the fine dust which had covered everything, despite having been wrapped in plastic bags.

When it was my turn to shower, I eagerly nipped up stairs and came out onto a flat roof, on which a large room containing half a dozen shower cubicles had been built.

Those who wear gasses will no doubt agree, there is nothing more annoying than getting your lenses splashed when washing or showering, so I removed mine as usual, and jumped into the shower. Needless to say the water ran a shade brown for the first few seconds, and I certainly felt pounds lighter when I eventually finished scrubbing.

Being myopic, or short-sighted, I can see things close-up very well, but anything over six feet away isn't sharp at all, and as I walked out of the shower to pick up my towel, I glanced towards the door and saw a bearded black man looking steadily in my direction.

I was taken by surprise, I hadn't heard anyone come in, but I thought if he's a hotel guest, he has the same right to use the showers as me, so I carried on.

As I bent to pick up my towel, so did he, and I suddenly realised I was looking at a frame-less mirror on the wall ten feet away, and the black man I saw was me.

I was as black as the ace of spades!

The recent days of warm wind and sunshine had burnt me the colour of mahogany, yet the others hadn't thought to mention it - it was strange how quickly you forget what you look like, especially after not seeing your face in a mirror for weeks!

The next day we decided to go sight seeing, and as a precaution against theft, I got permission to leave our vehicle in the police-station compound, I felt much happier with that task accomplished.

Bandar Abbas turned out to be a town of extreme contrasts, and being a large military base, there were army and navy personnel with their buildings and equipment everywhere. Despite this, there were very modern glass-fronted banks with superb rose gardens and orange trees for decoration, cheek by jowl with crumbling mudbrick houses of indescribable squalor.

The whole town was a heaving sea of people, interspersed with cars, lorries, pop-

pop bikes, taxis and noise. There was also a huge down-town bazaar or souk that seemed to go on for miles, where we rubbed shoulders with hundreds of interesting people, non more so than a couple of Indian naval officers in spotless white ducks, sporting nuclear submarine badges on their breast pockets.

While pushing through the souk, I had kept my eyes open in case I saw a sports shop where I might buy a face-mask and snorkel - I hoped we might do a bit of snorkelling on our way up the Persian Gulf, and seeing the two Indian officers coming towards me, I asked if they spoke English. They replied they certainly did.

I enquired if they knew where I could get a face-mask, or could they please write 'face-mask' in Farsi so I could ask in any likely looking shop for myself.

"We can do better than that" one said, "Why don't you go and see our commanding officer" - he wrote down his name, "at the naval barracks, and ask him if you can borrow one, I'm sure he wouldn't mind. By the way do you know Gosport in the UK?"

I replied that I had been there, but didn't know it all that well though.

"Oh well the next time you go there, you must call in at the 'Port-hole' club, and ask for Doris the waitress, she is my girlfriend you know, and would be very pleased to see you"

I nearly fell over backwards at the thought of meeting two Indian naval chaps in the bazaar at Bandar Abbas, one of whom had a girl friend in the UK - the world suddenly seemed a very small place!

When we had exhausted the sight-seeing and returned to our Landrover, I said to the others 'How about finding these barracks then, and seeing if this officer chap will lend us a face mask and snorkel?'

"Don't be so bloody daft, the bloke was only being polite, there's no such fella"

"Well if it's on our way out of town, I'd like to try, it might be a bit of a giggle anyway"

Passing through the dock area, our way was suddenly blocked by huge open-topped trucks grinding successively out of the gates, spilling enough grain from their tops, to feed the dozens of peasant women and children risking life and limb to glean the grains from the road with bare hands.

I was about to grab my camera and record the scene when I saw a sign in red letters on a white background saying in Farsi, and surprisingly in English too, 'Photography forbidden' and I left the camera alone. No point in asking for trouble round here!

Seeing a sailor on guard outside an imposing set of newly painted iron gates, I assumed we were passing the naval barracks, and asked Dick to stop.

"You're not really going in there to ask about that stupid face mask are you?" said Dick.

"Yes I ruddy well am, if he's here, we should be able to find him, if not there's nothing lost anyway"

Approaching the guard, I asked to speak with someone who spoke English, pointing to my self and saying "Ingloustan, ingloustan"

Without turning his head, he called to someone inside, and after a few minutes, a young chap came out, saying he spoke a little English as he was a university student doing his call-up service in the navy. I explained the purpose of my visit, and showed him the piece of paper with the naval officer's name written on it by our Indian friends in the bazaar.

"Oh yes, I know this officer, he is not here at the moment, but his second officer is here, I can take you to see him if you like"

I thought this is getting crazier and crazier by the moment, after all we ARE only tourists!

"Would you and your friends come with me, you can park your vehicle here, the guard will watch it, we will use our own transport around the camp"

Dick volunteered to stay with the Landrover, he didn't want any part of this nonsense, leaving Peter and I to follow our friend through the spotlessly 'bulled' guardroom towards a waiting Iranian jeep.

"I will take you to the officer's house, he is not on duty at the moment, but he will speak to you"

We drove slowly through beautifully kept gardens, where the detached living quarters for officers were set tastefully between groves of blossoming trees, until we reached the said officer's house.

Officer Mirzadeh spoke very good English, and enquired what we were doing in Iran, and where we were off to next. When I had answered his questions, I mentioned we were looking for somewhere I could get hold of a face mask and snorkel for a bit of underwater swimming in the Persian Gulf.

He replied, "No problem, I can do this for you"

We all piled into the jeep, and were taken to a huge compound topped with barbed-wire, situated on the water's edge next to some fighting craft.

"If you follow me, we will go to the stores and see what we can find for you, it's just through here"

I just couldn't believe it, here we were being taken into a military establishment just like that, no checks, no questions or passports, how come we were being taken completely at face value?

We threaded our way between rows of huge round mines sitting on their wooden cradles, and torpedoes in special racks, until we came to a large store, which he opened with his key. Inside, and along three walls, were about twenty sets of scuba equipment, each with it's own air cylinder, and in the corner about sixty pairs of rubber frog-feet.

"You are wanting to borrow one of these?" he asked without any surprise in his voice at all "How will you be able to re-charge the cylinder when it is empty, do you have a compressor?"

I just couldn't believe this, I had to be dreaming!

"No, no, we don't want air breathing equipment, Just a face-mask, snorkel tube and maybe a pair of frog-feet"

"That is no problem, help yourself, take two, one for your friend also, but I will ask you to do something for me too"

I couldn't think what he could possibly want from us, but he went on,

"My son has a digital watch like the one you have on, and the battery has gone dead. When you get back to England will you send me one, we cannot get them here"

Needless to say I agreed, and said that when I sent the equipment back to him, several batteries would be included - that was the least I could do!

Back at the Landrover, a worried looking Dick asked where the hell we'd been, and when I showed him the two sets of masks and flippers he was speechless, and said something about my luck which was totally un-printable!

# Chapter Twenty One

Leaving the depot, our route lay along a gravel and dirt road skirting the shores of the Clarence Strait, and we bottled along at a steady 40mph. passing the island of Qishm, designated a 'protected natural region' by the Environment office in Teheran, and apparently off limits to us visitors.

The sun sank with it's usual rapidity, leaving a royal blue sky streaked with red and orange like a flaming cauldron, indicating we had only a few minutes to find somewhere and pitch camp before darkness fell.

During the night I was woken by calls similar to those of a Tawny owl, and looking at my watch I saw it was 0250, perhaps we were hearing a Hume's owl and I didn't know it! I lay awake for another half-hour, but heard nothing else, and drifted off into a deep sleep again.

At 0400 all of us were suddenly woken by a deep rumbling tremor, the ground shook and heaved as though it were made of plastic. For several seconds a grinding groan vibrated through our bodies as we lay in close contact with the ground, and just as suddenly, it was all quiet again.

There was no doubt about it, we had experienced a small earth tremor, and if that WAS a small one, what the hell did a full size one feel like?

In the morning we explored the small date-palm grove we had camped in, and found a Syrian Woodpecker's nest hole drilled into a dead palm about twenty feet above ground. I thought it too good an opportunity to miss, and put up one of the hides for a while, hoping to get some shots of the adult birds with my 400mm. lens.

In two hours I managed to get twenty shots of both the male and female woodpecker at the nest, and left the hide so that Peter could have a crack at them too. After a quick lunch, we set off along the coastal track, with the sparkling blue waters of the Persian gulf a few yards away on our nearside, heading for our next marker, a town called Bandar Lengeh.

The thermometer swinging from the windscreen was registering a steady 40C. which prompted us to stop the vehicle by a suitable stretch of sandy beach, and plunge into the cool creamy rollers of the gulf. The place was so perfect with it's long sandy, palm-fringed beach, we decided to stay for a while and enjoy it to the full, you don't get luxuries like this very often!

In superlative comfort we bedded down for the night, the sleeping bags moulding perfectly to the warm sand, our heads poking out under the tent skirt, gazing up at the myriads of fiercely brilliant stars, background to a speeding satellite reflecting the rays of an invisible sun.

The next day we were on the road at 0700, passing the villges of Bandar Hamairan, Chah-i-Kuh and Kung, the dirt road getting more and more rugged by the mile.

On the outskirts of Lengeh itself, there was a profusion of birds in the small clumps of eucalyptus and casuarina, which seemed out of all proportion to the locale. There were Yellow-Throated Sparrows, Spotted Flycatcher, Common Babbler, various Phylloscopus, Turtle Dove, Red-Backed and Great-Grey Shrikes, Wheatears, and Red-rumped Swallows, it was an incredible gathering for such a harsh area.

While we were watching an Isabelline Shrike, a pale form of Lanner Falcon swished past and landed on a roadside boulder ten yards away, clutching it's dead prey. Before our eyes it began tearing up the catch, and both Peter and I frantically dived for our cameras to record the scene.

Just as we were about to take our first shots, an Iranian Mack diesel truck roared past, blaring his dual-tone horns in greeting, scaring off every bloody thing for miles, including our Lanner falcon.

If the driver could only have heard a fraction of our remarks about his ancestry, Anglo-Iranian relations would have been dealt a very serious blow.

The town of Bandar Lengeh was quite modern and well built, and it was only when we stopped on the far side of town to get petrol and water we found the reason why. The 'old' town nearby, was a massive area of dereliction, with collapsed buildings and walls left where they had fallen. It was obvious the place had been completely destroyed by an earthquake years before, and the locals had just moved along the coast a bit, and built a new town.

The track out of town ran along the top of a raised embankment about twenty feet higher than the surrounding land, and with the twinkling blue gulf a few yards away, was extremely pleasant route to drive on. The embankment ran for miles in an almost straight line, and in some places it had been built to a very high standard including an asphalt surface.

Whenever we came upon one of these 'improvements' or repairs, we found the road gang had covered the whole tarmac surface with boulders, making it impossible for a vehicle to drive on.

There were signs however that some of the ubiquitous pop-pops had threaded their way between the stones, travelling along un-impeded, but we, like other vehicles using the track, had to angle down the steep side of the embankment, and motor along the rough ground at the bottom, until we could climb back up again!

We couldn't figure out why traffic wasn't allowed to use the super new surface, but looking at the dirt accumulated under and around the rocks, it was obvious they had been blocking the road for some time. It was all a bit of a mystery.

Away on our right, at several miles distance lay the 4000'high Kuh-i-Khamir mountains, keeping pace with our slow progress, and were no doubt, the source of many winter rain run-offs, making their way into the Persian gulf.

It should have been obvious to anyone with half a brain, that if you build a raised dyke twenty feet high running parallel to the coast, and you have millions of gallons water galloping seawards on the inside, you have to find an easy way of letting it through to the seaward side.

The Iranians had obviously dealt with the problem of the run-off river meeting the dyke, by building a multi-arched stone bridge across the bed. Unfortunately someone, somewhere had got their sums sadly wrong, regarding the amount of water rushing through the arches, with quite hilarious consequences.

Arriving at the first of these 'junctions', we found the rushing waters must have piled up behind the inadequate bridge and overflowed, demolishing the earthen dyke for fifty yards at either end, leaving a small row of arches standing forlornly in the middle of a 200' river bed, like the last remaining wall of a Gothic church!

There were several of these little 'disasters' sprinkled along our route, and it was always a hazard to find somewhere to angle the Landrover off the dyke to pass these 'relics' without the risk of rolling over.

After covering forty clicks in this fashion, we came across a three-acre plantation of date palms, which appeared to be a haven for several species of birds trying to avoid the brain numbing 40C sunshine blazing from a cloudless blue sky.

Between the date plantation and the sea, a 30' high, wind-blown sand ridge stretched a mile along the shoreline, and climbing its summit, we saw a large gathering of terns and waders washing and preening in the shallows of the gulf.

I nipped back to the Landrover and grabbed my camera and 400mm lens, plus x2 converter and tripod, hoping that I might be able to get some reasonable photos of the unidentified tern species we had just seen.

During the next half-hour, we saw and photographed Sanderling, Turnstone and Dunlin, a Grey Plover in summer plumage, two Curlew of the Madagascariencis race, a dark-phase Reef Heron, 200 Bridled terns, and dozens of Common, Lesser and Great-Crested, White-Cheeked and Sandwich terns! Dwarfing this motley crowd of waders and terns were 21 Flamingoes, a truly fantastic sight, set against the royal blue backdrop of the sea.

After a bit of a make-shift meal we checked our maps with the surrounding terrain, and identified our position as being half-way between Ras-ash-Shias, the promontory jutting into the gulf behind us, and the village of Bustaneh, about five miles ahead.

On our right the 1750' Jebel Bustaneh reared into an azure sky, it's wind eroded foothills, and tortuous gorges seeming an ideal place to search for Hume's Tawny owl, perhaps we could start there?

The job of getting off the dyke was extremely difficult, and it took all our skill to prevent the vehicle from tipping over as we slid ignominiously to the bottom, before looking for a way through the sea of smashed rocks and boulders littering the area like a giant demolition site.

With Peter driving, and Dick navigating from his position on the bonnet, I walked a few yards in front 'route-finding' and getting us through the worst of the hazards. We were going 'against the grain' of dozens of dry water-courses descending from the Jebel, and I didn't want us to accidentally run into a dead-end.

In slow time we painstakingly made our way a couple of miles into the foothills, carefully dodging the myriad of deep ruts and fine gravel banks which just sat there waiting to cause trouble.

Some of these ruts were so deep the rear wheels of the Landrover virtually disappeared from sight, causing the spare-wheel bolted above the rear tow-ball to strike the ground, and bend the rear door outwards!

When we had gone as far as the rocky foothills, we found ourselves several hundred feet above sea-level, looking down on the huge empty panorama of the gulf coast, a sight which graphically reinforced our feelings of utter emptiness in an area as desolate as the moon.

Shortly after 1730 the sun dipped to the horizon and a strong, gusting wind came in off the sea, making it impossible to light our trusty petrol stove without windguards, and yet it wasn't the least bit cold.

As there was no moon, and we didn't know the area at all, we agreed it was far too dangerous to wander away from the vehicle in the dark. Our fluorescent strip-light, clipped to the outside of the Landrover gave insufficient illumination against twisting your ankle or falling heavily amongst the razor-sharp rocks piled all around.

For something to do, I sat on a huge boulder a few yards from camp, and kept my ears 'skinned' for any owl calls, but all I got for my pains was the distant yipping of a fox.

The next day dawned fine and clear with strong on-shore winds, and we decided to split up to see if between us, we could find some sign of Humes' in this terrible wilderness. If ever there was the feeling of looking for a needle in a haystack, this was it! Where did you start looking for owls in a place like this?

The only data I had, stated the bird 'Nests in holes in rocks or cliffs, and perhaps in old buildings near oases' - not really a lot to go on.

Setting out in line abreast, we were soon forced to separate as gullies running into the foothills grew deeper, and further apart, and pretty soon we lost contact altogether. In this area of massive shale slopes and gullies, dozens of Desert Larks were seen, and it was only by reference to the excellent illustrations in the Iranian field guide, I was able to identify them as the Bar-tailed variety, Ammomanes Cincturus, an entirely new species for me.

In most of the gullies we explored that morning, there were literally dozens of holes, the result of wind and rain erosion, some eminently suitable for owls to nest in, but empty, and others obviously used by mammals such as foxes to breed in, or lay up during the heat of day.

By mid-day the strong wind died away completely, leaving us to plod about under a cobalt sky in temperatures of 41C. The climbing and scrambling around dusty sandstone gullies searching for owl holes, was akin to running around an army assault course in a lime kiln.

When we met up again, it was unanimously agreed we retire into the relative shade of the cliff and the Landrover, and brew a large pot of tea. There, we could review our quest for the elusive Humes over lunch in relative comfort - there was an awful lot of space out here!

While Peter got on with the meal, Dick, ever the one to see a job needing doing and dealing with it, cajoled me into helping him remove the Landrover's rear door, prior to straightening it out. Once the door was off, Dick simply laid the door bowed side up across two flat rocks, and dropped the 80lb. spare wheel on it from head height, until it bent back to normal.

It all looked so easy!

Trying to ensure we shouldn't have the same problem again, Dick drilled four new 1/2" holes in the door with a hand drill, 8" higher than the old ones, which was enough to keep the wheel well out of reach of even the bumpiest terrain!

The dis-advantage of this alteration became apparent after re-mounting the wheel, when I found it impossible to insert the keys into the rear door lock - the tyre was in the way, so it was left unlocked for daily access.

During the afternoon we explored a section of foothills in the opposite direction to our morning scramble, but with virtually the same result. I had the distinct feeling this was not the best place to look for Humes' owl after all!

With our fresh water getting extremely low - the three of us used about three gallons a day - we decided to get back onto the coastal track and make for Bandar Moqam, in the hope of finding somewhere to fill our 5 gallon canisters, and of course continue our search for Hume's owl.

The descent from the foothills was, like the ascent, extremely hazardous, and required the same navigational technique to find a safe route through the amazing jumble of rocks and boulders, many of which were bright green or jet black, while others glinted like Galena.

It took an hour to get back to the dyke track, and find a safe place to ascend, before setting off along the dirt surface at speed, leaving a dust cloud behind that hung in the air for miles. Near the coastal village of Charak, the sight of huge gulf rollers breaking onto miles of deserted beach was just too much for our dehydrated bodies, and we deserted the vehicle there and then, plunging starkers into the cool refreshing sea!

Continuing our run towards Bandar Moqam, the surrounding habitat improved by the mile, with knee-high grasses by the hundreds of acres, interspersed with small thorn bushes and Zinjan trees. Eventually our maps indicated we were about five miles short of B. Moqam, and as it was early evening, it seemed to be a good time to stop for the night.

As Peter and I put up the tent a few yards off the track, an Iranian 'senior-citizen' cycled past on his rickety old bicycle, singing at the top of his voice and not giving us the slightest attention. It was obvious we couldn't be that far from human habitation after all.

After breakfast the next day I explored our little haven and found 10 Rufous Bush-Chats, 3 pairs of White-Cheeked Bulbuls, one lot with nest and eggs, two male and two female Cuckoos, Yellow-Throated Sparrows, Palm and Collared Doves, Nightingales, Redstarts, plus Great Grey and Red-Backed Shrikes. There is no doubt this grassy parkland dotted with thorn bushes and trees seems particularly suitable to Shrikes, and it didn't take long to add Lesser Grey, and Masked Shrike to our list as well.

Where the coastal track crossed smaller gullies running into the sea, colonies of Pale Crag Martins had built their mud nests under the stone bridges, most of which contained fully fledged young.

It was a pity really we didn't have more time to stay and photograph them.

In complete contrast to the last few miles, the track into Bandar Moqam deteriorated by the mile, and became little more than a rutted trail. At mid-day, with the temperature just over 42C. we arrived in the centre of 'town', to find the place absolutely lifeless and deserted, it was like a ghost town.

The only way forward appeared to be parallel with the coastline, but the trail just disappeared, and we found ourselves on a huge beach with rollers crashing in from the Persian Gulf, our wheels slowly sinking into the soft white sand.

The sound of our engine must have disturbed a few of the locals from their siestas, and a couple of gangly youths in striped night-shirts appeared from nowhere to stare at us with mouths agape in wonder.

It was pretty obvious we had missed whatever through route there was, and would have to back-track, skirting the peculiar two-storey mud houses fronting the beach, and their silent gawping occupants standing folornly at their doors.

In our very limited Farsi we attempted to question the two gangly youths as to how we might get to Neran, the next village along the coast, but we might just as well spoken to Martians for all the comprehension we got, they were definitely somewhere else!

Turning round in the village 'square', we discovered an obscure track leading off in the general direction we wished to go and followed that, although it seemed to go towards a mountain range several miles away that ran into the sea.

I hoped we had made the right decision!

For several miles we bumped along between low sand dunes on our left, and rocky outcrops on our right, which descended from unseen foothills, using the four-wheel drive to get us through the fine sand that had drifted across the track.

The track grew more and more rugged as we progressed along the coast, so much so that in several places we had to get the shovels off the roof-rack, and build ramps of earth and stones to get the Laandrover across the deep wadis that crossed our path.

"I've got a horrible feeling about this" I said to the other two.

"It just doesn't feel right does it?" said Peter "The track shows signs of use, but its in lousy condition, I wouldn't be surprised if it petered out altogether soon"

"Well we'd better soon find out" Dick replied "It'll be dark before long and I don't fancy grovelling about out here in these awful conditions"

"Amen to that" said Peter.

The sun had begun it's usual rapid descent, and was only just above the horizon, bathing everything in a warm pink glow like the city of Petra, and it felt for all the world as though we were on Mars.

Fifty yards to our left a rocky ridge shut off our view of the sea, and as the sun finally disappeared behind the mountains we were cast into deep gloom, forcing us to use the headlights in case we collided with rocky outcrops.

About a quarter of a mile ahead I noticed the slim outline of a 100' radio mast silhouetted against the last glow of the sun, and I was about to comment on it when Dick shouted "Look out - wires ahead!" and we skidded to a halt twenty feet short of a row of concrete posts carrying festoons of vicious looking barbed wire.

"What the blue blazes is this all about?" I began, but at that moment a dozen rifle toting Iranian soldiers appeared through a small gate in the wire, surrounding the Landrover in a distinctly menacing attitude. In a stream of harsh Farsi the Sergeant in charge obviously asked who the hell we were and what were we doing, and I cursed Hooshang Adami again, for holding onto our precious document, drafted for emergencies such as this.

Getting down from the Landrover I replied grumpily, "No understand, Ingloustan,

Ingloustan parandar chanas"

"Ingloustan, ingloustan?" he queried, and obviously told his men to guard us, while he went off somewhere for help. For about five minutes we sat immobile in the vehicle while the Iranian soldiery pointed their rifles at us menacingly, discussing things among themselves until the sergeant returned with another soldier.

"You English men?" he said without too much trouble "You please to get out of car and show your identity, you in big trouble, this is restricted military area"

"Oh shit" said Dick "That's all we needed to be arrested as spies, I knew I should have stayed at home"

"Look, let's just give them our passports to check, and we'll play it from there" I said "This chap seems to speak pretty good English, if we can convince him why we're here, we should be able to get out of this ok."

Once through the gate and into the compound, I spotted several small brick-built buildings deliberately designed to blend in with the rocks and shrubs so as to be almost invisible.

We were led into what in the British services would be regarded as a guard-room, and told to sit on a bench along one wall and wait.

Our details would be carefully checked with the 'general' in Teheran.

It might take some time.

Outside the door several armed guards precluded any attempt to wander off, while twenty nasty looking dogs of various ancestries roamed inside the wire, just looking for trouble.

For two hours we sat there, listening to the whistles and hums of radio transmitting and receiving equipment, little knowing that our 'case' was being discussed at the highest appropriate level in Teheran, eight-hundred miles away!

Just after midnight, our English speaking friend - incidentally another National Service schoolteacher, returned to tell us we could camp just outside the perimeter wire for the night - they would hold onto our passports until morning, when we would probably be taken under armed escort back to Bandar Moqam, and escorted out of the area.

We could consider ourselves very lucky if no further action was taken.

"Phew" said Dick, "That was pretty close, I felt sure we were for the chop or something, the way they pointed those bloody guns at us"

"Yeah, I wasn't too happy myself there for a while, if only that prat Adami hadn't held on to our document, none of this might have happened" I replied. Peter said nothing.

At gun point, and surrounded by snarling dogs on leads, we were escorted back to the gate in the wire, and told to sleep nearby, while the soldiers watched to see what we would do.

It all felt quite bizarre.

"Ok. let's get the tent up pronto, and cook ourselves a meal" I said. "I remember reading something ages ago that locals won't stand around and watch you if you are eating, it's not considered good manners, let's try it"

As soon as the petrol stove burst into life and the pans went on, our friends at the wire began to drift away, perhaps there was an element of truth in the old adage after all?

I suppose we had been snugged down in our sleeping bags for about half an hour, when a desert fox started yipping somewhere in the hills, causing the hounds in the compound to rush about in turmoil, upsetting the guards quite a bit.

"Bet you wouldn't dare do your vixen impression now" said a sleepy Dick from the depths of his sleeping bag "It would be more than your life's worth"

Needing no more than a dare to set me going, I did my best vixen calls on the spot, with quite astonishing results.

A tremendous howl went up from the pack inside the compound, and all hell broke loose as they broke from their handlers and shot through the wire, heading straight for our tent.

"Bloody hell" said Dick who was sleeping with his head in the tent doorway "You've certainly stirred up a hornets nest there!" and yanked the zip down smartly to close the tent door. To my surprise the pack roared past the tent, one or two colliding with the guy lines, before disappearing into the hills after my 'vixen', followed by a couple of irate guards waving their rifles and cursing. We laughed like drains.

At 0615 we rolled out into a beautiful sunny morning, and had just started our breakfast of porridge, scrambled egg, and tea, when a deputation of soldiers, headed by our English speaking friend appeared at the tent.

"We speak to General in Teheran this morning, and instructions are you can leave now, you take passports and go back to Bandar Moqam, not here - we send soldier with you to make sure"

He slapped the passports into my hand without any of the friendliness he had shown previously, and turned to go.

"What about the road to Asalu?" I asked, pointing in the direction we wanted to go.

"No road - finish, in sea, you go to Bandar Moqam, Gavbandi, and to Asalu, not this way" and I wondered if the coastal track had really been washed away, or was this an extremely sensitive military area they didn't want strangers to see?

The return trip to Bandar Moqam was just as diabolical as we remembered it from yesterday, I couldn't imagine how the radio unit got it's supplies in, unless they came by boat, it took us three hours driving at 8 mph. with our armed escort sitting on the bonnet to get back to the 'square' at Moqam.

As we entered the village, an army lieutenant complete with Sam Browne and holstered pistol, stepped into the road and pulled us to a halt.

"Passport, passport" he shouted loudly, demonstrating his importance in front of the few villagers present, keeping us captive for an hour while he carefully checked the vehicle and it's contents, asking if we had any whisky on board! Eventually he got bored with his little game, and said in passable English we could leave.

I asked him about the route to Gavbandi as we seemed to have missed the obvious route and made a silly mistake, and he told us that we had to strike north across the unmarked grassy parkland, passing the village of Goulshan before striking a track that would lead us to Gavbandi and Asalu. There was definitely no way along the coast we could use from here.

# Chapter Twenty Two

North of B. Moqam the route lay up the centre of a broad fertile valley, waist deep in rough grass, dotted with flat-topped thorn bushes and Zinjan trees, it looked more like photographs I had seen of game parks in Kenya.

It was certainly marvellous Shrike country, with dozens of Great-greys of the Syrian race perched on most suitable look-outs, interspersed with dozens of Red-backed and Masked Shrikes, Desert and Crested Larks, Wheatears and Rollers. As we drove slowly up the valley the trees got larger, and on top of one, about thirty feet tall I noticed a Spotted Little owl watching us with its brilliant yellow eyes.

The trunk of the tree, which was about a foot in diameter, had a large hole in it about four feet above ground, which on investigation contained a female owl, incubating an unknown number of eggs. I removed her gently from the nest, took some photographs to show the plumage pattern, and returned her to the nest without mishap - not exactly the Hume's owl we were looking for, but a vast improvement on anything found so far!

Within 3/4 mile we passed another large tree, complete with Little owl on top, and were quite surprised to find another hole containing a female sitting on five eggs. She too was carefully removed, photographed, and replaced without trouble, it was all getting rather interesting.

Our surprise knew no bounds when within a 1/4 mile another suitably sized tree yielded a third little owl nest, this time containing two well-grown youngsters, either the feeding was very good in the area or nest sites were hard to come by, but still no Hume's

The track to Gavbadi turned out to be our old friend the raised dyke of earth and stones 15' high, intersected at various points by bridges over gullies which we had met before, and again dozens of Pale Crag Martins and Red-Rumped Swallows had commandeered the arches for their mud nests. At one point the dyke ran onto a huge concrete causeway half a mile long spanning a wide river, whose rushing waters had long since subsided, leaving a chain of green stagnant pools gently simmering in the 41C. heat.

Not being overly fussy, we waded into the largest pool and flopped on our backs to enjoy the comparative luxury of a cool dip, only to be greeted by frantic 'Did ye do it, did ye do it?' calls of a pair of Red-Wattled Lapwing, desperate to draw us away from their newly hatched young. In a sand bank nearby, a dozen or more Rollers displayed and called loudly as they competed for nesting tunnels already dug in the soft red sand.

Much refreshed after our dip, I continued to drive along the track for a few miles, before seeing another of those tall radio masts like the one at Moqam, silhouetted against the skyline.

Was it yet another military establishment about to give us trouble?

I pulled gently to a halt, while we surveyed the scene through our binoculars and discussed how we might handle the situation.

It was decided to approach as quietly as possible, with the intention of trying to get past un-noticed in the heat of day, but as we drew near, a soldier who had been asleep with his rifle across his knees, jerked into consciousness, and dashed into the compound shouting to unseen comrades, that the Ingloustan were coming!

Giving the engine the gun, I accelerated rapidly, and as we passed the compound gate, several soldiers rushed out, led by their sergeant buckling on his revolver, shouting and waving at us to stop.

In answer to their waving, we waved back, all smiles and friendliness, as we fought to put as much distance as possible between them and us.

I suppose we must have made a mile or so before I became aware of another vehicle behind us sounding it's horn, and looking into the nearside mirror, I saw in the swirling dust, our army sergeant all red-faced and sweating, waving a pistol in his left hand, and driving his Honda pop-pop in our slipstream.

He was frantically waving at us to stop, and for a few seconds I was tempted to ignore him and keep going.

Looking again in the nearside mirror I could see he had drawn alongside, and was pointing his revolver at our nearside window, where Dick sat trying desperately not to look involved.

The sergeant's contorted features as he shouted and pointed his gun, convinced me he meant business, and feeling pretty helpless and angry, I slowed the vehicle down and pulled to a halt.

Our sergeant parked his Honda in front of our vehicle, and walked back to us, holstering his pistol deftly, and demanding 'passports' - there was no doubt he knew all about us from the previous night's radio messages, and he was going to have his two penn'orth as well.

"Ingloustan Police?" he demanded, and we all nodded.

"You go Asalu?" We nodded again, and getting a bit narked at the one sided conversation I said "You write your name on my paper - say Ingloustan very good - hilee-hob, Ok. yes?"

He scowled ferociously as if suspecting some hidden trap, but getting the message wrote a few lines in Farsi on my scrap of paper and handed it back to me.

"Ok. for us to go Asalu now?" I said in my best contrite voice, but for an answer, he just turned round, jumped on the motor-bike, and roared off back to camp. Again I cursed that ruddy Hooshang Adami for keeping our permit, this was a classic example where the document might have achieved everything we required, without all this agro.

Dick turned to me and said "I bet when that lot at Moqam radioed Teheran for advice concerning our presence on the Gulf, every service radio station for miles around was listening in, and as we're the most unusual thing to appear down here in years, we'll be fair game for every bugger from here to Bushire"

We had only gone another mile before we were stopped again, this time by two armed soldiers on a motor cycle, who blocked the road and refused to let us pass until we had produced our passports.

This time feeling quite narked, I got out of the car and handing over the passports, waved the piece of paper the sergeant had just given us, pointing to my watch and saying 'Pange' -five minutes ago sergeant - indicating three stripes on my arm with my fingers, say Ingloustan, hilee-hob - very good, why passports?

Obviously taken aback by my tirade, they read the sergeant's words, muttered something to each other, and handed the paper back, before getting their motorcycle out of the way and allowing us to proceed.

Behind me, Dick and Peter smiled grins of relief, and as I got back in the vehicle we all burst out laughing at our ludicrous situation. Here we were in the middle of nowhere, being asked to produce our passports every few minutes, as though we were spies in deepest Russia!

Dick said "How about we pull off the road for a while - perhaps go up into the mountains over there and have a look for Humes'? In that terrain at least we'd be away from the attentions of these silly buggers"

The track to Gavbandi meandered across baked and rutted ground, sparsely covered with a growth like the sueda found on salt marshes, which jolted the life out of us, and reduced our speed to about twelve miles an hour. Just before dark, we were still bumping along in the back of beyond, in fact according to our map we were between two mountain ranges near a village called Hashniz, but there was no sign of it yet.

"I vote we camp by that clump of trees over there" said Peter, "It doesn't really matter where the hell we are, we can check our direction by the sun as usual tomorrow, and perhaps we'll find this Gavbandi place then"

At this, I thought how funny it was to feel drawn to an insignificant bunch of trees when faced with an otherwise open space to stop, there's no more security there, than out in the open really, it just feels better!

The waist deep grass we had been driving through the last hour or so looked soft and inviting to sleep on, but on closer examination contained a carpet of viciously hooked and barbed seed heads, which grazed and scratched us badly when bedding down for the night.

After dinner, Peter and I decided to walk to the nearest foothills about a mile away, in an attempt to locate any Humes' owls that might be calling, but with no moon to illuminate the dark countryside it was very hard going.

The whole area seemed to be full of pot-holes and gullies, which jarred your teeth as the expected level of ground underfoot failed to materialise in the darkness.

For a couple of hours we wandered the foothills in stygian darkness, with only the calls of Little owl and desert fox to break the silence, if Humes was here, he was keeping a very low profile!

"I reckon it's time we made our way back" said Peter, "We can't be sure how far we've come really, it must be a couple of miles to the Landrover at least, and it's 2200hrs already"

In total darkness we trudged back down the last gorge we had recently explored, and made our way across a sea of gullies and pot-holes, looking for the tell-tale sign of the fluorescent light fixed to the side of the Landrover.

"Where the hell is it, I can't see it anywhere" Peter gasped.

"Its got to be somewhere out front if we haven't drifted too far to one side" I replied,

"Look, there's a large boulder just in front, if I climb up on that, I might get a better view ahead and see just where our light is"

With a subsequent increase in elevation, I just caught sight of the strip-light, a mere pin-prick of light, way ahead in the vast sea of blackness. It seemed an awfully long way off.

"I can see now we should have brought a compass with us, it's something you don't think you'll need out here in the darkness, anyway if you take a bearing from the direction I'm pointing in Peter, I'm sure we'll get there eventually"

Half an hour later as we topped a gentle rise in the jumbled terrain, we saw the steady light from the Landrover glowing brightly a quarter of a mile away. In the inky darkness, with little orientation as to up, down, or level, the light appeared to float just above head-height in a sea of inky blackness, and I had the mind boggling feeling astronauts must experience when returning to earth from space.

Here was our home, and somehow we had to cross this vast expanse of black void to get back to it, and safety.

How utterly fragile it looked!

At 0530 the next morning we were all jarred from sleep by the loudly repeated calls of a Little owl perched just above our tent, which only ceased when I put my arm outside the tent and shooed it away - obviously a case of the hunters being hunted!

Due to the actions of our 'alarm-clock' Little owl friend, we were able to make an early start on our resumed search for Hume's, driving along parallel with the distant foothills for a couple of miles, searching for suitable habitat to investigate.

The area between the rough track and the mountains two or three miles inland became more agricultural, and soon we were passing large acreages of wheat, onions, tomatoes and tobacco, it didn't look the least bit like Hume's country to me.

At one point, a wide path curved away from our track, heading through the cultivated fields towards the mountains, and we decided to take it, hoping it might lead to somewhere more interesting. After an hour's driving we stopped for a drink, and in the distance could hear the steady 'thump-thump-thump' of a diesel engine, commonly used in Iran to pump water from deep underground for irrigation.

Rounding a sharp bend in the path, we were suddenly confronted with a large mud-brick house with two Japanese pop-pops outside, and I mentally took my hat off to the sales force who had not only sold Japanese bikes to the UK. The traditional home of the motorbike, but even to farmers living way out here!

Stepping down from the Landrover, we were volubly greeted by an old man and his son sitting in the shade on the verandah. After our friendly 'hello'in reply, he courteously invited us out of the sun to partake of some tea. The occupants of the place appeared to be the old chap and his wife, the son and his wife, plus a couple of their children.

Fortunately for us, the son spoke one or two words of English, which, combined with our dreadful Farsi and sign language, enabled us to communicate after a fashion.

During tea, which we drank sitting cross-legged, Iranian style, round a beautiful Persian carpet, we managed to convey the reason for our presence, backed up by bird illustrations in the Collins Field Guide, some of which brought instant recognition from the son.

It was interesting to note the old man identified the Tawny owl as 'Bubo' but I'm sure he was confusing it with the Eagle owl which we had already seen and heard at Lake Perishan, and was pretty widespread throughout Iran. While we discussed the possible whereabouts of the owls, Dick was examining an old wasps' nest he had removed from the wooden door-frame, asking what I thought it was.

I explained it's function, and told him it wasn't being used at present, hence it's white appearance and the empty geodetic construction.

Seeing our interest in the little wasps' nest, the old chap leant across and took it from Dick's hand saying, amongst other things that it was 'Hilee-hob' which we knew meant it was fine, good, very acceptable. At that point the conversation was taken up by the son, and I lost sight of the old man - I presumed he must have had enough for one day, and had gone off for a siesta or something, so I dismissed him from my mind.

Half an hour later, when conversation was all but done, the old chap re-appeared with a large object wrapped in a piece of clean white muslin, and, placing it on a tray in front of me, said once more "Hilee-hob, hilee-hob"

To comply with his obvious request to unwrap the muslin, I took hold of the object and carefully unwrapped a huge section of honeycomb, it's cells full of delicious honey! He had obviously thought we were talking about honeycomb when we were looking at the old wasps' nest, and had rushed off outside somewhere to bring back this lovely present.

Waving his hand at the honeycomb and then at me, he pointed to his mouth and said again 'Hilee-hob' so I broke a piece off and stuffed it into my mouth, it was delicious, just as I remembered it from my days as a lad in Salcombe, I could go a bundle on this!

Smiling broadly, the old chap waved his arm at Peter and Dick, indicating they should do the same, at which I said "Yes do, it's absolutely wonderful, I haven't tasted honey like this in yonks"

Dick was quite au-fait with the honeycomb, but Peter seemed a bit non-plussed as how to deal with it. "Just pick a chunk off and pop it in yer mouth" laughed Dick, and proceeded to wrench another piece off for himself. With the whole family watching, the old chap indicated I should have another piece too, which I gladly did. The family, having held back out of courtesy to their guests, now ate huge chunks too, leaving little of the original comb behind.

Everyone was laughing and smiling, thoroughly enjoying the sweet honey, when I felt a harsh jab on my thigh, and I turned to find Dick's face close to mine, whispering in my ear. "Have a close look at the comb, I think you'll be surprised, I've got grubs in mine!"

In the dull light filtering into the room, I glanced at my piece to find I had exactly the same as Dick, I could see the white shapes inside their waxy tubes quite clearly once I knew.

Oh god! I thought, and suddenly the vision of the chap as guest of honour at the Bedouin feast, having to eat goat's eyeballs came to mind, and I all but retched. Before anyone present suspected anything amiss, Dick smiled, said 'Hilee-hob' and downed his remaining piece with a smile, looking at Peter and I to follow suit, which we did, although I must admit, it took a lot of will-power, knowing what I did.

At this point the lady of the house threw a handful of twigs on the glowing fire to boil the kettle again for tea, while her daughter in law, who had disappeared for a while, re-appeared carrying a very small baby.

In contrast to the lady of the house, the young mother wore a black leather Yashmak, which gave her the sinister appearance of Darth Vader, and I assumed she must have put it on due to our presence in their house.

The young husband explained that the two pop-pops parked outside belonged to his young wife and himself, his father and two other sons had to make do with another Japanese product, the Mazda pick-up truck. Apparently the main produce from the farm was tomatoes and onions, which were sent regularly to market, whilst the wheat and tobacco crop they kept for themselves, and, as if to emphasise the last point, the old chap began to set up an ornate looking hookah pipe.

Once he had got it going satisfactorily he offered us a puff, and I must admit, for a life-long non smoker like me, it tasted quite mild. With everyone fully refreshed, the old chap and two of his sons offered to show us the whereabouts of 'Bubu' in the mountains behind their home, an offer we gladly accepted, after all, who should know better where to find Humes' owl than one of the locals?

Their house was surrounded and shaded by rows of Eucalyptus and Casuarina trees, which held an amazing variety of birds for such an out of the way place, and we soon identified Upcher's warblers, Bulbuls, Scrub warblers, Babblers, Purple-Sunbirds and Rollers.

In complete contrast to this cultivated haven, the sparse slopes of the foothills behind the house, dotted with one or two Sinjed trees was positively arid. In the fierce mid-day heat it became a serious physical effort to reach the weirdly eroded gorges and cliffs which formed a curtain to the mountains behind, diamond etched against the vivid cobalt sky.

Unexpectedly, the old chap displayed the stamina of a mountain goat as he led us up the first rocky gorge, quickly pointing out two nest holes for us to examine in the first half-mile, but they both belonged to Spotted Little owl and not Humes'.

Checking the thermometer I had brought from the car, I found it already reading 42C. and understood why the three of us were feeling a bit the worse for wear, although it didn't seem to affect the old chap one little bit!

After an hour gadding about, following our leader here, there, and everywhere, it became obvious there was no way us three Brits were going to cover the myriad of holes and possible nest sites of Humes' without a small army of helpers.

It wasn't physically possible. It was as they say, like looking for a needle in the proverbial haystack.

The remorseless landscape was just as you would expect to find on some distant planet. In absolte silence and utter desolation, jagged peaks and crumbling buttresses soared into a stark azure sky, the only signs of life being the occasional Humes' and Desert Wheatears flicking away noiselessly at our approach.

As we moved along the gorges, hundreds of huge grasshoppers clattered away over the rocks on either side, a few getting caught in the 5' wide spider webs spanning the gullies at chest height. The spiders resting on these immensely strong webs were nearly 4" across at the legs, with a silver coloured, shell-like back similar to a spider crab, and while taking a few minutes well-needed rest, I managed to photograph a couple in close-up.

In an effort to cover more ground, I suggested that Peter and Dick together with the old chap, should cover the left wall of the gorge, while the other two and I covered the right, and call out if anything of interest was found.

After toiling for an hour amongst the rocks and rubble, I came up with a pair of Ravens feeding four large young in a huge stick nest, a pair of Kestrels with small young on a ledge in a cavern, two Rock-Nuthatch nests, both containing young, and a pair of Egyptian vultures at their nest in a cave, but of Humes' owl, not a sign.

While we were resting and taking a drink of water, one of the sons accompanying me pointed to an interesting looking hole ten feet up a rocky wall, and said 'Bubo, bubo' and looking through the binocs I tended to agree with him, it certainly looked promising, especially as there appeared to be some white droppings near the entrance. I'd have a closer look.

It was an easy climb, and soon I was looking into the hole's sandy entrance, where I could see signs of recent disturbance by the feet of some bird or other leading to the interior. I eased my head and shoulders into the hole, and waited a few seconds for my eyes to accustom to the gloom inside.

The hole was about three feet deep, curving gently to one side, and at the back I could see signs of a recent nest, in which there were lots of pellets (regurgitated remains of prey) and a few feathers. At full stretch I managed to hook a few pellets out, plus a couple of feathers, which I examined in daylight and found were, without doubt, those of a Tawny owl.

It seemed I had discovered our elusive quarry at last, but unfortunately far too late, the brood had fledged and gone!

The pellets I retrieved contained the remains of various rodents, one including a complete skull, and another contained part of a bird, probably a Babbler, it's skull, and leg remains giving a fair clue as to it's identity. These pellets and feathers would be very useful in establishing any claim of Hume's identity, once we got back to Teheran.

Back at our leader's place, we flopped out in an effort to recuperate from our recent rigorous exertions, before preparing ourselves for an evening wander around the gorges, listening for any calls of the recently departed Humes'.

Much revived after several cups of tea from our hosts, Dick asked about the diesel engine pump we could hear thumping away nearby, where was it? In answer, the eldest son took us across the yard to a huge hole in the ground, where steps cut into the soil led down to the murky depths.

Following him down about forty feet, we came across the engine slogging away noisily, sending precious water to the surface. He explained the pump drew water from much further down, and sent it all to the top where it was used to irrigate their crops, a massive undertaking.

Looking at the engine closely, I could see it was made in Britain, and built in Oldham in 1926 - old faithful here was still working and running well after all those years!

The following morning we said a sad goodbye to the delightful family who had made us so welcome, and continued our route towards Gavbandi and Asalu, places we knew existed from our maps, but nevertheless seemed reluctant to show themselves in the flesh.

We were back in the vast open spaces of the wilderness again.

A few miles away to our right, the endless backdrop of mountains that had paralleled our journey from Bandar Abbas, continued as far as the eye could see, broken occasionally by wide, boulder strewn gorges that were the outlet for winter melt-waters cascading from 3000' mountains towards the sea.

Interrupting a particularly long period of silence as we bounced along the track, Dick said "How about a final look around here for our old friend Humes' Owl then?, From the map this appears to be about the last big inlet into the mountains for miles, until we reach Asalu and Kangan in fact, after that it's all salt marshes"

In a re-run of our last incursion into the mountains, we made a careful approach through the maze of criss-cross water channels, which, combined with a look-out on the bonnet, gave us the best chance of keeping out of serious trouble. After covering roughly three miles toward the foothills at a tortuously slow pace, we found a tiny space under a cliff and pulled in.

We were nicely protected by the overhang from the hot sun, but with so many huge boulders scattered around, it wouldn't be easy to get out again, there was little room to manoeuvre.

That evening we went 'walk-about' in the foothills, using the new moon for guidance, but despite a long and diligent search heard nothing. It seemed as though the only contact we were going to make with Humes' was the one we had already made.

It was all a bit of an anti-climax, but we had given it our best shot.

The next day I was idly watching a Raven through binoculars as it drifted slowly along the coastal track we had quit yesterday, when I noticed a camouflaged helicopter flying at extremely low altitude just behind it, and it appeared to be looking for something.

As I watched, it covered a couple of miles in the direction of Asalu, then turning sharply, came back over it's previous route, barely skimming the small trees and shrubs bordering the track in places.

"Hey lads" I called. "There's a helicopter buzzing the coastal track down there, skimming backwards and forwards as though looking for something, do you think he's looking for us?"

"Bloody tough luck if he is" replied Dick. "There's no way they'll ever think of looking up here for us, so let 'em get on with it!"

Dick was right,our dark-green Landrover tucked snugly into the rocks would be invisible to most observers, while we, with our elevated position and unrestricted panoramic view of the coast, could see everything. We felt happy that unwittingly we had pulled a fast one on the annoying military, and it was now their turn to be mucked about!

A three hour jaunt into the mountains the next night produced nothing of note either, it would appear that if Humes' owl was present along this coast, it was very localised and quite specialised in it's diet - we didn't even hear a scavenging fox calling, so prey must be pretty thin on the ground.

Returning to the coastal track next day, our route towards Asalu lay across forty miles of unmarked salt wastes, the grey crystalline ground supporting only the hardiest growth. There were waxy looking plants similar to our English 'ice plant' and a convolvulus-like plant, with long running tendrils and purple, bell-shaped flowers which I photographed.

There was neither bird nor beast to be seen anywhere.

After covering miles and miles of grim salt flats we came unexpectedly upon the delightful fishing village of Nakhl-e Taqi, tucked idylically amongst date the palms on a broad, golden, sandy beach.

It looked just like a scene from a Seychelles travel poster except for the Arab dhow rolling gently in the creamy surf, huge circular fish-traps piled high on its back end. It was so photogenic we stayed for a while, watching and photographing the fishermen unloading their catch before selling it to the visiting agent. This relatively well-dressed chap weighed everything he chose from the fishermen's catch, before putting it into huge woven saddle-bags attached to the rear of his Honda motorcycle.

I nudged Dick and asked if he had noticed what the agent was using for weights on his portable beam scales.

There were a couple of U2 batteries strapped together for the 1/2lb weight, an old car water pump for the pounds - Lord knows how many, and what looked like a house brick wrapped in cloth and tied with string for the heaviest weight. It was all quite ingenious, and obviously worked fairly enough to everyone's satisfaction!

As we left the village to continue our journey, I noticed a two-storey house - in itself a rarity out here, which had beautiful fluted columns and ornate capitals supporting it's upper storey, even more out of place in this part of the world!

I stopped the Landrover, went over to the house and spoke to a man standing in the doorway, but he didn't speak English.

His friendhowever spoke a little, and through him I discovered the house had been built 25 years ago by a man who had once lived near Shiraz, and it was obvious he had been greatly influenced by the architecture seen at nearby Persepolis, it was quite amazing!

After the long hot haul from Gavbandi and Asalu, the imminent approach of Kangan, our next town, brought forth visions of ice-cold cokes drawn from fridges to slake our thirst, and we vied with each other as to who would see a Cola sign first.

There are however, times in life when, savouring a situation in the mind for some time, the mental picture bears no resemblance to the eventual reality, and life seems grossly disappointing.

Kangan was worse than that, it had absolutely nothing!

We stared in utter disbelief at the one horse, grotty, falling down filthy ruin of a 'town' that met our gaze. There were about six shops in the town which covered about

3/4 mile square, none of which had any drink whatsoever - 'nis Cola' was without doubt the order of the day!

It was as though the two or three people we did see, were the sole survivors of some vanished race.

The cluster of hovels on either side of the confluence of the dried up river and the track we had arrived on, were on their last legs, and everything swirled around in clouds of hot dust and rubbish.

I imagine in the wet period, one would have to travel several miles inland before finding a place to cross the fast flowing river, but now, in the dinging 42C heat, the river bed was bone-dry, cluttered unbelieveably with huge trees and rubbish swept down from the distant mountains.

It was like the aftermath of armageddon.

In absolute disgust we eased the Landrover down onto the dry river bed, and dodging carefully between the piles of rubbish and huge trees, made for the far bank, the sooner we left this bloody awful place the better!

Despite it's arid outlook, this part of the gulf appears to be a haven for thousands of Bee-Eaters. Ever since leaving Asalu we found them nesting in every available sandbank in their dozens, and at Deyyer, the next 'town' after Kangan, competition for nest sites was so keen, dozens of Little Green Bee-Eaters' nests were found in dry gully banks only a foot high!

That evening we camped beside the sea, and as we ate our meal I watched a couple of Egyptian Nightjars hunting to and fro along the huge sand dunes, which reminded me of a similar location on the dunes of Pylat near Arcachon in France.

The last section of our route to Bushire crossed the mighty Mand Rud, the same river we had crossed hundreds of miles away near Firouzabad, although here it was only a quarter-mile wide, emptying into the Persian gulf in a swirling muddy stream. Crossing the river, we were sandwiched on a narrow strip of sand between 2000' cliffs and the gulf, bundling along the dusty, rutted track at speed, until the offside rear tyre ballooned from it's casing, vibrating like a road drill until we found a place to stop and examine it.

Dick felt it wouldn't last much longer,so we'd have to be careful.

The scenery was pretty dismal too, with very little of interest anywhere, only a couple of farmers 'thrashing' their harvested corn by dragging a huge stone round and round behind a docile cow over the sheaves, broke the terrible sameness of it all.

Hadn't these people ever heard of hand-thrashing the sheaves of wheat into a bin for goodness sake?

As night fell, we were relieved to see the twinkling lights of Bushire appear in the far distance, and as we drew closer, I could see it was like a low-grade Bandar Abbas, with lots of garish lights and filth everywhere.

The two hotels we eventually located were both full-up, and in some desperation I drove round and round until we found ourselves at the end of a tarmac strip running down to a river, a few yards from the gates of a large campus.

In double quick time the tent was put up, and petrol stove lit for a well earned supper, we'd had enough exertion during the last few hours to last a lifetime, and we were starving!

The following morning I poked my head out of the tent into the glaring light of day, to find our campsite looking very different from the place I had envisaged in the dark - we were slap in the middle of dozens of houses, and right in front of a school or college!

Overhead dozens of swifts screamed loudly as they zoomed in and out of nest holes riddling the somewhat dilapidated buildings, while on a low stone wall a few feet away sat a row of young Iranians watching me watching them - what was going on?

Looking at my watch I saw it was just before 0530, but as the place was already coming to life, I thought we'd better get up and get mobile, in case we found ourselves arrested for loitering or something more sinister!

It was only after we had finished our breakfast, that the first of the Iranians got off the wall and came over to the car, and speaking broken English, asked if we could look at his work folder.

At this, the rest of them piled across, and within minutes Dick, Peter and I were inundated with dozens of questions concerning all manner of educational topics.

It was obvious they were high-school students, and we were outside their college.

The first chap to button-hole me must have been an agricultural student, and one of his questions concerned the keeping of various birds in aviaries for study, only he said 'Apiary' which of course is concerned with bee keeping.

"No no, birds are definitely in an apiary" he insisted after hearing my correction, so I wrote for him in English the two words - aviary and apiary, with a little drawing under each to represent the birds and bees.

Off he went, talking to himself, saying he was going to see his tutor right away and sort it all out. Rather thankfully I let him go, thinking that would be the last I would see of him, and turned to the next in line.

Just as we were putting the last bits and pieces on the roof of the Landrover before moving off, our friend re-appeared, and waving a piece of paper at me shouted "You English are wrong, you not know what you say. I speak to my tutor now, and he say birds are definitely in an apiary, he right - you wrong, you no good!"

I smiled, and wondered what chance any of them had to gain modern knowledge, if they were all as ill informed as our friend here, it seemed to me they had a rather tough uphill struggle to overcome!

# Chapter Twenty Three

The rear nearside tyre which had developed a nasty bulge at Bushire, gave up the ghost soon after we set off for Borajan - there was little doubt the severe hammering all our tyres had taken in the boulder filled river bed south of Lars and other places, had finally come home to roost!

Really, it was a good job we had two spare wheels on board, otherwise we would have been in real schtuck if we had suffered a puncture as well.

What came next was a surprise to all of us as we turned east at the Hilleh-Rud, and made our way through the mountain chain from Borajan towards our earlier starting point at Lake Perishan.

After a superb start, the asphalt road quickly deteriorated into a bumpy, stony track, passing the old bridge over the Dalaki-Rud and caravanserai, aiming itself in an apologetic manner at the base of the awesome 10,000'high Kuh-i-Dera mountain, a monstrous barrier stretching each side of us like an impenetrable wall.

Craning my head forward, I strove to see where on earth the track went next, mumbling to Dick in the navigator's seat, I didn't go much on the lousy approach to such a formidable feature as we were expected to climb.

"There's a couple of heavy lorries crawling along in front, plus one behind, I reckon if they can get across the mountains we can, let's go for it"

As we climbed the foothills, the mountain seemed to rise in front like the walls of a Crusader castle, and it was only by watching the stop lights on the lorry in front as it ground through the swirling dust clouds, I had any idea where the road went to next.

"I think with all this dust flying about, we'd better drop back a bit and let him get on with it, we can't pass him anyway it's far too steep, I'm in 4 wheel drive and second gear as it is"

The vehicle in front was at least a ten-tonner, and loaded to the gills, which made it's passage up the track agonisingly slow - I would just have to be patient. As we got higher, and the track steeper, the lorry in front often found it necessary to take two bites to get through the tight hairpins, which were at least a foot deep in dust.

"Bloody hell" said Peter from his kip-couch behind the front seats. "How much longer does this lark go on? it's getting dark already you know"

I craned forward again, looking upwards as far as I could, but the rock wall seemed to go up and onwards forever.

"I've looked and can't see an end to it yet Pete, at a guess I'd say we're about half-way up, so another hour might do it"

At just under the hour we turned the fiftieth hairpin, and saw clear sky and stars ahead, so we must be near the top at last, it had been a long hard haul.

Sandwiched in the middle of a small convoy and quite unable to stop, I pressed on, the descent if anything, being worse than the ascent! A couple of times I nearly lost it, as the Landrover slid with all wheels locked in thick dust on the hairpin bends, practically tail-gateing the chap in front - I didn't like this one little bit!

Descending into yet another of the steep hairpins and no retaining wall to stop us going to the bottom, hundreds of feet below, I skidded to a halt so violently, one of our five-gallon water canisters on the front broke loose, and cannoned off into space like a rocket.

I cursed loudly as I saw it go, we just couldn't afford to lose such a vital piece of kit at this stage of our trip.

After a while the roller-coaster downward track eased off a little, and it was a relief to drive normally again.

I knew it couldn't be far to Kazeroun 'city' and old Ali-Baba's Sandywich bar, we certainly needed to grab some food and drink before cracking the final stretch back to Lake Perishan.

I had more than finished my driving stint for the day, and Dick generously said he would drive the last few miles to our old campsite - he wanted something to do after that hellish nailbiting drive, and I gladly agreed.

Murphy though, had other ideas - after all the day wasn't finished yet, we still had a couple of hours 'til midnight! Gleefully he led us a merry dance through the wilds surrounding Perishan, until after twenty miles or so, we had to admit we were totally lost.

"Ok. that's bloody well it!" said Dick, banging the steering wheel in disgust. "We've had enough fun for one day, I say we put up the tent right here, and get our heads down. We can sort out where the hell we are in the morning"

Peter and I readily agreed, and got the tent down off the roof. The next morning after breakfast we turned the vehicle round, and retraced our steps in the direction we thought Perishan was, but the terrain was quite unrecognisable. There was no doubt about it, we were in unfamiliar territory, and totally lost.

The rough track ran between barren rocky ground on our left, and huge cultivated fields on the right, so we couldn't be too far from habitation to ask for directions.

As we bundled along something caught my eye, and I yelled "Hey Dick stop, stop! Can't you see what's growing in those fields, it's hundreds of acres of poppies - opium poppies!"

"How the hell do you know that?" Dick asked.

"I've photographed enough of the damn things in my job to know opium poppy heads when I see them, most of these are ripe for scouring already, hold on a minute while I take some photos will you?"

"What do you reckon the red flags on sticks at the corners of the fields are for?" said Peter, "Do you reckon they're to warn people off or what?"

As I began taking photographs of the fields, flags, and close-ups of the seed heads, a whistle started blowing somewhere in the far distance, as though a football match was going on.

"I don't know whether you've got friends out here or not" growled Dick in his usual laconic manner, "But through my binocs I can see a dozen soldiers carrying rifles coming this way through the poppy fields, and the chap in front is waving at us"

"Bloody hell!" said Peter "I think we've shit it this time, they obviously take great exception to you wandering among their opium poppies, and want to nick us. I think it's time we scarpered"

In a cloud of dust we roared away from our 'friends' and within half an hour located the track we should have found last night, leading to the lake, and our old campsite of three weeks ago.

It was like coming home.

It didn't take long to get ourselves organised as before, and while Dick ran the rule over the Landrover, Peter and I went off to the marsh, to ascertain what stage of breeding the local bird population had reached since our departure.

We had just finished lunch, and were getting some equipment sorted out for photography, when an army Landrover followed by a small open Russian truck, containing several soldiers roared into view, heading straight for our camp.

It looked rather ominous.

I had been setting up my portable tape recorder before lunch, checking the microphone and batteries, which were laid out on the Landrover's bonnet. At the army vehicles' approach, I turned the recorder on, pointed the microphone in the direction of our tent, and covered everything from view with my towel.

The Iranians pulled up just short of the tent, and the officer in charge - his badges suggested a lieutenant, strode purposefully towards us, demanding loudly "Passports, passports".

They were ruddy-well at it again!

We had a couple of camping chairs set up between the Landrover and the tent, and it was in these that we were reclining when the soldiers arrived. Peter got up and said "I know where the passports are from the previous fun and games, I'll get them, just give me a minute"

The lieutenant stood glaring at us, whacking a cane against his leg, eyes flicking over everything in view, he was no fool.

Taking our passports from Peter, he flicked through the pages, asking us questions in Farsi which we didn't understand, but to which we replied 'Ingloustan tourist, paranda shanass' and again I would love to have strangled that damned Hooshang Adami in Shiraz for hanging on to our letter.

The officer called a couple of his men over from their truck, and engaged in terse conversation concerning something he wasn't happy about, and although he mentioned parander shanass a couple of times, it was said in a tone which indicated he wasn't too keen on our explanation.

He walked over to Peter's camera and telephoto lens sitting on it's carrying case, and I hastened to describe it's use as a bird recording camera, with nothing sinister about it at all.

Watched closely by his men, he prowled around camp, looking first through the tent door, and then into the back of our Landrover, before examining it closely from all angles.

He was very thorough.

Returning to the front of our vehicle, he leant against the wing and regarded us intently for a few seconds, as though expecting us to say something. Then without a word, he leant forward and flicked my towel off the recorder and mike with his stick, pressed the key to stop the recording, and smiled.

I was flabbergasted, how had he even become aware of the recorder, and even more remarkable, how did he know where to switch it off?

Before any of us could move 'or say a word, he turned to his men, gave a sharp order, and they piled into their vehicles at the double and disappeared. It was all quite weird.

Despite all the excitement, the day wasn't quite finished yet, we had the unexpected arrival of Francis Argyle, one of the British ornithologists working for the Iranians in Teheran to contend with. It seemed to me, that all of a sudden we had gone from being pretty well the only creatures on Gods' earth in this empty wilderness, to the centre of attraction for miles around!

It was all getting a bit too much.

Although he tried to give the impression of travelling through the area, and deciding to look us up, something told me he'd made a deliberate effort to leave Teheran, and come hot-foot in a department vehicle, to see just what we were up to.

He didn't seem all that impressed by what we'd seen and done, apparently he'd been here a year ago, and knew the place quite well. Before he left though, he did tell us of a small island a mile or so down lake towards Famur, where a small colony of Collared Pratincoles nested most years - now that was interesting!

Over the next few days Peter and I got cracking on our bird photography, and began to get some nice stuff, including a species new to me, the White-tailed Plover, whose nests were appearing as quickly as the ground dried out from the winter rains.

Acting on Argyle's advice, all three of us decided to wade out to the island suspected of holding the nesting Pratincoles to see if they were there this year. We only had a general idea of the direction in which it lay, and as there were several large reed beds between our camp and the site, it would be hit and miss search until we found it.

From birds I'd watched earlier passing over our camp, I recognised the 'geer-luk geer-luk! calls of Pratincoles coming from somewhere ahead, and we soon found the 'island', a slight hump rising from the lake bottom, barely six inches above water.

Within a few minutes of wading ashore we had found twenty Pratincole nests,and two Black-Winged Stilt's nests, on an area of grassy mud, thirty feet long by twenty feet wide!

Elated by our find, we took a bearing on our position and began the long wade back to camp, which was at least two miles away in a straight line - if you could possibly manage such a thing!

The bottom of the lake consisted of soft, greyish mud in which you sank to the ankles, and the constant suction whilst walking, plus trying not to fall over with our cameras, made it a very exhausting journey.

While we were still some way offshore, Dick, who had been looking ahead through his binoculars said "Would you look at that, I don't bloody-well believe it, there's an army truck by our tent again, what the hell do they want now?"

Quite exhausted, we staggered ashore by the camp, and wearily hauled ourselves up the steep slope, where an army Landrover was parked, and before we had even had a chance to catch our breath, a Sergeant in charge of the group strode across and demanded 'passports!

Really narked by such cavalier and totally undeserved harsh treatment, I yelled back at him "Do you speak English? if you do you can ruddy well wait, we're fed up with your continual silly nonsense!"

Whether his command of English was good enough to understand me or not I don't know, but his expression changed from arrogant aggression to one of surprise, and he waited patiently while I went to the Landrover and got our passports.

Whist he took his time examining the papers, I wondered whether they had gone through our belongings while we were away, not that we had anything to hide, but we did have photographic equipment we could ill afford to lose.

With a cursory look around our camp, he handed the passports back, muttered something in Farsi, and strode off with his men to their Russian personnel carrier, and roared off in a cloud of dust.

This sort of treatment was definitely getting on our wick.

After a week of quite intensive photography, and exploring up and down the lake in mellors' punt, Dick said he would like to take a few days off sight-seeing in Shiraz, so I dropped him off at the police post to catch the Toyota truck-bus, collected our mail from the driver,and filled up with fresh water.

The letter I received from Teresa - brought from the Departments' office in Shiraz, told me she had been at her wits end the evening she woke me from my sleep. The Yard had apparently cocked up the arrangements for putting my salary cheque into the bank, and she had been completely out of cash!

With bills to pay, and the family to feed, she rang my colleague Frank at work,asking him if he would kindly sort out the cock-up, which he did in double quick time.

You wouldn't believe simple things like a pay cheque could go wrong - or would you?

Over the next couple of days I put a hide up on the little muddy island where the Pratincoles were nesting, and got Dick to drop me off one morning in Zammit's punt,for a photo session

The new hide overlooking one of several Pratincole's nests, had to be situated in a foot of water, six feet out from the island, which allowed me to get a good view of the sitting bird.

From the landward side, the bird would have been hidden by coarse vegetation and would have looked awful, so I had no choice but to shoot from the lake.

Working from 'wet' hides over the years, I had evolved a technique of putting all my photographic gear into a plastic bucket, and suspending it from the roof by a piece of rope, leaving the bucket to be supported by water at the bottom of the hide.

The only snag was if you dropped anything at all, it went straight in the drink, so utmost care was the order of the day!

Sitting on the bottom of the lake in water up to my waist, I centred the camera on it's tripod, and lined up my lens on the Pratincole's nest. It looked great.

From inside the hide I called "Thanks Dick, I'm ok. now, it's 1230, if you could come back for me at 1500, I should have all the pictures I want by then".

"Yeah, gotcha" replied Dick, and he was away, rowing mellors' punt in the snaking way we had grown accustomed to, due to it's lack of keel.

I don't suppose he had gone more than a hundred yards before the birds returned,totally accepting the hide now that the intruders had gone,and I got some beautiful shots of the female shuffling onto her eggs, using the 200mmm lens on my Pentax.

Finishing the roll of film, I reached into the bucket for a new one, and noticed through a peep-hole, the sun had disappeared. The sky was getting dull and murky, and nasty dark clouds were rolling in. Surely that wasn't the end of our good weather?

Within five minutes, the wind rose in short sharp gusts, and a steady rain began to fall, how could the weather change so darn quickly?

As the sky grew darker and blacker, a localised thunder and lightning storm tracked down the centre of the lake at about 10 mph, a black boiling cloud, rolling over and over like a huge dumpling, shot through with wicked flashes of lightning.

It was an awesome sight!

As the wind reached me, the hide began to lift from the soft mud of the lake, and began to rise into the air, which would have scared the living daylights out of the sitting birds around me, if I had suddenly appeared!

In desperation I hung on to the insides of the hide like grim death, fingers stiffening from cold, hoping to god I had the strength to outlast the storm.

Although the hide was flapping madly in the wind, I noticed when squinting through my peep-hole the Pratincole was apparently ASLEEP on its nest. It didn't seem to take a blind bit of notice of the mayhem going on all around!

As the storm raged, the temperature dropped considerably, and because I was wearing only my shorts, I began to get very cold.

My fingers were numb from holding on to the hide, and my legs cramped from clamping the tripod into the mud - I'd be more than glad when the damned weather quietened down a bit.

Checking the tripod between my legs, I could see several large dytiscus water beetles swimming in the calmer waters of the hide, and whilst I didn't mind them at all, I took great exception to an extremely large water-snake which tried the same trick, and gave him a fist on the snout for his trouble!

Gradually the storm abated, and glancing at my watch, I saw it was 1430. I had been holding the damned hide down for over an hour.

By now, I couldn't feel my hands at all, and my body was shivering with cold, I'd almost had enough. Ever so slowly, a weak sun appeared, and I carefully let go of the hide walls, peering out at the sitting Pratincole. It was still there, apparently unperturbed, sitting as though nothing had happened, it was incredible!

It was now 1600 and I was getting a bit worried - why hadn't someone made an attempt to reach me? After all I had agreed with Dick to be relieved at 1500, where was he. Had something gone wrong in camp?

Looking out of the side aperture for the hundredth time, I saw in the distance mellors' green punt making it's way slowly towards me, and I knew that rescue was on the way at last, but couldn't make out who was rowing.

Slowly Peter hove into view, explaining that Dick had gone down with the dreaded montezuma's revenge, and he, despite feeling shaky too, had finally made the attempt to come out and resue me, but it had been a close call!

It took several minutes to get to my feet, and leave the hide without falling over. I was frozen with cold, and suffering bad cramps from holding the hide in position for hours.

Sometimes bird photography could get beyond a joke!

One evening when we were filling our water canister near the Police post, Dick decided to see if the officers would appreciate the old trick of 'fly away Peter, fly away Paul, using pieces of paper stuck to his fingernails. In slow-time Dick gave his first demonstration, followed by a couple more in quick time, just to get the lads going.

In utter disbelief and perplexity, they made poor Dick repeat his trick over and over again, even examining his hands and wrists to see how it was done. They never did twig the swopping of fingers, and it was side-splitting to see them try to copy the trick themselves, without any success whatever!

By the 16th May, temperature in the open sunshine was 42C and in our plastic bird hides, a staggering 45C, and I was losing weight by the hour. Whilst this might be beneficial cosmetically, the down-side was that you needed to drink more to avoid de-hydration, and we were now using 5 gallons every two days.

That evening, it was my turn to cook the meal, and I thought it would be nice to have the tinned steak with rice, plus a few local courgettes and tomatoes. We were all as hungry as horses, so it should go down a treat.

As there had been considerable insect activity of late, I took the precaution of covering the pots and pans whilst things were cooking, I certainly didn't want any nasties dropping in un-announced.

By the time the meal was ready, darkness had fallen, and we were sitting alongside the Landrover with the neon strip-light for illumination, watching the antics of fire-flies as they switched their abdominal lights on and off.

In the darkness away from the strip-light, the flashing of fire-flies could even be seen through the bottom of our brown plastic washing up bowl, crawling around underneath, doing whatever it was they were doing!

I served Peter and Dick their share of the meal, and turned to get my own. It smelt delicious, and I couldn't wait to get stuck in.

As I moved the first spoonful towards my mouth, something unusual amongst the steak and gravy caught my eye.

Two long thin bristles stood up above the gravy in a totally alien way, what the hell was it?

Putting the spoonfull back on my plate, I fished under the bristles and hoicked out a Mole-Cricket over two inches long, its armour plated head and legs dangling obscenely over the edge of my spoon. Under most circumstances I would have got rid of the offending visitor and carried on with my meal, we'd had worse in Egypt, but this time something was different, and I rebelled.

"I'm not ruddy well eating that stuff now!" I shouted, and hurled the meal off my plate into the darkness, to the raucous laughs of Peter and Dick.

"Didn't think a little thing like a bug in your nosh would put you off" said Dick with a grin, "You never know, it might have given your rotten grub a bit more taste!"

"I don't care what it MIGHT have done, it MIGHT have been in there for ages for all I know, if so, you two will have extra vitamins too!"

"Doesn't matter a fig to me" said Peter, "I'd more or less finished mine when you flew into tantrums, its all gone down the hole now, and won't be coming back"

In a rotten mood at having been deprived of my eagerly awaited meal, I made do with some Iranian bread and Marmite, at least the bugs couldn't interfere with that!

The following evening after a hard day's photography, we came back to camp to find two Iranian school teachers from the nearby village waiting by our tent. Would we care to come to their place at Ayuzabad this evening to enjoy a meal and some conversation? Naturally we were always willing to share hospitality both ways, and it didn't take us long to wash and change, before piling into the Landrover.

It was a bit cramped inside with the two teachers, ourselves and Zammit - who had asked to be dropped off at the Police post on our way out. I'm sure the lift was mainly to get him another notch up the social scale, it was obviously something to be seen arriving in the Ingloustani's car!

Our visit to the teachers in the village was a very friendly affair, they produced a nice meal of stuffed peppers on a bed of beautifully fried rice, to which they added our contribution of tinned sardines.

We had also brought along a tin of sweet biscuits, which, with their home brewed coffee, we drank sitting cross-legged on the floor, discussing all sorts of things from football to politics.

They were extremely keen to discover how Iran was viewed by outsiders, and whether or not they would be allowed to study in Britain, just as some of their friends had been selected for courses in the USA.

When our discussion got into difficulties due to inadequacies of language, pencil and paper helped bridge the gap, and the point was eventually clarified, but all too soon it was time to go.

As we left the compound our teachers shared with a large family, I was intrigued to see the family already wrapped in their blankets lying in rows asleep on the compound floor, with only the sparkling stars for a canopy.

It seemed just right.

The next day, we all agreed a change of scenery was required, and the three of us, plus mellors, took off along the shoreline towards Famur, intent on seeing what bird life there was at that end of the lake compared with ours here.

There was mention in the notes given to us by the Department in Teheran, of a large colony of Pelicans nesting near Famur village which should be well worth seeing, plus several other interesting species, provided of course we could find them!

At the far end of the lake where it disappeared into dense reed beds, mellors spoke to a local shepherd, who informed him that the Pelican nesting colony we hoped to see didn't exist at that moment, even though we counted over 70 birds nearby. It had apparently been decimated by foxes taking the eggs (they would have to be excellent swimmers) the water rising and flooding the eggs - the nests were still dry and well above water, or the eggs had been taken by men in canoes,from Bushire!

We reckoned if you substituted 'locals' for 'men of Bushire' you might end up much nearer the truth!

The muddy shoreline on which the seventy-odd Pelicans and Marbled Teal rested was close by, and we persuaded Dick to drive closer to the water's edge, so that we could get some good photographs using the 400mm lens.

From a position on the roof, we were able to concentrate on our photography, leaving Dick to get on with the job of getting us really close, when suddenly the Landrover came to a halt, before sagging gently to the left. There was a frantic crunching of gears, as Dick fought to find reverse in a hurry but he was just too late.

"Oh shit! We're stuck, she's gone through the crust into the soft stuff underneath, I can't move her"

As Peter and I got down, we immediately saw the extent of our troubles - we were up to our hubs in black goo, and by the look of the trail behind us, had been on 'borrowed time' for some little while.

"I don't think the rule of 'who does it, gets it out and fixes it' applies this time" I said "We'd all better start looking for something to push under the wheels after we've dug them out, otherwise she might sink in further"

Fortunately there were several dead branches on the shoreline, and a few pieces of timber lying around the shepherd's hut, which he said we could use. After some very strenuous digging, we got the backs of the wheels cleared and chocked, and were ready to go.

"Ok. Dick, give her a try " I said, and he cautiously took up the drive while we stood by ready to feed in anything that would give the tyres extra grip.

Finding not a lot happening, Dick gave it a large dose of wellie, causing Peter and I at the rear end to be showered with stinking black mud from the wheel arches.

"Oh thanks a bleeding lot!" shouted Peter in disgust, as we staggered out of the firing line, "Perhaps YOU'D like to come out here and have a go at this little lot, while one of us does the easy bit, eh?"

"If you think you can do any better, you're welcome to have a go chum, jump in!" growled Dick.

"Hold on, hold on" I said, "Let's not get uptight about it, it's got to come out somehow, so let's dig gentle ramps away from each wheel for a few yards, and line them with lots of rushes and reeds, that way we might get a better run at it"

For the next hour we dug in the black ooze, feeding in huge amounts of vegetation for the wheels to grip on, while Mellors sat cross-legged looking in the opposite direction. He wasn't getting involved in any of this work stuff!

"Right, that seems as though it might do the trick, I'll give her a go this time, if you two plus mellors will give a push at the front, how about it?"

Retrieving Mellors from his mental trance, Peter and Dick took the strain under the bull-bar, as I let out the clutch.

For a few seconds I gave her half throttle, but not a lot seemed to happen, until Dick grimacing at me through the windscreen shouted "She's going, she's going, keep her moving for god's sake!"

As she began to claw out of the ooze and onto our bed of reeds, I gave her more throttle until I had the pedal to the floor, and in a shower of mud and leaves she charged violently backwards onto relatively dry ground, and stopped. We had done it!

"I think that deserves some sort of celebration, don't you?" said Dick.

"Yeah, I reckon so" agreed Peter, and went to his private locker in the Landrover, to bring out half a bottle of whisky, plus some undiluted orange squash.

"Cor, I reckon that should do us about fine" said Dick, and I had to agree. Within half an hour of sharing it out between the four of us, both bottles were empty, even Mellors, a supposed Muslim looked rather pleased, so that was something!

Back in camp the next day, Peter had a session in the Clamorous Reed warbler hide, while Dick and I went up into the hills to finish off a Red-Wattled Lapwing hide, where the bird was sitting on four eggs. I was keen to get a crack at the birds as soon as possible, in case the young hatched before we finished.

I had just carried another large rock to the site for the hide walls, when Dick observed in his usual droll manner, "Have you looked at the underside of those rocks you've been carrying lately?"

"Nope" I replied, I hadn't, "I've been too damn' busy hoicking them out of the ground to notice that much, why?".

"Well I think you ought to, there's a dirty great scorpion on the underside waving his claws at you"

I lowered the rock I had been carrying against my stomach, carefully on the ground, and looked closely at the underside. Yes, Dick was right, a large green scorpion sat there glinting in the sunshine, his claws all akimbo.

"I thought you'd like to know about that" he said off-handedly. "Do you think there were others on the previous rocks you were carrying?" I gave him a filthy look, but he just smiled.

Checking the next half-dozen boulders before lifting them, I found nearly every one had a scorpion underneath, no doubt keeping cool by hiding away from the blazing sun, they weren't silly!

It didn't take long to finish the hide, topping it off with inch diameter reed stems for the roof, and thatching it with green reed fronds. Providing we didn't get any storms during the next couple of days, the roof should hold out, and we could start photography almost anytime.

At the same time, I put up one of John Pryor's plastic 'loo' tents as a hide on a Crested Lark's nest near camp, hoping to get a few shots of them while waiting for the Lapwing to get accustomed to our 'rocky' hide.

It was a stinking hot day with no breeze whatever, and after an hour in the 'loo-hide', I just had to come out for a drink. The temperature inside was just over 45C, and the metal poles were so hot, you got a nasty burn if you accidentally touched one with your bare arm.

Returning to the Lark's hide after a suitable cooling off period, I noticed one of the large ants that were common round here, stuck in the saliva of one of the chick's mouths. Perhaps the adults had fed the chick with ants, and this one hadn't been swallowed?

Within a few minutes however, the mystery was solved in a most unusual way.

As I watched, an ant made its way over the rim of the Lark's nest, crawled onto the nearest chick, and made its way onto the head, and eventually into the chick's open mouth.

As the chick, in common with the rest of the brood was gaping in the heat, and cooling itself by evaporation, the ant appeared to take liquid from the chick's mouth, before scuttling back the way it had come, to be replaced by another!

Fully awake now, I watched carefully as a succession of ants indulged in the same behaviour, I was even able to pick up an ant several feet away from the nest, and watch its rapid progress towards the young larks in their nest, it was quite amazing.

Over the next week I photographed Pratincoles, Pied Kingfishers, Short-toed Larks, Red-Wattled Lapwing, Reed-Warblers, Crested Larks, Black-winged Stilts and White-Tailed Plover, a far greater variety of species than I could ever have imagined when planning our trip back in the UK.

There was a good indication of just how far we had been accepted by the indigenous bird population, when I looked out under the tent flap one morning to see a scurrying black and white bird stop, and settle down onto its nest, before its camouflage enabled it to 'disappear' in a sea of sand and stones. It was a Kentish Plover, and its nest, a mere hundred yards from our camp, contained four eggs.

I would have to do a few shots of that, with our tent in the background for the people back home to see, they just wouldn't believe it!

That evening, just as we were getting our meal ready, a jeep full of gendarmes from the post at Deh-i-Pul, roared erratically into camp, driven more or less, by the fat sergeant in charge. It was all totally unexpected, until Dick remembered on a recent trip to the water hole, he had invited the boys to come and see us whenever they had the time, and this was obviously it!

They had brought with them a huge bowl of 'mast', a sort of yoghourt/goat-cheese, and loads of fresh Iranian bread, which one of the men carried folded over his arm like a waiters' serviette. Our friend the sergeant, practically fell out of his Jeep, waving a couple of litre bottles of bourbon-type whisky in our direction, one of which had been started, hence his erratic driving!

In short time I grabbed some blankets from the tent, and laid them on the ground, while our friends put the goodies they had brought in the middle, and we all sat round the edges waiting to start.

I sensed we were going to have a right old time of it this evening!

Dick opened a large tin of Tuna, while Peter made a pot of strong coffee to supplement the stuff our friends had brought, and we all got stuck in.

With only our strip-light for illumination we ate, laughed, and listened, while they sang songs that were obviously new to us, and everyone got merrier and merrier, as the night wore on. It wasn't long before the sergeant, who had obviously taken a great shine to Dick, and was well gone, put his arms around Dick's shoulders, showing distinct signs of friendship that bordered on the unmentionable!

Just before 2300hrs the steam finally fizzled out of the proceedings, and they made moves to disappear, all laughs and sloppy movements, as they fell into their jeep.

Somehow the sergeant got it started and into reverse, roaring backwards at a high rate of knots laughing like an idiot, almost demolishing our tent in the process.

With a crunch of gears he roared off down the track towards Ayuzabad and Deh-i-Pul, and we hoped they wouldn't do anything stupid en-route and come to grief, they were quite nice chaps really.

It came as a bit of a shock to realise we only had a couple more days at Perishan, and I still had several shots I wanted to do, one being the Black bellied Sandgrouse, the other some nice close-ups of the Clamorous Reed Warbler at its nest, using my flash as fill-in. I would have to get cracking.

Next morning, getting my gear together, I made the awful discovery that 'sarge' and his merry friends, in their alcoholic exit, had reversed over my Mecablitz power pack lying on charge beside the Landrover, shattering the rechargeable battery and its housing like an eggshell.

How the hell was I going to manage photography of the Reed Warbler's nest, partly in shadow and bright sunshine, without a flash for fill-in?

Fortunately I remembered there were some U2 batteries in the Nagamichi recorder (which I had never used) and asked Dick to solder them together in a string, giving me the six volts I needed to drive the flash power pack. I lashed the batteries to the outside of the shattered power-pack with gaffer tape, and settled into the Reed-Warbler hide.

It was all or nothing.

The results I eventually achieved were a great success, something I could never have managed if I hadn't had the flash to fill-in on those very deep shadows.

At the crack of dawn on our last day, I got into our Sandgrouse hide parked a few yards out in the lake, and waited anxiously for the birds to arrive. Peter had been lucky on two earlier occasions and had the Sandgrouse plop down right in front of the hide to drink, but so far I had been completely unlucky. They were always too far away.

On the dot of 0630 a small knot of Sandgrouse flashed past the hide and plonked down fifty yards downwind, nowhere near close enough for my 400mm lens.

I cursed, and hoped they would come closer, when suddenly two more Sandgrouse whistled into view and plonked down directly opposite the hide, but ten yards inshore. Would they have the bottle to cover that distance to the water's edge and drink?

For five minutes the two Sandgrouse, male and female, stared at the hide, not quite sure of things, even though it had been in position for three weeks, before making their way cautiously to the water's edge.

Holding my breath, I began taking pictures each time they stopped and looked up, until finally they were at the edge. First one drank while the other watched, and then vice-versa, I hadn't realised before how shy and cautious these birds could be. They drank, and dipped themselves for a few seconds before flashing away over the lake, where they were joined by the others further down the shoreline.

Well, there it was, a couple of weeks' preparation all over and finished in a few seconds!

Packing up our gear at the end of the day for the last time was a hell of a wrench, we had got so used to the place it felt like home, who would inherit our carefully built, stone-lined cooking pit now?

The next morning at 0430, as if to show that nature could, and would have the last word, a violent storm exploded over the lake with crashing thunder, and bolts of lightning dancing wickedly along the tops of the mountains above Sharanjan. Unusually cold winds gusted with demonic force, probably reaching 50mph. and driving the rain horizontally before it like stair-rods, we were no strangers to this sort of stuff!

In desperation we lashed the tent to the Landrover to stop it blowing away, getting thoroughly soaked in the process - there wouldn't be much chance of getting any breakfast today! For two hours the storm crackled and banged, gusting winds crashing about with undiminished force, until at 0630 it suddenly fell away, leaving us with an uncanny silence.

But not for long.

At 0700 the storm hit again, with the same ferocity as before, continuing unabated until 1030, when slowly, and almost reluctantly, it began to blow itself out. Within minutes a pale blue sky and watery sun appeared as if to apologise for the recent mayhem, and we grabbed the chance to pack up the last of our things before making rapid tracks towards Shiraz.

Mellors insisted we take him to Kazeroun 'city' on our way out, as he wanted us to meet his immediate boss, Mr. Razi, no doubt to formally introduce his Ingloustani friends, and prove that he had been doing his overseeing job properly.

It was all quite touching.

It was strange being on the road again after so long in one place, each of us no doubt wrapped in his own thoughts, as we bundelled through the Arsinjan forest towards the fair city of Shiraz.

Chancing our arm a little, we went back to the Department's office in town, and were actually welcomed like long lost friends by the staff. Seizing the bull by the horns, we asked to use their hot showers, and did all our outstanding dhobying at the same time, before going out 'on the town' for hamburger and Pepsis!

In complete contrast to the utter tranquillity we had become used to at Perishan, the roar of city traffic at daybreak combined with the crowing of cockerels seemed insane, there was no point in trying to lay in bed with that infernal din going on, we just had to get up!

At 0700 the boss, Mr. Adami arrived, expressing no apparent surprise at seeing us in his building, and politely ushered us into his office for coffee. Whether he had been involved in the shenanigans caused by our trip up the gulf between Bandar Moqam and Bushire I don't know, but he did without asking, return our letter of approval from the Department in Teheran, thanking us for letting him see it.

I suppose that was some kind of apology!

At the same time he said if we were interested, he had a man going out to Lake Maharlu to check on the White Storks nesting there, and we could accompany him in their Landrover if we wished.

Dick said he would prefer to explore Shiraz if we didn't mind, so Peter and I accompanied Hidar Farhad, our driver and guide, to the villages of Kaftarak and Jareskan to see and photograph the White Storks of Maharlu.

The next day after a quick look round Shiraz for last minute presents, we left for Persepolis, the next most important part of the trip for me, after our wildfowl counts, and the Humes' owl hunt. After three hours driving along very pleasant roads, we entered a huge plain containing the ancient city of Persepolis, and were immediately overwhelmed by the sense of achievement and purpose that still pervaded the place, after all the intervening centuries.

I hadn't really known what to expect, especially after Pasargardae, which had almost disappeared, but here, at the seat of power which had shaped so much of our world today, a high degree of culture and progress were still evident, despite being ransacked by Alexander's troops in 330BC.

This was the spiritual centre of the Achaemenians, whose empire had once stretched from the Danube to Afghanistan and across into Egypt; whose Kings Darius and Xerxes, had marched against the Greeks leaving the sacred Acropolis sacked and burnt - no wonder Alexander took such terrible revenge!

During the last three hours of soft light before nightfall, I roamed over as much of the site as I could, photographing everything I saw. This was just too good a chance to miss and I used up three rolls of Kodachrome in no time!

That night we camped a few yards from the outer walls of the city, built on a huge rock terrace about a quarter of a mile wide by half a mile long, and I tried to visualise what it must have been like for the first Greek soldiers arriving beneath the twenty-foot walls for their attack.

How did they eventually get in?

As we were getting our heads down for the night, I said to Dick "How about you and I climbing the walls at dawn like the Greeks must have done 2000 years ago, to see if we can get in. There are still lots of photographs I want to take, as the direction of the sun across some of the cuneiform inscriptions this afternoon was all wrong, what do you say?"

"Yeah, that sounds great, count me in, what time shall we go 0430?"

"How about you Peter, are you game?"

"No, you can count me out" he replied. "I reckon you're both bloody mad, goodnight!"

This was the first time we hadn't done some major action in concert, and I didn't feel happy about that. Why was Peter against something which was different, and yet so interesting to do? After all, we would probably never come this way again, and you'd kick yourself for not giving it a go!

In the middle of a very pleasant dream, Dick kicked me into wakefulness with his great foot, saying "come on, get up you lazy bugger, it was your idea, let's go"

It didn't take long to make a quick cuppa, and, warmed against the cool wind of pre-dawn, make our way to the nearest bastion which rose before us like a sheer wall.

"If you come along here" I said to Dick "There's a crack running to the top in a diagonal line, I reckon we can get finger and toe-holds to reach the top if we're careful. If I go first and chuck a rope down, you can tie my camera bag on. I can haul it up whilst you're climbing"

As the first pink flush of dawn lifted across the vast open plain surrounding Persepolis, we made our way slowly up the wall, the first Englishmen in history to storm Persepolis!

Once over the wall we could see before us the main hall, the Apadana palace, with its tall, graceful columns reaching into the sky, and behind that, the fabulous hall of a hundred columns with its gate-like arches set in low walls. It was mind blowing in its magnificence.

In the slowly warming peach-light of dawn I began taking inspired photographs, this was definitely the time of day for best results, it was absolutely magical. During the next four hours we roamed over every inch of this magnificent site, the treasury, central palace, the Tachara - palace of Darius, ending up where the great platform on which Persepolis is built meets the Kuh-e-Rahmat, the mountain of Mercy.

Here, chiselled into to a solid rock face like Petra, are the magnificent tombs of Artaxerxes II and Artaxerxes III.

Exhausted after our exploration of one of the most beautifully preserved, and exciting places I had ever visited, we returned across the site to the entrance, walking for the last time down the magnificent northern staircase of the Apadana Palace, with its superb carving of the Iranian lion slaying the Assyrian bull at the base.

On this same staircase is an almost photographic carving of Phoenicians bringing gifts to the King, accompanied by two superb horses pulling a chariot, and I couldn't believe my eyes when I had a close look at the wheels. If you didn't know better, you would say the stonemasons who carved the chariot had chiselled an exact replica of a Dunlop tyre complete with treads on the wheels!

There was no doubt about it, the quality of the carvings throughout Persepolis was in a class of its own, and in my humble opinion, far superior to any of the Egyptian stuff.

We didn't have to climb the walls to get out - by now the site guards had opened the main gates to the public, and we were able to walk out as though we owned the place!

It was now the 24th. May - we had seventeen days to reach Calais by the 10th June, which seemed like acres of time, but with nearly 4000 miles to go, and several countries to cross, anything could happen, and probably would.

Our homeward route took us past Pasargardae for the second time, and we called in just to see how things were going since our previous visit. Had the storks been successful with their nesting on the one surviving column, and what about the Lesser Kestrels?

We found quite a few other birds nesting around the site this time, several Bee-eaters had their nest holes in the entrance to a fox's earth, and at least two pairs of Rock Nuthatch had nests on the ruined stonework. Solomon's Throne, the monumental oblong mound of stone blocks sported several pairs of nesting Lesser Kestrels, two pairs of little owls, and several pairs of Rollers, all occupying gaps between the large stones, while on the summit, a Long-legged Buzzard flapped away from a nest ready for eggs.

I had always wanted to see the beautiful Roller in close-up, and watching them dive into their nest holes while we stood twenty-five yards away gave me a cunning idea.

Rummaging through my mist-net bags, I found an old Kingfisher net, a compact job, five-feet square, which I fixed over the Roller's nest hole with small sticks. Lifting one corner, I left sufficient room for the birds to get in, and of course for me to close, once the bird was inside.

When the bird had entered and fed its young, it dived back out of the entrance, only to be held gently by the Kingfisher net mesh.

It worked first time.

There was no doubt, it was one of the most colourful birds in the country, the metallic sheen of its feathers was breath taking, and holding it carefully in my left hand, I took several close-ups using my macro lens, suffering a couple of vicious beak jabs to my wrist in the process.

We were just having a quick meal before moving off, when we were joined by Mr.and Mrs. Scurloch driving a long wheel-base Ford Transit, who told us they were bound for Australia via Quetta and Kathmandu, but just had to stop and see the wonders of Pasargardae and Persepolis.

What a fantastic journey they were undertaking!

In glorious sunshine we left Pasargardae and set off across the flat barren-looking plain near Sivand, bound for Deh-Bid and Abadeh, before heading off towards Esfahan, a city we all remembered well.

We had just cleared Abadeh, and were bowling along smooth tarmac when we gradually became aware of a drumming sound coming from the rear of the Landrover, and stopped to check.

Close examination showed the casing on the rear nearside tyre had a nasty bulge in it, so with two tyres out of action, we were down to our last four running tyres, and would need to drive carefully until we could get a replacement!

"It's 2130 now, we might as well pull in where we are for the night, and change the wheel in the morning" Dick mumbled from the kip-couch, and both Peter and I agreed. It was pretty cold, we were hungry, and needed a nice hot meal to liven us up.

In the morning, no-one was in any great hurry to get up. It had been a bitterly cold night, and we were just beginning to appreciate the comfortable warmth one experiences before having to get out of bed.

"As you're going to look at that tyre first thing, I'll make the tea and do breakfast, right?" I called across to Dick, but he only muttered something quite un-intelligible from the depths of his sleeping bag, and I had the satisfaction of kicking him from his sleeping-bag for a change.

In the cold light of early dawn, I could see we had turned off the road at Km.100 before Esfahan, a spot with nothing to commend it from any other section of the road for miles in either direction. Everywhere you looked was pretty desolate and un-interesting, it was just grotty old desert.

After changing the tyre, and eating a leisurely breakfast, we spent the rest of the day driving steadily north, through Esfahan and on towards Qom, getting 45 clicks north of Esfahan before the sun slid towards the horizon with a thump. There was nowhere in particular to stop, so we took the first gap between two sand dunes on our right, drove in a few yards and stopped.

This would do for the night, wherever it was!

At first light I saw we were camped amongst several large sand dunes, which were well stabilised with desert grasses and flowers. Several Short-toed Larks were obviously nesting in the area, and I thought it would be nice to have a quick look for them after breakfast.

While we were having our meal, I noticed a small black and white Lark making its way cautiously towards a tuft of grasses about 30 yards away, and grabbing my binocs, saw it was a Horned Lark, probably a female.

"Hey that's a new one, it's not the Shore Lark which normally breeds here, I know that species, this is different, we'll have to watch this bird and see if we can photograph it"

I managed to get a couple of distant shots with the 400mm lens, but they weren't nearly good enough for a proper identification.

As we watched, the bird disappeared behind a small tuft of grasses, and failed to re-appear.

"Do you know" I said to Peter, "I think that bird is nesting there somewhere, if so we've parked ourselves right on top of it during the night. We'll have to move the Landrover and tent back a bit sharpish to give the bird any chance of success"

As carefully as possible, we up-rooted the tent and started the engine, backing off as unobtrusively as possible, but as the engine sprang to life, the lark left its nest and flew a few yards away, watching us closely to see what we did next.

We managed to get about 50 yards away, and put the tent up in the lee of the car and watched - if the bird was going to return it had plenty of space now.

Within a few minutes a second bird appeared, it was the male, and for the next two hours both birds wandered backwards and forwards past the nest site, but without actually disappearing into the tuft of grasses.

I felt they must have been put off by us parking so close during the night, and the recent disturbance when we moved back, was just about the last straw.

Whilst watching the actions of the Horned Larks, I had plotted the nest sites of two pairs of Short-toed Larks, and as they were well away from the Horned Larks we were hoping might return, I decided to put up a half-height hide on one their nests containing small chicks. This proved to be a bonus for two reasons, one, I got some nice shots of the Short-toed larks feeding their young, and two, I discovered a second Horned lark's nest ten yards away to my right, and they appeared to be feeding young in their nest!

On being released from the hide, I walked over to the spot where I had seen the Horned larks disappearing, and found a nest containing three small chicks. With a bit of luck, I would now be able to photograph the adults in close-up for full identification.

Using the technique I had developed of digging a hole for one's legs and feet, and sitting on the ground to keep a low profile, I erected a half-height hide on the second pair of Horned larks, and covered it with vegetation. Within ten minutes both birds had accepted the hide and resumed feeding their young - it looked as if I could start photography as soon as we had eaten lunch.

Unfortunately, our old friend Murphy had other ideas.

Within a few minutes of sitting down to eat, a wind began to blow, slowly at first, and then with stronger gusts, until it was belting through the dunes at 40mph, thrashing the tent like a mad thing, and constantly extinguishing our petrol stove. No matter how we tried to shield the stove from the blast, it wouldn't stay lit, something we had never experienced before, and we made do with cold tinned spam, generously sprinkled with desert grit.

Very quickly the blue sky disappeared in the swirling red dust, while small stones whizzed viciously through the air, reminding me graphically of the Khamsins we used to suffer in Egypt, and I hoped the hides we had weighted down with heavy stones, would stay put.

Through odd gaps in the swirling dust and sand, we could see blue sky and bright sunshine overhead just like a summer's day, only the howling wind at ground level made things intolerable. There was little we could do except shut ourselves in the Landrover and watch the day slide slowly into dusk and disappear, it was infuriating.

The next morning dawned bright and clear, without the slightest trace of wind, and Peter and I were into the two hides sharp at 0730. We didn't want to be caught napping again!

I hadn't been in my hide very long, and had managed to get several nice shots of both Horned larks feeding their young, when I heard the tinkle of a sheep's bell, and the baa-ing of distant sheep, surely the stupid animals weren't coming this way?

Sure as eggs, the whole damn' herd of about a hundred sheep drifted slowly towards our hides, guided by a young lad in charge, who on seeing our hides, stood wondering what on earth they were.

As soon as the sheep got too close for comfort, and with the adult larks out of sight, I slid out the back of the hide, and shooed the stupid animals away, desperate to stop them treading on the Lark's nest.

To say the young lad was surprised to see me would be an understatement, he just stood there speechless, his mouth wide open, wondering where the hell I had suddenly sprung from.

I knew there wasn't a chance in hell of explaining what we were really doing, so I didn't bother, but something really caught my eye, the young lad was knitting a cable-stitch pull-over, using two bicycle spokes as knitting needles!

I indicated I would like to see his work closely, saying it was 'Hilee-hob'-very good, and he smiled appreciatively.

The knitting was so expertly done, using raw wool from his sheep, I asked if I could take a photograph of him and his work, and he readily agreed.

To help get him mobile, Dick and I gave him some of the hard-boiled sweets we kept for goodwill purposes, and he smiled broadly before moving off in the direction of the road. At least we had diverted his silly sheep away from our precious nests, and could get back to work!

The dust storm had already cost us a precious day already, and we only had a couple of hours before we had to move on. I was a bit disappointed really - I felt with more time I could have done some good work on the Temminck's Horned Lark's nest, a bird not mentioned in the Department's publication 'The Birds of Iran'

This was a species which as far as I knew, hadn't been recorded breeding in Iran before, and I made a note that we had discovered two pairs at Km.42 north of Esfahan, for the Department's records back in Teheran.

Averaging about 50mph on the excellent road, we quickly passed Delijan and Qom - the Iranian holy city, and I believe birth-place of ayatollah Khomenei, while far off to our right lay the vast expanse of Daryacheh Namak, a massive salt lake covering hundreds of square miles between Qom, Teheran, and the Dasht-i-Kavir to the east.

In the early evening, we entered the outskirts of Teheran, nose to tail behind a quagmire of vehicles crawling into the city centre, the bawling loud-speaker calls of mullahs and car horns merely adding to the bedlam!

Naturally we arrived in town on Friday, a public holiday, a feat we seemed to manage with unfailing regularity, and it took a further two hours to grind our way across Teheran and up Pahlavi Ave: to Lynn's flat in Tajrish.

On arrival we were royally welcomed by his wife, Rose Cornwallis - Lynn was apparently away on a field trip to Hamadan and wouldn't be back for a few days, so we made ourselves comfortable, dawdled under hot showers, and cooked a nice stewed-steak dinner for ourselves and Rose.

Before leaving the UK, I had agreed with Skol Lager to visit their manager George Haddad in Teheran at the end of our trip, to take a few photographs of their depot, so we decided to combine this with a visit to the Department's HQ. in Villa Ave:

While there, we could also pick up any mail there might be for us, as we had been out of touch with home for ages.

At the HQ we were greeted by Frances Argyle, who wagged his finger in mock admonishment concerning our escapade in Bandar Moqam, while I gave him my Humes' owl pellets and feathers to have confirmed by their lab.

Over cups of coffee he proceeded to take full notes and details of our two previously un-recorded species for Iran, the Paddyfield Warblers on the river Mand, and the Temminck's Horned Lark just north of Esfahan. He wasn't convinced at all by our sighting of the Olive-Tree warbler at Perishan, but I wasn't bothered whether he did or not, we had left our mark anyway.

At the Skol factory, we were met once again by a friendly George Haddad, who gave us a Cook's tour of the place, while I took our sponsors'photographs. During walkabouts Dick was propositioned by George to see if he was interested in staying on as maintenance trouble-shooter and Mr.Fixit, but Dick felt that the machinery had been running without proper maintenance for too long, and he would be on a good-hiding to nothing to keep it going.

He tactfully told George he would have to think about it and said he would let him know.

As good as gold, George said we could have the use of Skol's service bay the following day, and we made plans to do just that, after all, the Landrover's odometer was reading 19900 miles - it was 16850 the last time we were here, so there was urgent work to be done.

When Dick did the strip-down and service, he was surprised and pleased to see how clean the sump oil was, even the air filter was good, certainly full marks to Duckhams for their lubrication! Only the rear hub leak needed sorting out in the comfort of a service bay, plus a final clean and adjust of the brakes, and we were fit for the road again - apart from our tyres that is. There was nowhere in the immediate vicinity we could purchase a new Landrover tyre, so it would have to wait.

# Chapter Twenty Four

That afternoon I suggested to Peter and Dick, rather than go back the way we had come into Teheran, ie: through Tabriz, Mianeh and Qazvin, it might be a good idea to go north and have a look at the Caspian sea, following the coast until we could strike south again, picking up the road towards home at Mianeh, how about it?

"Do you think the roads shown on this map are good enough to get us across the mountains from the Caspian to Mianeh?" asked Peter.

"Well, although it looks a bit tortuous, it does show a reasonable route across, shall we give it a go?"

It was agreed that we'd give it a try, but if things got difficult, we would have to do a smart about-turn and come back, we couldn't risk tyre trouble, and we didn't have a lot of time to spare either.

Leaving Teheran at 1330hrs, we sped along Shahreza and Eisenhower Avenues to the Karaj freeway, which took us via a fantastic climb up the Karaj valley into the central Elborz mountains, giving us the feeling that we were in Switzerland, rather than Iran.

Despite being the last day of May, snow was still 8-9ft deep in places, although to be fair it was melting fast, but the air was still cold in comparison to the warmth of Teheran.

There was a feeling of exhilaration as we crossed the top of the mountains at 15000ft, and entered the Quruq pass, following the high Rud-e-Chalus road through tangled masses of rhododendrons where hundreds of Nightingales sang.

It was such a contrast to all we had met on the trip so far, we just had to stop and admire the scenery. There were stacks of different birds about too, Magpies, Hooded Crows, Starlings with young, Rollers, Rock Thrushes, Olivaceous warblers, Rock Bunting, Rufous Bush-chats, Choughs, the list seemed endless. It was certainly a great place.

Descending the steep northern side of the Elborz mountains turned out to be a different kettle of fish altogether, and we plunged into a thick mist which obscured the road for miles, making driving extremely difficult, and tiring on the eyes.

On the steep descent we had to stop a couple of times to cool the brakes down, the smell of hot metal, plus worrying brake-fade making us fully aware of how steep the descent really was.

"It's beginning to get dark" Dick observed. "I think we ought to pull in shortly, and try to find a place to put up the tent, otherwise we won't have time to sort things out and cook a meal"

I had been driving up 'til then and said "For the last umpteen miles it's been a steep drop-off on my side with nothing but tangled growth everywhere, we'll have to keep a sharp lookout, as there doesn't seem to be a flat space anywhere"

We had been descending continuously for about an hour, and I felt we must surely run onto flatter ground as we approached the Caspian, it couldn't be like this all the way to the bottom surely?

After a particularly steep descent through dense forest, the road flattened briefly, before crossing a natural stone bridge over a small stream, where a piece of ground about 40' long by 20' wide lay between the road and the river.

"That'll do us nicely" said Dick. "I've had enough of this rhubarb anyway, let's park here"

I drove on to the little bridge and reversed carefully onto the small plot of land, which represented the only flat spot we'd seen for absolutely miles.

"Good" said Dick "If you two can get the tent up behind the Landrover, I'll do the honours for grub, I'm sure you'll like that!"

Dick's effort wasn't that bad, at least it filled a hole, and we thankfully settled down to write up our notes, or read, whatever took our fancy until it was time for bed. The weather wasn't conducive to walking about anyway, it had turned quite cold and misty.

After half an hour of peace and quiet, the soft clonking of sheep bells heralded the approach of a flock of sheep and goats, and looking out the tent door, I watched in horror as two hundred animals crossed the little bridge and began to fan out onto 'our' plot of land.

In no time they were joined by four shepherds, three donkeys and several dogs, and the small area holding our tent and car began to disappear under a sea of heaving bodies.

In an effort to be sociable, we gave the shepherds some of our English tea and biscuits - I thought from the way they sat to one side and watched us eat, they probably didn't have much for themselves, and it was a cold night.

I noticed a couple of the men were wearing long waterproof coats with immensely wide shoulders, obviously supported on a piece of wood, a parody of a London spiv's overcoat.

By signs, I indicated we wanted to know what the strange coat was all about, why the broad shoulders?

One laughed and said something to his friends, before lying on the ground on his left side, and flipping the right side of the coat outwards a little, so as to form a triangle. He then withdrew his head into the large collar and disappeared inside, snug in his miniature bivouac tent!

Saying goodnight, we got into our tent, and made ourselves as comfortable as possible, the whole structure twanging and shaking as dozens of sheep tripped over the guy-lines, or pushed into the sides trying to keep warm. For ages we lay there unable to sleep, suffering the stink of wet sheep as they coughed, farted, and baa-ed continuously.

It was going to be a hard day's night!

Through that weird sensation of half waking and dreaming, I heard the shepherds whistling their sheep into action, and felt the thumps on the tent as the animals fought their way clear. I breathed a sigh of relief that they appeared to be up and leaving, yet it was still only 0500, and barely light.

With a bit of luck we could snuggle down and sleep in peace for a couple more hours yet!

In the dull misty yuk that passed for daylight, we turned out into a sea of sheep manure and churned up mud, the place looking as though we were camped at the bottom of a bomb crater!

Continuing down the Rud-e-Chalus valley in the early morning mist reminded me of driving across Dartmoor in the autumn, where, after heavy rain, everything is dripping wet and soggy. Where on earth was our old friend the sun?

The town of Chalus on the Caspian Sea turned out to be an interesting, relatively modern place, bustling with human activity, and lots of shops and houses. Stopping to look at some of the more interesting ones, we found a taxidermist's emporium, where dozens of wild birds stood transfixed in a travesty of their former lives, arranged into artistic poses by someone with no feeling for nature at all.

There were Rollers, Bee-Eaters, wildfowl, sea-gulls, waders, and birds of prey in profusion, and I took a couple of photographs to show someone like the WWF, what was happening to wildlife down here on the Caspian.

The proprietor, all smiles, thinking I was photographing his emporium as an example of excellence, stood munificently in the background nodding amicably, but I could cheerfully have burned the ruddy lot!

Before our trip, I had fondly imagined the shores of the Caspian to be something like the Persian Gulf, miles of sandy and muddy beaches, with Tamarisk overhanging, and stacks of sea birds and waders sprinkled along the shoreline.

It was nothing like that at all!

For miles we drove along the coastal road, where houses and cultivated plots stretched in an unbroken line, with hardly a sight of the sea at all. It was more like the approach to Fort Myers beach in Florida!

We tried several times to get down to the waterline, but each time we appeared to be on the point of trespassing on someone's private property, or a public landing slip for boats, so we gave up. The only place that seemed to offer any respite from the ribbon development along the shore was at Ramsar, the site of the first International Wildfowl conference. That at least was set in an area given over to some form of conservation, and looked quite promising.

At 1300 we arrived in Resht, and took the coastal road to Bandar Pahlevi, keeping a lookout for the turn off to Fowmen which we hoped would take us across the mountains to Mianeh. We didn't want to end up accidentally crossing the border into Russia, and being detained as spies again!

Three miles down the Fowmen road, Dick called out "Hey let's stop and look at that stall over there, they seem to have a fantastic collection of woven baskets, dishes and things, you never know there might be something worth taking home as a present"

It wasn't the usual tatty sort of display you might expect in a rural community, in fact the work was of a very high standard and beautifully done, with interesting ideas. Dick and I bought a couple of nice items, but Peter didn't bother, and we prepared to move off.

Starting the engine, I engaged first gear and let out the clutch, but apart from a whirring sound, nothing else happened. I dipped the clutch, engaged first again and let out the clutch, but we remained absolutely motionless.

“What’s going on?” I said, glancing at Dick in the navigator’s seat.

“Hold on a minute, keep the engine running while I look underneath, put her in gear when I tell you” and dived out to lay on the road, underneath.

“Ok. put her in gear!” he called, and I did it.

“Yep, we’ve got back axle trouble, probably stripped the half-shaft on our near-side, we’ll have to do a quick strip down and see. We’ve got spare half-shafts, but it might be that final drive hub again, and we’re plumb out of those “

I had always admired the way Dick dealt with our mechanical problems, he seemed to have inexhaustible experience and energy to solve whatever needed doing, and this time was no exception.

In no time he had the wheel off, and the offending item revealed, it was the final drive hub we had fitted new in Teheran 3500 miles ago, now stripped smooth and useless - not a good advert for Landrover spares!

Dick said “We’ll put her back together, and return to Resht, we might be able to get another hub there, after all Landrovers are quite common out here aren’t they?”

The only way we were going to get mobile was by engaging four wheel drive, and with the engine roaring away in high revs, we slowly limped back into Resht, tail between our legs.

It wasn’t funny.

As we entered Resht, I began looking for a sign, any sign, which might indicate where we could find motor spares, but it all looked quite unlikely, there were only food and clothing shops nearby.

After driving around for about ten minutes and getting nowhere, I saw a Landrover coming towards us driven by an Iranian, and thought he must be a good bet to get us out of trouble. Taking my life in my hands, I nipped through the busy traffic, and stood in front of the oncoming Landrover, waving my arms for him to stop, which he did with an expression of caution and fright.

“Ingloustan, ingloustan tourist, Landrover nis hob, nis hob!” I said pointing to one of his wheels, and then at our car across the street.

His expression changed immediately, and comprehension spread across his face with a grin. In Farsi he obviously said, you follow me, pointing to us and then to himself, and began to turn round in the street.

Dick, who had taken over the wheel, caught on immediately what was happening, and was already moving towards me so we wouldn’t lose our friend in the traffic.

It was a good job we had him with us, as in the myriad of back streets and alleyways, we would have been lost in seconds.

Eventually he pulled up outside a featureless corrugated iron building in the Pahlevi road, which he indicated sold lots of Landrover spares.

From our fast dwindling store of goodies, we gave him a couple of packs of cigarettes which he accepted all smiles, shook hands, and disappeared into the traffic. The rest was down to us.

“OK. once more into the breach dear friends...” said Dick, and within minutes the back-end of the Landrover was in the air, minus its nearside wheel, slap-dab in the busy main street of Resht.

Within minutes there was a crowd round us, all jabbering away in Farsi, the word Ingloustan being heard several times. A couple of little kids, bolder than the rest sat on our discarded wheel, sucking some sweets Peter had given them, telling Dick in detail how the job should be done.

"There you are mate, one clapped out hub, see if you can get me a new one" Dick said with a grin, and it was obvious I had to do my bit again, conversing with locals in an attempt to explain exactly what we wanted.

Inside the spare parts store, I found the usual oily and dented metal counter seen the world over, behind which an oily-faced Iranian stood in filthy overalls, rag in hand, waiting for me to speak.

Pointing to myself I said "Ingloustan tourist" and plonking the worn out hub on the counter continued, "Landrover hub, nis hob, ok?"

Without a word, or even a flash of recognition he turned, pulled an oil soaked wooden ladder along the tall racks of spares behind him, and climbed slowly to the top.

Reaching into the metal shelving he brought out a small cardboard box, before descending slowly down the ladder and plonking it on the counter in front of me.

You would have got exactly the same response from a store basher in Barking!

I read the label on the box, checking to see we had the right item, and saw written in English 'Genuine Landrover spares - Made in Japan' a right contradiction if ever there was one, but beggars can't be choosers. I took it.

Back outside, I found our impromptu repair situation causing great concern to the local police. An officer was trying to get the crowd of kids off the road as they were blocking the town's through traffic, but he wasn't having much success, just like home really.

"For best results we should leave the hub glued on the half-shaft with Locktite for a few hours and let it set, but as we haven't got the time, we'll have to take a chance that it will be ok" Dick told me, and I agreed.

In our present position we had to get a move on and cover as much ground as possible, despite our shaky tyre, every day was precious.

The road to Fowmen was interesting in that it passed through countless rice paddies, where the women were hard at work putting in the next crop. Over the flooded fields White-Winged Black Terns hovered as though nesting, while Little Egrets and Purple Herons stalked unseen prey in the shallows.

After Fowmen the track began to move inland, climbing alongside a rushing torrent of brown water that looked decidedly dangerous, especially if we mis-judged our crumbling path, towards the distant village of Masuleh.

It was in this village we hoped to find the track leading across the mountains to Mianeh, and the road home.

The track quickly disintegrated into a muddy, pot-holed dirt strip, containing some nasty 'tank-traps' of deep soft mud to snare the unwary, but old faithful in four-wheel drive got us safely through.

At one point where the track crossed a raging stream, the ground was like a quagmire, a huge bank of earth and stones had just been bull-dozed into place after being washed away by the rushing river, and was as soft as the proverbial.

After gingerly crossing the stream, the track climbed steeply until we were on a raised, flat-topped dyke wall, ten feet high, similar to the one we had used along the gulf, which ran for several miles before becoming a natural track once more.

The extreme hairiness of driving along the newly built earth wall, still soggy from the bulldozers, was amply demonstrated by seeing a newly crashed Iranian 3 ton truck on its roof at the foot of the embankment.

We'd have to be jolly careful not to end up the same way!

The track continued to climb steadily through extremely dense vegetation on all sides, the steep rocky cliffs were thick with tall pine trees so closely packed, there was hardly space between them, and reminded me of photos of British Columbia.

By this time the sun was beginning its inevitable dive towards the horizon, and it was clear we would have to find a space of some sort quickly, if we weren't to be caught unprepared in the dark.

By parking the car at a crazy angle under low, moss covered trees, we managed to make enough space to put up the tent, providing we didn't want any guy lines out, it was that tight!

As we ate, Nightingales burst into song around us, and we heard the mellow calls of a Tawny owl, it was almost like being back in England.

The following morning we were woken by Nightingales singing loudly at 0445, and as it was such a glorious beginning to the day, we decided to get up and explore, instead of laying in bed.

On large stones in the nearby boiling river, a family of young Dippers noisily begged for food, Pied and Grey Wagtails flitted about, whilst around the camp innumerable Chaffinches hopped amongst the leaves, looking for seeds.

Having got ourselves mobile so early, we were on the road again by 0530, something we had never managed before, and carried on up the beautiful valley towards Masuleh. We had covered about ten miles or so, when we met a team of Iranian engineers, complete with their bulldozer and heavy lifting crane, busily clearing away a huge rock-fall.

By the look of things, the rocks had until quite recently, blocked the whole track, which didn't look good. Bearing in mind the hazards we had experienced in getting the Landrover up here, I wondered how the hell they managed to muster their machinery here without some sort of disaster?

Guided by the foreman in his yellow plastic safety helmet, we managed to squeeze the Landrover between two huge boulders the size of a London bus, and continued up the valley.

Local traffic would have stood no chance if that lot had came down while they were passing, especially as the nearby river ran at the bottom of a gorge several hundred feet deep!

The track now became quite rocky, and in several places had been hacked out of vertical cliffs with a sheer drop to god knows where on our left - it was so deep, we couldn't even see the bottom!

Half-way along this stretch, we came to a spot where the track crossed a two-foot gap in the rocks, caused no doubt by earthquake movement and the constant passage of water into the depths below.

The locals, probably having only motorbikes and livestock to move, had bridged the gap with bundles of small trees laid over a couple of supporting poles underneath, which was obviously quite sufficient for them, but what about us?

As I was driving, Peter volunteered to get out and walk across to see if we could make safe passage over the flimsy bridge with our Landrover, after all we must weigh a ton and a half with all our gear!

Gingerly I offered our front end onto the bundles of trees, keeping the offside of the vehicle so tight against the rocky wall, our front wheel hub gouged a large groove in the soil.

Dick, who was sitting in the navigator's seat ostensibly to tell me how much room we had on that side, withdrew his head from the window and refused to look again, saying it made him feel sick.

Somehow the poles held our weight and we were across, I hoped it wouldn't get any worse than that, but considering the way the track was deteriorating by the minute, it didn't feel right.

I had a nagging ESP feeling we weren't doing things right at the moment at all.

About half a mile in front, a radio mast broke the skyline, and it looked as though we must be approaching the village of Masuleh, if so, we could soon be on the road to Mianeh and home. For a while the track improved a little, trees fell back, and we were running on huge platforms of natural rock, beautifully smooth, and only joined by narrow cracks to one another, it was like being on top of the world.

The radio mast now lay dead ahead, and as we drew up towards the few houses occupying both sides of the track, one or two people came out to see what was going on.

It was then I noticed with horror the track just petered out, stopping directly in front of a small house built in a hollow where the road ended, its roof more or less level with the track.

This was all very silly, where the hell had we gone wrong?

In a few minutes we had the whole population round the car, all twenty of them, and I looked for someone to converse with, someone who might tell us how the heck we get to Mianeh.

After repeating 'Ingloustan, ingloustan tourist, go Mianeh' and pointing vaguely in the direction I thought it should be, an old boy took the pipe out of his mouth and said 'Something, something, something, Mianeh nis hob'.

Seeing that I did not understand what he meant, he took my arm and walked me to a vantage point beside the track, pointing to a spot half a mile away on the opposite side of the gorge, saying 'Something, something, Mianeh nis hob, nis hob'

Suddenly it dawned on me what he meant, the bloody track had disappeared, fallen down, earthslide or something, it didn't exist any more!"

I drew a line in the dust on the ground, indicating our route, and wiped my hand across it obliterating the middle, and looked up at the old man. He smiled and nodded - that's it, we weren't going anywhere in that direction.

"Oh god!" said Dick, "If we've got to go back, there's that bloody awful crack to negotiate again. Well this time I'm WALKING across, you two can do the driving if you like!"

As I drew the short straw, I drove again, this time overlooking the sheer drop into the gorge - the mountains here are nearly 10,000ft high, but it was ok provided you concentrated fully on the job in hand!

In no time we were back at the rockfall, where a huge explosion had just taken place, and had to wait while the bulldozer pushed the shattered rocks off the track to let us through again.

There was definitely a feeling of deja-vous going back through Fowmen and Resht, but by getting our foot down to some serious motoring, we were soon belting through Chalus and on our way through the dreaded Elborz mountains, bound for Qazvin.

With the bit between our teeth, the miles seemed to fly past, and in quick succession we demolished Qazvin, Zanjan and Mianeh, getting to within 50clicks of Tabriz by 2200hrs - we were really making progress now!

The international currencies I needed to buy petrol were still working well, and I spent the last of my dollars buying petrol in Tabriz, which I expected should see us well into Turkey, but we still didn't see any tyre shops around selling Landrover tyres, which was worrying.

The next day saw us through Marand, Khoi and Maku, making our way steadily towards the Turkish border, arriving at Bazargan by 1730.

At the border control it was the usual chaotic circus, hundreds of people shouting and pushing, their goods piled high on trolleys, waiting hopelessly for some official to come and clear them through.

Putting into action our famous plan 'A' we located the nearest policeman, telling him we were English police visiting Turkey, and he whisked us through passport control in no time.

We had gone back to our previous system of two hours on - four off for the driving spells, and were, according to my daily log, making pretty good time and mileage. Leaving the Bazargan border post straight away, we drove non-stop through the night and arrived in Erzerum at 0630, almost out of petrol.

It didn't take long to transfer the last of our petrol from jerricans on the roof to the car's two tanks, and work out, that with care, we should make the next town, Erzincan quite easily.

I reckoned by the time we arrived there, the banks should be open, and I could buy some Turkish Lira with my dollars, and completely fill up with petrol again.

This of course is where Murphy had yet another field day.

Apparently there was a dispute of some kind with petrol companies in Iran, and for several days now, there had been no fresh supplies anywhere in Turkey. In desperation we toured all the garages in Erzincan, mindful we were burning our scarce reserves, but achieved no success at all. The standard reply was "Nis benzin, nis benzin, tomorrow, after midday - maybe!"

"What the hell are we going to do now, we can't wait here on the off-chance of some arriving, we'd be killed in the rush anyway" groaned Dick.

"I vote we go back towards Iran and see if we meet a tanker coming into Turkey, perhaps we can get some that way"

I'd never heard anything so daft and in-effectual in my life and said so, adding "We have had a fair amount of success getting to know police officers in various capacities, how about trying the local law to see if they can help us, they must have some pull round here"

"That sounds a good idea" said Dick. Any idea where the local cop-shop is?"

Our garage man soon gave us the requisite directions, and after driving a mile or so through town, the requisite Police HQ. came into view, on our offside.

"As it's your idea" said Peter "I suggest you go over there and see what you can do, I'm all for turning round and going back"

I didn't answer - I was too annoyed at his silly suggestion, and marched resolutely across the pavement towards a group of police officers sitting under a large umbrella, playing cards.

As I waited for the right moment to speak, I heard to my astonishment, they were all speaking German - at least we did have a better affinity with them than the Turks, so we might be lucky.

"Guten morgen" I began, "We are English police, we have no petrol, can you help us get some please?"

The chap I spoke to looked at me for a few seconds and said loudly for everyone's benefit "Sie haben nicht benzin? Wir haben kein benzin!" and roaring with laughter, grabbed me by the arm and took me to a nearby wall overlooking the police HQ. car park.

Pointing to the yard full of stationary BMWs and other official vehicles, he said "Turkei polizei hat kein benzin, sie hat kein benzin!" and still laughing like a drain, rejoined his colleagues at the table to play cards.

So much for that good idea!

"So what are we going to do now then?" said Peter in a sarcastic tone. We can't get any juice here, we'll HAVE to go back"

"No way!" I replied "I can see no point whatever in going back, we either wait here, or go on and see what the situation is like in Sivas, I reckon we've got enough petrol for about 60 clicks, that might be enough."

Dick, sensing things were getting a bit uptight said, "How about we have bets on how far we can get before running out of petrol, the one who is furthest away from the final figure buys beer all round at the next stop"

"Yeah, that sounds a good idea" said Peter "And as it was clever clogs here who had the bright idea about going on, he can do the driving!"

"Fine by me!" I replied sounding more confident than I felt, and off we went.

We had all written down what we thought the odometer reading would be when we conked out of petrol, and I had gone for the maximum of 60 clicks to show some faith in my outlandish decision.

The countryside was quite winding and hilly, so I treated the throttle as though it had an egg under it, and glided down every slope that gave us enough speed to roll.

In this way I hoped to stretch our small reserve of petrol to the absolute limit.

At 50 clicks Peter was out - it was obvious he would have to buy the beers, much to Dick's delight, and I gently pushed on, praying she would hold out to the next petrol station, wherever it was, this was like Russian roulette!

"Well that's me out too" said Dick, "I reckoned on 55 clicks and you've passed that now, so perhaps we might just make it"

The mileage was reading 77 clicks as we breasted a long slope, and there in the valley below us, we saw a petrol station, which if I was lucky, we could carefully glide to.

As I got down from the cab, an old chap came out of the shadows saying "Benzin, 10 litres only, finis!"

We protested that we needed more than that to continue our journey, but our pleadings fell on deaf ears, it was 10 litres or leave it, he didn't care.

With bad grace we paid for the piddling amount, and as we climbed aboard to move off he shouted, "You go Refahiye, 20 Kms.- plenty plenty benzin"

The 'garage' at Refahiye turned out to be a large corrugated iron shack beside the road, with a single hand pump standing folornly outside on a dusty forecourt.

As it came into view about a quarter of a mile ahead, we saw a small truck pull away from the pump, and someone disappear inside the shack, indicating to me at least, he had just served someone petrol.

We decided to try our luck there.

By the time we got to the pump, the place was shut and deserted, there wasn't a soul about.

"There's got to be someone here somewhere, we just saw the bugger go in" said Dick, and hammered heavily on the iron door, making the whole place vibrate like a drum.

"No benzin, no benzin" came a plaintive, muffled voice from somewhere inside.

"Go away, no benzin"

We continued to hammer on the doors, until the din inside must have been unbearable, and a scared looking face appeared at the small side window.

"No benzin, all finis, maybe tomorrow"

"We want some now, not tomorrow, we saw you sell petrol to a small truck just now, come on out and sell us some too"

He wouldn't come out, but continued to watch us closely through his little window.

"I know how we can smoke the little bugger out" I said.

"Dick, if you hop up and pass down the tent to Peter, and start putting it up on his forecourt, I'll get the petrol stove out and light it next to his pump. If I try and pump her too early, she'll go up like a ruddy flame-thrower, that'll bring him out of his hole"

The little face continued to watch us through the window, his eyes getting bigger by the minute as he watched the tent go up on his forecourt.

"We stay here, you sell us petrol, we stay until tomorrow"

When I lit the petrol stove and tried to pump her before the heat vaporised the petrol, a jet of flames shot into the air like a good 'un, and in two seconds flat, there was a rattle of keys from the inside, and chummy burst out shouting "No fire! no fire! petrol, no fire!"

Looking up from the stove I said, "You say you no have petrol here, fire ok. no problem, we stay"

"Ok. ok. I sell petrol, 20 litres only, all finis"

"Well that seems to have sorted that little lot out" Dick said "I thought you were a bit OTT with the flames though, you never know with these country chaps, whether there's a leak about or not"

I knew we still didn't have enough fuel to put our foot down and go at speed for Ankara, and we kept our eyes peeled for whatever petrol station might appear next.

We had covered another 20 clicks when Dick, who was driving shouted that he could see another petrol station ahead which boasted TWO hand pumps on the forecourt, it must be quite a joint!

Outside the front, an old boy with white whiskers, wearing an old jacket, baggy trousers and woolly hat, sat dozing in his chair. There was no-one else around.

"He looks such a typical old boy, I think I'll take a photograph of him sitting in his chair, before we ask him for some petrol" said Dick, and hopped out of the cab clutching his camera.

"Hello, can we have some benzine please?" I asked, and he pointed to a notice which said 'twenty litres each customer only'

"That's still not enough for what we need" said Peter, "We've got to have more than that, we can't keep stopping at every little tin-pot garage to pick up twenty litres or so, that's bloody stupid"

After Dick had taken his photograph, the old boy put the pump-nozzle in our tank and began turning the handle slowly, gradually pumping the precious fuel in. It was obviously all a bit too much for him.

"If I give him a hand to put the juice in, perhaps you would take your time Dick and take his photograph again, anything to take his mind off what we're doing as we turn the handle, that way we might get a tank full"

Dick performed like a trooper, smiling and gently cajoling the old boy to look at the camera just one more time, until we got a hundred litres on board, and still he hadn't looked at the gauge!

Meanwhile, Peter seizing on the opportunity like a trooper, wheeled two of our 5 gallon jerricans to the pump, and helped the old chap fill those as well, all in all quite a successful combined operation!

Feeling in an expansive mood now we had sufficient fuel on board for a good run, I gave him over the odds in Lira, and left him half smiling, half bemused as we drove smartly away.

I don't think he really knew what hit him!

To make sure we had plenty of time in hand, I suggested we continue driving two on, four off throughout the night, but before carrying on, we ought to stop for a meal break and a general tidy up.

The sun sank in a pink blaze over the snow covered hills on the road to Sivas and Ankara, and it really surprised us to see how much snow was still around even at the end of May.

It was obviously melting fast though, as vast sheets of water cascaded over grassy banks into rushing streams and low meadows, making everything extremely waterlogged.

The 'road' was just as bad as we remembered it from our outward journey, badly rutted with deep pot-holes full of water, which caused us to lurch and crash about madly, as the wheels fought for grip. There was no way you could travel faster than 25 mph. and we had to watch that tyre!

Half-way between Sivas and Ankara we stopped for a quick breakfast, before bashing on towards Yerkoy and Kirikkale, where we noted a very low Stork's nest beside the road containing two small chicks. I couldn't for the life of me see how they survived with all that passing heavy traffic.

The severe state of the track we had covered in the last few hundred miles, was taking its toll of our damaged tyre, and the bulge was beating a regular tattoo as and when we managed to get up a bit of speed. We'd have to watch it once we got on decent roads otherwise it wouldn't last long, then we'd be in real trouble!

We charged through Ankara at mid-day, and continued at good speed towards Adapazari and Izmit, passing huge flood lakes between Bolu and Duzce where large numbers of Cranes (grus) were resting.

Funny I thought, shouldn't they have been on their way across Europe by now?

The nearer we got to Adapazari, the worse the traffic became, especially the buses, which passed us as though we were standing still - they must have been doing seventy miles an hour in their manic dash to cut in between us and the vehicle in front.

In contrast to our outward journey, the last 10 click section into town was achieved with very little effort this time, as it was all madly downhill!

That evening, we cruised beside the sea of Marmara through Izmit and Uskadar which seemed to be one huge area of continuous suburbia, a shocking contrast to the last few hundred miles of relative wilderness.

Paying the extortionate rate of 10 Lira to cross the Bosphorus toll bridge, we moved quickly down the fantastically fast four-lane freeway to Edirne, and branched off towards Greece. I thought it might be a nice change instead of ploughing back through grim old Bulgaria.

Driving through the night we reached the customs post at Kipi at 0430, where the extremely efficient officers cleared us through in minutes.

In really heavy rain, the Landrover ploughed on to Alexandroupolis, where just before dawn Dick said it was time for a well earned brekkie and tea break, only to find we were completely out of sugar! Breakfast certainly wouldn't be the same until we got some!

Travelling through pleasant looking countryside now the rain had stopped, we passed Komotiri and Xanthu, and on to Kavalla, where we made a silly map reading boo-boo, and ended up in a place called Phillipi instead of Thessalonika.

"I remember this place from history lessons at school" I said. "It's a historic site relating to the ancient Greek culture, we ought to have a look at it while we're here"

Unfortunately we couldn't get to see much of the site as the place was closed to the public, and as there didn't appear to be anywhere to gain access, we moved on.

The road sign beside the Landrover now pointed to Drama, and when we got there I discovered from local tourist literature, we should expect to see a lovely amphitheatre set in a natural 'bowl' in the rocky hillside, and asking directions, found the site within minutes.

While Dick and I were clambering over the ruins taking photographs, the penny suddenly dropped. "Hey, this must be one of the very first oratories the Greeks used for their plays long ago, this place is called Drama, hence drama as in theatre or dramatic plays - it's fantastic!"

I was glad we had made the map reading error which led to seeing something we would otherwise have missed, it wasn't always doom and gloom when things went wrong!

"Hey!" said Dick, "There's some clown flashing us from behind in a white car, it could be the local fuzz, I'll have to pull over"

"Yeah, I think you ought to do that" said Peter, "I don't think we could outrun them in this, do you?"

After the usual passports game, the senior of the two policemen, George Korosidis by name, said he had stopped us because he could see our rear tyre was bulging, and if it wasn't replaced might cause an accident.

"We haven't got a spare tyre left at the moment" I replied. "We have come all the way across Turkey like that, we didn't find anywhere handy to get a Landrover tyre"

He didn't really understand what we were saying, and invited us to follow him into the nearby village of Nea Zinhi, where he introduced us to a Greek lady who taught English in the local school.

She was well able to translate our problems to him.

It turned out that the nearest place to get a Landrover tyre was a town called Serres, not too far away, which we could get to in the morning, meanwhile, we would be taken to a place to stop safely for the night - camping beside the road in Greece was strictly forbidden!

Following George and his friend along the road to Serres, he took us into the grounds of a football club, where we parked out of sight of the road. He indicated we had the use of team's dressing rooms and showers if we wished to use them, and at a push, could sleep on the benches.

Quite unknown to us, George had bought a bag holding 4-5lbs of sweet black cherries, which he gave us as a present, and we replied in kind, with half a dozen small jars of Nescafe which he said he liked, but couldn't get locally.

Dick said it was obviously time for a brew, and while Peter got the biscuits out, I made everyone a large mug of coffee. George leant over and said something quietly to his colleague, who sped off in their car, re-appearing ten minutes later with a box of fifteen fresh eggs.

They hoped we would enjoy them for our dinner tonight!

The next day at 0630 George and his friend appeared at the football club, joining us for a coffee, before leading the way into Serres to find our new tyre.

We were a bit early, even for these people, who didn't seem to sleep long hours, and had to wait patiently for the bank to open at 0800 and draw some much-needed cash.

The tyre cost 1700 drachmae, about £30, which I thought was a bit expensive, but in our position we didn't have much option - we had to have it.

Dick soon had the new tyre fitted and we shook hands with George and his friend, before hitting the road to Thessalonika.

Along both sides of the road there were hundreds of Nightingales singing from dense undergrowth, and I must say I've never heard that many before, not even in the Zagros mountains, it was delightful.

The Greek/Yugoslav customs at Evroni was a doddle, and we were through in minutes, pushing hard towards Skopje and Nis - we were well on the homeward run now!

A short while later, I saw a pathetic bundle of feathers flapping in the road ahead, and on investigation, found it to be a juvenile Kestrel. It had obviously been struck on the head by a vehicle, damaging the occipital ring round its eye, but the eye itself, appeared to be undamaged.

"What are you going to do with it then?" said Dick. "You can't feed it can you? It eats meat and stuff doesn't it?"

"That won't be problem" I said "If it comes to the worst, I'll buy a bit of meat from a butcher's, and as for feeding it's no great shakes, you hold it's beak open and push the food down with your finger, I've done it before"

As luck would have it, the next bird we saw lying in the road was a newly killed pigeon, and it didn't take long to strip the feathers from its breast, and cut a couple of juicy bits off for 'Kes', our latest acquisition!

Wrapping him gently in an old pullover to stop him struggling, I tweaked his beak open, and stuffed in some meat, which went straight down.

"There you are" I said to Dick "That's how you do it, it isn't difficult is it? I'm sure between us we can give him enough to get his strength back, and perhaps release him after a couple of days."

As we ran towards Skopje the rain came down in buckets, interspersed with weak bursts of sunshine throughout the day, making driving difficult - we hadn't experienced that sort of downpour in ages.

Since leaving Iran, we had been using the usual two on, four off system of driving, but since Turkey, I had noticed the daily log of distance covered was dropping back, and I wondered why.

Between the three of us we had been able to notch up about 700 miles a day - more if the roads were good, but lately this had dropped to just over 500.

I recalled the route hadn't been that bad overall, so why was the mileage so low? It was a bit of a mystery.

The whole way to Belgrade the rain bucketed down incessantly which, combined with a couple of nasty road accidents, caused us to stand stationary for over two hours at one point - it was really quite frustrating.

Eventually we made Zagreb at 10.00hrs, where I took my life in my hands, darting through the busy trafficand rain into the Jugobank for cash to buy petrol.

Fuel seems to be our main expense these days!

Just after Maribor, and before the customs with Austria, we stopped to stretch our legs and have a bite to eat - the long hours in the car were beginning to take their inevitable toll. Leaving Peter to tidy away after the meal, I walked over to where Dick was apparently looking at something through his binoculars.

"Do you know, there's something that's been puzzling me" I said.

"You know I keep a daily log on how far we travel each day, well it seems to be much less than I expected lately, any ideas why that might be?"

Turning round, and looking rather uncomfortable, he said hesitantly "I wondered how long it would be before you caught on, I'm surprised you haven't said something before, but because you and Pete were mates before I joined the scene, I didn't feel it was my place to say anything"

"Say what?" I asked, beginning to sense something awkward was coming out.

"Well lately, when you have done your shift, and are asleep in the kip-couch, Peter has driven for a while, before stopping for a brew up, a bite to eat and a chat, before carrying on. Sometimes we don't move for an hour or more, but it wasn't for me to say anything was it?

His answer hit me between the eyes like a sledge hammer.

How could a mate do such an underhand thing, knowing the tight schedule we had, and the deadline we had to meet. Was his action directed at getting back at me for some reason or other?

Trying not to blow my top, I went back to the car and fronted Peter. "I've just found out why we weren't doing as many miles as I expected during our daily run, what have you got to say about it then?"

He looked at me for a few seconds, and turned away without a word.

"Right, that's the last time you'll be asked to drive on this trip, I'll do your share, you can alternate with Dick sleeping and navigating, but you ain't driving this vehicle another mile mate!"

In a horrible silence we pushed on through sunny Austria, and reached Salzburg by late afternoon, and to save cooking a meal, ate in a restaurant. In stolid silence we ate our tasteless meal, and got under way in about half an hour bound for Munich, arriving at 2100hrs rather tired and grumpy.

Expeditions certainly bring out the best and worst in people!

I stuck rigidly to what I had said earlier about doing Peter's share of the driving, and felt rather knackered as we went through the night. I was more than pleased to reach Stuttgart in the early hours of morning, when it was Dick's turn to drive.

With only a quick stop for tea and a sandwich, we pressed on for Strasbourg and the crossing into France, aiming for Nancy, where we I expected to fill up with petrol, using the last of my French francs.

It was now the 9th.June, our penultimate day, we had to be at the Calais Hoverport at 0800 for the 0930 crossing tomorrow - come hell or high water, we didn't want any unexpected hiccoughs now!

With a sigh of relief, and quite bleary eyed I drove into Paris at 1730 - not a lot could go wrong now could it? Revelling in the glorious evening sunshine we did a quick 'rubber-neck' tour of Notre Dame, Arc de Triomphe, and Eifel tower, before getting ourselves hopelessly lost in the rush hour traffic somewhere north of Paris!

A lawyer, returning from court, led us in his car past the Gare du Nord, towards Lille and the Charles Degaulle airport, where he courteously waved us onto our correct route - what a gentleman!

From a roadside telephone we tried telephoning home to let them know we were on schedule, but couldn't get the pre-fix code right, and had to give up the idea - so near and yet so far!

Taking our time, we motored across the last bit of France and got to Calais at 0600, we had done it!

A quick check of the odometer showed that since we left Tabriz in Iran Wednesday night 2nd. June, until Paris Wednesday night 9th. June, we had covered 3372 miles, just over 480 miles per day.

Kes, our Kestrel had, in the few days on board, become quite tame, and would readily take food from the hand. He was mending nicely, and was almost ready to be released. Although I was aware he hadn't been taught to hunt by his parents, it was probably better he take his chance alone when released. His favourite perching place was on top of the curtain rail that shielded the sleeping couch from the front of the Landrover, where he would sit quietly for ages until he got hungry, then all hell let loose.

In a state of excitement now we were on the last leg of our trip, Dick drove us aboard the Hovercraft and parked in a bay, it wouldn't be long to home now.

As I sat in one of the cabin seats, I was amazed to see that Peter had, for reasons known entirely to himself, brought Kes into the passenger saloon of the Hovercraft, and was carrying him on his arm like a falconer.

"What the hell do want to do that for, why couldn't you leave him in the car, where he would be safe, the crossing only takes forty-five minutes" Dick asked.

"I thought I would bring him out for an airing" Peter replied "After all, he's been stuck in the car with us for a week"

As we took off, the stewardess came round to see if everyone was ok. and seeing Peter sitting with Kes on his arm said "Excuse me sir, is that a wild bird?"

"Yes it is" he replied. "We picked it up injured on the road a few days ago, and we're getting it well enough to be released"

"I'm afraid I'll have to report this to the Captain" she said curtly. "Don't you know about the movement of animals and birds order, forbidding the illegal importation of animals, which if broken can result in a heavy fine?"

Having been out of the country for three months, we were totally unaware of the hoo-ha and hysterical panic that was sweeping Britain concerning rabies etc; consequently we had dropped ourselves right in it.

"You've ruddy well done it now!" said Dick "If only you had left the darn' thing in the Landrover, we would have been ok. No-one would have noticed him in there"

After a few minutes the stewardess returned with the Captain, who told Peter firmly to take the Kestrel into the men's toilets and stay there until we arrived in Ramsgate. We were NOT to leave the Hovercraft without his express permission.

"Well you seem to have dropped us well in the crap this time" I said to Peter. "I don't know what they intend to do about it, but if it's a heavy fine we'll all be in schtook"

Sitting like some apprehended criminals, Dick and I waited while everybody got off with their vehicles, and then the Captain appeared.

"Right, you seem to have deliberately flouted the regulations governing the import of wild animals while the present emergency regulations are in place, and I intend to send you back to France without you getting off this craft. There you can get the necessary papers to import this bird, as it is you're lucky you haven't stepped ashore yet and committed an offence!"

"But there's no way the French are going to give us an export licence to export a wild bird, they might not even let us back in with it" I protested. I had visions of us going backwards and forwards like that dreaded ship of old, with a crew that couldn't ever come ashore.

"I can't help that, I can't see any other course of action at the moment"

"Look" I said in desperation. "This is a wild bird, lots of wild birds, this species included, migrate across the channel every year as a matter of course, you can't exclude them all, so why the trouble with this one?"

"Technically, if I let you ashore with this bird, in the current climate" he said, "I would be breaking the law relating to imported animals, but if you DON'T bring it ashore, you could be ok."

"What do you mean?" I asked.

"I mean, I'll give you a plastic bag to put the bird in, and I then want you to dispatch it, making sure that nothing escapes from the sealed bag, and I'll have it incinerated, it's either that, or back to France and see what they say"

The utter futility of trying to deal with a totally inflexible, and in this case, ridiculous situation sent my heart to my boots. We would have to kill the very bird we had so carefully restored to health.

"Ok. I suppose we have no choice" I said. Give me a plastic bag, and I'll do it straight away, it's not the answer, but I can't expect you to understand that"

I took Kes from Peter, and walked towards the nearby gent's toilets. I would do it with the door shut. Wrapping the unprotesting Kes gently in the bag, I took him by the feet and cracked his skull hard against the wash basin surround. He died instantly.

"There you are Captain, exactly as you requested, but in my opinion quite unnecessary"

"Ok. I'm satisfied, the bag is unbroken and the animal hasn't left this craft, you are free to go now"

Each of us, with thoughts of our own, didn't say a lot until we reached my place at Collier Row, where our wives and families were anxiously waiting. The trip was over.

There were some interesting details that came out of the figures I kept concerning the trip, and they were: Total petrol bought - 660 gallons. Cost in Iran @ 5 Rials per litre, £76. Total cost for fuel each way, £475. Miles covered: 11220. Miles per gallon overall 17mpg.

Having had the benefit of such wonderful weather for so long, I was convinced that back in England it would all be a terrible contrast, with cool miserable weather or poor sunshine the order of the day.

I couldn't have been more wrong, the weather was ruddy marvellous!

# Chapter Twenty Five

Within a few weeks of being back at the Yard, I was sent with a couple of lads to cover the Notting hill Carnival, which as far as the organisers were concerned, was to be a happy go lucky street display, with steel-bands and dancing the order of the day.

At first all went well, the super weather made the whole thing a grand spectacle, and then as the drinks got a hold in the warm afternoon, small groups of hooligans began throwing bottles and stones at police, until it all went ever so bolo.

I was on my own under the Westway flyover, taking photographs amongst the blacks as they threw stones at the oncoming police. For some reason the blacks took no notice of me, even though I was right close amongst them. Perhaps it was due to my heavy tan?

A white chap, dressed in khaki trousers, and carrying a cane, looking for all the world like a reporter observing the situation for a newspaper, was set upon by blacks and beaten over the head with a bottle, yet I was left alone, even though I was sporting a tasty looking Nikon camera.

The police, in an effort to close with the stone throwers, armed themselves with rubber dust-bin lids and such-like, in an attempt to deflect the rain of missiles flying thickly overhead as they advanced.

As the two opposing forces closed, the leading blacks turned, and ran from the advancing police towards their friends behind us, causing a crush of bodies going in two directions.

With several other bodies I was hurled towards the pavement in a sea of shouting people, all desperate to get out of the way of the mincer. The situation was beginning to turn very nasty.

Black re-inforcements quickly arrived, and it was now the turn of police to retreat as the vicious hail of bottles and stones in their direction increased.

With so much ammunition flying over our heads, it was a cruel joke when a cloud of feral pigeons rocketed out from under the arches, causing people to scream in fear, as they thought the birds were a shower of rocks coming straight for them. I don't mind saying I got down on the pavement with the rest of them, covering my head with my hands, I certainly didn't want a brick on my nut!

Still on my knees, I felt a sharp tug on my sleeve, and turned to find a young black lad close alongside me, anxiety written across his face.

"Hey man, do you want that fugging camera rammed down your throat? These boys mean business, if you've got any sense you'll get out of here fast!"

"Thanks very much for the warning" I replied without getting up, and he looked at me as though I was mad, before jumping up and disappearing into the crowd. You don't find too many black lads concerned for whites like that. As I was working with the standard 50mm lens on my Nikon, I could record faces and actions in close up, and I carried on taking pictures of rioters until police burst through the first line of throwers, and began clearing the street.

Funnily enough this was nearly my undoing as the first officer to reach my position, fired up with fear and anger, threatened to bring his truncheon down on my head, until he heard me shouting desperately, 'SO.3 photos, job photographer' and roared past me like a raging bull.

I continued roaming the streets, copping various faces I thought might be of interest to Demo control, gradually making my way back towards Westbourne Park railway station, and safety.

Suddenly, just in front of me a crowd of blacks surrounded a nondescript vehicle containing two officers in civilian clothes, and proceeded to hammer hell out of it.

Somehow, the officers managed to get clear, and legged it away from the scene, leaving the crowd to vent their anger by turning the car on its side, and smashing the windows.

Seeing this little lot going on forty feet away, I slid quietly into the first porch I found, and began clicking the camera round the edge of the wall, just as one of the crowd put a torch to the car.

In seconds it burst into flames, to the obvious delight of the cheering crowd, and I knew then, it would take ages to restore public order, and get this lot to push off home!

With daylight nearly gone, I concealed the camera under my jacket, and shoving hands in trousers pockets, sauntered casually past the shouting crowds towards Notting Hill police station, where I had left my van parked in the yard.

I could now 'Foxtrot-Oscar' back to the Yard, and go home, it had been a rather eventful day!

When the full extent of the riot became known, various intelligence groups waited anxiously to view the contents of the two films I had exposed, and as a result of their investigations, seventy-two people were identified and arrested for various disorder offences.

In court several weeks later, one defendant I had captured on film hurling a bottle at police, appeared with his brief - a fat little man in a scruffy black waistcoat, to protest his innocence.

"Tell me Mr. Parker" said the brief, "You say you were at Notting Hill for a considerable period of time, and saw my client on more than one occasion, did you make any notes at the time concerning these alleged actions?" He waved copies of my photos in the air in a peremptory gesture.

"Yes sir, I did"

"And may we see these notes you made at the time?"

"Yes sir you can, you're looking at them now"

It took a second or two before he fell in, then, in a gruff voice said, "Thank you, that will be all Mr. Parker", and I left the dock with a grin. Even the magistrate smiled a bit.

During the autumn of 1976 I felt at a bit of a loose end in the section, first I worked in the colour printing room, then the fingerprint room, and finally the studio, it was all a bit colourless and lacking in charisma after the Iranian trip.

Dave A. our boss, made another of his anti-social boo-boos, upsetting senior people in fingerprints, causing quite unnecessary friction between them and us. The umpty situation wasn't improved either, when Det.Insp.McMacken. who was the photographic instructor at Hendon Training college, informed Dave A. he was 'putting his papers in' and retiring to Australia - someone in the section would have to go and take his place.

Rounding up the five photographers who had passed me in the last promotion stakes, who held the requisite rank for the aforesaid job, Dave A. read them the riot act, saying he wanted a name for Hendon by the following Monday, otherwise he would depute someone to go.

The five, not wanting in the least to be sent off to Hendon - which was somewhere NORTH of London wasn't it? deliberated amongst themselves for ages, but still couldn't come up with a volunteer.

No, they informed Dave, no-one would volunteer, teaching students wasn't in their conditions of service etc; and no-way were they going to go into exile at the school for two years. Dave A. would have to go and whistle!

Thinking that reporting the situation to Gerry Lambourne, Commander of SO.3.dept. would scare one of the lads into volunteering, Dave A. nipped downstairs, only to be told in no uncertain terms that he was in charge of photographic section, and should sort out the problem for himself.

With the implacable five ranged before him once more, he ordered, cajoled, and blew his top, but to no avail, they weren't volunteering, and no-one was going.

It was pretty obvious there was a distinct lack of co-operation between himself and the men he had selectively promoted, and the atmosphere around his office was so thick, you could cut it with a knife!

I must admit I had a bit of a giggle to myself - he had hand picked his yes men, deliberately excluding me, only to find the ingrates said NO to a man!

As Gerry L. had more than a passing interest in the outcome of the exercise, he spoke to Dave A. during Friday, asking who was going to take over from DI.McMacken as he wanted the hand over to run in parallel for smoothness.

No doubt being told that a name wasn't yet forthcoming, he gave Dave the rest of the day to come up with someone, or he would come down personally, and see what the problem was.

By mid-afternoon, the rebel five had been approached one at a time in Dave's office, but the answer was still no, no-one was volunteering or going, it was a complete stand-off.

At five-o-clock, I had my motor-cycle gear on, and was just approaching the lift to go down to the garage, when the doors banged open, and an agitated, very angry looking Gerry L. appeared, bound for Dave A's office.

In mid-stride he stopped, looked me straight in the eye, and from a distance of about foot said angrily "If I asked you to go to Hendon College on Monday morning, what would you say?"

"I would expect to follow the last order guv'nor, and complain later, you know that"

"Right!" he said explosively "I'll speak to you again on Monday, goodnight!"

On the way home I wondered what the outcome of it all would be, I was glad I wasn't anywhere in the section when Gerry L. finished with Dave, it wouldn't be a pretty sight.

I don't suppose I had been in the section more than half an hour on Monday morning, when the imperious summons came - would I go to Dave A's office right away, as he wished to speak to me. What the hell was he doing in this early?

I soon found out!

Putting a brave face on it, and looking me straight in the eye he said "As you know, Det.Insp. McMacken is retiring from Hendon college shortly, and I want you to go up there and sit in, prior to someone else taking over and running the Overseas and Counties course.

Apparently you indicated to Gerry L. on Friday that you'd go, is that true?"

I said that it was, but refrained from saying just how it had come about, let him ruddy-well stew.

"What about the fact that I will be filling a Principal photographer's post, when I'm still only a Senior Photographer?" I said, rubbing salt into the wound.

"You'll be going up there as acting Principal - a promotion board will be held later, when you will be competing with others within the section for the post"

It was all I could do not to smile, he knew, and I knew, that his earlier terrible threat to screw me, was looking like so much snow in the sun, and was all going up in steam!

Just before Christmas I began the six-week 'sit-in' with DI.McMacken. at Hendon Police college, and it seemed like no time at all before he was away, Australia bound.

From my desk at the front of the class of nine students, I scanned their attentive faces, and heard myself begin to outline what I expected from them as students over the next six weeks.

I must admit I felt a bit nervous.

To add to my problems, Mr. Reid, Commandant of the Detective Training school informed me that it was one of the duties of an instructor to talk to the whole detective intake on their specialised subject, and to pass on such expertise as one had in these matters.

I was booked into the lecture hall for the following Monday morning!

Thinking the safest way to approach the problem of addressing sixty male and female detectives, was to acquaint them with the structure and operating procedures within SO.3. I worked out a detailed script, which I felt went rather well with the forty odd scenes of crime slides I had scrounged from visual aids.

I was first on before tea, and I watched in some trepidation as the lecture theatre quickly filled up, especially when I saw Mr.Reid the Commandant slip quietly into the back row, as I began my spiel.

Halfway through my stint there was a loud crash, and some pretty strong language, followed by ribald laughter, as one of the students having indulged in a heavy weekend, fell off his seat into gangway, fast asleep.

At the conclusion, I reckoned I had done a fair job, but didn't feel as though I had caught anyone's enthusiasm overmuch, but it was my first baptism of fire.

Mr. Reid came up to me and said "No, sorry Alan, that won't do, you were talking AT them, instead of TO them. With your years' of experience at scenes of crime, you should have shown them examples of how to do it, and how not to do it, with a few disasters thrown in, THAT'S want they wanted to hear. Never mind, I'm sure you'll get it right next time, let's go to tea"

It was sound advice, thoughtfully given, which I was later able to build on.

The photographic course lasted six weeks, and at the end of it I was pretty knackered. I had put a lot into it, and even after classes had finished, I found myself answering photographic questions when the students and I unwound over a beer in the college bar.

It was a bit like going back to photographic college all over again!

I received a call from the boss, Dave A. saying he would be arriving at the school next day to give my students their oral examination, and to look at the specimen work they had achieved, before taking it back to their forces as an aide memoir.

I felt this could be a bit harrowing all round!

One by one the students went into my office, where Dave A. shut the door and gave them their oral exam, while outside the rest of us nervously bit our nails and waited.

It was crunch-time for everyone.

"Well Alan" he said when we were alone, "I must say I am agreeably surprised, their negatives and printing were better than I expected, and they seem to have a reasonable grasp of photographic theory - we'll see if it continues through the next few courses, goodbye" and he was gone.

The atmosphere at the College was all that I remembered from my previous stint, and during the next week I was summoned before my peers, and ceremoniously presented with a Police Instructor's tie, a distinction given only to one other civilian before me, Terry Rockall I was extremely chuffed.

A few days later I was summoned to the Yard to attend a promotion board for the post of Instructor at the college, and took my place with the four other candidates Dave A. had selected.

"Its not exactly fair, is it?" said one of my competitors. "You've been up there, 'in-post' so to speak, while the rest of us have to go in cold, you've got it made"

"I didn't notice any of those who passed me in the promotion stakes over the last few years make any noises about going for the post did you, so what are you going on about?"

Happily I did pass the board, and a couple of days later was asked to attend the Yard once more, this time to receive congratulations from Gerry Lambourne head of SO.3. and of course sup a few beers with the lads.

I was beginning to feel I had cleared an enormous hurdle at last!

After lunch Dave A. called me into his office, and sitting behind his desk, fingertips together,said brusquely "I suppose some congratulations are in order, I don't know how you did it, but you managed to beat me, I didn't think you could, but you did"

I didn't bother to enlighten him, it wasn't worth wasting my breath on, I merely replied "Thank you very much" and left it at that - he hadn't been that difficult to beat in the long run.

There were I was told, sufficient applications from both provincial forces and overseas police, to fill the six-week courses right through 1977, therefore I had plenty of work to look forward to.

In the meantime I was able to update many of the set-pieces previously used for forensic photographic training, and bring them into line with current equipment and practice.

The photographic courses at Hendon continued to go down well, and I slid into a regular routine with my fellow police instructors, to the point where I felt entirely at home.

At the end of each course I had the customary visit from Dave A. so he could give his usual oral exam, and although I always felt apprehensive about his visits, I managed to pass muster each time, so I must have been doing something right!

I had to admit some of the courses were so demanding I was exhausted at the end, and needed every day of the week's break in between to recover. It was difficult to harmonise various technical aspects of the work between such varied students as those from Abu Dhabi, Belize,Oman and the English county forces.

In what appeared to be no time, the college summer break came round, and with it, the opportunity to take the family on holiday in the Volks camper - we were off to sunny Dorset for a few days.

In early September, Helen was born by caesarean section, and we began once again the routines necessary to bring a new baby into the family. It was all a bit hectic, but things soon settled down, and I thought ruefully I would be 66 by the time Helen was 21, and that sounded rather old!

With Teresa's severe medical condition dominating the scene, Christmas was a pretty quiet affair, and I for one was more than glad when the new year finally ushered itself in. We could confidently look forward to a letter from the specialist at London hospital, any day now.

When it finally did come, the letter said we should be at the hospital at 10am on the 4th May - it seemed an awfully long way off, bearing in mind the apparent seriousness of Teresa's condition.

I felt it should have been in January as initially suggested, but I was told the appointment couldn't possibly be changed.

The Churchill Trust people had written to me a few days previously, saying the medal presentation ceremony was coming up shortly at the Guildhall in London. It was to be a combined presentation between the 1976 winners, and all those who had yet to receive their medals, would I care to attend? The Queen mother was doing the honours.

Naturally I replied we would be honoured to attend, and subsequently received the entry tickets, but with Teresa so ill, I felt it would be quite out of the question for us to go.

Not so Teresa, she was determined we would.

On the due date, dolled out in our best bib and tucker, we drove to the Guildhall, and were duly ushered into the magnificent hall to begin the ceremony, although I was sure Teresa was hanging in there purely through some quiet inner strength.

My presentation to the delightful Queen mother was a great experience, and she showed by her questions, she had done some research into our individual projects, which I found quite remarkable and gratifying - it wasn't like being processed as a can of peas after all!

By the time we got to attend the London hospital in May, Teresa was suffering severe nausea from her condition each morning, and for some reason was beginning to put on weight round her abdomen.

I wasn't happy with the way things were shaping up at all. Her eventual examination consisted of an internal endoscopic check of the digestive tract whilst under anaesthetic, plus a biopsy of the stomach lining, which meant we had to wait until Teresa had recovered sufficiently, before travelling home in the car.

A week later we received the findings of the specialist which hit us like a hammer-blow. The biopsy apparently showed a very serious condition of the stomach - would we come in to see him right away?

Fortunately the hospital appointment was between courses, and I could take Teresa without disruption to the class, although I knew Mr.Reid the commandant, would have covered my absence without problem, nevertheless it was with great trepidation we made our way back to the London hospital.

The news was bad, Teresa had severe cancer of the stomach, which was inoperable, and in his opinion the specialist thought we had less than six months left. He couldn't understand why the team doing the caesarean operation at Helen's birth had failed to see the signs, which he thought should have been obvious.

In a state similar to one where you have received a severe blow to the head, and nothing really focuses or relates, I heard him say "We would like you to bring Mrs Parker in when she gets too big in the abdomen again, its called ascites, and must be drained away to give some relief to your wife.

Of course when it all gets too much, she'll have to come in to stay"

We looked at each other, and I felt tears of frustration and pity well up in my eyes. Why now for God's sake, when we had so much to do and enjoy, it was so bloody unfair!

I don't know how we managed to get through the next couple of days, things were a bit of a blur. It seemed as though every moment was geared to pushing the dreadful reality to the back of our minds, while trying to live a normal life, but the beast wouldn't go away, this was for real!

Although Teresa and I had always been very close, and able to discuss anything at all, our conversation became stilted, and we mentally sparred with each other, frantically trying to find common ground that wouldn't betray our deepest fears.

It was now early July, and although Teresa was at home, she was very weak due to the fact that she hardly ate anything, and often failed to keep even small amounts down. She spent much of the day resting on the settee, whilst kind friends came in to look after both her and Helen.

Returning to Hendon College to check all was ok. before the summer holiday break, I was astounded and saddened to hear that Mr.Reid Commandant of the Training school had just died of heart attack - the same compassionate man who had given me all the time I needed over the last couple of weeks was gone.

Life was definitely a bit of a bastard at times.

Somehow, Teresa had not only remembered my birthday on August 2nd, but got me a little present too, the indomitable spirit of her wonderful personality shone through in everything she did, despite her body failing to keep up - it was great to see her smile again.

The visiting MacMillan nurses were all that one could desire in their efforts to help us, a sheepskin rug to take the harshness off lying in the cot all day, plus all the bits and pieces necessary to nurse and comfort a seriously ill patient.

I was fortunate to have their help and advice.

On Sept.1st. I reached across to Teresa immediately I woke, and was jolted into consciousness by the terrible coldness of her arms and face, she was still breathing - but only just.

I felt her death was only a matter of hours away.

At ten o'clock, Teresa gave a last long sigh and passed away, whilst I still held her ice-cold hands.

It was done. We were finally parted. She was gone.

As though viewing the scene in a slow motion film, I watched the funeral parlour chaps take Teresa's body away - god, how many times had I seen that sight at a murder scene, when they carted the body away to the mortuary in a black tin coffin, and here it was happening to me!

That Christmas was a bit grim, trying to achieve those things a family expects in the festive season, but in our case, tempered by such a harsh loss, I had a lot of mental juggling to do.

At the end of one of the photo courses in February, Dave A. the boss, gave his usual exam, and just before departing said "You seem to have made a great success of your time here Alan, I think you ought to consider staying on for a few years, you don't really want the rough and tumble of scenes of crime at your time of life again do you?"

"Well, I've been here two years now, and I'm quite prepared to give it until the end of March, but after that I'll be looking for a change. I need the stimulus of other photographers, and different kinds of work to do, otherwise I'll get stale and out of touch"

"OK. we'll see about that nearer the time, but in the meantime bear in mind what I've said, after all you are your own boss here, with no-one to interfere in what you do"

Perhaps it was my wicked mind, but I read that to mean as long as I was comfortably side-lined here at Hendon, he could strut his stuff and do what he liked in the section without hassle from me.

It would mean I could also remain a Principal photographer for the rest of my service!

Not that I had any great desire for the top promotion, they could keep that, I just didn't like being passed out by people who had ten years less service than me, it wasn't right.

In no-time it was the first week of March, and I re-iterated to Dave A. my desire to return to the fold, and was told they were still having the same difficulty as before - there were no willing volunteers for Hendon.

Eventually I got a call from Frank Jones who had joined the section a year or so after me - and been promoted ahead of me, saying that to cut short the acrimonious dialogue developing between Dave A. and other Principals in the section, he was volunteering to come up to Hendon on a strict two-year posting to relieve me.

After that it was down to someone else, and I thought that was a very nice gesture.

The transitional 'sit-in' with Frank went without a hitch, and I was soon back in the frenetic dynamo that was scenes of crime, working alongside old colleagues, and a couple of youngsters who had joined the job since I was posted to Hendon.

One of the first scene of crime jobs I got, was to attend the exhumation of a young Jewish girl who had been found dead in a shared flat. It had been stated by the pathologist at the original post mortem, the girl had been hit on the back of the head with a heavy blunt instrument, probably a hammer, and killed.

Despite a thorough search, police failed to find anything fitting that description at or near the crime scene during the initial investigation, where was it?

The girl's boy friend had been seen legging it away from the flat by a neighbour, but despite extensive investigation had not been traced.

A month or so later, he wrote to a close friend saying, whilst staying in Belgium, he had read a recent newspaper article concerning his girlfriend's death, and wondered who would want to break in, and shoot her dead in their old flat?

As police had been told by the pathologist she had been struck viciously on the head, shattering her skull, with no mention of a shooting, the boy friend's letter subsequently taken to police by his friend, provoked a storm of controversy.

Why did the boyfriend say 'shot' when the pathologist made no mention of a shooting?

Six months after her burial, on a bitterly cold, sunny day in March, an exhumation at Waltham Abbey began, and I was there specifically to cover the job from the visual-aids/teaching aspect, carrying only a Nikon F2 with a couple of rolls of trannie film. Ralph R. a section colleague, had been deputed to attend from west London with our video equipment, and was asked to cover the job as fully as possible from an evidential point of view, in case of further proceedings.

As the JCB began removing the first scoops of soil, I looked round frantically for Ralph, but there was no sign of him or his van, so I started to cover the early aspects of the job as best I could.

It wasn't long before the coffin came into view, and due to some underground spring nearby, it was awash with water - I didn't give much for the state of the body it was supposed to contain after such an immersion!

With an obscene gurgle and dreadful sucking sound the JCB shovel lifted the coffin clear, and cascades of muddy water splashed those who stood too close, watching, and those taking un-official photographs who couldn't get out of the way!

The waterlogged coffin was carefully loaded into a funeral vehicle, and taken to the nearby mortuary, where a second post mortem was about to be held, and still there was no sign of Ralph and his video camera. This was beginning to get rather embarrassing!

There must have been a dozen people crammed into the small mortuary, and it became a right push and shove to get myself organised for the stills photography. Fortunately I had a couple of fully charged, trusty Mecablitz CT45's with me - I hadn't really expected to get involved with the full PM itself, but as there was no video camera present, it was down to Joe soap to hold the fort!

When the body was removed from the coffin, I was surprised to see how well preserved it was, there was still a lot of white flesh present, and very little sign of disintegration or decay, perhaps the icy cold water had helped to preserve the body?

Whatever the reason, she looked as if she had only been dead a few days, rather than several months.

The first thing the pathologist noticed was that the top of the skull, usually removed to examine the brain during a PM. was missing. It hadn't been replaced in the coffin as per normal practice, yet the brain area had been filled with wadding material so the scalp could be replaced for cosmetic reasons.

At this point I noticed the D/Supt looking at the original scenes of crime photos, taken by Alan C. - and in particular a full face photo of the deceased taken prior to the top of the skull being removed.

There, plain for all to see, was a ragged hole below her left cheek, surrounded by purple bruising, and the splatter of gun discharge material, typical of a weapon being fired at very close range.

She HAD been shot, and yet no-one had picked it up, least of all the pathologist who had undertaken the original PM!

This was deadly serious!

The pathologist went on. "I would like you to take particularly close views of these facial injuries Alan, and especially this hole through the cheek bone" which he demonstrated by skinning the face down to the upper jaw, leaving clean bone and the bullet hole.

"There is little doubt in my mind, this young girl was shot with a small calibre pistol at close range" he continued "And if we were to somehow discover what happened to the top of the skull, we should, I suspect, see the massive exit wound. She certainly was not killed by a violent blow to the back of the head"

In all my years attending deaths at mortuaries I had never seen anything like it, this was a shaker of the first order, and heads would certainly roll!

The sequel to this sorry tale was, the top of the skull was eventually discovered in a specimen drawer where the original PM had been carried out, and showed a typical 'punch-out' fracture directly in line with the wound through the cheek. Bearing in mind the nature of the boy friend's confession to his friend - that his girl had been shot when no-one else was aware of that fact, he was subsequently arrested and extradited for her murder.

When I got back to the section, I queried Ralph's lack of attendance with the video gear, and was told he had broken down on the North Circular near Hendon, and had asked our transport people to take his van to the nearest police garage, and had then gone home.

Naturally he got a terrific rollicking for not attending the exhumation, which did him no good in the popularity stakes at all.

Although the video equipment we currently used was only low-band U-matic stuff - a monstrous heavy recorder attached to the camera by a stout electronic umbilicus, it did give us the opportunity to try out this new method of filming, and compare it to our tried and tested method of 16mm cine.

I thought it had terrific potential.

I liked immensely the facility for instant picture playback, it certainly made life a lot easier when assessing awkward shots, and of course editing could be undertaken as soon as you returned to the section, there was no need for processing, matched prints, or cuts racks.

Now that I was back into the swing of things in the section, my time was fully stretched between working at scenes of crime, and managing with my daughter Ruth's help, to run the home and look after Helen.

I didn't have time to think too much about what may or may not have been in other circumstances, and time flew past.

We had a second serious incident in the family, when my uncle Arthur's boy, Richard Beckinsale died suddenly of a heart attack, leaving a wife and daughter at the height of his acting success.

Someone in the family said quietly, they hoped that bad things didn't always have to come in threes.

# Chapter Twenty Six

On Wednesday April 30th, a bunch of terrorists belonging to the Mohieddin al Nasser Arabistan martyr group, burst into the Iranian embassy in London and took a number of people hostage, including PC.Trevor Lock, whom I knew from occasional meetings at Dagenham Police station.

The embassy at Princes Gate was quickly surrounded by armed Police, who diverted all traffic away from the scene, and the situation developed into a stand-off.

Photographic were asked to cover the front of the embassy from a sandbagged position in the park opposite, and record anybody who showed themselves at the doors or windows.

Three Principal photographers were designated to organise a team of three photographers each, and given a two-day stints in the bunker - I copped the Sunday and Monday third slot, a bit of a bind really, but at least it was overtime, and of course Sunday was at DOUBLE time!

The first day of my groups' stint passed pretty boringly, the negotiators did their bit, with various comings and goings as various terrorist demands were acceded to, and the whole thing seemed to get locked into a bit of a stalemate.

The next day a call came over the communications link - would a photographer please attend Alpha control immediately, regarding an urgent matter.

Assuming that meant us, I left the bunker and made my way to the offices that were forward, or Alpha control, and enquired who wanted photographic.

A chap in civvies came forward, who was either MI.5 or military, and asked "Special Branch photographer?"

Immediately the thought flew through my mind - special branch photographer? What the hell does he think we've all been doing fifteen hours a day in the ruddy park, bird-watching or something? I answered "Yes, that's right"

"Good, I want you to go with this D.11 Firearms chap to a flat overlooking the rear of the embassy, and be ready with your camera to record whatever activity you observe at the windows there, concerning the terrorists"

I turned to the D.11 chap and said "I'll just go and collect my camera from our position in the park, and bring a back-up man, then we'll be ready to go, ok?"

Like the only people left in the world, the D.11 man, myself and 'Flogger' Flain crouched well below the wall in front of the embassy, awaiting the all clear from armed officers pointing their pistols at the embassy windows above. It was all un-naturally quiet, the only sound being the melodious song of a Blackcap warbler singing from the shrubbery in the nearby park, at least that was nice.

Given the 'go' by the officers, we sprinted along the pavement and into a building which allowed us to get into some flats at the rear of the Iranian embassy and up onto the second floor.

"We've managed to get a good overlooking position from a flat owned by Lord Knatchbull" said the D.11 chap. "I'll introduce you to the Chief Inspector in charge, then you can do the necessary for yourself"

Inside the sumptuous room, three armed D.11 officers sat on stools at the windows, their rifles fitted with telescopic sights, trained on the rear of the embassy a few yards away.

"Who are you, and what do you want here?" growled the terse and distinctly unfriendly Ch.Insp. as we went in, and I felt the usual attitude a civilian experiences, when you're not wearing blue trousers.

"We've been told by Alpha control to cover the rear of the embassy, and photograph anything that shows itself, until it's no longer possible to take photographs" I replied.

"Well you certainly AREN'T going to get in the way of my marksmen at the windows, I can tell you that for certain, so I don't know what you think you'll be doing"

Remembering once again what my old dad had told me years ago, that the only way to beat the system, is to use the system against itself, I replied.

"That's ok. if you say that you can't allow us access to any vantage point to take the photographs the Commissioner has requested that's fine, we'll return to Alpha control and let them know your decision"

I could see I'd got him on one foot, so I carried on. "However, if young Flain here could sit on a chair behind one of your marksmen, and be ready to move alongside if and when anything showed itself, that would be ok. wouldn't it? I could perhaps find another position nearby where I could squeeze in if necessary, without disturbing anyone"

"Ok. he can sit there in the corner behind that chap, and keep well out of the way until called forward, my man will have to protect him while he's vulnerable at the window"

"Thanks, I'm sure that will do fine" and I motioned flogger to sit with his Nikon, loaded with black and white, in the position indicated.

As there was nowhere else in the room I could usefully sit and poke my Nikon F2 out of a window, I went into the only other room with a view of the embassy, which was the kitchen.

It was rather poky, and had a small sash window situated above a stone butler sink, not as good as flogger's viewpoint, but it would have to do.

I went back into the main room and informed the Ch.Insp. what I wanted to do, and he agreed it was ok. provided I came away from the window at his command, he didn't want the responsibility of me being shot dead in his OP.

As there was very little happening at that point, I engaged him in conversation, in an attempt to inject a little more acceptance of our presence into his domain, and found out after some initial verbal fencing, the reason for his aversion to civil staff, and photographers in particular.

Apparently it all stemmed from an incident when he had been duty officer as an Inspector, and had harsh words with photographer Alan'C' who was known to be quite tactless at times.

I told him that as photographic duty officer, I had tangled with Alan C' myself, and once he realised that I had twenty-two years service in - more than he had, things got a little easier. At that moment two civvy types came into the room with some directional sound detecting gear, and made pointed remarks to the Ch.Insp. about who flogger and I were, and what we were doing there.

They plainly didn't want us to see what they were up to.

"We're from Box - if you've heard of us, what authority do you have for being here taking photographs?" one of them asked.

"We were asked by Alpha control to photograph anything that shows itself at the windows, if you're not happy about that, I suggest you contact Alpha control yourself, and maybe resolve the problem" I replied.

They set up their small parabolic reflector, muttering to themselves, and I heard the Ch.Insp. say quietly "You don't have to worry about these two, I have everything under control here" and with that, they left the room.

The Ch.Insp. and his team had a direct link to the control room running the show, and we had been listening closely to conversations the negotiators had been having with the terrorists, and were therefore party to what was going on, virtually by the second.

During the late afternoon things got really sticky when the terrorists shot Abbas Lavasani one of the hostages, and bundled his body out the front door, provoking a response the terrorists could hardly have imagined.

Things were definitely getting nasty now.

I nodded at flogger to be on the alert, and went into the kitchen to get into position for photography, my bum on the draining board and feet in the sink, camera at 90 degrees to my left through the open window.

As I looked through the viewfinder I noticed white ropes traversing the rooftop parallel to the ridge tiles, and looped around the chimney stack. For some peculiar reason I hadn't noticed them before, perhaps I hadn't been looking up there, but there they were, with several attachment points along their length, suggesting someone working on the roof needed secure support.

After killing the hostage, contact with the terrorists via the negotiator got more and more tense as they demanded transport away from the area, plus other concessions, while control carefully tried to assure them that everything they had asked for, was going to plan.

Suddenly through my Nikon viewfinder I saw the most bizarre sight imaginable - three or four grotesque heads moving along the roof ridge, each fitted with a shiny black gas mask, looking for all the world like creatures from another planet.

What the hell was going on?

The radio link, going nineteen to the dozen, now took on a slightly pleading air, as the negotiator tried desperately to assure Salim Towfigh - leader of the terrorists, that there was nothing in the fact that he could hear noises coming from the roof.

All was well he assured, and events proceeding exactly as requested.

Salim, obviously not convinced that all was well, must have been on the point of breaking off negotiations, even though the negotiator continued to insist that 'noises'off' were only in Salim's imagination.

The four men in masks were now quietly joined by a couple of others without their head gear, who proceeded to tie four long ropes onto the attachment points.

Suddenly a new command broke the air. "House-breaker one, house-breaker one, ready" and as I looked again at the menacing black figures on the roof adjusting their ropes, it suddenly dawned on me that an abseil assault was about to take place right before my eyes. They must be the SAS!

I focussed the 80-210 zoom on the group and started taking pictures, the only problem was, the setting sun coming in to view on my left was causing slight flare into the lens, and I had to draw back a little to let the window buttress shut off some of the rays.

Like a superbly choreographed team, the men, dressed from head to toe in black, and carrying sub-machine guns with a light on top, snicked on their carabiners in readiness for the assault.

This was absolutely fantastic, I was so close I could see every detail of the assault, and even hear what they said to one another.

Suddenly voices on the radio link disappeared as an almighty explosion rent the air, and Pago troop CRW assault team flicked their ropes down the embassy wall, and began a rapid descent.

Arriving at the balcony three floors down, they smashed their way through windows either side of the little door and lobbed in stun grenades, which detonated with an almighty roar and flash of flame, and they were in.

All except one poor chap that is, who fouled his ropes just short of the balcony, and was left hanging in front of the window, shouting to his comrades "Cut the ropes, cut the fugging ropes!" as he swung backwards and forwards through the inferno of flames roaring from the smashed window.

After what seemed an age, two lads cut him free, and disappeared inside to join the others in the staccato stutter of sub machine guns spewing instant death to Salim and his friends, it was absolutely incredible.

After a while, hostages began to appear from the back of the smoke-filled embassy, and were instantly grabbed by SAS men and cuffed - plastic ratchet binders on the wrists, and laid face down on the grass immediately below our windows.

I had run out of film at this point, and in the excitement of the moment was all fingers and thumbs loading a new one, but I was soon able to carry on, recording the hostages as they lay directly below me on the grass.

As I worked, I heard one of the SAS men say to his mate "This bloke is one of terrorists masquerading as a hostage, he's been identified by some of the others"

"Let's take the bastard back inside and shoot him then!"

"We can't, he's already been photographed by that bloke at the window up there!" so they hauled him to his feet and hustled him away from the main group of hostages into custody.

That was how Fowzi Bavadi Nejad became the only surviving terrorist to stand trial at the Old Bailey many months later.

He was a very lucky man!

A figure in blazer and slacks, left hand in jacket pocket appeared on the scene, strolling amongst the supine hostages with a magnificent air of authority - I think it must have been Col.Rose who was i/c operation Nimrod.

Seeing me taking photographs of the hostages from the window he called peremptorily, "You there, get back inside and stop taking photographs at once!"

Taking a leaf out of Nelson's book, I pretended I hadn't heard his remark, and carried on taking photographs regardless, I didn't rate him as the sole arbiter of whether police recorded the scene or not!

As the whole shebang came to an end, I ducked back into the room, in time to see the Ch.Insp. and his merry men drinking tea from flasks, and scoffing sandwiches from plastic boxes as though at a picnic or something, it did look funny.

"How did you get on flogger, did you get anything useful?"

"Yeah, I got some good stuff of the lads going in at ground level, and plenty of stuff all around, how did you do?"

I told him what I hoped I'd got, and we both felt well pleased with the way things had gone. I thanked the Ch.Insp. for letting us horn in, and promised to tell him about our results in due course.

I felt that in some small way we had been able to redress a bit of anti-civvy feeling that had unfortunately reared its ugly head, and hoped he might turn out to be more friendly towards photographic in the future.

When flogger and I returned to the section, there were, despite the late hour, quite a few staff about, and Ernie Whatmore in charge of machine processing, took my two colour trannie films and put them on the Colenta processor straight away.

Everyone was dead keen to see what I'd got at the siege.

The news that we had captured the SAS embassy assault on film, spread abroad like wildfire, and soon after my films came off the processor, DAC Dellow, responsible with Mr.Nievens for the police side of the operation, came into the section to examine the shots.

"Who took these?" he said, addressing people milling around the viewing box.

"I did Sir" I replied with a feeling of pride - the results looked pretty good from where I stood.

"Well, you could be the most famous photographer in the world at the moment, and if the press got hold of these, one of the richest, but you won't be either!"

"These photographs are subject to the highest security, and won't be seen by anyone except the anti-terrorist branch, but never mind, a very good result all the same" and with that he was off.

So much for fame and fortune!

The funny thing was, I later heard that Cmdr.Duffy, head of the anti-terrorist branch at the time, had attended a meeting of specialists in anti terrorism in the USA a week later, and had showed my slides as an example of how good we Brits were at this sort of thing - marvellous isn't it?

Although my VW camper had been an excellent choice for holidays or carrying bulky items we wanted moving around, it wasn't quite the vehicle for every day travelling to work. It was a bit too big for fighting through heavy rush-hour traffic in the city.

As a special concession, civil staff were allowed to park in a private car park near Victoria station, but the last leg of the journey across Westminster Bridge past the Yard was a right pain.  Sad as it was, our old VW bus would have to go, perhaps I should get something smaller and more manoeuvrable, like a motorbike?

There were some good deals going down at the motor-cycle shop in Romford, and after a bit of haggling, I came away with a 125cc. Kawasaki two-stroke trials bike, something I thought might get me to work a bit faster than my staid old Volks.

After my first week on the bike, I found you had to keep your eyes peeled and your responses electric if you wished to stay alive for long, on what must be the busiest commuter roads in the world.

There were an awful lot of idiot car drivers out there who didn't 'think bike' at all!

We were now a fairly settled lot at home, and a reasonable routine had evolved, which enabled us to achieve those things which had to be done, and still have some time left for relaxation.

I couldn't have managed it at all, if it hadn't been for young Ruth.

The awkward times came during my late-turn duty, Monday through to the following Monday, when I could be called out at any time during the night after working a full day. On the present rota this was coming round one week, every five or six weeks, which we could just about cope with.

It was under these conditions, when the kind arrangement made with Mary Boyer and her family came to the fore, with Helen being collected from us at 0830 to allow Ruth and Phillip to get off to school.

I was then able to collect Helen on my return from work during the evening.

At the Yard I had been invited to a pre-Christmas party do, and after doing the rounds plus a couple of drinks, was about to slide off, when one of the chaps I knew well from Special Branch, asked me how things were going with the family and so on. He was pleased to hear we were managing Ok. and that things were at last falling into shape.

"Have you been out socially with any friends, a woman maybe, since you lost your wife?"

I said I hadn't, I just didn't have the time for that, in fact I only attended the occasional function at the Yard because I was already there, and could nip off after a couple of quickies.

I had to get home as soon as I could, to see all was well, and to give my daughter Ruth a break.

"I've got a friend, a woman friend, who is in your position, although hers is from a divorce, she's well into photography and is an attractive and intelligent woman, you ought to meet her, how about it?"

"I don't know whether I'm into all that stuff at the moment" I said. "With a home and family to run, plus this job, my time is pretty full"

"Well she's coming here to the Yard next Friday, its with our lot for a 'do' in the office, naturally you're invited, how about it?"

"I'll have to let you know what happens during the week" I replied, "If it's Ok. with Ruth my daughter to hold the fort for the evening, I'll come along for a while, but I'm not making any promises regarding your friend"

"Well we'll see about that nearer the time" he smiled. In the meantime, look after yourself, and I'll contact you on Thursday to see if you're able to come"

I must admit I forgot all about the invitation until the phone rang on Thursday, and I said I'd be there if I could possibly make it - I still hadn't cleared it with Ruth.

Ruth was quite happy for me to go, she had her friend Tina from across the road she wanted to discuss things with, so I wouldn't be missed as long as I wasn't back too late, I felt a right Cinderella!

Although the 'do' was scheduled to last from 1730 until 2000, I deliberately held back until 1830, I wasn't happy about the situation at all.

I didn't need female company at present, they weren't a feature in my life, anyway, what if she were not my type, or I hers?

The place was jumping as I slowly eased my way to the bar between packed bodies, and the hubbub of noise was such, you couldn't understand a normal conversation - and I really hated that.

"Ah, there you are Alan, come and get yourself something to drink, and I'll introduce you to this dear friend of mine, I'm glad you could make it"

With a nice double Scotch and ginger for company, I followed him to a corner of the room, where a small group were jammed against a window, laughing and talking, amidst a sea of drinks and sandwiches.

"This is my friend Alan, Alan please meet Naomi" and I was standing in front of a very attractive woman in her mid-thirties, who was obviously enjoying herself immensely.

"Look after him will you love, while I circulate and do the necessary" and he was gone, swallowed up in a sea of laughing, jostling bodies.

"I understand you are in photographic" she said. "That must be interesting, I'm involved in a lot of photography myself, but not quite your style of things, mine is to do with promotional work. I'm an executive with a top car rental firm in London"

Despite the appalling rhubarb-rhubarb of conversation, we managed to make some sort of conversation concerning our mutual interests, but it was all a bit strained.

"Look I tell you what, I've got this problem concerning the use of flash to light one of our top BMW cars for a promotional handout, why don't you come to my place and help me sort it out?

"With your knowledge and experience it shouldn't take long, and I can drop you back here at the Yard afterwards, I only live at Hyde Park, how about it?"

In desperation I looked round for my friend, but in the sea of bodies he was nowhere to be seen, having done the intro, he'd skedadled and left me to it.

"Well yes, if you think I can help, of course, but I can't be too late as I have to get back to the family tonight"

Just inside the revolving doors of the Yard, I waited for her to appear outside, it was a bitterly cold night and I didn't have an overcoat with me. I had driven to work on the bike, and my protective gear was still in the office.

A gleaming metallic blue BMW saloon, no doubt the flagship of the company slid to a halt outside, and a smiling Naomi beckoned me to join her. As I got in, and sat behind a bank of dials and twinkling lights that wouldn't have been out of place on the flight-deck of the Enterprise, and I wondered what on earth I was letting myself in for.

Her flat was one of several in an exclusive communal development in Hyde Park, set in very pleasant surroundings, and within minutes I was sitting in a comfortable lounge, while she disappeared off somewhere to find the promotional photographs.

"Have a look at these while I get some coffee and biscuits on the go, tell me what you think, and how I can improve on them".

They weren't too bad as photographs went, but didn't exhibit anywhere near the expertise or 'eye' I would have expected from a prestigious organisation using such luxurious vehicles.

When she returned with the coffee I said. "You certainly have got problems here, the flash hasn't got anywhere near the coverage of the subject to give you control, you need much more power, and really, several flash guns".

Over the next half-hour we went through several promotional layouts and quite a few photographs, but something was bothering me, there didn't seem to be any really good photographs leading to a finished result.

Was this a case of the company getting an employee to do the work 'on the cheap?' - I would hardly think so, so what the hell was prickling my senses?

As we had finished our coffee some time ago, she asked if I would like another before we finished, and I said yes, it was good natural coffee - we only used Nescafe at home, purely out of convenience, so this was a real treat.

In a relaxed manner we sat on the carpeted floor drinking coffee and discussing the multitude of problems encountered by single adults, whilst still coping with a busy job.

All too soon it was 2300 and I said I ought to be getting back, and if going to the Yard was a problem at this late hour, I could easily get a bus or taxi.

"No, that's no problem, I'll run you back, and perhaps we can meet again soon, if you're free?"

It was obvious from our conversation that her life style and mine were miles apart, she went ski-ing in Switzerland during the winter, and had lots of friends abroad for summer visits, while I had a demanding job to do, plus trying to raise a family under difficult circumstances, really, I felt our lives were quite irreconcilable.

# Chapter Twenty Seven

That week the IRA made themselves a bloody nuisance again with an incident in Kensington, whereby the terrorist had the bomb he was carrying explode, as he bent to place the device under a car.

As I was the late bomb-duty photographer at the Yard, I copped the incident, and being almost 'next door' was on the scene within twenty minutes.

Getting out of my van, I saw the ambulance taking the badly injured terrorist to hospital was about to leave, so I was able to get cracking and record the bomb damage straight away.

It didn't take long to photograph the damage to cars and property using the 5x4 - the rest of the scene would have to be done in daylight tomorrow, and I prepared to leave.

The senior anti-terrorist squad officer on the scene came over to my van and said. "I'd like you to attend St. Stephen's Hospital right away if you will, and record chummy's injuries before they start surgery.

He won't be going into the operating theatre for a little while yet I'm told, so you should have time to make it."

"I've only got the 5x4 tripod mounted camera you saw me using earlier, which isn't really suitable for theatre photography, I'll have to nip back to the Yard and get a hand-held camera to do the job properly. You'd better tell them I'll be as quick as I can, and should be there in about forty-five minutes".

Giving my van lots of wellie on the deserted night-time streets, I roared back to the Yard, grabbed a 6x6 Bronica and some film from stores, and hared off to the hospital, hoping I wasn't going to be too late.

Suitably masked and gowned I presented myself in theatre, and saw our bomber friend lying on a trolley next to the operating table.

A team of three hospital staff at the table turned as I entered, and one of them, presumably the chief surgeon spoke.

"Ah, ok. now you're here we can get started, if you take hold of a leg please, the four of us can lift him gently onto the operating table, then you can start your photography as we clean him up"

I took hold of his left ankle and calf, and lifted carefully with the others, and it was immediately obvious to me the leg was cold and dead, I reckoned he'd lose that one for sure.

As the team went to work, I recorded the extent of the man's injuries, which were pretty horrific, his right hand was missing, and most of his abdomen and thighs had been stripped of flesh.

You certainly didn't stand that close to an exploding bomb and walk away laughing every day of the week!

As soon as I had done my bit, I left the theatre and drove back to the yard, thinking it was a dollop of justice for once, the terrorist getting exactly what he had hoped to dish out to others. Tough titty!

Months later, minus a hand and a leg he went for trial at the Old Bailey, and was sentenced to a lengthy term of imprisonment and I must say, I cheered.

Pity a few more of the IRA didn't blow themselves up like that, it might be a salutary lesson to the bastards!

Although I wasn't involved in the job, the IRA had another go at demoralising London, when they exploded a bomb at Chelsea barracks in early October, killing two and injuring dozens of bystanders.

Although bomb explosions among civilians have a devastating effect, I felt the IRA didn't understand British stoicism one little bit, if they thought terrorism would change people's views of their supposed cause.

Scenes of crime fully occupied my days at work, and although there were only so many variations on a theme, there was the odd time when I thought, 'Crikey, I've never even thought of that!'

One such time came in the company of several officers when raiding a brothel in west London at about 2000hrs.

Bursting in with a 35mm camera on motor-drive coupled to the faithful old Mecablitz flash, I recorded everything that presented itself.

In rapid succession I photographed various people in bed with each other, a room containing several people whom I supposed were male, but kitted out as hard-faced females, and another room where a couple of women were found sporting large false penises, the size of which would give most men a real inferiority complex!

Of course this wasn't the first time I had photographed a 'house of delights' and it certainly wouldn't be the last, but this one took the ruddy biscuit.

I marvelled at the superbly equipped 'perversion' room, complete with boxes of whips, rods, ropes, masks, rubber suits, whipping rack, knave-stock, and drawers full of assorted black and pink penises, it was certainly rather mind boggling!

One small room, illuminated by dull red light, and furnished with red furniture was optically mind-boggling to work in, and difficult, even when using the wide-angle lens and flash, but I suppose the jazzy effect, along with all the physical paraphernalia, gave the place its kinky appeal!

Christmas '81 came and went, during which time I met an attractive lady called Lisa, and as we appeared to have rather a lot of interests in common, decided to see each other, as and when we could.

Work was making heavy demands just then, and this, coupled with running a home and family, plus seeing Lisa, didn't leave me much time for bird photography.

So far, I hadn't even had the time to experiment with the first high-speed flash unit my brother Greg had designed and built for me.

A year ago I had said to Greg 'Build me a flashgun that goes off in 1/10,000sec, recycles in less than ten seconds, and has a 100 Joules output, working off a twelve volt battery'.

After doing some quick sums, he replied tersely 'It can't be done' but a year later, had somehow managed it, and here it was, waiting for me to try out.

Although the flash unit was a bit larger than I wanted - 10" x 8" and 6" deep, it put out 120 joules of power at a 1/30,000 sec, and re-cycled in about eight seconds, a formidable piece of equipment indeed!

It had its flash tube mounted directly onto the capacitor, cutting out the need for those potentially lethal connecting cables, while the power was generated from a battery via a transformer to produce the hefty 3Kv.the capacitor stored.

All I had to do now, was get another two units to go with it, and I was away, but at £500 a throw for components, plus Greg's time to build them, it was all pretty expensive!

One day, returning to the Yard from East Ham where I had been doing a particularly nasty GBH. I had just reached the Embankment by Blackfriars, when I got a call over the air to go immediately to Hyde Park.

There I was to join Alan C. who was dealing with a large bomb which had gone off, killing several Royal Cavalry officers and their horses.

Stamping the throttle to the floor, I was on the scene in about ten minutes, to be greeted by a scene of utter carnage and horror.

I had been in the job twenty five years now, and had seen pretty well everything crime-wise from A to Z, but the sight of so many horses lying in the road, blown to pieces, with piles of intestines and gallons of blood spread everywhere, plus the torn clothing and bodily remains of men, made a scene of such demonic madness, you couldn't attribute such an atrocity to human beings.

Alan C. and I worked mechanically through the scene in the silence of the park, recording everything of significance we could find.

The minute we were finished however, lorries and lifting cranes moved in, to drag the huge carcasses off the road, and our broom-sweepers began their arduous task of collecting every piece of debris for future forensic examination.

At this point a dull explosion rent the air - it was obviously another bomb going off somewhere, and within minutes a message over our radio asked for assistance in Regents Park, where a bomb had exploded in a bandstand, killing several soldier musicians.

"If you get over there and start work" said Alan C. "I'll arrange for someone to come out from the Yard and assist you, I've used all my film here and can't help, so I'll get back and get it processed, ok?"

Again, foot to the floor, the poor old mini roared out of Hyde Park, bound for God knows what in Regent's Park.

All it wants now is for a third bomb to go off, and we'll be in the cacky-poo for sure!

The sight which greeted me in Regent's Park was, if anything, more macabre than the one in Hyde Park.

This time lots of people had been blown to bits, and huge chunks of them lay scattered around the damaged bandstand amongst the obscenely twisted musical instruments and metal chairs.

I suppose I had been working for about half an hour when our film unit arrived, and began covering the scene in far greater detail than I ever could with my stills camera. It was a good job it was a bright day with plenty of light for our photography.

Having recorded everything I thought relevant, I let the mortuary people get started, picking up the hundreds of pieces of flesh and bone, arms and legs, even half torsos that littered the bandstand area. Sooner them than me!

A Superintendent walked over to where I was packing up my gear and said "We believe there might be some bodily or even forensically important debris on the bandstand roof."

"If I get the helicopter, which is nearby to drop in, can you do some close shots of it for me, we can't see anything from down here"

Within minutes India 99 touched down a few yards away, and I went over and got in. I knew the crew from countless flights we had made together in the past, and was familiar with the co-operation necessary to get the best from any given situation.

"I'd like you to slowly circle the bandstand from about a hundred feet altitude if you can" I said to the observer who was on intercom with the pilot - I hadn't had time to get a headset on.

"If there's nothing of importance lying on the roof, the shots will show the effect of the explosion, due to the debris on the ground, so the flight won't be wasted"

We were soon in position, and I experienced a moment of sheer cold panic when I realised there were only two shots left on the Bronica GS magazine from the earlier ground shots.

Fortunately though, whenever I went 'walkabouts' with a hand-held camera, I had adopted the habit of putting a couple of films into my trousers pocket, and I did a hasty run off of the film in the camera, before loading a new film.

There was very little on the bandstand roof, but the dispersion of debris and bodily remains, told a poignant tale of the force of the explosion. It was a nasty job.

About this time, I was involved with Garry B. in recording the actions of some highly dangerous paedophiles and their prey, working closely with a team of half a dozen officers from Tottenham Court Rd. nick.

We had the use of certain premises overlooking the insidiously named 'meat-rack'- the public safety railings on the north side of Piccadilly circus, where the rent boys plied their harrowing trade. Another location was a huge disused theatre in Victoria, overlooking a dingy café where rent boys and their clients could be observed from only a few yards distance.

We would normally be in position by late afternoon, and prepared to stay with cameras trained on the locations until midnight or later, building up a photographic dossier of who met whom.

Although it would have been easier for us to use an image intensifier coupled to a long focal-length lens to see what was going on, Garry and I found it far better definition-wise, to uprate our film as necessary and develop accordingly.

It wasn't unusual for us to push 800ASA film to 6400ASA or beyond, resulting in development times that allowed us to brew a cup of tea and have a sarnie whilst waiting!

The results when printed carefully, were, we felt far superior to those obtained by other means.

After a few weeks observation, Garry and I were as aware of our targets' behaviour patterns as the officers we were working with, and were able to respond to calls from 'trackers' to photograph the paedophiles as and when they moved around London.

On one such jaunt, I was whisked from Tower Bridge where I was working on a robbery, to Battersea Park, where one of the trackers had followed the main target, his associate and two boys in their car, which had just broken down in the roadway.

Target 2. was lying underneath the car, trying to fix whatever was wrong with it, while two of the rent boys sat on the grass nearby watching.

Target 1. meanwhile, had wandered off across the grass, and was sitting on a public bench by the river, dozing in the warm sunshine.

"I want some shots of Target 2. with the boys for evidence of association when we go to court, and it would be nice if we could get some good close-ups of Target 1. while you're at it."

Can you do that?" enquired D/I. H.

I had a Nikon fitted with an 80 - 200 zoom lens, and although the nearest trees and shrubbery were about 30 yards from the car, I felt if I did a bit of careful stalking through the undergrowth, I could get a good angle on Target 2. with the boys.

I must say it felt quite funny moving towards the group, just as though I was stalking some animal or bird for myself at the weekend, and after about five minutes I had a dozen shots of the three together, especially when 2. called the boys over to give him a hand with something by the door.

Returning to the D/I. I said "There's no way I'm going to get a covert shot of Target 1. I'll take the bull by the horns, and go over there and photograph him the same time as I take some shots of the river, just keep an eye on me from a distance, in case things go wrong"

Circling back, I approached the group from the roadway, taking a couple of shots of the road to show their position, before angling off across the grass towards our friend T1. I took a couple of scenic shots of the river looking towards Westminster, as any clicking tourist might do, noting that T1. took no notice of me whatever.

Stepping back a few yards as if to compose the shot a little better, I zoomed the lens to maximum focal length, giving me a lovely head and shoulders of T1. on the edge of the film.

I clicked the shutter again just for effect, before centring my man for a couple of mug-shots, checking that he took no notice of me whilst I worked.

"Nice day, and a lovely view of the river" I said to T1. but all I got was a mumbled reply, before he turned and looked the other way.

Never mind, I had the mug shots we wanted, and that's all that mattered just then.

Returning to the car, the D/I. said to me "Well, I suppose that's one way of doing it, what on earth did you say to target 1. wish him a happy bloody birthday or something?"

"You could say that" I replied, and we all dived back to Tower Bridge for lunch.

It wasn't long before we had enough evidence to get a search warrant for T1's address, which turned out to be a right stinker.

Filth and rubbish lay ankle deep everywhere, accompanied by that odour of urine and stale cheese which seems to pervade such horrible dwellings.

As soon as I had finished my photography, the unfortunate search team began their rotten job of stripping the place from top to bottom, in their search for evidence, you never knew what you might turn up in a dump like this.

As with a lot of the jobs you get to do, that was the last active photography concerning that case I undertook, and it was only much later after giving evidence in court, I learned the main defendants got six years imprisonment each, which of course means the obnoxious bastards would be out and about again in three or four years.

I didn't think that was half long enough, and felt they needed castration or hanging, I felt from my scant experience, these scum never give up preying on kids.

For the last year or so I had been getting occasional attacks of giddiness, when everything seemed to go round and round, and after one particularly nasty session, I decided to see the quack.

After hearing my tale of woe, he sent me of to St. Thomas' hospital in Westminster for tests, as he had no idea what the problem might be. The hospital staff spent a couple of days checking this, that and a lot of the other, before the doc finally said "We have a German lady professor here who has heard of your problem, and wants to do a special test on you, would you agree to that?"

Naturally I said yes, but had I known what was involved, I might well have declined. The next day, without breakfast, I was wheeled down to the basement, and in a cold, white-tiled room, asked to get onto a mortuary-like slab, and covered closely with a heavy rubber apron.

Suddenly into view came a middle-aged woman wearing rimless specs, who, staring down at my bewildered face, said in a heavily accented voice "I vant you to fix your gaze on zat light in zer ceiling, vhile I introduce hot and cold vater alternately into your ears, ok?"

In earlier years I had been the recipient of an ear-wax clean by my GP using a water squeezer, but this was something else!

As I fixed my gaze intently on the light bulb, a horrendous roar filled my head as ice-cold water surged into my eardrum from a rubber hose, and as though I was in the centre of a shrieking hurricane, the world began to revolve like a crazy merry go-round.

"Now zer hot Vater!" she warned, and a terrible nausea gripped my stomach as the room revolved faster and faster in a maelstrom of noise, and I was on the edge of passing out.

"Ok, now zer uzzer ear" and away we went again, producing the same giddy roundabout, followed by the feeling of terrible nausea as my eyes lost their focus on the ceiling light.

There's no doubt about it" she said as I came to. "It's a classic case of Meniere's syndrome, have any of your family ever suffered from zis?"

"Yes" I answered groggily "My mother has had these symptoms for years"

"Vell you also have it, probably brought on by some kind of stress, you'll have to learn to take things a bit easier, zere's no known cure for it"

And with that she was away, leaving me to be dried off, and wheeled back to the ward, feeling as sick as a dog.

Christmas 1982 wasn't one of the best I can remember, it wasn't easy trying to be festive in both the family home, and at Lisa's one after the other, and things felt a bit contrived, maybe this year though, things might improve.

Although I was still riding my Kawasaki 175 to work each day, I felt the need to update my normal mode of transport from the totally unsuitable Sierra estate I presently ran, and plonked for a snappy Ford XR2.

This delightful little car was quite capable of breaching the ton on a suitable stretch of road, and gave me the ludicrous feeling of being a carefree bachelor all over again!

Every few weeks or so, I made the trip down to Yelverton in Devon to see mum and Dad, sometimes covering the journey each way the same day. On one naughty occasion I left the clock tower in the centre of Plymouth at 1800hrs, and by putting my foot down, passed Big-Ben in Parliament square at 2130, AND I didn't use the M4 motorway!

That little car certainly had oomph, and drove like a dream.

At work, I continued to keep my head down and get on with scenes of crime, I was enjoying myself and getting a reasonable amount of overtime in, so I left the upper echelon power struggles to those that were interested in them, I certainly got less hassle that way!

There was no doubt the lack of scenes of crime video output was giving some cause for departmental concern. Ever since my CS gas film, we had sported a thriving film production unit, making instructional and visual aid presentations by the ton.

Something though, had gone sadly wrong scenes of crime video, but what was it?

I reckoned I had the answer to that one, but didn't make my thoughts public, but if I HAD been asked, I would have said they'd given the equipment to the wrong men.

You can't drive round London all day taking stills photos and leave the video kit stuck in its case. You had to get out and SELL the service, and that's just what the two incumbents hadn't been doing!

There must have been some serious head-scratching amongst the 'brains' of the section, because out of the blue I was told to get myself onto a week-long video course run by Sony at Staines, and familiarise myself thoroughly with video production techniques. All in a week?

The Sony course was quite an eye opener for someone like myself who had only picked up a scanty knowledge of video camera operation by talking to other users, and I was thrown in at the deep end using equipment and studio techniques I hadn't really appreciated existed until then!

We were given short film-making projects to script and complete in a day, leaving the final result to be analysed by the course instructor in the evening, and to me it was all rather hectic and demanding.

At the completion of the course, I wrote my report to the head of department, outlining what I had achieved etc; and sat back to await the results. Not a lot happened.

Two months later though, having gone back to scenes of crime and virtually forgotten about the Sony course, I was asked to present myself at the office forthwith, and pick up an issue of new video equipment.

I was being given the opportunity to see what kind of fist I might make of things at scenes of crime. Hallelujah!

The snag now of course was I was hoist on my own petard.

As a working Principal on area, and, like my contemporaries in charge of five staff covering everything on our patch, I had been used to doing my share of the jobs, no matter what they were.

Now though, despite our high workload, I had to accomplish both stills and video, depending on the type of job in hand.

My feelings had always been that one person couldn't properly apply both disciplines satisfactorily at one scene of crime, so I devised a system whereby I would video the whole scene from top to bottom in general detail, showing the relationship of one object to another, then cover just the prime scene of the incident with stills, for best record.

My 'issue' camera was a run of the mill Panasonic KY-1900, a single chip, low-band animal, not readily given to producing David Lean masterpieces, but it did give me an 'in' to the world of electronic imaging relating to crime, which seemed to me the way we ought to go in the future.

There were of course various obstacles to be overcome, the shot footage could not be edited to produce a 'tidy' result - the camera master could be demanded to be seen by the defence, and be compared with the submitted court copy.

Any observed edits could be used to insinuate other alterations or omissions of evidence, and cause the film to be thrown out of court.

With a microphone attached to the camera it was also essential to remind officers of the need for silence whilst filming, but even so, the odd juicy remark would be painfully clear on the master, and could only be hidden by leaving the sound track un-copied at that particular point!

There was also the matter of the sheer physical time it took to cover the scene twice, once for video, and again for stills, especially if the pathologist was jumping up and down at the mortuary, waiting for his body to arrive.

It would all take time to sort out satisfactorily.

In July I got my first chance to use the video gear in earnest at a nasty house fire in Ilford, where a woman and her three children had been burned to death. If we could prove arson, the main suspect, the husband, could be charged with murder, so it was a good one to start with.

There is no doubt, that to cover an arson at any location by means of stills photography, is a pain in the butt job, requiring careful work, lots of photographs, and lots and lots of flash.

The latter is often a real trial, as a jet-black room with very little daylight coming in, plus running water from our friends the fire service, soaks up all the light you throw at it, and more.

The final result isn't always as good as you might expect either.

Video would help change all that.

With a 100watt lamp clipped to the top, and the camera 'gain' wound up to 18db, a satisfactory overall impression of the fire scene could be achieved quite easily, leaving the detailed work to be done in close-up by the stills camera and flash.

A nasty arson now became something one could master with comparative ease, instead of the demanding ogre it had previously been.

Working closely with the Fire Investigation unit over the next two days, I was able to produce a record of their findings in detail.

It was very satisfying to video-record classical burning patterns on the floorboards, showing that cooking oil had been used to accelerate the fire, thus proving arson.

Subsequently, this was the first police video ever to appear at Crown Court as evidence, and we had to install a VCR player and television screens for the Judge, Counsel and Jury to view the prosecution's film.

It went down a real treat, and the defendant was found guilty.

Earlier, I had circulated hand-outs throughout my patch, which covered from the City along the Thames to Rainham, Essex, up to Potter's Bar and back to the City again, announcing that video filming at scenes of crime had started, but stressing that only serious crimes would be undertaken at present.

If the scheme really took off, there was no telling how the new medium might be used, it had pro's and cons, just like any other system.

Within a week I landed another serious arson, this time at St. Katherine's Dock, and I suspected that this was probably due to the delight our Fire Investigation branch expressed with the Ilford arson result.

I just hoped we might begin to branch out into something other than fires!

A week later I was called to the scene of a complicated fraud at Aveley in Essex, and on the second day of the investigation it was suggested that aerial photographs would be of great assistance in the enquiry, could I manage that?

The resulting job, complete with aerial video shot from India 99, the force helicopter, was received enthusiastically by the officer in the case, and I began to feel that there was even a place for aerial video to supplement the quality stills we had always produced.

On my birthday in August, I copped the murder of Robert Arne the American film actor, victim of a nasty homosexual slaying. I was able to demonstrate the ability of the video camera to provide a thorough overall picture of the murder scene, including several rooms and floors, without the 'gaps' inherent in a normal series of stills photographs, no matter how comprehensively they might be taken.

Further kudos was gained when I was able to nip back to the section, run off a quick copy of the video, and bring it back for viewing by the murder incident room team within two hours.

They couldn't believe they could view the scene of the murder in such detail without actually going there themselves.

We certainly sold ourselves that night!

Over the next couple of months I video-filmed four murder scenes, three more arsons, a rape scene, a brothel raid and an illegal drinking club raid.

It was all getting delightfully busy.

As I collected the various pieces of equipment needed to cope with the growing variety of jobs I was getting, the inside of my poor old mini began to resemble a boot sale.

It was obvious I would need to make a serious case for a much larger vehicle.

Over the months I had managed to get a VCR player and monitor of my own, which allowed me to demonstrate to the investigating team just what I had recorded at the scene, and through some fancy string pulling, also managed to acquire a couple of 'red-hat' 500watt lights and a petrol driven generator, to provide my own lighting.

All this extra gear, plus the stills and video equipment I normally carried, tended to drive the little mini to its knees!

At the end of November that year, just as dawn was breaking, I found myself waiting at a graveside in Bromley, Kent, where an exhumation was about to take place.

The reason for our early arrival was that certain religious convictions required the body to be re-buried before sunset, and we had to give the pathologist as much scope as possible to complete his second post mortem in time.

It was a good job I had been able to get hold of the 'red-hat' lights and generator, without them the job in the middle of the deserted cemetery would have been impossible.

I could have dragged the electrical engineers out of bed with their generator lorry, which may, or may not have been able to get to the remote spot where the grave was located, but in the main, I felt it better to be self-reliant.

The body was carefully exhumed, and we all went off to the mortuary, where the video proved ideal for showing every stage of the opening-up procedure, plus the verbal remarks of the pathologist as he worked.

It was the second time I had done a job where video alone was responsible for recording the information on an important case, and I wondered what procedural bugaboos might come to light as this particular job went along.

I was getting a bit of a reputation as 'Mr. Video' at most of the nicks I visited, but could obviously see, and well understand, the lack of trust many officers had, when told they wouldn't have a set of photographs in their hands for every crime.

After my video-filming, they would have to find a VCR to play my copy tape on, and view it on a TV screen.

"Do you really think the job is going to find the money to put VCRs into Divisional HQ's then?" I was often asked, and I assured my critics as best I could, that without some form of viewing video evidence when investigating a serious crime, officers would be at a distinct disadvantage, especially when possibly charging a defendant.

Station VCRs had to come.

At the end of January I was called to the scene of a very nasty murder involving some Vietnamese 'boat-people' in a typical three-storey block of flats off Stanway St. N1.

It was as one might expect, quite grotty location to work in.

I arrived a few minutes after Peter Palmer one of our photographers had started work, and was greeted by D/Supt. Paddy P. a huge wrestler of a man with a strong Irish accent.

"Morning guv'nor, Alan Parker SO3. Video, this looks a nasty one"

"What the hell do you want, I've already got a photographer here, I don't need you to clutter up the scene, go away"

I was well aware of Paddy P's. reputation for bluntness from the odd contact in the past, but this greeting had a bit more than the usual put down, but I decided to brazen it out.

"I've come to produce video coverage of the scene in conjunction with the stills photographer, it's a new addition to the service, and I have been told to attend"

"I already have all the services I need, Lab.liaison, photographic and fingerprints,

I don't need you to slow things down, and make us even later with the pathologist, buzz off"

"Nevertheless guv'nor, those are my instructions from the head of SO3. (not QUITE true) and I now have to record every scene of serious crime on video, because within a few years you won't have prints to look at, you'll only have a video"

His face went even redder than before, and I thought he would explode.

"Well hurry up and get on with it then, but if you cause me any delay with the pathologist I'll see you pay for it!" and he stormed off down the landing muttering to himself.

I hadn't exactly made a friend there!

Working with Peter, I managed to do the job without causing too much delay, and they all trailed off happily to the mortuary.

I wasn't going to push my luck by attending there just now, the crime scene video would have to do this time!

In early April I was asked to go to Barking, and video officers searching a large area of wasteland, where bodies of two missing men were expected to be found.

I spent the whole morning with them, without anything unusual coming to light, when a CID Sgt. rushed over to tell us we were wanted at the Kaleli restaurant opposite Barking railway station. Here, he said was the actual place the missing men had been murdered.

On arrival at the scene, I noticed the restaurant looked quite clean and tidy, certainly not the obvious scene of a murder, perhaps the men had been topped in the kitchen?

No, said one of the officers, a scared witness said they had been cut down with a sword, and killed just inside the main door. There was even a stab-hole in an overhead wooden beam, where the point of the sword had penetrated during the upswing of the killer's arm.

How come the place looked so clean and respectable then, if two murders had recently taken place?

Closer investigation showed the whole ground floor had been re-papered between the old wooden Tudor uprights in a white and yellow patterned wallpaper, so the blood stains, if any, were apparently underneath!

Likewise the floor had been carefully washed and cleaned, but you just can't hide traces of blood in small cracks between the tiles, and a chemical test with a paper probe soon showed the presence of human blood.

"Ok. everyone out!" said the guv'nor "I want you Alan, to video this place from top to bottom in great detail, before I get Lab. liaison to go over it with a fine toothcomb. After that I hope we can find a way to get this new wallpaper off, I want to see what's going on underneath!"

With new evidence slowly coming in, we were eventually given an address on the old A13 near Ford's, from where it was understood, a sword used to commit the murders had been taken.

The place was in fact a small club and restaurant, and along its walls were displayed various antique looking guns and swords.

One of the display bays had only its two supporting hooks left, the weapon itself was ominously missing, but the staff assured us it had previously contained a sword.

Not a lot more came to light that day, but rumours were rife, the dismembered bodies were sealed in 50 gallon drums and dumped off the end of Ford's Thames-side jetty.

They had been burned by the Mayesbrook, a little stream that ran under the A13 into the river Roding.

They were under water in the docks near Blackwall tunnel.

But where were they really hidden?

Nobody seemed to know for sure.

The next day I was back at the restaurant at dawn - I had been told over the phone, we had a good lead where the bodies were really hidden, and we had to move quickly.

They were, someone alleged, buried in the foundations of a recently built house extension in Blake Ave, Barking, and we were to go there, surprise the occupants, and dig up their extension's concrete floor.

There was the usual shouting and hassle one would expect from occupants roused at dawn by several business-like Police officers hammering on the doors, but we soon had the place to ourselves, and the lads examined everything minutely for clues as to what might have gone on.

The house was quite well furnished and maintained, but the back garden was an absolute tip. Apart from an extremely large, new timber shed on its fresh concrete base, the place was cluttered with junk left over from numerous building jobs.

The owner seemed to be running a small building business, and piles of rubbish brought home on his truck had accumulated throughout the whole sixty feet of back garden, leaving very little clear space for anything.

"Before anyone starts doing anything at all" I suggested to the D/I. "I want to video the place from top to bottom, we don't want any allegations of damage by police, except that which we have to do to locate the bodies. So if you could all disappear for about twenty minutes I'd really appreciate it"

I soon had the interior of the house covered, and asked a couple of the lads back in to remove the carpet covering the extension floor, to expose the wooden planking underneath.

I then recorded their actions as they prised up the floorboards to expose the new concrete foundations under those.

This was going to be a long old job.

While the chaps were waiting for the heavy mob and their pneumatic drills to be set up, I went into the back garden and filmed the outside of the extension base, which, due to the slope of the garden was at this point, about five feet thick. I followed this up by filming the rest of the garden from all angles, just in case something came to light there later on.

There is no doubt this is where video scores hands down over conventional stills photography. I would have been there for ever and a day photographing that lot, not to mention the mountain of colour printing the end result would have required.

And what would a jury have made of those innumerable photos?

I reckon they would have given up after the first dozen shots and gone to sleep!

It was such a nice day, I sat in the sunshine drinking a mug of tea one of the lads had made, listening to the merry clatter of road drills as the heavy mob blasted their way through the concrete floor. The way stuff was coming out of there, I hoped like hell they found something, otherwise we'd all be in schtook!

In the meantime, other lads had carefully unbolted the large new shed at the bottom of the garden, and stacked it against the fence, before demolishing its newly laid concrete base.

You never knew where the bodies might be hidden in a place like this!

When the last piece of shed base was lifted, and no sign of interment found, I began to have the feeling we might be on a bummer, if so, the Commissioner was going to have a heavy bill for damage on this one - and that could be embarrassing!

Returning once more to the drillers in the extension, I was surprised to see they had already got down to the clay and earth under the concrete, and a horrible smell wafted forth, had they struck gold so to speak?

The dog section were brought in, and the place given a thorough going over, but no, the smell came from the goo seeping below the topsoil from the nearby Mayesbrook stream. There was nothing for us here.

On waste ground bordering the stream, a partly burned out Ford pick-up sat rather forlornly - someone suggested it had been recently used by the owner whose property we were now searching - would I record it fully, prior to its removal to the Met.lab. for examination?

The removal vehicle was due almost anytime.

I had just completed filming the interior of the Ford, when a tow truck appeared, reversing along the riverbank towards the pick up, with the intention no doubt of hooking up the front end and hauling it away.

As I had just taken great care to record in detail the under chassis accumulation of peculiar-looking red shale, plus great blocks of the stuff under the wheel arches, I watched closely to see what our friends in the transport section were about to do.

The driver's mate got out and walked to the back of his tow-truck, and began to release the towing bar that would carry the front end of the pick-up, leaving the rear wheels to trundle along the road.

"I hope you're not thinking of towing this vehicle along the road to the Laboratory are you? Because if you are, you will dislodge all the mud and rubbish from underneath, which could be vital in determining where this vehicle has been driven lately"

"You're ruddy well joking aren't you mate?" said the driver.

"No I'm not, and if it means you have to go back to Lambeth for a low-loader, that's what you'll have to do"

"Isn't it bleedin'alright?" growled the driver's mate. "Why the hell didn't somebody tell us instead of wasting our flippin' time, it'll be an hour at least before we're back here again, I dunno" and off they went.

I informed the D/I. what I had done, but he seemed to have other things on his mind just then.

The sequel to this little saga was that the lab. did identify the peculiar soil under the chassis of the pick-up, and in conjunction with local CID, traced it to a specific loading yard near the Thames at Woolwich.

Would it turn out to be an important lead in our search for the missing bodies?

A few weeks after submitting the finished video to the murder squad, I received a call from the Yard's solicitors branch, asking if one of their senior staff could come and see me, concerning allegations of serious damage to property and belongings, sustained by the owner of Blake Ave. Barking.

"What can you tell me about what you personally saw at this address" the solicitor asked.

"This is a list of damaged property submitted by the complainant.

Its very detailed indeed. In fact it adds up to quite a few thousand pounds in damages over and above that incurred by digging"

"I can do better than tell you, I can show you, I presume you haven't seen the video I made of the place during the investigation?"

"No, I didn't even know one existed, I thought perhaps some ordinary photographs had been taken, but as no bodies had been found, they hadn't been printed"

I got a working copy of the video from the files, and put it on the VCR for him to see, watching his reactions as the scenario unfolded. Even I thought it was pretty comprehensive.

"Tell me, why did you think it necessary to cover the place in such detail, even that sea of rubbish described here as an attractive garden?"

"I felt that having video equipment to cover the scene as I usually do, and knowing what a horrendous case it would have been had we found the bodies in situ, I ought to do it"

"Are you available the day after tomorrow, at ten o'clock, to show this video when I ask you? The complainant and his solicitor want to hear our reactions to their claim, and as they obviously don't know about the video, it should be quite educational"

At the appointed time, the complainant and his brief arrived and sat down to discuss with our solicitor the basis for their claim, and their abhorrence of the conduct of Police officers who invaded the complainants' home and committed such terrible damage.

The brief then proceeded to go through his list, which described stuff I hadn't been aware of, ending with ' And damage to the recently laid green lawn and water fountain, which surely warranted no such attention at all'

I was gob-smacked - green lawn, water fountain, what bloody water fountain for goodness sake?

"May I stop you there" said our solicitor, "And show you some video film taken by our cameraman, Mr. Parker here, prior to police commencing any search of the premises whatsoever"

At his cue I rolled the video, and the brief's face was a picture to see as the camera panned slowly round the 'garden' and its terrible piles of rubbish.

The brief turned to his client and said in cold fury "You led me to believe that substantial damage had been done to your property by police, and it is patently not so, you and I have some hard talking to do"

Turning to our solicitor said, "Would it be possible for us to be alone for a few minutes please?"

Our solicitor nodded to me, and we left the room, I almost laughed out loud, what a farce, they'd been really shot up the arse by proper procedure, and I was quite chuffed.

Later our solicitor said to me "If only more of these jobs could be resolved so easily. Its nice to win the odd one now and again, well done, you've saved the Commissioner your year's wages at least"

Two weeks after the sword murders hit the press, the Station Officer at Harold Hill Police station was rudely awakened by something being thrown through the front doors into the foyer.

At 0600hrs on a Sunday morning that definitely wasn't funny!

Roused into action by the sound of raucous laughter, and the screech of squealing car tyres, he came round the counter to find a filthy sack tied with string on the floor, next to the public counter.

Gingerly cutting the string with scissors, he looked inside, to find two grotty human skulls grinning back at him, plus a note saying the coppers now had the missing heads they were looking for!

Despite it being Sunday, the pathologist and other interested parties were soon on the scene examining the nasty present, but came to the conclusion they were very old specimens, no doubt stolen from some cemetery or other.

I thought it quite funny that someone had gone to such lengths just to set up the old Bill!

A month later I was driving along the Victoria embankment when a call came over the air for me to get to St. James' Sq. just off Pall Mall as soon as possible, a WPC had been shot near the Libyan embassy, and assistance was urgently required.

It only took a few minutes to get there, by which time armed police where in position behind trees in the square, pointing their guns towards the embassy, while in the road a WPC's hat lay forlornly at the point where she had been shot.

Police had commandeered some buildings on the corner of Charles II St. one of which was the Natwest bank, and as the firearms group and serious crime squad were already in attendance.

I showed my ID. and went in.

The situation was apparently that the occupants of the embassy from whence the shot had come, were all entrenched behind heavily curtained windows and weren't in communication with police.

It was essential that police recorded everyone who showed themselves at doors or windows, with a view to identifying the said occupants.

To that end I staked claim to a first floor office which had a view of the front of the embassy 30 yards away, but only if you stuck your head out of the window!

I quickly set up a Nikon with a 200mm lens and angled it out of the window in the vertical format, so I could see through the viewfinder without sticking too much of my bonce out of the window.

That way we could at least get something if the situation warranted it.

Within half an hour, other members of photographic arrived and we were able to set up the Sony DX3000 video camera, and view the scene on a monitor without the need to stick any heads out of the window at all, which pleased the firearms lads no end.

Ernie Whatmore, our boffin photographer had the bright idea of unscrewing a good quality mirror off the managing director's toilet wall, and fixing it to the office window with gaffer tape.

When the window was opened to about 45 degrees, a stills photographer could see into it, and record anyone showing themselves at the embassy, without appearing at the window himself.

It would then be a simple matter to reverse the image of any interesting faces we managed to capture, during printing.

Throughout the days we occupied the bank, little or no business appeared to get done, and I wondered just how much a jaunt like this cost those whose businesses depended on continual access to bank files and records?

At the eventual conclusion of the siege, it was arranged that Libyan embassy staff and occupants should walk out one by one to their waiting transport, and I asked if I could go to the corner of Duke of York St. accompanied by a marksman, and photograph each of them as they came along the pavement.

It would be the only chance we had of recording each of them full face, and in colour.

Using a convenient lamp-post as a shield, I clocked each person head and shoulders as they came towards me, including the canvas bags of documents they carried, written all over in Arabic characters.

No doubt someone in Special Branch could interpret those later.

Although from a photographic point of view it had been a successful coverage of a serious situation, the fact that a foreign national had murdered a police officer in England and got away with it, left a nasty taste in our mouths.

On a lighter note, a subsequent display put on by the bank staff in the foyer, shows amongst other exhibits, the director's toilet mirror, minus a corner, broken off when it fell from the window, stating the important part it had played in the collapse of the Libyan embassy siege!

# Chapter Twenty Eight

As the scenes of crime video facility became more widely known in the Met. I was asked to record a growing variety of jobs, some of which suited the medium ideally, while others showed the need for a close link between stills and video, it was horses for courses.

In the middle of May, I was asked to accompany officers from Dagenham into Epping Forest, although unfortunately, it wasn't on a bird-watching trip.

They were taking a man there to reconstruct his actions concerning a kiddie called Maria P. who had gone missing from outside her home in Dagenham some time earlier.

He had been identified when a second attempted abduction of a policeman's child in West London went wrong, and his car index number and type were taken.

A subsequent search of his home revealed photo evidence that he was indeed involved with other children, including the disappearance of Maria P. from Dagenham.

He eventually told police he had hidden Maria's clothes in a hollow tree on the edge of a road leading through Epping forest.

By dint of careful searching and not a little luck, the tree was located, and the clothing retrieved.

It turned out to be Maria's.

However, no evidence of her burial could be found, even though police and dogs scoured every inch of dense undergrowth within 150 yards of the hollow tree. Where was the body hidden?

After further serious questioning, the man agreed to show police where he had buried the child several weeks before, which was the reason for our present visit to Epping Forest.

The road through the forest was closed to all traffic, and the man brought handcuffed to the hollow tree to explain his previous actions.

I had been asked to record whatever we found if the man co-operated with police, and as he appeared to take no notice of me and my video camera, I began filming immediately he began explaining to officers exactly what he had done.

He described how he had dumped the child's clothing in the nearby tree, and then, talking all the while, moved off through heavy undergrowth in a shallow arc, re-tracing his steps towards an unseen spot in the forest.

After walking about 200yards he stopped and said "Yes it was about here, I remember burying her near a heavy branch like that one there, and although it was dark and the place ankle deep in water, this looks like the place"

I felt a loathing for the man that could easily have escalated to a point where I could have belted him one, he was so matter of fact about the whole tragic affair, it was unbelievable!

D/Supt.L in charge asked the man again in front of the camera if this was the place he had brought Maria P. and when he answered it was, he nodded to me, and led the man back to the waiting cars.

Now we had to start digging.

As usual, I recorded the whole area before any work was done, then Sandy Sanderson, our Lab.liaison Sgt. and several police officers moved in with marker tapes to define the examination trenches they would have to dig, in the hope of discovering the exact location of the body.

The first two trenches, a foot deep and several yards long revealed nothing except tangled roots and old rotting branches, but the third trench, a mere five feet from the spot indicated earlier by our man, revealed a shallow grave containing human remains.

We had found what we were looking for, and it was all well documented on video.

At that point we took a break - we had to wait for the pathologist to arrive and do his bit, so we went back to the road, where our man sat quietly between two officers in the back of a police car.

What if anything, was going through his mind?

A DC. I knew well, came over and asked how it was going at the grave, and I told him about the man's actions prior to our finding the body, and how unnaturally cool and detached he appeared to be, especially when recounting such a horrendous act.

"That's nothing. Do you know, that lousy stinking bastard says he came back here the following night, dug up the body, and committed necrophilia with it.

Can you really believe any human being would do that?

I agreed with him it must be the lowest of the low in human(?) behaviour, I just couldn't begin to come to terms with such actions, despite my years of seeing the very worst of human nature first hand.

Over the next few hours we worked carefully to retrieve the remains from the ground, which, after such a long time in the earth, had the consistency of soft cheese, and was very difficult to extricate.

We had to try and slide the whole lot onto a piece of hardboard edged into the grave, without losing any evidence, and I felt sure there must be a better way of tackling it than this.

Perhaps small hydraulic scoops on either side, that took the soil and everything in one go might be the answer?

The post mortem was a bit grim, and I had to admire the pathologist, and indeed all his kind, who readily dived in to the most revolting scenarios, to ascertain the cause of death, in the cause of so called justice.

During the first week of September, I arranged things with my daughter Ruth to be away at the Natural History Photographers' convention - held this year in Wells, Somerset, where I was to demonstrate Greg's new High-speed flash unit to my colleagues.

It was a very good meeting with Eric Hosking and all the top natural history photographers attending, and lots of superb photographs and slides were shown.

Arriving back home late Sunday afternoon, I was met by a distraught Ruth, who told me Dad had died that morning, and Mum wanted me down in Yelverton straight away, would I go?

Stopping only to grab a quick cup of tea, I roared off back the way I had just come, thinking that if I had been able to leave a contact number with Ruth, I could have been with mum already.

When I got to Yelverton I found a very distraught mum being comforted by aunt Kath from nearby Plymouth, and I arranged to stay over for a couple of days until better arrangements could be made.

My fears concerning something happening to either mum or dad while I was 250 miles away in London, had unfortunately come true.

Dad's funeral was a very sombre affair, the only light part I felt was that his four sons were there to carry his simple coffin into the little chapel for cremation.

Although I had done quite a few jobs for Tottenham nick over the years, the area known as Broadwater Farm, with its high population of blacks hadn't featured much in my workload, and I sometimes wondered why.

Some people suggested it was a sort of 'no-go' area for police unless they went in prepared for trouble, if so, that's why I probably didn't get to go there very often.

All that changed when I received a phone call from Keith Clark, our duty officer during the early hours of October 6th, telling me to get myself down to Tottenham nick pronto, where a policeman had just been killed.

The nick was a hive of riot police and press activity when I arrived, and it took some time to gain access, and find the Det.Ch.Supt in charge.

Apparently this job was a very nasty one.

According to one chap I spoke to, the indigenous population of the estate had been sparked into a confrontation with police, and vicious rioting had ensued.

Gangs had run wild, and fires started, which necessitated the attendance of the Fire Service, who in the process of doing their job, were attacked in turn, by the rioting mob.

In one violent confrontation, the firemen were attacked so violently, police were called in to give assistance and protection.

PC. Blakelock who had been helping protect one small fire-fighting group, was surrounded on the stairs to an upper floor, and repeatedly struck with various weapons, only being dragged clear by a very brave fireman.

The mob, both black and white, with teenage youngsters among them, scenting blood, renewed their attack on the fallen officer in a frenzy, stabbing and hacking his body with anything to hand.

One account reported the leading antagonist saying he wanted to hack off the officer's head with his machete, and parade it around the estate on a pole!

It had got that bad.

By serious use of riot shield teams containing our photographers, some semblance of order had been enforced, leaving the burning, rubble-filled streets at last, under police control.

Det.Ch.Supt.Melvin told me to get down to the scene as soon as possible, and make a start on recording whatever I could, of the serious situation.

He was about to send a message to patrolling riot officers, telling them to look out for me, and give me whatever protection and assistance I needed.

As I entered the estate, clouds of smoke billowed from innumerable burning cars, and a couple of houses still smouldered through gaping holes in their roofs.

It was like the aftermath of a terrible battle, and I was the only white civvy walking around the place!

It wasn't the best of times to start photography, the sun hadn't begun to lighten the early morning gloom yet, so I started by recording the scene of PC Blakelock's murder, recording some of the discarded knives, sticks and iron bars that had been used as weapons.

Whilst working, I heard the familiar sound of a rubbish collecting lorry operating at the base of a nearby rubbish chute, and also saw a couple of chaps with a 'Council of Harringay' truck, begin to hitch up a burnt out motor vehicle, prior to dragging it off the road.

Stopping what I was doing, I ran over to the two men and asked "What do you think you're doing with that vehicle?"

One of them replied, "We've been told to get down here by the woman who runs the Broadwater Community centre, and clear this lot away, they're blocking the road"

"Don't you know a police officer has been murdered here, and this whole area is a murder scene?

If you carry on doing anything at all, I shall photograph you for identification, and have you arrested for interfering with a scene of crime"

His mouth opened in surprise, and he took a few seconds before saying "Who are you then guv?"

"I'm a Scotland Yard forensic photographer, helping to investigate this murder, if you're not happy with that, stay where you are, and I'll call some police colleagues over the radio, and get them across to deal with you"

"There's no need for that" he said anxiously, "We were just told to come here and clear it all away, if you say we can't, then we'll clear off, come on Fred" and away they went.

I immediately got on the radio to Information room at the Yard, asking them to pass an urgent message to Det.Ch.Supt Melvin at Tottenham, telling him that evidence at the scene was being removed, and that council lorries were taking away domestic rubbish at this un-earthly hour too.

It could well be that we were losing vital evidence of weapons and clothing disposed earlier, down the rubbish chutes after the riot.

As I moved about the area, several cars full of blacks roared out of the estate, loaded to the gunnels with toot.

It may all have been quite innocent, and probably was, but there was no concerted effort by police to shut the area down, and impose a blockade on all movement, which I thought was a very bad mistake.

Throughout the morning I attended various premises, schools and cars, which had been looted and destroyed by fire, but it was becoming clearer by the minute, this wasn't one of your two day murder scenes, this job was going to take a long, long time.

To save the hassle of trying to centre the enquiry at Tottenham police station - which didn't have the room anyway, Southgate was taken over as the centre of operations, and the support services told to report there.

Initially I was asked to share the local Scenes of Crime Officers (SOCO) office, but being equipped with just a single-phone, and a system of working quite different from ours, I said it was impracticable.

I needed an office with extra power points for our equipment, plus a couple of phones, exclusively for photographic's use, that way we could function properly.

By the end of the day, the full import of the terrible riot became clear, and it was gratifying to hear that civilian photographers employed among the riot-shield officers at the centre of trouble, had done a magnificent job, recording hundreds of participants in the fierce fighting.

Unfortunately they had not got nearer than about a hundred yards to Keith Blakelock's murder scene, otherwise some very interesting faces may have been recorded there too.

Our three lads had apparently exposed thirty, 35mm films using their riot flash cameras, and we had close on 800 colour photographs in need of urgent perusal and classification.

While printing teams in the section began the mammoth task of printing a dozen off each of the 800 negatives, we at Southgate managed to appropriate and set up a 'witness album' room, where all the photographs taken during the riot could be properly displayed.

This was done so that local officers could try and identify people shown in the photographs, and build up a dossier of who did what, and when.

To make sure we had all the photographs on the films in the correct order, I asked for a couple of rolls of 8" wide prints to be delivered uncut.

This was to enable us to display them on the wall in one long strip, protected by a roll of clear acetate laid over the top.

On this acetate, officers could then fix small dot stickers over suspects, each of which was given a consecutive number, relating to the identification of that particular suspect.

In keeping with the rules of evidence, officers were only allowed to view the prints on their own, and the room plus its contents were secured at the end of each day, by a combination lock.

As information and identification concerning suspects became clear, squads of male and female officers were deputed to raid certain premises on the estate, in an attempt to arrest people shown in the photographs, and take possession of their clothing for forensic examination.

This was the first time in the history of policing anywhere in the world, that riot photographs were used to arrest suspects photographed at the scene of a serious disturbance.

These raids, starting on the 10th Oct, four days after the horrific murder, were scheduled to go down from 0600hrs onwards, accompanied by a police photographer, who would initially photograph the whole house from top to bottom BEFORE officers searched the place, and again afterwards to obviate any allegation of police damage after we had finished.

In the event of an officer finding clothes identified in the riot photographs, the location of the clothes would be photographed before they were removed, along with the suspect.

I devised a system of working, whereby a Pentax 6x7 was mounted on a tripod, with a Mecablitz flash fixed alongside, leaving me free to direct a second flash into any area needing extra illumination, whilst firing the camera.

The agreed system of working was that once we gained entry by persuasion and warrant, and in company with a Det.Insp. plus owner of the house if possible, I would start photography.

The first shot from the front door, would show the hallway to the kitchen, the next would cover the first room on the left from either end, leaving it free to be searched by the first members of the search team.

Then in succession I would photograph the kitchen - one shot each way, and the dining room, same again, before plonking upstairs to do the rest.

Once I had covered the three rooms up there - one shot either way again, I would go to the front door and re-load.

At that point I would have taken about thirteen colour neg shots, and gone through two rolls of film after doubling up.

Only an idiot takes one shot of anything in this game!

If suspect clothing or shoes were found, they would also have to be photographed in position before being bagged and taken away for forensic examination, consequently each house took about two hours to complete if things went smoothly. Some did, many didn't.

When the search was complete, I went round again, repeating all the room shots I had done before, marking the films, to separate them from the first shots taken.

The final hurrah, was to take a photograph of the DI. standing with the house owners at the front door, to show that we left in relative peace, and that the front door was undamaged.

It was a heavy photographic undertaking at each address, but one which was to pay great dividends in the months to come.

As soon as one address was completed, it was off to the next, so that by lunchtime we had usually got through three addresses.

Having got the drift the way things were going, I asked for a good number two, to help me with the demanding early morning raids.

That way we could cover more addresses quickly, and I was given Steve D. or 'Donkeymoke' as he was known, as my No.2, a little workhorse of a fella.

Because we didn't have the facility to process and print at Southgate, all our films were dealt with on a requisition order, and sent down to the section each day by courier.

When I got my first negatives back, it was painfully obvious a system would have to be devised, whereby I knew exactly what address I was looking at, as a mistake in allocating the photographs to the wrong address would be disastrous!

Because our hands were full with the camera and flashes whilst working, writing notes was impossible, so I asked for a couple of sound activated personal tape recorders.

On these we could describe certain items in the various rooms, which would tie up visually with the prints coming back from the section, thus cutting out unnecessary errors.

It didn't take long for the arrested suspects to start 'coughing' as to who was standing on their left or right in a particular photo, and the prospective list of addresses for us to hit, got longer and longer.

It was all very well getting up at 0430 to be at Southgate for the 0530 briefing, and then hitting the first address at 0600, and finishing the day at 1800, but the old brain soon began to lag a bit, and was obviously in need of a rest!

On the 17th October, a hit team and I went to Newlyn Rd. the address of a suspect identified from photographs carrying an offensive weapon in the vicinity of a blazing car.

When we arrived at the address, armed police were already in position, trying to gain access for an arms search, and a loud argument was going on between police and a woman at a first floor window.

Eventually armed police gained access, and searched the place for weapons, and finding none, declared it safe for us to enter.

As usual I went in first, with DI.K. alongside, and explained what we intended to do, hardly getting through to the occupants, due to the frantic screaming and shouting going on all around.

It was pure bedlam.

The woman of the house, dressed in her dressing gown, was gradually quieting down, and began to appreciate that we weren't going to tear the place apart. I explained that she could stand alongside me as I took the photographs, so she could see exactly what I was doing.

After I had completed downstairs, I re-loaded the camera whilst standing in the hallway, and glanced towards the kitchen.

There, the mother stood with several cups handy, making a pot of tea, so I took her photograph with the flash, and she made no objection whatever.

It could be useful later on to show that she was relaxed enough to make tea for people, in the event of a claim for police damage or bad behaviour.

Leaving the search team to get on with the ground floor, I went upstairs unaccompanied, and immediately ran into a barrage of verbal abuse from a young teenage girl in her bedroom.

She trotted out the usual nonsense about racist oppression by police, human rights, and all the lefty rhubarb that goes with young student types, but I ignored her and carried on with the other rooms first.

I didn't need that sort of ear-bending just then.

Finally I came to her room, and asked if she would step outside for a minute while I took a couple of shots.

At that she exploded with "The last lot who came in here broke my wardrobe door off, look at the way its hanging, I bet you won't do anything about that!"

"Quite wrong lady" I replied. "I have every intention of recording anything I see in the way of damage, that's part of the reason for my photography, so if you let me in, I'll get cracking, and be out of your way"

With very bad grace, she reluctantly left the room, and I covered the place with two shots, including the damaged door.

On closer examination, I could see the detached bottom hinge damage was of long standing, there was no sign of either screws or new wood splinters on the floor.

I reckon the door had come adrift whilst being opened by the armed search team in the course of their search, and they hadn't been able to close it.

I had just left her room, and was standing on the landing outside re-winding my film, when I suddenly heard a thunderous crash of feet on the stairs, and a black man pounded into view.

"What the fuggin' hell is going on man, what are you doing here?"

From somewhere below came the mother's voice, explaining what was happening, and I began to open my mouth in explanation too, when he exploded into action.

Bellowing in blind anger, he lunged towards me and grabbed the camera and tripod saying "Get this lot out of here!" and threw the whole lot towards the head of the stairs.

Somehow I managed to catch it as it hit the wall, saving it from going down the stairs, at the same time shouting for assistance to the lads below.

Several uniform officers rushed up to assist me, trying to calm the man down, but this only seemed to make him worse, and they were forced to use arm-locks, and bundle him forcefully downstairs.

There was no doubt he was really going bolo, and it took several more officers to pin him down and put the cuffs on, before taking him away.

Once some semblance of order was established, the DI. asked the occupants to accompany us to the front door, so I could photograph police leaving with the occupants present, plus of course the front door, showing no signs of forced entry or damage.

If the rest of the searches were going to be as hairy as this one, we were in for a rough ride!

During the rest of that October, searches on suspects addresses' continued on a daily basis, sometimes three or four being 'hit' at the same time, causing us severe problems in attending.

To cover this situation, the duty office in photographic were informed the evening before the new searches took place, and senior photographers from scenes of crime were borrowed for the morning, to fill in.

One address, typical of many I attended, responded to the 0600 bang on the door, with screams and shouts from within, despite the DI. showing the requisite search warrant to the owners.

In absolute pandemonium, I struggled to take my photographs as the owners were held to one side by police, still trying desperately to explain what we were trying to do.

As I began to climb the stairs with my camera for the second part of the job, the woman of the house rugby tackled me, and brought me down hard, hitting my chin on the steps with a thud.

Behind me all hell broke loose as police and family fought, either to assist or deter my passage upstairs, but I twisted my legs free, got on my elbows, and staggered upstairs with camera and tripod.

This was like playing the All Blacks whilst trying to take photographs!

On completion of the upstairs rooms, I made my way cautiously downstairs, passing an old chap, probably the grandfather, sitting a couple of steps up from the bottom.

As I reached the hallway, I turned to see how the search team were doing, and saw the old chap rocking gently backwards and forwards, arms locked round his knees, quietly intoning as if in a trance "We is goin' to kill you all, yeah, kill you all"

I said to him as lightly as I could, "Surely you don't mean that do you?" but my words didn't seem to sink in, and he continued his monotonous chanting about our imminent demise.

This was a bewildering aspect of life I had never met before, and a bit depressing.

Once the addresses had been covered, I attended the charging station where the arrested people had been taken for questioning, and photographed them full length front, back and side views, enabling the officers to prove without doubt, whom they had in custody.

A weird spin-off to this was, the prisoners were often still wearing the clothing they had on when photographed during the riot days before, and to check this, a Polaroid shot was taken and immediately sent back to Southgate.

Now an immediate comparison could be made between the suspect and the display photographs in the witness room.

Occasionally a prisoner would refuse to have his photograph taken, and I would suggest it might be a good idea to get it done anyway, just in case he was subsequently assaulted, and needed proof he was ok. at the time of his arrest!

I know it was a bit naughty, and highly unlikely the prisoner would be assaulted whilst in custody, but it WAS a way of getting them all in the bag at once!

By the time donkeymoke and I reached the end of October, we had covered more than 60 addresses, and produced 600 negatives, which caused some people in the section to wonder what the hell we were playing at, deluging them with all that extra printing work!

Throughout November donkeymoke and I continued the early morning searches, and with the odd bit of help from the section, covered over 120 addresses, resulting in 1500 negatives, not a bad output at all!

One of the things that stood out after checking the riot photos against the arrested suspect's clothes was, the individual was usually the owner of easily identifiable trainers.

In fact some youngsters could tell us who a suspect in the photo was, despite his face being covered, because of the trainers he wore!

One morning as I sat in my van outside Tottenham nick, engine running, heater on full blast, waiting for the off, I felt my eyes beginning to close in sleep.

Frantically I rubbed my face hard, trying to keep my eyes on the vehicle in front, but it wasn't easy.

I was last in a convoy of four, and although I knew the address we were going to, I didn't quite know how to get there.

Suddenly I jerked into consciousness, not knowing I had even been asleep, and noticed with horror I was on my own, there were no vehicles in front of me!

Like a demon, I hared off in the direction I knew the address to be, and came to a skidding halt in the wrong half of the correct road - it was pedestrianised ahead!

Taking an inspired guess, I did a right at the end of my road, took thé next on the right, and right again, thankful to see on my left, the convoy of cars I had recently lost!

No words were said as I joined the lads scouring the address, either they were too good to say anything, or genuinely hadn't missed me, I don't know which, so I buckled down and got on with my photography.

Things were beginning to get really gutty.

One of the lads from the section brought the photographs of Keith Blakelock's PM for us to see, and I must say I was both shocked and depressed. The initial photographs taken of the officer in his uniform, riddled with artifacts like a hedgehog, were reminiscent of Richard III's hacking to death in Olivier's film, and were sickening.

It was like something out of mediaeval times.

Because of the pressure of work at Southgate, I hadn't seen my friend Lisa for a week or two, and when she did come round one evening, I was so shattered I could hardly string two words together in greeting, I felt a right idiot.

"What on earth are they doing to you up there, what's happening, why are you like this?"

My explanation that everyone was stretched to the absolute limit and doing their best, seemed incomprehensible to her, and she said it just wasn't good enough.

Over the last couple of weeks Lisa had been thinking we ought to take a holiday abroad in the warm sunshine, perhaps somewhere like Thailand.

She said I needed a break as soon as possible.

I agreed absolutely, saying it sounded both interesting AND warm!

As soon as this Tottenham riot investigation began to wind down we'd be off, sunshine bound, and to hell with all this grot for a while!

No doubt prodded by the need to keep the right political image, and see how his troops were doing 'in the field' the Commissioner, Sir Kenneth Newman, decided to grace us with his presence at Southgate Police station.

We were all prepared and 'standing to' in our respective sections as the great man came round, and soon it was my turn as photographer responsible for police response to the riot, to say his piece.

Det.Ch.Supt.Tony G. introduced me and said "Sir, this is Mr. Parker, civilian, SO.3 branch, who has been responsible for all our scene of crime photography, and the witness album room layout you see behind you"

I went through a quick spiel, describing how the lads in the section had attended the riot when it happened, producing the photographs covering the walls of the room in which we now stood.

Then I described how we went to various addresses after the local officers had identified suspects from the riot photographs, and showed him a typical search album.

Even as I spoke, I had the feeling I was talking to myself, the Commissioner was definitely somewhere else, he didn't ask a single question, or show any interest whatever in our vital work, and I found that quite disconcerting.

I don't suppose I kept him more than five minutes, but even so, walking away with the D/Ch.Supt. it seemed as if he couldn't get out fast enough.

Perhaps he had only come because it was politic to do so?

Throughout December and the run-up to Christmas, our daily searches continued, but fewer addresses were visited, as we began to scrape the bottom of the barrel.

Even so, by the 31st, we had recorded another 97 scene of crime visits, and due no doubt to my belt and braces policy of recording everything just before we left a scene - ensuring the photographer was the last person through the door, the Commissioner only received one complaint against police, despite our visiting nearly four hundred houses!

The solitary complaint surfaced eight years later, when the occupants of the house in Newlyn Rd, made a complaint against police for 'an unjustifiable length of time of detention' of the two men arrested in conjunction with the riot.

The two men were awarded payments of many thousands of pounds, and the mother was awarded £5000 for her stress, even though I had demonstrated her equable behaviour in the kitchen, by making a pot of tea!

The complaint went against police because two arresting officers of the arrested men were still unable to attend court due to psychological problems.

Det.Ch.Supt. Graham Melvin the officer in charge, was under suspicion of having falsified evidence in the main defendant Silcott's trial, (subsequently found to be a totally false allegation) and was also unable to give evidence due to being under suspension.

A right dog's dinner if ever there was one!

When I finally heard from the Yard's Solicitors branch, concerning the massive awards made to the Newlyn Rd family, I immediately wrote back, tongue in cheek, demanding MY award for the stress and agro endured from that family, and others, whilst going about my lawful job.

A few days later I received a nice letter from Solicitor's branch saying that while they fully understood the stress we had all been under during the Broadwater Farm riot, there was nothing they could do for me, it was all part of my job.

After all, I had been paid for my hours hadn't I?

In early February Lisa and I made arrangements for things to carry on at our homes, while we prepared to zot off to Thailand for a well earned break, no more getting up at un-godly hours for a couple of weeks thank goodness!

Our holiday in Thailand was a real eye opener, as we 'did' the sights round Bangkok before catching a bus down to the magical island of Phuket.

In the front of our bus next to the river, sat an armed soldier with an ouzi machine pistol across his lap at the ready.

Apparently bandits often made a habit of stopping tourist buses by blocking the road on lonely stretches, and relieving tourists of their valuables, hence our armed deterrent!

Twice during the long night journey to Phukhet, everybody was ushered off the bus for a free meal, which was usually rice floating in some thin, spicy soup which I didn't particularly like.

I was quite happy to forget the food, and continue our trip, I certainly didn't suffer from night starvation!

Each time we got on or off, the armed guard would video everyone in close up, no doubt checking to see that terrorists didn't sneak on board, and hold up the bus for friends down the road.

It was all very dramatic.

The island of Phukhet was a dream, with long golden beaches and clear blue seas, where no one but ourselves wandered during the heat of day.

We made one super excursion to Phi-Phi island, forty-five miles out in the Andaman sea, which was as near tropical paradise as I have ever seen.

It was absolutely pristine except for a small seasonal restaurant under the Palms, and the only people to be seen, apart from a couple of staff, were the Swift nest collectors on nearby island cliffs, climbing their amazing spindly bamboo structures in search of edible nests.

We also called in at the Muslim floating village, and the famous rock 'cave' which featured in a James Bond film, it was very warm, and restful.

All too soon our sojourn in paradise was over, and we were on our way back to dear old England, vowing we would return one day to look at the north of the country, where it joins Burma, the land of my ancestors!

At work, my urgent application for something better than the Mini to carry the mass of equipment I carried, had been taken on board by the 'transport procurement' section. I was promised a Leyland van big enough for all my gear, and more, plus a small video copying set-up inside too.

The new van would also have a portable generator and lights, plus a roof platform for elevated filming, it all sounded great, but would it really happen?

Somehow Christmas 86 came and went, and with mum now in a Yelverton nursing home, I wondered how long she would last in her present state. During the first week in January I had gone into her nursing home to find the patients, about forty in all, arranged in a huge semi-circle, utterly silent and immobile, just staring ahead.

Suddenly it hit me - they were all sitting there waiting to die, to move on, to make room for others on the great conveyor belt between life and death, it was rather depressing.

On a later visit, I wheeled her away from the dreaded semi-circle, and took her towards a large widow, where I sat, and began talking to her, my lips almost touching her ear.

After about ten minutes talking about anything I could think of that might get through to her, she suddenly gave a little smile and said "You sound just like my Alan" and that was it, she never said another word.

In early February the DC/I. at Bethnal Green, affectionately known as 'Black Adder' asked if I could video a murder for him, which, although it had started in a block of flats in Hackney, quickly escalated to cover a large part of the borough, plus neighbouring Chingford, and a gravel pit in East Tilbury.

The accused husband had killed his wife in a 'retaliatory attack' and then proceeded to dismember her body in the bath, at one point being interrupted by his six year old son, as he accidentally opened the door to go to the toilet.

To dispose of the remains, he wrapped small portions of his wife's body in plastic bags, before dropping them into litter-bins round Hackney, and along the river bank by Hackney marshes.

His piece de resistance however, was to encase her head in cement, and put the lot in a plastic shopping bag, before throwing it off Hungerford bridge into the Thames.

Later, I was on hand to film the Met.Underwater lads as they dived in to the river, and somehow within five minutes, retrieve the head in its bag from the Thames, where it had lodged on the muddy bottom without moving!

The torso and legs he had wrapped separately in old material, and dropped into roadside skips, which were later taken away by lorry, to be dumped on the rubbish landfill site at East Tilbury.

He had discovered a ready made disposal system for murder!

Over the next few days Black Adder and I plonked around East London, recording the various disposal sites confessed to by the defendant in his statement, but when it came to searching the rubbish site at East Tilbury, Black Adder had pressing business elsewhere.

After all it was bitterly cold, and snowing!

In freezing conditions laced with squally snow showers, I accompanied the poor dog-section chaps as they probed and searched the mountains of crap, swilling around knee-deep in glutinous mud and filth, dead scared to drop any equipment, or God forbid, slip, and fall over!

If we hadn't had the use of those great twenty-ton tippers to get us out onto the site, and a calor gas stove in a little tin hut to shelter in, I think there would have been four more bodies out there!

By a sheer miracle, the lads managed to locate the woman's torso, but that was due maimly to the operators keping a note of where each day's loads were dumped, and that was about it.

Subsequently the husband was sent for trial, and found guilty of manslaughter, being given all of six years for the offence.

Who says there's no such thing as justice?

As I was now getting more video work in a month than my two colleagues had collected in a year, I asked to take over one of the newer Sony DXC3000 cameras they carried.

The DXC was vastly superior to the old KY1900 I still plonked around with, and a real delight to use.

After a lot of humming and hah-ing, the boss eventually agreed I could do so, which put one chap's nose well out of joint, but I felt I could put his equipment to much better use, than have it trotted round London as ballast.

On the 28th April I got a call from the Yelverton nursing home to say mum had died that morning, and aunt Kath was making arrangements for the funeral to take place in a few days time.

Looking back on things, I could see this was the end of a long era of family memories, from now on, we were on our own.

# Chapter Twenty Nine

One day at the end of July, I was asked to accompany officers on a drugs raid involving a black Afro-club in Brixton, a sure area for potential trouble if ever there was one!

The premises were extremely difficult to approach to prove possession, being protected from street observation by a tall wooden fence, and surrounded on three sides by a wicked barbed wire fence.

A protective railway line also ran along an embankment at the back.

This scenario had inspired some bright spark to plan an ingenious assault, whereby a train loaded with police would stop at the rear of the premises, and disgorge its load of troops just as the barbed wire was being cut by two nearby 'track-workers'.

This incursion was timed to coincide with an assault by police piling in from a large furniture van stopped out front.

As the order was given over the air to go, the train disgorged its load of officers, who up till then had taken their helmets off, and kept well down below the windows to avoid discovery.

It was only when I took the leap off the carriage to the ground below, I realised how far off the ground the carriage door really was, and was lucky not to go base over apex down the steeply sloping embankment!

With camera running, we legged it through the cut barbed wire, and made for the back of the premises, where all hell was beginning to break loose.

The occupants, caught in a sledge-hammer, pincer movement, tried desperately to shuck their drugs down the sinks and toilets, but many were caught with their trousers well and truly down, and recorded on video.

It was by all accounts a highly successful action, which resulted in many prosecutions, and the nefarious club being closed down.

As I was now engaged in full-time video at scenes of crime, I carried only a basic stills kit, relying on my colleagues to attend the scene as well as me, and do the necessary in that direction.

Naturally, increased work at the scene, meant more work in the editing suite, making copies for the officer i/c. plus filing and annotation of the master, and the necessary paper work covering the job.

It all took time, but I enjoyed every minute of it.

There was a peculiar job running in the press that November, where a chap in prison was accused of the disappearance of his daughter under highly suspicious circumstances.

After several false clues, it was suggested she was incarcerated in a mausoleum in the derelict and grossly overgrown cemetery at Abney Park, in North London.

On a dull and miserable morning, officers in the case, plus lab.liaison, pathologist Peter Venessis, and myself, assembled outside the main entrance to the underground mausoleum, expecting to start work.

"There's no way into this place" said Peter V. "It's all bricked up, how long ago was that done?"

"A few months ago" replied a local CID officer. "The local hooligans used to come into the cemetery at night, pile into the mausoleum and hold rave parties amongst the coffins, so the local council bricked it up to keep them out"

"Well if you want us to look in there, you'll have to break it down again, won't you?" said Peter V.

A couple of council chaps with sledge hammers soon had a hole in the wall big enough to crawl through, and I poked the video camera in, complete with top light, to record whatever was inside, before we climbed in.

"If you'd like to go in first" said Peter V. "We'll pass your gear through, and you can film around down there before we disturb anything, Ok?"

Mausoleums and such never really bothered me, certainly not after some of the awful stuff we'd had to deal with in the past, so I put on some overalls, and climbed in.

It was a six foot drop to the floor, which appeared to be about a foot deep in debris, so it was a good job I had my wellies on.

With the camera and recorder passed through, I began filming, seeing in front of me long metal racks packed high with leaden coffins, the contents of which had oozed out over the shelves during the years, solidifying into long stringy stalactites resembling melted toffee.

It was quite bizarre.

The floor was deep in rubbish of unknown origin, and clouds of dust particles rose in my light beam as I moved about filming.

Suddenly, into the field of view came a brown coloured paper sack about three feet long, on the side of which was printed in red letters 'Confidential Waste Metropolitan Police' - I couldn't believe it!

"Hey! Do you know what I've found down here, a ruddy paper sack filled with something, and labelled Met.Police, how about that?"

"Don't be so bloody stupid and stop playing games" said Peter V. "We're coming in now anyway, so show your light over here, and give us a hand will you?"

"Bloody hell, he's right!" said Lab. liaison when I directed the video light back onto the sack. "What the hell's going on then?"

It turned out that local police officers getting a bit fed up with the hooligans chucking skulls and leg bones around the cemetery, had gathered them all into an official disposal sack, and seeing an opportunity to get rid of them without fuss, threw them into the mausoleum as it was being bricked up!

A complete search of the subterranean mausoleum failed to turn up anything else of interest, and we prepared to leave, I for one being quite pleased, as the dank, oppressive atmosphere was beginning to get to me, it was quite nasty.

Peter V. and I gave lab. liaison a lift to get him up and out of the small entrance hole, and next, I pushed Peter V. up, while he was pulled through by helpers on the outside.

Then there was silence, as everyone seemed to disappear.

In stygian darkness, apart from dull light filtering in through the hole, I waited for some sign that I was to be helped out next, but there was nothing doing.

I thought I'd wait a bit to see what happened, after all, I didn't want them to think I was scared to be down here.

It WAS only a hole in the ground full of dead people wasn't it?

A few minutes later Lab.liaison put his head through the hole and said "Sorry about that Al, we were all talking about something else, and completely forgot about you, pass up your gear and we'll get you out of there, ok?"

Back in the world of the living, and breathing relatively clean, fresh air, I refrained from saying what was on my mind.

I wasn't going to give them the satisfaction of my complaining, if leaving me down there hadn't been their intention all along!

That afternoon we were back at the cemetery again, this time armed with the knowledge that the girl was definitely there, but hidden away alongside one of the rough stone walls, amongst deep undergrowth.

With a dozen searchers engaged on the job, it didn't take long to find the girl's remains, a mere collection of bones and dried black skin, minus any skull, half buried in the soil.

Sifting through the detritus under the body, lab.liaison came up with a little crucifix necklace, which was later identified as belonging to the girl.

We had solved the mystery of her disappearance at last.

During the next few weeks, there was the usual run of murders, arsons, and club raids to attend, until I began to get involved in the Allison Day murder, a young girl murdered in December '85 at Hackney by an unknown killer, identified only as 'the railway murderer'.

In connection with this, I video filmed a community centre in north London where the killer was supposed to have taken Hap Ki Do Karate lessons, as one of his victims had possibly been killed by a Karate blow.

Apparently, police officers had been hunting the rapist/killer for three years now without success, and as his suspected victims now included Maartje Tamboezer in April, and Anne Locke in May 86, it was thought that Allison Day was a possible earlier victim too.

Over the next two weeks the impetus to find the killer was such, that a prime suspect for the rapes and murders was put under close surveillance, and was eventually seen stalking women in Copthall Park.

He was arrested and his home searched, but nothing incriminating was found, until officers searched his mother's home nearby and managed to find the incriminating evidence they were desperately looking for.

It was string, the same kind of string called Somyarn, used to tie the other victims' hands together before they were killed, a real clincher.

Some time later, I was present at Paddington Police station when the suspect, John Duffy was placed in an identification line-up, and the women who had been raped, came forward to try and identify their assailant.

Using all the equipment from our section's film production unit, plus my scenes of crime gear, we managed to cover the ID. parade in detail, one camera covering the parade Inspector and the complainant, to obviate any allegation of coercion or prompting by police.

Another camera covered the parade as a whole, while mine was at one end of the parade recording the complainant's actions during the ID. parade.

I reckoned we were bending over backwards to be more than fair, but because of the way defence counsel would exploit any weakness or imperfection in the law, we had to be absolutely watertight.

It was heartbreaking to see the women come in and face that terrible line up. You could certainly forgive them if they identified the wrong man, but a couple, in cold brutal silence pointed to Duffy, and left in tears.

At one point Duffy changed his place in the line-up so that he came almost opposite me, and I must say I have never seen such cold, evil intensity project from anyone's eyes like his, they were almost hypnotic.

The last woman witness entered with our cameras rolling, and when she came opposite Duffy, stopped dead as though she had run into a plate glass wall. She was absolutely devastated.

It was cruel to see her physically disintegrate before my eyes, her mouth opening soundlessly in tears as she tried to indicate Duffy.

He remained absolutely expressionless and unaffected, and I felt I could have killed the bastard myself.

At the end of it all I knew we had done a good professional job, and hoped to God he went down. I felt it was an absolute travesty that hanging wasn't in vogue any more, he certainly wouldn't be missed.

He got thirty years.

In Brompton Rd. Kensington, there are some premises known as the Safety Deposit Centre, and about lunch-time I received a call to get there pronto as a very large robbery had just taken place. Fingerprints and forensic were already on scene raring to go, but nothing could be done until the scene had been recorded in detail from top to bottom.

It was one of those very rare times when photographic weren't on scene first!

It was a very plush set-up, more like a Bond St. jewellers than a deposit centre, and DI.L from the robbery squad wanted everything covered, but everything, no messing!

During the next half hour, he and I re-enacted the robbery scenario in detail; filming everything just as it was supposed to have happened, but when we had finished at the back security door I began to get a smell of rotten cheese.

The foreign looking owner stated that he had seen two men at the back door on their security TV, and had let them in to the little foyer, as he was expecting them.

He then stated that he let them into the main part of the depository after using his special 'swipe' card, and surprise surprise, they pulled a gun on him, tied him up, and began to ransack the place!

The D.I asked me if I was happy with what I'd got, and I said yes, but I wasn't too impressed by the owner's story, I reckoned he'd done it himself, perhaps with accomplices.

"Yeah, well when I want your expert advice I'll ask for it" he replied, in a tone suggesting that was the last thing he wanted to hear, and disappeared.

After all, with a large crowd gathering outside on the pavement, and messages coming in from frantic depositors, it looked as though 20 or 30million quid could be involved, plus a lot of sensitive documentation.

One missing jewel alone was supposed to be worth over 4 million!

It could turn out to be a very tasty job.

There was no doubt, an awful lot of intelligence must have been gathered from the ankle deep papers strewn around the opened deposit boxes, and it was another full day before we got to the end of recording everything in the room.

It certainly was a big heist.

A couple of days later when I delivered the film to the squad, DI.L told me they had managed to get the owner to confess to setting the job up himself, describing how the scheme had been carefully prepared over two years, and costing over a million quid to set up.

What a cheeky scam!

In complete contrast, I received a request from Det.Supt.'Lee' Marvin - a wonderful character, who always reminded me of Michael Bentine, and socially just as whacky, to attend Elmers End cemetery at dawn, to film yet another exhumation.

Apparently we had to get cracking as soon as possible with the new post-mortem, as the body had to be re-interred before dark for religious reasons, just like last time.

In a chilly grey dawn spitting with rain, we got into position as the mechanical digger started work, and I filmed the scene as the coffin slowly emerged.

It had been down there some little time, and I didn't have a clue regarding what the pathologist hoped to find. I hadn't been told any of the background details, but he was quite welcome to this one!

With the coffin placed on the second mortuary slab, we all crowded into the comparative warmth of the small mortuary, waited while the lid was taken off, and the body removed to the main slab.

There were more than enough people interested in seeing first hand what the pathologist's examination might reveal, and having filmed the body from all sides, I pulled my camera and tripod out of the way, and let them get on with it.

I was in a funny mood, and didn't really worry if I had any further filming to do or not, I suppose it was all a bit too early in the day really!

After an hour paddling about in the disintegrating mess, the pathologist announced, "There's nothing special for you to record on this one photographer, as far as I am concerned you can go if you wish" and getting the nod from Lee Marvin packed up and left.

One body is very much like another really, it's only a matter of decomposition.

Not content with one early call, I got a another the next day at 0600 from Charley Farley of Limehouse nick, asking if I would care to attend Cantrell Rd. Bow right away, where a team of 'ringers' were knocking out bent BMW's and other tasty vehicles.

A raid was going down to put a spoke in their wheels, so to speak, and as the lads expected to turn over a rather tasty set-up, I was to record it all for posterity.

At 0800 sharp, half a dozen vehicles crammed with police descended on the scrap yard, and cordoned off the whole area, nobody but nobody was going anywhere today!

The timing was obviously spot on, and we nailed the main suspects in their office drinking tea, before going on to search the place yard by yard.

Apparently their speciality was BMW cars, and partly refurbished bodies were stacked all over the place, alongside rows and rows of car doors - there must have been a hundred of them at least.

There was another huge area where hundreds of car engines were lined up in neat rows awaiting sale or fitting, it was quite incredible.

In an adjacent area we found a black man sitting in the engine compartment of a Jaguar saloon, busily welding a commission plate into the bulkhead in place of the original, and he hadn't heard us come in.

For half a minute or so he carried on, his gas torch cracking and spluttering until, satisfied with the work, he pushed up his welding helmet and sat back, only to find himself surrounded by an admiring selection of the old Bill.

With eyes rolling in wild surprise, his only legible comment was a dejected "Oh shit!" and we all laughed like drains.

We heard India 99 clattering overhead, obviously making sure no naughty lads had it away on their toes over the roof-tops, and we began the onerous task of cataloguing everything we found in the place.

Naturally I was busy for the rest of the day, filming specialised remnants of identifiable cars, old index plates, commission plates, and chassis numbers, it was a right old Aladdin's cave, and by evening I felt quite knackered.

We kept the area closed for two days while we worked, and at the end of it all, had a load of evidence that showed a large number of expensive cars were being ringed and sold on to unsuspecting customers - the yard owners must have been making a fortune!

A week before the merry celebration of Christmas, I got a call to go to Romford, where a well known scrap dealer had been found murdered in his bed without apparent motive. The scene strangely enough, was well known to me, as just after the war we used to cycle there to try and get spares for our bicycles, which, due to the recent hostilities were in rather short supply.

The large country-style house in Crow Lane stood on an acre or two of ground, backing onto large marshy fields which we used to explore as kids, and unless the old chap had a stash of cash hidden under the floorboards, there didn't seem to be an obvious reason for his murder.

There wasn't the usual ransacking or disturbance within the house associated with burglary, and who steals scrap?

As the scene was quite large, especially the grounds out back, the D/I. asked me to go up in the helicopter and see if there were any tracks leading away from the house in the deep grass, and to cover the site photographically for future use.

I enjoyed the practice of covering the scene with both stills and video, and to renew my acquaintance with the helicopter crew, whom I hadn't seen for some little time.

According to lab. liaison, the dead man had been wearing a watch shortly before his death, the marks were still on his wrist, but where was it now?

Enquiries among his family revealed he had owned an expensive gold Rolex watch, which had obviously disappeared, but that alone would hardly be the reason for his murder, there must be something else!

Indeed there was, apparently a nasty family feud had erupted over cash required to finance a risky project abroad, and as it was not forthcoming from dad, he had been belted by his son and friends in an attempt to make him change his mind.

When that didn't happen, and he unfortunately snuffed it, the scenario was made to look like a robbery gone wrong, by removing his expensive watch, but it hadn't succeeded.

It was interesting to see how quickly pathologists caught onto the value of video at post-mortems, especially if they wanted some of their commentary recorded too.

I copped five of them in eight weeks, sharing the jobs with colleagues who were happily relieved of some of the arduous stills work, normally associated with PMs.

It was about this time that my daughter Ruth decided to do her own thing, and moved into a flat in my son Stephen's house, and although we had worked together for eight years since Teresa's death, I was happy to see Ruth start her own way in life.

Running the house with dad, hadn't always been a bed of roses!

Now that Helen and I were on our own so to speak, I had to make a better arrangement with Peter and Mary Boyer who had helped me bring up Helen, when no one was available during the day.

This meant that Mary picked Helen up from my place at 0730 enabling me to book on at Barkingside nick at 0800.

It was a stroke of luck that I was working on divisions and not in the section up town, otherwise it wouldn't have been easy to arrange things at all.

At the end of the day, whenever that happened to be, I would ring Mary and tell her my expected return time, and nip round there to collect Helen before going home to cook my dinner.

It was a bit hectic at times, but somehow it all seemed to work.

Work that is, until I began to cop a string of drugs raids in the East-end that were scheduled to go down around midnight.

I thought it would be well over the top to ask Mary at short notice to keep Helen for the night, as well as the day, and I couldn't think of anything else that might work, so I took her with me.

Behind the passenger seat, and under the video editing bench of the new Leyland van I now had, was a large space intended for the editor's feet, when the passenger seat was reversed.

This space, about four feet by three, was a snug place to put Helen in her duvet when I left home at 2300 to start the job.

I must admit I did have touch of the seconds about what would happen if anyone in the station yard heard a kiddie crying in my van, but as Helen had never stirred once she was asleep, I felt things should be Ok. and fortunately they were!

Over a period of two weeks, the local Ch/Insp. organised four raids on drugs-clubs, which, with loads of back up troops, plus the video camera churning away up front, produced some very satisfactory results.

Each time I went off filming, Helen slept in her little corner like a log.

With Lisa's daughter Nicky now living in Italy, and her son Dirk about to get married, Lisa suggested that after their wedding she would like to lend her place to the newly weds until they found a place of their own, and move in with me, how did I feel about that?

She wasn't sure how she would relate to Helen, but thought with a bit of give and take all round, it should work out fine.

One of the nastiest jobs I copped in a long time was the serious fire at King's Cross station in November, and I was directed to be there at first light, the morning following the fire.

The place was still in the hands of the Fire Service, reeking of smoke and steam, with salvage people dashing here, there and everywhere.

Coughing and spluttering, I followed our Fire Investigation chap down the unburnt escalator, to examine the damage at the bottom of the up escalator.

It looked as though a bomb had gone off.

Under his direction I filmed the fire damage that seemed to erupt from under the steps, and from both sides, before spiralling up the rest of the escalator to the top, and into the booking hall.

I filmed the path of the fireball as it had billowed upstairs, cutting across one of those advertisement frames as though slashed with a knife, the unburned portion still sitting grotesquely on a part of the undamaged wall.

It was so humid down there, I suggested we both go topside for a breath of fresh air, and whilst making our way through the devastated hall, were confronted by Prime Minister Maggie Thatcher, swinging briskly into view, followed by her faithful band of satellites.

Things must be pretty serious.

For the rest of the day, I recorded various manifestations of the horrendous fire, and was rather pleased when our fire investigation lad suggested we knock it on the head for now, and return the following morning.

We would then be examining the underside of the burnt-out escalator with all its nuts and bolts. That sounded tasty!

Although the passenger stairways seem quite spacious, easily taking two people side-by-side, the underside, where all the machinery lurks is a very different story.

Under the stairs there is a narrow service space just over three-feet wide, which descends via small concrete steps the whole length of the escalators, lit by small safety lights that disappear gradually into the gloom below.

"Ok. this is where we'll start" said our fire chappie.

"I want views showing how it all works, and in particular, certain parts I want you to cover in great detail, right down to fluff and dog-ends, can you give me that?"

Over the next hour we made our way slowly down the narrow tunnel, descending deeper and deeper, until we reached the point where the fire had apparently burst through to the outside.

"This is where I want you to give me the detailed stuff, this thick grease, fluff and dog-ends, matches and bits of paper, and of course these wheels which have been subjected to intense heat, Ok?"

It was a good job I had the Fujinon close-focussing wide-angle lens on camera, without that, I wouldn't have been able to even start the job.

I was within a foot of the subject in front of the lens, while the back of the camera banged against the escalator supports behind.

To add to my discomfort, everything was covered in thick black grease and grime, and I began to feel a little claustrophobic.

It seemed pretty obvious to me, that the large amount of debris and grease accumulating over a certain period of time, had become a very serious hazard.

If the machinery jammed or ran hot for any length of time, with the moving parts of escalator running over this debris, extreme heat could be generated, and the whole lot go up in flames.

I have to admit I'm no expert, but in my opinion very little if any cleaning maintenance had been carried out for ages down here, and I felt it would be very interesting to peruse any invoices submitted for payment, concerning date, time and place, of maintenance allegedly undertaken.

I was more than pleased to finish filming under those awful escalators, and had only a few upstairs shots to do, tying up with what we had discovered below, so I was nearly done.

It had been a grotty, dirty day, everything I touched was black and greasy, the camera and recorder would need to be thoroughly cleaned with white spirit.

At the end of it all, feeling quite knackered, I said to my friend that all I wanted was a good wash, something to eat, and a sit down, and he readily agreed.

It was a nice change to spend the next couple of days in the editing suite, making copies of the video, and despatching them to interested official parties.

I'd be very interested to hear the final outcome of this little lot, and see who would actually carry the can.

The trial had been running for some time concerning those who were charged with various offences at the earlier Broadwater Farm riot, and I was called to the Old Bailey to give evidence concerning a little hooligan accused of chucking a petrol bomb at police.

His brief pleaded that the print of his client submitted to the court could have been taken anywhere, and needed corroboration, how could he accept the photograph as genuine?

I explained to m'lud and the jury that the print was indeed one of a series taken at Broadwater Farm, and the uncut film was held in photographic's files, and could be viewed at any time.

"Have you got this film with you?" intoned m'lud, staring at me over his half glasses.

"No m'lud, the film is still being used to produce evidential photographs, but I can produce it tomorrow if necessary".

"As it is late afternoon, I'll adjourn the court until 1030 tomorrow morning. Will you please have the film with you, and an album of the entire film for us to see, so that we can clear up this matter".

We all left the Bailey, and I headed back to the office to locate a set of prints for tomorrow, and to see if I could borrow the BBS analyser, a German made piece of kit, that took a 35mm negative, and reversed it colourwise onto a TV screen.

I managed to get our TV lot to lend me a couple of monitors plus the BBS analyser, and in the few minutes before the court commenced, managed to wire them up, placing one for M'lud to see, and the other on defence counsel's table.

We were ready to go.

"Yesterday" defence counsel opened, "You were telling us that this single photograph was indeed one of a series on an uncut film, taken at Broadwater Farm on the night of October 6th, is that correct?"

"Yes sir, that is correct, I have brought along prints from that entire film, containing thirty-four exposures. The print we are interested in comes from negative number 28".

I waited while the albums were handed round to interested parties, and continued, "With the analyser I have here in front of me I can now demonstrate negative number 28 on the TV monitors in front of you"

I put on a pair of lint-less cotton gloves, and unwound the 35mm film, pulling it through the analyser until negative 28 showed on their screens.

I breathed a sigh of relief when I saw the TV image was exactly the same as the print defence counsel was looking at on his table.

Looking closely at counsel below me, I watched as he announced to the court "Yes, I suppose we must agree that negative 28 appears to be one of a series on this film from Broadwater Farm" and I watched even closer as he turned over the page and looked at the next photograph, which would be 29.

Out of habit, I glanced at the next negative on my film, and saw to my horror it wasn't the same as his, the corresponding shot on my film was number 27.

Somebody had made up the albums wrongly and transposed 27 and 29!

"Just to make absolutely sure, may we see negative 29 the photograph that follows the one in question please?"

Without looking at counsel I moved the film in the analyser backwards instead of forwards, presenting the court with the shot that matched his.

"Yes, thank you very much, that will be all Mr. Parker" and I breathed a sigh of relief that he hadn't asked to see negative 30 as well, otherwise I would have been well and truly in the mire!

Just when I felt we might have a reasonably easy run up to Christmas, I copped another exhumation.

This time it was at Plaistow, followed by a post mortem, performed by Dr.Grant, a likeable, but funny little chap, who reminded me of the Dormouse stuffed into the teapot in Alice in Wonderland.

His post-mortems always took ages.

As I had noticed on many occasions whilst working with him, he began after a while, to mutter little comments to himself about some aspect or other concerning the job, at the same time resting his rotund stomach on the edge of the slab.

Then, in a trance, he would gaze fixedly into the chest cavity or whatever, as though seeking some divine inspiration or guidance, often for several minutes.

Then, like the fabled Dormouse, he would stir, and click into action, often asking for something specific to be photographed, before going into the whole rigmarole all over again.

His PM's always seemed to last twice as long as anyone else's.

A few days before Christmas I was asked to meet a D.I from the Robbery squad, who was trying to formulate a new way of identifying suspects involved in serious crime, suspects who refused to attend an ID parade.

He felt that if we could video the suspect covertly and get a good likeness, his image could then be placed amongst other totally innocent 'stooges' and the resulting videotape shown to witnesses who would otherwise never get to view the suspect.

It seemed a good idea to me.

There was a particularly nasty villain, Wayne H. who had been involved in several bank hold-ups, where shots had been fired at police, and after a fight, had been arrested.

He was appearing at Lambeth Magistrates Court on the 10th, so it might be an excellent chance to get some video of him going into court.

We did a recce of the Court area the day before our man was due to appear, and decided the only practical place to work was the open yard at the rear.

We could get the prison van driver to park his vehicle over the far side, and I could video everyone as they got off and walked towards me, including our friend H.

Fortunately there was a barred window on the first floor of the court overlooking the yard, which I blacked out with a dark cloth, setting the camera behind it before going down into the yard to check if it all looked Ok.

It was fine, only a close scrutiny by someone actually looking up there, would reveal the lens tucked back inside the window.

It was 'all systems go' for tomorrow.

Naturally we had discussed what would happen if it rained, or there was some rubbish on the floor whilst filming the suspect, which didn't appear in the later shots of the 'stooges' so we kept our fingers crossed until we heard the prison van turning into the Court approaches.

Like a good 'un, the van driver parked his van on the far side of the yard with its exit door facing us, and I let the camera roll.

It was crunch time.

Behind me the D.I scanned the faces as they disembarked one at a time, before hissing "That's him, for God's sake don't lose him!" and I followed our friend as he walked across the yard before disappearing from view beneath us. He had taken ten seconds, a frighteningly short time, but with his return journey to the van, we could add a bit to that, so we should be Ok.

"On his return journey, could someone call out and get him to turn round for a couple of seconds, it could be useful if we're scratching for footage on the first take?" I asked.

The DI. disappeared from the room, and went off to make the necessary arrangements, it wouldn't be long before H. re-appeared, as he was only being further remanded in custody.

It was arranged for someone to give us the nod when H. was about to go through the doorway into the yard, so I could start filming again.

"He's on his way!" came a voice from outside the door, and even through the viewfinder I could see 'H' had a very distinctive build and heavy muscleman gait.

As he reached a point half-way across the yard, a voice called out, "Hey, are these your cigarettes?"

H. turned about, slapped his hands on his jacket pockets, and raised his hands palm upwards to indicate they weren't his, before turning back to the prison van, and was lost from sight.

It all seemed to have happened far too quickly to me, but the DI. seemed well satisfied.

"Well if you've done your job Ok. I think we've got him spot on, what do you reckon?"

I told him I'd feel a lot better when I had a working copy on the editor, and could tell him exactly how much useable footage we had, then I'd know what we needed to do, regarding our stooges.

Back in the section I found I had seven seconds walking towards the camera that showed H's face, and ten seconds of him walking away and turning round in the middle, not a lot of footage really.

However, when that seventeen seconds was sandwiched between eleven other similar sequences, plus the spaces in between, and an identifying number included for each clip, you have a film of over four minutes for witnesses to sit through, and that would be quite long enough.

Two weeks later I was back at Lambeth Court, this time in the company of a dozen actors, each of whom had been hired to copy H's walk from prison van to the Court and back again, including the bit where H. turned round for the ciggies.

I thought that should be fun.

I had brought along a copy of the master tape for the actors to see and emulate, and it was quite educational to see them practising H's walk and expression, as they saw it, and the Court yard took on the air of a film audition.

Fortunately, it all passed off Ok. and I now had the sheer slog of producing exactly the same footage for each of the twelve sequences, plus the spaces and identifying numbers in between.

Any variation whatsoever could be used by defending counsel - once they knew we had their client covertly on film, to allege we were favouring this or that image to the detriment of their client, creating an excuse for the film to be thrown out of court.

Once the twelve sequences had been timed and edited with their respective numbers, I had the tedious job of producing twelve further copies, EACH copy showing H. in a different position from the last!

It was a good job Paul Griffin from the Video production team offered to stay late one evening and give me a hand, otherwise I would have been there all night!

To make doubly sure that defence counsel could not allege that prosecution witnesses had seen the films prior to the trial, all copies were locked in a steel cabinet, and only booked out in the presence of an Inspector, who signed for it.

We also had defence counsel attend at the same time to select one of the dozen unmarked copies themselves, so that they were responsible for 'H's position on that film, and no-one else.

If the requirement to show the video at court went beyond one day, counsel were invited to select another copy for showing, so that a witness who knew the position of 'H' from the first day, could not communicate his knowledge to another witness for the following day. It was that tight.

At the end of it all, 'H' was found guilty and sent to prison.

As usual, Christmas came and went with its high level of activity, which seemed to have more to do with social spending, rather than celebrating the birth of Christ, and we burst through into the New Year.

Roll on 1988 and perhaps something a little bit better!

# Chapter Thirty

The facility offered by the video camera at scenes of crime was really beginning to take-off now, and jobs came in thick and fast.

Not that I minded too much, I felt the format had a lot to offer, especially in covering large scenes quickly, and on occasion, recording exactly what was said, and by whom.

During that January I covered four murders, a suspicious death, two drugs raids, an anti-abortion rally in Parliament Sq. and an Iraqi demo outside the embassy in Princes Gate.

A place I was quite familiar with, from spectacular events in the past!

If you had a weird sense of humour, then a job I covered for Limehouse nick would probably have tickled your fancy. Apparently the local dustmen had called to an address in Sturry St. off East India Dock Rd. and whilst emptying the bins, one of the lads decided to see just what was in the carefully wrapped, brownpaper parcels the householder was throwing away.

He should never have looked.

With a shout of terror he dropped the parcel and ran back to his mates shouting, "It's got a leg in it, it's got a leg in it!"

Subsequent examination by a Limehouse police officer confirmed the parcel did in fact contain a human leg, and by the feel of things, the other parcels contained something rather similar.

Setting up my camera next to the scenes of crime officer, I filmed the scene as he carefully unwrapped the other three parcels, using thin rubber gloves so that he didn't contaminate the wrappings with his own fingerprints.

They too contained human remains, another leg and two arms, making it necessary to check the rest of the rubbish the lads had just collected, in case we could find the missing head or torso.

With a bit of luck we might make up a complete body again!

During the next few days, a detailed forensic examination of the remains was undertaken, and extensive enquiries made, but nothing new came to light.

We couldn't go any further until we had more information, so until then, the limbs would have to stay as a 'body' found, without the rest of the body to go with them!

The weather was definitely improving by the day, and thankfully we seemed to be leaving the grotty grey stuff behind, it was much nicer doing 'outside' jobs in the weak spring sunshine, than pouring rain.

One job - it could be called a jammy one, was to attend North Weald airfield with officers from the driving school and the Met. Police Laboratory, to record the braking abilities of certain high-powered motor cars.

We spent most of the morning filming and measuring the stopping and skidding characteristics of the new Audi, the latest Jaguar, a couple of Porshe 924's, and an experimental Honda, which had the ability to turn the rear wheels in the opposite direction to the front ones, allowing it to turn corners faster without rolling over.

At the conclusion of all this technical stuff, we were told to try out whichever car took our fancy, and have a good sprint down the main runway. I could hardly believe my ears!

As there were two Porsches, I nabbed the 924S Turbo, and after a brief tuition from the organiser, moved carefully down the runway, trying to get the feel of this fantastic machine.

After a couple of minutes I felt confident enough to put my foot down a bit, and felt the awesome power as we purred through 60 in second gear.

Changing up, I switched in the turbo, and felt a kick in the back as we shot off down the asphalt like a scalded cat.

In a bit of a panic, I eased off the throttle and applied the brakes as the end of the runway seemed to be getting too darned close, and motored back to my starting point, acutely aware of the brute power lurking under the bonnet of this sophisticated looking car.

Naturally, there was a rush by the driving school bods to try all the cars, and I was swiftly elbowed out of the way, as vehicles went off this way and that, and I didn't manage to get a second drive.

Needless to say there was one clown - there always is, who goes too far, and behaves in a fashion which lets down all his colleagues.

This time it was a Det.Con. who had somehow managed to come along on the demo, and when it was his turn to drive, grabbed one of the Porsches, and took off with wheels spinning, in a cloud of smoke.

Needless to say on his return to the start point, he got a right bawling out from the chief organiser, who made it quite plain that he was lending his own cars to the Police as a favour, and didn't expect such hooligan treatment in return.

His behaviour certainly went down like a lead wellie.

With the continued destruction of wildlife habitat by the panjandrum of social progress, it was getting more and more difficult to find anywhere local for my natural history photography, but after a unique event in May, things were about to change.

Apparently, a husband in Fulham having killed his wife, decided the best way to get rid of her body was to cut it up, and distribute the pieces among several roadside rubbish skips in the area, similar to Black Adder's Hackney job.

These skips were then loaded into twenty-ton container boxes, and despatched down river to Stanford-le-Hope in Essex, where they were emptied into gravel workings, and compacted.

Det.Supt. H. of Fulham, having learned what had happened from the defendant, sent some of his troops down to Stanford-le Hope, in an attempt to locate the spot where the body parts might be buried.

Fortunately, Geoff Richmond and his staff at the Muckingford Tip, kept a log of where each day's loads were tipped, and was able to point out an area where a succesful search might be made, but to me it sounded mind-boggling.

To make sure any evidence found at the scene would be recorded before being taken away for forensic examination, I was asked to attend Muckingford, and meet the troops who were about to undertake the digging.

It sounded like a 'long wait' job with little to show at the end of it all, but at least it was a day out in the country.

It was a nice sunny day, and although the compacted rubbish was about fifteen feet deep at this point, a mechanical shovel, hired at great expense by police, got started on its first excavations, and we all crowded round.

As each huge shovel-full was lifted, its contents were carefully strewn to one side, and the troops went through it with their rakes and spades, looking for anything resembling a body.

It was very hard work.

At lunchtime, we all knocked off, and went back to the site HQ, where we were made welcome with tea and biscuits, but I had my sandwiches with me as usual, and was alright Jack.

Someone was designated to go off to nearby Stanford-le-Hope and buy a load of fish and chips, as a means of resuscitating the flagging diggers, who definitely needed reviving after their grotty work.

By mid-afternoon, the digger had made a darned great hole about twenty feet square, down to the original bottom of the pit, and was beginning to enlarge one wall when someone shouted "Hold it! I think I can see something" and grabbed a nearby ladder for a better look.

"Yep, we've hit it, I'm sure it's an arm, hey, photos get yerself over here and record it, so's we can take it out, will you?"

Commandeering the digger, I climbed into the shovel and had the driver hoist me up to point level with the dark brown, stick-like object, and was pleased to see it had some fingers on it, he was right, it WAS an arm!

I recorded it in detail, and went back to ground level to record the exact depth at which it had been found, after which Lab. Liason went up in the shovel, and removed it carefully for me to photograph on the ground, using a scale for reference.

Considering the mountain of rubbish that was being tackled, I felt this find was little short of a miracle.

It would be up to fingerprints now, to treat and soften the fingers so that a classification could be made and compared with fingermarks found at the deceased's known address.

Buoyed up by their discovery, the team kept digging and sorting, but nothing else came to light before knocking off time at six o'clock. We'd have to come back tomorrow.

Back at the pit HQ, I had time to look around before leaving, and noticed on some nearby run-down farm buildings, lots of white splashes on the roof gables, which indicated to me the presence of birds of prey, possibly owls.

Next to me while I was looking, stood an old chap, Fred, a resident of nearby Mucking Hall, who did odd jobs around the farm during the day.

"Excuse me, do you have any kind of owls round here?" I asked.

"Yeah, I reckon we do, mainly them old screech owls"

"Do you mean the white Barn Owl"

"Yeah, them's the ones, sees 'em of an evening, mainly between the church and the barn there" he indicated with a work-worn finger.

"Any chance I can have a look in the barn to see if they are in there?" I asked.

"'Fraid I don't have the key at the moment, but if you're keen tomorrow, I might be able to let you in then, you'll have to clear it with Geoff Richmond though, the barn belongs to the landfill people"

Hardly able to contain my excitement, I went home, looking forward to the next day when I could get a shufti into that barn, and perhaps find evidence of Barn Owls.

That would certainly be a turn up for the book!

The second day at the tip was like the first, warm, sunny and very pleasant to be working outside, and even though we were over our heads with evil smelling rubbish, it beat working in the office!

It was getting difficult now to find a fresh place to pile the stuff coming out of the hole, but even so, just before lunch another arm was discovered, and I recorded it in situ as before.

This was quite unbelievable, I hadn't expected anything from this monstrous pile of garbage, and yet here we had our second arm, roll on the rest!

That evening I managed to locate Fred again, and asked if he been able to get the key to open the two huge doors securing the barn.

"I don't suppose you'll find anything much in here" Fred growled, "Its hardly used at the moment, just full of farm machinery and stuff" and he began to undo the huge rusty padlock.

Inside the barn, the central area was taken up by a huge, funnel-shaped construction, which obviously allowed wheat to be bagged-up from a supply above, but what excited me most, was the abundant white splashes of owl droppings over everything, and the dozens of freshly regurgitated pellets all over the floor.

Walking round the back of the funnel, I found a set of steps going up into the roof, which at this point was boarded in, so that workers could get at the funnel.

"Can I go up, and have a look to see what's up there?" I asked.

"Yes I suppose so, but be careful, I don't want them police fellers coming round to see me, if you fall off"

I walked carefully up the twenty odd steps to the top, and as my head came level with the boarded floor, I was almost de-capitated by the whoosh of a Barn Owl as it flew past my head, and out of a nearby broken window.

Searching the area from which the Barn Owl had appeared, I saw in the dim light, eight white eggs nestling in a bed of old pellets on the timber floor, I'd done it, I'd found the owl's nest!

Down below Fred shouted "I just saw the owl go out the window"

"I know, she is nesting up here and has got eight eggs, I haven't seen a clutch that size in years, she must be a young bird, it's fantastic!"

As Fred locked up the barn once more, I asked what my chances were of gaining access to the barn during the evenings to photograph the owls. I would only be interested when they had young to feed.

I told him I had the Nature Conservation's permit to photograph owls, so I was 'legal' and after some thought he said. "Its ok by me, I have the only spare key, but you'll have to clear it with the Landfill people first".

The next day we assembled as usual by the gaping hole in the rubbish, and soon after eight, began digging and sifting in a pattern determined by the tipping log in the Landfill office. Luck certainly smiled on us early this time, as within an hour we recovered the woman's torso, or what remained of it.

I must confess you would have had to know what you were looking for, to recognise the blackened, dirt covered remains, but once we had washed it off, there was no doubt about it, we had a female torso.

Now that we were putting more pieces of the jigsaw together, the pathologist was able to start making comparisons between the saw-cut ends of the humerus, proving that the arms we had found earlier, belonged exclusively to this torso.

All we needed now was a bit more luck to turn up the head and legs, and we were home and dry!

In between recording the rapid progress of our diggers, I nipped back to the Landfill HQ, and found Geoff Richmond the site manager, who after a lengthy explanation of what I wanted to do, readily agreed to my request, stressing the need for me to return the key on completion of photography each evening to Fred, for security reasons.

I was in!

Over the next two days, the team managed to locate the woman's head and left leg, but even though digging continued until the end of the week, the remaining leg failed to turn up.

Bearing in mind the high cost of hiring the digger, and the mountains of rubbish shifted so far, Det.Supt.H felt we had achieved more than he'd ever expected, and called it a day.

For me, apart from the interest in the murder as a whole, I had 'discovered' an 800 acre site beside the Thames, which had lots of open water and reed beds, plus large areas of shingle which might hold breeding pairs of Oyster Catcher, Ringed and Little ringed Plover or even Lapwing.

I hadn't seen the likes of such a place for years, and couldn't wait to get out to explore what wildlife it might hold.

A few weeks after the Landfill job, I got a call from Professor 'taff' Cameron - one of our regular pathologists, who wanted me to film a murder/suicide post mortem, in conjunction with my old friend Det.Supt. 'Lee' Marvin.

Lee was a character with whom I had worked on many occasions, who soon had you in stitches from his collection of risque stories and jokes, making the job in hand seem almost incidental.

The job at the London Hospital took nearly three hours, but Lee's string of anecdotes concerning various colleagues, and the world at large, made the time fly, and on completion, we retired to taff's office to demolish the ritual bottle of hard stuff.

There was no doubt, when you were in the company of such a lovely pair of characters as these, your general education improved in leaps and bounds, and it was a wrench to go back to normal grotty jobs.

Down at Muckingford, the barn owls now had seven chicks, so I set up an Infra-Red camera trigger across the window they were using as access to the barn, hoping to record the prey they brought to their young.

To get some light on top of the flying bird, I had to suspend one of my flashes from the ceiling, pointing down at 45degrees, while the other two units were placed either side of the camera, to give a general lighting effect.

The camera with its 40mm lens was mounted on one of my sturdy Bilora tripods, which extended to a height of eight feet, the Hasselblad camera being accessed by using a twelve-foot folding ladder!

The Yuasa battery packs powering the flash-heads were attached to the flashes themselves, cutting out the need for power wires trailing everywhere, the only wires in use were those connecting the IR trigger to the camera, and the synch lead from the prime flash to the camera.

During a typical night's operation, I would get through a complete twelve exposure film, although I always triggered the first exposure myself, just to check the system was working correctly.

With the owls flying in and out, it was natural to expect that half the shots would be 'bum' shots, and un-useable, except perhaps to note the slight difference in plumage between the male and female.

I wished a few times that I had some device which only triggered the camera when the birds flew in!

In early July, I copped one of those jobs which start off suggesting an inconclusive result is likely, but ends up by being highly successful in quite a bizarre way.

Initially, the job started when a Canning Town disc-jockey, Bernie B. went to his wife's home in Ilford, to have serious words with the man she was living with, and was never seen again.

After trying for some weeks to locate him, relatives reported his disappearance to police, and he was eventually filed as a missing person.

For quite some time police made routine enquiries concerning his whereabouts, before word began filtering back that he had been killed at his wife's house, and the body 'got rid of'.

After further investigation and close questioning of witnesses by detectives, two men were arrested regarding B's disappearance, one denying any part in the killing, but stating he knew where the body could be found, the other man saying nothing.

The second arrested man was a right Rambo character, who had been captured by police after learning he was holed up in a deserted caravan, deep in the woods at Little Baddow in Essex.

He was apparently 'living off the land' by using snares and a crossbow to kill rabbits.

When officers finally located the derelict caravan, he sped off, and was only recaptured when an officer and his dog chased him into the vicinity of a stinking, black-water pond.

Seeing no immediate sign of the man, despite his dog going bolo at the water's edge, the officer scanned the pond closely, noticing a disturbance on the surface a few yards out amongst the reeds.

Wading into the stinking pond with his dog, he forced the suspect to the surface, and arrested him.

The suspect had tried unsuccessfully to escape capture by breathing through a hollow pipe whilst under water, but the rising bubbles gave him away.

Following the first prisoner's description of the burial site at Little Baddow, we all assembled at the edge of a small wood, and waited while Sandy our Lab.liason officer laid down a series of tapes for the search teams to follow.

With dense undergrowth making forward visibility impossible after just a few feet, I reckoned this was going to be a long old job.

For most of that sunny July day, officers searched along the plots removing loads of vegetation and roots, but finding nothing of interest.

At some stage, we were told, either en-route or at the wood, B's head and hands had been hacked off, to make identification difficult, before dumping his body into a deep hole.

Our informant then went on to say the severed head had been thrown into a nearby gravel pit, and I spent a couple of hours crawling through tangled vegetation and mud with our dog handlers, in an attempt to locate the darn' thing, but without success.

As the sun began it's dip towards the horizon, Det.Supt. John Grieve announced that as we hadn't got very far, we could leave it for today, and return at 0700 in the morning, when he hoped to have more for us to go on.

The next day dawned bright and clear - it was obvious we were in for a spell of fine weather, which was infinitely better than sploshing about in pouring rain under the trees, on this sort of job.

The search teams had been stripping back top vegetation in a repeat of yesterday's efforts for about an hour, when a car drew up, and John G. got out, came across to where we were working, and said "Any luck so far lads?"

On being given a negative reply he said "Ok, hold on a minute will you?" and went back to the car, where he had an earnest conversation with a handcuffed man in the rear.

As John and the handcuffed man got out, I heard him say "Right that's enough buggering about from you, this time I want it straight, you show us the right spot now, or I'm going to get very, very upset!"

They entered the wood, and immediately went a dozen yards to the right of where we had been digging, and, pausing under some trees the prisoner said, "I think this is it, yeah I'm sure this is it, it was dark then you know, but it looks about right to me"

"Well, you and I will go back to the car and wait shall we?"

"We'll see if the lads turn up anything, otherwise as I said, I'm going to be very upset"

With a new location to search, Sandy Sanderson laid out more pegs and tapes, and the lads began clearing off the top scrub, so that metal probes could be put down, and give the dogs a chance to sniff.

As usual, I filmed the scene completely before any work was done, and now that a search was in progress, I recorded the dog handlers pushing their long metal probes into the ground, before pulling them up for the dogs to sniff.

It was all good training stuff, which could be used later by the video production team if there was a dog training film to make.

It certainly wouldn't be wasted.

As the handler nearest me retrieved his probe and offered it to his dog, the animal yelped excitedly, and started scrabbling at the hole in the ground.

"This looks promising!" said the handler, and banged the probe in again about a foot to one side of the last hole.

Again the dog yelped, and started digging the earth, like he was bound for Australia.

"Ok. boy hold it. Hold it!" said the handler, and leashed his dog, while someone went to fetch John G.

"So you think you've got something then?" said John, his face wreathed in smiles "It's amazing what a little refreshment of the memory can do, ok Alan, you cover this area as the lads start to dig, and we'll see just what turns up"

At that moment, DC. Andy Millar grabbed the metal probe and put it to his nose, his eyes enlarging like gob-stoppers as he turned towards John G. saying in mock seriousness "Hey, guv'nor do you know what this really is?"

"No, what is it?" said John G. a puzzled look crossing his face.

"It's money guv'nor, fuggin' money, THAT's what it is!" and we all burst out laughing as the tension broke, trust that miserable Scots git to equate our find with overtime!

I got myself tucked into one corner while Sandy and an officer started to dig - I could see everything they were excavating, and wouldn't miss a thing, this could be very interesting.

One of the lads commented "The prisoner said they wrapped him in a red blanket when they carried him in here, so it should still be on the body"

"That'll be great if it's right" said Sandy, "We always like 'em wrapped up, it keeps the body in good condition, and stops the bluebottles getting in"

They continued to scrape like archaeologists at a dig, getting deeper and deeper until they were about three feet down.

"Bloody hell!" Sandy grunted as he scrabbled about, head first in the hole, "I hope we find something soon, this is bloody killing me" and I had to admit it did look funny seeing two men's bums sticking up in the air like burrowing badgers.

"If you'd like to take break" I called. "It's getting a bit dark down there, and I can hardly see what you're doing.

I'd like to get some extra lighting on the scene, Ok?"

I had the portable generator on board to power up a couple of 500watt lamps if we carried on 'til dark, but until then, I thanked PAG portable battery belts for their invention, and powered up the 100watt camera-top light with one of those.

Suddenly Sandy shouted, "What colour material did you say he was wrapped in, red? If so we've got it, I've just uncovered some material that looks red to me, and it's soft underneath too, could be the body"

I moved the camera so that I was looking straight down into the hole, and as the two lads got their heads out of the way, filmed the red material they had just uncovered. It seemed about right to me.

In just over an hour, they had the earth removed from around the body, and we were ready to lift everything out onto a stretcher.

The pathologist had been called, and as we waited for him to arrive, it seemed a good idea to brew a nice pot of tea.

As the pathologist and Sandy began carefully removing the red blanket from around the body, I began filming, it was amazing how well preserved our friend was, despite having been several feet under for quite some time.

This was probably due to the cool damp soil, and the almost mummifying effect the close wrapping had upon the body.

"Pity we haven't got the head or hands, but that shouldn't hold us back too much" said the pathologist.

"We should find plenty to go on for an identification, let's get him back to the mortuary for a proper look"

In no time we were off to St.Margaret's Hospital, Epping, for a nice little post-mortem to finish off the day.

A couple of days after the exhumation, the murder team received information that the head had actually been dumped in the West Thurrock Angling club pits near Rainham, while another source said it was buried in a graveyard at Danbury.

Naturally both sites had to be thoroughly investigated and cleared.

We were still enjoying nice sunny weather, so I relaxed on the bank of the angling pit, casually watching Coots and Great Crested Grebes on the' water, while the Met.Police underwater search team, swam this way and that, in an attempt to find the missing head, but without success.

Just after lunch they announced they were happy there was nothing for them in the pit, so we thanked them for their efforts, and made our way to Danbury, to search the graveyard there.

After ten minutes searching around, we couldn't find anyone in residence, and killed time waiting for some church-person to arrive, by having a quick shufti around the various graves, to see if there were any indications of recent operations.

There were a couple of those 'above ground' memorials protected by railings, which could be the hiding place, and others which had lids showing signs of recent removal, perhaps it was under one of those?

It wasn't a very big graveyard to cover, but if it was the hiding place for the missing head, it could be anywhere!

Apart from opening up everything that had a lid on it, or showing recently disturbed earth, I couldn't see how we were going to find the ruddy thing!

No doubt because we were all busy pottering around, nobody noticed the local vicar arrive on his bike, but all of a sudden he was amongst us, bristling and highly indignant, claiming police were ransacking his graveyard, without informing him first.

The D/S. took him to one side, and gently explained that nothing had been touched as yet, we were merely looking, if we did find anything suspicious, we would naturally go through the proper channels before going any further.

"Well I'm going to stay here as long as you are all present" he huffed. "Who on earth ever heard of a head being buried secretly in a cemetery?" and I heard someone quietly mutter, 'Someone who wanted a head start, that's who' and I smiled.

We gently lifted the tops off a couple of tombs that showed signs of being recently moved, but found nothing, and the search was put on hold, until more reliable evidence came in.

Apart from flying some aerial shots from India 99, which showed the approach to the little wood from the nearest road, and rambo's caravan buried deep in the nearby woods, I wasn't involved in any further investigative work, and went back to the section to put the film together in a way that would make sense to a jury.

It was an involved, but very interesting crime.

I had just finished editing the Bernie B. murder tape, when I got another phone call from Taff Cameron, saying how pleased he was with the last PM. film I sent him, could I come to the London Hospital and do another one?

There was no doubt about it, if you were a 'one man band' as I was, covering the thousand square miles of Metropolitan London with the video, producing copies for court, plus statements, and all the filing and paperwork involved, it sometimes got a bit much, and at times like this, felt I needed a good 'number two'.

Could I ever make a strong enough case to get one?

At the London, I was greeted by an affable Taff Cameron, and his accolyte in mirth, Det.Supt.Lee Marvin, saying this was a unique murder/suicide job, where a body had been recovered from the depths of a Swiss Lake.

I set up my gear as usual, and started filming as Taff began work, his comments going straight onto tape to reinforce his findings, which of course severely curtailed the funny stories that normally emanated from Lee.

"Well that's it, I think it's a fair job, we can wash and tidy up before going upstairs to my office for the closing summary of the film. Ok. with you, young Alan?"

Breaking the gear down, and humping it all up a flight of stairs to re-assemble for another shoot is always a bit of a bind, but with Taff and Lee for company, things went just that bit easier.

It didn't take long to film Taff's summary of the PM, and I noticed Lee was already in the corner, quietly supping a double of the hard stuff, as we came to the end.

"Tell me, did you hear about old so and so who .." Lee commenced, as Taff expertly doled out generous doubles for himself and me, and I could see, as the story rolled on, it was like letting the cork out of a bottle.

Lee had been silenced for far too long during the PM. and now it all had to come out.

As the glasses re-filled, I made an excuse to check the video camera still sitting on it's tripod, and switched to record, pushing up the microphone volume, hoping I could get some of Lee's stories on tape without him being aware.

"Did I ever tell you the one about the Japanese Kamikaze pilot who couldn't get a flight because..." and away he went on an absolutely hilarious tale concerning the unfortunate Kamikaze pilots' sexual exploits, and his eventual crash into scrap iron depot, everything sprinkled with F's and Zeds to emphasize certain situations.

Under those circumstances, it didn't take long to demolish the poor old bottle, but I stuck rigidly to my second glass - after all I was driving the job's vehicle, and didn't want any trouble if I had a 'touch'.

Taff Cameron was more than pleased with his second PM film, and asked for a copy to be sent to the Detective Training School at Hendon, with the intention of showing officers what a typical murder/suicide PM looked like.

I thought this would be a super chance to produce a gag which might surface sometime in the future.

I made the copy as requested, but after the final titles rolled, I waited five seconds before recording on sound only, the hilarious story of the unfortunate Kamikaze pilot, eloquently recited by Lee.

If the Instructor or whoever, was a bit slow in shutting down the VCR, all and sundry would be treated to the poor old Kamikaze pilots' serious physical defects and misfortunes!

It was about this time, a shuffle of responsibilities took place in the section, and I was given the opportunity to state my case for an assistant, which I did with great gusto, insisting on the best chap I knew for the job, Ian Nicholls, who happened to live near me at Hornchurch.

If I could get him, I knew I was onto a winner, he was a keen scenes of crime photographer, very knowledgeable regarding computers and electronics, and would tackle pretty well anything, but office politics being what they were, I didn't give much for my chances.

At the crucial meeting, I made my best case, and said whom I wanted, to be greeted with scorn from my peers, saying I was snaffling the best chap, and leaving other managers with less attractive choices.

I replied that was tough, but he was the only chap I considered suitable from the list available, who could be relied on to do the prestigious job properly, I didn't want any passengers.

The next day, as the list of new postings came out, I was both pleased and surprised to see I had got my man, Dave Teague, our first civilian boss, must have seen what I was trying to achieve, and had concurred.

Now we were going somewhere!

# Chapter Thirty One

In September, Ch.Insp.B. from Tottenham organised a return visit to Broadwater farm, with the intention of raiding addresses in Tangmere House, and arresting people for openly trading drugs on the estate.

We had two cameras on the go, both Ian's and mine, and we reckoned with those we could cover any eventuality that came up. About twenty police officers were involved in the hit, and we all crammed into a five-ton van, which rolled up to Tangmere House as though delivering goods.

At a command over the radio, the tailboard dropped, and we quickly got ourselves into the building - I went with one lot to the second floor, while Ian disappeared off with the second group to search an adjacent address.

For some unknown reason the estate 'lookout' system didn't work too well that day, and we managed to get outside the target's door, without being sussed, it was uncanny. I had the video running as we entered the building, but now I switched on the top light as the lads prepared to take out the door.

"Ok. now!" said the Insp. and two lads with sledge hammers swung to it with great gusto, the reverberating thuds sounding like an elephant dancing the two-step on the upstairs floor.

Like passenger's heads popping out of old-style train windows when a train reaches the station, blacks began popping their heads out of doorways to see what the hell was going on. I noticed a couple of little tackers whizzing away down the corridor at the far end, no doubt to warn all and sundry, the 'old-bill' were at it again!

The two men swung with fierce determination, twenty, and then thirty smashing blows, but still the door held firm, what was the heck was it made of, concrete?

"Ok. next two take over sharpish, give these lads a break, if he's in there with drugs, they'll be going down the toilet by now!"

I had stood a little to one side at the beginning, filming as the sledges started to go in, I thought it would only be a matter of minutes before it went, but this was getting silly.

With the second team exhausted, another pair attacked, and the brickwork round the edges of the door finally began to crumble, revealing the door firmly set in an angle iron frame bolted into the wall.

You weren't going to get past that in a hurry!

I was getting distinctly embarrassed filming the apparently ineffectual efforts of the lads to get us in, and was in two minds to stop filming. However, the thought of questions flying around concerning that course of action, on top of the present fiasco, prompted me to leave it running.

At last with a great crash the door went down, and I stepped across the rubble alongside the Insp, filming as we went in.

It turned out to be a bit of an anti climax really - there was no-one at home!

"I suppose you filmed that bloody fiasco?" said one of the exhausted hammer swingers.

“Yes I’m afraid I did, it’s all part and parcel of the raid, but never mind, I’m sure it will give someone, somewhere, a damn’ good laugh”

We didn’t find any great drugs ‘stash’ as expected, only a few bits and bobs that weren’t really worth all that effort, and I hoped Ian had been more successful with his address.

A little while after my birthday in August, Lisa said as things between us had settled into a nice stable pattern, wouldn’t it be a good idea to get married?

Helen, who was now eleven, seemed very happy with the idea, so on September 17th. we tied the knot at the Brentwood registry office - each of us for the second time.

For some weeks prior to the wedding, Lisa and I had been planning a three-week holiday in Peru, hoping to see Machu Picchu, and some of the other sights such as the Nazca lines, Lake Titicaca, and perhaps Tiwanaku on the Bolivian border.

We thought the holiday could double as our honeymoon, and felt we had to try the adventure now before we got too old, you never knew how much time you had left!

At the Yard I was pleased to see how quickly Ian got his feet ‘under the table’ and was well able to do things the way I liked them done, the service certainly wouldn’t come to grief while I was away, and we wouldn’t lose impetus.

I remembered from past experience, there was always some bugger hiding somewhere, who wanted to alter things as soon as your back was turned, but we shouldn’t suffer that nonsense now.

The sixteen hour flight to Caracas in Venezuela and on to Lima, was a bit of a drag, but Lisa and I did what we always did when travelling long distance, and accepted the local time scale on arrival.

If it was breakfast time, then treat the day as a new one, and DON’T go to sleep, wait until the evening.

That way we had never suffered the so-called ‘jet-lag’.

Our first couple of days in Lima were a real eye-opener, the extreme poverty, cheek-by-jowl with affluence, reminded me of my time in Egypt, and the whole place had a brooding air of oppressive menace. This was visibly accentuated by steel-helmeted, AK-47 toting soldiers, posted at intervals along the pavements, and on every street corner, making tourist photography difficult.

As Lisa and I walked in the main square thronged with people, a saloon car screeched to a halt ten feet in front of us, the door swung open, and a man, an arm’s length away, was bundled into the car by two pistol toting civilians.

Nobody around us seemed to react as the car swished off, and I wondered for a minute if I’d imagined it all!

Walking along by the ‘Palace’, it’s ugly, cast-iron railings reminiscent of Buckingham palace, I felt quite intimidated by the line of steel helmeted soldiers, one every ten feet or so, standing with their AK-47’S across their chest, like automatons.

Each man stood to attention behind a white line painted on the road, six feet out from the railings, no doubt to define his area of patrolling.

Whilst looking at the soldiers, I noticed the roof of the Spanish style palace had several Black Vultures perched on it, and I stepped forward to get a better view.

Immediately there was an ear-splitting blast on a whistle, and I nearly jumped out of my skin, as the nearest soldier pointed to the pavement at my feet, blowing furiously.

Frozen to the spot, I vainly tried to make out what had got him so excited, but he continued to blast away, his face purpling as he stabbed his finger repeatedly at my feet.

Suddenly I saw what he was getting at, my toe was on his white line, obviously a VERY serious offence!

As soon as I stepped back, he let the whistle dangle on it's lanyard, and resumed his rigid posture, gazing fixedly ahead while gripping his rifle. They certainly were a weird lot!

It wasn't particularly relaxing walking round the sights of Lima either, especially in the busy shopping centre, as we were soon to discover.

A woman with two small children walking behind us, tapped Lisa on the shoulder, saying "Pigeon. Pigeon!" in broken English, indicating by her actions that a pigeon must have messed on her shoulder.

At the same time a man and a boy suddenly appeared in front of us, and tried to snatch Lisa's bag, as she turned to examine her shoulder.

The instant it became clear that something was amiss, Lisa covered her bag with both hands, and backed into a convenient shop doorway, leaving the would be thieves nothing else to do but leg it away, empty handed. It had been a narrow escape.

After that incident, we began to read 'body-language' as people came towards us, and we could see after a while, they never looked you in the face, only at what you carried or wore.

You were the prey, and they were out hunting you!

With such overt aggression, it was impossible to take any photographs of interesting shop fronts or local people, and I had to keep the Nikon hidden under my jacket, only taking a photograph when shielded by Lisa.

We became quite paranoid by it all, and couldn't get away quickly enough from Lima to start the rest of our trip.

The traffic in Lima had to be seen to be believed, there were of course the nice shiny Mercs, owned by those who had the power and the dosh to buy them, but in the main, the ramshackle heaps that tottered round town could be bettered by anyone walking into any English scrapyard, and buying the first car he saw.

There were cars without windows, many without doors, others with no roof or mudguards, all chuntering around and breaking down in the most inconvenient places.

On one major round-about in town, a ten-ton, flat-bed lorry had broken down, something was seriously wrong with the rear axle by the look of things, but there it stood, totally unattended, it's wheel off and lying in the road.

A great pool of black oil spread lazily across the carriageway, and by the look of tyre tracks patterning through the goo, the lorry had been there for some time, but nobody seemed to care.

We hailed a taxi, intending to visit one of the Ceramica museums outside town, and flagged down an old Mk.1 Cortina, which rattled and hissed like an old Emmett steam engine as it came to a halt.

Having got our destination and fare sorted out, our man got the shaking wreck into gear, and juddered off.

I whispered to Lisa I didn't think we had any great hopes of getting to our destination at all, and within minutes, I was proved right!

After about three or four miles, the poor car crunched to a halt, and our man hopped out, trying to spot what the trouble might be.

He didn't have far to look as the engine didn't have a bonnet, but he seemed to be twiddling with something lashed with string to the carburettor.

"How far museum?" I asked in my best Spanish.

"Car Ok. we go soon museum"

"How far museum, how many kilometres?"

"Two kilometres, car take, you wait"

I said to Lisa, "I'm sure this thing isn't going any further, let's get out and walk, the area doesn't look too rough, we should be Ok"

As we got out, our man rushed round to what remained of the door saying "You give Intis, more Intis to fix car, we go museum"

Laughing at his ruddy cheek, I gave him the agreed fare, and we walked off, I didn't think his car would move from that spot in ages!

Our coach left Lima that afternoon, bound for Pisco, via Chincha Alta, and as we bundled along in the golden sunshine, a lolloping rumble developed under our seat, which I recognised straight away as coming from the rear wheels.

"Hold on tight, I think we're going to have a puncture any minute now!"

I had hardly finished speaking, when there was an almighty bang, followed by the coach leaning to the left, and we came to a bumpy halt.

"How on earth did you know that was going to happen?" Lisa asked.

"Quite simple really, I remember having exactly the same thing happen to us in Iran with the Landrover, so I knew what to expect"

After some heated Spanish dialogue between the driver and our guide, the driver got out, and went round to examine the burst tyre. I could see by his face as he stood outside our window, he was thoroughly pissed off about the job he had to do next.

"Would everyone get off the coach please?" asked our guide "The driver wants the bus as light as possible, so that he can jack up the vehicle and change the tyre, we shouldn't be too long"

I watched as our man got the bottle jack out and fixed it under the chassis, prior to getting the wheel off.

I could see he had the spare already alongside, so after undoing the nuts and removing the old wheel, it would be a simple matter of putting the new wheel on to get us rolling again, yes? Not so.

As he pushed the punctured wheel to one side, and offered up the new one, I let out a howl of laughter - I just couldn't believe what I was seeing.

The old wheel had five stud holes, while the new one had four.

There was no way he was going to fix it on that hub for sure!

I bet his spare hadn't been bolted to the chassis as it should have been - it was probably stowed in the luggage space under the coach, so no one actually noticed it was the wrong type of wheel for that particular coach.

It was a good job the bus had twin wheels at the rear, and we were able to drive slowly on the remaining good tyre to get a repair done.

The 'repair depot' turned out to be a roadside shack built of corrugated iron, about twenty feet square, with a great chimney in the centre, belching black smoke.

"We are going to be here for some time while the puncture is repaired" said our guide, "I'm sorry for the delay, but there's nothing else I can do"

Out of interest, I went over to the shack, and saw it was divided into two parts, one containing a huge vulcanising machine plus the owner, while the other half contained a woman and her three children.

They were sitting on the straw covered ground eating a meal.

It was obviously their home.

In double quick time the owner had his hacksaw at work on the old tyre, cutting away the damaged portion, before sticking thick layers of rubber goo on the inside.

Applying the same rubber goo on the outside, he slotted in a new piece of tread, before bundling the whole lot into the autoclave for cooking.

As it was dark, there wasn't a lot to see or do, so we waited, and waited and waited, until at last, the driver reappeared with his mended wheel, and stuck it back on the bus.

I couldn't believe it. Here we were in the middle of nowhere, and a chap and his family living in a solitary shack, had been able to repair a serious blow-out, and get us back on the road again in a few hours. It was quite remarkable.

The rest of the journey to Pisco was quite uneventful, and our guide whisked us into some very basic accommodation for a quick meal and bed, saying the next day she was taking us on an excursion to the nearby Balesto guano islands, where we would see fantastic Seal and seabird colonies.

When we eventually approached the islands, the roar I had taken to be pounding surf, turned out to be the combined barking of hundreds of seals crowding the stony beaches in huge colonies.

They were pretty tame though, and came to within a few feet of the boat, looking at us with great gob-stopper eyes, or rushing past like jet black torpedoes, it was wonderful stuff, and I managed to get some really good photographs.

Our journey continued during the late afternoon using a public bus, we had roughly 300 miles to cover to Arequipa, a town we were staying at for a couple of days to sight-see, and acclimatise ourselves to the high altitude.

Our ever present friend Murphy had other ideas though.

Somewhere round about ten o'clock that night, our 'new' bus conked out, and refused to go any further, but our resourceful guide said we should all get our luggage off, and wait by the roadside.

She fully expected another lorry or bus to pass during the night, and with a bit of luck she might get us a lift.

I suppose it was something new to sit by the road and gaze at the stars, after all it was clear bright night, with fiercely burning stars, but it was quite chilly too.

We must have been there for about two hours without even the sound of a plane, when lights appeared in the distance, and our guide called out "Ok. get ready, if I say go, get onboard as soon as possible, we might not get a second chance".

As the lights drew near, I could see it was another bus, and our guide stepped into the road to flag it down, but even at that distance it looked pretty full to me.

As it screeched to a halt, she went up to the driver's door, and after several minutes intense conversation turned to us and said "I've arranged that if we each give him a couple of pounds - which he'll split with the conductor, they'll take us on to Arequipa.

Other than that we'll be stuck out here all night"

The ten of us piled onboard, only to find every seat taken, so we stood in the gangway with our cases and bags, until we arrived in Arequipa some hours later, totally exhausted.

Through the weird sensation of an early rising following a hectic night, we awoke to the frantic screaming of swifts, whizzing round our hotel in their hundreds, obviously enjoying the bright sunshine heralding the dawn of a new day.

Before leaving home, we had read a pamphlet describing accommodation standards in rural Peru, which stated that in the hotel we were now staying, you had to be careful about switching on the electric light in the one and only shower.

They went into some detail about the switch being broken, bare wires visible etc; and the need for great care.

Considering the pamphlet had been written by a visitor at least a year before our visit, it was absolutely hilarious to find the same switch still broken and lethal, as faithfully described in the tourist literature!

One of the things both Lisa and I had wanted to do whilst in Peru was to visit the ancient Nazca lines, and we took advantage of an excursion leaving Arequipa the next day.

I had always thought Von Danniken's explanation of the lines as 'space-guides' a lot of silly rhubarb, and wanted to see them for myself.

Apparently the best way to see them is by air, so we hired a single engine aircraft from the airstrip at Nazca, and took to the air.

The 'lines' etched in the soil by removing the dark stones were all that I hoped they would be, and we circled the area taking photographs of the spider, humming bird, and other weird designs, until our time was up.

I felt the explanation that the designs were meant to indicate to the gods in the sky, what was important to the local people in their time of need, a far more plausible tale than Von Danniken's.

The next leg of our trip ended at Puno, on the edge of Lake Titicaca, a place I never dreamed I would ever visit, but here it was, the highest lake in the world, and although I felt only slightly nauseous, poor Lisa was feeling the effects of extreme altitude quite badly.

During our couple of days stay, we did the touristy bit by visiting and photographing the reed island people far out on the lake, and suffered the quite unfathomable peculiarities of meals and drinks served at our hotel.

We usually got a character I knicknamed 'Manuel', as he was the spitting image of John Cleese' bete noir in Fawlty Towers, but in complete contrast, was utterly silent. He didn't even said 'Que?'

Manuel was totally unable to make a cup of tea the same way twice running, and in desperation we settled for the coca-leaf tea, as drunk by the locals, and quickly left the hotel to eat somewhere else!

An excursion to the fabled city of Tiwanaku, often thought to have been a major centre of civilisation prior to the Inca, proved be both awe inspiring, and at the same time a little depressing.

The city lay in a vast expanse of barren land, with very little else to see, except a low hill nearby which could have been a buried temple.

The one thing I had previously read about, the Sun Gate, did come up to expectations with its intricate pictograms and hieroglyphs reputedly working out in detail forthcoming events, up to thousands of years in the future.

As we walked amongst the ruins, children hasseled us, trying to sell artifacts allegedly looted from the city, most looked like recently made clay images chucked into a fire to make them look old and authentic.

One or two did look rather genuine though.

The quality of the stonework that remained was mind-blowing in it's accuracy, and if the ancients only had non-ferrous tools to work with, I just couldn't see how on earth they achieved it.

Leaving Puno, we travelled by bus to Copacabana, situated on the border between Peru and Bolivia, where we disembarked by the lake, staggering along the beach with our cases between the various money changers' stalls, towards the whitewashed customs post.

Then it was back onto another bus bound for La Paz.

It was all chatter and chaos, a bit like Hampstead Heath during the holidays, and a bit of a laugh.

I quite liked La Paz, it seemed a vibrant, modern city, but exhibiting the usual third world affluence alongside desperate poverty.

One evening, as our party made it's way on foot from our hotel to a nearby fashionable restaurant, we passed several children huddled in doorways out of the cold wind, crying, and begging for food.

It made me feel quite guilty that I was about to eat a good meal, while these youngsters apparently had nothing.

I spoke to our guide about the children, who replied that there were literally hundreds of youngsters like them with nowhere to go, and little to eat, staying on the streets all night, or anywhere else they could find.

There were of course some who made begging their 'profession' and returned home at the end of the day with a few coins, but most of these looked genuine to me.

Having heard the music of Paco Pena and the Inti Illimani group, it was fascinating to see at last the actual Mt. Illimani towering like a huge backdrop behind the city of La Paz, it certainly looked a magnificent sight, and well worth photographing.

As I took my first photograph, I noticed a couple of shoe-shine boys plying their trade next to a fountain, so I changed to the 200mm lens and began recording them at work, they were magic.

I stayed focussed on them for about fifteen minutes, getting some nice local touches, when I felt a hand on my shoulder, and a smart-suited chap flashed me his ID saying something in Spanish about photos.

In English I replied I was a tourist, and taking photos of the people and places in La Paz, what was wrong with that?

He asked to see my passport, and went across to a colleague who stood nearby, looking occasionally in my direction.

In fair English he said it was ok. to photograph the views and buildings, but he didn't like me photographing their poor people, that wasn't good.

To me it was a typical example of high-handed interference in personal affairs, which didn't endear me to their regime one little bit.

An unusual excursion from La Paz was to visit Mt. Chacaltaya, a snow covered mountain well outside town, which supposedly contained the highest ski slope in the world. It was apparently a must see.

As our little bus zig-zagged it's way through the tortuous foothills, it was obvious how difficult travel was in this area, and with the altitude reading well over 10,000ft, the lack of oxygen made us breathless, whenever we exerted ourselves.

At last our bus came to a halt outside a building not unlike a French Alps Ski station, and we all piled out into the dazzling snow covered scenery.

On our right, a huge bowl set in the mountain flank contained the ski slope, which started several hundred feet above us, and continued down the mountain for half a mile or so, before ending in a jumble of rocks and boulders as big as busses.

God help anyone flashing down the length of the slope at speed and not being able to stop in time, they'd be splattered to pulp on the rocks!

"You can continue to the top of the mountain if you wish" our guide informed us.

"It is a bit steep, but if you keep to the ridge you should make it alright, but do remember we are just over 16,000' altitude at the moment, so take it easy, and don't overdo it"

Lisa and I struggled about a hundred feet up the jagged ridge before flopping exhausted onto a conveniently placed seat.

This was damned hard work, and our lungs seemed to receive little useful air, despite our great searing gulps.

"If you want to go on, do so, I can't go any further" Lisa said, and I thought she had done remarkably well, considering she had part of her lung removed several years ago.

"I'll see if I can get a bit further then, wait for me here, Ok?"

At that moment, an old lady of about sixty who had been on our trip from the beginning, came up and said, "Are you going to the top? Our guide says it's a wonderful view from there, and don't forget to bring your camera to record the mountains"

Without waiting for a reply, she forged steadily upwards and disappeared out of sight, what a woman!

I took several deep breaths to try and hyper-ventilate, but the sub-zero air temperature scoured my throat like a knife, even though we were in brilliant sunshine.

I couldn't take too much of that!

Slowly, with legs like lead, I fought my way up the ridge, just in time to see the old lady disappearing over a snow covered shoulder two-hundred yards ahead, how the hell did she do it?

I used to think I had a good lung capacity, after all, I had been able to go down to forty-feet depth in the Red Sea, and stay down for three minutes, but this was something else, I felt as weak as a baby!

With my head reeling like a new-year drunk, I fell to my knees, unable to take another step forward, I had only gone a hundred feet since leaving Lisa and I was done, this was a real cruncher!

With my tail metaphorically between my legs, I staggered down to where Lisa sat in the bright sunshine, and collapsed onto the seat next to her, puffing like a grampus.

"Did you make it to the top then?" she asked.

I shook my head in reply, I was still too puffed to answer.

As I sat there recovering, the old lady re-appeared, striding out as though on a country walk, not appearing to be overly worried by the steep descent.

"Didn't manage the top then?" she said, "Don't worry too much about it though, I've done a lot of high climbing, and I'm quite used to it, there's nothing to it really" and away she went, down to the Ski station, leaving me feeling totally inadequate.

Back in Puno, our party made ready to board the train for Cuzco, a journey which went up into the high country and through the mountains, some of which climbed to 20,000ft.

The scenery was fantastic, huge areas of brown sunburned grass swooped up to the foothills of jagged mountains, with only the occasional Vulture or Condor to break the emptiness, it was nature in the raw.

About halfway between Puno and Cuzco, our train slowed to a walking pace before grinding to an ominous halt. Apparently a train coming the other way on the single line system, had come off the rails, and we had to stop.

After a long time doing nothing, our loco was de-coupled, and in a cloud of blue smoke, disappeared into the distance, no doubt going to the assistance of the other train.

As there was nothing else to do, most people got down from the carriages, and either sat beside the track, or wandered off a few yards into the wilderness, but nobody actually came and told us what was happening.

I walked back down the track a hundred yards or so, and took a photograph of our carriages standing ludicrously alone in this vast wilderness. It reminded me of a scene from a spaghetti western, where the baddies steal the loco, and drive off, leaving the passengers stranded in the middle of nowhere. It was almost funny.

I suppose we must have been stuck there three or four hours, before we saw our loco bundling towards us in the distance, if they'd managed to put the other loco back on the line in that short time, I reckoned they'd done a pretty fair job!

Cuzco was all we had expected it to be, a mixture of Spanish architecture brutally imposed over the natural stonework of the Inca, but an interesting city none the less.

Near the stereotype, Spanish-style Cathedral was a super little restaurant run by a German chap who played classical music all day long.

In complete contrast to the pan-pipes of our surroundings, he played Tchaikovsky,

Mozart, Bach, Mahler and other European composers, while his customers enjoyed their meals!

Just after dawn the next day, as we pushed and shoved with locals and other tourists on the steps to the station, Lisa became aware for the second time since being in Peru, that her bucket bag had been slashed with a Stanley knife, and travel brochures and papers fell to the ground.

It was fortunate that we both used body belts for our passports and money, consequently nothing of value was taken.

Mentioning this incident to one of our fellow travellers he replied "Yes, we've seen that, that's why the local women here line their bags with chicken wire, cuts out all that agro"

Our route to Machu-Picchu lay up the valley of the Urubamba river a few miles north of Cuzco, and was usually approached by rail, although to get there, the train had to leave the station in a most peculiar way.

Our loco, sounding as if nothing was oiled, screeched it's way out of the station, hauling our carriages up a steep incline until it could go no further. At this point, the guard at the back got off and pulled a lever beside the track to change the points.

The train now reversed up the next section of track until it could go no further, and our driver then got off at the front.

Pulling a second track-side lever next to his engine he changed the points, which allowed us to ascend the next steep incline.

In this amazing manner, we zig-zagged our way to the top of the hills surrounding Cuzco, before trundling off towards Machu-Picchu with a triumphant whistle!

At a lovely little place named Agua Calientes (hot water) we got off, and were given rooms in a small, but unfinished guest house, run by a friendly English couple. Everything was quite laid-back and easy going, it didn't seem very Peruvian at all.

Nearby was a Banos, or open air baths, filled with hot water bubbling naturally from the ground. You could, if you were that sort of person, go from the quite hot water of the pool, into the freezing cold waters of a nearby stream, and flagellate your body into submission.

Not this fella though, I just stuck with the hot bath!

To get to Machu-Picchu it was necessary to walk along the rail track for about a mile, entering tunnels cut through the mountain above, and dodging into special safety alcoves when a train came past.

Then came the ascent to Machu-Picchu itself, a city hidden somewhere above us in the clouds, but if you had limited time at your disposal, as we did, a small bus was available to save you the hideous ascent to the top.

It was no wonder the lousy Spaniards failed to find the place, it was totally invisible from below, but once at the top, the town with it's fantastic stone buildings and architecture was amazing to behold, it was a photographer's paradise.

Ever since Cuzco, I had been astounded by the sheer precision of stone cutting and joining, and this place was no exception.

It was as if the ancient stonemasons had said 'We can do anything in stone, you name it, we can do it' and the resulting expertise was mind boggling to behold.

There were 'windows' set in walls three feet thick, where the cill instead of being the top of the existing wall, and the sides, square blocks laid to that, they had incorporated part of the cill into a section of the side wall in a graceful curve, the whole piece weighing a ton or more.

How and why did they do it?

It didn't seem practical when the other three corners were square, were they just 'showing off' their considerable expertise?

The whole place was a marvel of construction and stonemasonry, coupled with a very sophisticated system of terrace culture, which allowed the residents to grow food in seemingly inaccessible places.

The next day we explored a similar place known as Ollantay tambo, once again set high above the Urubamba valley floor, and sadly sacked by the Spanish.

To gain access to the place, a track had been cut into the side of an ascending ridge of rock, with a sheer ascending cliff on the nearside, and an awful drop into a gulley on the right.

To keep out intruders, the Inca had built a massive 'gate' halfway up the track, consisting of two huge pillars of rock, each about two-feet square, forming the gateposts, while on the top sat a massive stone lintel, six feet long and two feet square.

I imagine the door itself must have been made of logs, and pulled up into the closed position from inside, like a drawbridge.

As we passed through the gate pillars, and stepped around the now unseated lintel, our guide informed us that the invading Spaniards had eventually fought their way in and levered off the lintel, so they could fight the Inca on horseback without dismounting, as they appeared more formidable that way.

I looked at the inside face of the pillars, and noticed there were boxes cut into the stone, each of which contained a stone roller standing on it's end.

I grabbed hold of one, and slowly revolved it in it's box, and suddenly realised they must have been the means by which the Inca raised and lowered the heavy door.

There was space behind each roller for a heavy hauling rope to pass, but how had they got the oversize rollers into the boxes, resting in their shallow 'cups'?

Close inspection revealed the pillars were made in two halves, top and bottom, joining at the exact spot where the box held it's roller, the hairline join being hardly visible.

The craftsmanship was amazing!

Turning to the dislodged lintel, I saw that the surface which had rested on top of the pillars was extremely smooth, so I reasoned the top of the pillar must be the same.

Despite fears for my safety from Lisa, I climbed on top of the pillar set in the rock face, and was amazed to see it absolutely smooth, polished in fact, but you could still see the multi-pronged, star-shaped impact points of the labourer's obsidian chisel as he dressed it off, it was as though time had stood still.

I got my camera with the macro lens, and took several photographs of this amazing work, before getting down, to be told by Lisa the rest of the party had gone ahead, and were well out of sight.

At the top of the track, we were confronted with yet more amazing craftsmanship in stone, three huge blocks of stone set in a row, each weighing several tons, were said to be part of a religious building.

The stones were about six feet square, each one fitting to the next with the usual hair line join, but in one instance, earth-tremors had separated two of the stones by an inch, and it was possible to see right through.

I remembered then, reading the hypothesis of one learned chap, who said he thought the stones were only hair line joined at the face edge, and behind that it was all rough and didn't matter.

I looked closely at these two monster blocks to see if that was indeed true, and found it was not.

Even where one block had a slight warp or twist to it, the adjacent block followed that contour exactly, matching the profile right the way through, and I took some photographs to prove it.

How on earth had the ancient craftsmen achieved such an amazing result?

On what was to be our last day in Cuzco, Lisa and I went off on our own to explore the ruins of Secsuwayman, or sexy-woman as we heard it described, and were again astounded by the sheer brilliance of the stonework, where acre upon acre of construction showed just how superb these ancient artisans had been.

Massive stones, graduating from huge ones at the bottom to smaller ones at the top, fitted together with knife-like precision on the straights and curves in a display which was quite incredible.

From our elevated position above Cuzco, we could look down on the city and it's airport, the very place we should be flying from tomorrow morning, despite a report on the radio saying that one of the BAC111's taking off the day before had flipped over and crashed, killing 17 passengers on board!

We hoped it wasn't a bad omen.

The next day, Lisa and I were the last to get aboard our BAC111, and as we walked down the gangway toward our seats, the pilot gunned the engines and moved onto the runway for take off.

Against the pull of full acceleration, we staggered forward with our hand luggage, collapsing into the seats just as the aircraft left the ground.

What kind of Fred Karno's army was running this outfit anyway?

The seats were pretty tatty and dirty, with food trays broken and hanging by one corner, in fact the whole interior of the aircraft looked well used and shoddy. We could only hope the engines and other bits necessary to keep us in the air were working better than this lot aappeared!

The flight back to Lima was fortunately uneventful, and after a day's walking round the city's shops for last minute gifts, we were on our way back to the UK. listening to the pilot's report of the raw weather we could expect on our return to London.

# Chapter Thirty Two

Perhaps it was a coincidence, maybe not, but on Nov.5th. my friend DCI. Albert Patrick - now posted to Limehouse, asked me to attend a big drugs bust going down on a pleasure boat moored on the Thames, saying there could easily be fireworks ahead!

Apparently there were two main offenders running the acid-house party, but to keep the lid on security, no-one was being told the exact location, until the final briefing that very evening.

"Well chaps" said our DCI. "This will be a big do, and I want the best job possible, remember we have Mr. Parker from SO.3. along with his video gear, and I want as much evidence of prisoners and their drugs as we can.

Call him to your prisoner, and demonstrate what you have found so Alan can film it, before you both leave the boat, Ok?"

Thus, on a bitterly cold night, our breath billowing like smoke, and ice all over the ground, we piled into a couple of large box vans and made our way to the rendezvous south of the river.

In complete darkness and silence, we waited for the signal to move forward, and I checked once again that I was ready to go, top light working, tape colour-barred, and three spare tapes stuffed into the front of my top jacket.

I carried the PAG-Light battery belt cinched tight round my waist - it weighed four kilos, and with the recorder and camera at another fifteen Kilos, I wasn't exactly kitted out for speed.

For safety, I had arranged beforehand with the two chaps jumping off first to grab my elbows and support me as I hit the deck, the old knees weren't up to that sort of rough maltreatment any more!

Quietly our small convoy edged forward, until we were a short distance from the jump off point with everybody wound up, and ready to go.

Suddenly the engine roared into life and we were off at full throttle, swinging rapidly round an unseen corner that threw everyone against one side of the van.

The chap behind me, knowing the load I carried, grabbed me by the scruff of the neck and held on as we skidded to a halt, and the rear shutter slammed up.

"Ok. go, go, go!" said the DS. and we hit the road at the run following the chap in front who hopefully knew where the hell we were going.

By now I was in the first six as we arrived at the top of a ramp which descended sharply towards the jetty below, and I saw below us a large river boat lit by carnival lights absolutely jumping with people.

The down ramp was made of diamond pattern steel sheet, and due to the freezing night was covered in a thin layer of ice, causing the first two lads to go base over apex to the bottom.

Seeing them go, I abandoned any attempt at running, and deliberately slid, legs apart schoolboy style, until I reached the bottom, somehow remaining upright.

Turning left to gain access to the boat, I ran into the backsides of the first wave of officers trying to get aboard, and came to a halt. I wouldn't get on there un-assisted.

"Let the photographer on, let the photographer on!" someone shouted, and I was bodily lifted between the pushing, shoving bodies of police trying to get on, and the panicking party goers trying to get off.

I managed to record the first few officers and their captures, complete with ecstasy or whatever they had, but the scrummage was so bad I got off again, and filmed everyone who left the boat with an officer, whether they were arrested or not.

That way I felt we had a facial record of all those on board, and if they had been found to have substances in their possession, or had previous for handling, then we were covered.

I had never seen so many people get off one boat, until I realised there was a second boat moored immediately behind the Royal Princess, and I had to change tapes to get everybody recorded.

Once the boats were clear of people, I went back on board, filming the dozens of pills, packets and containers littering the floor, and of course the toilets - there were enough goodies shucked down there to keep a whole regiment quiet!

The two main suspects were already in custody and being questioned by police, I don't think they knew what hit them.

It must have seemed of late as though police were turning a blind eye to acid house parties, but this one had definitely come apart at the seams!

It was now 0300, and as I had been on duty since 0800 yesterday, I was feeling a bit knackered, and was less than pleased to hear the DCI. say "Ok. Alan, I want you to go with these lads and the prisoners to search their home addresses, film anything they find."

Both prisoners live locally so it shouldn't take you long"

The first address was no problem, it was quite an ordinary sort of flat and was quickly filmed and searched, but nothing was found, and we moved on to the next.

I must say as we went in, I was totally thrown by the opulence the second address exuded, you would never have believed such a luxurious pad could exist behind the facade of a London E.14 address.

With its obvious architect design and fittings, it wouldn't have looked out of place in 'Homes and Gardens'.

The owner was asked to sit down while I filmed the place from top to bottom prior to our search, and requested a cigarette while he happily answered questions put to him by the officers.

Surely we weren't going to find anything here I thought, and although the interior decor was still under construction, there didn't seem to be anywhere suitable to stash a load of drugs.

"Alan, can you come here a minute?" called one of the lads from the elegantly marbled shower and bathroom.

"Could you film this tile while I take out what's behind it?" and he bent down to remove a facing tile from the pedestal under the handbasin, exposing an area behind, that went quite a way back.

Inserting his hand, he gently withdrew a paper package, and laid it on the floor.

At that point the DI. who had come in quietly behind me, leant over my shoulder and said "What have you got there then?"

"We're just about to unwrap it guv" said the DC. "As soon as Alan is ready to go, we'll see just what we've got" and undoing the paper, he exposed a load of round, whitish-looking tablets.

Over his shoulder the DI. Called out, "Bring D.in here will you?" and as I finished filming, D. came in.

"I'd like you to look at what we've just found hidden behind those tiles there, what do you have to say about that?" said the DI.

In fact D. didn't have a lot to say about anything at that moment, he just went berserk, shrieking and shouting, and lashing out with his feet at anyone who was near.

"You lousy stinking bastards, you've fitted me up, you put that stuff there, it's got nothing to do with me, you lousy fucking bastards!" and it took three officers to pin him to the floor and hold him still.

Back at the nick, the DCI. appeared quite pleased with our efforts, and turned to me saying "Thanks a lot Alan, I'm sure you've got all we need on this job, buzz off home now and get some kip" and I left them to it. It was after all, 0530, and I had been working for 22 hours!

Two years later I received an official commendation from Deputy Assistant Commissioner Taylor, for 'professional abilities leading to the arrest of persons supplying' etc. a nice end to a rather demanding job.

A few days after the Royal Princess escapade, I got a call from DI. S. asking if I would go with him to Yorkshire to undertake another VFI (video film identification) as the first one at Lambeth Court had gone down so well, resulting in a good conviction.

Naturally I was dead keen to expand this new venture, and get the necessary practice in setting up the video camera in covert situations.

Really, it was like natural history filming in reverse, capturing people instead of birds!

The new venue was the town of Keighley in Yorkshire, and the target was a local chap, who once again refused to attend an identity parade, but had to sign on at Keighley Police station every night.

The nick was obviously the best place to capture him on film, but we couldn't work from the outside as there was no cover - he would have to be recorded inside the building.

Keighley nick was one of those old fashioned buildings which get darker the further you travel from the main door, and with it's polished wooden counter, resembled a gloomy ticket kiosk at a railway station.

Customers were obliged to stand in front of a small opening through which all business was done, and the business side of the counter could only be seen by looking over the attending PC's shoulder.

This cramped set-up was about the best place to get our man on film, so I went round behind the counter to see where I might hide the video camera.

The short distance between the back edge of the counter and the office wall was approximately four feet, and already contained a couple of tall filing cabinets, and a grossly overloaded coat stand.

With the duty PC doing the necessary business at the counter, the space would be full!

With so little choice of manoeuvre, I placed the video camera directly behind the coat stand, and fitted the trusty wide-angle lens, which gave me a nice head and shoulders of anyone standing at the pigeon hole.

All I had to do now, was poke the lens forward carefully under an overcoat sleeve, drape the tripod legs with a black cloth, and we were ready to go.

Earlier, I had asked the duty PC if he would disappear from the counter for a few minutes once our man came in, and when he did attend the counter, place the signing-on book the wrong way round, and walk away as though busy.

That way I reckoned we should have a bit more filming time, with our man well framed in the pigeon hole.

The camera's recording cable ran to my video-recorder in the back room, where a small monitor showed us exactly what was going on at the front counter.

When we eventually got the nod that chummy was approaching the nick, all I had to do was switch on the recorder and wait.

Good as gold, he came in, and waited patiently at the counter for the duty PC. but almost as though he suspected something fishy, kept well back from the pigeon hole, allowing us only a view of his nose mouth.

Our PC appeared, and placed the book as requested, but keeping it a little further back, so chummy would have to lean in and get it.

As the PC walked away, talking to a mythical person out of sight, chummy leant in, turned the book around, and signed his name and the time.

We had got him.

Although he was wearing a typical Yorkshireman's flat cap, his face was plainly visible, and he hadn't clocked a thing!

All we needed now were a dozen stooges in flat caps to repeat the same actions, and we were home and dry.

Casting around the station for people to take part in the stooges' line up, I was amazed to learn that one of the volunteers, a relative of our counter PC, was such a dead ringer for the man we had covertly recorded, it was unreal!

An hour later, having got everything we wanted 'in the can' so to speak, we were invited to sample the nick's hospitality by accompanying a couple of their chaps to Harry Ramsden's fish and chip emporium situated just outside of town.

With previous knowledge of the culinary delights to be had at the legendary establishment, I was ready in two seconds flat!

The meal was all that folklore described, superb fish, and a monstrous helping of chips, plus a huge mug of tea, and all for a quid, it was unbelievable!

A little while later I understood the reason for the unique taste of Harry's fish and chips, they had been cooked the old fashioned way in lard fat, which left a fatty deposit on your lips after the meal.

It was quite different from our oil fried food, but it WAS delicious!

Back in London, I stupidly thought that after editing the Keighley stuff, we might, just for once have a quiet run up to the weekend, but it was not to be.

An old friend from many previous public order demonstrations, Insp.D. of TO(20). rang to say they wanted video cover of a National Union of Students breakaway march starting from two separate venues, one at Malet St, near University College, the other from Vincent Square near Victoria.

It was a job requiring two cameras, so Ian Nicholls and I tossed up to see who got what - he won, and I got Vincent Square.

My part of the march started off with no problems at all, the students were in a good mood, keeping to the route prescribed by police, heading towards Lambeth bridge and the Embankment.

The students, forbidden by law to march or demonstrate within the precincts of Parliament whilst it was sitting, had been deliberately routed away from Parliament Square, across Lambeth bridge to the south bank, to keep the Thames between themselves and Parliament.

After filming hundreds of students crossing Lambeth bridge, I tagged along in the middle, following the crowd towards Lambeth Palace on the far side, and although everyone was shouting and waving banners, they still faithfully followed police directives.

As our lot reached the middle of the bridge, students up front began bunching ominously outside Lambeth Palace, forcing everyone else to a halt, and causing local traffic chaos.

It was now 1500hrs.

We heard over a nearby officer's radio that Westminster Bridge had been closed by police at the junction with the Embankment, and there appeared to be a large gathering of students forming at the southern end of Westminster Bridge by St. Thomas' hospital.

Pushing through the crowd towards Lambeth Palace, I noticed behind me a cordon of police forming across our end of Lambeth bridge, sealing it off now the students had passed through, and thought if there was going to be any confrontation at all, it would come from the southern end of Westminster bridge towards Parliament.

Turning to my 'minder,' an officer in plain clothes, I said "I think we ought to get back over Lambeth bridge, and high-tail it to Parliament square, we would be behind police lines there in case the students try crossing the bridge, Ok?"

"I don't think that's a good idea at all" he replied.

" I think we ought to stay where we are and see what happens don't you?"

"We don't know what has happened to the other half of the march" I answered, "But if they come into Parliament square from Whitehall or the Embankment, we'll be shut out, and won't be able to gain access anywhere, I'm going to Parliament square to cover whatever happens there"

I could see he wasn't happy about that, and felt he only wanted to tackle the job from the perimeter, but you can't clock faces at half a mile, so off I went with him reluctantly in tow.

Getting out his miniature tape recorder, my minder frantically dictated notes into the microphone, while I broke into a lolloping trot, hoping to get into the square before things really started popping.

Lugging the heavy video gear was a bind, and it took twenty minutes hard yomping to get to Big Ben, only to find the place still occupied by traffic and tourists, and the first group of mounted police making their way slowly towards to the cordon across Westminster bridge. It was 1535.

Foot Police were beginning to clear the area around Big Ben, persuading people not to cross the bridge, and I felt certain that this is where a confrontation was expected, despite the ruling of Parliament.

A strong police cordon was thrown across the Embankment next to Boadicea's statue, and a row of mounted police took up position across the middle of the bridge facing south, causing people to stop and look about with an air of uncertainty.

They didn't appear to know what was going on, and certainly no-one was telling them.

It was pretty obvious to anyone standing there watching, students were 'infiltrating' Parliament square from across the bridge by posing as members of the public, and if someone didn't wake up to it soon, there would be enough students behind police lines to cause a lot of trouble.

As dozens of students calmly walked through the police vehicle barricade at the southern end of the bridge, and past the mounted police line in the middle, my minder continued to put his observations on tape.

I hoped he was getting it all down in detail - it was obvious as hell, someone 'up top' had goofed, and there was no question as to who were streaming through our lines, as cries of "Maggie, maggie, maggie, out out out !" rent the air.

And still no-one moved to stem the tide.

Several Police personnel carriers were now sandwiched between the crowds at the far end of the bridge, and the horse-line across the middle, and were forced to make a slow, undignified retreat, pulling loads of chanting students towards Big Ben.

A new cordon of vehicles was hastily strung across the bridge by the famous 'White lion' next to the old County Hall, causing hundreds of students to mass on the Embankment steps, chanting and haranguing police like demons.

It was all going ever so slightly pear-shaped.

In the failing light, street lights came on and it started to feel quite cold, would the silly buggers please get fed-up now, and go home?"

The shouting, chanting crowd pushed forward waving their banners, and were literally face to face with the row of mounted police dispersed in front of blockading personnel carriers, and people were getting crushed.

Jeering, chanting masses, egged on by their own excitement, surged forward like a football crowd, causing police horses to back up, virtually sitting on the vehicles immediately behind them.

It was definitely getting very nasty.

To get a better view of things I jumped up on the nearest personnel carrier and filmed the mad scramble going on right under my nose, filming both police and protesters being wrestled from the melee, noting some were on the point of physical collapse.

The sixty or so police holding the crowd, backed up by two rows of mounted colleagues struggled manfully to contain things, but like the power in a surging stream, it was obvious the dam would soon be washed away, and people would be hurt against the blockading vehicles.

Dozens of men and women police officers were fed in through the vehicle cordon to back up their colleagues barely holding the line, but something else had to be done, and quickly.

It was still only 1550.

Behind me I noticed two rows of police horses forming up a few yards behind the vehicle cordon, and thought that a new defence line was being drawn to ease pressure on the forward troops.

Suddenly at 1600 the forward vehicle cordon split into two halves and moved back, revealing a line of approximately thirty mounted police officers strung across the centre of the bridge, looking to me as if they meant business!

At a signal they broke into a trot, and advanced swiftly on the student mob, closely followed by running policemen and women on foot, obviously intent on containing the demonstration by County Hall, once and for all.

My minder, who had been advocating constantly that I come back to the kerb and stay clear, was beginning to get up my nose, so while he was looking elsewhere, I dodged through the cordon of police vehicles and came up behind the officers penning the students into the space directly under the side of County Hall,

I could work far better without my minders' continual constraints at my elbow.

As the students gradually realised they had 'lost it', a lethal barrage of wooden spears showered the containing officers, made by shucking the poster attached to the three foot carrying pole, and then hurling these poles viciously at the police and me.

I was graphically reminded of an attack by Australian aborigines with their spears and woomeras!

Snatch squads went in amongst the shouting, screaming mob, taking out the worst offenders, while encircling police vehicles gradually tightened the cordon behind foot police.

It was nearly over.

Around County Hall the street was ankle deep in discarded pamphlets and posters, resembling a landfill garbage dump, and through it all waded police and demonstrators, horses and vehicles, in a swirling kaleidoscope of madhouse action.

By now the light was fading fast, and I looked across at Big Ben to check the time and saw it was 1605, what a gay day!

Foot-police had dispersed several hundred students from the White Lion area down onto the Embankment, where, with clenched fists and contorted faces, they screamed slogans at police, while the last of their colleagues were removed from the Lion statue.

Police with loud-hailers now directed the remaining demonstrators to clear the area between St. Thomas' Hospital and County Hall, and escorted them through the cordon at the south side of the bridge.

It was all over.

I made my way back to the White Lion, where a Ch/Insp. asked me to video the huge sea of rubbish and spears, but before I could start, I was button-holed by a pompous

Ch.Supt. who gave me right rollicking for daring to stand on the bonnet of one of his carriers to film the demo. I couldn't believe my ears!

I don't suppose for one moment he worried about the damage done to the vehicles by demonstrators, or even the heavy police horses, I think he just wanted to have a go at someone, and I was it.

I told him that if ever I needed a vantage point to film from, I would use whatever came to hand as I thought fit, in the interest of gathering evidence of assaults against police, which left him fuming, silly bugger!

Checking Big Ben again I saw it was 1630 and quite dark, so I made my way over to Canon Row canteen for a bite of something to eat and a cuppa. I felt I had seen enough excitement for one day.

When I got into the section next day, TO.20 asked me what film I had managed to get, and on seeing my results, asked for a copy straight away, as some lefty twit in Parliament was claiming heavy handed use of horses and police against poor defenceless students had caused injuries, ha!

I reckoned my films when seen in the cold light of day would throw an entirely different light on the whole matter!

I suppose the now famous 'train-raid' on the drugs Afro-centre in Brixton, had remained etched in some clever bugger's memory, because a similar approach was planned for an acid party expected to be held in a large building next to the Elephant and Castle Underground station.

Apparently one of the station exits was only yards from the party venue, and it was thought we could catch the organisers flat-footed, provided we could gain rapid access.

As we sat on an Underground train at midnight, waiting for the 'off', I thought this was the first time I had ever gone to a scene of crime by underground train, and in such comfort too!

The journey from Charing Cross to the Elephant only took a few minutes, and in complete silence, sixty officers and I, piled off the train to take our places quietly, behind large steel doors leading directly onto the street.

The Ch/Insp. quietly reminded everyone to call the photographer over to film their prisoner, and his or her substances before anything else was done, so that a record of who had what could be seen as well as documented.

After a tense ten-minute wait, the doors were quietly opened, and we doubled towards a large building where the thump-thump of reggae music announced the 'do' was well under way.

As usual, I had the camera running as we approached the door, and only switched on the top-light once we were inside, there was no point in alerting any clever clogs look-outs, we were coming.

The place was quite large, it looked in the dim light like a derelict warehouse, there must have been at least two-hundred people crammed into it, most of whom didn't twig the old Bill were there for about ten seconds, then all hell broke loose!

Fortunately for me, a P/Sgt. who designated himself as my liaison officer, was able to direct me to the most pressing confrontations quickly, and the prisoners were rapidly wheeled away outside to the nick.

Buzzing this way and that, I quickly filmed prisoners full-length, close-up of head and shoulders with arresting officer, plus whatever substance they were being arrested for, and moved on to the next.

I stopped briefly to change tape cassettes, and prayed the PAG belt driving the top light would hold out, I hadn't brought a second one along - I had enough to carry as it was.

After half an hour we had covered everything, all I had to do was film the complete display of substances confiscated that night, plus the most lethal-looking lash up of mains wiring for lighting and sound amplification I had ever seen, and we could go home. The spaghetti convolutions of taped and bare wires trailing from the roof looked horribly lethal, and was no doubt the product of some lads' warped expertise at extracting electricity without actually paying for it!

It was obviously a time for doing jobs associated with trains, because two days later I got an urgent message, whilst working at West Ham, to get down to Spencer Rd. Clapham pronto, where a serious train crash had just occurred.

The emergency services were well into their work when I arrived, and I quickly made contact with the Major Incident officer, to find out what had happened, and how I could best get into the scene without disrupting essential medical services.

Apparently a passenger train had gone through safety lights which should have indicated a stationary train ahead, and had piled into the rear of that train, just as another passenger train was coming in the opposite direction.

The resulting carnage was quite horrific.

With terrible impetus, the ramming train had managed to force it's way along the off-side of the stationary train for three carriage lengths, before the on-coming train ploughed through it's first two coaches head on, shearing them open like a tin-opener.

And it all happened in the confines of a narrow cutting.

To gain access to the tangled coaches below, the rescue services had laid a mat of fence posts in a series of steps from the roadway above, and by stepping carefully down this makeshift walkway, I was able to get onto the roof of the nearest carriage, and start work.

It is under such circumstances, when all about you other people are frantically beavering to assist the trapped and dying, you feel like an intruder, and quite surplus to requirements.

I had to forcefully clear my mind of sentiment, in order to get on with the privileged job I had of recording the terrible scene.

Above us, the roadway round the little tri-angular green adjacent to the crash scene, was snowed under with rescue vehicles.

I counted at least forty ambulances and twenty fire engines gridlocked with police vehicles, and special services helping at the shocking scene.

It was a huge response to a terribly tragic accident.

A short distance from the green, a hall had been taken over as a temporary examination centre, where the bodies of those killed in the accident could be identified and photographed, before going off to the mortuary.

A couple of the lads from SO.3 had the unenviable job of photographing everything in detail, so that no mistakes would be made when subsequently presenting evidence of the deceased at Coroner's Court.

Mid-way through the afternoon, a massive 'Cherry-Picker' mobile crane arrived, and took up prime position on one corner of the small green.

There was no doubt a superb overall picture of the scene could be obtained from the top of that, if I could get the Incident officer to allow me aboard.

The small platform affixed to the end of the jib looked as though it would only take two or three people at most, but on the first ascent, I was packed in with four others, including the Major Incident Officer, and slowly hoisted aloft.

I know they say if you concentrate on what you're doing, and use logic that the thing is made of steel and won't break in half, you'll be Ok, but as we passed the sixty foot mark, a definite feeling of vertigo took over, as the ground disappeared somewhere below.

With a faint hydraulic hiss, and slight judder, we came to a halt with the crane jib pointing almost vertically into the air, and I took a nervous peek between my shoes, seeing nothing between me and the ground ninety-feet below, it was revolting!

The old knees went all tingly and funny, and there was that weird sensation of wanting to jump off, but I swallowed hard, and concentrated on filming everything from the bridge ahead of the crash, to well down the line and the signal gantry, the one which the errant train had recently passed.

"Have you got all you want?" asked the Incident Officer, and getting my silent nod, waved to the controller far below, and we began our descent.

I know it's totally illogical, but when we got to within twenty or thirty feet of the ground, the vertigo quickly disappeared, and I felt Ok.

It's not as though you couldn't be killed falling from thirty feet, but at ninety feet you know if you do go, it's curtains!

It was such a vast scene to cover I had to return the next day, filming the damaged track, the signal gantry, and other technical points of interest, and I felt this was only the beginning of what was to be a long and serious enquiry as to what had gone wrong.

By the last day of the year, I found we had covered just over 200 video scenes in 1988, compared to 27 in 1986, and 74 in 1987, we were really beginning to motor now!

# Chapter Thirty Three

One day in the office Frank Jones pulled me aside and said, "Do you remember how long ago it was that you were in Iran?"

"Yes of course I do, it was twelve years ago, why?"

"Well I was looking up some staff records yesterday, and saw that you're due to retire in '92, that's just a quarter of the time since you went to Iran. Makes you think a bit doesn't it?"

I didn't know whether he was trying to depress me, or merely indicate the speedy passage of time, if the latter, he needn't have bothered, I knew well enough how damn' fast that went!

A couple of weeks into 1989, I was asked to attend a briefing, where the object of the exercise was a raid on a notorious Pub near Blackwall Tunnel, where drugs were being openly sold to members of the public.

The raid was to be known as operation 'Block'

To make sure everyone knew what the premises looked like from the outside, I was asked to produce a short film, showing the approaches to the pub, and relevant points of access into the building, but there was a slight snag.

I couldn't do it openly as someone would clock me from one of the pub's top windows.

To get round this, I asked one of the DC's to drive my van to the scene, whilst I lay on the rooftop filming platform, covered with a large piece of canvas. That way he could drive in like a prospective punter, stop a reasonable distance back from the front of the pub whilst I filmed, before slowly touring the front of premises, and leaving.

A couple of days after the initial film had been seen by troops mounting operation Block, Insp. S. asked me if I would cover the same location again, this time filming after dark when the dealers and punters were known to be well at it.

We got the 'off' by radio from an observer at the scene, and in a light drizzle, headed for the pub, only to discover the whole forecourt was jam-packed with parked vehicles, and we couldn't get in as close as I wanted to show the dealers actually dealing.

We had to stand off at thirty yards distance and do the best we could, but it certainly looked a 'go-er' to me.

While I awaited the final call from the operation Block lads, I copped an early morning return visit to Stapleford House on the dreaded Broadwater Farm estate, this time, in an attempt to catch a certain Keith W. in possession of drugs.

I hoped like hell it wasn't going to be a repeat of the last farce, and that this time the information would be 'good'

It was a bit of a drag getting up at 0300 to get to Tottenham nick for 0400, and waiting for the latest intelligence to come in, but at least I was being paid!

The final briefing over a welcome cuppa, pushed the time to 0500, when we piled into a box van taking everyone onto the Broadwater estate.

After a bouncing, juddering ride the vehicle slowed to a halt, and we stood silently in the dark, waiting for something to happen.

"It's clear to go " said a voice from somewhere behind me "Don't forget, I want it nice and quiet up the stairs, and no talking!"

In Indian file, we ran briskly up two flights of stairs, checking each landing as we arrived, in case some somnambulent character spotted us and blew the whistle, but it was all clear.

A bit puffed from the early morning exertions, our group arrived outside the correct address without being discovered, and everything was looking good.

At a nod from the D/S. I switched on the video camera just as the hydraulic door opener went in.

With a whine and a crash the door was off, and we were in, no messing.

As we made for the bedroom, the D/S called out "This is the Metropolitan Police, please stay where you are, you will come to no harm!"

I thought, the last time we had entered premises like this was during the riot, and we had been backed up by armed police then, but with this incumbent being wakened violently from his sleep, weren't we at risk of being repelled as mobsters or enemies?

As the bedroom light snicked on, I saw Keith W. just as I remembered him from 1985, except now his eyes were as big as gob-stoppers, as he tried to take everything in, mouth opening and closing silently like a fish out of water.

"Hey man, what's all this hassle?" he suddenly exploded. "What am I supposed to have done for fucks sake man?"

"Get yourself up and get dressed, then come into the other room, and I'll explain what we are about to do, ok?"

When he had been told the reason for our rather early disruption of his slumbers, he visibly relaxed, and said he was quite happy for us to go ahead, provided he was able to see us all the time, as he didn't want to be 'stitched up'

"Our photographer here will film your place before we start searching, then anything we find will be recorded in situ, and everything again afterwards when we leave, so there can be no allegations of damage on your part, ok?"

The flat was quite well furnished with good quality gear, which included some expensive sound mixing and recording equipment, plus several musical instruments.

As the special search team began to take the place carefully apart, the D/S asked W. "Are you really into all this music business then?" and W explained that he was well known in the musical writing and publishing business, something which left him little time for anything else these days.

From my position by the door I could see the search team were being very thorough indeed, and no possible hiding place was left unchecked in their search for hidden drugs.

As we had all been up and about for some time, and the video gear was beginning to drag on my shoulder, I sat on the arm of the settee next to the D/S and W. gently cradling the camera across my lap and relaxed.

Looking at W. closely, I was intrigued to see him apparently quite unconcerned by the shindig going on around him, and I wondered if we had picked ourselves a 'bummer' again.

If we had, the crap would hit the fan and someone's head would definitely roll!

Switching on the camera, I unobtrusively back-zoomed the wide-angle lens until I had a full side-face of W. as he spoke calmly to the D/S, and covertly started filming.

It could be useful later on, if things went badly wrong.

"Nearly finished here Sarge" called one of the search team, "Just this corner and the book-cupboard to check, then we're done. Nothing so far I'm afraid"

Apart from a slight smile, W. didn't interrupt his conversation, or betray the slightest hint of anxiety by his body language, and I felt sure we must have blown it. It didn't look good.

As the search chap opened the cupboard doors, I could see it contained the usual toot normally associated with such a convenient parking place, papers, books, magazines, and most of the odds and sods people wanted popped out of sight.

The first object to hand was a Phillips' screwdriver, and the minute he picked it up, the searcher looked up at the two huge bass-reflex speakers on top of the cupboard, and said, "Aha!"

I started filming.

In less than a minute he had removed the four screws securing the bass speaker to it's fascia, and carefully lowered the speaker and it's wiring onto the cupboard top.

Rolling up his sleeve, he carefully put his arm deep inside the speaker cabinet and felt around.

As he withdrew his hand, I saw he held a couple of plastic bags sealed with sticky tape, and W's calm demeanour disappeared in a flash.

"Oh, fuckin' hell man, what did you want to go and do that for?"

"Up 'til now everything was goin' fine, now you've blown it!"

The best part was, I had captured it all on tape, with W's voice-over completing the damning picture!

Once W. had been read his rights and taken off, I spoke to the searcher and said "What made you look at the speakers then, why did you suspect the stuff was hidden in there?"

"Well it was his own fault really, there were no other tools anywhere else in the flat, and immediately next to the open-fronted speakers was this Phillips screw driver, the rest was easy".

I must say, I was most impressed.

Three days later operation Block was planned to roll.

"To make sure we have the best element of surprise" said Insp.S. "I intend our convoy to form up in the south-bound section of the Blackwall Tunnel - which will be closed to the public just before midnight, and make our way to within a half mile of the venue before going in.

Once we get the go, it's straight into the pub and grab your dealers, Alan from SO.3 will be on hand to film your prisoners and any substances you find, ok?"

At 2330 we left the tunnel one after the other, there must have been at least twenty vehicles in the convoy, and lord knows how many officers on board.

When you consider how much an operation like this costs the taxpayer, I hoped to goodness we got a worthwhile result!

Just short of the pub. our convoy pulled in, while the latest intelligence informed us of the state of play, then it was off like Custer's cavalry.

Although the chaps were keen to get in first, I was bundled forward with the first wave, filming as we went, it was all arms, legs, and shoving.

Once the initial filming of arrests had been done, and prisoners taken away, filming of the stuff dumped on the floor and in the toilets began.

It was all going down nice and easy - there was no aggro. and I felt we should be able to wrap things up quite quickly.

I was taking a breather, and talking about the apparent success of the operation to Insp.S. when two lads in their early twenties came over saying "Is i' awrigh' if we take our san' gear?"

Insp. S. and I looked at each other in puzzlement, quite incapable of understanding this epiglottal, East-London jargon - what sand?

"Could you say that again please?" said Insp. S. "I didn't quite get you"

"Can we take our san' gear, thas i' over there" said one, and pointed to a couple of speaker boxes mounted on chromium stands, complete with amplifier and turntable deck.

"I think he means sound gear" I said.

"Providing the Publican vouches that it's yours, and you show my officers some form of identification, yes of course"

The next day, the raid was pronounced a great success, and the pub. immediately closed down.

Over the next couple of years I looked at the building each time I passed on my way to Erith or somewhere south of the river, seeing it become more and more run down, and felt although it had been a good job, it seemed a sad end to a fine looking building.

During a rather cold period in late February, I set up the Mark 2 high-speed flash units Greg had built, with the intention of trying to capture some Starlings in flight.

I had noticed that when the weather forced birds to feed from the bird table, Starlings would fight furiously over the food, and 'tower' into the air for several feet, battling face to face until one of them won.

The winner would then fly back to the table and feed.

I felt that if you restricted the Starlings to a small feeding post, it should be possible to predict fairly accurately the spot they would rise to in the air, and if the camera was correctly focussed, the speed of the flash would capture their rapid actions perfectly.

I set up the infra red trigger horizontally, so that the beam went through a spot, a foot or so above the bait, and focussed the camera on this point from six feet away, all I had to do now was wait.

It didn't take long for the Starlings to come down to the bait I had set out, and trigger the camera as expected.

The problem was however, they broke the beam from different angles to the one I wanted, and I acquired lots of photographs of birds doing silly things, or being cut off on the edge of my film.

It was a 'nearly' result.

Over the next couple of weeks I set up the flash-guns whenever it was cold enough to entice the Starlings within range, but I was still getting lots of heads and tails shots, rather than the fighting poses I wanted, I wasn't winning at all!

All too soon it was spring, and the birds weren't interested in playing stooge any more, they were more interested in other things.

I would have to try again next winter.

Although I wasn't on duty, the duty officer rang during the first weekend in March, asking me to get down to Purley as soon as possible as there had been a serious train crash there.

They wanted it covered by video and stills whilst everything was in position, but the stills duty photographers were well tucked up on other serious jobs, and couldn't attend.

I replied, the only way I was going to get there in double quick time was to ask the Helicopter Unit at Lippett's Hill to pick me up somewhere, and drop me and my equipment at the scene of the crash, could he organise that?

Five minutes later he was back on the phone - India 99 would pick me up from Chigwell Police sports club cricket pitch in half an hour - just be there!

The flight to Purley didn't take long, and I was soon looking down on another scene of crash chaos, asking the pilot to go round a few times at zero altitude, so I could get some stills shots done on the Bronica while I was still in the air.

The pilot skilfully put us down on a nearby school playing field, and a local police car took me the short distance to the scene, where fire engines, emergency services, and ambulances already filled the street.

This time, a moving train had run into the rear of a stationary one, ricocheting off the crumpled rear coach and careering down a steep embankment towards the houses below, demolishing everything in it's path.

In one garden, an old chap was standing in his shed looking out of the window, drinking a cup of tea, just as the second and third coaches jack-knifed down the embankment, folding themselves neatly round his shed, leaving him unhurt, but scared witless!

The fact that none of the people living near the track had been killed seemed a small miracle to me, even though one of the huge sets of double bogie-wheels had ended up well away from the train, crashing against the side of the nearest house.

There was no doubt about it, if any of us photographers had been asked to cover disaster scenes such as this using stills photography alone, we would have been tucked up for ever and a day.

Not only that, the resulting mass of prints needing to be viewed by the Coroner or some investigating committee would be almost too much to take in, and I was glad we had the video camera to make life a lot easier for everyone.

It had always been a tenet of mine to cover on video, every possible aspect of a particular crime, so that in the ensuing days and weeks of the investigation, we would be able to determine exactly where everything of note had originally been.

I would video the top of an office desk, complete with all it's papers, plus one or two close-ups of phone-numbers or memo jottings, just in case it was alleged that police had 'planted' certain information.

Also in the scenario where a party had got out of hand and ended in murder, the position of every bottle and glass on a coffee table, plus whether the curtains were drawn, lights working, doors open etc; were all recorded, it was so easy to cover with video.

The importance of being as thorough as possible when video filming a major scene, was brought home with a thump after a particularly vicious murder of two black chaps in Wardour St, Soho.

Apparently the owner of an amusement arcade had got severely on the wrong side of some local 'heavies', and they sent their lads along to teach him some manners.

Having smashed his place up, and roughed up the staff, they took two black chaps down into the basement, and after tying them up, locked them in a brick-built alcove fitted with wooden doors.

The wooden doors occupied the centre of the low, arch-shaped alcove, leaving two-foot spaces on either side, which had been filled in with heavy - duty wire mesh.

Upstairs, just to make sure chummy got the message, the heavies set fire to the place, and someone, with a very wicked mind, went downstairs and poured Paraffin over the two black chaps in the alcove, before throwing a match inside and shutting the doors.

When I got to the scene, I did everything upstairs first, to enable the Fire Investigation lads to get started, before I tackled the basement fire damage and the bodies.

To get a decent view of the two dead men, I had to sit on the basement floor and hand-hold the camera between my knees, it was that cramped for space.

Because of the lack of lighting it was necessary to use the video top light for filming, and the heat from this, plus the smell emanating from the paraffin soaked bodies, made the cellar a bit yukky, so I started breathing through my mouth in the approved fashion.

When I had completed the two bodies, I carefully filmed the rubbish-strewn spaces behind the wire mesh on both sides of the doors, making sure there wasn't an inch of the alcove that wasn't recorded, one way or another.

At the finish, I crawled out of the cramped, dirty scene, and went upstairs to the sunshine of the 'other world' for a breath of fresh air, and a refreshing cuppa.

Despite breathing through my mouth most of the time, I had a nasty taste on my tongue as though I had been sucking old pennies, and the tea was most welcome.

A week after the event, I received a call from the senior Fire Investigator at the Met. Lab. asking if I had attended the Wardour St. fire, and if so, could he come over right away and see what film I had shot.

He said it was rather important.

Fortunately I had a copy of the tape handy, and was able to sit him at the editing suite, while I ran it through.

"Ah, this is the bit we're interested in" he said as the edit monitor showed the two burnt men.

"We are more than keen to see various items amongst the rubbish on the right-hand side of the alcove, yes, there it is, can you hold that bit there?"

As it was a copy, and not the master, I re-ran the tape and freeze-framed the bit he was interested in.

“Can you see that plastic bottle over by the back wall?”

“Well that bottle is the bone of some serious contention, inasmuch that a local officer visited the scene a couple of days after the murder, and, poking about amongst that rubbish, found the plastic bottle with accelerant in it.

It will probably turn out to be Paraffin, and fingerprints say there are some very good marks on the outside for a possible ident too”.

“If you hadn’t recorded that bottle on film at the time of the fire, I doubt whether we could have introduced it as evidence. Even now it’s going to cause some rather red faces, but that’s better than it being missed altogether, wouldn’t you say?”

It turned out that a positive identification was made from fingermarks on the bottle, and an arrest made for murder.

It had always struck me as strange, that criminals who go out to commit armed robberies using guns, never seem to take into account the skills of armed police they might meet in the course of their robbery.

Having worked closely with the firearms lads, producing training films for many years and noting at first hand, the high level of expertise they acquire during training, I wouldn’t have swopped shots with these experts any time!

And yet in April ‘89, a nasty armed robbery went badly wrong, ending in the deaths of three armed men near Rayners Lane, Harrow. I arrived soon after the incident, and had the job of recording the scene, whilst the area was still closed to the public.

Guns, bullet cases, and pools of blood were mute testimony to the short, sharp, bloody exchange that had taken place on the housing estate, and people were still looking out of their windows in shock.

I could already see the aggro coming from the ‘do-gooders’ and civil rights lot, no doubt howling once again for the removal of armed police from the streets.

A lot of them don’t seem to realise or care that someone else has to face these violent robbers on their behalf!

A few days after this harsh event, I was asked to go on an early morning counterfeiting and forgery raid in Baldock, deepest Hertfordshire, which sounded a nice change from the grotty stuff I had been getting lately.

The premises were situated in a small modern complex, masquerading under the guise of producing silk-screen signs and notices, everything looking quite innocuous from the outside.

Once we gained entry, I quickly video-filmed the place from top to bottom, so that after ten minutes, the searchers were able to get on with their business with customary zeal.

“I’d like you to get me some shots of this printing machine in situ” the DI. Said. “In particular showing this printing plate and some of the discarded printing proofs made from it, can you get all that in the one shot?”

“No problem at all” I said. “I’ll just go and get the wide-angle lens and we can get started”

As my van was parked a few yards away, I took the video camera complete with it’s tripod to the van, and brought out the spanking new super wide-angle lens and put it on.

Although the tripod was fitted with an excellent rubber 'spider'- a device for holding all three legs equi-distant apart, the concrete path the tripod was standing on was only just wide enough to take all three legs.

After carefully fitting the new wide-angle, I placed the lens I had been using back in the van, and turned to pick up the camera and tripod, when Murphy smiled, and let me have a loud raspberry, broadside.

In horribly slow motion, the tripod leg furthest from me slid off the edge of the path, and the out of balance camera began it's lazy descent to the ground.

Frantically I dived full length to stop the camera hitting the concrete, but only got my hand under the end of the lens as it whacked down hard.

The force of it hitting the concrete despite being cushioned by my hand was enough to snap the aluminium lens barrel in half, leaving me looking at two halves of a £5000 lens!

"Oh, shit, shit, shit!" I managed to blurt out. "That's all I need, in all the years I've never broken a bloody thing until now, and it has to be this!"

Fortunately, the other DXC3000 used by Ian was away for service, and I had his super wide-angle on board, and I fitted that instead, but I didn't let it out of my hands for a second - I wasn't giving Murphy a second chance!

Despite Murphy, the gods smiled on me after all - having submitted a full report concerning the accident, I found I wasn't being assessed for the expensive damage, but it had better be my one and only transgression, or else!

In July, there was an armed robbery at the Natwest bank in Tottenham, where the gunman, baulked from escape by patrolling police, had taken the employees hostage, and shut the main door.

Armed police were quickly on the scene, and after the usual loud hailer appeals for surrender, and the inevitable non-compliance, the whole thing degenerated into a stand off.

Although the bank was situated in the High St. the area had been completely sealed off, and a cordon of police kept the excited public several hundred yards away.

DCI.Albert Patrick, now a bluff, no-nonsense C8 robbery squad man was in charge, and quickly convinced the gunman by loud-hailer, it would be to his advantage to accept a field telephone, wired into a shop opposite, where several members of the firearms unit covered the bank's main door.

The negotiator soon got on talking terms with the gunman, and managed to convince him to let the hostages go. and I was able to film them coming out of the bank, apparently un-harmed.

It looked as if this siege was about to go down satisfactorily after all.

" Alan,I want you to go with these two officers to the bank's main door, and do exactly as they say.

Keep right behind them out of harms way, and film our man when he comes out" said the DC.I.

"And I don't want any cock-ups!"

We crossed the road well out of any possible danger, before moving back along the pavement to a position by the bank door, and waited for what might happen next.

"He's going to open the door and throw out his gun", someone called from across the road, and within a minute it was done, and all recorded on film.

"Ok. now come out with your hands on your head, and get down on the pavement!" shouted one of the D.11 men, and the door opened slowly to reveal a slim person in jeans, looking not in the least like a hardened bank robber.

Once he was cuffed, searched, and led away, we entered the bank still filming, so I could have an accurate record of everything as it was before police started their examination.

Although there was no doubt that our apprehended gunman was the robber, I still kept myself to the fringes of the area behind the counters whilst filming.

There was no point in adding extra shoe marks or fingerprints to the scene for the poor old DFO to find and mark up, or us to photograph!

For some time I watched DCI. Patrick and the bank manager re-enact the scenario of the hold-up, and it was obvious that Albert, our DCI. wasn't entirely happy with what was coming out.

For some reason they couldn't locate the missing cash, which was supposed to amount to several thousand pounds, and I reckoned Albert was having second thoughts, thinking someone in the bank must be telling porkies.

As I had just run out of tape, I went back across the road to pick up my hold-all from the shop, containing spare tapes, batteries and stuff, and tucked myself and the camera well out of the way in a small corridor leading to the bank's back door.

I felt it was far better to leave the area clear for Lab.liaison to get on with their bit unhindered, while I reloaded and awaited further developments.

I suppose I sat there for about an hour, while things were checked and sorted out, and when Albert came towards me, I asked if he was happy as far as I was concerned.

"Yes, that's fine Alan, you can clear off now, just send me a copy of the tape as soon as you can will you?"

One of the D.11 firearm lads I knew well, was standing nearby, and hearing our conversation, offered to give me a lift with my gear to the van, which I gratefully accepted.

"If I bring the camera, tripod and holdall, can you manage the video-recorder, spare tapes and stuff, that way we'll manage the lot in one go"

"No trouble at all" he said, "You know where you left your van, lead on"

As we left the main door, I turned to see how my friend was coping, and noticed that apart from the recorder and a box of tapes, he was carrying a green, service-style hold-all too.

"What have you got there?" I asked "That holdall's not mine, I've got my black one here, where did you get that one from?"

"It was next to your gear in the passage and I thought it was yours, so I brought it along. You sure it's not yours?"

Putting his load down, he gently un-zipped the green hold-all to reveal a great wodge of bank-notes stuffed inside.

It was the missing cash.

"Oh fuck!" he said in a hoarse whisper, "I'm a bleedin' bank robber now, that's all

I need - better call the DCI. and explain"

Albert was of course very understanding, and rather pleased the missing dosh had been found, adding in a school-masterly tone, "I'm not entirely convinced you weren't trying to have it away on your toes with this, you young bugger, now clear off!"

I hadn't been up in the police helicopter since the Purley rail crash, consequently it was nice to get a job which required some interesting flying over a large part of east London.

During a late evening drinkies at the Horn of Plenty PH. in Mile End road, a murder had taken place, after which the suspect had taken off at high speed down Cambridge Heath Rd. towards Hackney in a van.

Police were called, and the description and index of the vehicle passed by Information Room to all traffic units in the area.

It wasn't long before the van containing the suspect was picked up, travelling at high speed down the Lea Bridge Rd. bound for nearby Epping Forest.

As police gave chase, the driver got his foot hard down, roaring the wrong way round the huge Waterworks roundabout over the A406, before continuing through Woodford Green, and on to the Epping New Rd.

By now both vehicles were flashing through Epping Forest towards the Robin Hood roundabout, which the suspect took at such speed, he clipped the centre island and burst his off-side front tyre.

Not the least deterred, the suspect continued to give his van the gun, belting towards the Wake Arms roundabout, the front wheel giving off a fiery cascade of sparks as he shredded the tyre to the rim.

Somehow he managed to get through the Wake Arms roundabout, with one police vehicle behind, and another manoeuvring alongside to head him off, but things were still pretty hairy, as they sped along at over sixty mph.

The road ahead into Epping town had just been blocked off by Essex police, and as the suspect van finally became boxed in by police vehicles, he decided enough was enough, and slowed to a halt.

For over fourteen miles he had led police a merry dance, from the Mile End Rd to the Wake Arms, the last two miles completely without a front tyre, it had been a very hairy ride!

My job now, was to show the route from the air, allowing the Court to appreciate the length and complexity of the route, and the danger to other road users posed by the speeding van.

Starting off from just above the Horn of Plenty P.H. I asked our pilot to 'crab' the chopper along at an angle so I could lean out of the side door to film, whilst still having some vision ahead.

The observer sitting alongside called out the various landmarks as we approached, outlining the general twists and turns of the route to me like a rally driver's navigator.

With one eye glued to the viewfinder and the other seeing more or less what was coming up, it would have been impossible over the maze of streets around Hackney to know exactly where you were, without the observer's valuable assistance.

Things went very well, until we hit the Waterworks roundabout over the A406 where the roadway immediately disappeared under the leaf canopy of roadside trees.

This frustrating situation continued more or less until we cleared the Robin Hood roundabout, leaving us with a large chunk of the route totally unrecorded.

Back at the nick, I acquainted the DI. with our unforseen problem, and suggested we retrace the route using a vehicle with a camera mounted inside, looking through the windscreen.

He replied. "We can do better than that, if we use my car with the sun roof open, you can put your camera and head through the hole, and film the whole route from there, how about that?"

I must confess the thought of standing with my head stuck out of a car sun roof for twenty minutes while we chugged through east London didn't exactly turn me on, but I went along with it.

At least I could turn the camera into the junctions as we turned left or right - it had always annoyed me that a fixed position camera gave a false idea of a driver's view, especially when cornering.

In the event, I made a combination copy of both the aerial and car viewpoints, clipping the car shots in when the road disappeared from view under the trees, and the final result was well received, anyway, it had been an interesting aerial exercise!

During the first few days of August one of our foreign 'dissidents' decided to take lodgings in deepest Paddington, holing up at the Beverley House Hotel in Sussex gardens, where he proceeded to construct an explosive device.

For some reason or other, as he was putting the finishing touches to his little device, it blew up, completely destroying the upper floor of the hotel, and sending him heavenwards in small pieces.

Hearing of this, I thought that Murphy, or maybe even Allah has an eye for justice, especially when dealing with these wicked bastards.

At the scene, the only way to get into to the wrecked upper floor was by fireman's turntable ladder, crawling in through what was left of one of the windows, and moving about carefully so you didn't fall through to the floors below.

Fortunately it was a nice warm, sunny day, and the blue sky made a nice backdrop to what remained of the roof.

The spot where chummy had been working on his bomb was quite obvious, and wasn't too badly damaged, the scale of carnage seemed to increase the further you went from the source of the explosion, something I had noticed at other bomb scenes.

Rather grotesquely, one of our bomber's legs , severed at the hip, swung gently to and fro from the rafters, like a man in a one-legged race, but that was the biggest piece of him we found, the rest must have been dispersed far and wide over Sussex Gardens!

I was there most of the day whilst the bomb squad lads gave the place a thorough going over, searching for evidence to show what type of device it had been, and perhaps identify the bomber himself, and I wondered if this was the beginning of another hate 'campaign'?

Fortunately it didn't turn out to be the precursor to a period of terrorist violence, but I did collect over the next month four murders, two drugs manufacturing raids, a child abuse case, and a return to Broadwater farm, for yet another drugs raid on Tangmere

House.

Life was getting hectic again.

As before, we made our way onto the Broadwater farm in a couple of box vans, but none of the bystanders seemed greatly surprised as we let the tailgates go with a crash, and made a dash for the shops on the first level.

"Hey man, what kept yuh?" shouted one cheeky young herb.

"We knew you was coming ages ago, did yuh get lost or somethin'? said another.

We spent an hour or so pulling various places to bits, finding the odd stash of Cannabis here and there, but not much else.

I suppose our visit helped keep the druggies on their toes.

In October I did a very sad, and sickening job involving paedophilia at the Woodfield boy's school in Kenton near Harrow.

A senior master had consistently abused the boys in his care over many years, and now everything had come to light with subsequent public furore.

I video-filmed the master's office, where certain offences had apparently taken place, and of course the communal showers, where he stood watching the lads as they washed themselves down after sports and cross country running.

If there is one thing that gets right up my nose, it's the sexual abuse of youngsters by the scum in whose power they have been innocently placed, and this was a bad one.

A couple of days after filming various venues where offences had taken place, I was asked by the child abuse investigation team at Kingsbury Police station, to film one of the lads from the Woodfield school in their private interview suite.

I had been there several times before, and although we didn't have one-way glass, or even remotely controlled cameras to record the youngsters' tragic stories, I had evolved a technique whereby I sat on the floor of the suite some fifteen feet away from the child, and only after he or she had accepted my presence as part of the scenery, did the gentle questioning start, and the camera begin to roll.

There were many times when the body language of the children gave away a lot more than they were able to express in words, and it was useful to home in on this in close-up, while the dialogue could still be heard over picture.

If the child was extremely nervous, and didn't settle easily, I arranged for the interviewer to give me a nod when he or she thought the child was ready, and I would switch on the camera and leave the room.

The only problem with this technique was, the tape only lasted twenty minutes, and I had to keep a close eye on the clock and warn the interviewer when time was running out.

This time the youngster being interviewed was nearly seventeen, and from his actions and speech, appeared to be mentally retarded, but this apparently was not the case.

He had been so affected by constant abuse from the master, and possibly another man, he had been totally destroyed as a person, only mustering enough ability to get a job stacking goods in a local supermarket.

His stutter to get words out was painful to hear, words often repeated ten or a dozen times in an effort to communicate, and I thought if there was a hell where people went after death, the scumbag who had been this boy's destroyer, should certainly go there!

As with quite a few jobs we did at scenes of crime, I didn't get any follow up details after completing the work. I would dearly have loved to hear this swine had been weighed off for a hundred years or so, plus the cat o' nine tails.

It would have made my day.

It certainly might have gone some way to recompense for the years of work someone was going to have to undertake, to bring that young lad back from hell.

That poor chap wasn't the only youngster I had to film at the child abuse suite connected with that infamous school regime, and I was glad when it was all finished.

I found the whole business utterly depraved and depressing.

# Chapter Thirty Four

In November, the security chaps at Heathrow, having gone through various scenarios concerned with terrorist and Hi-jacking incidents, asked if was possible for us to produce a film from the helicopter, showing every aspect of the airport in detail.

I replied we certainly could!

Naturally with such a demanding task to hand, I attended a couple of briefings, so that I knew exactly what they had in mind.

It was quite a huge undertaking, and we would be required to fly in and out of a nearby holding area, as and when airliners needed the airspace we currently occupied.

The area they wanted covered was limited in the North by the Bath Rd. between Cranford and Colnbrook, in the East by the Parkway Cranford and down to North Feltham, along the South from North Feltham to Staines Moor, and back up to the North along the M25 to Harmondsworth, a really huge area!

Discussing the situation with our pilot, I suggested we fly all along the outside of the boundaries looking in towards the centre, and then do a couple of passes up and own the whole complex, parallel with No.1 and No.5 runways, before doing a couple of slow spins round the central Tower complex to finish it all off.

He said although it sounded a good idea, he would have to put it to air traffic control, and if they didn't object, we would go ahead.

It was decided that early Saturday morning was the best time for us to avoid absolute airport chaos, and in bright sunshine we stooged along over the Bath Rd, side door open, camera suspended on rubber bungees, but also fixed to the aircraft by carabiners and a steel wire.

We didn't want the damn thing falling out and causing an incident among the unsuspecting public below!

Apart from having to retreat to a holding area designated by air traffic control to allow intercontinental jets to roar past us west-bound, we accomplished the outside shots without incident, and asked permission to move in over the main runways at about 600 feet.

We had just done our first pass over No.1 runway when we got the call to move in towards the control tower, as an aircraft was approaching from the east, and we were in, but above it's line of flight.

Our pilot was obviously listening in to instructions given by ATC. and indicated there was some really choice language emanating from the in-coming aircraft as to exactly what 'that silly bugger in the chopper thought he was playing at'

As the huge jet glided in directly under us, I realised just how good everyone had to be at their job controlling this lot, and that really, I had the easiest job of all.

For the next half hour we flew back and forth over the control tower complex, looking down from a ridiculously low altitude at all the aircraft, and people going about their daily tasks, even Concorde, that superb example of aviation design, sat under us like a resting falcon glinting in the sunshine.

I felt we were very privileged to have such unrestricted access to the airport, something which had never been granted to anyone else before, and was rather sad when the job finished.

Every so often a job comes along which allows you to practice a technique you have tried before in a different format, but now broadens your experience in video.

There had been many instances over the years where I had to use image intensifiers on stills cameras during night surveillance, and in my opinion the results were usually a bit 'iffy'.

If there was no light at the scene at all, the addition of an Infra-red light source undoubtedly improved subject definition, but where there was some level of light, and you could see figures, it was often better to uprate the existing 800 ASA film to 1600, 3200, or even 6400 ASA, if you didn't mind suffering the extended development time, and grain like footballs!

Such a job came through when under-cover officers asked us to cover the scene of serious street drugs dealing on the Lovelinch estate in Deptford.

Garry B. one our most experienced surveillance photographers was sporting a 300mm F.4 lens on his Nikon, attached to an image intensifier, and I had a similar intensifier mounted behind a 200mm specially adapted 35mm lens, attached to the low-band DXC3000 Video camera.

Whereas Garry's set-up was about 20 inches long, my outfit was well over two feet long, and resembled a mini bazooka, requiring a really hefty tripod to support the whole thing securely.

The designated observation point (OP) was the inside of a tall church tower, where the spire joined the roof, and from there we were able to see down into the street, and even the front door of one of the main targets.

To get our gear into the church undetected, we had some local officers dress up as painters and decorators, and transport our tripods and cameras in hold-alls and sacks, disguised as painting gear.

You never knew with villains of this sort, what clever-clogs look-outs they might have posted around the place to keep cavey.

As dusk fell, the weevils came out of the woodwork, and we saw the first 'runners' leaving the flat with their supplies for street sale, and the first of the punters rolling up to the front door to buy.

It was a good thing the blacks didn't appreciate we could follow their every move on film, via the image intensifier, and it wasn't long before we were able to recognise certain characters for ourselves, and know pretty well what they would get up to next.

We ran the set-up until just after 0200 when things seemed to slow down a bit, and carefully made our way, one at a time out the rear of the OP. to our transport.

I was certainly ready for a good night's kip after that little lot!

Four days later we were back at the OP again, setting up for another night's surveillance on our black friends.

Apparently the officers running the job had been well pleased with our earlier efforts, and this second session was designed to show the first surveillance results were not just a 'one-off' but a regular feature.

It was quite remarkable the definition you could achieve with the video camera set on 18db gain whilst coupled to the intensifier, and I thought how useful it could be when photographing owls at night, at least you'd know for certain when the owl was in front of the camera!

As we got to the week before Christmas, arrangements for a special section 'do' were being finalised, practically everyone in the section was attending, plus a guest list of nearly sixty people. Even by using our large film studio, it would be pretty crowded with a hundred and fifty people celebrating, with plenty to eat and drink. It was something not to be missed.

I was on late turn duty that week, plus the week end, and prayed that the villains had all jetted off to Spain or somewhere similar, leaving us in relative peace and quiet to enjoy the festivities.

I suppose we had got about half an hour into the super party, when the duty officer called over the Tannoy for the duty video man to attend the office, he had a fatal accident scene for me to attend.

Murphy had caught up with me again!

"Pity you won't be here to enjoy your chicken drumsticks and sausage rolls" grinned a smug Derek Cook.

"Never mind, I'll have yours while you're out in the cold, cold snow - on yer bike!"

"Thanks a bunch!" I growled back.

"All the way to ruddy Biggin Hill, ugh! but if it is a Helicopter that's crashed, it must be serious - on my way"

There was quite a lot of traffic about as I bashed along through Lewisham, Catford, across Bromley Common and onto the Westerham Rd. where my sparse knowledge of the 'far south' was beginning to run out, and I was flying by the seat of my trousers.

Fortunately Biggin Hill airfield was sign posted, and after buttonholing a poor bemused pedestrian for instructions, I found myself rattling down Jail Lane, looking for the site of the crash. Through the open window I could see nothing but inky darkness, and with my breath making clouds of smoke in the cold night air, I cursed my luck at having drawn the short straw.

Suddenly, a police car whizzed past me, and slid into an almost invisible road, giving me the clue which way to go, and in front I saw the flashing blue lights of vehicles attending a serious accident, like bluebottles round a piece of meat.

"You photographic?" shouted a figure coming towards me in the car headlights.
"Yes, where is the scene of the crash then?"

"Bring your gear with you and I'll take you up there, it's not easy to get to, you'll need wellies, and some lights, we've only got hand torches at the moment"

Leading off into darkness under the trees, we began climbing a steep muddy bank which seemed to go on and on, until after about five minutes he said "Well here we are, the helicopter, or what's left of it, is over there."

In the dim light of his torch I saw a mass of twisted aluminium barely visible amongst the trees and thick undergrowth.

"Any idea where you want me to start?" I asked in some dismay, "I'll get what I can now, but the rest will have to wait until tomorrow if you want to see everything in detail".

"The duty officer asks if you can show the human remains that are immediately visible, as well as the position of the fuselage before anything gets moved around, and that'll do fine, the rest as you say, can be done tomorrow"

In the bright beam of the camera's top-light, I could see pieces of flesh caught in the trees, and parts of badly severed limbs laying amongst the twisted metal, which I recorded in detail before they were placed in plastic bags for removal.

Like some ungainly bear, I lumbered through the waist-high vegetation in a rough circle, filming the wreckage as I went, noticing there didn't seem to be an awful lot of the chopper left.

"Ok. I think I've got all I can usefully get tonight, I'll be back at 0900 in the morning to do the rest, make sure you tell the duty officer I'm coming before they start taking anything away, ok?"

Digging my heels in, and walking slowly down the steep muddy incline, I suddenly lost my footing and hit the ground hard with my bum, jarring my teeth through my skull.

Cursing and swearing, I slid ignominiously to the bottom on my back, hoping to god the camera was still in one piece.

Fortunately nothing was broken or damaged, and I made my way back to the section in Walworth Rd, hoping some decent soul had remembered to leave me a few drops of something at the bottom of a bottle.

I needn't have worried though, Shirley, our office clerk had put aside a nice plate of goodies, plus half a bottle each of white and red wine, which went down a real treat after my little jaunt into the cold, dark countryside.

Those poor devils in the chopper wouldn't be getting any Christmas tucker this year, that's for sure!

The next day I was back at the crash scene at 0900, and was pleased to see some enterprising soul had made a walk-way up the steep muddy slope, by placing heavy fenceposts sideways like a ladder, making climbing much safer and easier!

In daylight, I began to appreciate the terrible desiccation of vegetation and machinery that had taken place as the helicopter hit the ground, its rotors thrashing at high speed.

Trees four inches in diameter had been sliced off in a circle approximating the rotor's turning circle, leaving an area of stumps about three feet high, indicating to my mind, the aircraft might have been upside-down when it hit the ground.

There wasn't a lot left of the fuselage, and without the remains of the shattered rotors it would have been difficult to say just what kind of aircraft it had once been.

Dave Shapland and one of our young female photographers, had been allocated the un-enviable task of photographing every large chunk of debris, and human remains, complete with an identifying number tag, so that a full identification could be made of each piece, once everything had been collected for examination.

Although I made several phone enquiries to the local station over the next couple of weeks, I never did find out the official cause of this tragic air accident.

Christmas came and went, closely followed by the next event on the festive calendar, New Year's eve.

Because of trouble in the past, Public Order section decided that it would be a good thing if photographic could mount a couple of video cameras part-way up Nelson's column in Trafalgar Sq. and video any crowd trouble, as and when it occurred.

We could also pick out and film the trouble making 'steamers' as they crashed their way through the crowds, bullying and robbing revellers as they went.

Steel scaffolding was erected to get us well above the crowd, and three cameras, complete with 5K spotlights were positioned to enable us to cover in detail, an area from Pall Mall, across the National Gallery, St. Martins in the fields, to the Strand and Charing Cross Station.

Plus of course, everyone in the square below.

Wrapped in warm clothing and woollen hats, we tested our gear as the crowds began to fill the square, our pictures being relayed to nearby monitors where police observers noted what they saw, and were able to direct colleagues by radio to any individual who was causing trouble.

It all seemed to be working just fine.

As the celebrations progressed, our cameras recorded the scene for subsequent crowd control analysis, plus several individuals in close-up, who were seen to snatch bags or property from revellers.

The villains obviously thought they had got away with their thuggery by hiding amongst the crowd, but ran headfirst into the arrest squads sent in to get them.

They were completely gob-smacked at their arrest, and subsequent pleas of innocence and false arrest were easily refuted by the close-up evidence recorded on our videos.

The whole operation was deemed to be a great success by those who knew about these things, and from our point of view it was quite a success too - a full day's work from 0800 until 0200 the next day at double-time rates.

I deemed that as highly acceptable by anyone's standards!

It had been an idea of mine for some time, not only to get Starlings fighting in the air over food at a bird table - which was difficult enough, but to get them fighting whilst it was actually snowing.

I also wanted to see what snow flakes looked like when 'frozen' by the flash.

Lisa thought I was nuts, and asking for the impossible.

As the weather got colder, I set up my bits and pieces in the garden, and waited patiently for the hoped for snow to appear, but no joy.

I was getting quite skilled at triggering the camera manually, using a long electrical lead, and had several good photographs already.

All I needed now, were the right weather conditions to put everything into practice, and I could have a winner.

But the snow just wouldn't come!

At work it was a very different story however, and jobs came in by the bucket load, so that by the end of February 1990, I had covered four drugs raids, three child abuse cases, one rape, seven murders, another covert video identification, and a brothel raid.

There was one hilarious job I went on, where the station briefing indicated we were about to hit premises in Oakdale Rd. Leytonstone E.11, where a pornographic tape duplicating set-up was operating.

In a slick, well drilled operation, the station van with four officers on board, plus a

CID car and my video van slid to a halt outside private premises, and we all burst in.
To say I was surprised by what I saw inside, was an understatement, it was quite bizarre!
Where were the ranks of copying VCRs, and stacks of tapes for distribution that I expected to see, in fact where was anything pornographic?
Standing just inside the front door of the house, we were confronted by a lounge buried waist-high, under piles of books and magazines, tables covered in masses of electrical items such as old radios, irons, record players, TVs, clocks etc; piles of clothes, spin dryers and washing machines.
It looked more like Steptoe's yard gone mad!
Are you sure we're in the right place?" I asked the D/S.
"Of course we are!" he replied irritably "A couple of the DCs kept obbo on it for a while, so we know we're in the right place!"
Wending my way through a narrow walkway between the piles and piles of stuff, I came to a small clearing in front of the TV set, where two old VCRs were lashed together, back to back, indicating that someone was crudely copying video tapes.
"Is this it then?" I said turning to the DS. just behind me, "You really mean this is the porno tape duplicating set-up you were after, a ONE AT A TIME cottage industry job, that would have to be running day and night to make a living?"
"Our informant tells us that he helped shift over sixty tapes last week at a tenner apiece, which isn't bad for starters"
Having filmed the place as best I could from various points around the room, plus the copying set-up in great detail, I went out the front door and left them to search the place thoroughly, it all seemed a bit over the top to me.
Shortly afterwards, a WPC came out to where I was sunning myself on the front porch and said "Would you please come inside and record what I have just found, the D/S. said it was very important"
Wondering what on earth it could be, I followed her to the far side of the lounge, where an old washing machine stood with it's front door half open.
"I want you to film every item the WPC pulls out of the machine. She'll unwrap each one in front of the camera and then pass it to me. That way we'll have a complete record of all the property found in it, ok?"
The WPC leant into the open door, drew out a brown envelope, and opened it in front of the camera, it contained money, lots of money.
"There's a hundred pounds in this one" she said to camera, and handed the envelope to the DS. before reaching in for the next one.
"There's a hundred and twenty in this one" she said, before reaching for the next, and in a short time we had emptied the machine of some twenty envelopes.
"Well unless the lady of the house and her son can tell us where this little lot came from, I think we can assume these envelopes contain the proceeds from recent porno-tape sales, not bad eh, Mr. photographer?"
The British National Party, represented in the main by blokes who wouldn't look out of place in a wrestling ring, decided to hold a noisy meeting at the Weaversfield school, Valance Rd E2, to air their xenophobic grievances.

It was my bad luck to be asked to cover the proceedings on video, whilst a couple of the lads from the section wandered incognito through the crowd, clocking faces on camera for subsequent identification.

The whole shindig was expected to be quite boisterous but that was about it, no serious disorder was expected.

At the end of the proceedings, having clocked all and sundry, we went home, eventually submitting our work for the public order lads to interpret.

The word came back we had clocked Jordan their self-styled leader, getting very close to uttering sedition to the assembled masses, and in consequence, our presence was sought to cover another Nationalist meeting scheduled for July. I couldn't wait.

Those cowards the IRA, hiding behind anonymity, let off a couple more bombs to try and get their warped views across, this time at the Army recruiting offices in Eltham, and the Army recruiting office in Wembley, giving us a few days intensive forensic work in rather nice summer weather.

Close on the heels of that little lot, and no doubt just to make sure I earned my crust, Murphy landed me with six murders in the space of four weeks, giving me the run through Hackney, Finsbury Park, Ilford and Leyton.

In July, a car dealer from Kent was reported missing by his family, and after intensive police enquiries, was suspected of being 'removed' by business acquaintances, for unknown transgressions.

Rather similar to the time in 1953 when Setty the car dealer had disappeared from the East-End, and his severed head had been found by us birdwatchers on the marshes at Bradwell in Essex, the Kent car dealer's body was found by a bird watcher roaming the wastes of Rainham marshes.

Who else would be daft enough to go poking around such remote places?

Having spent many hours at Rainham marshes over the years, I knew exactly where at the end of Ferry Lane I needed to go, and was soon trundling through familiar territory, looking for the incident team.

Apart from the place being used as a communal dumping ground, not a lot appeared to have changed over the years.

The huge sewage dispersal pans were virtually dry, and covered in dense vegetation, but it was still a miniature 'wilderness' adjacent to London, where dozens of Herons roamed, Short-Eared Owls could be seen in the winter, and many a rare species of wader still lurked, if you looked hard enough.

"I suppose you'll be off doing a bit of birding if we don't keep your foot nailed to the floor?" said Sandy our Lab.liaison man, as I rolled up.

"You've got to admit a job like this is a real gift, where else would you get paid to go into the open country on a sunny day, and listen to the birds. You've got it made mate"

"If I had known before hand I was coming here" I replied, "I would have brought my binocs, but as I didn't, I'll forgo the pleasure. Why don't you just show me what we've got to do, and let me get on with it, hmm?"

"Well get your wellies on and follow me, keep to the path I've marked out, and we'll record the scene in detail before we move him to the mortuary".

"He is rather far gone I'm afraid, and extremely messy"

Sandy was damn'right.

Our man lay face down amongst the tangled thistles and weeds, and appeared to have been dead for some time.

His bottom half was reasonably intact, and I could see below his jeans he had no shoes on, but his top half was a writhing sea of maggots, and disappearing fast.

I recorded everything from the back that I could, before Sandy had the un-enviable job of turning him over onto the body sheet tucked in tight alongside.

"Right here we go then" said Sandy, and applying gentle pressure to the man's hips, gradually rotated him face up onto the body sheet.

With a slurp like wellies pulling loose from deep mud, the body rolled over onto the sheet, emptying the chest contents in a flood of brown Windsor soup, liberally laced with wriggling maggots.

"Bloody hell!" said Sandy, "This is a bit ripe, get it recorded a bit sharpish, so's we can get it wrapped up and away, will you?"

It was amazing what the forces of nature could do in so short a time, there were no facial features to compare with the photograph of the dead man we had, just a bare, earth-stained skull with matted brown hair.

The maggots must have been working overtime!

Alongside the place where the body had been dumped, were a couple of good tyre impressions, plus several walking-boot impressions, which I photographed using the Bronica GS-1 set vertically on a tripod, using a two dimensional scale for accuracy.

With a bit of luck, and some good detective work on the part of the Kent police, our tyre and shoeprint photos might produce suspects, if there were any in the offing.

Like a lot of jobs one does, unless you are asked to attend court and give evidence at a subsequent trial, or meet the officer in the case soon afterwards, that's the last you heard about it, unless you read something later in the newspapers.

That was the case here.

In early July, the next political meeting of the National Front party took place as expected, this time the venue was the Old Ford school in Bethnal Green.

Somehow they had managed to get permission to hold their meeting inside the school, and they were making sure that only the faithful, and accredited supporters were allowed inside.

No-one, but no-one else, was going to get a sniff at it!

Because of the hairyness of the job, and the fact that if they'd sussed us as old Bill, we would have been rough-handled out of it, I prominently displayed in my shirt breast-pocket, a couple of their distinctive pamphlets, indicating that I was perhaps sympathetic to their cause, and not a dire threat.

As the party elite arrived at the venue, dozens of anti NF party supporters began violent protests, right on the toes of the ring of heavies guarding the entrance to the school, and punch-ups became the order of the day.

Police deployed on public order duty did their best to keep the fighting factions apart, and after a lot of effort, managed to clear the pavement directly outside the school main door.

Turning to my plain-clothes minder, I said "I'd like to get along there by the door, to film close-up, Colin Jordan and his guest speaker, just for the record"

"I don't think that's a good idea" he replied. "If they cop we're old Bill, it'll get rather umpty"

"Well let's give it a go anyway, if it does go pear-shaped, we'll have given it our best, and can have it away on our toes, ok?"

Dressed in working clothes, and no doubt being seen by police as yet another pain in the butt to be dealt with, we were both man-handled into the crush of people swirling around on the pavement, and told to keep back.

As soon as Jordan and his guest entered the door, I moved forward filming as I went, closely followed by my minder, and somehow we found ourselves inside the hall surrounded by the cheering, shouting faithful as the leader took his place on the stage.

The school doors slammed shut, and one of the heavies standing next to me said "If you want to see better, you'd better stand on this chair", and praying he didn't ask who the heck I was, I did just that.

There was virtually no room to move, I was jammed against the green painted school wall, recorder between my feet, camera on shoulder, wedged in a sea of fist waving, chanting fanatics, which had all the hallmarks of a pre-war Nazi rally.

It was potentially very hairy.

As the meeting got under way, I began filming, keeping the camera as steady as I could, filming the podium a few yards away, while the guest speaker was introduced.

Suddenly a man a few feet away jumped to his feet, shouting anti-Nationalist party rhetoric towards the stage, and was immediately set upon by bully boys, who punched and kicked him to the floor, before dragging him away, and throwing him outside.

Discretion being the better part of valour, I kept the camera rigidly focussed on the stage, not giving the least hint that I was interested in recording any such naughty goings on.

As soon as the first man had been ejected, a second, and then a third gave vent to their violent re-actions to the meeting, and were summarily beaten into submission, and ejected.

I hoped to god they never sussed us, or it would be quite painful, we had no friends in here!

For twenty minutes I listened to the carefully orchestrated tirade, there was no doubt it contained a lot of material which was bread and butter to anyone who felt pro-British, and deplored the retreat from national pride the public had to endure from our crummy politicians, but it was well over the top too.

Several times I thought they were going to lay themselves open to a charge of sedition or worse, but somehow they appeared to stay a gnat's cock clear of actually breaking the law.

When a rallying statement was made, and the audience responded with cheers and clapping, I took the opportunity to turn round and pan slowly up and down the rows of seats, recording the faces of everyone I could clap eyes on.

I hoped they felt I was filming their reaction to the gems of nationalist wisdom tumbling forth from the speakers, and not their facial idents!

I had been standing on that ruddy chair for an hour now, used three twenty-minute tapes, and was beginning to get the muscular shakes.

My shoulder was absolutely numb from the weight of the camera, and I felt we'd recorded more than enough material, why didn't the silly buggers pack it in and go home?

At last the meeting broke into nationalist inspired songs, and it became clear we could soon get out of the damn' place.

I still couldn't figure out why we had never been challenged as to who we were, and allowed to carry on!

Perhaps someone somewhere thought we were friendlies, and our attendance was authorised, I don't know, but I clocked a lot of interesting faces anyway.

The continuing investigation into the paedophile murders of Mark Tildesley, Jonathan Swift and others, lured off the streets by perverts Cooke, Bailey and Smith and tortured to death, led us to re-examine the murder scene of Barry Lewis at Waltham Abbey in Essex.

I was asked to video the scene where Barry's body had been buried at Clapgate, and cover the entire journey as stated by one of the defendants, Bailey, as he walked back into nearby Waltham Abbey.

I mentioned to DC.Supt. Roger Studeley, officer in the case that I had filmed the route of a previous murder, using both helicopter and vehicle, as this seemed much easier for investigators to interpret than a series of still photographs, and he agreed.

The defendant's statement had been that he had walked along the road from Clapgate to a petrol station in Waltham Abbey, a distance of just over a mile, carrying the boy in his arms, filled a can with petrol, and returned along the same route.

Unless Bailey was built like an all-in wrestler, I felt it impossible for anyone to carry a six year old kiddie two miles, the second mile with a can of petrol as well, which must have weighed at least ten pounds!

Bailey also stated that he had not buried the boy where he had been found, so there were a couple of mysteries there that needed answering, for my money.

To cover the route, I asked one of the DC's to drive my van at a steady pace along the route into Waltham Abbey, while I lay on the roof platform, filming as we went along.

It wasn't a difficult task, but one thing became abundantly clear to me as we bowled along, there was NO pavement or walkway on the nearside for practically the whole journey!

There was only a narrow strip of rough grass between the road and the hedge.

Anyone walking along that route with a child in his arms must have caused overtaking traffic to swerve around him, and I couldn't imagine anyone failing to stop and help, seeing a man carrying a child under such circumstances.

Later I asked if there had been any reports of drivers seeing a man carrying a child along that route, but apparently there were none, and I felt certain things just didn't add up.

At the end of July I was asked to attend a Caribbean music festival being held in Finsbury Park, where intelligence had it, some of the revellers would be in the business of pushing drugs.

I would be given a protective 'escort' of two plain clothes officers, who would watch my back as I recorded suspects in the crowd, while ostensibly filming for TV.

Although it was Saturday and I should have been off, it was a nice sunny day, and the thought of eight hours at time and a half went some way to make it all seem worth while.

In a relaxed mood I arrived at the local nick in good time for a bite to eat before attending the festival, and found my two 'minders' in the canteen having a cuppa.

"We don't expect any serious trouble here today" said the PS. "However, I've got a serial of troops standing by with their carrier at Highbury Vale just in case, so shall we get started?"

"You aren't going into the park in your uniform are you?" I asked the second minder, a woman PC.

"I'm quite happy to have you as minders a short distance back in the crowd, but not obviously as the old Bill if you don't mind!"

"What's wrong with a casual, low profile police presence then?" she replied snottily.

"We are readily accepted at such functions you know"

"You may very well be accepted by the public at large at such gatherings, but if we are here to get on film people who are dealing, I could get a knife in my back if I'm associated with you, so would you kindly go off and change?"

I could see we had got off on the wrong foot already, but I wasn't risking my neck out there with someone who didn't appreciate how nasty things could get in a matter of seconds.

I'd rather not do the job.

Leaving our vehicles in Green Lanes, I took just the camera, recorder, and a couple of spare tapes in my jacket pockets, and let them lead off towards the park, while I followed fifty yards behind, visually clocking the people around me as we hurried along.

There seemed to be a lot of people about, all apparently heading for the shindig in the park, and just to make things a little more arduous while carrying my heavy gear, the organisers were only allowing the public in through the Endymion Rd. entrance, half a mile away!

Hot and sticky, and feeling that things weren't getting off to a good start, I squeezed through the gates, and walked towards some tents where loud music was booming from huge, megawatt speakers. The base output was so intense it made my diaphragm resonate, and was a real physical assault on the ears!

Standing back a little way, I pretended to film the group that was responsible for the din, and then began filming for real, picking up some unsavoury looking characters who were huddled in a group to one side of the display.

Shutting off the camera, I turned round casually, and saw my minders standing under some trees fifty yards off, as they stood watching me, so I wandered along to the next musical group, and repeated the procedure.

I knew I was getting a few funny looks, and heard the odd cat-calls as I worked, but having had plenty of that in the past, I ignored it, and carried on filming.

There were of course hundreds of people just enjoying the music, buying food and drink from the stands, or sitting on the grass and relaxing in the warm sun, but there were also a few who seemed to be worth recording as they huddled together, trying to keep a low profile.

I suppose I only became aware things weren't quite tickety-boo when a vicious fight broke out just in front of me, and blood stared to flow.

Naturally I kept the camera running, until the defeated party ran off, and it was then I realised there was no-one within 25 yards of me, except my minders, who were looking anxiously in my direction.

Suddenly it hit me, in this sea of black people, most of whom were just out enjoying themselves for the day, we were the only whites to be seen.

We must have stood out like nuns at a rock festival!

There was no doubt about it, we had been 'blown-out,' and would get nothing of any use today.

We might as well pack it in and get the hell out of there while we still could.

Looking at my minder in the light of our sticky situation, I could see by his clean-shaven face and shortish hair, he must epitomize 'old bill' to the blacks, and obviously by association, the WPC too.

A dozen or so young blacks jeered at our embarrassment, and loosely encircled us as we made our way back to the exit, exulting in their command of the situation by seeing us off their premises. I felt if we had in fact observed the drug activities we had come to record, the whole scenario might have ended up very differently, and with perhaps, rather serious consequences.

# Chapter Thirty Five

There had been rustlings amongst certain senior staff in the section ever since Frank Jones had succeeded Dave Teague as head man, and it was common knowledge he was looking for a reliable No.2, to help put in place ideas which were not always palatable to his other two Chief Photographers.

Who might that be?

There were a couple of 'in-house' contenders for the post, who made no secret of their eminent suitability for the job, on the grounds that working in the section daily for the past umpteen years must surely count for something.

Whereas a person like myself, eligible on all counts except one - I was a scenes of crime 'freebooter', was a twenty-to-one outsider.

Anyway, any thoughts I may have had about nobbling the opposition, or trying to formulate answers as to WHY I thought I might be suitable for the post, were swept away in a tide of jobs that saw me attend five murder scenes, a gross indecency job in public toilets, and a grotty 'Keep Britain out of Saudi Arabia' demonstration in a week.

So much for tactics!

The day of the selection board dawned, and with some trepidation, I went over in my mind all the things I could usefully say that might put me in with a fighting chance.

I didn't necessarily want the job for it's own sake, but I DID draw the line at a couple of the lads who had many years less service than me, thinking that on past performances under Dave A. I could be passed over yet again.

On the whole the interview went quite smoothly, and I managed to answer everything confidently, including some of the senior management scenarios I had recently read up on, which I now answered like an old hand.

As so often happens when you come out, you have a touch of the seconds, and clearly remember some of the things you should have said, and perhaps one or two you shouldn't, anyway the die was cast now, and I could get back to work again!

I couldn't believe it when I was asked to accompany a big vice raid on private premises in swanky Earls Court Square, apparently prostitution was rife in the place, and anything was catered for.

During the briefing it was made clear that everyone who was found on the premises had to be photographically recorded and questioned, and his reason for being there ascertained.

I wondered if someone had 'put the bubble in' hoping to catch some prominent person 'in flagrente' so to speak!

That evening, the lead car, with me in the passenger seat, ready to go, plus a couple of carriers full of officers, screeched to a halt outside an imposing residence in Earls Court Square.

After gaining swift access through the massive front door, I piled inside with camera running, clocking all and sundry as the inmates slowly realised the old Bill were now visiting in force.

In a couple of rooms, we caught fellers in bed with their women, and it was hilarious to see how the men tried to hide under the sheets out of view, while the women just sat there shouting abuse.

Once we had covered all the rooms and their occupants, with I think, the madam in tow to observe exactly what we were doing, I started to cover each of the rooms again in detail, to show just what had been going on with the clients.

Some of it was quite amazing.

There were rackfulls of whips and canes, rubber capes and masks, huge plastic strap-on penises, rubber dolls, whipping racks, sadistic torture equipment, everything you could possibly think of, and one or two that were quite new to me!

There was even a tea and coffee making set-up with small table and chairs, where the hard-working girls could nip out between jobs and seek refreshment.

In this respect it was obvious they were better organised than we were!

I thought we had more or less covered everything, until one of the lads discovered a cupboard door leading to a below floor 'dungeon' where an even more bizarre set-up was found.

When the lights were put on, everything down there was bathed in a deep orange glow, making the place seem like a scene from hell, with it's various pieces of equipment designed to induce pain, fear, bliss, or whatever into the recipient.

The ceiling, which was really the floor above, was so low, I couldn't stand upright to film the place at all, and I ended up on my knees in damp grotty stuff littering the floor, it was disgusting.

At last we trooped out the front door, and prepared to leave, but not before I had done my usual bit, filming all the cars and their index numbers within fifty yards of the address.

You never knew whom you might turn up on the police national computer!

When I got into the office next day, I was summoned, along with other candidates for the Chief Photographer's post, to Frank Jones' office, where we would be told the result of the recent board.

Looking closely at the faces of the other contenders, I tried to see if any of them had that smug look on his face which might indicate he had been selected, but I couldn't be sure.

Who the hell had got it then?

"As you must be aware, I've asked you all to come to my office to hear the result of the recent board for Chief Photographer, and I am very happy to tell you that Alan Parker has been successful, although you all did very well, congratulations Alan", and Frank shook my hand.

I was in a complete daze, and taken completely by surprise at his words, I felt sure that one of the others, having been party to all the internal politics and in-fighting over the years must have been selected, but no, I had eventually done it!

I breathed a great sigh of relief, feeling it was all unreal, and I would wake up and find it a dream, but it was real enough, and now my life style at work would change drastically.

Gone were the days of double time overtime - senior ranks got plain time rates if they did any at all.

To compensate for this though, my annual salary as Chief was now the same as my previous rank with overtime, so theoretically I was better off, with more time to myself.

Gone too, were the days when I ran my own ship, and travelled the Met. like a freebooter, would I regret it?

Later, when we alone in his office Frank said quite seriously, "Now that you're a Chief, I want you here in the office with me, your days of gallivanting around the MPD as a one man band are over, you've got two good men in Ian Nicholls and Paul Griffin, so leave it all to them"

"Let them get on with the graft for a while, you'll have plenty of paperwork to keep you busy here, I'll see to that!"

My heart sank into my boots at this, this was definitely the downside of promotion!

I had been as free as a Lark for the last twenty years, and now the hobbles were being put on, could I take it?

I now divided London into two halves, Ian covered the East, while Paul covered the West, with strict instructions that if they incurred any serious jobs like murders, sieges or demos I was to be informed immediately, day or night, so that I could keep a 'hands on' approach.

Needless to say the first big job to come up was the Anti Poll-Tax demo in Brixton, which needed all hands anyway, as it was expected to be a rough old do.

Ian and I took one video kit, Paul and Derek the second, giving us the chance to cover the demo from both ends, and it was fortunate we did so, because during the day, things went ever so pear-shaped.

To make sure we were recognised by our own troops, we were issued with arm bands, saying 'Police' in blue letters, all very nice and proper, but a bit of a disadvantage when clocked by the 'rent-a-mob' gang, or up-tight demonstrators, who saw anyone associated with the old bill as fair game for a whacking.

It was a rough couple of hours, with more than a little action thrown in, but eventually law, and some sort of order returned, and we were all stood down.

It was certainly better than being in the office!

Five days later, with Ian tucked up on a long job, I attended our old venue, Broadwater Farm, for yet another drugs raid.

This time it was centered on the Launderette, and I thought that either some of the residents must be getting very bold, or our patrolling chaps were keeping an unduly low profile, whichever it was, search teams were required.

Again we did the stealthy approach, with everyone concealed in a box van, and as the tail-board went down, I leapt off the rear, gallantly supported by two uniformed officers as my knees buckled under the weight of camera and recorder.

I was definitely getting a bit fragile in some places, for this lark!

With camera running, we reached the Launderette on the first level, and went in, clocking everyone in the place as it was quickly secured, so far, so good.

There was the usual shouting and scuffling, as someone was arrested and taken to the custody van, but things soon settled down and the search teams started their onerous work.

The crowds of black kids who had been watching us suspiciously, broke up, moved off, and began playing games.

I sat on the concourse wall in the weak sunshine, waiting to be called to film whatever the searchers found, and thought how different the atmosphere was, compared to the shrieking hate and violence we had encountered here during the riot in 1985.

Perhaps that in itself was some sort of progress?

The search teams turned up several small stashes of cannabis which I recorded before it was taken away as evidence, and unless there were a few prisoners taken away for possession that I hadn't seen, it didn't seem to me to be an overly productive result for the amount of energy expended.

As the Christmas festivities marking the end of 1990 began to roll, we made preparations to film the new year shindig in Trafalgar square once again, although it didn't seem a year ago we set up the system for the first time.

Didn't someone, somewhere say, time goes much faster the older you get? Now there's food for thought!

At my insistence, Greg had been working hard for months to produce a more compact version of the first high-speed flash units, and had come up with a Mark 2 prototype which was 8"x6"x6"in size.

This was a third smaller than the previous ones, but with the same hefty 120Joules output, and 1/30,000sec flash duration.

It sounded too good to be true.

It was a double flash-tube job, weighing in at 6lbs, a bit lighter than the originals, and consequently a bit easier to handle when fixing to trees or buildings, and I couldn't wait to try them out.

Although the weather was cold, I desperately needed some snow, I couldn't photograph the Starlings in mid-air, fighting over food scraps if it wasn't cold enough.

I still wanted to catch them in the air at the same time as it was snowing, and see what happened to snowflakes when they hit the bird's wings or bodies.

Did the snowflakes break up, or just get knocked out of the way?

After one memorable week-end of snow, when the protected camera and watertight flash units were under several inches of snow, I got a couple of good results, which although not perfect, showed me I was on the right lines, and the snowflakes just got pushed out of the bird's way.

The downside was the dark, under-lit background was still causing serious problems, especially combined with dark-coloured birds like Starlings.

Unless I could afford to have at least one flash dedicated solely to lighting the background, Starlings tended to merge into the background, making it difficult to see exactly what was going on.

I would have to provide my own 'manufactured' background, the correct colour and distance behind the birds, so that a balanced photograph would result, and I felt the whole set-up was getting like an outdoor studio!

In early March I paid a long overdue visit to Hainault Lodge, checking to see whether the Tawny Owls were still using their old nesting site, and was lucky to find the bird present sitting on two eggs.

Although it was a difficult site to work, I decided to have a go, using the high-speed flash units mounted on brackets screwed into the tree, some thirty feet up.

It meant though, I would have to leave my equipment in situ overnight, and come back early the following morning to make sure no-one did a runner with my gear!

After all, the Hasselblad plus my three flashes were probably worth something over £3000!

There was a six-inch diameter branch extending horizontally from the oak tree just below the nest hole, so it was fairly easy to fix one half of the infra-red trigger there, while I fixed the sensor device to the end of a rod, and positioned it directly above the nest.

This would enable me to photograph the Tawny as it flew in towards it's nest hole, catching the bird in mid-flight.

The only snag was, the horizontal branch below the nest on which I rested the double-extension ladder, was 30 feet above ground, which left the top of the ladder absolutely level with the top of the branch.

Any small amount of sinking into the soft ground below whilst I climbed with the heavy equipment would leave precious little of the ladder leaning against the tree!

I waited until the Tawny's eggs hatched before starting any photography, so that disturbance could be kept to the minimum, and on a Friday evening drove to the Lodge and set everything in place.

Whenever I set the gear up in awkward places for the first time, it seems to take a heck of a time, and I felt that perhaps I should have found an easier site than this!

Unfortunately places where you can work relatively undisturbed are getting scarcer and scarcer around London, so you have to deal with what you are lucky enough to find.

Because the Lodge is overgrown and disused, I had to leave my van by the entrance - normally closed to prevent access, inviting passers-by to ask, 'what is going on in there at this time of night?'

Consequently I have to work quickly in case a Police vehicle comes nosing by!

After the first night's photography, I found the camera had been triggered twice - it was quite possible for the birds to swing in from one side and miss the sensor beam, which I didn't mind too much, so long as they played fair, and gave me at least a couple of shots for my trouble!

When I developed the film, I found I had two super shots of the owl, but it's wings were in a forward, braking position, obviously checking the birds' momentum, leaving the head and body totally obscured.

It was the classic 'almost' result!

The following week-end I was more fortunate, and got four exposures, but despite moving the trigger forwards a bit to get a different wing position, I still only got one good shot for all my efforts, but at least I was making progress!

On the last weekend I was able to undertake photography, the largest of the two Tawny owl chicks was ready to leave the nest, in fact he sat in the nest entrance, snapping his beak at me as I fixed the camera in position.

I knew from previous experience that young tawnies leave the nest and climb amongst the branches well before they can fly, so I knew I was fast running out of time.

When I returned to pick up my camera the following morning, I was amazed, and very happy to see all twelve exposures on the film had been used, but wondered what sort of activity could have triggered so many exposures?

Did I have a fantastic series of mind blowing flight shots?

I most certainly did not!

On developing the film I saw a good shot of the owl flying back to the nest with a Sparrow in it's beak, and the next, a young Tawny making it's first flight from the nest.

The rest of the film showed the top of the youngster's head as it stood next to the trigger receiver on the branch, breaking the beam every second or so with it's tail, until the film ran out!

A very interesting job came in as a result of two young lads computer hacking into businesses and institutions. They left a trail of damage and chaos behind them costing many thousands of pounds to put right, and putting a lot of people at risk of an unnecessary early death.

Some of their 'fun' consisted of hacking into a major hospital in Copenhagen, and obliterating case histories and records, dialling a firm in Japan, and leaving their phone open on international calls over the whole weekend, and finally hacking into a secure section of the Pentagon in the USA, causing the authorities to say enough was definitely enough.

It had reached a point where the President of America had spoken to Margaret Thatcher direct, saying if the Brits didn't shut this lot down we'd be off the information exchange network forthwith.

Our computer fraud department at the Yard was shunted into full speed mode to deal with it, and photographic were asked to give technical support.

After carefully monitoring hundreds of telephone calls, British Telecomm's investigation dept. had narrowed the origin of the hacking to two places in the midlands, and the one I was expected to cover with our squad was in Manchester.

Listening to detailed briefing concerning the action to be taken once the identity of the hackers was known, it seemed to me a terrible loop-hole existed where someone could use his modem to capture a selected business telephone number, and use this number to dial around the world, hacking into other firms' computers.

"We should know final details in the next day or so after BT have tracked these two down, and we'll move straight in to the addresses to catch them actually operating if we can"

The next day I was asked to get my gear together and accompany officers to Chadderton, Oldham, near Manchester, where we would be the guests of the local police until required for action.

None of the locals knew what we were there for, and speculation ran rife amongst local officers, necessitating absolute schtum as the order of the day.

During a briefing the following day, we learned the hackers had been well at it during the night, and BT were confident they would get a fix for us when they started up again that evening.

All we had to do was wait.

Just before midnight everyone piled into a couple of cars and drove off into the suburbs, parking in a quiet side-street to await further instructions.

For the umpteenth time I switched on the video camera resting on my lap, and checked that everything was ready to go, I couldn't afford any slip-up on this one, it was far too serious a job for mistakes even to be considered.

"Cars at location A-Alpha, are you receiving me, over"

"Loud and clear, over"

"Your man has just started his calls, will you go to the next position and wait? Over"

It was now just before 0100hrs, and we slid forward a hundred yards before coming to a halt, engine running.

"Ok. Alpha, go go go!" and we moved quickly round the corner before pulling up outside what appeared to be a row of private houses.

"Ok lads, now keep it quiet, no talking, we want to make the front door without being clocked"

In single file we walked up the path to the front door and waited, while the chaps with the hydraulic door-opener got themselves into position.

I switched on the camera, but left the top light off until we were in, I didn't want anyone inside seeing a bright light outside their front door, and blowing the works.

At a swift nod from the guv'nor, our man applied the opener to the door, and with a whine, and crunch of splintering wood, we were in.

I was third in line behind two officers deputed to find the computer operator and hold him in front of his PC until I got there. Switching on the light as we went in, I ran for the stairs, thinking the computer would be in the boy's upstairs room.

As I reached the bottom step, a man in his pyjamas hurled himself downstairs shouting and cursing like a madman, obviously thinking he was being burgled, or something worse!

"In the downstairs lounge Alan, not upstairs!" came an urgent shout, and I turned right, leaving the swinging, punching pyjama clad man to those behind me.

Entering the lounge I saw a young lad seated at a computer, his hands resting on the table, a look of stark fear and horror on his face as we caught him bang to rights!

Zooming the camera onto his face, I recorded him in detail before shooting over his shoulder to record the details on his monitor screen.

Moving back a couple of paces I panned around the room before coming back again to the young lad, held by his arresting officers.

"Ok, that should do for the minute, you can let him up if you want, I'll cover in detail what's written on the papers covering his desk" and he was wheeled away to one side to watch as I worked.

In the meantime, the pyjama clad man, who turned out to be the lad's father, having been acquainted with who we were, and what his son was being charged with, had calmed down considerably.

I think I would have re-acted rather violently too, had I been on the receiving end of our entry into his home, it must have been quite frightening!

Once I had covered everything from top to bottom, the computer and all associated equipment was removed for analysis, and the thought struck me as a rather simple computer person - why didn't his parents question the large phone bill that must have been incurred while he was up and running, surely something must have clicked?

The other raid on the second hacker also went down 100% and we felt very pleased at the successful outcome. We had stopped two young lads, too young even be at work, from creating a serious international incident, and untold damage and expense to hundreds of ordinary people.

"Don't worry" said the DI. when I mentioned my disgust at their criminal actions "As soon as this is all over, and the courts dole out whatever punishment they see fit, you can bet your bottom dollar these kids will be head-hunted by the top businesses in the country to protect their systems from other hackers."

"Their future is made"

With Ian now covering most of what I used to do in the eastern half of the Met, and Paul covering the west, I was much less involved in the day to day scenes of crime work as Frank had promised, and more into managing my sectional responsibilities.

I had seventeen staff to look after, and with the paper work that entailed, plus attending various meetings, I felt I was rapidly becoming a 'paper-pusher,' something I had energetically tried to avoid all my life!

Earlier in the year I had written to Ray Connor, my colleague in the 'egg photography' saga, who now lived in Spain, and fixed up a visit to his place in the foothills of the Sierra Nevada to photograph Woodchat Shrike, Hoopoe and any other species we might find.

I naturally expected to use 35mm on some species, but was keen to use the 6x6 Bronica and my high-speed flashes on something like the Hoopoe in flight if possible.

The main fly in the ointment was the weight of all my gear when flying by charter flight. I was strictly limited to 20 kilos of hold luggage, and 10 kilos of cabin luggage - a piddling amount!

I needed to take a hide with me, (minus poles etc; I could get those locally) two camera kits, a tripod, stands for the high speed flashes, and of course the bulky flash units themselves.

That lot weighed in at more than 50 kilos. how on earth could I get round that?

When I carefully read the advertising blurb that arrived with my flight tickets, I was astounded to see the airline were actually allowing golfing equipment to travel free, as an inducement to patrons of the sport to go there and play!

This gave me the wicked idea to borrow a capacious golf bag from a friend, and stuff it to the gills with my tripod, stands for the electronic flashes, and anything else that could pass muster for golf clubs, before locking it securely from prying eyes.

The flash-heads I packed into a chippies canvas holdall, which I hoped would go into the aircraft cabin marked 'glass - with care' while the hide and my clothes made makeshift packing for the photographic equipment, except for the Bronica which hung round my neck.

On the day of departure, I nervously presented myself at the check-in, and pointing to the golf bag, which seemed to weigh a ton, enquired "This goes free doesn't it?"

"Yes, that's correct, would you do me a favour and put it with the rest of the golf stuff on that trolley over there, and save me coming round the counter?"

Too right I would, if it would get the bag on board without being assessed as far too heavy for golfing equipment!

The smiling hostess indicated where I could park the 'glass- with care' container for the flight, and I breathed a sigh of relief as I took my seat by the window. So far, so good.

Ray met me at Malaga, and took me to his home in the hills by Jeep. It was very remote and quiet, but with majestic scenery all around.

Over the next ten days I photographed Black-eared Wheatear, Blue Rock Thrush, Nightingale, Woodchat-Shrike and Hoopoe, the last being a super below-ground nest-site, where I was able to set up the high-speed flash units to good advantage.

All too soon it was time to lug all my stuff back to the airport, and say goodbye to Ray for his hospitality.

It had been a valuable experience for me, setting up the flash units in the field, and I came back with some good stuff.

Despite my promotion, there were still a couple of jobs I liked to have a 'handle' on, and one of them was aerial video.

During May I was asked to spend a couple of days evaluating the possibilities of using a small airship over London as a filming platform, to supplement the work we did using the Police helicopter.

The pilot, a Swedish chap, and an expert in manoeuvring such craft, welcomed me aboard at the launch site near Rickmansworth, and after strapping me and my gear securely into the bucket seat, we swept aloft.

It was a bit like sitting in a world war one, canvas and string aircraft, with a large part of the gondola open to the windy skies.

It all seemed slightly ridiculous after the job's purposeful Jet-Ranger Helicopter, but given time, and not too strong a headwind, we were able to chunter round north London, and get our filming tests done.

The Public Order section, hearing of this new opportunity to get a view of what joe public were up to at large open air functions, asked if I would go up again and film the crowd control procedures put in place for the cup final at Wembley.

They wanted the crowd approaches covered, coach parking facilities prior to the game, and after, and the dispersal of the home-going crowds and traffic.

It was quite an order.

According to the pilot once we were aloft, there was to be no landing between the beginning and the end of the match,

"That means we'll be in the air for three hours at least" I said in surprise.

"That's right" he replied "And don't drink too much beforehand, we don't have any toilets on board you know!"

Fortunately the day was bright and sunny, although at 600 feet the wind was pretty chilly, and I wished I had brought some thin leather gloves with me, to help handle the camera.

For a couple of hours we gently stooged around Wembley, watching the game from on high, there was no doubt about it, when the airship was heading gently into the wind, it was as stable a camera platform as you could wish for, but there were times on turning around, when she wallowed a bit in the turbulence, and was quite hopeless.

Although I had suffered from Meniere's syndrome for a number of years now, and prolonged flights in the helicopter caused me to become quite nauseous, I didn't get that horrible sensation in the airship, it was obviously a far gentler form of transport!

Covert filming of suspects for identification had really taken off during the last year, both Ian and Paul were well tucked up trying to fit everything in, and each of them needed a number two purely for their video work.

VFI was becoming an industry in itself.

As the year came to an end, we began our annual pilgrimage to Trafalgar Square, to film festivities taking place there, and of course record the hooligans and villains who couldn't let an opportunity pass without making trouble.

You might have thought they'd learned something by now?

The first week into January 1992 saw me back at the Cory Landfill site at Stanford-le-Hope, searching for more human remains in a case of murder, this time with Ian and Derek.

They were the video men now, and I was just over-seeing, keeping a watching brief you might say, and of course getting myself well and truly away from the office and paperwork!

As in the previous murder hunt, we were fortunate to have the accurate rubbish tipping records for reference, and after two days of hard digging, recovered a couple of identifiable pieces of the dismembered torso, but nowhere near as successfully as our previous excavation.

You can't win them all.

During February I decided it might be a good idea to try photographing some Rooks again, I hadn't photographed them since Hainault Lodge in 1955, and as there was a thriving Rookery of about 120 pairs at Cory's landfill site, I thought I could start there.

Looking closely at the trees which still held some of last years' nests, I chose one which overlooked a group of about twenty nests, which I felt should give me a great view of things, if all went according to plan.

I banged a few six inch nails into the Ash and began to climb, it wasn't too bad, even though I hadn't been up a tall tree for ages, and soon I was fifty feet up, looking across at the nearby nests, getting a great view.

With a bit of care I could build a hide platform in the tree I was standing in, and put the covering material on top later, once the birds had returned to breed.

I had taken the precaution of bringing a thin, sixty-foot rope with me, so I tied it on where I stood, and dropped the remainder to the ground.

Now I could tie on anything I wanted hauled to the top, without having to climb up with it first, nothing like saving the old muscles!

At home,I still nurtured ideas about capturing Starlings in flight whilst it was snowing, and as the cold weather approached, renewed the feeding station in the garden to entice birds in front of the camera.

I had used bread as bait in the past, but knew Starlings couldn't resist cheese, so I wrote to our local Tesco Stores, asking if they would let me have some of their unsold stale cheese to use as bait.

They came up trumps by letting me have 5lbs!

The weather suddenly got a lot colder and I was able to set up the camera and high-speed flashes around the feeding station, using the infra red beam to trigger the camera as before.

The birds quickly became used to the studio set up, and I began to get results, not by any means world beaters, but good enough to show me the lighting and camera position was about right, all I needed now was a fair dollop of snow.

After I had shot a couple of rolls of film on the Starlings, I came to the same conclusion as last year, that the IR trigger wasn't the answer to getting the shots I wanted at all.

The birds were breaking the beam at weird angles, and I was getting rear views, side views, and birds on the edge of the film, albeit sharp and well lit, but not what I had in mind.

I would have to go back to manual control, using an electrical lead operated from the kitchen.

At the end of the month, I visited the rookery again, and was pleased to see there was a fair amount of activity from the returning birds, and better still, they seemed to be clustered around the general area I wanted to work.

Over the next couple of hours I hauled several long pieces of 4x2 and some thinner pieces of wood into my tree, plus a plastic bucket containing hammer, saw, nails and wire. It didn't take long to fashion a floor and some uprights, and I sat back to admire my handywork, a hide frame, four feet by three, and about four feet high.

All I had to do now was cover the darn thing with canvas or some such weather-proof material, so I wouldn't get wet if it rained!

My intention was to go for photographs of individual birds this time, plus some Hi-8 video-filming.

I had already done plenty of close-up nest photography at Hainault Lodge, so I wasn't particularly interested in doing that stuff again.

I thought if I could get the birds to accept the huge 300mm 2.8 lens sticking out the front of the hide, with a x2 doubler on the back, I would have a '600' F5.6 to play with, and hopefully get some frame-filling portraits of Rooks.

By the time I returned the following week-end, about sixty pairs of Rooks were in residence, cawing and flapping noisily as they tried to get their first nesting sticks into position.

Quite a few were in the trees immediately in front of the hide, indicating that my woodwork hadn't put them off the area in the least.

Despite scouring most places on the in-fill site, I couldn't find a suitable piece of green canvas to cover the hide, and had to make do with some rather bright blue plastic sheeting.

It didn't look very professional, but it was all I could get, so on it went. When I climbed down at the conclusion of the cutting and stitching and saw the results of my labours, I had a touch of the seconds, it looked incongruous!

Would the birds really accept a bright-blue shape lodged in the top of a neighbouring Ash tree, or would I have problems?

Packing up my tools, I left the wood, and as soon as I had cleared the immediate area, the Rooks returned, and I watched from a distance to see what they made of it all.

If they shunned the hide area, it would all have to come off, and I'd have to start again!

Within five minutes the birds were back in the branches near the hide, cawing and bowing like mad. It was obvious the bright blue hide hadn't made a scrap of difference at all, I was ok.

The only trouble with working on your own is that when you want to get into a hide, someone has to put you in, otherwise the birds won't return.

The same goes for the moment you wish to leave the hide, someone has to let you out.

If you were to suddenly appear amongst the birds near their nests, all hell would break loose, and the birds would almost certainly desert.

You would certainly have labelled the hide as something to do with humans, and therefore a device to keep well clear of.

To overcome this problem on my next visit, I persuaded one of the landfill workers to accompany me to the foot of the tree containing the hide, and wait while I hauled my photographic gear up in the bucket, and got settled in.

"Can either yourself or one of your mates come back just after lunch and let me out, all you have to do is come to the bottom of the tree, how about two o'clock?"

As he disappeared off under the trees, I hoped he would remember to come back, otherwise I would be stuck up here in a silly situation, and would have to think of something drastic to get out!

He hadn't been gone five minutes before most of the Rooks came back, and I began looking for the best spots in the open where I could get clear views of the birds.

I particularly wanted a shot of a bird facing me, calling, with it's beak open and tail fanned, but as the action only lasted a second or two, you had to be very lucky to capture it.

I had covered the lens hood on the huge 2.8 lens with camouflage material so that no metal parts would glint in the sun, and provided I moved the lens slowly on the tripod's fluid head, the Rooks accepted it quite happily, which was a great relief.

I had taken about twenty shots before the alarm calls of disturbed Rooks announced the imminent approach of my relieving man, and, feeling a bit stiff after a four hours in the hide, I lowered my gear in the bucket, and climbed slowly down.

"How did you get on then?" he asked. "Not much sun about for good pictures is there?"

"It's not too bad, but you do need some sunshine to capture that lovely metallic sheen the birds have on their wings, never mind, it's early days yet, and the weather can only improve"

The Barn owls were showing an interest in Muckingford church again, flying in and out through a broken section of leaded window, thirty feet above ground.

I asked Grahame, the owner of the property, if I could possibly photograph the owls as they flew in, and he kindly agreed, asking me how on earth I was going to get my camera up to that level.

"That's where I need your permission to erect a scaffolding tower inside the old church, so I can get my camera and flashes level with the window, without the birds being disturbed by my photography." I explained.

"That's no great problem, I've got a lot of scaffolding here, you tell me what you want done, and I'll build it"

During the next few days, Grahame built a tower platform thirty feet high, tucked well to one side of the Owl's path through the window, and I climbed up to try it for size.

It seemed absolutely perfect.

"If you don't mind, I'll leave the tower for a while, and let the birds get used to it, before I find a way of covering the broken window with my IR. trigger.

I also have to find a way to suspend a flash over the owls when they fly in, to get the necessary top lighting effect"

"That's alright by me, the scaffolding isn't in my way, you get on and take whatever time you want"

By using Grahame's forty-foot ladder at maximum extension, I was just able to fix the IR trigger across the broken leaded window and take the connecting wire across to the top of the scaffold tower.

The next problem was, how to fix the top flash over the owls?

Fortunately the old bell rope was still hanging down the wall, although it wasn't attached to any of the huge bronze bells in the loft, so I attached one of my flashes to that, hauling it into position each time I needed it.

At last came the time to set it up for real, and crossing my fingers that everything would work, passed a long stick through the IR beam from where I stood on top of the tower, and pow! the three flashes went off with a crack. We were in business.

Grahame had kindly supplied me with a spare key to the church, and I was able to let myself in and out without bothering him, which was a good thing, as I had to pick up my camera at 0600 the following morning.

When I retrieved the camera, there appeared to be no exposures left on the film, and I got quite excited at what I may have captured during the night.

Equipment wise, the 12volt, 4amp/hr Yuasa batteries drove the flashes quite happily for about 12 hours, so there was no need to worry about the power going down.

It was the twelve exposure film which was the limiting factor, and, without being able to tell WHEN the exposures were made, I didn't know if I was getting photographs during the early part of the evening, or spaced evenly throughout the night.

At work, I watched anxiously as my colour neg film came off the processor, it looked as though I had a full set of exposures, and they looked ok. for density, but were they any good?

On the neg viewer I stuck the magnifier over the film and studied the photographs closely, yes, they looked pretty good, one of the shots showing the bird coming towards the camera with food in it's beak looked promising, and I couldn't wait to make a print.

When I studied the 12x10 print in detail, I saw it was one of those 'almost' results, the depth of field was a shade off, and the bird's face was unsharp.

I would either have to stop down the lens to increase the depth of field, and use a faster film - with consequent loss of image quality, or jiggle the point of focus forwards a bit, and let the tail go soft. I chose the latter.

It graphically demonstrated to me how important it was to leave your triggering set-up 'in situ', only removing the camera for security reasons.

That way one could fine tune either the IR triggering point, or the camera focus point as necessary.

To make sure I got the same point of focus each time, I carefully marked the focus scale on the lens barrel, so all I had to do was sight the camera correctly, stop the lens down to F16. turn the lens to the marked focus point, and we were ready.

It certainly made life a lot easier, whilst working in the gloom of the old church.

A week later I was able to set up again, and this time hit the nail on the head, all my shots were pin sharp.

The next problem was that only every other shot was a head-on view, the owls triggered the camera both on entering, and leaving the window, but even so, I did have six good frontal shots per film!

If Greg could have built in a different 'chip' to give me more than the ten seconds delay I presently had before the camera wound on, I might have had even more frontal shots.

On the other hand, if two birds came in a few seconds apart, I could easily miss the second one, so you pays your money, and takes your choice!

We were well into the month of June, when I suddenly realised that with young Barn owls taking an average of seventy days to fledge, they would be just about be flying when I retired in August!

I was mainly interested to see what prey items the owls brought for their young, so I set the camera up three times a week, usually Sunday, Wednesday and Friday nights, enabling the birds to have a break from my photography in between.

At work the chances of escaping the office grew fewer, and fewer, and I began to experience that funny, slightly depressed feeling one experiences during the last days of a super holiday, it was all ending far too quickly!

Changes in the section were afoot, my lads were out visiting major video equipment manufacturers, evaluating which system we might buy next, while somewhere in the Commissioner's echelons, some misguided quango was suggesting that to save money (?) they could give cameras to certain groups of policemen!

Can you imagine, amateurs handling professional equipment at TWICE the salary of a professional civilian, to save money?

I would love to have heard the police uproar to any suggestion that civilians, because they were cheaper, could more economically set about detecting the perpetrators of some serious crime, ha!

Why on earth had they employed us professionals to undertake specialist photographic work - leaving police free to 'man the beat' for the past thirty five years then?

Talk about re-inventing the wheel!

Down at Mucking, the Barn owls were coming along fine, I could hear their cat-like hissing as I came into the church at dusk to set up the camera, and by the sound of it there were at least three chicks.

I was getting some really nice stuff now I had succeeded in nailing down the depth of field problem, and had a couple of rolls of transparency film exposed, as well as colour neg material.

My natural history picture agency should be well pleased with those!

It was now the last week in July, and I had been clearing my office of years of accumulated junk, until the waste bin was full, only the bare essentials remained.

It was almost like moving house!

A quick tot up of serious jobs I had covered since early 1956 showed that I had attended approximately 3000 murders, although the CPS loved to downgrade some of those into 'Suspicious death' or 'Unlawful killing' categories, to reduce the unpalatable statistics for public consumption.

My final day in the job was a hectic affair, there was so much to organise, but with the willing help of our office girls, and a couple of the lads, enough food and drink was laid on in the film studio to satisfy the hundred and fifty guests I expected.

It was going to be a good old send off!

At the end of it all, when the speeches were done, and various hairy exploits re-told with howls of laughter, Lisa, Helen and I left the place as the last few bottles were being drained, it had been a really good 'do'.

We were now free to organise our relaxing trip to Australia for Christmas, and visit my brothers on the Gold Coast in their manor, and maybe take photographs of what I wanted, in my own time and at my own pace.

My Police photography days at the Yard were definitely over and done!

**Black and white map of Iran and internal journey.**